MONOGRAPH PUBLISHING
SPONSOR SERIES

ANTONY AND CLEOPATRA
CYMBELINE
PERICLES

SHAKESPEARE AS SPOKEN
A Collation of 5000 Acting Editions
and Promptbooks of Shakespeare

Volume 12

By

WILLIAM P. HALSTEAD
Professor Emeritus of Theatre
University of Michigan

Published for
AMERICAN THEATRE ASSOCIATION
by
UNIVERSITY MICROFILMS
INTERNATIONAL
1979

Produced and distributed by
University Microfilms International
Ann Arbor, Michigan 48106

Library of Congress Cataloging in Publication Data

Halstead, William Perdue.
  Shakespeare as spoken.

  (Monograph publishing : sponsor series)
  Includes bibliographies.
  1. Shakespeare, William, 1564-1616–Dramatic
production. 2. Shakespeare, William, 1564-1616–Stage
history. I. American Theatre Association. II. Title.

PR3091.H34   792.9   77-84909
ISBN 0-8357-0494-7 (v. 12)

CONTENTS.

GLOBE EDITION and SHAKESPEARE AS SPOKEN

TABLE OF CONTENTS OF VOLUME 12

SPECIAL ABBREVIATIONS IN BIBLIOGRAPHIES AND COLLATIONS

J   Jaggard's Shakespeare Bibliography, 1911
S   Charles Shattuck, The Shakespeare Promptbooks, 1966
SS   Shakespeare as Spoken, (the present work)
JPKPB   John Philip Kemble Promptbooks, edited by Charles Shattuck, 1974

X   Line omitted
aX   First part of line omitted
bX   Final part of line omitted
cX   A middle portion of line omitted
abX   First and final portions of line omitted, leaving a center portion
R   Line revised but retained
B   Line containing a substitute word or two as a Bowdlerization of a
            religious, sex or scatalogical reference
N   Name change of speaker or similar alteration of line
Tr   Words transposed within line without change of meaning
ADD   Lines added to Shakespeare text

Ac   Acquisition number (in call numbers of BPL, Nuffield, and NYPL TC)
Bd   "Bound in"(used in library call numbers)
f   "folio"(as part of acquisition number at Nuffield)
n d   "no date" given for publication
n l   "no location" given for publication
n p   "no publisher" listed
PB   Promptbook or similar work
Th   "Theatre"
v   "Version"(as part of call number at Nuffield)
vol   "volume"

STC   Short Title Catalog, 1475-1640; microfilm reproduction indicated
            by number and reel number
Wing   Short Title Catalog, 1640-1700; microfilm reproduction indicated
            by number and reel number

BM   British Museum
BPL   Birmingham Public Library
BUS   Boston Public Library
Folger Folger Shakespeare Library, 201 E. Capitol, Washington, D.C.
Harvard U TC Theatre Collection of Harvard University Library
MCNY   Library of Museum of the City of New York
Nuffield Library of the Birthplace Trust, formerly Shakespeare Centre
            Library
NYPL   New York Public Library, 42nd St.
NYPL TC Theatre Collection of NYPL, Lincoln Centre
Players The Players, Gramercy Park, New York City
V&A   Victoria and Albert Museum (Forster Library, Enthoven Theatre
            Collection, Print Room, etc.)
WPH   Personal library of the author
Cal, Conn, etc. State abbreviations

A back-reference to an edition is by an edition sigla followed by a
        "J," "S," or "SS" number.
Introduction in Volume 1 gives a full explanation of all terms used

BIBLIOGRAPHY FOR A N T O N Y A N D C L E O P A T R A

J W1   Mr William Shkespeare, Comedies, Histories and Tragedies.
             London: Jaggard, 1623 (J "The First Folio")
         Kokeritz facsimile. New Haven: Yale U Press, 1954
         Divergence from Globe: 27: 137N; 44: 6N, 8N

J W2   London: Cotes for Smethwick, 1632
         Folger: Proclamation Case
         pp 363 and 365-366
         Unmarked fragment

J AC1   'Sir Charles Sedley, Baronet.' 'Licensed Apr 24, 1677,
             Roger L'Estrange.' London: Tonson, 1677
         U Mich RBR PR3671/S4/A7; Nuffield 50.02/162/ vers 1677
         Different play

J AC2   All for Love John Dryden. London: Herringman, 1678
         BPL S312/3/1678/Case (Ac 16350)
         Different play, though follows Shakespeare's outline

J AC1b   'Sir Charles Sedley.' London: Bentley, 1696
         BPL S312/33/SAFE (Ac 3348)
         Identical with Tonson, 1677, Sedley(J AC1)

SS AC307 Beauty the Conquorer, or the Death of Mark Antony,Sir
             Charles Sedley. 1702
         Folger PR3671/S4/1702/Cage
         Recognized no lines

J AC8   All for Love, John Dryden. London: Tonson, 1709
         BM 11763/f6
         Duplicate of Herringman, 1678(J AC2)

J AC11   Caesar in Egypt Mr Cibber. London: Watts, 1736(J "1725")
         Nuffield 50.02/1623/vers 1735; BPL S312/32 (Ac 113664)
         Different play (Julius, not Antony)

J AC12 and W19 London: Tonson, 1734
         U Mich RBR uncataloged, vol 7
         Full text

J AC13   London: Walker, Dramatic Works of William Shakespeare,   Wal
             1734, vol 3
         Folger PR2802/1734a/Copy 1/Sh Col

J AC15   'Garrick and Capell.' London: Tonson, 1758   GCa
         U Mich RBR PR2802/A22/C23; BM 162/b69; Philadelphia Free
             Public Library P 822.33/S1017; Folger PR2802/1758/Copy
             1/Sh Col
         I included in cuts passages marked with apostrophes

SS 910c ANTONY Biblio

J AC15b Dublin: Peter Wilson, 1759
    BM 640/h29
    Duplicate of Tonson 1758(J AC15--GCa)

S AC1 "David Garrick, Drury Lane, 1759"(S) "In hand of Edward Cap
     Capell"(Hand)
    Folger PB Antony 3

J AC17 and W59 London: Bell, Bell's Edition of Shakespeare's Plays, Bel
     1773-74, vol 6
    U Mich RBR uncataloged

J AC17b London: Bell, 1776, vol 11
    Folger Bd in PR1241/347/Cage/vol 11; BUS K38.78
    Identical with Bell(J AC17--Bel)

SS AC417 "Gilbert"(Hand)
    BUS RBR K38/78
    PB in Bell 1776(J AC17b--Bel); ADD·1 after 33: 29, 1 after
     52: 34

SS AC300 'Henry Brooke.' 'reprint from Collection of Pieces former-
     ly published by Henry Brooke, Esq.' London, n p, 1778
    U Mich RBR uncataloged
    Very free adaptation--few reconizeable lines

J AC25 and W142 'Mrs Inchbald.' London: Longman, n d (J "1808") Inc
    U Mich PR1243/I37/vol 4; BM 1345/a1; BM 1345/a4(single)
    (U Mich cast:Garrick-Yates(Inc) BM cast:Young-Fauct(In2) In2
J AC29 "J P Kemble.' London: Barker, 1813
    U Mich RBR uncataloged; Cornmarket (facsimile of BPL S312/
     1813)
    Duplicate of Inchbald(J AC25--Inc) except: CUT: 12: 172b-
     173a; 4-11: all; 4-14: 1-3; RESTORE: 14: 62-63; 36: 69-
     76; ADD: 1 after 14: 36, 1 after 14: 37; DOES NOT MOVE:
     22: 3-10 to 33

S AC2 "J P Kemble"(S)
    Nuffield 50.02/vers 1813, Folger facsimile of it FILM Ac
     479
    PB in Barker(J AC29--Bar); CUT: 14: 40a; 8 Dryden lines

S AC3 "J P Kemble"(S)   JKP
    Folger S a 125

J AC25b 'Mrs Inchbald.' London: Hurst, 'New Edition, n d ("1816"
     BUS)
    BUS *6551.54
    Identical with Inchbald(J AC25--Inc)

J AC34 London: Cowie, Cowie's British Theatre, 1833
    Ind U, Libby Library
    Full text

S AC4   "William Charles Macready Prompt, Nov 21, 1833"(Hand)   **WMP**
    Folger S a 130 and microfilm of it Ms S a 130
    PB in manuscript(S "in Macready's hand")

S AC5   "Samuel Phelps"(S) "Sadler's Wells Th, 1849"(Hand)   **SP1**
    Folger PB AC8
    PB in unidentified full text

S AC5b   "Samuel Phelps, Sadler's Wells Th, Pepper Williams,Prompter,
        1849"(S)
    NYPL TC *NCP 343411
    PB in "text of Mr Steevens last edition"(Hand), no notes

J AC36   London: Cumerland, n d, vol 44 (J "1848," BM Catalog "1850")Cum
    BM 642/a23 (single); U Mich set stops before this

J AC36b   London: Davidson, Cumberland's British Theatre, n d
    U Mich RBR PR2802/A22/D18/ n d; BPL S312/1848 (Ac 1786)
    Identical with Cumberland(J AC36--Cum)

S AC6   "Isabelle Glyn"(Hand, S "1852")
    Folger PB AC2
    PB in unidentified full text; CUT: 11: 10B, 13B; 12: 27b-
        28a, 33-42, 47-82, 103b-108a, 115b-119, 121b, 167b-171a;
        14: 61b-63a; 15: 7-18a; 21: all; 22: 54b-71a; 24: all;
        25: 5-9a, 58b-59a, 71-72a; 26: 31b-34a; 31: all; 36: 5b-
        8a, 68b-76a, 94-96a; 37: 6b-10, 30-41; 3-11: 25-50; 3-13:
        132b-133; 42: all; 43: all; 4-14: 31-34a; 4-15: 12b-13,
        21b-38, 78b-84a; 52: 74-75a, 112, 157b-158a, 160-164a,
        174b-175a, 184b-187, 317, 323b-327, 331-332a, 340b-360,
        363b-366a

J AC40   London: Lacy, Cumberland's British Theatre (incorporating
        Duncombe's British Theatre), n d (J "1866")
    Nuffield 39/183-/186- (Ac 916)
    Identical with Lacy 1867(J AC42--Lac). I cannot distinguish
        except by library dates

J AC40b   London: Frenchm.
    Nuffield 39/183-/186- (A.c 916)
    Identical with Lacy 1866 and 1867(J AC42--Lac)

J AC41   'Charles Calvert.' Edinburgh: Schenck, n d "1866"(Hand, J   ChC
        "1867")
    Folger PR2802/A31/Sh Col; U Mich RBR uncataloged; Nuffield
        50.02/vers 1867 (Ac 9196, f 60); BPL S312/1867 (Ac 64317;
        Harvard U TC 13484/6/10*; Nuffield 50.02/vers 1869 (Ac
        2196, f 60)

S AC7   "Charles A Calvert, Manchester, 1866"(S) "George Becks"(Hand)
    NYPL TC *NCP 164539
    PB in Calvert (J AC41--ChC) · · · : CUT: 12: 115b-199a; 13:
        45b-54a, 91b-95a; 14: 17, 47b-55a, 61b-63a; 15: 27b-34a;

22: 15-17a, 46b-51a, 54b-71a, 156-160a, 162b-163a, 170-
171a; 23: all; 25: 4a, 64b, 94-95a; 27: 65b-66, 127-142;
33: 41a; 36: 19b-27a, 8 added after 68b; 37: 6b-10a; 39:
27-30, 32-35a; 3-11: 27-35a; 3-12: all; 3-13: 105; 44:
4 added after 19; 4-12: 4b-6 which had been inserted
after 37: 71a; 4-14: 24a, 31-34a; 4-15:1-6a; 52: 193-
194a, 197-204, 211b-213a, 221b-222, 233, 241a, 272-279,
284b-285

J AC42   London: Lacy, n d (J "1867")   Lac
          U Mich 822.08/L15/vol 75; BM 2304/f20; BPL 822.08/LAC
            (Ac 80434)

S AC8   "Anonymous"(S)
          Harvard U TC 13484/6/10*
          PB in Calvert(J AC41-ChC); no cut

S AC9   "Anonymous"(S) "E Edwards"(Hand)
          U Bristol, Drama Library, Tree Coll, Box 199
          Edwards says cuts from various versions; not collated

S AC10   "Anonymous"(S Furness "near affinity to Phelps . . .
            Miss Glyn in 1805s")
          U Penna, Furness Coll, C59/Sh 1/an
          PB in vol 7 of Works "Does not appear to have been used
            for a production"(S); CUT: 12: 27b-28a, 32-82, 92-98a,
            103b-108a, 115-121, 163-164, 167b-171a, 190b-198a; 13:
            45b-54a; 14: 41-55a, 61b-63a; 15: 7-18a, 27b-29a; 21:
            all; 22: 15-17a, 20b-35a, 45b-51a, 54b-71a, 98b-116,
            133b-137a, 141b-146, 154b-160a, 163b-167, 172b-176, 179-
            180a, 233, 243b-248a; 23: all; 24: all; 25: 4-9a, 25B,
            73b-74, 88N, 107-108, 118b-119; 26: 8b-29a, 31b-34a,
            53b-60, 91-107; 27: 24b-26, 42-45, 59-60, 63, 65b-66,
            68b; 36: 19b-34, 68b-86a, 91, 93-96a; 37: 6b-10, 30-41,
            55N, 62N, 71b-79; 38: all; 39: all; 3-10: 4N, 14-15;
            3-11: 8b-17a, 70b-71a; 3-13: 34b-37a, 48-52, 68-69, 89-
            80, 132b-139a, 195-201; 41: 6N; 42: 1-13a; 43: 12b-23;
            44: 18N; 45: all; 46: 1-18a, 20N; 47: all; 49: 1-5a,
            23b-28, 30b-31, 32b-33; 4-10: all; 4-11: all; 4-12:
            1-9a, 13b-17; 4-14: 25b, 31-34a, 39b-43, 45b-50a, 114b-
            115, 123b-124a, 133-134; 4-15: 11b-13, 21b-40, 56b-57a,
            69, 71, 78b-84a; 51: all; 52: 35, 42b-46a, 74-75, 78b,
            81b, 112-113, 137, 157b-158a, 160-164a, 167b-170a, 174b-
            179a, 218b-221a, 223b-224a, 233N, 245b-258, 263-281,
            323N, 245b-258, 263-281, 323N, 327-328a, 333b-334a, 338,
            340b-369

J AC45   'Andrew Halliday.' London: Tinsley Bros, 1873   Hal
          BM 11766/b25; U Mich RBR PR2802/A22/H17; Nuffield 50.02/
            vers 1873 (Ac 1075)

S AC11   "Jean Davenport Lander, Brooklyn Th, Brooklyn, 1874"(S) JL1
            "George Becks"(Hand)
          NYPL TC *NCP 342921
          PB in Halliday1873(S)

S AC12   "Jean Davenport Lander, 1874"(S)
        NYPL TC *NCP 346654
        Role books for many roles, "made by W H Crampton, Pitts
          burgh Opera House"(Had); not collated

S AC13   "Jean Davenport Lander, 1874"(S) "George Becks"(Hand)
        NYPL TC *NCP 342925
        Divergence from Lander(S AC11--JL1); CUT: 13 71c; 14: 12-15a,
          41-55a, 15: 7b-18a; 22: 75b-76; 25: 117b-118a, 119b; 27:
          59-60, 126-167; 3-13: 41-46a, 80-81a, 105, 173-176, 178-
          182a; RESTORE: 12: 97-115a; 27: 65b-66; 4-14: 60b-62a;
          4-15: 78b-85a; DOES NOT MOVE 23: 2b-50 to follow 25: 108a;
          49: 7-23a to follow 4-14: 140

S AC14   "Jean Davenport Lander, 1974"(S) "George Becks"(Hand)
        Folger PB AC1
        Divergence from Lander(S AC11--JL1): CUT: 12: 27b-28a; 14:
          12-15, 41-55a, 61b-63a; 15: 7b-18a, 47b-50a; 22: 15-17a,
          22b-25a, 46b-51a, 61b-71a, 174-176, 179-180a; 25: 118-119;
          26: 80-82, 84-91, 96b-101, 107-116, 118-121, 126-127; 27:
          all; 3-10: 31-33a; 3-11: 31, 33, 35b-38a, 42-46; 3-13:
          61b-62a, 68-69, 79-81a, 105; 44: 24-25; 45: 2-17a; 46:
          23b-24a; 4-13: 4-6; 4-14: 82b-84a, 133-134; 4-15: 78b-
          84a; 52: 42b-46a, 74-75; RESTORE: 12: 83, 97-115a; 22:
          52b-54a, 248b-250; 37: 24b-31; 3-10: 22-24, 29b-30; 3-11:
          9-10, 16-17, 21; 3-13: 186b-187, 191b-194; 46: 13b-15a;
          49: 10b-11; 4-14: 60b-62a; ADD: 8 after 4-15: 36a; DOES
          NOT ADD: 2 after 12: 204; DOES NOT MOVE: 26: 63-79 and 84-
          127 to follow 27: 8; 33: 26-50 to follow 25: 158; 3-11:
          1-70a to follow 44: 34; 3-13: 1-2 to follow 4-12: 49;
          3-10 8b, 4b-8a, add 7, 26b-35a to follow 4-14: 140; 49:
          7-23a to follow 4-14: 140

S AC15   "Lander"(S) "Recollections of Mrs F W Lander and James
          Taylor, 1867"(Hand)
        Harvard U TC *61-2354
        Notes in Lacy(J AC42--Lac); not collated because of
          "memory after 15 years," and confusion of lines boxed
          for movement, but location not indicated

S AC47   Antony and Octavius in Works of W S Landor. London: Chap-
          man, 1876
        BPL S 878/7 (Ac 78876)
        No resemblance

J W1070   Henry Irving Shakespeare, Henry Irving and Frank A Marshall. HIM
          London: Blackie, 1888
        U Mich RBR 822.9/S53.1888-90/I7

SS AC301
        'Kyrle Bellew.' NY: Koppel, n d(copyright 1889)   KyB
        U Mich RBR PR2802/A22/B44; Folger PR2802/A39/Sh Col;
          Princeton U, RBR, in PB of AC

S AC16   "Kyrle Bellew, Palmer's Th, NY, 1889"(S)
          Princeton U RBR, Seymour Coll, PB Antony
          PB in Koppel(SS AC301--KyB); CUT: 48: 19b-22a

SS AC302 "Mrs Langtry.' London: Leadenhall Press, n d (Production   LiL
               1890)
          U Mich RBR PR2802/A2/L29

J AC59   Memorial Th Edition, C E Flower. London: French, n d, and   MTh
               other publishers in Stratford-upon-Avon and Birmingham
               (J :1891")
          U Mich RBR uncataloged, filed at 1894

S AC17   "Edmund Teare's Co in 1890s--PB" (Hand)   EdT
          Nuffield 72.02/TEA (Ac 9010)
          PB in Cassell's full text

SS AC400 "William Winter, 1896"(Folger catalog)
          Folger PB AC9
          PB in Temple(Dent), 1896; CUT: 11: 58-59, 62b; 12: 27b-30,
               33-42, 47-82, 118-119, 192b-199a; 13: 45b-49a; 14: 44b-55a,
               62a; 15: 8-18a; 21: all; 25: 3b-9a, 58b-59, 74; 26: 12b-14a,
               29b-34a, 57b-60, 91b-106; 27: 1-19, 112-119, 126-142; 31:
               all; 32: all; 34: all; 36: 5b-8a, 19b-27a, 76b-86a; 37: 6b-
               10; 3-10: 14; 3-11: 25-30, 31, 34-41; 3-12: all; 3-13: 34b-
               37a, 79-81a; 42: all; 43: all; 47: all; 49: 23b-27a; 4-10;
               all; 4-12: 1-9a; 4-15: 12b-13a, 21b-37; 51: all; 52: 42b-
               46a, 74-75, 112-113, 247b-248, 252b-258a, 317-323a, 325-368

J AC63   'Louis Calvert and Richard Flanagan.' Manchester: Broad,1897 LoC
          U Mich RBR PR2802/A22/C17; Folger PR2802/A41/Sh Col; BPL
          S312/1897 (Ac 194166)

SS AC401 Antonia Y Cleopatra
          Folger PB AC12
          PB in Barcelona, 1849. Text and notes in Spanish

A AC18   "Charles B Hanford, 1900(S)
          Folger PB AC6
          PB in Temple; CUT: 11 40b-41a; 12: 4-5, 40-41a, 60-64a, 69c,
               73b-76, 79B, 94N, 121b, 128, 131, 146c, 205b-208a; 13: 62-
               70a; 14: 18b-80, 86-97; 15: 4, 11-22a, 27-29a; 21: all;
               22: 18b-22a, 66, 70b-79a, 85-90a, 101-102, 107a, 197b-202,
               207a, 230-240, 278b; 23: 5b-11, 47-49; 24: all; 25: 5a,
               7-8a, 67b-69a, 73R, 74, 83-84, 88b-91, 116-118, 124b-131,
               150b-151; 26: all; 27: 1-24, 38-142; 31: all; 32: 1-30;
               34: all; 35: all; 36: 12N, 47-98; 37: 9b12; 38: all; 39:
               all; 3-10: 35b-37; 3-11: 17b-19a, 22b-26a, 27-37a, 48b-
               52a; 3-12: all; 3-13: 97-99a , 146b-148a, 199b-200a; 3-14:
               8b-9a, 22b-23a, 36-42; 41: all; 42: all; 43: all; 44: 2b-
               3, 15-16; 46: all; 47: 1-3, 10b-21; 49: all; 4-10: 5b-10;
               4-11: all; 4-12: 1-11a, 23-27a, 28b-31, 34, 42, 49-53a;
               4-13: 2b-3a, 5-7a; 4-14: 57b-62a, 65-67, 75b-125a, 131-
               133, 137, 141-167, 170-177; 4-15: 1-8a, 10-1, 15b-21, 26-
               44, 50-53, 70b-73a, 76b-77, 80b-81a, 86, 90b-99a, 103b-
               105a; 51: all; 52: 1-8, 26-31a, 40-44, 55b-62a, 72b-83

85-129, 136-233a, 241-246a, 249b-251, 263b-271a, 286b-287,
294-297, 342b-344, 350-355, 358-361a; ADD: 7 after 13:
132, 14 after 22: 297, 82 after 33: 92; MOVE: 22: 1-250,
23: 1-5, 32: 31-86, 23: 13-46 to follow 14: 85; 27: 25-
37 to follow 22: 229; 33: 1-72 to follow 25: 53; 44: 30b-
48 to follow 45: 26; 48: 1-10, 47: 4-10a, 48: 11-46 to
follow 4-10: 1b

S AC20 "Hanford, 1900"(S)
Folger Pβ AC4 and 5
Rolebooks; not collated

S AC21 'Herbert Beerbohm-Tree.' London: Warrington, 1907   BT1
BM 11785/a49

S C22 "H Beerbohm-Tree, 1906"(S)
U Bristol, Drama Library, Tree Coll, Box 199
Workbook in unidentified full text; not collated

S AC23 "H Beerbohm-Tree, 1906"(S)
U Bristol, Drama Library, Tree Coll, Box 193A
PB in Temple; not collated on assumption it was a duplicate

S AC24 "Beerbohm-Tree, 1906"(S)
U Bristol, Drama Library, Box 193A
Partially cut book(Scene 12 in normal order); not collated

S AC25 "Beerbohm-Tree, 1906"(S)
U Bristol, Drama Library, Tree Coll, Box 193A
Role books for many roles

S AC26 "Beerbohm-Tree, 1906"(S)
U Bristol, Drama Library, Tree Coll, Box 193
Role book for Antony; not collated

S AC27 "Beerbohm-Tree, 1906"(S)
U Bristol, Drama Library, Tree Coll, Box 193A
Partially developed PB on proof-sheets of Tree(S AC21--BT1);
not collated; similar to S AC28

S AC28 "H Beerbohm-Tree, 1906"(S)
U Bristol, Drama Library, Tree Coll, Box 199
Final PB(S) on proof-sheets of Tree(S AC21--BT1); Deviations
from Tree(S AC21--BT1); CUT: 11: 26-31a, 56-624-11: 20-23a;
4-12: 1-9a, 36b-47a; 52: 229b-230; RESTORE: 11: 35b-36a;
12: 4-5, 41-42, 80-85, 167b-171; 15: 29b-78; 22: 23-42a;
25: 58b-59a, 99-100; 52: 1-5, 8-11, 269-271; DOES NOTADD:
4 after 23: 7; 2 after 3-13: 31a

S AC29 "Beerbohm-Tree, 1906"(S)
U Bristol, Drama Library, Tree Coll, Box 193
Uncompleted PB, starts identically with Tree(S AC28); not
collated

S AC30   "Beerbohm-Tree, 1906"(S)
         U Bristol, Drama Library, Tree Coll, Box 194
         Tech materials; no text

S AC31   "Beerbohm-Tree,¦ "Tallulah Bankhead"(Hand)
         NYPL TC *NCP 328654B (S "44x545")
         Carbon of typed script, "produced at Mansfield Th, NY, Nov
           10, 1937"(Hand.) Deviations from Tree(S AC21--BT1)L CUT:
           34: 19-20a, 21-22a; 3-13: 41-46a; 52: 193-196; RESTORE:
           11: 28; 37: 69-74a, 76b-82; 3-11: 10b-11, 16-17a, 18-20a;
           3-13: 141b-143; 4-10: 1, 3b-4a; 4-12: 27; 4-14: 47b-49;
           52: 269-271, 289-290; ADD: 7 after 4-12: 3a

S AC32   "Sothern and Marlowe, 1909"(S) "Winthrop Ames, presented
           at New Th"(Hand)
         NYPL TC *NCP
         Preparation copy(S) in Temple; not collated

S AC33   "Edward H Sothern and Julia Marlowe Sothern Coll"(Hand)
           "1909"(S)
         NYPL TC *NCP 44x220
         "Preparation copy"(S) in unidentified full text; CUT: 22:
           174-175, 180b; 25: 59a, 77; 52: 386b-389

S AC34   "E H Sothern production at New Th, NY"(Hand) "1909"(S)   SM1
         MCNY 43/430/621
         "Preparation copy"(S) in unidentified full text

S AC35   "E H Sothern"(Hand)
         MCNY 43/340/622
         Role book for Antony; not collated

S AC36   "Winthrop Ames, 1909"(Hand)   WA1
         NYPL TC *NCP 51624B
         PB in typed script(p 39 missing)

S AC36b   "Winthrop Ames"(S) 'for presentation ˉ at the New Th,1909"
           (Hand)
         NYPL TC *NCP 516255B (38x111)
         PB in unidentified text; divergence from Ames(S AC36--WA1);
           CUT: 12: 83b-91, 95-98a, 101-103, 113b-115a, 132-134a,
           186b-198a; 13: 12-13, 30-31a, 57-61; 14: 25b-33a; 15:
           27b-37, 67-75; 22: 156-160a; 25: 86b-88a; 47: 4-6a; 48:
           all; RESTORE: 12: 27b-28a, 40, 45-46, 59-60, 168b-176a;
           14: 12-15, 40b-44, 47b-55a, 61b-63a; 15: 39-42a; 22: 15-
           17a. 19b-24, 135,174-176; 23: 26-30a; 26: 82; 27: 7-9,
           16-19, 126-142; 36: 60b-63, 68b-76a, 93-97; 37: 14b-16a,
           54b-58a; 3-13: 48-52, 147b-151; 4-14: 17-18, 97b-99a,
           116-128a. 131-134. 138b-140; 52: 193-196, 256b-259, 265-
           271, 363b-366a; MOVE: 22: 1-250 and 23: 1-43 to follow
           13: 106; 14: 1-83 to open play; 25: 10-119a to follow
           15: 75; 42: 1-44a to follow 3-13: 167; 33: 1-51 to fol-
           low25: 119a; 32: 25-37 to follow 23: 59; 43: 1-26 to
           follow48: 39; DOES NOT MOVE: 22: 190-246 to follow 11:
           10; 22: 176-188 to follow 22: 298

S AC37   "Winthrop Ames"(S) "for presentation at the New TH, 1909"
       (Hand)
       NYPL TC *NCP 516225B (38x111)
       PB in unidentified text: Deviations from Ames(S AC36--WA1);
         CUT: 12: 43-44, 55-60; 22: 61b-66; 25: 109; 26: 82; 43:
         16-23; 4-15: 41-46; RESTORE: 12: 141-144a; 14: 12-15; 22:
         135; 36: 46b-50a; 37: 54b-58a; 3-10: 31-33a; 3-11: 47-
         48; 47: 11-12a; 4-12: 3-9a; 4=13: 2-3a; 4-14: 102b-103a;
         52: 327, 332b-335a, 363b-366a; ADD: 7 after 12: 32; DOES
         NOT MOVE 32: 24-37 to follow 23: 7a

SS AC303   Cleopatra in Judaea, Arthur Symonds(Typed) "c1910"(Folger)
       Folger N b 27
       24p typed ms of a different play

SS AC402   Cleopatra in Judaea, Symonds(Typed)
       Folger S b 27
       Rolebooks in French

S AC38   "Oscar Asche and Lily Brayton"(Hand. Program of Th Royal   OA1
       Melbourne, Australia, 1917)
       Nuffield 72.903/ASC (Ac 5403, f92)

SS AC304   Players Shakespeare, J H Walker. London: Heinemann, n d
       (BM "c1920")
       BM 11768/k7
       Full text; 'reading in classroom'

J W1130b   Henry Irving Shakespeare, Henry Irving and Frank A Marshall.
       London: Gresham, 1922
       BM 11763/t7
       Identical with Irving-Marshall(J W1130--HIM)

S AC39   "W Bridges-Adams, 1931"(Hand)   STRATFORD-UPON-AVON   BA1
       Nuffield 71.21/1931A (Ac 2179, f 90)
       PB in Temple

SS AC403   "Nugent Monck, Maddermarket Th"(Hand. Productions 1924,   NM1
       1934)
       Nugent Monck Coll, Jack Hall
       Memorial PB in Methuen, 2nd ed, 1930

S AC40   "Ben Iden Payne, 1935," "Marked originally for W Bridges-   IP1
       Adams, 1931; change in pencil to Payne"(Hand)
       Nuffield 71.21/1935A (Ac 7925) STRATFORD-UPON -AVON

S AC41   "Tallulah Bankhead, Mansfield Th, NY, 1937"(Hand)   TaB
       NYPL TC *NCP 494168
       Typed script in prose

SS AC404   "Nugent Monck"(Hand)
       British Drama League (but they say 1979, "Never had it")
       PB in unidentified full text. Notes lost

S AC42   "Robert Atkins, 1945," "Originally used for 1935 product-   RA1
            ion"(Hand)   STRATFORD—UPON—AVON
            Nuffield 71.21/1945A (Ac 5366, f 91)

SS AC415   "James Sandoe, 1950"(Hand)   ASHLAND   JS1
            Ore Shakespeare FestivAL Archives

SS AC305   NY: Dodd Mead, n d (printed with George Bernard Shaw's
            Caesar and Cleopatra, presumably in 1952 when Olivier-
            Leigh did double-bill
            U Mich 822.8/S535c/1952
            Full text

S AC43   "Glen Byam Shaw, 1953"(Hand)   STRATFORD—UPON—AVON   GS1
            Nuffield 71.21/1953A (Ac 8551)
            PB in Temple

S AC44   "Glen Byam Shaw, 1953 Prince's Th and Continental Tour"
            (Hand)   STRATFORD—UPON—AVON
            Nuffield O S 71.21/1953A (Ac 8552)
            Identical with Shaw (S AC43--GS1)

S AC45   "1953-1954"(Hand)   STRATFORD—UPON—AVON
            Nuffield O S 71.21/1953-54 (Ac 8612)
        [ue book, with text selectively cut; not collated
S AC46   "Robert Helpman, 1957"(S) "Michael Benthall"(Hand)   RH1
            Old Vic Archives
            PB in New Temple

SS AC411   "Bernard Hepton, 1961"(Hand)
            Birmingham Repertory Th Archives
            PB in unidentified full text

SS AC405   "Joseph Papp, Delancourt Th, 1963"(Hand) SHAKESPEARE IN   JP1
            NY Shakespeare Festival Archives   THE PARK
            PB in Penguin, "edited by M Mack". Also a text "adapted
            by Kornfeld, and a Pengin casually and incompletely
            cut

SS AC414   "Allen Fletcher, 1963"(Hand)   SAN DIEGO   AF1
            San Diego National Shakespeqare Festival Archives
            PB in unidentified text

SS AC406   "Michael Langham, 1967"(Hand)   ONTARIO   ML1
            Stratford Shakespeare Festival Archives

SS AC407   "Michael Langham, Exposition 1967"(Hand)   ONTARIO
            Stratford Shakespeare Festival Archives
            Duplicate of Langham(SS AC406--ML1) except: CUT: 25: 2b;
            31: 23R, 28R, 29R; 34: 35R, 36R, 37R; 35: 19a; RESTORE:
            24: 19b; 31: 34 in place of 34R; 35: 19b-20a; 37: 76b;
            4-12: 28b; 52: 65, 328a

SS AC412 "Jerry Turner, 1967"(Hand)   ASHLAND
          Ore Shakespeare Festival Archives
          CUT: 12: 123-124, 196b-201a; 14: 57b-58a, 60a, 65-66a; 24:
          all; 27: 116b-118; 31: all; 32: 1-6a, 51-59a; 34: 15-20a;
          35: L0b-12a; 36: 8b-11a, 68b-76a ; 37: 71b-75a, 78b-80;
          38: all; 3-12: 2b-6a; 3-13: 7-12a, 16b-17a, 143b-151, 160b-
          161a, 165, 169-171; 44: 33b-34a; 47: 1-3, 16b; 48: 32-35a;
          4-12: 20b-24a; 4-14: 135-138a; 51: 26a

SS AC306 'George Skillan.' London: French, 1970
          B M 11791/71735 or 1739
          CUT: 12: 80-82; 14: 65-68a; 15: 9b-12a; 23: 23-27a, 35b-38a;
          25: 5-9a, 58b-59a; 27: 13-18; 49: 23h-34; 4-10: move 3b-4
          to follow 7, 6-7; 4-14: 133-134a to follow 52: 353

SS AC413 "Ellia Rabb, 1971"(Hand)   SAN DIEGO   ER1
          San Diego National Shakespeare Festival Archives
          3 scripts in unidentified text

SS AC413 "Michael Kahn, 1972"(Hand)   CONNECTICUT
          American Shakespeare Festival Archives
          CUT: 22: 166b-167a; 23: 43b-44a; 24: all; 25: 7; 26: 53b-
          57a, 104-106, 125b-130a; 27: 1-19, 116R, 133b-134a, 138;
          32: 6b-20a, 51b-53a; 33: 51; 35: move 14-16a to follow
          25; 36: 69-76a; 37: 7b-10, 36-38, 41b-47, 58, 71b-82;
          38: all; 39: all; 3-10: 13, 24b; 3-13: 22b-25a, 31b-
          34a, 41-46a, 50b-52, 115b-122a, 143b-147a, 173-177; 42:
          12c; 44: 18n-23, 31-32a; 47: 1-3, 15-16; 48: 1-2a, 4b-
          7a, 11b-13a, 31-35a; 4-10: 4b-9; 4-11: all; 4-14: 25b;
          4-15: 26b-29a; 51: 26N; 52: 124, 341b-349a

SS AC409 "Larry Kornfeld, 1972"(Hand) SHAKESPEARE IN THE PARK LK1
          NY Shakespeare Festiv al Archives
          Typed ms. Apparently not done in Park

SS AC410 "Trevor Nunn with Buzz Goodbody and Euan Smith, 1972"   TN1
          (Hand)   STRATFORD-UPON-AVON
          Nuffield 71.21/1972/ANT (Ac 1293 and 1294)
          2 identical texts in unidentified full text

ALPHABETICAL LIST OF SIGLA FOR ANTONY AND CLEOPATRA

BA1 W Bridges-Adams, 1931
Bel London: Bell, 1773
BH1 Bernard Hepson, 1961
BT1 Herbert Beerbohm-Tree, 1907
Cap David Garrick-Edward Capell PB 1759
Cum London: Cumberland, 1848
EdT Edward Tear e, 1890
ER1 Ellis Rabb, 1971
GCa 'David Garrick and Edward Capell.' London: Tonson, 1758
GS1 Glen Byam Shaw, 1953
Hal 'Halliday.' London: Tins y, 1873
HIM Henry Irving-Frank A Marshall, 1888
Inc 'Mrs Inchbald.'London: Longman, 1808, Garrick-Yates cast
In2 'Mrs Inchbald.' London: Longman, n d, Young-Faucit cast
IP1 Ben Iden Payne, 1935
JKP John Philip Kemble PB, 1813
JL1 Jean Davenport Lander, 1874
JP1 Joseph Papp, 1963
JS1 James Sandoe, 1950
KyB 'Kyrle Bellew.' NY: Koppel, 1889
Lac London: Lacy, 1867
LiL 'Mrs Langtry.' London: Leatherhall Press, 1890
LK1 Larry Kornfeld, 1972
LoC 'Louis Calvert.' Manchester: Broad, 1897
ML 1 Michael Langham, 1967
MTh <u>Memorial Theatre Edition</u>, 1891
NM1 Nugent Monck, 1924
OA1 Oscar Asche, 1917
RA1 Robert Atkins, 1945
RH1 Robert Helpman, 1957
SM1 Sothern and Marlowe, 1909
SP1 Samuel Phelps, 1833
TaB Tallulah Bankhead, 1937
TN1 Trevor Nunn, 1972
WA1 Winthrop Ames, 1909
WM1 William Charles Macready PB 1833

ANTONY AND CLEOPATRA.

DRAMATIS PERSONÆ.

MARK ANTONY,
OCTAVIUS CÆSAR, } triumvirs.
M. ÆMILIUS LEPIDUS,
SEXTUS POMPEIUS.

DOMITIUS ENOBARBUS,
VENTIDIUS,
EROS,
SCARUS, } friends to Antony.
DERCETAS,
DEMETRIUS,
PHILO,

MECÆNAS,
AGRIPPA,
DOLABELLA,
PROCULEIUS, } friends to Cæsar.
THYREUS,
GALLUS,

MENAS,
MENECRATES, } friends to Pompey.
VARRIUS,
TAURUS, lieutenant-general to Cæsar.
CANIDIUS, lieutenant-general to Antony.
SILIUS, an officer in Ventidius's army.
EUPHRONIUS, an ambassador from Antony to Cæsar.
ALEXAS,
MARDIAN, a Eunuch, } attendants on Cleopatra.
SELEUCUS,
DIOMEDES,
A Soothsayer.
A Clown.

CLEOPATRA, queen of Egypt.
OCTAVIA, sister to Cæsar and wife to Antony.

CHARMIAN,
IRAS, } attendants on Cleopatra.

Officers, Soldiers, Messengers, and other Attendants.

SCENE: *In several parts of the Roman empire.*
ACT I.

1,+1   SCENE I.   *Alexandria. A room in Cleopatra's*
palace.

2   *Enter* DEMETRIUS *and* PHILO.

3–4	*Phi.* Nay, but this dotage of our general's	1
5	O'erflows the measure: those his goodly eyes,	2
6	That o'er the files and musters of the war	3
7	Have glow'd like plated Mars, now bend, now	
8	turn,	4
9	The office and devotion of their view	5
10	Upon a tawny front: his captain's heart,	6
11	Which in the scuffles of great fights hath burst	7
12	The buckles on his breast, reneges all temper,	8
13	And is become the bellows and the fan	9
14	To cool a gipsy's lust.	

15   *Flourish. Enter* ANTONY, CLEOPATRA, *her*
16   *Ladies, the Train, with Eunuchs fanning her.*

17	Look, where they come: **10**	10
18	Take but good note, and you shall see in him	11
19	The triple pillar of the world transform'd	12
20	Into a strumpet's fool: behold and see.	13
21	*Cleo.* If it be love indeed, tell me how much.	14
	Ant. There's beggary in the love that can be	
22	reckon'd.	15
23	*Cleo.* I'll set a bourn how far to be beloved.	16
	Ant. Then must thou needs find out new	
24–5	heaven, new earth.	17

26   *Enter an* Attendant.

27	*Att.* News, my good lord, from Rome.	
28	*Ant.* Grates me: the sum.	18
29	*Cleo.* Nay, hear them, Antony:	19
30	Fulvia perchance is angry: or, who knows **20**	20
31	If the scarce-bearded Cæsar have not sent	21
32	His powerful mandate to you, 'Do this, or this;	22
33	Take in that kingdom, and enfranchise that;	23

<u>Insert</u> 14: 1-83: KyB, LiL <u>Insert</u> 22: 177-232, <u>11</u>: 1-81a: TaB <u>Insert</u>
 <u>41</u>: 1-2a, 9-12, 18a, 29b-34a, 36b-37, <u>add</u> 12, <u>22</u>: 191-192, 196-
 295:: LiL
1 X: LK1; <u>N</u>: LoC; <u>MOVE</u> 1-13 to follow 55: BTl
2 X: LK1; <u>b</u>X: TaB, ER1
3 X: TaB, ER1, LK1

4 same as 3
5 same as 3
6 X: LK1; <u>a</u>X: TaB, ER1; <u>b</u>X: Inc, Cum, Hal, JL1
7 X: Inc, Cum, Hal, JL1, LK1
8 same as 7
9 same as 7, KyB

10 R: WM1; <u>a</u>X: Inc, Cum, Hal, JL1, KyB, LK1; <u>b</u>X: SP1, SM1, TaB, AF1*
11 X: LK1; <u>Insert</u> 22: 238-244a, 190-221a: JKP
12 X: LK1
13 R: WM1; <u>ax</u>: LK1; <u>B</u>: ChC, Hal, KyB, EdT, LoC, BA1; <u>ADD</u> 6: WM1
14

15
16

17 <u>ADD</u> 1: ML1, LK1

18 <u>R</u> : Cap; <u>N</u>: Hal, JP1
19
20
21
22 <u>b</u>X : Cum
23 X: Cum

*11:10 ER1; <u>Insert</u> 22: 190-295: SM1, WA1

34	Perform't, or else we damn thee.'	
35	*Ant.* How, my love!	24
36	*Cleo.* Perchance! nay, and most like:	25
37	You must not stay here longer, your dismission	26
38	Is come from Cæsar; therefore hear it, Antony.	27
39	Where's Fulvia's process? Cæsar's I would say? both?	28
40	Call in the messengers. As I am Egypt's queen,	29
41	Thou blushest, Antony; and that blood of thine	30
42	Is Cæsar's homager: else so thy cheek pays shame **3I**	31
43	When shrill-tongued Fulvia scolds. The messengers!	32
44	*Ant.* Let Rome in Tiber melt, and the wide arch	33
45	Of the ranged empire fall! Here is my space.	34
46	Kingdoms are clay: our dungy earth alike	35
47	Feeds beast as man: the nobleness of life	36
48	Is to do thus; when such a mutual pair	37
48+1	[*Embracing.*	
49	And such a twain can do't, in which I bind,	38
50	On pain of punishment, the world to weet	39
51	We stand up peerless.	
52	*Cleo.* Excellent falsehood! **40**	40
53	Why did he marry Fulvia, and not love her?	41
	I'll seem the fool I am not; Antony	42
54	Will be himself.	
55	*Ant.* But stirr'd by Cleopatra.	43
56	Now, for the love of Love and her soft hours,	44
57	Let's not confound the time with conference harsh:	45
58	There's not a minute of our lives should stretch	46
59	Without some pleasure now. What sport to-night?	47
60	*Cleo.* Hear the ambassadors.	
61	*Ant.* Fie, wrangling queen!	48
62	Whom every thing becomes, to chide, to laugh,	49
63	To weep; whose every passion fully strives **50**	50
64	To make itself, in thee, fair and admired!	51
65	No messenger, but thine; and all alone	52

24   X: Cum; $\underline{b}$X: LoC
25   X: LoC, $\overline{BT1}$
26   X: LoC
27   X: LoC

28   X: LoC, BT1, RH1
29   X: LoC; $\underline{aX}$: JKP, OA1
30   X: LoC

31   X: LoC; $\underline{bX}$: BT1

32   X: LoC; $\underline{R}$: ML1; $\underline{aX}$: BT1

33
34   $\underline{bX}$: TaB
35   $\overline{bX}$: In2, JKP, BT1, RA1
36   $\overline{aX}$: In2, JKP, BT1, RA1
37   $\overline{bX}$: In2

38   X: In2; $\underline{bX}$: ML1
39   X: In2, $\overline{ML1}$

40   $\underline{a}$X: In2, ML1; $\underline{bX}$: ChC, LoC
41   $\overline{X}$: ChC, LoC
42   X: JKP, WM1, LoC, TN1; $\underline{aX}$: ChC; $\underline{bX}$: RH1

43   X: JKP, WM1, RH1, TN1; $\underline{bX}$: In2
44   X: JL1

45
46
47

48
49   X: ChC, LoC
50   X: ChC, LoC
51   X: ChC
52   $\underline{bX}$: In2

	To-night we'll wander through the streets and	
66	note	53
67	The qualities of people. Come, my queen;	54
68	Last night you did desire it: speak not to us.	55
69	[Exeunt Ant. and Cleo. with their train.	
70	Dem. Is Cæsar with Antonius prized so slight?	56
71	Phi. Sir, sometimes, when he is not Antony,	57
72	He comes too short of that great property	58
73	Which still should go with Antony.	
	Dem. I am full sorry	59
74	That he approves the common liar, who 60	60
75	Thus speaks of him at Rome: but I will hope	61
	Of better deeds to-morrow. Rest you happy!	62
76	[Exeunt.	

76+1	**Scene II.** *The same. Another room.*	
77	*Enter* Charmian, Iras, Alexas, *and a* Sooth-	
78–9	sayer.	
	Char. Lord Alexas, sweet Alexas, most any	1
80	thing Alexas, almost most absolute Alexas, where's	2
81	the soothsayer that you praised so to the queen?	3
82	O, that I knew this husband, which, you say,	4
83–4	must charge his horns with garlands!	5
85	*Alex.* Soothsayer!	6
86	*Sooth.* Your will?	7
	Char. Is this the man? Is't you, sir, that	
87	know things?	8
	Sooth. In nature's infinite book of secrecy	9
88–9	A little I can read.	
90	*Alex.* Show him your hand. 10	10

90+1	*Enter* Enobarbus.	
	Eno. Bring in the banquet quickly; wine	
91	enough	11
92	Cleopatra's health to drink.	12
93	*Char.* Good sir, give me good fortune.	13
94	*Sooth.* I make not, but foresee.	14
95	*Char.* Pray, then, foresee me one.	15
96	*Sooth.* You shall be yet far fairer than you are.	16
97	*Char.* He means in flesh.	17
98	*Iras.* No, you shall paint when you are old.	18
99	*Char.* Wrinkles forbid!	19
100	*Alex.* Vex not his prescience; be attentive.	20
101	*Char.* Hush! 21	21

53 X: Inc

54 X: Inc

55 X: Cap; aX: In2; ADD 1: LK1; Insert 12: 11-12: AF1; Insert 11-13:
       BT1; Insert 22: 189-250, add 4: GCa; Insert 22: 189-243: Inc; In-*

56 X: GCa, Cap, Inc, In2, SP1, Cum, OA1, JP1, LK1; N: WM1, LoC

57 same as 56, TN1; same N

58 same as 57; less N

59 same as 58, less Inc, RA1; aX: Inc, RA1; bX: BT1; N: BT1

60 X: GCa, Cap, SP1, Cum, OA1, JP1, LK1; aX: TN1

61 same as 60; less aX; bX: AF1

62 same as 60, AF1; less aX; aX: TN1; bX: Ha1, RA1; Insert 12: 92-
       204: BT1

Scene 12

1   X: Cap, Be1, Inc, In2, JKP, Cum, ChC, Ha1, LiL, LoC, TaB; Insert 11*

2   same as 1; less Insert

3   same as 2

4   X: Cap, Be1, Inc, In2, JKP, SP1, Cum, ChC, Ha1, LiL, LoC, BT1, SM1*

5   same as 4, KyB, BA1, GS1; less bX; ADD 3: WM1

6   X: Cap, Be1, Inc, In2, JKP, WM1, Cum, ChC, Ha1, LiL, LoC, TaB

7   same as 6; N: JP1

8   same as 6

9   same as 6

10 same as 6

11 same as 6, BT1, LK1; MOVE 11-12 to follow 1: TN1; MOVE 11-12 to*

12 same as 11; less MOVEs

13 same as 12, less BT1

14 same as 13

15 same as 13, GS1

16 same as 15, GCa, BH1

17 same as 16

18 same as 16

19 same as 16

20 same as 16, less RH1

21 same as 20, TN1

*11:55 sert 22: 238-243a: in2   *12: 1 -12: TN1
*12: 4 WA1, NM1, TaB, RH1, AF1, ML1; bX: KyB, BA1, GS1
*12:11 follow 11: 55: AF1

Sooth. You shall be more beloving than beloved. 22

103 *Char.* I had rather heat my liver with drinking. 23
104 *Alex.* Nay, hear him. 24
Char. Good now, some excellent fortune! Let 25
105 me be married to three kings in a forenoon, and 26
106 widow them all: let me have a child at fifty, to 27
107 whom Herod of Jewry may do homage: find me 28
108 to marry me with Octavius Cæsar, and compa- 29
109 nion me with my mistress. 30 30
Sooth. You shall outlive the lady whom you
110 serve. 31
Char. O excellent! I love long life better
111 than figs. 32
Sooth. You have seen and proved a fairer
112 former fortune 33
113 Than that which is to approach. 34
Char. Then belike my children shall have no 35
114 names: prithee, how many boys and wenches 36
115 must I have? 37
Sooth. If every of your wishes had a womb, 38
116-17 And fertile every wish, a million. 39
118 *Char.* Out, fool! I forgive thee for a witch. 40 40
Alex. You think none but your sheets are 41
119-20 privy to your wishes. 42
121 *Char.* Nay, come, tell Iras hers. 43
122 *Alex.* We'll know all our fortunes. 44
Eno. Mine, and most of our fortunes, to-night 45
123-4 shall be—drunk to bed. 46
Iras. There's a palm presages chastity, if no- 47
125 thing else. 48
Char. E'en as the o'erflowing Nilus presageth 49
126-7 famine. 50
Iras. Go, you wild bedfellow, you cannot 51
128 soothsay. 52
Char. Nay, if an oily palm be not a fruitful 53
129 prognostication, I cannot scratch mine ear. Pri- 54
130-1 thee, tell her but a worky-day fortune. 55
132 *Sooth.* Your fortunes are alike. 56
133 *Iras.* But how, but how? give me particulars. 57
134 *Sooth.* I have said. 58
Iras. Am I not an inch of fortune better than 59
135 she? 60
Char. Well, if you were but an inch of fortune 61
136-7 better than I, where would you choose it? 62
138 *Iras.* Not in my husband's nose. 63

```
22   same as 21
23   same as 21
24   same as 21
25   same as 21, ML1, less GCa, GS1, LK1, TN1; aX: GCa; bX: NM1
26   same as 25, NM1, RH1; less aX, bX; bX: EdT
27   same as 26, MTh; less bX; aX: EdT; bX: SP1, KyB, WA1, OA1, RH1
28   same as 27, KyB; less aX, bX; aX: SP1, WA1, OA1, NM1, RH1
29   same as 28; less aX
30   same as 29


31   same as 29, less KyB, BT1, ML1


32   same as 31, less MTh


33   X: Cap, Bel,  Inc, In2, JKP, WM1, SP1, Cum, ChC, Lac, Hal, JL1, HIM*
34   same as 33
35   same as 33, KyB, EdT
36   X: GCa, Cap, Bel, Inc, In2, JKP, WM1, SP1, Cum, ChC, Lac, Hal, JL1*
37   same as 36
38   same as 36, BA1; bX: BT1
39   same as 36; R: BT1; aX: BA1
40   same as 36, less KyB, LoC, OA1; bX: BA1
41   same as 40, EdT, BT1, OA1, BA1, less Inc; less bX
42   same as 41, less GCa
43   X: Cap, Bel, In2, JKP, WM1, SP1, Cum, ChC, Lac, Hal, JL1, HIM, LiL*
44   same as 43
45   same as 43, BT1, WA1
46   same as 45; ADD 1: KyB
47   X: Cap, Bel, In2, JKP, WM1, SP1, Cum, ChC, Lac, Hal, JL1, HIM, KyB*
48   same as 47
49   same as 47
50   same as 47, NM1

51   same as 50, BA1
52   same as 51, GS1
53   same as 52, RA1, AF1, ER1, TN1, less GS1; aX: GS1
54   same as 53, less SM1, BA1, NM1, ER1, TN1; less aX; aX:SM1,BA1,NM1,ER1,TN1
55   same as 54, less WA1, RA1, AF1; less aX
56   same as 55, less EdT
57   same as 56, TN1
58   same as 57
59   same as 57
60   same as 57, OA1
61   same as 60, Inc, EdT, SM1, WA1, BA1, NM1, IP1
62   same as 61
63   same as 61
```

```
*12:33 LiL, MTh, LoC, SM1, WA1, TaB, GS1, BH1, ML1, ER1, TN1
*12:36 HIM, KyB, LiL, MTh, EdT, LoC, SM1, WA1, OA1, NM1, TaB
*12:43 MTh, LaC, TaB, LK1              *12:47 LiL, MTh, EdT, LoC, BT1,SM1
   WA1, TaB, LK1
```

139	*Char.* Our worser thoughts heavens mend!	64
	Alexas,—come, his fortune, his fortune! O, le	65
140	him marry a woman that cannot go, sweet Isis!	66
141	beseech thee! and let her die too, and give him	67
142	a worse! and let worse follow worse, till the wors	68
143	of all follow him laughing to his grave, fifty-fol	69
144	a cuckold! Good Isis, hear me this prayer, though	70
145	thou deny me a matter of more weight; good	71
146	Isis, I beseech thee!	72
	Iras. Amen. Dear goddess, hear that prayer	73
147	of the people! for, as it is a heart-breaking to see	74
148	a handsome man loose-wived, so it is a deadly	75
149	sorrow to behold a foul knave uncuckolded: there-	76
150	fore, dear Isis, keep decorum, and fortune him	77
151	accordingly!	78
152	*Char.* Amen.	79
	Alex. Lo, now, if it lay in their hands to make	80
153	me a cuckold, they would make themselves	81
154–5	whores, but they'ld do't!	82
157	*Eno.* Hush! here comes Antony.	
158	*Char.* Not he; the queen	83

156	*Enter* CLEOPATRA.

159	*Cleo.* Saw you my lord?	
160	*Eno.* No, lady.	
161	*Cleo.* Was he not here!	84
162	*Char.* No, madam.	85
163	*Cleo.* He was disposed to mirth; but on the sudden	86
164–5	A Roman thought hath struck him. Enobarbus	87
166	*Eno.* Madam?	88
167	*Cleo.* Seek him, and bring him hither. Where's Alexas?	89
168	*Alex.* Here, at your service. My lord ap-	
169	proaches.	90
171	*Cleo.* We will not look upon him: go with us	91
172	[*Exeunt.*	

170	*Enter* ANTONY *with a* Messenger *and* Attendants

173–4	*Mess.* Fulvia thy wife first came into the field	92
175	*Ant.* Against my brother Lucius?	93
	Mess. Ay:	94
176–7	But soon that war had end, and the time's state	95
	Made friends of them, jointing their force 'gainst	
178	Cæsar;	96
179	Whose better issue in the war, from Italy,	97

64   same as 61, TN1, less BT1, SM1, OA1, NM1, IP1; aX: BT1, SM1, OA1,*
65   same as 64, less LK1; less aX; bX: GS1
66   same as 65, GS1; less bX
67   same as 66; bX: ML1
68   same as 66, ML1
69   same as 68
70   same as 68, RH1; bX: BH1
71   same as 70, SM1, RH1
72   same as 71, BA1
73   same as 72, BT1, OA1, less BA1, ML1; bX: BH1
74   same as 73, BH1; less bX: bX: RA1
75   same as 74, RA1; less bX
76   sae as 75; B: NM1
77   same as 75, ML1
78   same as 77
79   same as 77, less RA1, ML1
80   same as 79, NM1, SFr, less OA1, BH1
81   same as 80, less SFr; bX: OA1
82   same as 81, OA1

83   X: Bel, Inc, In2, JKP, WM1, Cum, ChC, Ha1, JL1, KyB, LiL, LoC, BT1,
      TaB; bX: SM1, OA1, LK1

84   X: Bel, In2, ChC, Ha1, JL1, KyB, LiL, LoC, BT1, SM1, OA1, TaB;R: Cap*
85   same as 84, less R, bX; aX: JKP; N: Inc

86   same as 85; less aX, N
87   same as 86; bX: LK1; ADD 13: WM1
88   same as 87, WM1, LK1; less bX, ADD; ADD 1: Cum

89   same as 88, Cum, less LK1; less ADD; bX: LK·

90   same as 89, less WM1; less bX; aX: Cap, WM1, LK1
91   same as 90, less Cum; less aX

92   X: ER1; N: KyB; MOVE 92-204 to follow 11: 62: BT1
93   X: ER1
94   X: ER1; N: LoC
95   X: ChC, KyB, LiL, LoC, ER1, LK1; R: ML1

96   X: ChC, KyB, LiL, LoC, ER1, aX: ML1, LK1
97   X: ChC, JL1, KyB, LiL, LoC, AF1, ER1, LK1

*12:64 NM1, IP1, GS1   *12:84 bX: JKP

180	Upon the first encounter, drave them.	
181	*Ant.* Well, what worst?	98
	Mess. The nature of bad news infects the	
182	teller. 99	99
183	*Ant.* When it concerns the fool or coward. On:	100
184	Things that are past are done with me. 'Tis thus;	101
185	Who tells me true, though in his tale lie death,	102
186	I hear him as he flatter'd.	
	Mess. Labienus—	103
187-8	This is stiff news—hath, with his Parthian force,	104
	Extended Asia from Euphrates;	105
189	His conquering banner shook from Syria	106
190	To Lydia and to Ionia;	107
191	Whilst—	
192	*Ant.* Antony, thou wouldst say,—	
193	*Mess.* O, my lord!	108
194	*Ant.* Speak to me home, mince not the gene-	
	ral tongue:	109
195-6	Name Cleopatra as she is call'd in Rome; 110	110
197	Rail thou in Fulvia's phrase; and taunt my faults	111
198	With such full license as both truth and malice	112
	Have power to utter. O, then we bring forth	
199	weeds,	113
	When our quick minds lie still; and our ills	
200	told us	114
201	Is as our earing. Fare thee well awhile.	115
202(3)	*Mess.* At your noble pleasure. [*Exit.*	116
	Ant. From Sicyon, ho, the news! Speak	
204	there!	117
205	*First Att.* The man from Sicyon,—is there	
206	such an one?	118
207	*Sec. Att.* He stays upon your will.	
208	*Ant.* Let him appear.	119
209	These strong Egyptian fetters I must break, 120	120
210	Or lose myself in dotage.	
211	*Enter another* Messenger.	
212	What are you?	121
213	*Sec. Mess.* Fulvia thy wife is dead.	
214	*Ant.* Where died she?	122
	Sec. Mess. In Sicyon:	123
215	Her length of sickness, with what else more	
216	serious	124
217	Importeth thee to know, this bears.	
217+1	[*Gives a letter.*	
218	*Ant.* Forbear me.	125

98   X: JL1, KyB, LiL, LoC; a̲X̲: ChC, AF1, ER1, LK1; c̲X̲: ML1

99   X: JL1, TN1
100   X: JL1, ML1, TN1
101   X: ChC, JL1, KyB, LoC, SM1, RA1, BH1, TN1; b̲X̲: ER1
102   X: JL1, KyB, RA1, BH1, ER1, TN1

103   X: JL1; a̲X̲: KyB, RA1, BH1, ER1, TN1
104   X: JL1; R̄: Bel, Inc, Cum, ML1; a̲X̲: GCa, Cap, In2, EdT, TN1; b̲X̲:ER1
105   X: JL1, ĒR1; R: In2, ML1
106   X: ChC, JL1, L̄oC; R: In2
107   X: ChC, JL1, LoC, ĒR1

108   X: JL1

109   X: JL1 ; a̲X̲: Cap
110   X: JL1
111   X: JL1
112   X: JL1

113   X: JL1; b̲X̲: Cap, In2, KyB, BT1, OA1, BA1, NM1, RH1, JS1, GS1, RH1,
       BH1, J̄P̄1, AF1, ML1, ER1, LK1
114   X: Cap, In2, JL1, KyB, BT1, OA1, BA1, NM1, RA1, JS1, GS1, RH1, BH1*
115   X: In2, JL1, BT1, NM1, JS1, RH1, JP1, ML1; a̲X̲: Cap, KyB, OA1, BA1*
116   X:In2, Lac, Hal, JL1, HIM, EdT, BT1, SM1, NM̄1, JS1, RH1; a̲X̲: JP1

117   X: Lac, Hal, JL1, HIM, EdT, NM1, JS1, RH1, AF1, ML1; b̲X̲: KyB, BT1,
       WA1, BA1, RH1, JP1
118   X: Lac, Hal, JL1, HIM, KyB, EdT, BA1, NM1, RA1, JS1, RH1, JPL, AF1,
       ML1; b̲X̲: LoC, WA1; N: Cum
119   same as 118, less OA1; less b̲X̲, N; a̲X̲: BT1; N: LiL; A̲D̲D̲ 2: Inc
120   X: Lac, Hal, JL1, HIM, EdT, N̄M1, JS̄1, RH1, J̄P̄1

121   X: Hal, JL1, NM1, JS1, RH1, JP1; a̲X̲: Lac, HIM, EdT

122   b̲X̲: TN1; N̲: LoC, JP1
123   X̄: TN1

124

125

*1̲2̲:̲1̲1̲4̲ JP1, AF1, ML1, ER1, LK1   *1̲2̲:̲1̲1̲5̲ RH1, GS1, BH1, AF1
   ER1, LK1; b̲X̲: Lac, Hal, HIM, EdT, SM1

218+1	[*Exit Sec. Messenger.*	
	There's a great spirit gone! Thus did I de-	
219	sire it:	126
220	What our contempt doth often hurl from us,	127
221	We wish it ours again; the present pleasure,	128
222	By revolution lowering, does become **129**	129
223	The opposite of itself: she's good, being gone;	130
	The hand could pluck her back that shoved	
224	her on.	131
225	I must from this enchanting queen break off:	132
226	Ten thousand harms, more than the ills I know,	133
227,29	My idleness doth hatch. How now! Enobarbus!	134

228	*Re-enter* ENOBARBUS.	
230	*Eno.* What's your pleasure, sir?	135
231	*Ant.* I must with haste from hence.	136
	Eno. Why, then, we kill all our women: we	137
232	see how mortal an unkindness is to them; if they	138
233–4	suffer our departure, death's the word.	139
235	*Ant.* I must be gone. **140**	140
	Eno. Under a compelling occasion, let women	141
236	die: it were pity to cast them away for nothing;	142
237	though between them and a great cause, they	143
238	should be esteemed nothing. Cleopatra, catch-	144
239	ing but the least noise of this, dies instantly;	145
240	I have seen her die twenty times upon far poorer	146
241	moment: I do think there is mettle in death,	147
	which commits some loving act upon her, she	148
242–3	hath such a celerity in dying.	149
244	*Ant.* She is cunning past man's thought. **150**	150
	Eno. Alack, sir, no; her passions are made	151
245	of nothing but the finest part of pure love: we	152
246	cannot call her winds and waters sighs and tears;	153
247	they are greater storms and tempests than alma-	154
248	nacs can report: this cannot be cunning in her:	155
249	if it be, she makes a shower of rain as well	156
250	as Jove.	157
251	*Ant.* Would I had never seen her!	158
	Eno. O, sir, you had then left unseen a won-	159
252	derful piece of work; which not to have been	160
253–4	blest withal would have discredited your travel.	161
255	*Ant.* Fulvia is dead.	162
256	*Eno.* Sir?	163
257	*Ant.* Fulvia is dead.	164
258	*Eno.* Fulvia!	165
259	*Ant.* Dead.	166

```
126
127   X: JS1
128   X: JS1; bX: In2, JKP, WM1, KyB, SM1, WA1, OA1, BA1, IP1, RA1, GS1*
129   X: In2, J̄KP, WM1, KyB, BT1, SM1, WA1, OAI, BA1, IP1, RA1, JS1, GS1*
130   X: BT1; aX: In2, JKP, WM1, KyB, SM1, WA1, OA1, BA1, IP1, RA1, JS1,
          GS1, R̄H̄1, BH1, ML1, TN1
131   X: JKP, BA1
132   X: Ky₤
133   X: KyB
134   R: GCa ; aX: KyB; bX: Cum; cX: Cap; ADD 1: LK1


135
136   R: In2
137   b̄X: In2, BA1, IP1, RH1, GS1
138   X̄: BA1, RH1; aX: In2, IP1, GS1
139   X: BA1, RH1
140   X: JKP, BA1
141   X: JKP, SM1, WA1, BA1, TaB, RH1, ML1, LK1
142   same as 141; bX: In2, IP1, TN1
143   X: In2, JKP, S̄M̄1, WA1, BA1, IP1, TaB, RA1, RH1, ML1, LK1, TN1
144   aX: In2, JKP, SM1, WA1, BA1, IP1, TaB, RA1, RH1, ML1, LK1, TN1
145
146   R: In2; bX: GCa, Inc, JKP, WM1, Cum, LiL, EdT, LoC, BA1, GS1
147   X: GCa, Īnc, In2, JKP, WM1, Cum, LiL, EdT, LoC, BA1, GS1;bX: Cap,ChC
148   same as 147, Cap, ChC, less BA1; less bX; aX: BA1
149   same as 148; less aX
150
151   X: GCa, Cap, Inc, In2, JKP, WM1, Cum; bX: TN1
152   same as 151; less bX; aX: TN1
153   X: GCa, Cap, Inc, Īn2, J̄KP, WM1, Cum, BT1, BH1
154   same as 153
155   same as 153; aX: WM1, BT1; bX: GS1, ML1, TN1
156   same as 153, W̄M̄1, ML1, TN1
157   same as 153, less BT1
158   X: GCa, Cap, Inc, In2, Cum; bX: Cap
159   X: GCa, Cap, Inc, In2, JKP, C̄um
160   same as 159; bX: BA1, GS1, TN1
161   X: GCa, Inc, Īn2, JKP, Cum, BA1, GS1, TN1
162   X: JKP
163   X: In2
164   X: In2
165   X: JKP
166   X: JKP

+12:128  RH1, BH1, ML1, TN1            *12:129 RH1, BH1, ML1, TN1
```

Eno. Why, sir, give the gods a thankful sacrifice. When it pleaseth their deities to take the wife of a man from him, it shows to man the tailors of the earth; comforting therein, that when old robes are worn out, there are members to make new. If there were no more women but Fulvia, then had you indeed a cut, and the case to be lamented: this grief is crowned with consolation; your old smock brings forth a new petticoat: and indeed the tears live in an onion that should water this sorrow.

Ant. The business she hath broached in the state
Cannot endure my absence.   179

Eno. And the business you have broached here cannot be without you; especially that of Cleopatra's, which wholly depends on your abode.

Ant. No more light answers. Let our officers
Have notice what we purpose. I shall break
The cause of our expedience to the queen,
And get her leave to part. For not alone
The death of Fulvia, with more urgent touches,
Do strongly speak to us; but the letters too
Of many our contriving friends in Rome
Petition us at home: Sextus Pompeius   190
Hath given the dare to Cæsar, and commands
The empire of the sea: our slippery people,
Whose love is never link'd to the deserver
Till his deserts are past, begin to throw
Pompey the Great and all his dignities
Upon his son; who, high in name and power,
Higher than both in blood and life, stands up
For the main soldier: whose quality, going on,
The sides o' the world may danger: much is
     breeding,   199
Which, like the courser's hair, hath yet but life,
And not a serpent's poison. Say, our pleasure,
To such whose place is under us, requires
Our quick remove from hence.

Eno. I shall do 't.   [*Exeunt.*

SCENE III. *The same. Another room.*

Enter CLEOPATRA, CHARMIAN, IRAS, *and*
          ALEXAS.

Cleo. Where is he?

167
168
169
170
171
172
173
174
175
176
177
178
179
180
181
182
183
184
185
186
187
188
189
190
191
192
193
194
195
196
197
198
199
200
201
202
203
204

260
261
262
263
264
265
266
267
268-9
270
271
272
273-4
275-6
277
278
279
280
281
282
283
284
285
286
287
288
289
290
291
292
293
294
295
296
297
297+1
298
298+1
299

167   X: Bel; b̲X̲: GCa, Inc, In2, WM1, SP1, Cum, BT1, SM1, BA1, IP1, JS1*
168   X: GCa, C̲ap, Bel, Inc, In2, JKP, WM1, SP1, Cum, BT1, SM1, BA1, IP1*
169   same as 168, WA1, BH1, ER1; less b̲X̲
170   same as 169
171   X: Cap, Bel, In2, JKP, SP1, BT1, WA1, BH1, ML1, ER1; a̲X̲: GCa, Inc*
172   X: Bel, EdT, LoC, WA1, NM1; a̲X̲: Cap, BH1, ML1, ER1, TN1;b̲X̲:ChC,JL1
173   X: Bel, ChC, JL1, EdT, LoC, W̲A̲1, NM1
174   same as 173, In2, SM1, less NM1; a̲X̲: NM1; b̲X̲: JKP, Cum
175   same as 174, Cum, less SM1; less a̲X̲, b̲X̲; a̲X̲: JKP, SM1; b̲X̲: GS1, BH1
176   X: Bel, ChC, EdT, LoC, GS1, BH1; a̲X̲: J̲L̲1, W̲A̲1; b̲X̲: ML1
177   same as 176, ML1, less Bel; less a̲X̲, b̲X̲

178   X: In2, JKP, BH1
179   X: In2, JKP
180   X: Bel, In2, JKP, TN1
181   same as 180
182   X: Bel, In2, JKP
183   a̲X̲: Bel; b̲X̲: JKP, TN1
184   a̲x̲: JKP, T̲N̲1; b̲X̲: ChC, LiL, LoC; A̲D̲D̲ 2: JKP
185   X̲: ChC, LiL, LoC
186   X: In2, ChC, LiL, LoC; R: ML1; b̲X̲: Cap, JL1, KyB, BA1, JS1, GS1, JP1*
187   X: Cap, In2, ChC, JL1, K̲yB, LiL, LoC, BA1, JS1, GS1, JP1, ER1, TN1*
188   same as 187, ML1; less b̲X̲; a̲X̲: BT1, IP1; b̲X̲: LK;
189   same as 188, LK1; less a̲X̲, b̲X̲
190   X: Cap, In2, KyB, BA1, J̲S̲1, G̲S̲1, JP1, ER1, LK1; a̲X̲: ChC, JL1, LiL,*
191   same as 190, RA1, less JS1; less a̲X̲, b̲X̲
192   same as 191; b̲X̲: ChC, Lac, JL1, L̲i̲L̲, M̲T̲h, EdT, LoC, OA1
193   X: Cap, In2, C̲hC, Lac, JL1, HIM, KyB, LiL, MTh, EdT, LoC, OA1, BA1*
194   same as 193
195   same as 193
196   same as 193; b̲X̲: JKP, WM1, IP1, RH1, TN1; A̲D̲D̲ 8: JKP
197   X: CaP, In2, J̲KP, WM1, ChC, Lac, JL1, HIM, K̲yB, LiL, MTh, EdT, LoC*
198   same as 187, ML1, less WM1, RH1, TN1; less b̲X̲; a̲X̲: WM1, RH1, TN1;
      b̲X̲: SM1, WA1
199   X: C̲ap, In2, JKP, KyB, SM1, WA1, BA1, IP1, RA1̇, GS1, JP1, ML1, ER1*
200   X: Cap, In2, WM1, KyB, BT1, SM1, WA1, BA1, IP1, RA1, JS1, GS1, RH1*
201   X: Cap, ER1; a̲X̲: In2, WM1, KyB, BT1, SM1, WA1, BA1, IP1, RA1, J
202   X: ER1
203   X: ER1
204   X: BT1, ER1; A̲D̲D̲ 1: OA1; A̲D̲D̲ 2: JL1; A̲D̲D̲ 3: WM1

Scene 13

*12:167 GS1, BH1, TN1   *12:168 JS1, GS1, RH1, ML1, TN1; b̲X̲:
  WA1, BH1, ER1   *12:171 Cum, SM1, BA1, IP1, JS1, GS1, RH1; b̲X̲:
  LoC, NM1   *12:186 ER1, TN1   *12:187 b̲X̲: BT1,
  IP1, ML1   *12:190 LoC, ML1, TN1; b̲X̲: RA1
*13:193 RA1, GS1, JP1, ER1, L̲K̲1   *12:197 BT1, OA1, BA1, IP1,RA1,
  GS1, PH1, JP1, ER1, LK1, TN1;b̲X̲: ML⟩ *12:199 a̲X̲: ChC, Lac, JL1, HIM,
  LiL, MTh, EdT, LoC, OA1, LK1;b̲X̲: TS̲I̲*12:200 BH1, JP1, ML1, ER1, LK1, TN1
             TN1

300	*Char.* I did not see him since.	1
301	*Cleo.* See where he is, who's with him, what	
302	he does:	2
303	I did not send you: if you find him sad,	3
304	Say I am dancing; if in mirth, report	4
305	That I am sudden sick: quick, and return.	5
305+1	[*Exit Alexas.*	
306	*Char.* Madam, methinks, if you did love him dearly,	6
307	You do not hold the method to enforce	7
308	The like from him.	
309	*Cleo.* What should I do, I do not?	8
310	*Char.* In each thing give him way, cross him in nothing.	9
311	*Cleo.* Thou teachest like a fool; the way to lose him. 10	10
312	*Char.* Tempt him not so too far; I wish, forbear:	11
313	In time we hate that which we often fear.	12
315	But here comes Antony.	
314	*Enter* ANTONY.	
316	*Cleo.* I am sick and sullen.	13
317	*Ant.* I am sorry to give breathing to my purpose,—	14
318	*Cleo.* Help me away, dear Charmian; I shall fall:	15
319	It cannot be thus long, the sides of nature	16
320	Will not sustain it.	
321	*Ant.* Now, my dearest queen,—	17
322	*Cleo.* Pray you, stand farther from me.	
323	*Ant.* What's the matter?	18
324	*Cleo.* I know, by that same eye, there's some good news.	19
325	What says the married woman? You may go: 20	20
326	Would she had never given you leave to come!	21
327	Let her not say 'tis I that keep you here:	22
328	I have no power upon you: hers you are.	23
329	*Ant.* The gods best know,—	
330	*Cleo.* O, never was there queen	24
331	So mightily betray'd! yet at the first	25
332	I saw the treasons planted.	
333	*Ant.* Cleopatra,—	26
334	*Cleo.* Why should I think you can be mine and true,	27
335	Though you in swearing shake the throned gods,	28

```
 1    X: WM1; aX: BH1; bX: JL1; ADD 2: JL1

 2    X: WM1
 3    X: WM1
 4    X: WM1
 5    X: WM1

 6    X: WM1
 7    X: WM1

 8    X: WM1; bX: NM1

 9    X: WM1, NM1

10    X: WM1, NM1

11    X: WM1, KyB, NM1, ML1, TN1; bX: In2, BA1, JS1, GA1, RH1
12    X: In2, WM1, KyB, BA1, NM1, JS1, GS1, RH1, ML1, TN1



13    aX: WM1, JS1

14

15
16

17

18

19
20    ADD 1: WM1
21
22
23

24    X: JKP, WM1
25    X: JKP, WM1

26    X: JKP, WM1

27    X: JKP, WM1
28    X: JKP, WM1, JS1, GS1, BH1, TN1
```

336	Who have been false to Fulvia? Riotous mad-	
337	ness,	29
338	To be entangled with those mouth-made vows, 30	30
339	Which break themselves in swearing!	
340	*Ant.* Most sweet queen,—	31
	Cleo. Nay, pray you, seek no colour for your	
341	going,	32
342	But bid farewell, and go: when you sued	
343	staying,	33
344	Then was the time for words: no going then:	34
345	Eternity was in our lips and eyes,	35
346	Bliss in our brows' bent; none our parts so poor,	36
347	But was a race of heaven: they are so still,	37
348	Or thou, the greatest soldier of the world,	38
349	Art turn'd the greatest liar.	
350	*Ant.* How now, lady!	39
	Cleo. I would I had thy inches; thou shouldst	
351	know **40**	40
352	There were a heart in Egypt.	
353	*Ant.* Hear me, queen:	41
354	The strong necessity of time commands	42
355	Our services awhile; but my full heart	43
356	Remains in use with you. Our Italy	44
357	Shines o'er with civil swords: Sextus Pompeius	45
358	Makes his approaches to the port of Rome:	46
359	Equality of two domestic powers	47
	Breed scrupulous faction: the hated, grown to	
360	strength,	48
361	Are newly grown to love: the condemn'd Pompey,	49
362	Rich in his father's honour, creeps apace **50**	50
363	Into the hearts of such as have not thrived	51
364	Upon the present state, whose numbers threaten:	52
365	And quietness, grown sick of rest, would purge	53
366	By any desperate change: my more particular,	54
	And that which most with·you should safe my	
367	going,	55
368	Is Fulvia's death.	56
	Cleo. Though age from folly could not give	
369	me freedom,	57
370	It does from childishness: can Fulvia die?	58
371	*Ant.* She's dead, my queen:	59
372	Look here, and at thy sovereign leisure read **60**	60
373	The garboils she awaked; at the last, best:	61
374	See when and where she died.	
375	*Cleo.* O most false love!	62
376	Where be the sacred vials thou shouldst fill	63

```
29   X: JKP, WM1; bX: JS1, RH1
30   X: JKP, WM1, KyB, JS1, RH1

31   X: KyB; aX: JKP, WM1, JS1, RH1

32

33
34
35
36   bX: Cum
37   X: Cum; bX: In2
38   X: In2, Cum

39   X: In2, Cum; bX: Cap, JKP, WM1

40   X: Cap, In2, JKP, WM1, Cum

41   aX: Cap, In2, JKP, WM1, Cum
42
43
44   bX: RA1
45   X: RA1; bX: Cap, In2, JL1, HIM, KyB, MTh, EdT, OA1
46   X: Cap, In2, Lac, JL1, HIM, KyB, MTh, EdT, SM1, WA1, OA1, RA1, BH1
47   X: Cap, In2, WM1, ChC, Lac, Ha1, JL1, HIM, KyB, MTh, EdT, LoC, BT1,
        SM1, WA1, OA1, BA1, IP1, RA1, JS1, GS1, BH1, ML1, TN1
48   same as 47, less LoC, BT1; aX: BT1
49   same as 48, less WA1, RA1; less aX; aX: WA1, RA1; bX: JKP, BT1
50   X: Cap, In2, JKP, ChC, Lac, Ha1, JL1, HIM, KyB, MTh, EdT, BT1, OA1, BA1*
51   same as 50, LoC; R: ML1
52   same as 51, ML1; less R; bX: SM1, WA1
53   X: Cap, In2, JKP, WM1, Lac, JL1, HIM, KyB, MTh, EdT, LoC, BT1, SM1, WA1*
54   X: Lac, EdT, TN1; aX: Cap, In2, JKP, WM1, JL1, HIM, KyB, MTh, LoC, BT1,
        SM1, WA1, OA1, RA1

55
56   X: EdT

57   X: JKP, KyB, EdT; R: In2
58   X: JKP, EdT; aX: In2; KyB
59   X: JKP, EdT
60   X: In2, JKP, KyB, EdT, LK1, TN1
61   same as 60, BA1

62   X: In2, EdT; aX: LK1
63   X: JKP, EdT
```

*13:50 IP1, JS1, GS1, TN1   *13:53 OA1, RH1, TN1; aX: ML1

377	With sorrowful water? Now I see, I see,	64
378	In Fulvia's death, how mine received shall be.	65
	Ant. Quarrel no more, but be prepared to	
379	know	66
380	The purposes I bear; which are, or cease,	67
381	As you shall give the advice. By the fire	68
382	That quickens Nilus' slime, I go from hence	69
383	Thy soldier, servant; making peace or war 70	70
384	As thou affect'st.	
385	*Cleo.* Cut my lace, Charmian, come;	71
386	But let it be: I am quickly ill, and well,	72
387	So Antony loves.	
388	*Ant.* My precious queen, forbear:	73
389	And give true evidence to his love, which stands	74
390	An honourable trial.	
391	*Cleo.* So Fulvia told me.	75
392	I prithee, turn aside and weep for her:	76
393	Then bid adieu to me, and say the tears	77
394	Belong to Egypt: good now, play one scene	78
395	Of excellent dissembling; and let it look	79
396	Like perfect honour.	
397	*Ant.* You'll heat my blood: no more. 80	80
	Cleo. You can do better yet; but this is	
398	meetly.	31
399	*Ant.* Now, by my sword,—	
400	*Cleo.* And target. Still he mends:	82
	But this is not the best. Look, prithee, Char-	
401	mian,	83
402	How this Herculean Roman does become	84
403	The carriage of his chafe.	85
404	*Ant.* I'll leave you, lady.	
405	*Cleo.* Courteous lord, one word.	86
406	Sir, you and I must part, but that's not it:	87
407	Sir, you and I have loved, but there's not it:	88
408	That you know well: something it is I would,—	89
409	O, my oblivion is a very Antony, 90	90
410	And I am all forgotten.	
411	*Ant.* But that your royalty	91
412	Holds idleness your subject, I should take you	92
413	For idleness itself.	
414	*Cleo.* 'Tis sweating labour	93
415	To bear such idleness so near the heart	94
416	As Cleopatra this. But, sir, forgive me;	95
417	Since my becomings kill me, when they do not	96
418	Eye well to you: your honour calls you hence;	97
419	Therefore be deaf to my unpitied folly,	98

64 X JKP, EdT
65 X: JKP, EdT

66 X: JKP, EdT; b̲X̲: Cap, TN1
67 X: Cap, JKP, E̅d̅T̅, TN1; b̲X̲: JS1
68 X: EdT, JS1; a̲X̲: Cap, J̅K̅P̅, TN1
69 X: EdT; R̲: Cap; a̲X̲: JS1
70 X: EdT

71 X: EdT; b̲X̲: JKP, WM1, Cum, ChC, LoC
72 X: JKP, W̅M̅1, Cum, ChC, EdT, LoC; b̲X̲: Bel

73 X: Bel, JKP, WM1, Cum, EdT; a̲X̲: ChC, LoC
74 X: Bel, JKP, WM1, EdT

75 X: Bel, WM1, EdT; a̲X̲: JKP
76 X: Bel
77 X: Bel
78 X: Bel
79 X: Bel; b̲X̲: WM1

80 X: Bel; a̲X̲: WM1; b̲X̲: Cum

81 X: Bel, Cum

82 X: Bel, Cum

83 X: Bel, Cum; b̲X̲: WM1
84 X: Bel, WM1, C̅u̅m̅; R̲: ML1
85 X: Bel, WM1, Cum, M̅L̅1; B̲: SM1

86 X: Bel; a̲X̲: Cap
87 X: Bel
88 X: Bel
89 X: Bel
90 X: Bel, Cum

91 X: Bel, Cum; b̲X̲: Cap, JS1
92 X: Cap, Bel, C̅u̅m̅, JS1

93 same as 92; b̲X̲: In2, BT1, NM1
94 X: Cap, Bel, I̅n̅2, Cum, BT1, NM1, JS1
95 XL Cap, Bel, In2, JS1; a̲X̲: Cum, BT1, NM1
96 X: Cap, Bel, In2, KyB, E̅d̅T̅, BT1, JS1
97 a̲X̲: Cap, Bel, In2, KyB, EdT, BT1, JS1
98

420	And all the gods go with you! upon your sword	99
421	Sit laurel victory! and smooth success **100**	100
422	Be strew'd before your feet!	
423	*Ant.* Let us go. Come;	101
424	Our separation so abides, and flies,	102
425	That thou, residing here, go'st yet with me,	103
426	And I, hence fleeting, here remain with thee.	104
427	Away! *[Exeunt.*	105
427+1	**SCENE IV.** *Rome. Cæsar's house.*	
428	*Enter* OCTAVIUS CÆSAR, *reading a letter,*	
429	LEPIDUS, *and their* Train.	
	Cæs. You may see, Lepidus, and henceforth	
430	know,	1
431	It is not Cæsar's natural vice to hate	2
432	Our great competitor: from Alexandria	3
433	This is the news: he fishes, drinks, and wastes	4
434	The lamps of night in revel; is not more manlike	5
435	Than Cleopatra; nor the queen of Ptolemy	6
436	More womanly than he; hardly gave audience, or	7
	Vouchsafed to think he had partners: you shall	
437	find there	8
438	A man who is the abstract of all faults	9
439	That all men follow.	
440	*Lep.* I must not think there are **10**	10
441	Evils enow to darken all his goodness:	11
442	His faults in him seem as the spots of heaven,	12
443	More fiery by night's blackness: hereditary,	13
444	Rather than purchased; what he cannot change,	14
445	Than what he chooses.	15
	Cæs. You are too indulgent. Let us grant, it	
446	is not	16
447	Amiss to tumble on the bed of Ptolemy;	17
448	To give a kingdom for a mirth; to sit	18
449	And keep the turn of tippling with a slave: **19**	19
450	To reel the streets at noon, and stand the buffet	20
	With knaves that smell of sweat: say this becomes	
451	him,—	21
452	As his composure must be rare indeed	22
	Whom these things cannot blemish,—yet must	
453	Antony	23
454	No way excuse his soils, when we do bear	24
455	So great weight in his lightness. If he fill'd	25
456	His vacancy with his voluptuousness,	26
457	Full surfeits, and the dryness of his bones,	27

99
100

101   b<u>X</u>: LiL
102   <u>X</u>: LiL
103   X: LiL
104   X: LiL
105   X: In2, ChC, LiL; <u>ADD</u> 2: LK1; <u>ADD</u> 5: ChC, LoC; <u>Insert</u> <u>15</u>: 1-78:WM1

<u>Scene 14</u>

<u>ALL</u> <u>CUT</u>: EdT, BT1
  1   X: Hal, JP1; <u>MOVE</u> 1-25a to follow <u>15</u>: 15: OA1; <u>MOVE</u> 1-83 to open:*
  2   X: JP1
  3   X: JP1
  4   X: JP1
  5   X: JP1
  6   X: JP1
  7   X: JP1; b<u>X</u>: WM1, BA1

  8   X: WM1, JP1; a<u>X</u>: BA1; b<u>X</u>: JS1
  9   X: WM1, Hal, <u>JS1</u>, JP1

10   a<u>X</u>: WM1, Hal, JS1, JP1
11
12   X: ChC, LiL, LoC, WA1, ER1; b<u>X</u>: In2
13   same as 12; less b<u>X</u>; a<u>X</u>: In2; b<u>X</u>: IP1
14   same as 12, IP1; <u>less b<u>X</u></u>, b<u>X</u>: A<u>F1</u>
15   same as 14, AF1; less b<u>X</u>

16   X: Hal; b<u>X</u>: Cum
17   X: In2, Cum, Hal, JL1
18   X: Cum, Hal, BA1; b<u>X</u>: WM1, LiL
19   X: WM1, Cum, Hal, <u>LiL</u>, BA1
20   X: WM1, Cum, ChC, Hal, JL1, LiL, LoC; b<u>X</u>: In2, TaB

21   X: Cum, Hal, TaB; a<u>X</u>: In2, WM1, ChC, JL1, LiL, LoC; b<u>X</u>: TN1
22   X: SP1, ChC, Hal, <u>JL1</u>, LoC, BT1, WA1, TaB, BH1, <u>E</u>R1, <u>TN1</u>

23   X: Hal, BT1, WA1, TaB; a<u>X</u>: CP1, ChC, JL1, LoC, RH1, ER1, <u>T</u>N1
24   X: Hal, BT1, WA1; R: ML<u>1</u>; b<u>X</u>: In2
25   X: In2, JKP, Hal, <u>BT1</u>; a<u>X</u>: <u>WA1</u>, ML1; b<u>X</u>: JKP, WM1, ChC, JL1, LiL, LoC*
26   X: In2, JKP, WM1, ChC, <u>Hal</u>, JL1, KyB, <u>LiL</u>, LoC, BT1, OA1, NM1, TaB, RA1*
27   same as 26

*<u>14</u>: 1 KyB, LiL, BT1, TaB   *<u>14:25</u> OA1, NM1, TaB, RA1, JS1,
   RH1, AF1, ER1, LK1, TN1   *<u>14:26</u> <u>JS1</u>, RH1, AF1, ER1, LK1, TN1

458	Call on him for't: but to confound such time,	28
459	That drums him from his sport, and speaks as loud	29
460	As his own state and ours,—'tis to be chid 30	30
461	As we rate boys, who, being mature in know-ledge,	31
462	Pawn their experience to their present pleasure,	32
63	And so rebel to judgement.	

464	*Enter a* Messenger.	
465	*Lep.* Here's more news.	33
	Mess. Thy biddings have been done; and every hour,	
466		34
467	Most noble Cæsar, shalt thou have report	35
468	How 'tis abroad. Pompey is strong at sea;	36
469	And it appears he is beloved of those	37
479	That only have fear'd Cæsar: to the ports	38
471	The discontents repair, and men's reports	39
472	Give him much wrong'd.	
473	*Cæs.* I should have known no less.	40
474	It hath been taught us from the primal state, 41	41
475	That he which is was wish'd until he were;	42
476	And the ebb'd man, ne'er loved till ne'er worth love,	
477		43
	Comes dear'd by being lack'd. This common body,	
478		44
479	Like to a vagabond flag upon the stream,	45
480	Goes to and back, lackeying the varying tide,	46
481	To rot itself with motion.	
482	*Mess.* Cæsar, I bring thee word,	47
483	Menecrates and Menas, famous pirates,	48
	Make the sea serve them, which they ear and wound	
484		49
485	With keels of every kind: many hot inroads 50	50
486	They make in Italy; the borders maritime	51
487	Lack blood to think on 't, and flush youth revolt:	52
488	No vessel can peep forth, but 'tis as soon	53
489	Taken as seen; for Pompey's name strikes more	54
490	Than could his war resisted.	
491	*Cæs.* Antony,	55
492	Leave thy lascivious wassails. When thou once	56
493	Wast beaten from Modena, where thou slew'st	57
494	Hirtius and Pansa, consuls, at thy heel	58
495	Did famine follow; whom thou fought'st against,	59
496	Though daintily brought up, with patience more	60

28 same as 26, less In2; aX: In2

29 same as 28; less aX
30 X: JKP, WM1, Ha1, KyB, BT1, OA1, NM1, TaB, RA1, RH1, ER1, LK1, TN1;
  R: ML1; aX: ChC, JL1, LiL, LoC, JS1, AF1
31 same as 30, ML1; less R, aX
32 same as 31, less BT1

33 X: JKP, Ha1, OA1, NM1; aX: WM1, KyB, BT1, TaB, RA1, RH1, ML1, ER1,
  LK1, TN1
34 X: In2, Ha1, OA1, LK1; bX: JS1; N: JKP, LiL, LoC, WA1, JP1
35 same as 34, BT1; less bX, N
36 X: Ha1, OA1, LK1; aX: In2, BT1, JS1
37 same as 36; less aX
38 same as 37; bX: JKP, AF1, ML1, ER1; ADD 1: JKP
39 X: JKP, Ha1, OA1, AF1, ML1, ER1, LK1, TN1

40 X: JKP, Ha1, OA1, LK1; aX: AF1, ML1, ER1, TN1; bX: In2, ChC, LoC,*
41 X: In2, JKP, ChC, Ha1, LiL, LoC, BT1, WA1, OA1, BA1, RA1, BH1,JP1,LK1
42 same as 41, JS1, ML1, TN1

43 same as 41, ML1; aX: TaB, RA1

44 X: In2, JKP, ChC, Lac, Ha1, LiL, LoC, WA1, OA1, BA1, JP1, ML1, LK1*
45 X: In2, JKP, WM1, SP1, Cum, ChC, Lac, Ha1, HIM, KyB, LiL, MTh, LoC*
46 same as 45

47 X: Lac, Ha1, HIM, LiL, MTh, WA1, OA1, TaB, JP1; aX: In2, JKP, WM1,SP1*
48 same as 47, BT1; less aX, bX; aX: ML1; ADD 2: AF1

49 same as 48, AF1; less aX, ADD; bX: In2, WM1, JS1, ML1, ER1, TN1
50 X: In2, Lac, Ha1, HIM, LiL, MTh, BT1, WA1, OA1, TaB, JS1, JP1, AF1,ML1*
51 same as 50, ChC, LoC; less bX; R: ML1; bX: JKP, WM1, IP1, RA1
52 same as 51, WM1, RA1; less bX: aX: JKP, IP1
53 X: Lac, Ha1, HIM, LiL, MTh, BT1, WA1, OA1, TaB, RA1, GS1, JP1, AF1,LK1
54 same as 53, less MTh, AF1; aX: MTh, AF1; bX: TN1

55 X: BT1, OA1; R: ML1; aX: Lac, Ha1, HIM, LiL, WA1, TaB, RA1,GS1,JP1,LK1*
56 X: OA1; bX: TaB, GS1, ML1
57 X: OA1, TaB, GS1, ML1; R: In2; bX: RA1, JS1, LK1, TN1; Tr: JKP
58 X: OA1, TaB, ML1; aX: In2, RA1, JS1, GS1, LK1, TN1
59 same as 58; less aX; bX: MTh, IP1, RA1, GS1
60 X: MTh, OA1, IP1, TaB, RA1, GS1, ML1

*14:40 BT1, WA1, BA1, JP1   *14:44 R: Inc; aX: BT1, BH1; bX:
 WM1, SP1, Cum, HIM, KyB, MTh, TaB, AF1   *14:45 WA1, OA1, BA1,
 TaB, JP1, AF1, LK1   *14:47 Cum, ChC, KyB, LoC, BA1, AF1, MORE
*14:50ER1, TN1; bX: ChC, LoC   *14:55 TN1; MOVE 55b-73a to follow
 22: 13: Ha1   *14:47(continued) LK1; bX: BT1, NM1

497	Than savages could suffer: thou didst drink	61	61
498	The stale of horses, and the gilded puddle		62
	Which beasts would cough at: thy palate then		
499	did deign		63
500	The roughest berry on the rudest hedge:		64
501	Yea, like the stag, when snow the pasture sheets,		65
502	The barks of trees thou browsed'st: on the Alps		66
503	It is reported thou didst eat strange flesh,		67
504	Which some did die to look on: and all this—		68
505	It wounds thine honour that I speak it now—		69
506	Was borne so like a soldier, that thy cheek	70	70
507	So much as lank'd not.		
508	*Lep.* 'Tis pity of him.		71
509	*Cæs.* Let his shames quickly		72
510	Drive him to Rome: 'tis time we twain		73
511	Did show ourselves i' the field; and to that end		74
512	Assemble we immediate council: Pompey		75
513	Thrives in our idleness.		
514	*Lep.* To-morrow, Cæsar,		76
515	I shall be furnish'd to inform you rightly		77
516	Both what by sea and land I can be able		78
517	To front this present time.		
	Cæs. Till which encounter,		79
518	It is my business too. Farewell.	8o	80
	Lep. Farewell, my lord: what you shall know		
519	meantime		81
520	Of stirs abroad, I shall beseech you, sir,		82
521	To let me be partaker.		
	Cæs. Doubt not, sir;		83
522	I knew it for my bond. *[Exeunt.*		84

522+1 **SCENE V.** *Alexandria. Cleopatra's palace.*

523 *Enter* CLEOPATRA, CHARMIAN, IRAS, *and*
523+1 MARDIAN.

524	*Cleo.* Charmian!	1
525	*Char.* Madam?	2
	Cleo. Ha, ha!	3
526	Give me to drink mandragora.	
527	*Char.* Why, madam?	4
	Cleo. That I might sleep out this great gap of	
528	time	5
529	My Antony is away.	
530	*Char.* You think of him too much.	6
531	*Cleo.* O, 'tis treason!	
532	*Char.* Madam, I trust, not so.	7

61   X: MTh, OA1, TaB, GS1, ML1; aX: Cum, IP1, RA1; bX: In2, SP1, Lac,Hal*
62   X: In2, SP1, ChC, Lac, Hal, HIM, KyB, LiL, MTh, LoC, WA1, OA1, BA1,
       NM1, TaB, GS1, BT1, ML1; aX: Inc, WM1
63   X: In2, ChC, OA1, TaB, GS1, ML1; aX: SP1, Lac, Hal, HIM, KyB, LiL,*
64   X: OA1, TaB, GS1, ML1
65   same as 64
66   same as 64; bX: In2, WM1, BA1, NM1, TN1
67   X: In2, WM1, OA1, BA1, NM1, TaB, GS1, ML1, TN1
68   X: OA1, NM1, TaB, GS1, ML1; aX: In2, WM1, BA1, TN1
69   X: In2, OA1, NM1, TaB, GS1, ML1, LK1
70   X: OA1, TaB, GS1; R: ML1

71   X: OA1, GS1; aX: TaB; bX: WM1, LK1; ADD 14: WM1
72   X: WM1, OA1; R: Hal
73   X: WM1, OA1; bX: Hal, LK1; ADD 1: Hal, LK1
74   X: WM1, Hal, OA1, LK1
75   same as 74; bX: TaB, ER1, TN1

76   X: WM1, Hal, OA1, TaB, ER1, LK1, TN1; bX: JKP
77   same as 76, JKP, less TN1; less bX
78   same as 77; R: ML1

79   X: WM1, Hal, OA1, WR1, LK1; aX: JKP, TaB; bX: AF1
80   same as 79; less aX, bX; aX: JKP, TaB

81   X: Hal, OA1, ER1, LK1; aX: WM1; bX: BT1, WA1, BA1, TaB
82   X: Hal, BT1, WA1, OA1, BA1, TaB, ER1, LK1

83   same as 82
84   same as 82, KyB

Scene 15

1   MOVE 1-78 to follow 13: 105: WM1; MOVE 1-65a to follow 23: 44: Hal*
2
3   X: In2

4   X: In2

5

6

7   X: Inc, In2, WM1, SP1, Cum, KyB; bX Cap, ChC, Lac, Hal, HIM,LoC,TaB
*14:61 HIM, LiL, LoC, WA1, BA1, NM1, BT1   *14:63 MTh, LoC, WA1,
   BA1, NM1, BH1   *15: 1 EdT; MOVE 1-78 to follow 21: 52:
   ChC, KyB, LiL; MOVE 1-29a to follow 23: 41: BT1; MOVE 1-75 to follow
   25: 2: SM1; MOVE 1-75a to follow 27: 137: TaB

533	*Cleo.* Thou, eunuch Mardian!	
534	*Mar.* What's your highness' pleasure?	8
535	*Cleo.* Not now to hear thee sing; I take no pleasure	9
536	In aught an eunuch has: 'tis well for thee, 10	10
537	That, being unseminar'd, thy freer thoughts	11
538	May not fly forth of Egypt. Hast thou affections?	12
539	*Mar.* Yes, gracious madam.	13
540	*Cleo.* Indeed!	14
541	*Mar.* Not in deed, madam; for I can do nothing	15
542	But what indeed is honest to be done:	16
543	Yet have I fierce affections, and think	17
544	What Venus did with Mars.	
545	*Cleo.* O Charmian,	18
546	Where think'st thou he is now? Stands he, or sits he?	19
547	Or does he walk? or is he on his horse? 20	20
548	O happy horse, to bear the weight of Antony!	21
549	Do bravely, horse! for wot'st thou whom thou movest?	22
550	The demi-Atlas of this earth, the arm	23
551	And burgonet of men. He's speaking now,	24
552	Or murmuring 'Where's my serpent of old Nile?'	25
553	For so he calls me: now I feed myself	26
554	With most delicious poison. Think on me,	27
555	That am with Phœbus' amorous pinches black,	28
556	And wrinkled deep in time? Broad-fronted Cæsar,	29
557	When thou wast here above the ground, I was 30	30
558	A morsel for a monarch: and great Pompey	31
559	Would stand and make his eyes grow in my brow;	32
560	There would he anchor his aspect and die	33
56;	With looking on his life.	
562	*Enter* ALEXAS, *from* CÆSAR.	
563	*Alex.* Sovereign of Egypt, hail!	34
564	*Cleo.* How much unlike art thou Mark Antony!	35
656	Yet, coming from him, that great medicine hath	36
566	With his tinct gilded thee.	37
567	How goes it with my brave Mark Antony?	38
568	*Alex.* Last thing he did, dear queen, 39	39
569	He kiss'd,—the last of many doubled kisses,—	40
470	This orient pearl. His speech sticks in my heart.	4;
571	*Cleo.* Mine ear must pluck it thence.	

```
8    X: Cap, Be1, Inc, In2, JKP, WM1, SP1, Cum, ChC, Lac, Ha1, HIM, KyB,
        LiL, MTh, BT1, SM1, WA1, OA1, NM1, TaB; aX: EdT; MOVE 8-18a to fol-*
9    same as 8; less aX, MOVE; bX: EdT
10   same as 9, EdT; less bX ; bX: TN1
11   same as 10, TN1; less bX
12   same as 10; less bX: aX: TN1
13   same as 10; less bX; aX: Cum
14   same as 10, less Inc; less bX

15   same as 10, GCa; less bX
16   same as 15, TN1
17   sam eas 15

18   X: Be1, JKP; aX: GCa, Cap, Inc, In2, WM1, SP1, Cum, ChC, Lac, Ha1,HIM,
        KyB, LiL, MTh, EdT, LoC, BT1, SM1, WA1, OA1, NM1, TaB
19   X: Be1
20   X: Be1
21   X: Be1, JKP, WM1, BT1

22   X: Be1, BT1, OA1
23   same as 22
24   X: Be1; aX: BT1, OA1; ADD 1: TaB

25   X: Be1
26   X: Be1, In2; bX: SP1
27   X: Be1, In2, SP1; bX: Cap, Inc, WM1, Cum, Lac, Ha1, HIM, KyB, MTh,SM1*
28   X: Cap, Be1, Inc, In2, WM1, SP1, Cum, Lac, Ha1, JL1, HIM, KyB, MTh,*
29   same as 28, less SP1, Lac, HIM, MTh; aX: SP1, Lac, HIM, MTh; bX: BT1
30   same as 29, BT1; less aX, bX
31   same as 30

32   same as 30
33   same as 30; Tr: JKP



34   X: BT1, SM1; aX: Cap, Be1, Inc, In2, WM1, Cum, Ha1, JL1, KyB,NM1, RA1*
35   X: JKP, KyB, BT1, SM1
36   same as 35
37   same as 35
38   X: BT1, SM1
39   X: BT1, SM1, WA1
40   same as 39
41   same as 39; bX: WM1, TaB, RA1

*15:8 low 25: 9; JP1                    *15:27 WM1, RA1, ER1
*15:28 SM1, NM1, RA1, ER1          *15:34 ER1; ADD 1: JKP
```

572	*Alex.* 'Good friend,' quoth he,	42
573	'Say, the firm Roman to great Egypt sends	43
574	This treasure of an oyster; at whose foot,	44
575	To mend the petty present, I will piece	45
576	Her opulent throne with kingdoms: all the east,	46
577	Say thou, shall call her mistress.' So he nodded,	47
578	†And soberly did mount an arm-gaunt steed,	48
579	Who neigh'd so high, that what I would have spoke	49
580	Was beastly dumb'd by him.	
581	*Cleo.* What, was he sad or merry? 50	50
582	*Alex.* Like to the time o' the year between the extremes	51
583	Of hot and cold, he was nor sad nor merry.	52
584	*Cleo.* O well-divided disposition! Note him, Note him, good Charmian, 'tis the man; but	53
585	note him:	54
586	He was not sad, for he would shine on those	55
587	That make their looks by his; he was not merry,	56
588	Which seem'd to tell them his remembrance lay	57
589	In Egypt with his joy; but between both:	58
590	O heavenly mingle! Be'st thou sad or merry,	59
591	The violence of either thee becomes, 60	60
592	So does it no man else. Met'st thou my posts?	61
593	*Alex.* Ay, madam, twenty several messengers:	62
594	Why do you send so thick?	
	Cleo. Who's born that day	63
595	When I forget to send to Antony,	64
596	Shall die a beggar. Ink and paper, Charmian.	65
	Welcome, my good Alexas. Did I, Charmian,	66
597-8	Ever love Cæsar so?	
599	*Char.* O that brave Cæsar!	67
600	*Cleo.* Be choked with such another emphasis!	68
601	Say, the brave Antony.	
602	*Char.* The valiant Cæsar!	69
603	*Cleo.* By Isis, I will give thee bloody teeth,	70
604	If thou with Cæsar paragon again 71	71
605	My man of men.	
606	*Char.* By your most gracious pardon,	72
607	I sing but after you.	
608	*Cleo.* My salad days,	73
609	When I was green in judgement: cold in blood,	74
610	To say as I said then! But, come, away;	75
611	Get me ink and paper:	76
	He shall have every day a several greeting,	77
612-13	Or I'll unpeople Egypt. [*Exeunt*	78

```
42   X: BT1, SM1, RA1; aX: WM1, WA1, TaB
43   same as 42; less aX
44   X: In2, BT1, SM1, RA1; aX: WM1
45   X: BT1, SM1, RA1
46   same as 45
47   same as 45; bX: ChC, LoC, BA1, TaB, RH1, AF1, ER1, TN1
48   X: ChC, LoC, BT1, SM1, BA1, TaB, RA1, RH1, AF1, ER1, TN1; R: EdT

49   same as 48, WM1; less R

50   X: BT1, SM1; aX: WM1, ChC, LoC, BA1, TaB, RA1, RH1, AF1, ER1, TN1

51   X: BT1, SM1
52   X: BT1, SM1
53   X: BT1, SM1

54   X: BT1, SM1; bX: JS1, ER1
55   X: BT1, SM1, JS1, ER1
56   same as 55
57   same as 55
58   same as 55; bX: RA1
59   same as 55, RA1; bX: TN1
60   same as 59, TN1; less bX
61   X: BT1, SM1; aX: RA1, JS1, ER1, TN1
62   X: BT1, SM1; bX: IP1

63   X: BT1, SM1, IP1
64   same as 63
65   same as 63; R: WM1; bX: ChC, Hal, LiL, LoC
66   X: Inc, In2, SP1, Cum, ChC, Hal, LoC, BT1, IP1; R: WM1; aX: SM1; bX:
       KyB
67   same as 66, WM1, KyB; less R, aX, bX; R: JKP
68   same as 67, less WM1, IP1; less R; aX: IP1; ADD 1: JKP

69   same as 68, JL1; less aX, ADD; bX: JKP
70   same as 69, JKP, less SP1; less bX
71   same as 70, less JKP, JL1

72   same as 71

73   same as 71
74   same as 71, less Cum; aX: Cum
75   X: In2, Hal, KyB, LoC, BT1; aX: Inc, JKP, ChC; bX: OA1, TaB, RA1;*
76   X: In2, WM1, Hal, BT1, SM1, OA1, TaB, ML1
77   X: Hal, BT1, SM1, OA1, TaB
78   same as 77
```

*15:75 Insert 14: 1-25a: OA1

ACT II.

SCENE I. *Messina. Pompey's house.*

Enter POMPEY, MENECRATES, *and* MENAS,
in warlike manner.

Pom. If the great gods be just, they shall assist 1
The deeds of justest men.
Mene. Know, worthy Pompey, 2
That what they do delay, they not deny. 3
Pom. Whiles we are suitors to their throne, decays 4
The thing we sue for.
Mene. We, ignorant of ourselves, 5
Beg often our own harms, which the wise powers 6
Deny us for our good; so find we profit 7
By losing of our prayers.
Pom. I shall do well: 8
The people love me, and the sea is mine; 9
My powers are crescent, and my auguring hope 10
Says it will come to the full. Mark Antony 11
In Egypt sits at dinner, and will make 12
No wars without doors: Cæsar gets money where 13
He loses hearts: Lepidus flatters both, 14
Of both is flatter'd · but he neither loves, 15
Nor either cares for him.
Men. Cæsar and Lepidus 16
Are in the field: a mighty strength they carry. 17
Pom. Where have you this? 'tis false.
Men. From Silvius, sir. 18
Pom. He dreams: I know they are in Rome together, 19
Looking for Antony. But all the charms of love, 20
Salt Cleopatra, soften thy waned lip! 21
Let witchcraft join with beauty, lust with both! 22
Tie up the libertine in a field of feasts, 23
Keep his brain fuming: Epicurean cooks 24
Sharpen with cloyless sauce his appetite; 25
That sleep and feeding may prorogue his honour 26
Even till a Lethe'd dulness!

Enter VARRIUS.

How now, Varrius! 27
Var. This is most certain that I shall deliver: 28

Scene 21

ALL CUT: GCa, Cap, Inc, In2, JKP, Cum, ChC, Lac, Hal, JL1, HIM, MTh, EdT, LoC, SM1, WA1, OA1, NM1, TaG, GS1: JP1, ER1, LK1

1   X: WM1; <u>MOVE</u> 1-50a to follow <u>33</u>: 49: BT1

2   <u>a</u>X: WM1; <u>b</u>X: BA1, AF1; <u>MOVE</u> 2b-43 to follow <u>22</u>: 248a: WM1
3   X: BA1, AF1, TN1

4   X: BA1, JS1, ML1, TN1

5   same as 4; <u>b</u>X: LiL, AF1
6   X: LiL, BA1, JS1, AF1, ML1
7   same as 6; <u>b</u>X: BT1

8   R: WM1; <u>a</u>X: LiL, BT1, BA1, JS1, AF1, ML1
9   R: WM1; <u>ADD</u> 1: WM1
10 X: WM1; <u>b</u>X: AF1
11 X: WM1; <u>a</u>X: AF1
12 X: WM1
13 X: WM1
14 X: WM1
15 X: WM1; <u>b</u>X: AF1

16 X: WM1; <u>a</u>X: AF1; <u>b</u>X: BT1
17 X: WM1, BT1

18 X: WM1, BT1; <u>c</u>X: TN1

19 X: WM1, BT1
20 X: WM1, BT1
21 X: WM1; <u>a</u>X: BT1; <u>b</u>X: LiL
22 X: WM1
23 X: WM1
24 X: WM1; <u>b</u>X: LiL, BA1, AF1
25 X: WM1, LiL, BA1, AF1
26 same as 25

27 X: WM1; <u>a</u>X: LiL, BA1, AF1; <u>b</u>X: ML1
28 X: WM1, BT1, AF1

651	Mark Antony is every hour in Rome		29
652	Expected: since he went from Egypt 'tis	30	30
653	A space for further travel.		
654	*Pom.* I could have given less matter		31
655	A better ear. Menas, I did not think		32
	This amorous surfeiter would have donn'd his		
656	helm		33
657	For such a petty war: his soldiership		34
658	Is twice the other twain : but let us rear		35
659	The higher our opinion, that our stirring		36
660	Can from the lap of Egypt's widow pluck		37
661	Th· se'er-lust-wearied Antony.		
662	*Men.* I cannot hope		38
663	Cæsar and Antony shall well greet together:		39
664	His wife that's dead did trespasses to Cæsar:		40
665	His brother warr'd upon him; although, I think,		41
666	Not moved by Antony.		
667	*Pom.* I know not, Menas,		42
668	How lesser enmities may give way to greater.		43
669	Were't not that we stand up against them all,		44
	'Twere pregnant they should square between		
670	themselves;		45
671	For they have entertained cause enough		46
672	To draw their swords: but how the fear of us		47
673	May cement their divisions and bind up		48
674	The petty difference, we yet not know.		49
675	Be't as our gods will have't! It only stands	50	50
676	Our lives upon to use our strongest hands.		51
677	Come, Menas. [*Exeunt.*		52

677+1	**Scene II.** *Rome. The house of Lepidus.*

678	*Enter* ENOBARBUS *and* LEPIDUS.	
679	*Lep.* Good Enobarbus, 'tis a worthy deed,	1
	And shall become you well, to entreat your cap-	
680	tain	2
681	To soft and gentle speech.	
682	*Eno.* I shall entreat him	3
683	To answer like himself: if Cæsar move him,	4
684	Let Antony look over Cæsar's head	5
685	And speak as loud as Mars. By Jupiter,	6
686	Were I the wearer of Antonius' beard,	7
687	I would not shave't to-day.	
	Lep. 'Tis not a time	8
688	For private stomaching.	
	Eno. Every time	9
689-90	Serves for the matter that is then born in't. 10	10

```
29   X: WM1
30   X: WM1; bX: BT1, BA1, RA1, AF1, ML1, TN1

31   X: WM1; aX: BT1, BA1, RA1, AF1, ML1, TN1
32   X: WM1; bX: TN1

33   X: WM1, TN1
34   X: WM1; aX: BT1, TN1
35   X: WM1; bX: BA1
36   X: WM1, BA1
37   X: WM1, BA1

38   aX: WM1, BA1; bX: BT1
39   X: BT1
40   X: BT1
41   X: BT1; bX: TN1

42   X: TN1; aX: TN1
43   X: BT1
44   X: WM1, BA1, RA1, AF1, TN1

45   X: WM1, RA1, AF1, TN1; R: ML1
46   X: WM1, BT1, RA1, ML1, TN1
47   aX: BT1, RA1, ML1, TN1
48   X: WM1
49   X: WM1; bX: AF1, TN1
50   X: WM1; bX: BT1, AF1
51   X: WM1, BT1, AF1
52   X: WM1, BT1; Insert 15: 1-78: KyB, LiL
```

Scene 22

```
1    X: EdT, LK1

2    X: EdT, LK1

3    X: EdT, LK1
4    X: EdT, LK1; bX: LiL
5    X: LiL, EdT, LK1
6    same as 5; bX: JKP, KyB, AF1, ML1
7    X: JKP, KyB, LiL,  EdT, TaB, AF1, ML1, LK1

8    X: KyB, LiL, EdT, TaB, LK1; aX: JKP, AF1, ML1; bX: TN1

9    same as 8, TN1; less aX, bX
10   same as 9
```

Lep. But small to greater matters must give 11
691 way.
692 *Eno.* Not if the small come first.
Lep. Your speech is passion: 12
693 But, pray you, stir no embers up. Here comes 13
694 The noble Antony.

695 *Enter* ANTONY *and* VENTIDIUS.

696 *Eno.* And yonder, Cæsar. 14

698 *Enter* CÆSAR, MECÆNAS, *and* AGRIPPA.

698 *Ant.* If we compose well here, to Parthia: 15
699 Hark, Ventidius.
Cæs. I do not know, 16
700 Mecænas; ask Agrippa.
701 *Lep.* Noble friends, 17
That which combined us was most great, and let
702 not 18
703 A leaner action rend us. What's amiss, 19
704 May it be gently heard: when we debate **20** 20
705 Our trivial difference loud, we do commit 21
706 Murder in healing wounds: then, noble partners, 22
707 The rather, for I earnestly beseech, 23
708 Touch you the sourest points with sweetest terms, 24
709 Nor curstness grow to the matter.
710 *Ant.* 'Tis spoken well. 25
711 Were we before our armies, and to fight, 26
712 I should do thus. [*Flourish.* 27
713 *Cæs.* Welcome to Rome.
714 *Ant.* Thank you.
715 *Cæs.* Sit.
716 *Ant.* Sit, sir.
717 *Cæs.* Nay, then. 28
Ant. I learn, you take things ill which are
718 not so, 29
719 Or being, concern you not.
Cæs. I must be laugh'd at, **30** 30
720 If, or for nothing or a little, I 31
721 Should say myself offended, and with you 32
Chiefly i' the world; more laugh'd at, that I
722 should 33
Once name you derogately, when to sound your
723 name 34
724 It not concern'd me.
Ant. My being in Egypt, Cæsar, 35

11 same as 9, JKP

12 X: KyB, LiL, EdT, LK1; aX: JKP, TaB, TN1
13 X: LiL, EdT, LK1; ADD: Hal

14 X: EdT, LK1; R: BT1; bX: JKP, Hal, KyB; ADD 26, insert 36: 1-18 and
        14: 55b-73: Hal

15 X: JKP, Lac, Hal, HIM, KyB, MTh, EdT, BT1, SM1, WA1, OA1, TaB, JP1,LK1

16 same as 15; bX: RH1; N: GCa, Cap, In2, WM1, Cum, LoC

17 X: Hal, EdT, OA1; aX: JKP, Lac, HIM, KyB, MTh, BT1, SM1, WA1, JP1, LK1;
        bX: In2; N: WM1, LoC
18 X: In2, JKP, Hal, EdT, OA1, ER1; R: ML1
19 same as 18, less JKP; less R; aX: JKP; bX: WA1, TaB
20 X: In2, Hal, EdT, WA1, OA1, TaB; aX: ER1; bX: JKP, WM1, ChC, Lac, JL1*
21 X: In2, JKP, WM1, ChC, Lac, Hal, JL1, HIM, KyB, LiL, EdT, LoC, BT1,SM1*
22 X: In2, JKP, Lac, Hal, HIM, KyB, LiL, EdT, SM1, WA1, OA1, BA1, TaB;*
23 same as 22, ChC, LoC, BT1, BA1, ER1; less aX
24 X: In2, Lac, Hal, KyB, EdT, SM1, WA1, OA1, BA1, TaB; aX: HIM

25 X: In2, Hal, KyB, EdT, OA1; aX: Lac, BT1, SM1, WA1, BA1, TaB
26 same as 25; less aX
27 X: EdT, OA1; aX: In2, Hal, KyB

28 XL JKP; ADD 12: In2

29

30 bX : Hal, JL1, LK1
31 X: Hal, JL1, LK1
32 same as 31

33 same as 31; bX: JKP, KyB, BA1, TaB, ML1, TN1

34 X: JKP, Hal, JL1, KyB, BA1, TaB, ML1, LK1, TN1

35 X: JKP; aX: Hal, JL1, KyB, BA1, TaB, ML1, LK1, TN1

*22:20 KyB, LiL, LoC, SM1, BA1, IP1, ML1   *22:21 WA1, OA1, BA1,
    IP1, TaB, ML1   *22:22 aX: WM1, ChC, JL1, LoC, IP1, ML1

725	**What was't to you?**	36
726	*Cæs.* No more than my residing here at Rome	37
727	Might be to you in Egypt: yet, if you there	38
728	Did practise on my state, your being in Egypt	39
729	Might be my question.	
730	*Ant.* How intend you, practised? 40	40
731	*Cæs.* You may be pleased to catch at mine intent	41
732	By what did here befal me. Your wife and brother	42
733	Made wars upon me; and their contestation	43
734	Was theme for you, you were the word of war.	44
735	*Ant.* You do mistake your business; my brother never	45
736	Did urge me in his act: I did inquire it;	46
737	And have my learning from some true reports,	47
738	That drew their swords with you. Did he not rather	48
739	Discredit my authority with yours;	49
740	And make the wars alike against my stomach, 50	50
741	Having alike your cause? Of this my letters	51
742	Before did satisfy you. If you'll patch a quarrel,	52
743	As matter whole you have not to make it with,	53
744	It must not be with this.	
745	*Cæs.* You praise yourself By laying defects of judgement to me; but	54 / 55
746	You patch'd up your excuses.	
747	*Ant.* Not so, not so:	56
748	I know you could not lack, I am certain on 't,	57
749	Very necessity of this thought, that I,	58
750	Your partner in the cause 'gainst which he fought,	59
751	Could not with graceful eyes attend those wars 60	60
752	Which fronted mine own peace. As for my wife,	61
753	I would you had her spirit in such another:	62
754	The third o' the world is yours; which with a snaffle	63
755	You may pace easy, but not such a wife.	64
	Eno. Would we had all such wives, that the	65
756-7	men might go to wars with the women!	66
758	*Ant.* So much uncurbable, her garboils, Cæsar,	67
759	Made out of her impatience, which not wanted	68
760	Shrewdness of policy too, I grieving grant	69
761	Did you too much disquiet: for that you must 70	70
762	But say, I could not help it.	
	Cæs. I wrote to you	71
763	When rioting in Alexandria; you	72

```
36  X: JKP
37  X: JKP
38  X: JKP
39  X: JKP

40  X: JKP

41  X: JKP, KyB, BT1, TaB

42  X: KyB; aX: JKP, BT1, TaB
43  X: KyB; R: ML1
44  X: KyB

45  X: KyB
46  X: KyB; bX: In2, JKP, Lac, Hal, HIM, LiL, MTh, EdT, BT1, SM1, WA1,OA1*
47  X: In2, JKP, Lac, Hal, HIM, KyB, LiL, MTh, EdT, BT1, SM1, WA1, OA1,
       BA1, IP1, TaB, RA1, JS1, GS1, AF1, ER1, TN1
48  X: In2, JKP, Lac, Hal, HIM, KyB, LiL, MTh, EdT, BT1, SM1, WA1, OA1,TaB*
49  same as 48, RH1, TN1; less aX, bX
50  same as 49, less TN1
51  X: KyB, LiL, TaB, ER1; aX: In2, JKP, Lac, Hal, HIM, MTh, EdT, BT1, SM1*
52  X: KyB, LiL, BA1, TaB, ER1, LK1; aX: TN1; bX: JKP, JL1
53  X: JKP, JL1, KyB, LiL, BT1, SM1, BA1, TaB, JS1, AF1, ML1, ER1, LK1,TN1

54  X: JKP, JL1, KyB, LiL, BA1, TaB, ER1, LK1; bX: Cap, Lac, HIM, MTh, EdT*
55  X: Cap, JKP, Lac, JL1, HIM, KyB, LiL, MTh, EdT, SM1, WA1, OA1, BA1, IP1,
       TaB, ER1, LK1, TN1
56  same as 55; aX: AF1
57  same as 55, BT1, JS1; R: ML1
58  same as 57; less R
59  same as 58, less BT1
60  same as 59; R: ML1
61  X: Lac, HIM, KyB, MTh, EdT, SM1; R: ML1; aX: Cap, JKP, JL1, LiL, WA1,*
62  same as 61, TN1; less R, aX

63  same as 62, less TN1
64  same as 63
65  X: Bel, In2, Lac, Hal, HIM, KyB, MTh, EdT, SM1
66  same as 65

67  X: Cap, Bel, In2, JKP, Lac, Hal, HIM, KyB, MTh, EdT, BT1, SM1, WA1OA1*
68  same as 67, BA1, less ML1; less aX; bX: ER1
69  same as 68, less BA1, LK1; less bX; aX: BA1, ER1, LK1
70  same as 69; less aX

71  X: Bel; aX: Cap, In2, JKP, Lac, Hal, HIM, KyB, MTh, EdT, BT1, SM1,WA1*
72  X: Bel
```

*22:46 BA1, TaB, RA1, JS1, GS1, AF1, ER1, TN1   *22:48 GS1; aX:
   BA1, IP1, RA1, JS1, AF1, ER1, TN1   *22:51 WA1, OA1, GS1, RH1;
   bX: BA1, LK1, TN1   *22:54 SM1, WA1, OA1, IP1, TN1
*22:61 OA1, BA1, IP1, TaB, JS1, ER1, LK1, TN1   *22:67 BA1, IP1, TaB,
   RA1, GS1, ML1, ER1, TN1;;aX: ER1   *22:71 OA1, BA1, IP1, RA1, GS1, TN1

764 Did pocket up my letters, and with taunts 73
765 Did gibe my missive out of audience.
      Ant.   Sir, 74
766 He fell upon me ere admitted: then 75
767 Three kings I had newly feasted, and did want 76
768 Of what I was i' the morning: but next day 77
769 I told him of myself; which was as much 78
779 As to have ask'd him pardon.   Let this fellow 79
771 Be nothing of our strife; if we contend,   80 80
772 Out of our question wipe him.
      Cæs.   You have broken 81
773 The article of your oath; which you shall never 82
774 Have tongue to charge me with.
775   *Lep.*   Soft, Cæsar!
      Ant.   No, 83
776 Lepidus, let him speak: 84
777 The honour is sacred which he talks on now, 85
778 Supposing that I lack'd it.   But, on, Cæsar; 86
779 The article of my oath. 87
780   *Cæs.* To lend me arms and aid when I required
          them; 88
781 The which you both denied.
782   *Ant.*   Neglected, rather: 89
783 And then when poison'd hours had bound me up 90
784 From mine own knowledge.   As nearly as I may, 91
785 I'll play the penitent to you: but mine honesty 92
786 Shall not make poor my greatness, nor my power 93
787 Work without it.   Truth is, that Fulvia, 94
788 To have me out of Egypt, made wars here: 95
789 For which myself, the ignorant motive, do 96
790 So far ask pardon as befits mine honour 97
791 To stoop in such a case.
792   *Lep.*   'Tis noble spoken. 98
    Mec. If it might please you, to enforce no
793   further 99
794 The griefs between ye: to forget them quite 100 100
795 Were to remember that the present need 101
796 Speaks to atone you.
797   *Lep.*   Worthily spoken, Mecænas. 102
    Eno. Or, if you borrow one another's love 103
798 for the instant, you may, when you hear no more 104
799 words of Pompey, return it again: you shall 105
800 have time to wrangle in when you have nothing 106
801 else to do. 107
802   *Ant.* Thou art a soldier only: speak no more. 108
    Eno. That truth should be silent I had almost 109

73 X: Be1

74 X: Be1
75 X: Be1, LiL
76 X: Be1, LiL
77 X: Be1, LiL; b̲X̲: JKP, GS1
78 X: Be1, JKP, L̅i̅L, GS1
79 X: Be1, LiL; a̲X̲: JKP, GS1; b̲X̲: AF1
80 X: Be1, LiL, A̅F̅1; b̲X̲: TN1

81 X: Be1, LiL; a̲X̲: AF1, TN1
82

83
84
85 X: BT1
86 a̲X̲: BT1
87

88

89 R̲ : ML1
90 X̲: GS1
91 a̲X: GS1
92 b̅X̅: BA1, IP1, RH1, ML1, TN1
93 X̅: BA1, IP1, RH1, ML1, TN1; b̲X̲: In2, BT1, ER1
94 a̲X̲: In2, BT1, BA1, IP1, RH1, M̅L̅1, ER1, TN1
95
96
97

98 b̲X̲ : Be1, KyB

99   X: Be1, In2, KyB, LK1; b̲X̲: JS1; N̲: JP1
100 X: Be1, In2, KyB, JS1, L̅K̅1; b̲X̲: B̅T̅1; N̲: Ha1
101 X: Be1, In2, KyB, LK1; a̲X̲: B̅T̅1̅, JS1

102 same as 101; less a̲X̲; b̲X̲: JKP, SM1; N̲: Ha1, OA1
103 X: Be1, In2, JKP, K̅y̅B, L̅K̅1
104 same as 103
105 same as 103
106 same as 103
107 same as 103
108 same as 103
109 same as 103

803-4	**forgot.** **110**	110
	Ant. You wrong this presence; therefore	
805-6	speak no more.	111
807	*Eno.* Go to, then; your considerate stone.	112
808	*Cæs.* I do not much dislike the matter, but	113
809	**The** manner of his speech; for't cannot be	114
810	**We** shall remain in friendship, our conditions	115
811	**So** differing in their acts. Yet, if I knew	116
	What hoop should hold us stanch, from edge **to**	
812	edge	117
813	**O'** the world I would pursue it.	
814	*Agr.* Give me leave, Cæsar,—	118
815	*Cæs.* Speak, Agrippa.	119
	Agr. Thou hast a sister by the mother's side,	120
816	**Admired** Octavia: great Mark Antony **121**	121
817	**Is** now a widower.	
	Cæs. Say not so, Agrippa:	122
818	**If** Cleopatra heard you, your reproof	123
819	**Were** well deserved of rashness.	124
	Ant. I am not married, Cæsar: let me hear	125
820-1	**Agrippa** further speak.	126
822	*Agr.* To hold you in perpetual amity,	127
823	**To** make you brothers, and to knit your hearts	128
824	**With** an unslipping knot, take Antony	129
825	**Octavia** to his wife; whose beauty claims	130
826	**No** worse a husband than the best of men:	131
827	**Whose** virtue and whose general graces speak	132
	That which none else can utter. By this mar-	
828	riage,	133
829	**All** little jealousies, which now seem great,	134
	And all great fears, which now import their	
830	dangers,	135
831	**Would** then be nothing: truths would be tales,	136
832	**Where** now half tales be truths: her love to both	137
833	**Would,** each to other and all loves to both,	138
834	**Draw** after her. Pardon what I have spoke;	139
835	**For** 'tis a studied, not a present thought, **140**	140
836	**By** duty ruminated.	
837	*Ant.* Will Cæsar speak?	
838	*Cæs.* Not till he hears how Antony is touch'd	141
839	**With** what is spoke already.	142
840	*Ant.* What power is in Agrippa,	
841	**If** I would say, 'Agrippa, be it so,'	143
842	**To** make this good?	144
843	*Cæs.* The power of Cæsar, and	
844	**His** power unto Octavia.	145

110 same as 103, Cum

111 X: Be1, In2, JKP, Cum, Ha1, KyB, EdT, TaB, LK1
112 same as 111, Inc, less Ha1
113 X: JKP, KyB, LK1
114 same as 113
115 same as 113; bX: BA1, ML1
116 X: JKP; aX: KyB, BA1, ML1; bX: LK}

117 X: JKP; aX: LK}

118 aX: JKP; bX: Be1
119 X: Be1, JKP, LK1; bX: JL1; N: LiL
120 X: Be1
121 X: Be1; ADD 4: WM1

122 X: Be1; N: LiL
123 X: Be1
124 X: Be1
125 X: Be1
126 X: Be1; N: LiL
127
128 X: In2, JKP
129 aX: JKP
130 bX: JKP, WM1, SP1, KyB, BH1, AF1
131 X :JKP, WM1, SP1, KyB, BH1, AF1
132 X: JKP, WM1, SP1, ChC, JL1, HIM, LiL, BH1, AF1

133 X: WM1; aX: JKP, SP1, ChC, JL1, HIM, LiL, EdT, BH1, AF1; bX: ER1
134 X: In2, WM1, BA1, ER1

135 X: In2, JKP, WM1, ChC, JL1, HIM, LiL, LoC, SM1, WA1, IP1, JS1, ER1*
136 X: In2, WM1, BA1, ER1; bX: Be1, Inc, SP1, Cum, ChC, HIM, KyB, LiL,LoC*
137 X: Be1, ChC, HIM, KyB, LiL, LoC, BA1, IP1, GS1, AF1, TN1; aX: Inc, In2*
138 X: Be1, Cum, ChC, JL1, HIM, KyB, LiL, LoC, IP1, GS1, AF1, TN1; aX: BA1
139 X: AF1; aX: Be1, ChC, HIM, KyB, LiL, LoC, BT1, TN1; bX: BT1
140 X: AF1

141 aX: BT1, AF1; bX: JKP, WM1
142 X: JKP, WM1

143 X: JKP; R: Lac; aX: WM1; bX: Be1; N: Cum, LiL
144 X: Be1, CKP; N: Cum, LiL

145 X: Be1, JKP

*22:135 bX: BA1   *22:136 BT1, RH1, JS1, GS1, AF1, ML1, TN1
*22:137 WM1, SP1, Cum, BT1, JS1, ML1, ER1; bX: JL1

845	*Ant.* May I never	146
846	To this good purpose, that so fairly shows,	147
847	Dream of impediment! Let me have thy hand:	148
848	Further this act of grace; and from this hour	149
849	The heart of brothers govern in our loves 15	150
850	And sway our great designs!	
851	*Cæs.* There is my hand.	151
852	A sister I bequeath you, whom no brother	152
853	Did ever love so dearly: let her live	153
854	To join our kingdoms and our hearts; and never	154
855	Fly off our loves again!	
856	*Lep.* Happily, amen!	155
	Ant. I did not think to draw my sword	
857	'gainst Pompey;	156
858	For he hath laid strange courtesies and great	157
859	Of late upon me: I must thank him only,	158
860	Lest my remembrance suffer ill report;	159
861	At heel of that, defy him.	
862	*Lep.* Time calls upon's: 160	160
863	Of us must Pompey presently be sought,	161
864	Or else he seeks out us.	
865	*Ant.* Where lies he?	162
866	*Cæs.* About the mount Misenum.	163
867	*Ant.* What is his strength by land?	164
868	*Cæs.* Great and increasing: but by sea	165
869	He is an absolute master.	
870	*Ant.* So is the fame.	166
871	Would we had spoke together! Haste we for it:	167
872	Yet, ere we put ourselves in arms, dispatch we	168
873	The business we have talk'd of.	
874	*Cæs.* With most gladness:	169
875	And do invite you to my sister's view, 170	170
876	Whither straight I'll lead you.	
	Ant. Let us, Lepidus,	171
877	Not lack your company.	
	Lep. Noble Antony,	172
878–9	Not sickness should detain me.	173
880	[*Flourish. Exeunt Cæsar, Antony,*	
881	*and Lepidus.*	
882	*Mec.* Welcome from Egypt, sir.	174
	Eno. Half the heart of Cæsar, worthy Mece-	175
883–4	nas! My honourable friend, Agrippa!	176
885	*Agr.* Good Enobarbus!	177
	Mec. We have cause to be glad that matters	178
886	are so well digested. You stayed well by 't in	179
887	Egypt. 180	180

146 <u>aX</u>: Be1, JKP; <u>bX</u>: AF1
147 <u>X</u>: AF1
148 <u>aX</u>: AF1; <u>bX</u>: ER1
149 <u>X</u>: ER1
150 X: ER1

151 <u>aX</u>: ER1; <u>bX</u>: In2, ML1
152 <u>X</u>: TaB
153 X: TaB; <u>bX</u>: TN1
154 X: TaB, TN1

155 X: TaB, TN1; <u>aX</u>: JS1; <u>bX</u>: In2, JKP, Lac, Ha1, JL1, HIM, MTh

156 X: Cap, JKP, Lac, Ha1, JL1, HIM, KyB, LiL, MTh, OA1, TaB, ML1, LK1*
157 same as 156,TN1; less <u>MOVE</u>
158 same as 157; <u>bX</u>: GS1
159 same as 157, GS1; less <u>bX</u>; <u>aX</u>: MTh

160 X: KyB, LiL, OA1, GS1, LK1, TN1; <u>aX</u>: Cap, JKP, Lac, Ha1, JL1, HIM,*
161 X: WM1, KyB, LiL, OA1, GS1, LK1, TN1

162 same as 161, less GS1, TN1; <u>aX</u>: GS1, TN1; <u>bX</u>: Lac, Ha1, JL1, HIM,*
163 X: WM1, JL1, KyB, LiL, OA1, TaB, ER1, LK1; <u>R</u>: Cum; <u>aX</u>: Lac, Ha1,HIM*
164 X: WM1, KyB, LiL, OA1, LK1
165 same as 164

166 same as 164; <u>bX</u>: BT1, SM1, WA1, BA1, JS1, ML1, ER1
167 X: In2, JKP, LiL, OA1, LK1; <u>aX</u>: WM1, KyB, BP1, SM1, WA1, BA1,ML1,ER1
168 X: KyB, LiL, OA1

169 X: OA1; <u>aX</u>: KyB
170 X: OA1

171 X: KyB; <u>R</u>: WM1; <u>aX</u>: OA1, AF1; <u>bX</u>: TaB; <u>ADD</u> 3: TaB

172 X: KyB
173 X: KyB; <u>ADD</u> 3: Cap

174 X: GCa, Cap, Inc, In2, Cum, Lac, Ha1, HIM, EdT, WA1, LK1; N: LoC,TaB;*
175 X: GCa, Cap, Inc, In2, Cum, Lac, Ha1, HIM, EdT, SM1, WA1, TaB, JP1*
176 X: GCa, Cap, Inc, In2, JKP, WM1, Cum, Lac, Ha1, HIM, EdT, WA1, OA1,*
177 X: GCa, Cap, Inc, In2, Cum, OA1, LK1; N: Ha1; <u>ADD</u> 1: AF1
178 same as 177, TaB, less OA1; less N, <u>ADD</u>; N: Lac
179 X: GCa, Cap, Inc, In2, Cum, Ha1, HIM, LK1; <u>aX</u>: Lac, TaB; N: JKP, LiL*
180 X: GCa, Cap, Inc, In2, Cum, LK1; <u>aX</u>: Lac, Ha1, HIM, LoC; <u>bX</u>: JKP, SM1

*22:156 <u>MOVE</u> 156-160a to follow 162: SM1   *22:160TaB, ML1;
   bX: WM1   *22:162 TaB, ER1   *22:163 insert 156-160a:SM1
*22:174 <u>MOVE</u> 174-232a to open play   *22:175 LK1; <u>aX</u>: AF1; N: LiL,
  LoC; <u>Insert</u> 26: 122-135: JKP   *22:176 LK1; N: LiL, TaB
*22:179LoC; <u>MOVE</u> 179-180 to follow 290: WA1

Eno. Ay, sir; we did sleep day out of counte- 181
888-9 nance, and made the night light with drinking. 182
Mec. Eight wild-boars roasted whole at a 183
890 breakfast, and but twelve persons there; is this 184
891 true? 185
Eno. This was but as a fly by an eagle: we 186
892 had much more monstrous matter of feast, which 187
893-4 worthily deserved noting. 188
Mec. She's a most triumphant lady, if report 189
895-6 be square to her. 190 190
Eno. When she first met Mark Antony, she 191
897-8 pursed up his heart, upon the river of Cydnus. 192
Agr. There she appeared indeed; or my re- 193
899-900 porter devised well for her. 194
901 *Eno.* I will tell you. 195
902 The barge she sat in, like a burnish'd throne, 196
903 Burn'd on the water: the poop was beaten gold; 197
904 Purple the sails, and so perfumed that 198
905 The winds were love-sick with them; the oars
906 were silver, 199
907 Which to the tune of flutes kept stroke, and made 200
908 The water which they beat to follow faster, 201 201
909 As amorous of their strokes. For her own person, 202
910 It beggar'd all description: she did lie 203
911 In her pavilion—cloth-of-gold of tissue— 204
912 O'er-picturing that Venus where we see 205
913 The fancy outwork nature: on each side her 206
914 Stood pretty dimpled boys, like smiling Cupids, 207
915 With divers-colour'd fans, whose wind did seem 208
916 To glow the delicate cheeks which they did cool, 209
917 And what they undid did.
918 *Agr.* O, rare for Antony! 210 210
919 *Eno.* Her gentlewomen, like the Nereides, 211
920 So many mermaids, tended her i' the eyes, 212
921 And made their bends adornings: at the helm 213
922 A seeming mermaid steers: the silken tackle 214
923 Swell with the touches of those flower-soft hands, 215
924 That yarely frame the office. From the barge 216
925 A strange invisible perfume hits the sense 217
926 Of the adjacent wharfs. The city cast 218
927 Her people out upon her; and Antony, 219
928 Enthroned i' the market-place, did sit alone, 220 220
929 Whistling to the air; which, but for vacancy, 221
930 Had gone to gaze on Cleopatra too 222
931 And made a gap in nature.
932 *Agr.* Rare Egyptian! 223

181 X: GCa, Cap, Inc, In2, JKP, Cum , SM1, LK1
182 same as 181
183 same as 181, AF1
184 same as 183, BT1, NM1
185 same as 184
186 same as 184; b̲X: TN1
187 same as 184, T̄N̄1
188 same as 187
189 X: GCa, Cap, In2, JKP, LK1; R: Inc; a̲X̲ Inc; MOVE 189-245 to follow*
190 XL Cap, In2, JKP, LK1; R̲: GC̄a, Cum; a̲X̲: GS1; MOVE 190-246 to follow*
191 X: Cap, In2; R̲: GCa, Inc, Cum; MOVE 191-192 to open: LK1; MOVE 191-*
192 X: Cap, Inc, Īn2; R̲: GCa, Cum
193 X: In2, JKP; R̲: GC̄a; N̲: Cap, Cum
194 X: In2, JKP
195 a̲X: In2; N̲: Vap, Inc; MOVE 195-245 to open: LK1
196 MOVE 196-2̄10a to follow 4̄8̄: 39: In2
197
198

199
200
201
022
203
204
205
206
207
208
209

210 b̲X: In2; N̲: Inc
211 X̲: In2
212 X: In2
213 X: In2
214 X: In2
215 X: In2
216 X: In2
217 X: In2
218 X; In2
219 X: In2
220 X: In2
221 X: In2
222 X: In2

223 X: In2, Lac; b̲X: Bel

*22:189 1̲1̲: 10a: SM1; MOVE 189-243a to follow 1̲1̲: 55: In2
*22:190 1̄1̄: 10: WA1; MOVE 190-243a to follow 1̄1̄: 55: GCa, Cum; MOVE 190-
    244a to follow 1̄1̄: 10a:JKP   *22:191237 to follow 1̲1̲:
    109: JKP

933	*Eno.* Upon her landing, Antony sent to her,	224
934	Invited her to supper: she replied,	225
935	It should be better he became her guest:	226
936	Which she entreated: our courteous Antony,	227
937	Whom ne'er the word of 'No' woman heard speak,	228
938	Being barber'd ten times o'er, goes to the feast,	229
939	And for his ordinary pays his heart 230	230
940	For what his eyes eat only.	
941	*Agr.* Royal wench!	231
942	She made great Cæsar lay his sword to bed:	232
943	He plough'd her, and she cropp'd.	
944	*Eno.* I saw her once	233
945	Hop forty paces through the public street:	234
946	And having lost her breath, she spoke, and panted,	235
947	That she did make defect perfection,	236
948	And, breathless, power breathe forth.	237
949	*Mec.* Now Antony must leave her utterly.	238
950	*Eno.* Never: he will not:	239
951	Age cannot wither her, nor custom stale 240	240
952	Her infinite variety: other women cloy	241
953	The appetites they feed: but she makes hungry	242
954	Where most she satisfies: for vilest things	243
955	Become themselves in her: that the holy priests	244
956	Bless her when she is riggish.	245
957	*Mec.* If beauty, wisdom, modesty, can settle	246
958	The heart of Antony, Octavia is	247
959	A blessed lottery to him.	
	Agr. Let us go.	248
960	Good Enobarbus, make yourself my guest 249	249
961	Whilst you abide here.	
962	*Eno.* Humbly, sir, I thank you. [*Exeunt.*	250

962+1	**SCENE III.** *The same. Cæsar's house.*

963	*Enter* ANTONY, CÆSAR, OCTAVIA *between them,*
963+1	*and* Attendants.

964	*Ant.* The world and my great office will sometimes	1
965	Divide me from your bosom.	
	Octa. All which time	2
966	Before the gods my knee shall bow my prayers	3
967	To them for you.	
968	*Ant.* Good night, sir. My Octavia,	4
969	Read not my blemishes in the world's report:	5

224   X: Bel, In2, BT1
225   same as 224
226   same as 224
227   same as 224

228   same as 224
229   same as 224
230   same as 224

231   same as 224; bX: WM1, ChC, JL1, LoC
232   X: Bel, In2, JKP, WM1, ChC, JL1, KyB, LoC, BT1, NM1; bX: LiL,Tab

233   X: Bel, In2, WM1, SP1, ChC, Hal, JL1, HIM, LiL, LoC, BT1, SM1, BA1*
234   X: GCa, Cap, Bel, Inc, In2, WM1, SP1, Cum, ChC, JL1, LiL, LoC, BT1*
235   same as 234
236   same as 234
237   same as 234
238   MOVE 238-243a to follow 11: 55: In2
239
240

241   bX: ChC, JL1, LiL, MTh, LoC
242   X: ChC, JL1, LiL, MTh, LoC; bX: HIM
243   same as 242; less bX; bX: GCa, Cap, Inc, In2, JKP, SP1, Cum, Lac*
244   X: GCa, Cap, Inc, In2, JKP, SP1, Cum, ChC, Lac, Hal, JL1, HIM,KyB*
245   same as 244, WM1
246   X: GCa, Cap, Inc, In2, SM1, LK1; N: VhC
247   same as 246; less N

248   same as 247, less SM1; aX: SM1; bX: WM1, Hal, JL1; N: JKP, LoC;*
249   X: GCa, Cap, Inc, In2, WM1, JL1, LK1; Insert 179b-188: WA1

250   same as 249; less Insert; bX: OA1; ADD 3: Cum; Insert 32: 24-50:LiL;
      Insert 32 : 22-61: ChC; ADD 2: JJK

Scene 23

ALL CUT: GCa, Cap, Inc, In2, WM1, Cum, Lac, JL1, HIM, MTh, TaB, LK1
1   X: JKP, Hal, KyB

2   same as 1
3   same as 1

4   same as 1; bX: LiL; cX: BT1, SM1, WA1, OA1
5   same as 1, LiL

*22:233 NM1, TaB; aX: JKP, KyB, WA1; bX: GCa, Cap, Inc, Cum
*22:234 BA1, NM1, TaB   *22:243 Hal, HIM, KyB, OA1, ML1
*22:244 LiL, MTh, LoC, OA1, ML1; bX: WM1   *22:248 Insert
   21: 2b-43, add 5, 26: 1-145: WM1; Insert 26: 134-144: Hal; Insert
   26: 122-141a, 142-144: OA1

970	I have not kept my square; but that to come	6
	Shall all be done by the rule. Good night, dear	
971	lady.	7
972	**Good night, sir.**	8
	Cæs. Good night.	9
973	*[Exeunt Cæsar and Octavia.*	
974	*Enter* Soothsayer.	
975	*Ant.* Now, sirrah; you do wish yourself in Egypt?	10
	Sooth. Would I had never come from thence,	11
976	nor you	
977	**Thither!**	12
978	*Ant.* If you can, your reason?	
	Sooth. I see it in	13
979	**My motion, have it not in my tongue: but yet**	14
980	**Hie you to Egypt again.**	
	Ant. Say to me,	15
981-2	**Whose fortunes shall rise higher, Cæsar's or mine?**	16
	Sooth. Cæsar's.	17
983	**Therefore, O Antony, stay not by his side:**	18
984	**Thy demon, that's thy spirit which keeps thee, is**	19
985	**Noble, courageous, high, unmatchable,** 20	20
986	**Where Cæsar's is not; but, near him, thy angel**	21
987	**Becomes a fear, as being o'erpower'd: therefore**	22
988	**Make space enough between you.**	
989	*Ant.* Speak this no more.	23
	Sooth. To none but thee; no more, but when	
990	to thee.	24
991	**If thou dost play with him at any game,**	25
992	**Thou art sure to lose; and, of that natural luck,**	26
	He beats thee 'gainst the odds: thy lustre	
993	thickens,	27
994	**When he shines by: I say again, thy spirit**	28
995	**Is all afraid to govern thee near him;**	29
996	**But, he away, 'tis noble.**	
997	*Ant.* Get thee gone: **30**	30
	Say to Ventidius I would speak with him:	31
998	*[Exit Soothsayer.*	
999	**He shall to Parthia. Be it art or hap,**	32
1000	**He hath spoken true: the very dice obey him;**	33
1001	**And in our sports my better cunning faints**	34
1002	**Under his chance: if we draw lots, he speeds;**	35
1003	**His cocks do win the battle still of mine,**	36
1004	**When it is all to nought; and his quails ever**	37
1005	**Beat mine, inhoop'd, at odds. I will to Egypt:**	38

6 same as 5

7 same as 5; bX: SM1; ADD 4: BT1; Insert 32: 24-37: SM1, WA1
8 X: JKP, Hal, KyB
9 X: JKP, Hal

10 X: Bel, JP1; N: Hal, WA1; MOVE 10-40a to follow 25: 119: JKP; MOVE
    10-40a to follow 27: 112: ER1
11 X: Bel, JP1; N: WA1
12 X: Bel, JP1

13 X: Bel, JKP, SM1, JP1; N: WA1
14 same as 13 including N

15 X: Bel, JP1; aX: JKP, SM1
16 X: Bel, JP1
17 X: Bel, JP1
18 X: Bel, JKP, JP1
19 X: Bel, JP1
20 X: Bel, JKP, JP1
21 X: Bel, JP1
22 X: Bel, JP1; bX: JKP

23 X: Bel, JP1; aX: JKP

24 X: Bel, JP1; bX: TN1
25 X: Bel, LiL, SM1,   GS1, JP1
26 same as 25, WA1; bX: BA1, IP1, ML1

27 X: Bel, LiL, SM1, WA1, BA1, IP1, GS1, JP1; aX: ML1; bX: BT1
28 X: Bel, BT1, SM1, WA1, GS1, JP1; aX: LiL, BA1, IP1; bX: TN1
29 X: Bel, BT1, SM1, WA1, GS1, JP1, TN1

30 X : Bel, JP1; aX: BT1, SM1, WA1, GS1, TN1
31 X: Bel, JKP, Hal, KyB, OA1, RH1, JP1, AF1, TN1

32 X: Bel, JKP, JP1, ML1; aX: Hal, KyB, OA1, RH1, TN1
33 X: Bel, JP1; bX: ChC, AF1, TN1
34 X: Bel, ChC, RH1, JP1, AF1, TN1
35 same as 34; bX: JKP, KyB, LiL, IP1, GS1, BH1, ML1, SFr
36 X: Bel, JKP, ChC, KyB, LiL, IP1, GS1, RH1, BH1, JP1, AF1, ML1,TN1
37 same as 36, less JKP; bX: JKP, BA1
38 X: Bel, JP1, AF1; aX: JKP, ChC, KyB, LiL, BA1, IP1, GS1, RH1, BH1,
    ML1, TN1

1006	And though I make this marriage for my peace,	39
1007a	I' the east my pleasure lies.	
1008	*Enter* VENTIDIUS.	
1007b	O, come, Ventidius, 40	40
1009	You must to Parthia: your commission 's ready:	41
1010	Follow me, and receive 't. [*Exeunt.*	42

1010+1   SCENE IV. *The same. A street.*

1011   *Enter* LEPIDUS, MECÆNAS, *and* AGRIPPA.

1012	*Lep.* Trouble yourselves no further: pray you, hasten	1
1013	Your generals after.	
	Agr. Sir, Mark Antony	2
1014-15	Will e'en but kiss Octavia, and we'll follow.	3
1016	*Lep.* Till I shall see you in your soldier's dress,	4
1017	Which will become you both, farewell.	
	Mec. We shall,	5
1018	As I conceive the journey, be at the Mount	6
1019	Before you, Lepidus.	7
	Lep. Your way is shorter;	8
1020	My purposes do draw me much about:	
1021	You'll win two days upon me.	
1022	*Mec.* }	
	Agr. } Sir, good success!	9
1023	*Lep.* Farewell. [*Exeunt.* 10	10

1023+1 SCENE V. *Alexandria. Cleopatra's palace.*

1024	*Enter* CLEOPATRA, CHARMIAN, IRAS, *and*	
1024+1	ALEXAS.	
1025	*Cleo.* Give me some music; music, moody food	1
1026	Of us that trade in love.	2
1027	*Attend.* The music, ho!	

1028   *Enter* MARDIAN *the Eunuch.*

1029	*Cleo.* Let it alone; let's to billiards: come, Charmian.	3
1030	*Char.* My arm is sore; best play with Mardian.	4
	Cleo. As well a woman with an eunuch play'd	5
1031	As with a woman. Come, you'll play with me,	
1032	sir?	6
1033	*Mar.* As well as I can, madam.	7
1034	*Cleo.* And when good will is show'd, though 't	

39 X: JP1; bX: NM1, AF1, ER1, TN1; ADD1: AF1

40 X: JP1; aX: Be1; bX: JKP, Hal, KyB, LiL, EdT, SM1, WA1, OA1, NM1, AF1*
41 X: JKP, Hal, KyB, LiL, EdT, SM1, WA1, OA1, NM1, JP1, AF1, ER1, TN1
42 same as 41, BT1, less Hal; Insert 15: 1-209 and 26: 1-145: BT1; ADD
        2, insert 22: 24-37 and 15: 1-65: Hal

                                Scene 24

ALL CUT: GCa, Cap, Inc, In2, WM1, SP1, Cum, ChC, Lac, Hal, JL1, HIM, KyB,
    LiL, MTh, EdT, LoC, BT1, SM1, WA1, OA1, BA1, IP1, TaB, RA1, JS1, RH1,
    JP1, AF1, ER1, LK1, TN1
  1

  2
  3

  4 X: JKP, BH1

  5 aX : JKP, BH1
  6
  7
  8

  9
10 ADD 8: JKP

                            Scene 25

  1 X: JS1; MOVE 1-119 to follow 27: 137: TaB
  2 X: JS1; bX: In2, ChC,, EdT, LoC : ADD 1: In2; Insert 15: 1-75: SM1

  3 X: In2, SM1, WA1, NM1; bX: JKP, WM1, LiL, BT1, ML1
  4 X: Inc, In2, JKP, WM1, SP1, Cum, Lac, Hal, JL1, LiL, MTh, BT1, SM1,WA1*
  5 X: Inc, In2, JKP, WM1, SP1, Cum, ChC, Lac, Hal, JL1, HIM, KyB, LiL, MTh,
        EdT, LoC, BT1, SM1, WA1, OA1, NM1, SP1; Insert 15: 11-22: JP1
  6 same as 5, less EdT, OA1; less Insert; aX: EdT, OA1; bX: BA1
  7 same as 6, BA1; less aX, bX

*23:40 ER1, TN1; ADD 1: AF1; Insert 15: 1-65: KyB; Insert 15: 1-78:EdT
*25: 4 NMo; bX: ChC, HIM, EdT, LoC

1035	come too short,	8
1036	The actor may plead pardon. I'll none now:	9
1037	Give me mine angle; we'll to the river: there,	10
1038	My music playing far off, I will betray **11**	11
1039	Tawny-finn'd fishes: my bended hook shall pierce	12
1040	Their slimy jaws, and, as I draw them up,	13
1041	I'll think them every one an Antony,	14
1042	And say 'Ah, ha! you're caught.'	
	Char. 'Twas merry when	15
1043	You wager'd on your angling: when your diver	16
1044	Did hang a salt-fish on his hook, which he	17
1045	With fervency drew up.	
1046	*Cleo.* That time,—O times!—	18
1047	I laugh'd him out of patience; and that night	19
1048	I laugh'd him into patience: and next morn, **20**	20
1049	Ere the ninth hour, I drunk him to his bed:	21
1050	Then put my tires and mantles on him, whilst	22
1051a	I wore his sword Philippan.	
1052	*Enter a* Messenger.	
1051b	O, from Italy!	23
1053	Ram thou thy fruitful tidings in mine ears,	24
1054	That long time have been barren.	
1055	*Mess.* Madam, madam,—	25
1056	*Cleo.* Antonius dead!—If thou say so, villain	26
1057	Thou kill'st thy mistress: but well and free,	27
1058-8	If thou so yield him, there is gold, and here	28
1060	My bluest veins to kiss: a hand that kings	29
1061	Have lipp'd, and trembled kissing.	30
1062	*Mess.* First, madam, he is well.	
1063	*Cleo.* Why, there's more gold	31
1064	But, sirrah, mark, we use	32
1065	To say the dead are well: bring it to that,	33
1066	The gold I give thee will I melt and pour	34
1067	Down thy ill-uttering throat.	35
1068	*Mess.* Good madam, hear me.	
1069	*Cleo.* Well, go to, I will:	36
1070	But there's no goodness in thy face: if Antony	37
1071	Be free and healthful,—so tart a favour	38
1072	To trumpet such good tidings! If not well,	39
1073	Thou shouldst come like a Fury crown'd with snakes,	40
1074	Not like a formal man.	
1075	*Mess.* Will 't please you hear me!	41
	Cleo. I have a mind to strike thee ere thou	
1076	speak'st:	42

8   same as 7, OA1, RA1, JP1, TN1
9   X: In2, SP1, SM1, WA1, JP1; $\underline{aX}$: Inc, JKP, WM1, ChC, Lac, Ha1, JL1, KyB,
10 X: SP1, $\overline{Cum}$; $\underline{aX}$: In2
11 X: WM1, SP1, $\overline{Cum}$; $\underline{aX}$: In2
12 same as 11; less $\underline{aX}$; $\underline{bX}$: In2
13 same as 11; less $\underline{aX}$; $\underline{aX}$: In2
14 same as 11; less $\underline{aX}$

15 X: SP1, Cum; $\underline{aX}$: WM1; $\underline{bX}$: JKP, Ha1
16 X: JKP, WM1, $\overline{SP1}$, Cum, $\overline{Ha1}$
17 same as 16, less WM1

18 sameas 17
19 same as 17
20 same as 17; $\underline{bX}$: WM1
21 same as 17, $\overline{WM1}$
22 X: WM1, SP1, Cum, Ha1; $\underline{aX}$: JKP, SP1

23 $\underline{aX}$: WM1, Cum, Ha1; $\underline{bX}$: In2
24 $\overline{X}$: In2, ChC, LoC

25 $\underline{aX}$: In2, ChC, LoC; $\underline{N}$: In2, JP1
26
27
28 $\underline{R}$: Cum
29 $\underline{aX}$: Cum
30

31 N: SP1
32 $\overline{X}$: WM1
33 X: WM1, Cum; $\underline{bX}$: In2
34 X: WM1, Cum; $\overline{R}$: In2
35 X: In2, WM1, $\overline{Cum}$

36 X: In2, JKP, Cum, KyB; $\underline{aX}$: WM1; $\underline{bX}$: BT1
37 X: JKP, KyB, BT1; $\underline{aX}$: Cum; $\underline{bX}$: $\overline{In2}$, RA1, OA1
38 X: In2, JKP, KyB, $\overline{BT1}$, RA1, $\overline{TN1}$
39 same as 38

40 X: JKP, WM1, KyB, BT1, RA1, TN1

41 X: WM1, BT1; $\underline{aX}$: JKP, KyB, RA1, TN1; $\underline{bX}$: Be1, Cum

42 X: Be1, JKP, 'WM1, Cum

1077	Yet, if thou say Antony lives, is well,	43
1078	Or friends with Cæsar, or not captive to him,	44
1079	I'll set thee in a shower of gold, and hail	45
1080	Rich pearls upon thee.	
1081	*Mess.* Madam, he's well.	
1082	*Cleo.* Well said	46
1083	*Mess.* And friends with Cæsar.	
1084	*Cleo.* Thou'rt an honest man	47
1085	*Mess.* Cæsar and he are greater friends than ever.	48
1086	*Cleo.* Make thee a fortune from me.	
1087	*Mess.* But yet, madam—	49
1088	*Cleo.* I do not like ' But yet,' it does allay	50
1089	The good precedence; fie upon ' But yet'!	51
1090	'But yet' is as a gaoler to bring forth	52
1091	Some monstrous malefactor. Prithee, friend,	53
1092	Pour out the pack of matter to mine ear,	54
1093	The good and bad together: he's friends with Cæsar;	55
1094	In state of health thou say'st; and thou say's free.	56
1095	*Mess.* Free, madam! no; I made no such report:	57
1096	He's bound unto Octavia.	
1097	*Cleo.* For what good turn!	58
1098	*Mess.* For the best turn i' the bed.	
1099	*Cleo.* I am pale, Charmian	59
1100	*Mess.* Madam, he's married to Octavia.	60
1101-2	*Cleo.* The most infectious pestilence upon thee! [*Strikes him down*	61
1103	*Mess.* Good madam, patience.	
1104	*Cleo.* What say you? Hence, [*Strikes him again*	62
1105	Horrible villain! or I'll spurn thine eyes	63
1106	Like balls before me: I'll unhair thy head:	64
1107	[*She hales him up and down*	
1108	Thou shalt be whipp'd with wire, and stew'd in brine,	65
;;09	Smarting in lingering pickle.	
1110	*Mess.* Gracious madam,	66
1111	I that do bring the news made not the match.	67
112	*Cleo.* Say 'tis not so, a province I will give thee,	68
1113	And make thy fortunes proud: the blow thou hadst	69
1114	Shall make thy peace for moving me to rage;	70

43 X: Bel, WM1
44 X: Bel, WM1; bX: LiL
45 X: Bel, WM1

46 aX: Bel, WM1

47

48

49
50 bX: BA1
51 aX: BA1, TN1; bX: In2, WM1
52 X: In2, WM1, KyB
53 aX: In2, WM1, KyB
54

55

56

57 bX: JKP

58 X: JKP; bX: GCa, Cap, Bel, Inc, In2, WM1, SP1, Cum, ChC, Lac, Hal, JL1,
   HIM, KyB, LiL, MTh, LoC, BT1, OA1, BA1, TaB
59 X: GCa, Cap, In2, JKP, Cum, Lac, KyB, SM1; aX: Bel, Inc, WM1, SP1, ChC*
60 X: In2, KyB, SM1

61 X: Bel

62 X: Cap, Bel; bX: JP1, OA1; cX: Cum; Insert 74: WM1

63 X: Cap, Bel, In2, JS1; bX: WM1
64 same as 63; less bX; aX: WM1; bX: Cum, JL1, ML1

65 X: Cap, Bel, In2, WM1, Cum, ChC, JL1, LoC; bX: JKP

66 X: Bel, WM1, Cum; aX: Cap, In2, JKP, ChC, JL1, LoC; bX: SP1
67 X: Bel, WM1, SP1, Cum

68 X: WM1, SP1, Cum, KyB

69 same as 68; bX: In2, JKP, ChC, JL1, LoC, IP1, TaB, RA1, JS1, ML1, TN1
70 X: Cap, In2, JKP, WM1, SP1, Cum, ChC, JL1, KyB, LoC, IP1, TaB, RA1, JS1,
   ML1, TN1

*25:59 Hal, JL1, HIM, LiL, MTh, EdT, LoC, BT1, WA1, OA1, BA1, TaB

1115	And I will boot thee with what gift beside	71
1116	Thy modesty can beg.	
1117	*Mess.* He's married, madam.	72
	Cleo. Rogue, thou hast lived too long.	
1118	*[Draws a knife.*	
1119	*Mess.* Nay, then I'll run.	73
	What mean you, madam? I have made no fault.	74
1120	*[Exit.*	
	Char. Good madam, keep yourself within	
1121	yourself:	75
1122	The man is innocent.	76
1123	*Cleo.* Some innocents 'scape not the thunderbolt.	77
1124	Melt Egypt into Nile! and kindly creatures	78
1125	Turn all to serpents! Call the slave again:	79
1126	Though I am mad, I will not bite him: call. 80	80
1127	*Char.* He is afeard to come.	
1128	*Cleo.* I will not hurt him.	81
1128+1	*[Exit Charmian.*	
1129	These hands do lack nobility, that they strike	82
1130	A meaner than myself; since I myself	83
1131a	Have given myself the cause.	
1132	*Re-enter* CHARMIAN *and* Messenger.	
1131b	Come hither, sir.	84
1133	Though it be honest, it is never good	85
1134	To bring bad news: give to a gracious message	86
1135	An host of tongues; but let ill tidings tell	87
1136	Themselves when they be felt.	
1137	*Mess.* I have done my duty.	88
1138	*Cleo.* Is he married?	89
1139	I cannot hate thee worser than I do, 90	90
1140	If thou again say 'Yes.'	
1141	*Mess.* He's married, madam.	91
1142	*Cleo.* The gods confound thee! dost thou hold	
1143	there still?	92
1144	*Mess.* Should I lie, madam?	
1145	*Cleo.* O, I would thou didst,	93
1146	So half my Egypt were submerged and made	94
1147	A cistern for scaled snakes! Go, get thee hence:	95
1148	Hadst thou Narcissus in thy face, to me	96
1149	Thou wouldst appear most ugly. He is married?	97
1150	*Mess.* I crave your highness' pardon.	
1151	*Cleo.* He is married?	98
	Mess. Take no offence that I would not offend	
1152	you:	99

71   same as 70, less In2

72   X: WM1, SP1, Cum, KyB; aX: Cap, JKP, ChC, JL1, LoC, IP1, TaB, RA1,JS1,
      ML1, TN1; bX: In2

73   X: Bel, In2, WM1, SP1, Cum, bX: JKP, ChC, Lac, Hal, JL1, HIM, LiL,EdT*
74   X: Bel, In2, JKP, SP1, Cum, ChC, Lac, Hal, JL1, HIM, KyB, LiL, LoC,
      BT1, AF1, TN1; bX: GS1; MOVE 74 to follow 62: WM1

75   X: Bel, In2
76   X: Bel, In2
77   X: Bel, In2, ChC, LoC, SM1, WA1
78   X: Bel, In2, ChC, LoC
79   same as 78, NM1; bX: WM1, Cum
80   X: Bel, In2, JKP, WM1, Cum, ChC, LoC; bX: LiL

81   X: Bel, In2, JKP, Cum, ChC, LoC; aX: WM1, LiL

82   X: Bel, In2, Cum, ChC, LoC
83   same as 82; bX: BT1

84   XL Bel, Cum , ChC, LoC; aX: In2, JKP, BT1
85   X: In2, Cum, ChC, LoC
86   same as 85; R: LiL; bX: WM1, KyB, BT1, TN1
87   X: In2, WM1, Cum, ChC, KyB, LoC, BT1, TN1

88   X: WM1, Cum, ChC, LoC; aX: In2, KyB, BL1, TN1; bX: JL1; cX: EdT
89   X: Cum; bX: LiL
90   X: Cum, KyB

91   X: Cum, KyB; bX: In2

92   X: Cum , KyB; R: In2; aX: JKP

93   X: WM1, Cum; R: In2; bX: JL1
94   X: In2, WM1, Cum, JL1, KyB, TN1
95   same as 94, less JL1; aX: JL1; bX: JS1, ML1
96   X: In2, WM1, Cum, KyB, JS1, ML1, TN1
97   X: In2, WM1, Cum, KyB; R: LoC; aX: JS1, ML1, TN1; bX: ChC, LiL; Insert
      33: 6-49a, and 32: 5-16, 19b-67: Hal
98   X: Cap, In2, JKP, Cum, ChC, Hal, KyB, LiL, LoC; aX: WM1

99   X: Cap, In2, JKP, Cum, ChC, Hal, JL1, KyB, LoC, BT1, JS1, BH1, ML1,TN1

*25:73 LoC, BT1, SM1, WA1, TaB, RA1, AF1

1153	To punish me for what you make me do 100	100
1154	Seems much unequal: he's married to Octavia.	101
	Cleo. O, that his fault should make a knave	
1155	of thee,	102
1156	That art not what thou'rt sure of! Get thee hence:	103
	The merchandise which thou hast brought from	
1157	Rome	104
1158	Are all too dear for me: lie they upon thy hand,	105
1159	And be undone by 'em! [*Exit Messenger.*	
1160	*Char.* Good your highness, patience.	106
	Cleo. In praising Antony, I have dispraised	
1161	Cæsar.	107
1162	*Char.* Many times, madam.	
	Cleo. I am paid for't now.	108
1163	Lead me from hence:	109
1164	I faint: O Iras, Charmian! 'tis no matter. 110	110
1165	Go to the fellow, good Alexas; bid him	111
1166	Report the feature of Octavia, her years,	112
1167	Her inclination, let him not leave out	113
1168	The colour of her hair: bring me word quickly.	114
	[*Exit Alexas.*	
1169	Let him for ever go:—let him not—Charmian,	115
1170	Though he be painted one way like a Gorgon,	116
1171	The other way's a Mars. Bid you Alexas	117
1171+1	[*To Mardian.*	
	Bring me word how tall she is. Pity me, Char-	
1172	mian,	118
1173	But do not speak to me. Lead me to my chamber.	119
1174	[*Exeunt.*	

1174+1	**SCENE VI.** *Near Misenum.*	
1175	*Flourish.* *Enter* POMPEY *and* MENAS *at one*	
1176	*door, with drum and trumpet: at another,*	
1177	CÆSAR, ANTONY, LEPIDUS, ENOBARBUS, ME-	
1177+1	CÆNAS, *with* Soldiers *marching.*	
	Pom. Your hostages I have, so have you	
1178	mine;	1
1179	And we shall talk before we fight.	2
	Cæs. Most meet	3
1180-1	That first we come to words; and therefore have we	4
1182	Our written purposes before us sent;	5
1183	Which, if thou hast consider'd, let us know	6
1184	If 'twill tie up thy discontented sword,	7
1185	And carry back to Sicily much tall youth	
1186	That else must perish here.	

100   same as 99, IP1, less JS1, ML1, TN1
101   X: Cap, In2, JKP, Cum, ChC, Hal, JL1, LiL, LoC; aX: KyB, BT1,BA1,IP1

102   X: Cap, In2, JKP, WM1, Cum, ChC, Hal, JL1, KyB, LiL, LoC, BT1, SM1*
103   X: Cap, In2, JKP, Cum, ChC, Hal, JL1, KyB, LiL, LoC, SM1; R: Ne1,WM1;
       aX: EdT, BT1, BA1, IP1, RA1, RH1, JP1, ML1, TN1
104   same as 103, BT1, WA1, JS1; less R, aX
105   same as 104, IP1

106   X: Cum, Hal, JL1, KyB; aX: Cap, In2, JKP, ChC, LiL, LoC, BT1, SM1,
       WA1, IP1, JS1; ADD 1: ChC
107   X: In2, WM1, SP1, Cum, ChC, Hal, JL1, KyB, LoC

108   X: In2, SP1, Cum, Hal, KyB, LoC; aX: WM1, ChC, JL1; Insert 33: 26-50:JL1
109   X: Hal, KyB
110   X: Hal, KyB
111   X: Hal, KyB
112   X: Hal, KyB
113   X: Hal, KyB
114   X: Hal, KyB; bX: ML1

115   X: Hal, KyB; bX: In2
116   X: In2, Hal, KyB
117   same as 116; bX: LoC

118   X: ChC, Hal, KyB; aX: In2, LoC; bX: WM1
119   X: WM1, Hal, KyB; bX: ChC, LoC, BT1, SM1, WA1, OA1; ADD 18: JKP; In-
      sert 35: 1-20, and 34: 1-28, and 23: 10-40: JKP, WM1; Insert 34:
      1-32, add 56: In2; Insert 33: 6b-51, and 26: 84-115, add 7: ChC, LoC;
      Insert 33: 1-516: SM1, WA1, OA1

Scene 26

ALL CUT: Inc, In2, Cum, KyB, LiL, EdT, NM1, LK; ALL CUT EXCEPT TRANSFER:
Hal, OA1

1   X: GCa, Cap, JKP, ChC, JL1, LoC, RH1; MOVE 1-144 to follow 21: 43:*
2   same as 1; less MOVEs; bX: WM1
3   same as 1; less MOVEs; R: WM1
4   same as 1; less MOVEs
5   same as 4
6   same as 4
7   same as 4

*25:102 BA1, IP1, RA1, JS1, RH1, ML1, TN1   *26: 1 WM1; MOVE
   1-145 to follow 23: 49: BT1

1187	*Pom.* To you all three,		8
1188	The senators alone of this great world,		9
1189	Chief factors for the gods, I do not know	10	10
1190	Wherefore my father should revengers want,		11
1191	Having a son and friends ; since Julius Cæsar,		12
1192	Who at Philippi the good Brutus ghosted,		13
1193	There saw you labouring for him. What was't		14
1194	That moved pale Cassius to conspire ; and what		15
1195	Made the all-honour'd, honest Roman, Brutus,		16
1196	With the arm'd rest, courtiers of beauteous free-dom,		17
1197	To drench the Capitol ; but that they would		18
1198	Have one man but a man? And that is it	19	19
1199	Hath made me rig my navy ; at whose burthen		20
1200	The anger'd ocean foams ; with which I meant		21
1201	To scourge the ingratitude that despiteful Rome		22
1202	Cast on my noble father.		
1203	*Cæs.* Take your time.		23
1204	*Ant.* Thou canst not fear us, Pompey, with thy sails ;		24
1205	We'll speak with thee at sea : at land, thou know'st		25
1206	How much we do o'er-count thee.		
1207	*Pom.* At land, indeed,		26
1208	Thou dost o'er-count me of my father's house :		27
1209	But, since the cuckoo builds not for himself,		28
1210	Remain in't as thou mayst.		
1211	*Lep.* Be pleased to tell us—		29
1212	For this is from the present—how you take	30	30
1213	The offers we have sent you.		
1214	*Cæs.* There's the point.		31
1215	*Ant.* Which do not be entreated to, but weigh		32
1216	What it is worth embraced.		
	Cæs. And what may follow,		33
1217	To try a larger fortune.		
1218	*Pom.* You have made me offer		34
1219	Of Sicily, Sardinia ; and I must		35
1220	Rid all the sea of pirates ; then, to send		36
1221	Measures of wheat to Rome : this 'greed upon,		37
1222	To part with unhack'd edges, and bear back		38
1223	Our targes undinted.		
1224	*Cæs. Ant. Lep.* That's our offer.		
	Pom. Know, then, 40		40
1225-6	I came before you here a man prepared		41
1227	To take this offer : but Mark Antony		42
1228	Put me to some impatience : though I lose		43

```
 8  same as 4; bX: RA1, JP1
 9  same as 4, RA1, JP1
10  same as 9
11  same as 9
12  same as 9; bX: Lac, MTh, BT1, SM1, WA1, TaB
13  X: GCa, Cap, JKP, ChC, Lac, JL1, MTh, LoC, BT1, SM1, WA1, TaB, RA1*
14  same as 13, less Lac, MTh; aX: Lac, MTh
15  same as 14; less aX
16  same as 15

17  same as 15, BA1; R: WM1
18  same as 15; R: WM1
19  X: GCa, Cap, JKP, ChC, JL1, LoC, RA1, RH1, JP1; R: WM1; aX: BT1, SM1*
20  same as 19, WM1; less R, aX
21  same as 20
22  same as 20

23  same as 20, less WM1, RH1; aX: WM1, RH1

24  same as 23, less RA1; less aX

25  same as 24

26  same as 24; bX: Bel, SP1, IP1
27  same  as 24, Bel, SP1, IP1
28  same as 27, WM1, AF1

29  X: GCa, Cap, Bel, JKP, ChC, JL1, LoC, GS1; aX: WM1, SP1, LoC, IP1, AF1
30  same as 29; less aX; aX: SP1, IP1

31  same as 30; less aX; bX: SP1, Lac, HIM, BA1, TN1
32  X: GCa, Cap, Bel, JKP, WM1, SP1, ChC, Lac, JL1, HIM, LoC, BT1, BA1,GS1
      TN1; bX: MTh
33  same as 32, MTh; less bX: R: ML1; bX: IP1

34  X: GCa, Cap, JKP, ChC, JL1, MTh, LoC; aX: Bel, WM1, SP1, HIM, BT1, GS1*
35  same as 34, RA1, less MTh; less aX; aX: MTh; bX: WM1
36  same as 35; less aX, bX; R: WM1; bX: TN1
37  same as 35, WM1; less aX, bX; aX: TN1
38  same as 37; less aX; bX: ML1
39  same as 37; less aX; aX: ML;

40  X: GCa, Cap, JKP, ChC, JL1, LoC; aX: WM1
41  same as 40; less aX
42  same as 41; bX: SP1, TaB
43  X: GCa, Cap, JKP, SP1, ChC, JL1, LoC, TaB
```

*26:13 RH1, JP1   *26:19 WA1, TaB   *26:34 ML1, TN1

1229	The praise of it by telling, you must know,	44
1230	When Cæsar and your brother were at blows,	45
1231	Your mother came to Sicily and did find	46
2132	Her welcome friendly.	
1233	*Ant.* I have heard it, Pompey;	47
2134	And am well studied for a liberal thanks	48
2135	Which I do owe you.	
1236	*Pom.* Let me have your hand:	49
1237	I did not think, sir, to have met you here. 50	50
	Ant. The beds i' the east are soft; and thanks	
1238	to you,	51
1239	That call'd me timelier than my purpose hither;	52
1240	For I have gain'd by't.	
	Cæs. Since I saw you last,	53
1241	There is a change upon you.	
1242	*Pom.* Well, I know not	54
1243	What counts harsh fortune casts upon my face;	55
1244	But in my bosom shall she never come,	56
1245	To make my heart her vassal.	
1246	*Lep.* Well met here.	57
	Pom. I hope so, Lepidus. Thus we are	
1247	agreed:	58
1248	I crave our composition may be written,	59
1249	And seal'd between us.	
1250	*Cæs.* That's the next to do. 60	60
	Pom. We'll feast each other ere we part;	
1251	and let's	61
1252	Draw lots who shall begin.	
1253	*Ant.* That will I, Pompey.	62
	Pom. No, Antony, take the lot: but, first	63
1254	Or last, your fine Egyptian cookery	64
1255	Shall have the fame. I have heard that Julius	
	Cæsar	65
1256	Grew fat with feasting there.	
1257	*Ant.* You have heard much.	66
1258	*Pom.* I have fair meanings, sir.	
1259	*Ant.* And fair words to them.	67
1260	*Pom.* Then so much have I heard:	68
1261	And I have heard, Apollodorus carried—	69
1262	*Eno.* No more of that: he did so.	
1263	*Pom.* What, I pray you? 70	70
1264	*Eno.* A certain queen to Cæsar in a mattress.	71
	Pom. I know thee now: how farest thou,	72
1265	soldier?	
	Eno. Well:	73
1266	And well am like to do; for, I perceive,	74

44 same as 43
45 same as 43
46 same as 43

47 same as 43
48 same as 43

49 X: GCa, Cap, JKP, SP1, JL1, TaB; aX: ChC, LoC
50 same as 49; less aX

51 same as 50
52 same as 50

53 same as 50; bX: WM1, BH1

54 same as 50, WM1, BH1; bX: TN1
55 same as 54, TN1
56 same as 55

57 X: GCa, Cap, JKP, WM1, SP1, JL1, TaB; aX: BH1, TN1; bX: LoC

58 X: GCa, Cap, JKP, Lac, JL1, HIM, MTh; aX: WM1, SP1, LoC, TaB; bX: TN1
59 X: GCa, Cap, JKP, Lac, JL1, HIM, MTh, TN1

60 same as 59

61 X: GCa, Cap, JKP, JL1, TN1; R: SM1; bX: SP1, LoC, WA1

62 X: GCa, Cap, JKP, SP1, ChC, JL1, LoC, SM1, WA1, JS1, TN1; R: WM1
63 X: GCa, Cap, Bel, JKP, WM1, SP1, ChC, LoC, WA1, JS1, BH1, TN1; MOVE 63-*
64 X: GCa, Cap, Bel, JKP, WM1, SP1, TN1

65 same as 64

66 same as 64

67 same as 64, ML1
68 same as 64
69 same as 64

70 same as 64
71 same as 64
72 same as 64, less WM1

73 same as 72
74 same as 72

*26:63 79 to follow 27: 8: JL1

1267	**Four feasts are toward.**	
1268	*Pom.* Let me shake thy hand:	75
1269	**I never hated thee: I have seen thee fight,**	76
1270	**When I have envied thy behaviour.**	
	Eno. Sir,	77
1271	**I never loved you much: but I ha' praised ye,**	78
1272	**When you have well deserved ten times as much**	79
1273	**As I have said you did.**	
1274	*Pom.* Enjoy thy plainness, 80	80
1275	**It nothing ill becomes thee.**	81
1276	**Aboard my galley I invite you all:**	82
1277	**Will you lead, lords?**	
1278	*Cæs. Ant. Lep.* Show us the way, sir.	
	Pom. Come.	83
	[Exeunt all but Menas and Enobarbus.	
1279	*Men.* [*Aside*] Thy father, Pompey, would	84
1280	ne'er have made this treaty.—You and I have	85
1281	known, sir.	86
1282	*Eno.* At sea, I think.	87
1283	*Men.* We have, sir.	88
1284	*Eno.* You have done well by water.	89
1285	*Men.* And you by land. 90	90
	Eno. I will praise any man that will praise	91
1286	me; though it cannot be denied what I have d...	92
1287	by land.	93
1288	*Men.* Nor what I have done by water.	94
	Eno. Yes, something you can deny for y...	95
1289-90	own safety: you have been a great thief by sea	96
1291	*Men.* And you by land.	97
	Eno. There I deny my land service. P...	98
1292	give me your hand, Menas: if our eyes h...	99
1293	authority, here they might take two thie...	100
1294	kissing. 101	101
	Men. All men's faces are true, whatsome'e	102
1295-6	their hands are.	103
	Eno. But there is never a fair woman ha...	104
1297-8	true face.	105
1299	*Men.* No slander; they steal hearts.	106
1300	*Eno.* We came hither to fight with you.	107
	Men. For my part, I am sorry it is turned...	108
1301	a drinking. Pompey doth this day laugh aw...	109
1302	his fortune. 110	110
	Eno. If he do, sure, he cannot weep't ba...	111
1303	again.	112
	Men. You've said, sir. We looked not f...	113
1304	Mark Antony here: pray you, is he married...	114

```
75   X: GCa, Cap, JKP, SP1; aX: Bel, TN1; ADD 5: WM1
76   same as 75; less aX, ADD

77   same as 76
78   same as 76
79   same as 76

80   same as 76
81   same as 76; ADD 34: WM1
82   same as 76, WM1


83   X: GCa, Cap, JKP, WM1, JL1, LoC; aX: ChC

84   X: Cap, Bel, JKP, WM1, JL1, BT1, BA1, JP1; MOVE 84-115 to follow 25:*
85   X: Cap, Bel, JKP, JP1; aX: WM1, BT1., BA1
86   same as 85; less aX
87   same as 86; R: GCa
88   same as 87 including R
89   X: GCa, Cap, Bel, JKP, ChC, LoC, JP1
90   same as 89
91   same as 89, BH1; bX: TN1
92   X: GCa, Cap, Bel, JKP, ChC, JL1, LoC, BT1, BH1, JP1, TN1
93   same as 92
94   same as 92
95   same as 92
96   X: GCa, Cap, Bel, JKP, ChC, LoC, BH1, JP1; aX: JL1, BT1, TN1
97   same as 96; less aX
98   same as 97, TN1; aX: BT1; bX: JS1
99   same as 98, JS1, less BH1; less aX, bX; bX: BT1, GS1, BH1
100  X: GCa, Cap, Bel, JKP, ChC, LoC, BT1, JS1, GS1, BH1, JP1, TN1
101  X: GCa, Cap, Bel, WM1, ChC, LoC, BT1, SM1, BA1, RA1, JS1,GS1, RH1,BH1*
102  X: GCa, Cap, Bel, WM1, ChC, JL1, LoC, BT1, SM1, WA1, BA1, RA1, JS1,*
103  same as 102
104  same as 102
105  same as 102, TaB, less TN1
106  sam as 105
107  X: Bel, WM1, ChC, BT1, BA1, RA1, RH1, JP1, ML1
108  X: Bel, WM1, BT1, RA1, JP1
109  same as 108
110  same as 108
111  same as 108
112  same as 108, less WM1
113  same as 112
114  X; Bel, BT1, JP1; bX: ChC
```

```
*2684  119: ChC, LoC              *26:101  JP1, ML1, TN1
*26:102  GS1, RH1, BH1, JP1, ML1, ER1, TN1
```

1305	Cleopatra?	115
1306	*Eno.* Cæsar's sister is called Octavia.	116
	Men. True, sir; she was the wife of Caïs	117
1307	Marcellus.	118
1308	*Eno.* But she is now the wife of Marcus Antonie.	119
1309	*Men.* Pray ye, sir?	120
1310	*Eno.* 'Tis true.	121
	Men. Then is Cæsar and he for ever knit to	122
1311	gether.	123
	Eno. If I were bound to divine of this unity.	124
1312=13	I would not prophesy so.	125
	Men. I think the policy of that purpose made	126
1314-15	more in the marriage than the love of the parties	127
	Eno. I think so too. But you shall find, the	128
1316	band that seems to tie their friendship together	129
1317	will be the very strangler of their amity: Octavia	130
1318-19	is of a holy, cold, and still conversation.	131
1320	*Men.* Who would not have his wife so?	132
	Eno. Not he that himself is not so; which is	133
1321	Mark Antony. He will to his Egyptian dish	134
1322	again: then shall the sighs of Octavia blow the	135
1323	fire up in Cæsar; and, as I said before, that which	136
1324	is the strength of their amity shall prove the im	137
1325	mediate author of their variance. Antony will	138
1326	use his affection where it is: he married but his	139
1327	occasion here.	140
	Men. And thus it may be. Come, sir, will	141
1328-9	you aboard? I have a health for you.	142
	Eno. I shall take it, sir: we have used our	143
1330-1	throats in Egypt.	144
1332	*Men.* Come, let's away. [*Exeunt*	145

1332+1	**SCENE VII.** *On board Pompey's galley, of*
1332+2	*Misenum.*

1333	*Music plays. Enter two or three* Servants with	
1334	*a banquet.*	
	First Serv. Here they'll be, man. Some of	1
;335	their plants are ill-rooted already; the least wind	2
1336-7	i' the world will blow them down.	3
1338	*Sec. Serv.* Lepidus is high-coloured.	4
	First Serv. They have made him drink alms	5
1339	drink.	6
	Sec. Serv. As they pinch one another by the	7
1340	disposition, he cries out 'No more;' reconciles	8
1341-2	them to his entreaty, and himself to the drink.	9

115 X: Bel, ChC, BT1, JP1
116 X: Bel, ChC, LoC, BT1, JP1
117 same as 116, JL1
118 same as 116
119 same as 116
120 same as 116
121 same as 116
122 same as 116, JL1; MOVE 122-141a to follow 22: 248: OA1; MOVE 122-134a*
123 same as 22; less MOVEs
124 X: Bel, ChC, JL1, LoC, BT1, TaB, JP1, TN1
125 same as 124, less TaB
126 X: Bel, JKP, WM1, ChC, LoC, BT1, OA1, BA1, RA1, JS1, GS1, RH1, JP1*
127 same as 126
128 X: Bel, JKP, ChC, JL1, LoC, BT1, BA1, RA1, GS1, RH1, JP1, ML1; aX:WM1*
129 same as 128; less aX
130 X: Bel, ChC, JL1, LoC, BT1, RA1, JP1, ML1; aX: JKP, BA1, GS1, RH1
131 same as 130; less aX
132 same as 131
133 same as 131; MOVE 133-144 to follow 22: 248: Hal
134 X: Bel, ChC, JL1, LoC, BT1, JP1; aX: RA1, ML1; bX: JKP; ADD 1: JKP
135 same as 134, ChC; less aX, bX, ADD
136 same as 135; R: ML1; bX: RH1, TN1; cX: BA1, RA1, GS1
137 same as 135, GS1, RH1, TN1; R: ML1
138 same as 137, including R; bX: BA1
139 same as 137, BA1, ML1; less R, bX
140 same as139
141 X: Bel, JKP, ChC, JL1, LoC, JP1; aX: BT1, TN1; bX: OA1
142 same as 141; less aX, bX; aX: OA1; MOVE142-144 to follow 22: 250a:Hal
143 same as 141; less aX, bX
144 same as 143
145 X: GCa, Cap, Bel, JKP, WM1, ChC, JL1, LoC, WA1, OA1, JP1, TN1

Scene 27

ALL CUT: Bel. Inc, Tn2, JKP, WM1, Cum, ChC, Hal, KyB, LiL, EdT, OA1, NM1,
LK1

1 X: SP1, Lac, HIM, MTh, LoC, BT1, SM1, BA1, IP1, RA1, BH1, JP1, AF1, ML1*
2 same as 1; less R
3 same as 2
4 same as 2
5 X: GCa, Cap, SP1, Lac, HIM, MTh, LoC, BT1, SM1, BA1, IP1, RA1, BH1,JP1*
6 same as 5, RH1
7 X: GCa, Cap, SP1, Lac, HIM, MTh, LoC, BT1, SM1, WA1, BA1, IP1, RA1,GS1*
8 same as 7; Insert 24: 63-79: JL1
9 same as 7, JL1

*26:122 to follow 22: 177: JKP   *26:126 ML1, TN1
*26:128 OA1, JS1, TN1   *27: 1 ER1; R: Cap   *27: 5 AF1,
  ML1, ER1, TN1   *27: 7 RH1, BH1, JP1, AF1, ML1, ER1, TN1

	First Serv. But it raises the greater war be-	10
1343–4	ween him and his discretion. **11**	11
	Sec. Serv. Why, this it is to háve a name in	12
1345	reat men's fellowship: I had as lief have a reed	13
1346	hat will do me no service as a partisan I could	14
1347	at heave.	15
	First Serv. To be called into a huge sphere,	16
1348	nd not to be seen to move in't, are the holes	17
1849	where eyes should be, which pitifully disaster	18
1350	he cheeks.	19
1351	*A sennet sounded. Enter* CÆSAR, ANTONY,	
1352	LEPIDUS, POMPEY, AGRIPPA, MECÆNAS, ENO-	
1353	BARBUS, MENAS, *with other captains.*	
	Ant. [*To Cæsar*] Thus do they, sir: they take	
1354	the flow o' the Nile **20**	20
1355	By certain scales i' the pyramid; they know,	21
1356	By the height, the lowness, or the mean, if dearth	22
1357	Or foison follow: the higher Nilus swells,	23
1358	The more it promises: as it ebbs, the seedsman	24
1359	Upon the slime and ooze scatters his grain,	25
1360	And shortly comes to harvest.	26
1361	*Lep.* You've strange serpents there.	27
1362	*Ant.* Ay, Lepidus.	28
	Lep. Your serpent of Egypt is bred now of	29
1363	your mud by the operation of your sun: so is your	30
1364	crocodile. **31**	31
1365	*Ant.* They are so.	32
	Pom. Sit,—and some wine! A health to Le-	33
1366	pidus!	34
1367	*Lep.* I am not so well as I should be, but I'll	35
1368	ne'er out.	36
	Eno. Not till you have slept; I fear me you'll	37
1369–70	be in till then.	38
	Lep. Nay, certainly, I have heard the Ptole-	39
1371	mies' pyramises are very goodly things; without	40
1372–3	contradiction, I have heard that. **41**	41
1374	*Men.* [*Aside to Pom.*] Pompey, a word.	
	Pom. [*Aside to Men.*] Say in	
1375	mine ear: what is't?	42
	Men. [*Aside to Pom.*] Forsake thy seat, I do	
1376	beseech thee, captain,	43
1377	And hear me speak a word.	44
1378	*Pom.* [*Aside to Men.*] Forbear me till anon.	
1379	This wine for Lepidus!	45

```
10    same as 9
11    same as 9
12    same as 9, JS1, less GS1
13    same as 12; bX: TN1
14    same as 12, TN1
15    same as 12
16    same as 12
17    same as 12
18    same as 12
19    same as 12, less Lac, JS1




20
21
22
23
24
25
26
27
28
29    X: JL1
30    X: JL1
31    X: JL1
32    X: JL1
33    X: JL1
34    X: JL1
35
36    X: GCa; bX: BA1
37    X: GCa, BA1
38    X: BA1
39    aX: BA1
40
41    X: JL1


42    X: GCa, Lac, JL1, HIM, BT1, JP1

43    same as 42
44    same as 42

45    same as 42
```

1380	*Lep.* What manner o' thing is your crocodile?	46
	Ant. It is shaped, sir, like itself; and it is as	47
1381	broad as it hath breadth: it is just so high as it	48
1382	is, and moves with it own organs: it lives by	49
1383	that which nourisheth it; and the elements once	50
1384	out of it, it transmigrates. 51	51
1385	*Lep.* What colour is it of?	52
1386	*Ant.* Of it own colour too.	53
1387	*Lep.* 'Tis a strange serpent.	54
1388	*Ant.* 'Tis so. And the tears of it are wet.	55
1389	*Cæs.* Will this description satisfy him?	56
	Ant. With the health that Pompey gives him,	57
1390-1	else he is a very epicure.	58
	Pom. [*Aside to Men.*] Go hang, sir, hang!	
1392	Tell me of that? away!	59
1393	Do as I bid you. Where's this cup I call'd for?	60
	Men. [*Aside to Pom.*] If for the sake of merit	
1394	thou wilt hear me, 61	61
1395	Rise from thy stool.	
	Pom. [*Aside to Men.*] I think thou'rt mad.	
1395	The matter? [*Rises, and walks aside.*	62
	Men. I have ever held my cap off to thy for-	
1397	tunes.	63
	Pom. Thou hast served me with much faith.	
1398	What's else to say?	64
1399	Be jolly, lords.	
1400	*Ant.* These quick-sands, Lepidus,	65
1401	Keep off them, for you sink.	66
1402	*Men.* Wilt thou be lord of all the world?	
1403	*Pom.* What say'st thou?	67
1404	*Men.* Wilt thou be lord of the whole world?	
1405	That's twice.	68
1406	*Pom.* How should that be?	
	Men. But entertain it, 69	69
1407	And, though thou think me poor, I am the man	70
1408	Will give thee all the world.	
1409	*Pom.* Hast thou drunk well?	71
	Men. No, Pompey, I have kept me from the	
1410	cup.	72
1411	Thou art, if thou darest be, the earthly Jove:	73
1412	Whate'er the ocean pales, or sky inclips,	74
1413	Is thine, if thou wilt ha 't.	
1414	*Pom.* Show me which way.	75
	Men. These three world-sharers, these com-	
1415	petitors,	76
1416	Are in thy vessel: let me cut the cable;	77

46
47
48
49
50
51
52
53
54
55
56   X: GCa, BA1, IP1
57   same as 56
58   same as 56

59   X: Lac, HIM, BT1, JP1; bX: IP1, ML1
60   same as 59; less bX; aX: ML1; bX: LoC, TN1

61   X: GCa, BT1, JP1

62   sameas 61

63   X: BT1, JP1; bX: TN1

64   X: GCa, BT1, JP1, TN1

65   X: TN1; aX: BT1, JP1; bX: Lac, JL1, HIM, LoC
66   X: Lac, JL1, HIM, TN1; aX: LoC

67   X: BT1

68   X: GCa, BT1, JP1

69   X: GCa, BT1, GS1, JP1
70   same as 69

71   X: GCa, BT1, JP1; aX: GS1

72   X: GCa, BT1, JS1, JP1
73   same as 72, TN1
74   sameas 73

75   X: GCa, BT1, JP1, TN1; aX: JS1

76   X: GCa, BT1
77   X: GCa, BT1

1417	And, when we are put off, fall to their throats:	78
1418	All there is thine.	
1419	*Pom.*. Ah, this thou shouldst have done,	79
1420	And not have spoke on 't! In me 'tis villany; 8ɔ	80
	In thee 't had been good service. Thou must	
1421	know,	81
1422	'Tis not my profit that does lead mine honour;	82
1423	Mine honour, it. Repent that e'er thy tongue	83
1424	Hath so betray'd thine act: being done unknown,	84
1425	I should have found it afterwards weil done;	85
1426	But must condemn it now. Desist, and drink.	86
	Men. [*Aside*] For this,	87
1427-8	I'll never follow thy pall'd fortunes more.	88
	Who seeks, and will not take when once 'tis	
1429	offer'd,	89
1430	Shall never find it more.	
1431	*Pom.* This health to Lepidus! 9o	80
1432	*Ant.* Bear him ashore. I 'll pledge it for him,	
1433	Pompey.	91
1434	*Eno.* Here's to thee, Menas!	
1435	*Men.* Enobarbus, welcome!	92
1436	*Pom.* Fill till the cup be hid.	93
1437	*Eno.* There's a strong fellow, Menas.	94
1437+1	[*Pointing to the Attendant who carries*	
1437+2	*off Lepidus.*	
1438	*Men.* Why?	95
	Eno. A' bears the third part of the world, man;	96
1439-40	see'st not?	97
	Men. The third part, then, is drunk: would	
1441	it were all,	98
1442	That it might go on wheels!	99
1443	*Eno.* Drink thou; increase the reels. 1oo	100
1444	*Men.* Come.	101
1445	*Pom.* This is not yet an Alexandrian feast.	102
	Ant. It ripens towards it. Strike the vessels,	
1446	ho!	103
1447	Here is to Cæsar!	
	Cæs. I could well forbear 't.	104
1448	It's monstrous labour, when I wash my brain,	105
1449	And it grows fouler.	
1450	*Ant.* Be a child o' the time.	106
	Cæs. Possess it, I 'll make answer:	107
1451	But I had rather fast from all four days	108
1452	Than drink so much in one.	
	Eno. Ha, my brave emperor! [*To Antony.*	109
1453	Shall we dance now the Egyptian Bacchanals,	110

78 X: GCa, BT1

79 XL GCa, BT1
80 X: GCa, BT1

81 X: GCa, BT1; b̲X̲: BA1, JS1, GS1, JP1
82 X: GCa, BT1, $\overline{\text{BA1}}$, JS1, GS1, JP1
83 same as 82
84 X: GCa, BT1, BA1, JP1; a̲X̲: JS1, GS1; b̲X̲: TN1
85 X: GCa, BT1, BA1, JP1, $\overline{\text{TN1}}$
86 XL GCa, BT1, JP1; a̲X̲: BA1, TN1
87 same as 86; less a̲X̲
88 XL GCa, BT1, JP1, $\overline{\text{TN1}}$

89 X: GCa, SP1, BT1, GS1, JP1; a̲X̲: TN1

90 X: GCa; a̲X̲: SP1, BT1, GS1, JP1

91

92 X: JP1
93 X: BT1,   JP1
94 X: JP1

95 X: JP1
96 X: JP1; b̲X̲: BT1
97 X: BT1, $\overline{\text{JP1}}$

98 X: BT1, JP1
99 X: BT1, JP1
100 X: BT1, JP1
101 X: BT1, JP1
102 X: JP1

103 X: JP1

104 X: JP1; b̲X̲: SP1
105 X: SP1, $\overline{\text{JP1}}$

106 X: SP1,   JP1
107 X: GCa, Cap, SP1, RH1, JP1
108 X: GCa, Cap, SP1, SM1, JP1, TN1; a̲X̲: RH1

109 a̲X̲: GCa, Cap, SP1, SM1, TN1
110 X̲: JP1

1454	And celebrate our drink?	
1455	*Pom.* Let's ha't, good soldier. **111**	111
1456	*Ant.* Come, let's all take hands,	112
	Till that the conquering wine hath steep'd our	
1457	sense	113
1458	In soft and delicate Lethe.	
1459	*Eno.* All take hands.	114
1460	Make battery to our ears with the loud music:	115
1461	The while I'll place you: then the boy shall sing;	116
1462	The holding every man shall bear as loud	117
1463	As his strong sides can volley.	118
1464	[*Music plays. Enobarbus places them*	
1464+1	*hand in hand.*	

1465	THE SONG.	119
1466	Come, thou monarch of the vine, **120**	120
1467	Plumpy Bacchus with pink eyne!	121
1468	In thy fats our cares be drown'd,	122
1469	With thy grapes our hairs be crown'd:	123
1470	Cup us, till the world go round,	124
1471	Cup us, till the world go round!	125

1472	*Cæs.* What would you more? Pompey, good	
1473	night. Good brother,	126
1474	Let me request you off: our graver business	127
1475	Frowns at this levity. Gentle lords, let's part:	128
	You see we have burnt our cheeks: strong Eno-	
1476	barb	129
1477	Is weaker than the wine: and mine own tongue	130
	Splits what it speaks: the wild disguise hath	
1478	almost **131**	131
	Antick'd us all. What needs more words? Good	
1479	night.	132
1480	Good Antony, your hand.	
1481	*Pom.* I'll try you on the shore.	133
1482	*Ant.* And shall, sir: give's your hand.	
	Pom. O Antony,	134
1483	You have my father's house,—But, what? we are	
1484	friends.	135
1485	Come, down into the boat.	
	Eno. Take heed you fall not.	136
	[*Exeunt all but Enobarbus and Menas.*	
1486	Menas, I'll not on shore.	
	Men. No, to my cabin.	137
1487-8	These drums! these trumpets, flutes! what!	138
1489	Let Neptune hear we bid a loud farewell	139
	To these great fellows: sound and be hang'd,	

111 X: JP1
112 X: JS1, JP1

113 X: JS1, RH1, JP1, TN1

114 X: JS1, RH1, JP1; aX: TN1; bX: ML1
115 X: JS1, RH1, JP1, ML1
116 same as 115; bX: AF1, TN1
117 X: BT1, BA1, JS1, RH1, JP1, AF1, ML1, TN1
118 same as 117; ADD 2: JL1

119 X: JS1, RH1, JP1, AF1, ML1
120 same as 119
121 same as 119
122 same as 119, TaB
123 same as 119
124 same as 119
125 same as 119; ADD 12: GCa

126 X: Lac, HIM, MTh, WA1, JP1
127 X: Lac, HIM, MTh, BT1, WA1, JP1, TN1
128 same as 127; bX: SP1, GS1

129 X: SP1, Lac, HIM, MTh, BT1, WA1,   , JP1; aX: GS1
130 same as 129; less aX

131 same as 130; bX: BA1, IP1, GS1, RH1, TN1

132 X: Lac, HIM, MTh, BT1, WA1, BA1, GS1, JP1; aX: SP1, IP1, RH1, TN1

133 X: Lac, HIM, MTh, WA1, JP1; aX: GCa, Cap, BT1, GS1; bX: BA1

134 same as 133; less aX, bX; aX: BA1; bX: BT1, IP1; cX: Cap; ADD 2:GCa,
     Cap
135 X: Lac, HIM, MTh, BT1, WA1, IP1, JP1

136 X: Lac, HIM, MTh, WA1, JP1; aX: GCa, Cap, RH1, ML1; bX: BT1

137 X: Lac, HIM, MTh, BT1, WA1, RH1, JP1, TN1
138 same as 137, AF1
139 X: Lac, HIM, MTh, LoC, BT1, WA1, RH1, JP1; aX:GCa

1490-1	sound out! [*Sound a flourish, with drums.*	140
1492	*Eno.* Ho! says a'. There's my cap. **141**	141
1493	*Men.* Ho! Noble captain, come. [*Exeunt.*	142

1493+1	# ACT III.
1493+2	## SCENE I. *A plain in Syria.*

1494	*Enter* VENTIDIUS *as it were in triumph, with*	
1495	SILIUS, *and other* Romans, Officers, *and* Sol-	
1495+1	diers: *the dead body of* PACORUS *borne before*	
1495+2	*him.*	
	Ven. Now, darting Parthia, art thou struck;	
1496	and now	1
1497	Pleased fortune does of Marcus Crassus' death	2
1498	Make me revenger. Bear the king's son's body	3
1499	Before our army. Thy Pacorus, Orodes,	4
1500	Pays this for Marcus Crassus.	
1501	*Sil.* Noble Ventidius,	5
1502	Whilst yet with Parthian blood thy sword is warm,	6
	The fugitive Parthians follow; spur through	
1503	Media,	7
1504	Mesopotamia, and the shelters whither	8
1505	The routed fly: so thy grand captain Antony	9
1506	Shall set thee on triumphant chariots and	10
1507	Put garlands on thy head.	
1508	*Ven.* O Silius, Silius,	11
1509	I have done enough; a lower place, note well,	12
1510	May make too great an act: for learn this, Silius;	13
1511	Better to leave undone, than by our deed	14
	Acquire too high a fame when him we serve's	
1512	away.	15
1513	Cæsar and Antony have ever won	16
1514	More in their officer than person: Sossius,	17
1515	One of my place in Syria, his lieutenant,	18
1516	For quick accumulation of renown,	19
1517	Which he achieved by the minute, lost his favour.	20
1518	Who does i' the wars more than his captain can	21
1519	Becomes his captain's captain: and ambition,	22
1520	The soldier's virtue, rather makes choice of loss	23
1521	Than gain which darkens him.	24
1522	I could do more to do Antonius good,	25
1523	But 'twould offend him; and in his offence	26
1524	Should my performance perish.	
1525	*Sil.* Thou hast, Ventidius, that	27
	Without the which a soldier, and his sword,	28

140   same as 139; less a<u>X</u>: b<u>X</u>: AF1
141   same as 139, RH1, <u>T</u>N1; less a<u>X</u>; b<u>X</u>: AF1
142   X: Lac, HIM, M<u>T</u>h, LoC, BT1, <u>WA1, B</u>A1, RH1, JP1; <u>ADD</u> 10: AF1; <u>ADD</u> 13:
       JL; <u>Insert</u> 23: 11–40a: ER1; <u>Insert</u> 15: 1–15a and <u>25</u>: 1–119 and <u>33</u>:
       <u>1</u>–50: TaB

Scene 31

<u>ALL CUT</u>: GCa, Cap, Inc, In2, JKP, WM1, Cum, ChC, Lac, Hal, JL1, HIM, KyB,
<u>Li</u>L, MTh, EdT, LoC, BT1, SM1, WA1, OA1, NM1, TaB, RA1, JS1, GS1, RH1,
JP1, AF1, ER1, LK1, TN1

 1   X: SP1, ML1
 2   X: SP1,   ML1
 3   X: SP1, ML1; b<u>X</u>: BH1
 4   X: SP1, BH1, <u>ML</u>1

 5   X: SP1; a<u>X</u>: BH1, ML1
 6   X: SP1

 7   X: SP1; b<u>X</u>: BH1
 8   X: SP1, <u>BH</u>1
 9   X: SP1 , BH1
10   X: SP1 , BH1

11   X: SP1; a<u>X</u>: BH1
12   X: SP1
13   X: SP1
14   X: SP1

15   X: SP1
16   X: SP1, ML1
17   X: SP1, ML1
18   X: SP1, BA1, ML1
19   same as 18
20   same as 18
21   X: SP1
22   X: SP1
23
24
25
26

27   <u>R</u>: ML1
28   <u>R</u> : ML1

1526	Grants scarce distinction. Thou wilt write e	
1527	Antony?	29
1528	*Ven.* I'll humbly signify what in his name, r	30
1529	That magical word of war, we have effected:	31
1530	How, with his banners and his well-paid ranks,	32
1531	The ne'er-yet-beaten horse of Parthia	33
1532	We have jaded out o' the field.	
1533	*Sil.* Where is he now'	34
	Ven. He purposeth to Athens: whither, s:	
1534	what haste	35
1535	The weight we must convey with 's will permit	36
	We shall appear before him. On, there; pas	
1536–7	along! [*Exeunt*	37

1537+1   **SCENE II.** *Rome. An ante-chamber in*
1537+2   *Cæsar's house.*

1538   *Enter* AGRIPPA *at one door,* ENOBARBUS
1538+1   *at another.*

1539	*Agr.* What, are the brothers parted?	1
	Eno. They have dispatch'd with Pompey, 2	
1540	is gone;	2
1541	The other three are sealing. Octavia weeps	3
1542	To part from Rome; Cæsar is sad; and Lepis	4
1543	Since Pompey's feast, as Menas says, is trouble	5
1544	With the green sickness.	
1545	*Agr.* 'Tis a noble Lepidus.	6
	Eno. A very fine one: O, how he love	
1546	Cæsar!	7
	Agr. Nay, but how dearly he adores Mar	
1547	Antony!	8
1548	*Eno.* Cæsar? Why, he's the Jupiter of me	9
1549	*Agr.* What's Antony? The god of Jupiter.	10
	Eno. Spake you of Cæsar? How! the nx	
1550	pareil!	11
1551	*Agr.* O Antony! O thou Arabian bird!	12
	Eno. Would you praise Cæsar, say 'Cæsar	
1552	go no further.	13
	Agr. Indeed, he plied them both with excel	
1553	lent praises.	14
	Eno. But he loves Cæsar best; yet he love	
1554	Antony:	15
1555	Ho! hearts, tongues, figures, scribes, bards	
1556	poets, cannot	16
1557	Think, speak, cast, write, sing, number, ho!	17
1558	His love to Antony. But as for Cæsar,	18

```
29   X: ML1
30
31
32
33

34   ADD 1: ML1

35   bX: BH1
36   X̄: BH1; R: ML1

37   X: ML1
```

Scene 32

ALL CUT: GCa, Cap, Inc, In2, JKP, WM1, Cum, Lac, JL1, HIM, KyB, EdT, MTh
  BT1, OA1, TaB.   CUT ALL EXCEPT TRANSFER: ChC, Hal, LiL, LoC, SM1, WA1
```
 1   X: Bel, BA1, GS1, ER1, LK1

 2   same as 1
 3   X: Bel, BA1, GS1, LK1; aX: ER1
 4   same as 3; less aX
 5   same as 4; cX: BH1, ML1

 6   same as 4; bX: JP1

 7   X: Bel, BA1, GS1, RH1, JP1, LK1

 8   same as 7
 9   X: Bel, BA1, NM1, GS1, RH1, JP1, LK1, TN1
10   same as 9

11   same as 9, BH1, ML1, less TN1
12   same as 11

13   same as 11, TN1

14   same as 13

15   same as 11

16   same as 13
17   same as 13
18   same as 13, less BH1; aX: BH1
```

1559   Kneel down, kneel down, and wonder.

1560   *Agr.*   Both he loves.   19

     Eno. They are his shards, and he their beetle.

1561   ' [*Trumpets within.*] So: **20**   20

1562 This is to horse. Adieu, noble Agrippa.   21

     Agr. Good fortune, worthy soldier; and fare-

1563   well.   22

1564   *Enter* CÆSAR, ANTONY, LEPIDUS, *and* OCTAVIA.

1565   *Ant.* No further, sir.   23

1566   *Cæs.* You take from me a great part of myself;   24

1567 Use me well in 't. Sister, prove such a wife   25

As my thoughts make thee, and as my farthest

1568   band   26

1569 Shall pass on thy approof. Most noble Antony,   27

1570 Let not the piece of virtue, which is set   28

1571 Betwixt us as the cement of our love,   29

1572 To keep it builded, be the ram to batter   **30**   30

1573 The fortress of it; for better might we   31

1574 Have loved without this mean, if on both parts   32

1575 This be not cherish'd.

     Ant.   Make me not offended   33

1576 In your distrust.

1577   *Cæs.*   I have said.

1578   *Ant.*   You shall not find,   34

p579 Though you be therein curious, the least cause   35

1580 For what you seem to fear: so, the gods keep you,   36

1581 And make the hearts of Romans serve your ends!   37

1582 We will here part.   38

     Cæs. Farewell, my dearest sister, fare thee

1583   well: 39

1584 The elements be kind to thee, and make   **40**   40

1585 Thy spirits all of comfort! fare thee well.   41

1586   *Oct.* My noble brother!   42

     Ant. The April's in her eyes: it is love's

1587   spring,   43

1588 And these the showers to bring it on. Be cheerful.   44

     Oct. Sir, look well to my husband's house;

1589   and—

     Cæs.   What,

1590 . Octavia?   45

1591   *Oct.* I 'll tell you in your ear.   46

     Ant. Her tongue will not obey her heart,

1592   nor can   47

1593 Her heart inform her tongue,—the swan's down-

1594   feather,   48

19   same as 18; less aX; bX: AF1

20   same as 19, AF1; less bX
21   X: Be1, BA1, GS1, JP1, AF1, ER1, LK1

22   same as 21; ADD 1: LK1

23   X: BA1, JP1, ER1; ADD 1: LK1; MOVE 23-61 to follow 22: 250: ChC
24   MOVE 24-50 to follow 22: 250: LiL; MOVE 24-37 to follow 23:47:Hal;*
25   bX; IP1, RH1; MOVE 25-37 to follow 23: 5a: WA1

26   X: RA1; aX: IP1; bX: BA1, RH1, ML1
27   X: RA1; aX: BA1, RH1, ML1
28   X: RA1
29   X: RA1
30   X: RA1
31   X: RA1; bX: RH1
32   X: RA1, RH1

33   aX: RA1, RH1; bX: BA1

34   aX: BA1; bX: RA1
35   X: RA1
36   X: RA1; bX: GS1
37   X: RA1, GS1
38   X: RA1, GS1

39   X: GS1, ML1
40   X: GS1, ML1, TN1
41   same as 40
42   X: BA1, TN1

43   X: JP1, TN1
44   X: JP1, TN1

45

46

47   X: RA1, JP1

48   X: RA1, JP1; bX: ER1, TN1

*32:24   MOVE 24-161a to follow 22: 250: LoC; MOVE 24-37 to follow 23:
         7: SM1

1595	That stands upon the swell at full of tide,	49
1596	And neither way inclines. **50**	50
1596	*Eno.* [*Aside to Agr.*] Will Cæsar weep?	
1598	*Agr.* [*Aside to Eno.*] He has a cloud in 's face.	51
	Eno. [*Aside to Agr.*] He were the worse for	
	that, were he a horse;	52
1599–1600	So is he, being a man.	
1601	*Agr.* [*Aside to Eno.*] Why, Enobarbus,	53
1602	When Antony found Julius Cæsar dead,	54
1603	He cried almost to roaring: and he wept	55
1604	When at Philippi he found Brutus slain.	56
	Eno. [*Aside to Agr.*] That year, indeed, he	
1605	was troubled with a rheum:	57
1606	What willingly he did confound he wail'd,	58
1607	Believe 't, till I wept too.	
1608	*Cæs.* No, sweet Octavia,	59
1609	You shall hear from me still: the time shall not	60
1610	Out-go my thinking on you.	
1611	*Ant.* Come, sir, come; **60**	61 +
1612	I'll wrestle with you in my strength of love:	62
1613	Look, here I have you: thus I let you go,	63
1614	And give you to the gods.	
1615	*Cæs.* Adieu: be happy!	64
1616	*Lep.* Let all the number of the stars give light	65
1617	To thy fair way!	
1618	*Cæs.* Farewell, farewell! [*Kisses Octavia.*	
	Ant. Farewell!	66
1619	[*Trumpets sound. Exeunt.*	

1619+1	**Scene III.** *Alexandria. Cleopatra's*	
1619+2	*palace.*	

1620	*Enter* Cleopatra, Charmian, Iras, *and*	
1620+1	Alexas.	

1621	*Cleo.* Where is the fellow?	
1622	*Alex.* Half afeard to come.	1
1623a	*Cleo.* Go to, go to.	

1624	*Enter the* Messenger *as before.*	

1623b	Come hither, sir.	
	Alex. Good majesty,	2
1625	Herod of Jewry dare not look upon you	3
1626	But when you are well pleased.	
	Cleo. That Herod's head	4
1627	I'll have: but how, when Antony is gone	5
1628	Through whom I might command it? Come	

+ Number used in 1891

49 X: RA1, JP1, ER1, TN1
50 X: JP1, ER1; aX: RA1, TN1

51 X: Be1, GS1, JP1, ML1, TN1; bX: BA1, IP1, AF1

52 X: Be1, BA1, IP1, GS1, RH1, JP1, AF1, ML1, LK1, TN1

53 X: Be1, GS1, JP1, ML1, LK1; aX: BA1, IP1, RH1, AF1, TN1; bX:RA1,ER1
54 X: Be1, RA1, GS1, JP1, ML1, ER1, LK1
55 same as 54
56 same as 54

57 same as 54
58 X: Be1, BA1, IP1, RA1, GS1, RH1, BH1, JP1, AF1, ML1, ER1, LK1

59 X: BA1, IP1; aX: Be1, RA1, GS1, RH1, BH1, JP1, AF1, ML1, ER1, LK1
60 bX: TN1

61 aX: TN1
62
63

64
65

66

Scene 33

ALL CUT Inc, JKP, WM1, Cum
1 X; In2, ChC, Ha1, JL1, KyB, LoC; MOVE 1-50 to follow 27: 137: TaB;
    MOVE 1-51 to follow 35: 119: SM1, WA1, OA1

2 X: ChC, Ha1, KyB, LoC; R: EdT; aX: JL1; bX: LiL, SM1, RH1, JS1, RH1
3 X: ChC, Ha1, KyB, LiL, LoC, SM1, RA1, JS1

4 same as 3; bX: BT1, WA1, TaB
5 X: ChC, Ha1, KyB, LiL, BT1, SM1, WA1, TaB, RA1, JS1; aX: LoC;MOVE
    5b-50 to follow 25: 119: LoC

1629	thou near.	6
1630	*Mess.* Most gracious majesty,—	7
1631	*Cleo.* Didst thou behold Octavia?	8
1632	*Mess.* Ay, dread queen.	9
1633	*Cleo.* Where? **10**	10
	Mess. Madam, in Rome;	11
1634	I look'd her in the face, and saw her led	12
1635	Between her brother and Mark Antony.	13
1636	*Cleo.* Is she as tall as me?	
1637	*Mess.* She is not, madam.	14
1638	*Cleo.* Didst hear her speak? is she shrill-	
1639	tongued or low?	15
	Mess. Madam, I heard her speak; she is low-	
1640	voiced.	16
	Cleo. That's not so good: he cannot like her	
1641	long.	17
1642	*Char.* Like her! O Isis! 'tis impossible.	18
	Cleo. I think so, Charmian: dull of tongue,	
1643	and dwarfish!	19
1644	What majesty is in her gait? Remember, **20**	20
1645	If e'er thou look'dst on majesty.	
	Mess. She creeps:	21
1646	Her motion and her station are as one;	22
1647	She shows a body rather than a life,	23
1648	A statue than a breather.	
1649	*Cleo.* Is this certain?	24
1650	*Mess.* Or I have no observance.	
	Char. Three in Egypt	25
1651	Cannot make better note.	
	Cleo. He's very knowing;	26
1652-3	I do perceive 't: there's nothing in her yet:	27
1654	The fellow has good judgement.	
1655	*Char.* Excellent.	28
1656	*Cleo.* Guess at her years, I prithee.	
	Mess. **Madam,**	29
1657	She was a widow,—	
1658	*Cleo.* Widow! Charmian, hark. **30**	30
1659	*Mess.* And I do think she's thirty.	31
	Cleo. Bear'st thou her face in mind? is't long	
1660	or round?	32
1661	*Mess.* Round even to faultiness.	33
	Cleo. For the most part, too, they are foolish	
1662	that are so.	34
1663	Her hair, what colour?	35
1664	*Mess.* Brown, madam: and her forehead	36
1665	As low as she would wish it.	

6 X: KyB, JS1; aX: ChC, Ha1, LiL, BT1, SM1, WA1, RA1; MOVE 6b-49a to*
7 X: KyB; aX: JS1
8 aX: KyB, BA1; ADD 3: KyB
9
10
11
12 X: ChC, AF1
13 X: ChC, AF1

14

15

16 ADD 1: In2

17 aX: In2
18 R: In2

19 bX: In2
20

21 R: In2
22 X: In2
23

24 bX: Ha1

25 X: Ha1; bX: In2, BA1

26 X: In2, Ha1; aX: BA1
27 X: Ha1; aX: In2

28 X: Ha1

29 X: In2; ADD 1: Be1

30 X: In2
31 X: In2, KyB

32
33

34
35
36 bX: AF1

*33: 6 follow 25: 98: Ha1; MOVE 6b-51 to follow 25: 119: ChC

1666	*Cleo.* There's gold for thee.	37
1667	Thou must not take my former sharpness ill:	38
1668	I will employ thee back again; I find thee	39
1669	Most fit for business: go make thee ready; 40	40
1670	Our letters are prepared. [*Exit Messenger.*	
1671	*Char.* A proper man.	41
1672	*Cleo.* Indeed, he is so: I repent me much	42
1673	That so I harried him. Why, methinks, by him,	43
1674	This creature's no such thing.	
1675	*Char.* Nothing, madam.	44
	Cleo. The man hath seen some majesty, and	
1676-7	should know.	45
	Char. Hath he seen majesty? Isis else defend,	46
1678-9	And serving you so long!	47
	Cleo. I have one thing more to ask him yet,	
1680	good Charmian:	48
1681	But 'tis no matter; thou shalt bring him to me	49
1682	Where I will write. All may be well enough. 50	50
1683	*Char.* I warrant you, madam. [*Exeunt.*	51
1683+1	**SCENE IV.** *Athens. A room in Antony's house.*	
1684	*Enter* ANTONY *and* OCTAVIA.	
1685	*Ant.* Nay, nay, Octavia, not only that,—	1
1686	That were excusable, that, and thousands more	2
1687	Of semblable import,—but he hath waged	3
	New wars 'gainst Pompey; made his will, and	
1688	read it	4
	To public ear:	5
1689-90	Spoke scantly of me: when perforce he could not	6
1691	But pay me terms of honour, cold and sickly	7
1692	He vented them; most narrow measure lent me:	8
1693	When the best hint was given him, he not took't,	9
1694	Or did it from his teeth.	
1695	*Oct.* O my good lord, 10	10
1696	Believe not all; or, if you must believe,	11
1697	Stomach not all. A more unhappy lady,	12
1698	If this division chance, ne'er stood between,	13
1699	Praying for both parts:	14
1700	The good gods will mock me presently,	15
	When I shall pray, 'O, bless my lord and hus-	
1701	band!'	16
1702	Undo that prayer, by crying out as loud,	17
	'O, bless my brother!' Husband win, win	
1703	brother,	18
1704	Prays, and destroys the prayer; no midway	19

37 aX: AF1
38 X̄: In2
39 X: In2, Ha1, AF1
40 same as 39

41 X: Ha1; aX: In2, JL1, OA1, AF1
42 X: Ha1; b̄X̄: In2
43 X: Ha1; ā̄X̄: In2

44 X: Ha1

45 X: Ha1, LiL
46 X: Ha1, LiL, BT1
47 same as 46

48 X: KyB, TN1
49 X: KyB, TN1; bX: Ha1; Insert 21: 1-50 and 26: 1-145, and 35: 1-25:BT1
50 X: Ha1; aX: KȳB̄, TN1; ADD 10: JL1
51 X: Ha1, J̄L̄1, EdT, LoC, T̄aB; ADD 48: LK⅟; ADD 144: In2; Insert 36: 39-
       86: RH1

Scene 34

ALL CUT: GCa, Cap, Inc, WM1, Cum, ChC, Lac, Ha1, JL1, HIM, KyB, LiL, MTh,
   EdT, LoC, SM1, WA1, OA1, GS1, RA1, LK1

1 MOVE 1-38 to follow 25: 119: JKP; MOVE 1-32 to follow 25: 119: In2
2 b̄X̄ : TN1
3 R̲: In2; aX: TN1 ; ADD 1: In2

4 bX: ER1, TN1
5 X̄: TN1
6 bX: RA1, TN1
7 X̄: RA1, TN1; bX: AF1
8 X: RA1, AF1; āX̄: TN1; bX: BT1, BA1, IP1, ER1
9 X: BT1, BA1, R̄A1, AF1, ̄ER1

10 aX: BT1, BA1, RA1, AF1, ER1
11 b̄X̄: BT1
12 āX̄: BT1
13
14
15 X: In2, ER1; R̲: Be1

16 X: In2, ER1; R̲: Be1; bX: IP1
17 X: In2, IP1, ̄ER1

18 X: IP1, ER1; aX: In2; bX: JKP, BA1
19 X: JKP, BT1, B̄A̅1, IP1, ̄ER1; bX: ML1

1705	'Twixt these extremes at all.	
1706	*Ant.* Gentle Octavia, 20	20
	Let your best love draw to that point, which	
1707	seeks	21
1708	Best to preserve it: if I lose mine honour,	22
1709	I lose myself: better I were not yours	23
	Than yours so branchless. But, as you re-	
1710	quested,	24
1711	Yourself shall go between 's: the mean time, lady,	25
1712	I'll raise the preparation of a war	26
	Shall stain your brother: make your soonest	
1713	haste:	27
1714	So your desires are yours,	
1715	*Oct.* Thanks to my lord.	28
	The Jove of power make me most weak, most	
1716	weak,	29
1717	Your reconciler! Wars 'twixt you twain would be	30
	As if the world should cleave, and that slain	
1718	men 31	31
1719	Should solder up the rift.	32
1720	*Ant.* When it appears to you where this begins,	33
1721	Turn your displeasure that way; for our faults	34
1722	Can never be so equal, that your love	35
	Can equally move with them. Provide you	
1723	going;	36
	Choose your own company, and command what	
1734	cost	37
1725	Your heart has mind to. [*Exeunt*	38
1725+1	Scene V. *The same. Another room.*	
1726	*Enter* Enobarbus *and* Eros, *meeting.*	
1727	*Eno.* How now, friend Eros!	1
1728	*Eros.* There's strange news come, sir.	2
1729	*Eno.* What, man?	3
	Eros. Cæsar and Lepidus have made war	4
1730	upon Pompey.	5
1731	*Eno.* This is old: what is the success?	6
	Eros. Cæsar, having made use of him in the	7
1732	wars 'gainst Pompey, presently denied him rival-	8
1733	ity: would not let him partake in the glory of the	9
1734	action: and not resting here, accuses him of	10
1735	letters he had formerly wrote to Pompey: upon	11
1736	his own appeal, seizes him: so the poor third is	12
1737	up, till death enlarge his confine.	13
	Eno. Then, world, thou hast a pair of chaps,	

20 aX: JKP, BT1, BA1, IP1, ML1, ER1

21 X; BT1, ER1, TN1; bX: IP1
22 X: IP1; aX: BT1, ER1, TN1
23 X: BA1, IP1

24 aX: BA1, IP1
25 bX: JKP
q6 X: JKP

27 X: JKP

28 X: JKP; aX: TN1

29 MOVE 29-32 to follow 38: JKP
30

31 X: TN1
32 X: TN1
33 X: In2, JKP, BT1, RA1; bX: AF1
34 X: In2, JKP, BT1, RA1, AF1; bX: BA1, ML1
35 X: In2, JKP, BT1, BA1, RA1, ML1; aX: AF1

36 X: In2; aX: JKP, BT1, BA1, RA1, ML1

37 X: In2
38 X: In2; Insert 30b-32, 29-30a: JKP

Scene 35

ALL CUT: GCa, Cap, Bel, Inc, In2, Cum, ChC, Lac, Hal, JL1, HIM, KyB, LiL,
  MTh, EdT, LoC, SM1, WA1, OA1, BA1, TaB, RA1, GS1, RH1, ER1, LK1, TN1
 1 X: JP1; MOVE 1-20 to follow 26: 98: WM1; MOVE 1-20 to follow 25:119:*
 2
 3 X: JP1
 4 X: BH1
 5 X: BH1; R: WM1
 6 X: RH1, JP1; R: WM1; aX: JKP
 7 R: WM1
 8 X: JKP, WM1; bX: BH1
 9 X: WM1, RA1
10 X: WM1; R! ML1; aX: BH1; cX: JKP
11 X: WM1, ML1
12 X: WM1, ML1; ADD 1: AF1
13 X: WM1

*35: 1 JKP; MOVE 1-25 to follow 33: 49: BT1

1738	no more;	14
	And throw between them all the food thou hast,	15
1739-40	They'll grind the one the other. Where's Antony?	16
	Eros. He's walking in the garden—thus; and	
1741	spurns	17
	The rush that lies before him; cries, 'Fool	
1742	Lepidus!'	18
1743	And threats the throat of that his officer	19
1744	That murder'd Pompey.	
1745	*Eno.* Our great navy's rigg'd. 20	20
1746	*Eros.* For Italy and Cæsar. More, Domitius;	21
1747	My lord desires you presently: my news	22
1748	I might have told hereafter.	
	Eno. 'Twill be naught:	23
1749	But let it be. Bring me to Antony.	24
1750	*Eros.* Come, sir. [*Exeunt.*	25

1750+1   SCENE VI. *Rome. Cæsar's house.*

1751   *Enter* CÆSAR, AGRIPPA, *and* MECÆNAS.

	Cæs. Contemning Rome, he has done all this,	
1752	and more,	1
1753	In Alexandria: here's the manner of't:	2
1754	I' the market-place, on a tribunal silver'd,	3
1755	Cleopatra and himself in chairs of gold	4
1756	Were publicly enthroned: at the feet sat	5
1757	Cæsarion, whom they call my father's son,	6
1758	And all the unlawful issue that their lust	7
1759	Since then hath made between them. Unto her	8
1760	He gave the stablishment of Egypt; made her	9
	Of lower Syria, Cyprus, Lydia, 10	10
1761	Absolute queen.	
1762	*Mec.* This in the public eye?	11
	Cæs. I' the common show-place, where they	
1763	exercise. .	12
1764	His sons he there proclaim'd the kings of kings:	13
1765	Great Media, Parthia, and Armenia,	14
1766	He gave to Alexander; to Ptolemy he assign'd	15
1767	Syria, Cilicia, and Phœnicia: she	16
1768	In the habiliments of the goddess Isis	17
1769	That day appear'd; and oft before gave audience,	18
1770	As 'tis reported, so.	
	Mec. Let Rome be thus	19
1771	Inform'd.	
1772	*Agr.* Who, queasy with his insolence 20	20
1773	Already, will their good thoughts call from him.	21

14 R: JP1
15 X: IP1
16 bX : ML1

17 X: AF1, ML1; bX: BH1

18 X: AF1, ML1; aX: BH1
19 X: AF1, ML1

20 X: ML1, aX: AF1 ADD 2: WM1
21 X: JKP, WM1, AF1, ML1; bX: JP1
22 X: JKP, WM1, JP1, AF1, ML1

23 X: JKP, WM1, ML1; aX: JP1, AF1
24 X: JKP, WM1, ML1; bX: BT1, JP1, AF1
25 X: JKP, WM1, AF1, ML1

Scene 36

ALL CUT: JL1, LK1
1   R: Cap; MOVE 1-18 to follow 22: 14: Ha1
2   X: JKP
3   X: JKP
4   X: JKP
5   X: JKP; bX: WM1, SP1, Cum, ChC, Lac, KyB, LoC, SM1, WA1, TaB, ER1
6   X: JKP, WM1, SP1, Cum, ChC, Lac, KyB, LoC, SM1, WA1, TaB, ER1
7   same as 6; R: Ha1
8   X: JKP, SP1, Ha1, SM1; aX:WM1, Cum, ChC, Lac, KyB, LoC, WA1, TaB, ER1
9   X: JKP, Ha1; aX: SP1, SM1
10 X: JKP; aX: Ha1

11 X: JKP

12 X: JKP; R: Ha1
13 X: JKP, SP1, Ha1, TaB, RA1
14 X: JKP, SP1, Ha1, KyB, EdT, IP1, TaB, RA1, AF1
15 same as 14
16 X: JKP, EdT, TaB, AF1; aX: SP1, Ha1, KyB, IP1, RA1; bX: ML1
17 same as 16, ML1; less aX, bX
18 same as 17; R: Ha1; bX: TN1

19 X: Ha1; aX: JKP, EdT, TaB, AF1, ML1, TN1; bX: Lac, HIM, MTh

20 X: Lac, Ha1, HIM, MTh, TN1; bX: SP1, Cum, TaB, RH1, ER1; N: JKP, LoC
21 X: SP1, Cum, Lac, Ha1, HIM, MTh, TaB, RH1, ER1, TN1

1774	*Cæs.* The people know it; and have now re- ceived	22
1775	His accusations.	
1776	*Agr.* Who does he accuse?	23
1777	*Cæs.* Cæsar: and that, having in Sicily	24
1778	Sextus Pompeius spoil'd, we had not rated him	25
1779	His part o' the isle: then does he say, he lent me	26
1780	Some shipping unrestored: lastly, he frets	27
	That Lepidus of the triumvirate	28
1781	Should be deposed; and, being, that we detain	29
1782	All his revenue.	
1783	*Agr.* Sir, this should be answer'd. 30	30
1784	*Cæs.* 'Tis done already, and the messenger gone.	31
1785	I have told him, Lepidus was grown too cruel;	32
1786	That he his high authority abused,	33
	And did deserve his change: for what I have conquer'd,	34
1787		
1788	I grant him part; but then, in his Armenia,	35
	And other of his conquer'd kingdoms, I	36
1789	Demand the like.	
1790	*Mec.* He'll never yield to that.	37
1791	*Cæs.* Nor must not then be yielded to in this.	38

1792   *Enter* OCTAVIA *with her train.*

	Oct. Hail, Cæsar; and my lord! hail, most	
1793	dear Cæsar! 39	39
1794	*Cæs.* That ever I should call thee castaway!	40
	Oct. You have not call'd me so, nor have you	
1795	cause.	41
	Cæs. Why have you stol'n upon us thus? You	
1796	come not	42
1797	Like Cæsar's sister: the wife of Antony	43
1798	Should have an army for an usher, and	44
1799	The neighs of horse to tell of her approach	45
1800	Long ere she did appear; the trees by the way	46
1801	Should have borne men; and expectation fainted,	47
1802	Longing for what it had not; nay, the dust	48
1803	Should have ascended to the roof of heaven, 49	49
1804	Raised by your populous troops: but you are come	50
1805	A market-maid to Rome; and have prevented	51
1806	The ostentation of our love, which, left unshown,	52
1807	Is often left unloved: we should have met you	53
1808	By sea and land: supplying every stage	54
1809	With an augmented greeting.	
1810	*Oct.* Good my lord,	55
1811	To come thus was I not constrain'd, but did	56

```
22   X: Lac, Hal, HIM, MTh

23   X: Lac, Hal, HIM, MTh; bX: JKP, KyB
24   X: JKP, Lac, Hal, HIM, MTh; R: ML1; bX: RA1
25   X: JKP, Lac, Hal, HIM, MTh, RA1, AF1; R: ML1
26   same   as 5; less R; ; bX: WM1, OA1, TaB, GS1, ER1, TN1
27   X: JKP, Hal, RA1, AF1; aX: WM1, Lac, HIM, MTh, OA1, TaB, GS1, ER1, TN1
28   X: JKP, Hal, RA1, AF1
29   same as 28; R: ML1; bX: TaB

30   X: Hal; aX: JKP, TaB, RA1, ER1
31   X: Hal, ER1, TN1
32   same as 31, JKP
33   same as 32, TN1

34   same as 32
35   same as 32
36   same as 32, SM1

37   same as 32
38   same as 32




39   X: Hal, KyB; MOVE 39-86 to follow 33: 51: RH1
40   X: Hal, KyB; ADD 5: In2

41   X: In2, Hal, KyB

42   same as 41; bX: TaB
43   X: Hal, KyB, TaB
44   same as 43; bX: JKP
45   X: JKP, Hal, KyB, TaB
46   same as 45; bX: In2, ChC, LoC, SM1, WA1, BA1, RA1, GS1, BH1, ML1, ER1
47   X: In2, JKP, ChC, Hal, KyB, LoC, SM1, WA1, BA1, TaB, RA1, GS1, BH1,*
48   same as 47, less BH1; less bX: aX: WM1, BH1; bX: TN1
49   same as 48, TN1, less RA1; less aX, bX: aX: RA1
50   X: Hal, KyB, TaB; aX: In2, JKP, ChC, LoC, SM1, WA1, BA1, GS1, ML1,ER1*
51   X: WM1, Hal, KyB, IP1, TaB, RA1, AF1; bX: In2, BA1, GS1, ML1, ER1
52   X: In2, WM1, Hal, KyB, BA1, IP1, TaB, RA1, GS1, ML1, ER1; R: Cap; bX*
53   X: WM1, Hal, KyB, TaB, RA1, GS1, ML1, TN1; aX: In2, BA1, IP1, TaB*
54   X: WM1, Hal, KyB, GS1, ML1, TN1; aX: RA1

55   X: Hal, KyB; aX: WM1, TaB, ML1, TN1
56   X: Hal, KyB
*36:47  ML1, ER1; bX: WM1              *36:50 TN1; bX: WM1, IP1, RA1
*36:52 RH1, TN1          *36:53 RH1, ER1
```

k8k2	On my free will. My lord, Mark Antony,	57
1813	Hearing that you prepared for war, acquainted	58
1814	My grieved ear withal; whereon, I begg'd	59
1815	His pardon for return.	
1816	*Cæs.* Which soon he granted, 60	60
1817	Being an obstruct 'tween his lust and him.	61
1818	*Oct.* Do not say so, my lord.	
1819	*Cæs.* I have eyes upon him,	62
	And his affairs come to me on the wind.	63
1820	Where is he now?	
1821	*Oct.* My lord, in Athens.	64
1822	*Cæs.* No, my most wronged sister; Cleopatra	65
	Hath nodded him to her. He hath given his	
1823	empire	66
1824	Up to a whore; who now are levying	67
1825	The kings o' the earth for war: he hath assembled	68
1826	Bocchus, the king of Libya; Archelaus,	69
1827	Of Cappadocia; Philadelphos, king **70**	70
1828	Of Paphlagonia; the Thracian king, Adallas;	71
1829	King Malchus of Arabia; King of Pont;	72
1830	Herod of Jewry; Mithridates, king	73
1831	Of Comagene; Polemon and Amyntas,	74
1832	The kings of Mede and Lycaonia,	75
1833	With a more larger list of sceptres.	
1834	*Oct.* Ay me, most wretched,	76
1835	That have my heart parted betwixt two friends	77
1836	That do afflict each other!	
	Cæs. Welcome hither:	78
1837	Your letters did withhold our breaking forth; **79**	79
1838	Till we perceived, both how you were wrong led,	80
1839	And we in negligent danger. Cheer your heart:	81
1840	Be you not troubled with the time, which drives	82
1841	O'er your content these strong necessities;	83
1842	But let determined things to destiny	84
1843	Hold unbewail'd their way. Welcome to Rome;	85
1844	Nothing more dear to me. You are abused	86
1845	Beyond the mark of thought: and the high gods,	87
1846	To do you justice, make them ministers	88
1847	Of us and those that love you. Best of comfort;	89
	And ever welcome to us. **90**	
1848	*Agr.* Welcome, lady.	90
1849	*Mec.* Welcome, dear madam.	91
1850	Each heart in Rome does love and pity you:	92
1851	Only the adulterous Antony, most large	93
1852	In his abominations, turns you off;	94
1853	And gives his potent regiment to a trull,	95

```
57   X: Hal, KyB
58   X: Hal, KyB
59   X: Hal, KyB

60   X: Hal, KyB; bX: HIM, WA1
61   X: Hal, HIM, KyB, WA1

62   same as 61
63   same as 61

64   X: Hal, KyB; R: Cap
65   X: Hal, KyB

66   X: Hal, KyB; bX: Inc, In2, SP1, Cum
67   X: Inc, Cum, Hal, KyB; R: JKP; aX: In2, SP1; bX: ChC, LiL, EdT, LoC,*
68   X: Inc, Cum, ChC, Hal, KyB, LiL, LoC, TaB, RA1; bX: GCa, Cap, In2,JKP*
69   X: GCa, Cap, Inc, JKP, WM1, SP1, Cum, ChC, Lac, Hal, HIM, KyB, LiL*
70   same as 69 including R
71   same as 69 including R; bX: ML1
72   same as 769, ML1; same R
73   same as 72, In2; less R
74   same as 73
75   same as 73, TN1, less Inc, In2, ML1; aX: Inc, In2

76   X: JKP, SP1, ChC, Lac, Hal, HIM, KyB, MTh, RH1; aX: GCa, Cap, WM1, Cum*
77   X: Lac, Hal, HIM, KyB, MTh

78   same as 77; bX: EdT, BT1, SM1, WA1, BA1, IP1, GS1, RH1, JP1, ML1ER1,TN1
79   X: Lac, Hal, HIM, KyB, MTh, EdT, BT1, SM1, WA1, BA1, IP1, GS1, RH1, JP1*
80   same as 79
81   X: Lac, Hal, HIM, KyB, MTh, EdT, SM1, WA1, GS1, RH1, JP1, TN1; aX: BT1*
82   X: JKP, ChC, Lac, Hal, HIM, KyB, LiL, MTh, EdT, LoC, BT1, SM1, WA1, GS1*
83   same as 82 including R
84   same as 82, less GS1; same R
85   X: JKP, ChC, Lac, Hal, HIM, KyB, MTh, EdT, RH1, TN1; R: WM1; aX: LiL*
86   X: JKP, Hal, KyB; aX: WM1, Lac, HIM, MTh, EdT, Go1, RH1, JP1, TN1; MOVE*
87   X: Hal, KyB; bX: ER1
88   X: Hal, KyB, ER1
89   same as 88; bX: JKP, BA1, IP1, GS1, TN1

90   X: Hal, KyB; aX: JKP, BA1, IP1, ER1, TN1; bX: ChC, LiL, LoC
91   X: ChC, Lac, Hal, KyB, LiL, LoC, WM1, JP1
92   X: ChC, Hal, KyB, LiL, LoC
93   X: In2, Cum, ChC, Hal, HIM, KyB, LiL, MTh, LoC, WA1, BA1; N: JKP
94   same as 93; less N
95   same as 94, Lac
```

*36:67 TaB, RA1; R: ChC, Lac, LiL, LoC, Insert 86b-90a: EdT   *36,68 WM1,
   SP1, Lac, HIM, MTh, WA1, BA1, IP1, JS1, GS1, RH1, BH1, AF1, ER1
*36:69 MTh, EdT, LoC, WA1, BA1, IP1, TaB, RA1, JS1, GS1, ER1, BH1, AF1, ER1;
   R: In2   *36:76 LiL, EdT, LoC, WA1, BA1, IP1, TaB, RA1, JS1,
   GS1, BH1, AF1, ER1; bX: ML1   *36:79 ML1, ER1, TN1
*36:81BA1, IP1, ML1, ER1; bX: WM1, LiL, LoC, BH1, AF1   *36:82 RA1,
   BH1, JP1, AF1, TN1, R: WM1   *36:85 LoC, BT1, SM1, WA1, BH1, AF1;
   bX: GS1   *36.86 86b-90a to follow 88a: EdT

1854	That noises it against us.	
1855	*Oct.* Is it so, sir?	96
1856	*Cæs.* Most certain. Sister, welcome: pray you,	97
	Be ever known to patience: my dear'st sister!	98
1857	- [*Exeunt.*	

1857+1   SCENE VII. *Near Actium. Antony's camp.*

1858   *Enter* CLEOPATRA *and* ENOBARBUS.

1859	*Cleo.* I will be even with thee, doubt it not.	1
1860	*Eno.* But why, why, why?	2
	Cleo. Thou hast forspoke my being in these	
1861	wars,	3
1862	And say'st it is not fit.	
1863	*Eno.* Well, is it, is it?	4
	Cleo. If not denounced against us, why should	
1864	not we	5
1865	Be there in person?	6
	Eno. [*Aside*] Well, I could reply:	7
1866	If we should serve with horse and mares together,	8
1867	The horse were merely lost; the mares would bear	9
1868	A soldier and his horse.	
1869	*Cleo.* What is't you say? 10	10
1870	*Eno.* Your presence needs must puzzle Antony:	11
	Take from his heart, take from his brain, from's	
1871	time,	12
1872	What should not then be spared. He is already	13
1873	Traduced for levity; and 'tis said in Rome	14
1874	That Photinus an eunuch and your maids	15
1875	Manage this war.	
1876	*Cleo.* Sink Rome, and their tongues rot	16
	That speak against us! A charge we bear i' the	
1877	war,	17
1878	And, as the president of my kingdom, will	18
1879	Appear there for a man. Speak not against it:	19
1880	I will not stay behind.	
	Eno. Nay, I have done. 20	20
1882	Here comes the emperor.	

1881   *Enter* ANTONY *and* CANIDIUS.

1883	*Ant.* Is it not strange, Canidius,	21
1884	That from Tarentum and Brundusium	22
1885	He could so quickly cut the Ionian sea,	23
1886	And take in Toryne? You have heard on't, sweet?	24
1887	*Cleo.* Celerity is never more admired	25
1888	Than by the negligent.	

96 X: Cum, ChC, Hal, NIM, KyB, LiL, MTh, LoC, WA1, BA1; aX: In2, Lac, EdT
97 X: ChC, Hal, HIM, KyB, LiL, LoC, WA1; aX: Cum, MTh; bX: WM1, ML1, TN1*
98 X: WM1, ChC, Hal, KyB, LoC, WA1, ML1; aX: LiL; bX: TN1; Insert 36: 1-
       16: OA1; Insert 3-12: 1-36: EdT

                          Scene 37

CUT ALL: LiL
  1 X: Hal, JL1; ADD 1: In2
  2 X: Hal, JL1

  3 X: Hal, JL1

  4 X: Hal, JL1; bX: TaB

  5 X: JL1; aX: SP1, TaB; MOVE 5-19a to follow 25: 97: Hal
  6 X: JL1; bX: Bel, Inc, In2, JKP, SP1, Cum, Lac, HIM, MTh, BT1, SM1, OA1
  7 X: Bel, Inc, In2, JKP, WM1, SP1, Cum , Lac, JL1, HIM, KyB, MTh, BT1*
  8 X: Bel, Inc, In2, JKP, WM1, SP1, Cum, ChC, Lac, JL1, HIM, KyB, MTh,LoC*
  9 X: Bel, Inc, In2, JKP, WM1, SP1, Cum, ChC, Inc, JL1, HIM, KyB, MTh,BT1,
       SM1, WA1, OA1, BA1, NM1, TaB, RH1, ML1; aX: LoC, RA1, GS1, TN1
 10 X: Bel, Inc, In2, JKP, Cum, Lac, JL1, HIM, MTh, BT1, SM1, WA1, OA1,TaB*
 11 X: Bel

 12 X: Bel
 13 X: Bel
 14 X: Bel; bX: WA1
 15 X: Bel, JKP, ChC, JL1, HIM, LoC, SM1, WA1, RA1; aX: In2; B: WM1

 16 X: Bel; R: Hal; aX: JKP, ChC, JL1, HIM, LoC, SM1, WA1, RA1; bX: Cum

 17 X: Bel, Cum; R: Hal; bX: JL1; ADD 4: JL1
 18 X: Bel, Cum, JL1, TaB
 19 X: Bel, JL1; R: WM1; aX: Cum, TaB; MOVE 19b-56 to follow 44: 17a: Hal

 20 X: Bel, JL1; R: WM1; aX: Hal, TN1; bX: JKP

 21 X: In3, JKP; aX: Bel, JL1, ML1, TN1; bX: Hal
 22 X: In2, JKP, OA1
 23 X: In2, JKP; R: Hal
 24 X: In2, JKP; bX: Hal, JL1
 25 X: In2, JKP, Hal, JL1

*36:97 Insert 4-11: 53-56: ChC; ADD 6, insert 25: 1-118a: WM1
*37: 7 SM1, OA1, NM1, RH1, ML1, TN1; bX: WA1, TaB   *37: 8BT1,SM1,
    WA1, OA1, NM1, TaB, RA1, RH1, ML1, TN1; bX: BA1, GS1
*37:10 aX: WM1, ChC, KyB, BA1, NM1, IP1, RH1, ML1

1889	*Ant.* A good rebuke,	26
1890	Which might have well becomed the best of men,	27
1891	To taunt at slackness. Canidius, we	28
1892	Will fight with him by sea.	
1893	*Cleo.* By sea! what else?	29
1894	*Can.* Why will my lord do so?	
1895	*Ant.* For that he dares us to't. 30	30
1896	*Eno.* So hath my lord dared him to single fight.	31
1897	*Can.* Ay, and to wage this battle at Pharsalia,	32
1898	Where Cæsar fought with Pompey: but these offers,	33
1899	Which serve not for his vantage, he shakes off;	34
1900	And so should you.	
1901	*Eno.* Your ships are not well mann'd;	35
1902	Your mariners are muleters, reapers, people	36
1903	Ingross'd by swift impress; in Cæsar's fleet	37
1904	Are those that often have 'gainst Pompey fought:	38
1905	Their ships are yare; yours, heavy: no disgrace	39
1906	Shall fall you for refusing him at sea, 40	40
1907	Being prepared for land.	
1908	*Ant.* By sea, by sea.	41
1909	*Eno.* Most worthy sir, you therein throw away	42
1910	The absolute soldiership you have by land;	43
1911	Distract your army, which doth most consist	44
1912	Of war-mark'd footmen; leave unexecuted	45
1913	Your own renowned knowledge; quite forego	46
1914	The way which promises assurance; and	47
1915	Give up yourself merely to chance and hazard,	48
1916	From firm security.	
1917	*Ant.* I 'll fight at sea.	49
1918	*Cleo.* I have sixty sails, Cæsar none better. 50	50
1919	*Ant.* Our overplus of shipping will we burn:	51
1920	And, with the rest full-mann'd, from the head of Actium	52
1921	Beat the approaching Cæsar. But if we fail,	53
1922a	We then can do 't at land.	
1923	*Enter a* Messenger.	
1922b	Thy business?	54
1924	*Mess.* The news is true, my lord; he is descried;	55
1925	Cæsar has taken Toryne.	56
1926	*Ant.* Can he be there in person? 'tis impossible;	57
1927	Strange that his power should be. Canidius,	58
1928	Our nineteen legions thou shalt hold by land.	59

```
26   same as 25
27   same as 25
28   X: JKP, JL1; R: OA1; aX: In2, Ha1; N: ML1

29   X: JL1; aX: JKP

30   X: JL1; N: JP1, ML1
31   X: JKP, JL1, BT1, NM1, TaB
32   X: JKP, JL1, KyB, BT1, NM1, TaB, RH1, AF1, ER1; R: ML1; N: ML1

33   X: JKP, KyB, BT1, NM1, TaB, AF1; aX: JL1, BH1, ML1, ER1
34   same as 33; less aX

35   X: JKP, KyB; aX: BT1, NM1, TaB, AF1
36   X: JKP, KyB, RA1, AF1, ER1; cX: WM1
37   X: JKP, KyB, RA1; R: ML1; aX: AF1, ER1; bX: WM1
38   X: JKP, WM1, KyB, RH1
39   X: JKP, KyB; aX: WM1
40   X: JKP, KyB; R: In2

41   X: JKP; aX: In2, KyB; bX: WM1, RA1
42   R: In2, WM1
43   R: WM1; ADD 1: AF1
44   X: KyB, BA1, IP1, GS1, AF1, ER1; R: WM1; bX: In2
45   X: KyB, BA1, IP1, GS1, AF1, ER1; R: WM1; aX: In2; bX: TN1
46   X: ChC, KyB, LoC, BA1, IP1, GS1, AF1, ER1, TN1; R: WM1; bX: BT1, ML1
47   X: ChC, LoC, BT1, BA1, IP1, GS1, ML1, ER1, TN1; R: WM1
48   X: ChC, LoC, GS1, ML1, TN1; R: WM1

49   X: TN1; R: WM1, ML1; aX: ChC, LoC, BT1, GS1, AF1, TN1; ADD 1: LK1
50   R: WM1
51   X: AF1; R: WM1; bX: RA1

52   X: WM1, RA1, AF1
53   X: WM1, RA1; bX: JKP, TaB

54   X: JKP, TaB, RA1; aX: WM1; bX: ChC, KyB, LoC, WA1, OA1, NM1,JS1,AF1,LK1

55   X: JKP, ChC, KyB, LoC, WA1, NM1, TaB, RA1, JS1, AF1, LK1; R: In2; N: JP1
56   same as 55, WM1; less R, N ; ADD 1: BT1

57   X: JKP, KyB, LoC, WA1, NM1, TaB, RA1, JS1, AF1, LK1; R: In2; aX: ChC
58   X: JKP, KyB, NM1, RA1, AF1, LK1; aX: In2, LoC, WA1, TaB, JS1, TN1
59   same as 58, less JKP; less aX
```

1929	**And our twelve thousand horse. We'll to our ship:**	60
1930	**Away, my Thetis!**	
1931	*Enter a* Soldier.	
1932	How now, worthy soldier! 61	61
1933	*Sold.* O noble emperor, do not fight by sea;	62
1934	**Trust** not to rotten planks: do you misdoubt	63
1935	This sword and these my wounds? Let the Egyptians	64
1936	And the Phœnicians go a-ducking: we	65
1937	Have used to conquer, standing on the earth,	66
1938	And fighting foot to foot.	
1939	*Ant.* Well, well: away!	67
1939+1	[*Exeunt Antony, Cleopatra, and Enobarbus.*	
1940	*Sold.* By Hercules, I think I am i' the right.	68
	Can. Soldier, thou art: but his whole action	
1941	grows	69
1942	**Not** in the power on't: so our leader's led, **70**	70
1943	And we are women's men.	
	Sold. You keep by land	71
1944–5	The legions and the horse whole, do you not?	72
1946	*Can.* Marcus Octavius, Marcus Justeius,	73
1947	Publicola. and Cælius. are for sea;	74
	But we keep whole by land. This speed ↄ	
1948	Cæsar's	75
1949	Carries beyond belief.	
1950	*Sold.* While he was yet in R⌐⌐	76
1951	His power went out in such distractions as	77
1952	Beguiled all spies.	
1953	*Can.* Who's his lieutenant, hear yơ⁷	78
1954	*Sold.* They say, one Taurus.	
1955	*Can.* Well I know the man	79
1956	*Enter a* Messenger.	
1957	*Mess.* The emperor calls Canidius. ↆ	80
1958	*Can.* With news the time's with labour, aꭓ throes forth,	81
1959	Each minute, some. [*Exeu⌐*	82

1959+1	SCENE VIII. *A plain near Actium.*	
1960	*Enter* CÆSAR, *and* TAURUS, *with his army,*	
1960+1	*marching.*	
1961	*Cæs.* Taurus!	1
1962	*Taur.* My lord?	2
1963	*Cæs.* Strike not by land; keep whole: p⌐	

60   X: KyB, AF1; aX: In2, NM1, LiL; bX: EdT; ADD 7: In2

61   X: In2, KyB, AF1, ER1; aX: EdT; bX: OA1, TaB, JP1, TN1; N: SP1, BT1
62   X: In2, TaB, JP1; aX: ML1; N: Hal, LoC
63   same as 62; less aX, N; bX: KyB

64   same as 63; less bX; aX: KyB
65   same as 63; less bX; aX: AF1
66   same as 63; less bX

67   same as 66; bX: Inc; ADD 1: EdT, BT1; ADD 3, insert 3-12: 1-36:KyB;
        ADD 7: WM1
68   X: Bel, In2, Hal, KyB, BT1, TaB, JP1; MOVE 68-82 to follow 39: 4: EdT

69   same as 68; less MOVE; bX: BA1, AF1, ML1, ER1, TN1; N: WM1
70   same as 68; less MOVE; aX: BA1, AF1, ML1, ER1, TN1

71   same as 68; less MOVE; bX: JKP, WM1, ChC, Lac, JL1, HIM, MTh, LoC, SM1*
72   X: Bel, In2, JKP, ChC, Lac, Hal, JL1, HIM, KyB, MTh, LoC, BT1, SM1, WA1*
73   same as 72, RH1; same R
74   same as 73 including R

75   same as 73, less IP1, RH1, ML1, TN1; same R; aX: IP1, ML1, TN1

76   same as 75; less R, aX; R: WM1; bX: IP1, TN1
77   same as 75, WM1, IP1, TN1; less R, aX

78   same as 77, BA1, less IP1; aX: IP1; bX: RH1

79   same as 78, RH1; R: ML1

80   X: Bel, In2, WM1, ChC, Hal, JL1, KyB, BT1, SM1, WA1, OA1, BA1, NM1,TaB,
        JP1, AF1, TN1; N: JKP, LK1
81   same as 80, LK1; R: ML1; N: JKP
82   same as 81; less R, N

Scene 38

ALL CUT : Inc, In2, WM1, SP1, ChC, Lac, Hal, JL1, HIM, KyB, LiL, EdT, LoC,
    BT1, SM1, WA1, NM1, TaB, RA1, RH1
 1   X: JKP, LK1; N: ML1; MOVE 1-6 to follow 39: 4: IP1; MOVE 1-6 to follow*
 2   X: JKP, LK1; bX: AF1; N: ML1

*37:71 WA1, OA1, NM1, IP1, AF1, ML1, ER1, LK1, TN1; ADD 4: JL1; Insert 4-12:
    3b-6: ChC   *37:72 OA1, NM1, IP1, TaB, JP1, AF1, ML1, ER1,
    LK1, TN1; R: WM1   *38: 1 36: 98: OA1

1964	— voke not battle,	3
1965	Till we have done at sea. Do not exceed	4
1966	The prescript of this scroll: our fortune lies	5
1967	Upon this jump. *[Exeunt*	6

1967+1   **SCENE IX.** *Another part of the plain.*

1968   *Enter* ANTONY *and* ENOBARBUS.

	Ant. Set we our squadrons on yond side	
1969	the hill,	1
1970	In eye of Cæsar's battle; from which place	2
1971	We may the number of the ships behold,	3
1972	And so proceed accordingly. *[Exeunt*	4

1972+1   **SCENE X.** *Another part of the plain.*

1973	CANIDIUS *marcheth with his land army*
1974	*way over the stage; and* TAURUS, *the lieu-*
1975	*tenant of* CÆSAR, *the other way. After their*
1976	*going in, is heard the noise of a sea-fight.*

1976+1   *Alarum. Enter* ENOBARBUS.

	Eno. Naught, naught, all naught! I can	
1977	behold no longer:	1
1978	The Antoniad, the Egyptian admiral,	2
1979	With all their sixty, fly and turn the rudder:	3
1980	To see't mine eyes are blasted.	

1981   *Enter* SCARUS.

	Scar. Gods and goddesses	4
1982	All the whole synod of them!	
1983	*Eno.* What's thy passion?	5
1984	*Scar.* The greater cantle of the world is lost	6
1985	With very ignorance; we have kiss'd away	7
1986	Kingdoms and provinces.	
1987	*Eno.* How appears the fight?	8
1988	*Scar.* On our side like the token'd pestilence	9
	Where death is sure. Yon ribaudred nag of	
1989	Egypt,—	10
1990	Whom leprosy o'ertake!—i' the midst o' the fight	11
1991	When vantage like a pair of twins appear'd,	12
1992	Both as the same, or rather ours the elder,	13
1993	The breese upon her, like a cow in June,	14
1994	Hoists sails and flies.	15
1995	*Eno.* That I beheld:	16
1996	Mine eyes did sicken at the sight, and could not	17

```
3    X: AF1
4    X: AF1; bX: TN1
5    X: AF1; aX: TN1
6    X: AF1
```

Scene 39

ALL CUT: Cap, Inc, JKP, WM1, SP1, Cum, ChC, Lac, Hal, LJ1, HIM, KyB, LiL, LoC, BT1, SM1, WA1, OA1, NM1, TaB, BA1, GS1, RH1, ER1

```
1
2
3    ADD 5: In2; Insert 37: 68-82: EdT; Insert 38: 1-6: IP1
4
```

Scene 3-10

ALL CUT: Inc, Cum

```
1    X: TaB; R: In2; bX: OA1; Insert 4b-8a, add 1: Hal
2    X: OA1, TaB, AF1; aX: ER1; bX: ML1
3    X: OA1, TaB, AF1

4    aX: OA1, TaB; bX: Bel, JKP, RA1, JP1; MOVE 4b-8a to open 3-10: Hal;
        Insert ?  : 226-229, 233-235: Hal
5    X: Bel, In2, JKP, JP1; aX: RA1; bX:  AF1
6    X: Bel
7    X: Bel

8    X: Bel; R.: In2; bX: OA1, ER1; ADD 7: JL1
9    X: Bel, Hal, JL1, OA1, AF1, ER1

10   X: Bel, Hal, JL1; R: Cap, KyB; aX: OA1, AF1, ER1
11   X: Bel, Hal, JL1; bX: LiL
12   X: Bel, JKP, Hal, JL1, LiL, BT1, SM1, WA1, AF1
13   X: Bel, JKP, Hal, JL1, KyB, LiL, EdT, BT1, SM1, WA1, AF1, TN1
14   X: Bel, In2, WM1, ChC, Lac, Hal, JL1, HIM, KyB, LiL, EdT, BT1, SM1,WA1
15   X: Bel, Hal, JL1; bX: TN1
16   X: Bel, In2, Hal, JL1, OA1, AF1, TN1
17   X: Bel,  In2, Hal, JL1, AF1; aX: TN1; bX: ML1
```

1997	:dure a further view.	
1998	*Scar.* She once being loof'd,	18
1999	The noble ruin of her magic, Antony,	19
2000	Laps on his sea-wing, and, like a doting mallard,	20
2001	Leaving the fight in height, flies after her: **21**	21
2002	I never saw an action of such shame:	22
2003	Experience, manhood, honour, ne'er before	23
2004	Did violate so itself.	
2005	*Eno.* Alack, alack!	24
2006	*Enter* CANIDIUS.	
2007	*Can.* Our fortune on the sea is out of breath,	25
2008	And sinks most lamentably. Had our general	26
2009	Been what he knew himself, it had gone well:	27
2010	O, he has given example for our flight,	28
211	Most grossly, by his own!	
	Eno. Ay, are you thereabouts?	29
2012-13	Why, then, good night indeed. **30**	30
2014	*Can.* Toward Peloponnesus are they fled.	31
2015	*Scar.* 'Tis easy to't; and there I will attend	32
2016	What further comes.	
2017	*Can.* To Cæsar will I render	33
2018	My legions and my horse: six kings already	34
2019	Show me the way of yielding.	
2020	*Eno.* I'll yet follow	35
	The wounded chance of Antony, though my reason	
2021	reason	36
2022	Sits in the wind against me. [*Exeunt*	37
2022+1	SCENE XI. *Alexandria. Cleopatra's*	
2022+2	*palace.*	
2023	*Enter* ANTONY *with* Attendants.	
	Ant. Hark! the land bids me tread no more	
2024	upon't:	1
2025	'tis ashamed to bear me! Friends, come hither:	2
2026	I am so lated in the world, that I	3
2027	Have lost my way for ever: I have a ship	4
2028	Laden with gold; take that, divide it; fly,	5
2029	And make your peace with Cæsar.	
2030	*All.* Fly! not we.	6
	Ant. I have fled myself; and have instructed cowards	
2031	cowards	7
	To run and show their shoulders. Friends, be gone;	
2032	gone;	8
2033	Have myself resolved upon a course	9

18 X: Be1, Ha1, JL1; aX: In2, AF1, ML1
19 same as 18; less aX̲
20 same as 19
21 same as 19, AF1
22 same as 19, IP1
23 same as 19, LiL

24 X: Be1, Ha1, JL1, LoC; R̲: JKP; b̲X̲: In2, AF1; MOVE 24b-35a to follow 44:
      34: JL1

25 X: Ha1, JL1, KyB, LiL, OA1, JP1, AF1, ER1, TN1; N: ML1
26 X: KyB, LiL, OA1, JP1, ER1; R̲: TN1; a̲X̲: Ha1, JL1, AF1
27 same as 26; less R, a̲X̲; ADD 6̲: JKP
28 X: JKP, KyB, LiL, OA1, JP1

29 same as 8, GCa; b̲X̲: JL1, AF1, ER1
30 X: GCa, JKP, Ha1, JL1, KyB, LiL, OA1, JP1, AF1, ER1
31 same as 30, SM1, WA1, less GCa; ADD 6: In2
32 X: In2, JKP, Ha1, KyB, LiL, SM1, WA1, OA1, JP1. ER1; a̲X̲: AF1

33 X: In2, JKP, KyB, LiL, JP1; a̲X̲: Ha1, SM1, WA1, OA1, ER1; b̲X̲: WM1, AF1
34 same as 33, NM1, AF1; less a̲X̲, b̲X̲; N̲: Ha1

35 X: JKP, KyB; a̲X̲; In2, LiL, NM1, JP1, AF1; b̲X̲: Ha1, JL1

36 X: JKP, Ha1, JL1, KyB
37 same as 36; ADD 13, insert 3-12: 6-25a, add 20: In2; Insert 3-12: 1-
      33: ChC, LoC

Scene 3-11

1   MOVE 1-24 to follow 44: 18a: Ha1; MOVE 1-71a to follow 3-12̲3̲3̲+ LiL*
2
3
4
5

6

7   X: RA1

8   aX: RA1; bX: In2, SP1, JP1
9   X̲: In2, SP1, Ha1, JL1, IP1, RA1, RH1

*3-11: 1 MOVE 1-70a to follow 44: 34: JL1

2034	...ch has no need of you: be gone:	**10**	10
2035	...s treasure's in the harbour, take it. O,		11
2036	...ow'd that I blush to look upon:		12
2037	...y very hairs do mutiny: for the white		13
2038	...prove the brown for rashness, and they them		14
2039	...x fear and doting. Friends, be gone: you shall		15
2040	...ave letters from me to some friends that will		16
2041	...eep your way for you. Pray you, look not sad,		17
2042	...r make replies of loathness: take the hint		18
2043	...ich my despair proclaims: let that be left		19
2044	...ich leaves itself: to the sea-side straightway:		20
2045	...will possess you of that ship and treasure. **21**		21
2046	...ave me, I pray, a little: pray you now:		22
2047	...y, do so; for, indeed, I have lost command,		23
	...erefore I pray you: I'll see you by and by.		24
2048	*[Sits down.*		

2049	*Enter* CLEOPATRA *led by* CHARMIAN *and* IRAS;		
2049+1	EROS *following.*		
	Eros. Nay, gentle madam, to him, comfort		
2050	him		25
2051	*Iras.* Do, most dear queen.		26
2052	*Char.* Do! why: what else?		27
2053	*Cleo.* Let me sit down. O Juno!		28
2054	*Ant.* No, no, no, no, no.		29
2055	*Eros.* See you here, sir?	**30**	
2056	*Ant.* O fie, fie, fie!		31
2057	*Char.* Madam!		32
2058	*Iras.* Madam, O good empress!		33
2059	*Eros.* Sir, sir,—		34
2060	*Ant.* Yes, my lord, yes; he at Philippi kept		35
2061	His sword e'en like a dancer; while I struck		36
2062	The lean and wrinkled Cassius; and 'twas I		37
2063	That the mad Brutus ended: he alone		38
2-64	Dealt on lieutenantry, and no practice had		39
2065	In the brave squares of war: yet now—No matter.		40
2066	*Cleo.* Ah, stand by.	**41**	41
2067	*Eros.* The queen, my lord, the queen.		42
2068	*Iras.* Go to him, madam, speak to him:		43
2069	He is unqualitied with very shame.		44
2070	*Cleo.* Well then, sustain me: O!		45
2071	*Eros.* Most noble sir, arise; the queen approaches:		46
2072	Her head's declined, and death will seize her, but		47
2073	Your comfort makes the rescue.		48

```
10   same as 9; bX: KyB, BT1, AF1
11   X: In2, SP1, KyB, LiL, BT1, JP1, AF1; aX: ER1
12   XL In2, LiL
13   X: Cap, In2, WM1, LiL, RA1, ER1, TN1
14   same as 13

15   X: Cap, In2, LiL, ER1, TN1; aX: WM1, RA1; bX: JKP, SP1, Ha1, KyB,IP1,JP1
16   X: Cap, In2, JKP, SP1, Ha1, JL1, KyB, LiL, BT1, IP1, JP1, AF1,ER1,TN1
17   X: In2, SP1, KyB, LiL, JP1, TN1; R: Ha1; aX: Cap, JKP, JL1, BT1, IP1,*
18   X: In2, SP1, KyB, LoC, BT1, SM1, WA1, OA1, JP1, TN1; aX: AF1; bX:Cap,IP1
19   X: Cap, In2, KyB, LiL, BT1, SM1, WA1, JP1, TN1; aX: SP1, OA1, IP1
20   same as 19, BA1, less BT1, JP1; less aX; aX: BT1, JP1; bX: AF1
21   X: Cap, In2, Ha1, JL1, KyB, LiL, SM1, WA1, AF1, TN1
22   X: In2, KyB, LiL, OA1; bX: JKP, JP1
23   same as 22; less bX; aX: JKP, JP1
24   X: In2, KyB, LiL, BA1, JP1, AF1; ADD 37: WM1



25   X: In2, Lac, Ha1, HIM, LiL, MTh, EdT, TaB; N: LoC
26   same as 25; less N
27   X: In2, JKP, Lac, Ha1, JL1, HIM, LiL, MTh, EdT, TaB
28   same as 27; aX: BA1, IP1
29   same as 27, less JKP, JL1
30   same as 27, less JKP
31   X: In2, Lac, Ha1, HIM, MTh, EdT, TaB
32   same as 31, JKP, JL1
33   same as 31, JKP
34   X: In2, Lac, Ha1, JL1, HIM, MTh, EdT, TaB
35   same as 34, RA1, less JL1; aX: JL1
36   same as 35, JKP
37   same as 35
38   same as 35; bX: ChC, JL1, LoC, SM1, WA1, IP1, GS1
39   X: In2, ChC, Lac, Ha1, JL1, HIM, MTh, EdT, LoC, SM1, WA1, IP1, TaB*
40   X: In2, Lac, Ha1, JL1, HIM, MTh, EdT, TaB, RA1; aX: ChC, LoC, SM1, WA1*
41   same as 40; less aX
42   same as 41, less JL1
43   X: In2, JKP, Lac, Ha1, HIM, EdT, TaB, RH1
44   same as 43
45   same as 43

46   same as 43, less RH1
47   X: In2, JKP, Lac, Ha1, JL1, HIM, EdT, SM1, WA1, TaB, TN1
48   same as 47
```

*3-11:17 AF1, ER1; bX: OA1   *3-11:39 RA1, GS1
  *3-11:40 IP1, GS1

2074	*Ant.* I have offended reputation,	49
2075	A most unnoble swerving.	
2076	*Eros.* · Sir, the queen. 50	50
	Ant. O, whither hast thou led me, Egypt?	
2077	See,	51
2078	How I convey my shame out of thine eyes	52
2079	By looking back what I have left behind	53
2080	'Stroy'd in dishonour.	
2081	*Cleo.* O my lord, my lord,	54
2082	Forgive my fearful sails! I little thought	55
2083	You would have follow'd.	
2084	*Ant.* Egypt, thou knew'st too well	56
2085	My heart was to thy rudder tied by the strings,	57
2086	And thou shouldst tow me after: o'er my spirit	58
2087	Thy full supremacy thou knew'st, and that	59
2088	Thy beck might from the bidding of the gods 60	60
2089	Command me.	
2090	*Cleo.* O, my pardon!	
2091	*Ant.* Now I must	61
2092	To the young man send humble treaties, dodge	62
2093	And palter in the shifts of lowness; who	63
	With half the bulk o' the world play'd as I	
2094	pleased,	64
2095	Making and marring fortunes. You did know	65
2096	How much you were my conqueror; and that	66
2097	My sword, made weak by my affection, would	67
2098	Obey it on all cause.	
2099	*Cleo.* Pardon, pardon!	68
2100	*Ant.* Fall not a tear, I say; one of them rates	69
2101	All that is won and lost: give me a kiss; 70	70
2102	Even this repays me. We sent our schoolmaster;	71
2103	Is he come back? Love, I am full of lead.	72
2104	Some wine, within there, and our viands! For-	
2105	tune knows	73
	We scorn her most when most she offers blows.	74
2106	[*Exeunt.*	

SCENE XII. *Egypt. Cæsar's camp.*

2107	*Enter* CÆSAR, DOLABELLA, THYREUS, *with*
2107+1	*others.*

2108	*Cæs.* Let him appear that's come from Antony.	1
2109	Know you him?·	
2110	*Dol.* Cæsar, 'tis his schoolmaster:	2
2111	An argument that he is pluck'd, when hither	3
2112	He sends so poor a pinion of his wing,	4

49 same as 47, less SM1, WA1

50 X: In2, JKP, Ha1, JL1, EdT, TN1; aX: Lac, HIM, TaB

51 X: In2, TN1; bX: JS1, GS1, ER1; MOVE 51-68 to follow 45: 18: Ha1
52 X: In2, JKP, WM1, JS1, GS1, RH1, ER1, TN1
53 same as 52; R: ML1

54 X: JS1; aX: In2, JKP, WM1, GS1, RH1, ER1, TN1
55

56
57
58 bX: In2
59 X: In2
60 X: In2

61 X; In2
62 X: In2
63 X: In2

64 X; In2
65 X; In2; bX: JKP, BT1, ER1
66 X: In2, JKP, BT1, ER1
67 same as 66

68 aX: In2, JKP, BT1, ER1
69 X: ChC, Ha1, LoC
70 X: ChC, LoC; aX: Ha1; bX: WM1, JL1; MOVE 70b-74 to follow 3-13:167:Ha1
71 X: WM1, ChC, JL1, LoC; R: Cap, JP1; bX: In2, JKP, Ha1, HIM, LiL, OA1*
72 X: ChC, JL1, LiL, LoC, TaB; R: JP1; aX: In2, JKP, WM1, Ha1, HIM, OA1

73 X: WM1, ChC, JL1, LiL , LoC, TaB; R: In2; bX: ML1; cX: ER1
74 same as 73, ML1; less R, bX, cX; R: In2

Scene 3-12

ALL CUT: Lac, Ha1, JL1, HIM, MTh, BT1, SM1, WA1, OA1, TaB, AF1, ER1, LK1
1   X: In2, WM1, JP1; MOVE 1-36 to follow 36: 18: EdT; MOVE 1-33 to follow
        3-10: 37: ChC, LoC; MOVE 1-36 to follow 37: 67: KyB, WA1, LK1
2   X: In2, WM1, JP1; R: Cap; bX: JKP, ChC, LiL, LoC; N: JKP
3   X: In2, WM1, ChC, LiL, LoC, JP1, TN1
4   same as 3

*3-11: 71 TaB; N: EdT

2113	Which had superfluous kings for messengers	5
2114	Not many moons gone by.	
2115	*Enter* EUPHRONIUS, *ambassador from Antony.*	
2116	*Cæs.* Approach, and speak.	6
2117	*Euph.* Such as I am, I come from Antony:	7
2118	'I was of late as petty to his ends	8
2119	As is the morn-dew on the myrtle-leaf	9
2120	To his grand sea.	
2121	*Cæs.* Be't so: declare thine office. 10	10
	Euph. Lord of his fortunes he salutes thee, and	
2122		11
2123	Requires to live in Egypt: which not granted,	12
2124	He lessens his requests; and to thee sues	13
	To let him breathe between the heavens and earth,	
2125		14
2126	A private man in Athens: this for him.	15
2127	Next, Cleopatra does confess thy greatness;	16
2128	Submits her to thy might; and of thee craves	17
2129	The circle of the Ptolemies for her heirs,	18
2130	Now hazarded to thy grace.	
2131	*Cæs.* For Antony,	19
2132	I have no ears to his request. The queen 20	20
2133	Of audience nor desire shall fail, so she	21
2134	From Egypt drive her all-disgraced friend,	22
2135	Or take his life there: this if she perform,	23
2136	She shall not sue unheard. So to them both.	24
2137	*Euph.* Fortune pursue thee!	
2138	*Cæs.* Bring him through the bands.	25
2138+1	[*Exit Euphronius.*	
	[*To Thyreus*] To try thy eloquence, now 'tis time: dispatch;	
2139		26
2140	From Antony win Cleopatra: promise,	27
2141	And in our name, what she requires; add more,	28
2142	From thine invention, offers: women are not	29
	In their best fortunes strong; but want will perjure 30	
2143		30
	The ne'er-touch'd vestal: try thy cunning, Thyreus;	
2144		31
2145	Make thine own edict for thy pains, which we	32
2146	Will answer as a law.	
2147	*Thyr.* Cæsar, I go.	33
2148	*Cæs.* Observe how Antony becomes his flaw,	34
2149	And what thou think'st his very action speaks	35
2150	In every power that moves.	
2151	*Thyr.* Cæsar, I shall. [*Exeunt.*	36

5   X: In2, WM1, ChC, LiL, LoC, JP1; aX: TN1

6   X: JP1; aX: In2, WM1, ChC, LiL, LoC; ADD 2: WM1; MOVE 6b-25a to fol-*
7   X: JP1; R: WM1; N: Cap, JKP, Cum
8   X: JKP, SP1, Cum, ChC, LoC, JS1, JP1; R: WM1
9   same as 8, WM1; less R

10 X: JKP, WM1, SP1, Cum, JS1, JP1; aX: ChC, LoC

11 X: WM1, JP1; N: Cum
12 X: WM1, JP1; bX: SP1, Cum
13 X: In2, JKP, WM1, SP1, Cum, JP1

14 same as 13, less In2; aX: In2
15 X: JKP, WM1, JP1; aX: SP1, Cum
16 X: WM1, JP1; bX: In2
17 X: WM1, JP1; R: In2; bX: BA1
18 X: WM1, BA1, JP1; R: In2

19 X: WM1, JP1; aX: BA1
20 X: WM1, JP1
21 X: WM1, JP1; R: ML1
22 X: WM1, JP1
23 X: In2, WM1, JP1
24 same as 23

25 X: WM1, JP1; bX: In2; N: Cum

26 X: In2, WM1
27 X: In2, WM1
28 X: In2, WM1; bX: GS1, ML1
29 X: In2, WM1; aX: GS1, ML1

30 X: In2, WM1; bX: GS1

31 X: In2, WM1; aX: GS1; bX: JKP
32 X: In2, JKP, WM1, BA1; R: ML1

33 X: In2, JKP, WM1, BA1, GS1; R: ML1; aX: GS1; Insert 3-11:1-72:LiL
34 X: In2, WM1, ChC, LiL, LoC, BA1, JS1; R: ML1
35 same as 34, TN1; same R

36 same as 34, less BA1; same R; aX: BA1, TN1; bX: JKP
*3-12: 6 low 3-10: 37: In2

2151+1   **SCENE XIII.** *Alexandria. Cleopatra's*
2151+2   *palace.*

2152   *Enter* CLEOPATRA, ENOBARBUS, CHARMIAN,
2152+1   *and* IRAS.

2153	*Cleo.* What shall we do, Enobarbus?	
2154	*Eno.* Think, and die.	1
2155	*Cleo.* Is Antony or we in fault for this?	2
2156	*Eno.* Antony only, that would make his will	3
2157	Lord of his reason. What though you fled	4
	From that great face of war, whose several	
2158	ranges	5
2159	Frighted each other? why should he follow?	6
2160	The itch of his affection should not then	7
2161	Have nick'd his captainship; at such a point,	8
2162	When half to half the world opposed, he being	9
2163	The †meered question: 'twas a shame no less 10	10
2164	Than was his loss, to course your flying flags,	11
2165	And leave his navy gazing.	
2166	*Cleo.* Prithee, peace.	12

2167   *Enter* ANTONY *with* EUPHRONIUS, *the*
2167+1   *Ambassador.*

	Ant. Is that his answer?	13
2168	*Euph.* Ay, my lord.	14
	Ant. The queen shall then have courtesy, so	
2169	she	15
2170	Will yield us up.	
2171	*Euph.* He says so.	
	Ant. Let her know't.	16
2172	To the boy Cæsar send this grizzled head,	17
2173	And he will fill thy wishes to the brim	18
2174	With principalities.	
2175	*Cleo.* That head, my lord?	19
2176	*Ant.* To him again: tell him he wears the rose	20
	Of youth upon him; from which the world should	
2177	note	21
2178	Something particular: his coin, ships, legions,	22
2179	May be a coward's; whose ministers would prevail	23
2180	Under the service of a child as soon	24
2181	As i' the command of Cæsar: I dare him therefore	25
2182	To lay his gay comparisons apart,	26
2183	And answer me declined, sword against sword,	27

Scene 3-13

```
1   X: In2, Hal, OA1, RH1; R: WM1; MOVE 1 to follow 28: TaB; MOVE 1-2 to*
2   X: In2, Hal, OA1, TaB, RH1
3   same as 2, JL1
4   same  as 3; bX: ChC, LoC

5   X: In2, ChC, Hal, JL1, LoC, SM1, WA1, OA1, TaB, RH1; bX: BT1, BA1
6   X: In2, ChC, Hal, JL1, LoC, SM1, WA1, OA1, TaB, RH1, AF1;aX: BT1, BA1
7   X: In2, JKP, ChC, Hal, JL1, LoC, BT1, OA1, TaB, GS1, RH1, AF1
8   same as 7, less BT1; aX: BT1; bX: SM1, BA1, IP1, JS1, ML1
9   X: In2, JKP, WM1, ChC, Hal, JL1, LoC, SM1, WA1, OA1, BA1, IP1, TaB,*
10  X: In2, WM1, ChC, Hal, JL1, LoC, SM1, WA1, OA1, TaB, JS1, RH1; aX:JKP*
11  same as 10; less aX

12  X: In2, Hal, JL1, OA1, TaB, RH1; aX: WM1,ChC, LoC, SM1, WA1; bX:Inc


13  X: In2, Hal, JL1, ER1
14  same as 13; ADD 9: LK1

15  same as 13


16  X: In2, Hal, JL1; R: Inc; aX: ER1; bX: JKP; ADD 1: Cap
17  X: In2, Hal, JL1
18  same as 17

19  same as 17
20  same as 17

21  same as 17; bX: BT1, GS1, ER1
22  X: In2, Hal, JL1, BT1, GS1; aX: ER1; bX: RA1
23  same as 22, RA1; less aX, bX; bX: RH1, ML1
24  X: In2, Hal, JL1, BT1, RA1, GS1, RH1, ML1
25  X: In2, Hal, JL1; aX: BT1, RA1, GS1, RH1, ML1
26  same as 25; less aX
27  same as 26; R: ML1
```

*3-13: 1 follow 4-12: 49: JL1   *3-13: 9 JS1, GS1, RH1, AF1
*3-13:10 BA1, IP1, GS1, AF1, ML1

2184	Ourselves alone. I'll write it: follow me.	28
2184+1	*[Exeunt Antony and Euphronius.*	
	Eno. [*Aside*] Yes, like enough, high-battled	
2185	Cæsar will	29
2186	Unstate his happiness, and be staged to the show,	30
2187	Against a sworder! I see men's judgements are	31
2188	A parcel of their fortunes; and things outward	32
2189	Do draw the inward quality after them,	33
2190	To suffer all alike. That he should dream,	34
2191	Knowing all measures, the full Cæsar will	35
	Answer his emptiness! Cæsar, thou hast sub-	
2192	dued	36
2193	His judgement too.	

2194   *Enter an* Attendant.

2195	*Att.* A messenger from Cæsar.	37
	Cleo. What, no more ceremony? See, my	
2196	women!	38
2197	Against the blown rose may they stop their nose	39
2198	That kneel'd unto the buds. Admit him, sir. *c*	40
2198+1	*[Exit Attendant.*	
	Eno. [*Aside*] Mine honesty and I begin to	
2199	square.	41
2200	The loyalty well held to fools does make	42
2201	Our faith mere folly: yet he that can endure	43
2202	To follow with allegiance a fall'n lord	44
2203	Does conquer him that did his master conquer,	45
2204	And earns a place i' the story.	

2205   *Enter* THYREUS.

2206	*Cleo.* Cæsar's will?	46
2207	*Thyr.* Hear it apart.	
2208	*Cleo.* None but friends: say boldly.	47
2209	*Thyr.* So, haply, are they friends to Antony.	48
2210	*Eno.* He needs as many, sir, as Cæsar has:	49
2211	Or needs not us. If Cæsar please, our master	50
2212	Will leap to be his friend: for us, you know	51
2213	Whose he is we are, and that is, Cæsar's.	
	Thyr. So.	52
2214	Thus then, thou most renown'd: Cæsar entreats	53
2215	Not to consider in what case thou stand'st,	54
2216	Further than he is Cæsar.	
2217	*Cleo.* Go on: right royal	55
2218	*Thyr.* He knows that you embrace not Antony	56
2219	As you did love, but as you fear'd him.	
2220	*Cleo.* O!	57

28   same as 26; <u>Insert</u> 1: TaB

29   X: GCa, In2, Hal, JL1, TaB, RA1
30   same as 29
31   X: GCa, In2, Hal, JL1, TaB; <u>aX</u>: RA1, AF1; <u>bX</u>: JKP, WM1, SP1, ChC*
32   X: GCa, In2, JKP, WM1, SP1, C̄h̄C̄, Hal, JL1, K̄yB, LoC, BT1, SM1, WA1*
33   same as·32, BA1, GS1, RH1, ML1; less b̄X̄
34   X: GCa, In2, JKP, WM1, ChC, Hal, JL1, K̄yB, LoC, BT1, TaB, TN1; <u>aX</u>:*
35   X: GCa, In2, JKP, WM1, ChC, Lac, Hal, JL1, HIM, KyB, LiL, MTh,LoC,
      BT1, IP1, TaB, AF1, TN1
36   X: GCa, Inᴄ, Lac, Hal ,JL1, HIM, KyB, MTh, BT1, TaB, TN1; <u>aX</u>: JKP,
      WM1, ChC, LiL, LoC, IP1, AF1

37   X: GCa, BT1; <u>aX</u>: In2, Lac, Hal, JL1, HIM, KyB, MTh, TaB, TN1; <u>bX</u>: ML1;
      N: SP1
38   X: B̄T̄1, ML1; <u>bX</u>: WM1, BA1, TN1
39   X: WM1, BT1, B̄Ā1, AF1, ML1, TN1; R: In2
40   X: BT1, ML1, TN1; <u>aX</u>: WM1, BA1, ĀF1; <u>bX</u>: JKP, JP1

41   X: GCa, Inc, In2, JKP, Cum, ChC, LoC, SM1, WA1, BA1, TaB, TN1; *
42   same as 41; less <u>MOVE</u>
43   same as 42, less ĀF̄1̄; <u>aX</u>: AF1; <u>bX</u>: KyB, ML1; <u>ADD</u> 1: KyB
44   same as 43, KyB, ML1; l̄ess <u>aX</u>, <u>b̄X̄</u>, <u>ADD</u>
45   same as 44

46   X: GCa; <u>aX</u>: Inc, In2, JKP, Cum, ChC, KyB, LoC, SM1, WA1, BA1, TaB,ML1;
      N: C̄ap, JP1
47   N: C̄ap, JP1
48   X̄: In2, ChC, KyB, LoC, WA1, LK1
49   same as 48, RH1
50   same as 49, ER1, TN1; <u>bX</u>: RA1, GS1, RH1, JP1
51   X: In2, JKP, ChC, KyB, L̄oC, WA1,BA1, RA1, GS1, RH1, BH1, JP1, ER1, LK1,
      TN1; <u>bX</u>: EdT
52   X: In2, J̄KP, ChC, KyB, LoC, WA1, BA1, JP1, ER1, LK1, TN1; <u>aX</u>: RA1, GS1*
53   X: BA1, LK1
54   X: LK1; <u>ADD</u> 1: In2

55   X: LK1; <u>bX</u>: ML1
56

57

*3-13:31 KyB, LoC, BT1, SM1, WA1, BH1, TN1; <u>ADD</u> 2: BT1   *3-13:32 TaB,
   BH1, TN1; <u>bX</u>: BA1, GS1, RH1, ML1   *3-13:34 SP1, S̄M̄1̄, W̄Ā1̄,BA1,
   GS1, RH1, B̄H1, ML1; <u>bX</u>: Lac, HIM, LiL, MTh, IP1, ĀF̄1̄
*3-13:41<u>MOVE</u> 41-46a to f̄ollow 37:JP1   *<u>3-13:52</u> BH1

	Thyr. The scars upon your honour, therefore, be	
2121		58
2122	Does pity, as constrained blemishes,	59
2123	Not as deserved.	
2124	*Cleo.*　　　He is a god, and knows　6o	60
2125	What is most right: mine honour was not yielded,	61
2126	But conquer'd merely.	
2127	*Eno.*　　[*Aside*] To be sure of that,	62
2128	I will ask Antony. Sir, sir, thou art so leaky,	63
2129	That we must leave thee to thy sinking, for	64
2130	Thy dearest quit thee.　　　[*Exit.*	
2131	*Thyr.*　　　Shall I say to Cæsar	65
2132	What you require of him? for he partly begs	66
2133	To be desired to give. It much would please him,	67
2134	That of his fortunes you should make a staff	68
2135	To lean upon: but it would warm his spirits,	69
2136	To hear from me you had left Antony,　　7o	70
	†And put yourself under his shrowd,	71
2137	The universal landlord.	
2138	*Cleo.*　　　　What's your name?	72
2139	*Thyr.* My name is Thyreus.	
2140	*Cleo.*　　　　Most kind messenger,	73
2141	Say to great Cæsar this: in deputation	74
2142	I kiss his conquering hand: tell him, I am prompt	75
2143	To lay my crown at's feet, and there to kneel:	76
2144	Tell him, from his all-obeying breath I hear	77
2145	The doom of Egypt.	
2146	*Thyr.*　　　'Tis your noblest course.	78
2147	Wisdom and fortune combating together,	79
2148	If that the former dare but what it can,　8o	80
2149	No chance may shake it. Give me grace to lay	81
2150	My duty on your hand.	
2151	*Cleo.*　　　Your Cæsar's father oft,	82
2152	When he hath mused of taking kingdoms in,	83
2153	Bestow'd his lips on that unworthy place,	84
2154	As it rain'd kisses.	
2155	*Re-enter* ANTONY *and* ENOBARBUS.	
	Ant.　　　Favours, by Jove that thunders!	85
2156	What art thou, fellow?	
2157	*Thyr.*　　　One that but performs	86
2158	The bidding of the fullest man, and worthiest	87
2159	To have command obey'd.	
2160	*Eno.*　　　[*Aside*] You will be whipp'd.	88
	Ant. Approach, there! Ah, you kite! Now,	
2161	gods and devils!	89

```
58   X: JKP
59   X: JKP


60   aX: JKP
61   bX: In2, ChC, LoC

62   X: GCa, In2, ChC, LoC; bX: SM1, TaB
63   X: GCa, In2, ChC, LoC, SM1, TaB; bX: Inc, Cum, KyB, GS1, AF1
64   X: GCa, Inc, In2, Cum, ChC, KyB, LoC, SM1, TaB, GS1, AF1

65   X: GCa, ChC, LoC; aX: Inc, In2, Cum, KyB, SM1, TaB, GS1, AF1
66   X: ChC, LoC; bX: BT1, SM1, WA1, IP1, AF1
67   X: BT1; aX: ChC, LoC, SM1, WA1, IP1, AF1; bX: WM1, ML1
68   X: WM1, Lac, Hal, HIM, KyB, BT1, OA1, AF1, ML1
69   X: Lac, Hal, HIM, KyB, OA1, AF1; R: WM1; aX: BT1, ML1
70
71   R: Cap

72   R: JP1; bX: JKP, WM1, TaB; N: JP1

73   X: JKP; aX: WM1, TaB; N: Bel, Inc
74   bX: BT1, ML1
75   aX: BT1, ML1
76
77


78
79   X: JKP, WM1, ChC, Lac, Hal, HIM, KyB, MTh, LoC, BT1, SM1, WA1, OA1*
80   same as 79
81   X: JKP; aX: WM1, ChC, Lac, Hal, HIM, KyB, MTh, LoC, BT1, SM1, WA1,
        OA1, TaB, RA1, RH1, ML1, ER1, TN1
82
83
84



85   aX: WM1; bX: LK1; ADD 1: In2

86   X: AF1, LK1
87   X: AF1, LK1

88   X: GCa, AF1; aX: LK1; bX: In2, WM1, ChC, LoC, BT1, SM1, WA1

89   X: In2; aX: AF1

*3-13:79  TaB, RA1, RH1, AF1, ML1, ER1, TN1
```

	Authority melts from me: of late, when I cried	
2262	'Ho!' 90	90
2263	Like boys unto a muss, kings would start forth,	91
2264	And cry 'Your will?' Have you no ears? I am	92
2265a	Antony yet.	
2266	*Enter* Attendants.	
2265b	Take hence this Jack, and whip him.	93
	Eno. [*Aside*] 'Tis better playing with a lion's	
2267	whelp	94
2268	Than with an old one dying.	
2269	*Ant.* Moon and stars!	95
	Whip him. Were't twenty of the greatest tribu-	
2270	taries	96
2271	That do acknowledge Cæsar, should I find them	97
	So saucy with the hand of she here,—what's her	
2272	name,	98
2273	Since she was Cleopatra? Whip him, fellows,	99
2274	Till, like a boy, you see him cringe his face, 100	100
2275	And whine aloud for mercy: take him hence.	101
2276	*Thyr.* Mark Antony!	
2277	*Ant.* Tug him away: being whipp'd,	102
2278	Bring him again: this Jack of Cæsar's shall	103
	Bear us an errand to him.	104
2279	[*Exeunt Attendants with Thyreus.*	
2280	You were half blasted ere I knew you: ha!	105
2281	Have I my pillow left unpress'd in Rome,	106
2282	Forborne the getting of a lawful race,	107
2283	And by a gem of women, to be abused	108
2284	By one that looks on feeders?	
2285	*Cleo.* Good my lord,—	109
2286	*Ant.* You have been a boggler ever: 110	110
2287	But when we in our viciousness grow hard—	111
2288	O misery on't!—the wise gods seel our eyes:	112
	In our own filth drop our clear judgements;	
2289	make us	113
2290	Adore our errors; laugh at's, while we strut	114
2291	To our confusion.	
2292	*Cleo.* O, is't come to this?	115
2293	*Ant.* I found you as a morsel cold upon	116
2294	Dead Cæsar's trencher: nay, you were a fragment	117
2295	Of Cneius Pompey's: besides what hotter hours,	118
2296	Unregister'd in vulgar fame, you have	119
2297	Luxuriously pick'd out: for, I am sure, 120	120
2298	Though you can guess what temperance should be,	121
2299	You know not what it is.	

90 X: In2
91 X: In2; <u>a</u>X: ML1
92 <u>aX</u>: In2

93 X: GCa, In2

94 X: GCa, Inc, In2, Cum, OA1, GS1; <u>MOVE</u> 94-95a to follow 104: TN1

95 X: In2; <u>a</u>X: Inc, Cum, OA1, GS1

96 X: In2
97 X: In2

98 X: In2
99 X: In2; <u>b</u>X: ML1, ER1
100 X: Cum, M̄L1, ER1
101 X: ER1; <u>a</u>X: ML1; <u>b</u>X: WM1, OA1

102 X: Cum, TaB; <u>b</u>X: In2, JKP, WM1, LoC, AF1
103 X: JKP, ChC, T̄aB, AF1; <u>a</u>X: In2, Cum, LoC
104 X: JKP, ChC, TaB, AF1; <u>aX</u>: LoC; <u>Insert</u> 94-95a: TN1

105 X: In2, KyB
106 X: In2, AF1
107 X: Inc, In2, WM1, SP1
108 X: In2, AF1; <u>a</u>X: Inc, WM1, SP1

109 X: In2; <u>a</u>X: AF1
110 X: Cap, Īn2, JKP
111 X: Cap, In2, JKP, ChC, LoC, RA1, BH1
112 same as 111

113 same as 111, LiL, OA1; R: Ha1, KyB; <u>a</u>X: Cum, Lac, HIM; <u>b</u>X: BT1
114 same as 111; <u>a</u>X: LiL, B̄T1

115 X: Cap, JKP, ChC, LoC; <u>a</u>X: In2, RA1, BH1; <u>b</u>X: Cum, JL1
116 X: Bel, In2, JKP, Cum, L̄ac, JL1, HIM, KyB, M̄Th
117 same as 116
118 same as 116; <u>b</u>X: Ha1, LiL
119 same as 116, H̄a1, LiL
120 same as 119, less Cum; R: Ha1; <u>a</u>X: Cum; <u>b</u>X: BT1, TaB
121 same as 120, TaB; less R̄, <u>a</u>X, b<u>X</u>; <u>a</u>X: MTh

2300	*Cleo.* Wherefore is this?	122
2301	*Ant.* To let a fellow that will take rewards	123
2302	And say 'God quit you!' be familiar with	124
2303	My playfellow, your hand: this kingly seal	125
2304	And plighter of high hearts! O, that I were	126
2305	Upon the hill of Basan, to outroar	127
2306	The horned herd! for I have savage cause;	128
2307	And to proclaim it civilly, were like	129
2308	A halter'd neck which does the hangman thank	130
2309a	For being yare about him.	
2310	*Re-enter* Attendants *with* THYREUS.	
2309b	Is he whipp'd? **131**	131
2311	*First Att.* Soundly, my lord.	
2312	*Ant.* Cried he? and begg'd a' pardon?	132
2313	*First Att.* He did ask favour.	133
2314	*Ant.* If that thy father live, let him repent	134
	Thou wast not made his daughter; and be thou	
2315	sorry	135
2316	To follow Cæsar in his triumph, since	136
	Thou hast been whipp'd for following him: hence-	
2317	forth	137
2318	The white hand of a lady fever thee,	138
2319	Shake thou to look on 't. Get thee back to Cæsar,	139
2320	Tell him thy entertainment: look, thou say **140**	140
2321	He makes me angry with him: for he seems	141
2322	Proud and disdainful, harping on what I am,	142
2323	Not what he knew I was: he makes me angry;	143
2324	And at this time most easy 'tis to do 't,	144
2325	When my good stars, that were my former guides,	145
2326	Have empty left their orbs, and shot their fires	146
2327	Into the abysm of hell. If he mislike	147
2328	My speech and what is done, tell him he has	148
2329	Hipparchus, my enfranched bondman, whom	149
2330	He may at pleasure whip, or hang, or torture,	150
2331	As he shall like, to quit me: urge it thou: **151**	151
2332	Hence with thy stripes, begone! [*Exit Thyreus.*	152
2333	*Cleo.* Have you done yet?	
	Ant. Alack, our terrene moon	153
2334	Is now eclipsed; and it portends alone	154
2335	The fall of Antony!	
2336	*Cleo.* I must stay his time.	155
2337	*Ant.* To flatter Cæsar, would you mingle eyes	156
2338	With one that ties his points?	
2339	*Cleo.* Not know me yet?	157
2340	*Ant.* Cold-hearted toward me?	

122   X: Bel, In2, JKP, Lac, HIM, KyB; <u>aX</u>: JL1, LiL, BT1, TaB; <u>bX</u>: ER1
123   X: Bel, AF1, ER1
124   same as 123
125   X: Bel, WM1, AF1, ER1
126   X: Bel, WM1, ER1; <u>aX</u>: AF1; <u>bX</u>: GCa, Cap, Inc, In2, JKP, Cum, KyB*
127   X: GCa, Cap, Bel, Inc, In2, JKP, WM1, Cum, KyB, JS1, ER1
128   same as 127; <u>bX</u>: IP1, GS1, RH1, BH1
129   X: GCa, Cap, Bel, Inc, In2, JKP, WM1, Cum, KyB, BT1, WA1, BA1, IP1*
130   same as 129

131   X: Bel, In2, JKP, WM1, WA1, TaB; <u>aX</u>: GCa, Cap, Inc, Cum, KyB, BT1,
     BA1, IP1, JS1, AF1, ML1, ER1, TN1; <u>bX</u>: ChC, LoC, RA1, GS1, RH1,BH1
132   X: Bel, In2, JKP, WM1, ChC, JL1, LoC, TaB; R: Cum; <u>bX</u>: Lac, Hal,HIM*
133   X: Bel, In2, JKP, WM1, Cum, ChC, Lac, Hal, JL1, HIM, KyB, MTh, LoC*
134   X: Cap, Bel, In2, JKP, WM1, ChC, Lac, Hal, JL1, HIM, KyB, MTh, LoC,
     BT1, SM1, WA1, TaB, RA1, ER1, EdT
135   same as 134; <u>bX</u>: ML1, TN1
136   same as 134, ML1, TN1; less <u>bX</u>

137   same as 136, less BA1, TN1; <u>aX</u>: RA1, TN1
138   X: Cap, Bel, WM1, ChC, Lac, Hal, JL1, HIM, KyB, MTh, EdT, LoC, BT1*
139   X: Bel, ChC, LoC, TaB; <u>aX</u>: Cap, WM1, Lac, Hal, JL1, KyB, MTh, EdT*
140   same as 139; less <u>aX</u>; <u>bX</u>: BA1
141   X: Bel, ChC, LoC, BA1, TaB; <u>bX</u>: In2, WM1, BT1, SM1
142   X: Bel, WM1, ChC, LoC, BT1, SM1, WA1, TaB; <u>aX</u>: In2
143   same as 142, less WM1; less <u>aX</u>; <u>aX</u>: WM1; <u>bX</u>: SP1, RA1
144   X: Bel, SP1, ChC, LoC, BA1, TaB, RA1, JS1
145   same as 144, OA1, BH1
146   same as 145; <u>bX</u>: IP1
147   X: Bel, ChC, LoC, TaB, RA1, JS1, RH1; <u>aX</u>: SP1, OA1, BA1, IP1; <u>bX</u>:Cap*
148   X: Cap, Bel, In 2, JKP, WM1, ChC, Lac, Hal, JL1, HIM, KyB, MTh, EdT*
149   same as 148
150   same as 148
151   X: Cap, Bel, In2, JKP, WM1, ChC, Lac, Hal, JL1, HIM, MTh, EdT, LoC*
152   X: Bel, ChC, LoC, TaB

153   X: ChC, LoC; <u>aX</u>: Bel, WM1
154   X: ChC, LoC

155   <u>aX</u>: ChC, LoC; <u>bX</u>: JKP, AF1, TN1
156   X: JKP, AF1, TN1

157   X: JKP; <u>R</u>: ML1; <u>aX</u>: AF1, TN1; <u>bX</u>: WM1, JL1; <u>ADD</u> 4: WM1

*3-13: 129 TaB, RA1, JS1, GS1, RH1, BH1, AF1, ML1, ER1, TN1
*3-13:126 JS1; <u>ADD</u> 1: JKP   *3-13:132 KyB, MTh
*3-13:133 TaB   *3-13:138 SM1, WA1, TaB, ER1
*3-13:139 BT1, SM1, WA1, ER1   *3-13:147 In2, JKP, WM1, Lac, Hal,
    JL1, HIM, KyB, MTh, EdT, SM1, WA1, RH1, AF1, ML1, ER1, TN1
*3-13:148 EdT, LoC, SM1, WA1, TaB, RA1, JS1, RH1, BH1, AF1
*3-13:151 BT1, SM1, WA1, TaB, BH1, AF1, ML1, TN1; <u>aX</u>: KyB, RA1, RH1, ER1

2341	*Cleo.* ·Ah, dear, if I be so,	158
2342	From my cold heart let heaven engender hail,	159
2343	And poison it in the source; and·the first stone	160
2344	Drop in my neck: as it determines, so 161	161
2345	Dissolve my life! The next Cæsarion smite!	162
2346	Till by degrees the memory of my womb,	163
2347	Together with my brave Egyptians all,	164
2348	By the discandying of this pelleted storm,	165
2349	Lie graveless, till the flies and gnats of Nile	166
2350	Have buried them for prey!	
2351	*Ant.* · I am satisfied.	167
2352	Cæsar sits down in Alexandria: where	168
2353	I will oppose his fate. Our force by land	169
2354	Hath nobly held; our sever'd navy too 170	170
2355	Have knit again, and fleet, threatening most sea- like.	171
2356	Where hast thou been, my heart? Dost thou hear, lady?	172
2357	If from the field I shall return once more	173
2358	To kiss these lips, I will appear in blood:	174
2359	I and my sword will earn our chronicle:	175
2360	There's hope in't yet.	176
2361	*Cleo.* That's my brave lord!	177
2362	*Ant.* I will be treble-sinew'd, hearted, breathed,	178
2363	And fight maliciously: for when mine hours	179
2364	Were nice and lucky, men did ransom lives 180	180
2365	Of me for jests; but now I'll set my teeth,	181
2366	And send to darkness all that stop me. Come,	182
2367	Let's have one other gaudy night: call to me	183
2368	All my sad captains; fill our bowls once more;	184
2369	Let's mock the midnight bell.	
2370	*Cleo.* It is my birth-day:	185
2371	I had thought to have held it poor; but, since my lord	186
2372	Is Antony again, I will be Cleopatra. ·	187
2373	*Ant.* We will yet do well.	188
2374	*Cleo.* Call all his noble captains to my lord.	189
2375	*Ant.* Do so, we'll speak to them; and to-night	
2376	I'll force 190	190
2377	The wine peep through their scars. Come on,	
2378	my queen;	191
2379	There's sap in't yet. The next time I do fight,	192
2380	I'll make death love me: for I will contend	193
	Even with his pestilent scythe.	194
2381	[*Exeunt all but Enobarbus.*	
	Eno. Now he'll outstare the lightning. To	

158   cX: JL1
159   X̄: BT1
160   X: BT1; bX: OA1
161   X: BT1, ŌA1, BA1; bX: ML1
162   aX̲ : OA1, ML1; b̲X̲: In2, Cum, KyB, TaB
163   X: In2, Cum, KyB̄, TaB
164   X: In2, TaB
165   X: In2, WM1, KyB, BT1, OA1, BA1, TaB, BH1
166   X: In2, KyB, TaB

167   aX: In2, KyB, TaB; A̲D̲D̲ 9, insert 3-11: 70b-74: Hal
168   X̄: Hal, SM1, WA1, ER1; R: W̄M1; M̲O̲V̲E̲ 168-194 to follow 45: 17: BT1
169   X: Hal, ER1; R: WM1; aX̲: SM1, W̄A̲1̲; bX: Cap, JL1, GS1; A̲D̲D̲ 3: JL1; M̲O̲V̲E̲*
170   X: Cap, Hal, JL1, GS1, ER1; R̲: WM1

171   same as 170; less R̲; R: WM1, ML1; bX: BA1; I̲n̲s̲e̲r̲t̲ 177: JKP

172   R: WM1
173   R̄: In2, WM1
174   X̄: JKP; R: WM1
175   X: JKP; R̄: WM1; A̲D̲D̲ 2: WM1
176   X: JKP; aX̲: WM1
177   M̲O̲V̲E̲ 177 to follow 171: JKP
178   X̄: RA1
179   X: RA1; bX: WM1, KyB
180   X: WM1, K̄yB, RA1
181   X: WM1, RA1; aX̲: KyB; bX: ML1; A̲D̲D̲ 3: TaB
182   aX̲: WM1, RA1, M̄L1; bX: JL1, TaB
183   X̄: Hal, JL1, TaB; bX̲;WM1; A̲D̲D̲ 16: WM1
184   X: WM1, JL1, WA1, T̄aB

185   same as 184; bX̲: Cum, ChC, LoC, BT1, OA1

186   X: WM1, ChC, Hal, JL1, LoC, OA1, TaB; aX̲: Cum, BT1
187   same as 186; less aX̲
188   X: JKP, WM1, ChC, H̄al, JL1, KyB, LoC, BT1, SM1, OA1, TaB
189   X: WM1, Hal, JL1, KyB, BT1, SM1, OA1, TaB

190   same as 189, less OA1; aX̲: OA1

191   X: WM1 , Hal, JL1, KyB, TaB; aX̲: BT1, SM1
192   same as 191; less aX̲; aX: JKP, WM1, Cum, BT1
193   same as 191, less W̄M1; less aX̲; bX: AF1, ML1
194   X: Hal, JL1, Ky3, TaB, AF1, M̄L1; A̲D̲D̲ 2: LiL, BT1, OA1; A̲D̲D̲ 267: In2

*3-13:169 169b-194 to follow 4̲2̲: 46: SM1; M̲O̲V̲E̲ 169b-194 to follow 4̲3̲: 41a:
  WA1

2382	be furious,	195
2383	Is to be frighted out of fear: and in that mood	196
2384	The dove will peck the estridge: and I see still,	197
2385	A diminution in our captain's brain	198
2386	Restores his heart: when valour preys on reason,	199
2387	It eats the sword it fights with. I will seek 200	200
2388	Some way to leave him. [*Exit*.	201

2388+1

ACT IV.

2388+2   SCENE I. *Before Alexandria. Cæsar's camp.*

2389   *Enter* CÆSAR, AGRIPPA, *and* MECÆNAS, *with*
2390   *his Army;* CÆSAR *reading a letter.*

Cæs.   He calls me boy; and chides, as he had
2391   power   ;
2392   To beat me out of Egypt: my messenger   2
He hath whipp'd with rods; dares me to personal
2393   combat,   3
2394   Cæsar to Antony: let the old ruffian know   4
2395   I have many other ways to die; meantime   5
2396   Laugh at his challenge.   6
Mec.   Cæsar must think,
2397
2398   When one so great begins to rage, he's hunted   7
2399   Even to falling.   Give him no breath, but now   8
2400   Make boot of his distraction: never anger   9
2401   Made good guard for itself.
Cæs.   Let our best heads   r
2402
2403   Know, that to-morrow the last of many battles   10
2404   We mean to fight: within our files there are,   11
2405   Of those that served Mark Antony but late,   12
2406   Enough to fetch him in.   See it done: 13
2407   And feast the army; we have store to do't,   14
2408   And they have earn'd the waste.   Poor Antony. 15
                                        [*Exeunt*   16

2409+1   SCENE II. *Alexandria. Cleopatra's palace.*

2409   *Enter* ANTONY, CLEOPATRA, ENOBARBUS, CHAR-
2410   MIAN, IRAS, ALEXAS, *with others.*

2411   *Ant.*   He will not fight with me, Domitius
2412   *Eno.*   Na   1
2413   *Ant.*   Why should he not?   2
Eno.   He thinks, being twenty times of better
2414   fortune,   3
2415   He is twenty men to one.

195   X: In2, Lac, Ha1, JL1, HIM, KyB, MTh, EdT, BT1, SM1, WA1, OA1, TaB;*
196   same as 195, BA1, IP1; less bX, <u>MOVE</u>
197   same as 195; <u>aX</u>: BA1, IP1
198   same as 195
199   same as 195; <u>bX</u>: ML1
200   same as 195, <u>aX</u>: ML1
201   same as 195; <u>ADD</u> 20: LiL

Scene 41

<u>ALL CUT</u>: GCa, Cap, Be1, Inc, In2, JKP, Cum, Ha1, JL1, LiL, SM1, WA1, TaB
1   <u>MOVE</u> 1-16 to follow <u>45</u>: 26: KyB; <u>MOVE</u> 1-14 to follow <u>45</u>:17: WM1, OA1*
2

3
4
5

6   <u>bX</u>: JS1, LK1
7   <u>X</u>: JS1, LK1
8   X: JS1, LK1; <u>bX</u>: GS1
9   X: JS1, GS1, <u>LK1</u>; <u>bX</u>: BA1, BH1, ML1, TN1

10   X: LK1; <u>aX</u>: BA1, JS1, GS1, BH1, ML1, TN1; <u>bX</u>: ChC, KyB, LoC, BT1,OA1
11   X: ChC, <u>KyB</u>, LoC, BT1, OA1, LK1
12   X: ChC, LoC, BT1, LK1; <u>aX</u>: KyB, OA1
13   same as 12; less <u>aX</u>
14   same as 13; bX: O<u>A1</u>
15   X: WM1, ChC, <u>KyB</u>, LoC, BT1, OA1, AF1, LK1
16   X: WM1, ChC, LoC, BT1, LK1; <u>aX</u>: KyB, OA1, AF1

Scene 42

<u>ALL CUT</u>: GCa, Cap, Inc, In2, WM1, SP1, Cum, Lac, Ha1, JL1, HIM, KyB, LiL,
  MTh, EdT, BT1, OA1, TaB, RA1, GS1, RH1, BH1, ER1, TN1
1   X: ChC, LoC
2   X: ChC, LoC

3   X: ChC, LoC

*3-13:195 bX: BA1, IP1; <u>MOVE</u> 195-201 to follow 42: 45: ChC, LoC
*41: 1<u>MOVE</u> <u>1</u>-10a to follow <u>44</u>: 38: ChC, LoC; <u>MOVE</u> 1-10a to follow <u>45</u> 17:
  BT1

2416	*Ant.* To-morrow, soldier,	4
2417	By sea and land I'll fight: or I will live,	5
2418	Or bathe my dying honour in the blood	6
2419	Shall make it live again. Woo't thou fight we:	7
2420	*Eno.* I'll strike, and cry 'Take all.'	
2421	*Ant.* Well said; come c:	8
2422	Call forth my household servants: let's to-nig:	9
2423a	Be bounteous at our meal.	

Enter three or four Servitors.

2423b	Give me thy hand, r	10
2425	Thou hast been rightly honest;—so hast thou:—	11
2426	Thou,—and thou,—and thou:—you have serve me well,	12
2427	And kings have been your fellows.	
2428	*Cleo.* [*Aside to Eno.*] What means th:	13
2429	*Eno.* [*Aside to Cleo.*] 'Tis one of those o: tricks which sorrow shoots	14
2430	Out of the mind.	
2431	*Ant.* And thou art honest too.	15
2432	I wish I could be made so many men,	16
2433	And all of you clapp'd.up together in	17
2434	An Antony, that I might do you service	18
2435	So good as you have done.	
2436	*All.* The gods forbid!	19
2437	*Ant.* Well, my good fellows, wait on me t- night:	20
2438	Scant not my cups; and make as much of me	21
2439	As when mine empire was your fellow too,	22
2440	And suffer'd my command.	
2441	*Cleo.* [*Aside to Eno.*] What does he mean:	23
2442	*Eno.* [*Aside to Cleo.*] To make his followe: weep.	
2443	*Ant.* Tend me to-night:	24
2444	May be it is the period of your duty:	25
2445	Haply you shall not see me more; or if,	26
2446	A mangled shadow: perchance to-morrow	27
2447	You'll serve another master. I look on you	28
2448	As one that takes his leave. Mine honest frien:	29
2449	I turn you not away; but, like a master	30
2450	Married to your good service, stay till death:	31
2451	Tend me to-night two hours, I ask no more,	32
2452	And the gods yield you for't!	
2453	*Eno.* What mean you, :	33
2454	To give them this discomfort? Look, they wee:	34
2455	And I, an ass, am onion-eyed: for shame,	35

```
 4   aX: ChC, LoC
 5
 6
 7

 8   bX: BA1
 9   X: BA1; R: JKP


10   R: JKP; aX: BA1; bX: JP1
11   X: JP1

12   X: JP1

13   X: JP1

14   X: JP1

15   X: JP1; bX: JKP
16   X: JKP, JP1
17   X: JKP, JP1
18   X: JKP, JP1

19   X: JKP, JP1

20   X: JP1
21   X: JP1
22   X: JP1

23   X: JP1


24   X: JP1
25   X: JP1
26   X: JP1
27   X: JP1
28   X: JP1
29   X: JP1; bX: BA1, IP1
30   X: BA1, IP1, JP1; bX: NM1
31   X: BA1, IP1, JP1; aX: NM1
32   same as 31; less aX

33   X: JP1; aX: BA1, IP1
34   X: JP1
35   X: JP1
```

2456	Transform us not to women.	
2457	*Ant.* Ho, ho, ho!	36
2458	Now the witch take me, if I meant it thus!	37
	Grace grow where those drops fall! My hearty	
2459	friends,	38
2460	You take me in too dolorous a sense;	39
	For I spake to you for your comfort; did desire	
2461	you **40**	40
2462	To burn this night with torches: know, my hearts,	41
2463	I hope well of to-morrow; and will lead you	42
2464	Where rather I 'll expect victorious life	43
2465	Than death and honour. Let's to supper, come,	44
2466	And drown consideration. [*Exeunt.*	45

2466+1   **SCENE** III. *The same. Before the palace.*

2467   *Enter two* Soldiers *to their guard.*

	First Sold. Brother, good night: to-morrow	
2468	is the day.	1
	Sec. Sold. It will determine one way: fare	
2469	you well.	2
2470	Heard you of nothing strange about the streets?	3
2471	*First Sold.* Nothing. What news?	4
	Sec. Sold. Belike 'tis but a rumour. Good	
2472	night to you.	5
2473	*First Sold.* Well, sir, good night.	6

2474   *Enter two other* Soldiers.

2475	*Sec. Sold.* Soldiers, have careful watch.	7
2476	*Third Sold.* And you. Good night, good night.	8
2477	[*They place themselves in every corner of*	
2477+1	*the stage.*	
2478	*Fourth Sold.* Here we: and if to-morrow	9
2479	Our navy thrive, I have an absolute hope **10**	10
2480	Our landmen will stand up.	
	Third Sold. 'Tis a brave army,	11
2481	And full of purpose.	
2482	[*Music of the hautboys as under the stage.*	
2483	*Fourth Sold.* Peace! what noise?	
2484	*First Sold.* List, list!	12
2485	*Sec. Sold.* Hark!	
2486	*First Sold.* Music i' the air.	
2487	*Third Sold.* Under the earth.	13
2488	*Fourth Sold.* It signs well, does it not?	
2489	*Third Sold.* No.	
	First Sold. Peace, I say!	14

```
36   X: JP1
37   X: JP1

38   X: JP1
39   X: JP1

40   X: JP1
41   X: JS1, JP1
42   X: JP1
43   X: JP1
44   X: JP1; bX: SM1
45   X: SM1, JP1; Insert 3-13: 195-201: ChC, LoC; Insert 3-13: 169-194:
        SM1, WA1
```

Scene 43

ALL CUT: GCa, Cap, Bel, Inc, In2, JKP, WM1, SP1, Cum, ChC, Lac, Hal, JL1,
  HIM, KyB, LiL, MTh, EdT, SM1, OA1, TaB, RA1, BH1, JP1
```
 1   X: LoC; MOVE 1-23 to follow 46: 39: BT1; MOVE 1-26 to follow 48:39; WA1,
        RH1
 2   X: LoC; aX: BT1
 3   X: LoC
 4   X: LoC

 5   X: LoC
 6   X: LoC


 7   X: LoC, JS1
 8   X: LoC, JS1


 9   X: LoC, WA1, BA1, JS1, ER1, TN1
10   same as 9

11   same as 9


12   aX: LoC, WA1, BA1, ER1, TN1; MOVE 12b-23 to follow 4-14:140: LoC


13


14
```

2490	˜at should this mean?	15
	Sec. Sold. 'Tis the god Hercules, whom An-	16
2491	tony loved,	
2492	˜w leaves him.	17
2493	*First Sold.* Walk; let's see if other watchmen	18
2494	˜o hear what we do?	
	[*They advance to another post.*	
	Sec. Sold. How now, masters!	
2495	*All* [*Speaking together*] How now!	19
2496	How now! do you hear this?	
2497	*First Sold.* Ay; is't not strange? 20	20
	Third Sold. Do you hear, masters? do you	
2498	hear?	21
	First Sold. Follow the noise so far as we have	
2499	quarter;	22
2500	let's see how it will give off.	
2501	*All* Content. 'Tis strange. [*Exeunt.*	23

2501+1	Scene IV. *The same. A room in the palace.*
2502	*Enter* ANTONY *and* CLEOPATRA, CHARMIAN,
2502+1	*and others attending.*

2503	*Ant.* Eros! mine armour, Eros!	
2504	*Cleo.* Sleep a little.	1
	Ant. No, my chuck. Eros, come; mine ar-	
2505	mour, Eros!	2
2506	*Enter* EROS *with armour.*	
2507	Come, good fellow, put mine iron on:	3
2508	If fortune be not ours to-day, it is	4
2509	Because we brave her: come.	
2510	*Cleo.* Nay, I'll help too.	5
	What's this for?	
2511	*Ant.* Ah, let be, let be! thou art	6
2512	The armourer of my heart: false, false; this, this.	7
2513	*Cleo.* Sooth, la, I'll help: thus it must be.	
	Ant. Well, well:	8
2514	We shall thrive now. Seest thou, my good fellow?	9
2515	Go put on thy defences.	
2516	*Eros.* Briefly, sir. 10	10
2517	*Cleo.* Is not this buckled well?	
2518	*Ant.* Rarely, rarely:	11
2519	He that unbuckles this, till we do please	12
2520	To daff't for our repose, shall hear a storm.	13
2521	Thou fumblest, Eros; and my queen's a squire	14
2522	More tight at this than thou: dispatch. O love,	15

15

16
17
18 b<u>X</u>: JS1, ER1

19 X: JS1; <u>a</u>X: ER1

20 X: JS1

21 X: JS1; b<u>X</u>: TN1

22 b<u>X</u>: AF1

23

<u>Scene 44</u>

<u>ALL CUT</u>: Be1, In2, LiL, BT1
 1 X: JKP; <u>R</u>: WM1

 2 X: JKP; <u>R</u>: WM1; <u>a</u>X: Cum

 3 X: JKP; <u>R</u>: WM1
 4 X: JKP; <u>R̄</u>: WM1

 5 X: JKP; <u>R</u>: WM1

 6 X: JKP; <u>R</u>: WM1; <u>a</u>X: RA1; <u>N</u>: GCa, Inc, Cum
 7 X: JKP; <u>R̄</u>: WM1

 8 X: JKP, WM1, OA1; <u>a</u>X: Cum
 9 same as 8; less <u>aX</u>

10 same as 9, TN1

11 same as 9
12 same as 9
13 same as 9
14 X: Cap, JKP, WM1, Cum, OA1
15 X: Cap, JKP, WM1; <u>a</u>X: Cum, OA1

2523	That thou couldst see my wars to-day, and knew'st	16
2524	The royal occupation! thou shouldst see	17
2525	A workman in't.	

Enter an armed Soldier.

2527	Good morrow to thee; welcome:	18
2528	Thou look'st like him that knows a warlike charge:	19
2529	To business that we love we rise betime, **20**	20
2530	And go to't with delight.	
	Sold. A thousand, sir,	21
2531	Early though 't be, have on their riveted trim,	22
2532	And at the port expect you.	23
2533	[*Shout. Trumpets flourish.*	

Enter Captains *and* Soldiers.

2535	*Capt.* The morn is fair. Good morrow, general.	24
2536	*All.* Good morrow, general.	
2537	*Ant.* 'Tis well blown, lads:	25
2538	This morning, like the spirit of a youth	26
2539	That means to be of note, begins betimes.	27
2540	So, so; come, give me that: this way; well said.	28
2541	Fare thee well, dame, whate'er becomes of me:	29
2542	This is a soldier's kiss: rebukeable [*Kisses her.*	30
2543	And worthy shameful check it were, to stand 31	31
2544	On more mechanic compliment; I'll leave thee	32
2545	Now, like a man of steel. You that will fight,	33
	Follow me close; I'll bring you to't. Adieu.	34
2546	[*Exeunt Antony, Eros, Captains, and*	
2546+1	*Soldiers.*	
2547	*Char.* Please you, retire to your chamber.	
2548	*Cleo.* Lead me.	35
2549	He goes forth gallantly. That he and Cæsar might	36
2550	Determine this great war in single fight!	37
2551	Then, Antony,—but now—Well, on. [*Exeunt.*	38

2551+1 **SCENE V.** *Alexandria. Antony's camp.*

2552	*Trumpets sound. Enter* ANTONY *and* EROS; *a*
2552+1	Soldier *meeting them.*

	Sold. The gods make this a happy day to	
2553	Antony!	1
	Ant. Would thou and those thy scars had	
2554	once prevail'd	2
2555	To make me fight at land!	
2556	*Sold.* Hadst thou done so,	3
2557	The kings that have revolted, and the soldier	4

16 same as 15; less aX
17 same as 16

18 X: Cum; aX: Cap, JKP; bX: SP1, ChC, Ha1, LoC, BA1, JS1, JP1, ER1,TN1*
19 X: SP1, Cum, ChC, LoC, OA1, BA1, RA1, JS1, JHP , ML1, ER1, TN1
20 same as 19, GS1, less ML1

21 same as 20, less OA1, GS1; aX: OA1, GS1; bX: JKP
22 same as 21, AF1
23 same as 21

24 X: JKP, ChC, LoC, OA1, JS1, JP1

25 X: JKP, RA1, JS1, JP1, ER1; aX: WM1; bX: AF1
26 X: Cap, JKP, KyB, OA1, JS1, JP1
27 same as 26, JL1
28 X: JKP, JL1, OA1, JP1, ER1; bX: Cap, WM1, TN1
29 X: JKP, JL1; R: WM1, KyB
30 X: JKP, WM1, JL1; bX: ChC, KyB, LoC, SM1, WA1, OA1, BA1, IP1, GS1,*
31 X: Cap, JKP, WM1, ChC, JL1, KyB, LoC, SM1, WA1, OA1, BA1, IPi , GS1*
32 X: JKP, WM1, JL1, KyB, BA1, ER1; aX: Cap, ChC, LoC, SM1, WA1, OA1,IP1*
33 X: JKP, WM1, JS1, ER1; aX: JL1, KyB, BA1, AF1; bX: RA1
34 same as 33; less aX, bX; aX: RA1; bX: AF1

35 X: JKP, WM1, JL1, EdT, JS1; MOVE 35-38 to follow 45: 17: BA1, ER1
36 same as 35; less MOVE; bX: ML1
37 same as 36; less bX
38 same as 35, TaB; less bX; Insert 3-11: 51-68: Ha1; Insert 47: 1-
        100: ChC, LoC; Insert 3-10: 4b-8a, add 7, 26b-27, and 3-11: 1-70a:
        JL1

Scene 45

ALL CUT: Bel, In2, ChC, Lac, HIM, LiL, EdT, LoC, SM1, WA1, TaB
 1 X: JL1; N: SP1

 2

 3
 4

*44:18 ADD 4: ChC; Insert 48: 13-16: LoC; ADD 10, insert 37: 19b-67, and
    48: 13b-16a, add 16, insert 3-13: 1-24: Ha1   *44:30 OA1, BH1,
    JP1, ML1, ER1, TN1   *44:31 BH1, JP1, AF1, ML1, ER1, TN1
*44:32 GS1BH1, JP1, AF1, ML1,TN1; bX: JS1; MOVE 32b-38 to follow 35 17:OA1

2558	**That** has this morning left thee, would have still	5
2559	**Follow'd** thy heels.	
2560	*Ant.* Who's gone this morning?	
	Sold. Who!	6
2561	**One** ever near thee: call for Enobarbus,	7
2562	**He** shall not hear thee; or from Cæsar's camp	8
2563	**Say** ' I am none of thine.'	
2564	*Ant.* What say'st thou?	
	Sold. Sir,	9
2565	**He** is with Cæsar.	
	Eros. Sir, his chests and treasure 10	10
2566	**He** has not with him.	
2567	*Ant.* Is he gone?	
	Sold. Most certain.	11
2568		
2569	*Ant.* Go, Eros, send his treasure after; do it;	12
2579	**Detain** no jot, I charge thee: write to him—	13
2571	**I** will subscribe—gentle adieus and greetings;	14
2572	**Say** that I wish he never find more cause	15
2573	**To** change a master. O, my fortunes have	16
	Corrupted honest men! Dispatch.—Enobarbus!	17
2574	*[Exeunt.*	

2574+1 **SCENE VI.** *Alexandria. Cæsar's camp.*

2575	*Flourish. Enter* CÆSAR, AGRIPPA, *with* ENO-	
2576	BARBUS, *and others.*	
2577	*Cæs.* Go forth, Agrippa, and begin the fight:	1
2578	**Our** will is Antony be took alive;	2
2579	**Make** it so known.	3
2580	*Agr.* Cæsar, I shall. *[Exit.*	4
2581	*Cæs.* The time of universal peace is near:	5
	Prove this a prosperous day, the three-nook'd	
2582	world	6
2583	**Shall** bear the olive freely.	
2584	*Enter a* Messenger.	
	Mess. Antony	7
2585	**Is** come into the field.	
2586	*Cæs.* Go charge Agrippa	8
2587	**Plant** those that have revolted in the van,	9
2588	**That** Antony may seem to spend his fury 10	10
2589	**Upon** himself. *[Exeunt all but Enobarbus.*	11
2590	*Eno.* Alexas did revolt; and went to Jewry on	12
2591	**Affairs** of Antony; there did persuade	13
2592	**Great** Herod to incline himself to Cæsar,	14

5

6
7
8   b<u>X</u>: ML1

9   a<u>X</u>: ML1

10

11
12   b<u>X</u>: OA1
13
14   X: JKP
15
16
17   a<u>X</u>: BT1; B<u>X</u>: JL1, ML1; <u>ADD</u> 5: JKP; <u>ADD</u> 15, insert <u>41</u>: 1-14: WM1 ;
         <u>Insert</u> A<u>I</u>: 1-16: KyB; <u>Insert</u> 3-13: 168-194 and 4<u>1</u>: 1-9: BT1; <u>Insert</u>
         <u>44</u>: 32b-38, and <u>41</u>: 1-16: OA1; <u>Insert</u> 25-30: BA1; <u>Insert</u> 44: 35-
         38: ER1

Scene 46

<u>ALL CUT</u>: Be1, KyB, SM1, WA1, TaB; <u>CUT ALL BUT TRANSFER</u>: Hal
1   X: ChC, JL1, LiL, LoC, LK1
2   same as 1
3   same as 1
4   same as 1; <u>R</u>: JKP
5   X: JKP, ChC, JL1, LiL, LoC,LK1

6   same as 5, BT1

7   X: JL1, LiL, LK1; a<u>X</u>: JKP, ChC, LoC, BT1; <u>N</u>: SP1

8   same as 7, less a<u>X</u>, <u>N</u>; b<u>X</u>: LoC
9   same as 7, less a<u>X</u> <u>N</u>
10   same as 9
11   same as 9, NM1; <u>ADD</u> 11: In2; <u>ADD</u> 3: JKP
12   X: In2, ChC, JL1, LoC, BT1, N<u>M1</u>, JP1, AF1, LK1; <u>R</u>: ER1; b<u>X</u>: Lac, HIM,*
13   same as 12, ML1, ER1; less <u>R</u>, b<u>X</u>, <u>N</u>, <u>MOVE</u>; a<u>X</u>: Lac, HIM; <u>bX</u>: BH1
14   same as 13, BA1, less ML1; less a<u>X</u>, b<u>X</u>; a<u>X</u>: ML1

*46:12 ML1; <u>N</u>: LiL; <u>MOVE</u> 12-39 to follow <u>49</u>: 11: JKP

2593	**And** leave his master Antony: for this pains	15
2594	**Cæsar** hath hang'd him. Canidius and the rest	16
2595	**That** fell away have entertainment, but	17
2596	**No** honourable trust. I have done ill:	18
2597	**Of** which I do accuse myself so sorely,	19
2598	**That** I will joy no more.	

2599	*Enter a* Soldier *of* CÆSAR'S.		
2600	*Sold.* Enobarbus, Antony	20	20
2601	**Hath** after thee sent all thy treasure, with		21
2602	**His** bounty overplus: the messenger		22
2603	**Came** on my guard: and at thy tent is now		23
2604	**Unloading** of his mules.		
2605	*Eno.* I give it you.		24
2606	*Sold.* Mock not, Enobarbus.		25
2607	**I** tell you true: best you safed the bringer		26
2608	**Out** of the host; I must attend mine office,		27
2609	**Or** would have done't myself. Your emperor		28
2610	**Continues** still a Jove. [*Exit.*		29
2611	*Eno.* I am alone the villain of the earth,	30	30
2612	**And** feel I am so most. O Antony,		31
2613	**Thou** mine of bounty, how wouldst thou have paid		32
2614	**My** better service. when my turpitude		33
2615	**Thou** dost so crown with gold! This blows my heart:		34
2616	**If** swift thought break it not, a swifter mean		35
2617	**Shall** outstrike thought: but thought will do't I feel.		36
2618	**I** fight against thee! No: I will go seek		37
2619	**Some** ditch where'n to die; the foul'st best fits		38
2620	**My** latter part of life. [*Exit*		39

2620+1	**SCENE** VII. *Field of battle between the camp*	
2621	*Alarum. Drums and trumpets. Enter* AGRIPPA	
2622	*and others.*	
2623	*Agr.* Retire, we have engaged ourselves to far:	1
2624	**Cæsar** himself has work, and our oppression	2
2625	**Exceeds** what we expected. [*Exeunt*	3
2626	*Alarums. Enter* ANTONY, *and* SCARUS	
2627	*wounded.*	
2628	*Scar.* O my brave emperor, this is fought'a deed!	4
2629	**Had** we done so at first, we had droven them home	5

```
15    same as 14, less ER1; less aX; aX: ML1, ER1
16    X: In2, JP1, AF1, LK1; aX ChC, JL1, LoC, BT1, BA1, NM1; N: EdT, ML1;*
17    same as 16; less aX, N, MOVE
18    X: In2, JP1, LK1; aX: A F1
19    X: In2, JP1, ML1, LK1


20    X: In2, JP1; aX: LK1; N: SP1, LoC
21    X: In2, JP1; R: ML1
22    X: In2, JP1; aX: ML1; bX: OA1, AF1
23    X: In2, OA1, JP1, AF1

24    X; In2, JP1; aX: OA1, AF1
25    X: In2, JP1
26    X: In2, JP1; bX: BT1, RA1, AF1, ML1, ER1, TN1
27    X: In2, BT1, RA1, JP1, ML1, ER1, LK1, TN1; aX: AF1
28    X: In2, JP1, ER1; aX: BT1, RA1, AF1, ML1, LK1, TN1
29    X: In2, JP1, ER1
30    X: In2, JP1; MOVE 30-39a to follow 4-15: 91: Hal
31    X: In2, JP1; ADD 1: WM1
32    X: In2, JP1
33    X: In2, JP1

34    X: In2, JP1
35    X: In2, BA1, JP1, TN1

36    same as 35
37    X: In2, JP1
38    X: In2, JP1
39    X: In2, JP1; ADD 2: WM1; Insert 43: 1-23: BT1
```

Scene 47

ALL CUT: Bel, Inc, In2, SP1, Cum, ChC, Lac, Hal, JL1, HIM, KyB, LiL, MTh,
   EdT, LoC, BT1, SM1, OA1, BA1

```
1    X: JKP, WA1, RH1, BH1, AF1, ER1, TN1
2    same as 1
3    same as 1




4    X: NM1, JP1; MOVE 4-6 to follow 48: 4: JKP
5    X: WM1, NM1, JP1; bX:TN1
```

*46:16 MOVE 16b-39 to follow 4-14: 140: JL1

2630	With clouts about their heads.	
2631	*Ant.* Thou bleed'st ~~~	6
2632	*Scar.* I had a wound here that was like a I.	7
2633	But now 'tis made an H.	
2634	*Ant.* They do retire.	8
	Scar. We'll beat 'em into bench-holes: I h~	
2635	yet	9
2636	Room for six scotches more. ~	10

2637 *Enter* EROS.

	Eros. They are beaten, sir; and our adv~	
2638	age serves	11
2639	For a fair victory.	
2640	*Scar.* Let us score their backs.	12
2641	And snatch 'em up, as we take hares, beh~d:	13
2642	'Tis sport to maul a runner.	
2643	*Ant.* I will reward the~	14
2644	Once for thy spritely comfort, and ten-fold	15
2645	For thy good valour. Come thee on.	
2646	*Scar.* I'll halt after. [*Ex~*	16

2646+1 **SCENE VIII.** *Under the walls of Alexa~ir~*

2647	*Alarum. Enter* ANTONY, *in a march;* SC~	
2648	*with others.*	
	Ant. We have beat him to his camp: ru~ ~	
2649	before,	1
2659	And let the queen know of our gests. To-m~~	2
2651	Before the sun shall see 's, we'll spill the ~~~	3
2652	That has to-day escaped. I thank you all:	4
2653	For doughty-handed are you, and have f~~~	5
2654	Not as you served the cause, but as 't had ~~	6
	Each man's like mine; you have show~ ~	
2655	Hectors.	7
2656	Enter the city, clip your wives, your friend~	8
	Tell them your feats; whilst they with jo~	
2657	tears	9
	Wash the congealment from your wounds, ~	
2628	kiss	10
2659	The honour'd gashes whole. [*To Scar~s*] G~	
2661	me thy hand;	11

2660 *Enter* CLEOPATRA, *attended.*

2662	To this great fairy I'll commend thy acts,	12
	Make her thanks bless thee.· [*To Cleo.*] O ~	
2663	day o' the world,	13

6   X: NM1, JP1; aX: WM1, TN1; bX: WA1, LK1
7   X: JKP, WM1, W̄A1, NM1, JP1, L̄K1

8   X: JKP, WM1, WA1, NM1, JP1; aX: LK1

9   X: JKP, WM1, WA1, NM1, IP1, JP1; bX: ML1, LK1
10 X: JKP, WM1, WA1, NM1, IP1, JP1, ML̄1, LK1

11 X: JKP, WM1, WA1, NM1, JP1; bX: OA1

12 X: JKP, WA1, NM1, JP1; aX: WM1; bX: IP1, AF1, TN1
13 X: JKP, WA1, NM1, IP1, ŌA1, JP1, ĀF1, TN1; R: WM1

14 X: JKP, WM1, WA1, NM1, IP1, JP1, TN1; aX: AF1; bX: RA1
15 X: JKP, WM1, WA1, NM1, IP1, RA1, JP1, T̄N1; aX: ŌA1; bX: AF1

16 same as 15; less aX, bX; bX: TaB, BH1; ADD 2: WM1

Scene 48

ALL CUT: ChC, JL1, LiL, EdT, BT1, SM1, OA1, NM1; ALL BUT TRANSFER: Ha1
1   X: RA1, LK1; aX: BH1; bX: BA1, ER1
2   X: RA1, ER1; aX: BH1, L̄K1
3   X: WM1, RA1, ĒR1
4   X: RA1, ER1; aX: WM1; bX: JKP; Insert 47: 4-7, add 2: JKP
5   X: Cap, BA1, R̄A1, RH1, ĒR1, TN1; aX: In2
6   same as 5; less aX

7   same as 6, less RH1; aX: RH1; bX: TaB
8   X: JKP, TaB, RA1, ER1

9   same as 8; bX: WM1, KyB

10 X: JKP, WM1, KyB, TaB, RA1, ER1

11 X: JKP, TaB, ER1; aX: WM1, KyB, RA1; bX: JP1, ML1, LK1, TN1

12 X: In2, JKP, TaB, JP1, ER1, LK1, TN1

13 X: TaB, ER1; aX: In2, JKP, JP1, LK1, TN1; MOVE 13b-16a to follow 44:
      17b: Ha1, LoC

2664	Chain mine arm'd neck; leap thou, attire and all,	14
2665	Through proof of harness to my heart, and there	15
2666	Ride on the pants triumphing!	
2667	*Cleo.* Lord of lords!	16
2668	O infinite virtue, comest thou smiling from	17
2669	The world's great snare uncaught?	
2670	*Ant.* My nightingale,	18
2671	We have beat them to their beds. What, girl!	
2672	though grey	19
	Do something mingle with our younger brown,	
2673	yet ha' we 20	20
2674	A brain that nourishes our nerves, and can	21
2675	Get goal for goal of youth. Behold this man:	22
2676	Commend unto his lips thy favouring hand:	23
2677	Kiss it, my warrior: he hath fought to-day	24
2678	As if a god, in hate of mankind, had	25
2679	Destroy'd in such a shape.	
2680	*Cleo.* I'll give thee, friend,	26
2681	An armour all of gold; it was a king's.	27
2682	*Ant.* He has deserved it, were it carbuncled	28
2683	Like holy Phœbus' car. Give me thy hand:	29
2684	Through Alexandria make a jolly march: 30	30
	Bear our hack'd targets like the men that owe	
2685	them:	31
2686	Had our great palace the capacity	32
2687	To camp this host, we all would sup together,	33
2688	And drink carouses to the next day's fate,	34
2689	Which promises royal peril. Trumpeters,	35
2690	With brazen din blast you the city's ear:	36
2691	Make mingle with our rattling tabourines;	37
	That heaven and earth may strike their sounds	
2692	together,	38
2693	Applauding our approach. [*Exeunt.* 39	39

2693+1	SCENE IX. *Cæsar's camp.*
2694	Sentinels *at their post.*

	First Sold. If we be not relieved within this	
2695	hour,	1
2696	We must return to the court of guard: the night	2
2697	Is shiny; and they say we shall embattle	3
2698	By the second hour i' the morn.	
	Sec. Sold. This last day was	4
2699	A shrewd one to 's.	

2699+1	*Enter* ENOBARBUS.

14 X: TaB, ER1
15 X: TaB, ML1, ER1; <u>bX</u>: WH1

16 X: TaB, ER1; <u>aX</u>: WM1, ML1; <u>bX</u>: In2, LoC
17 X: LoC, TaB, $\overline{ER1}$

18 X: LoC, TaB; <u>aX</u>: ER1

19 X: LoC, TaB; <u>bX</u>: Cap, In2, RA1

20 X: Cap, In2, JKP, LoC, TaB, RA1
21 same as 20, less RA1; <u>aX</u>: RA1
22 X: JKP, LoC, TaB; <u>R</u>: $M\overline{L1}$; <u>aX</u>: Cap, In2; <u>bX</u>: JP1
23 X: LoC, TaB, JP1
24 same as 23
25 same as 23

26 same as 23; <u>bX</u>: ML1
27 same as 23, $\overline{ML1}$
28 same as 27; <u>bX</u>: TN1
29 X: LoC, TaB; <u>aX</u>: JP1, ML1, TN1; <u>ADD</u>: In2
30 X: LoC, TaB

31 X: JKP, LoC, IP1, TaB, RA1, ML1
32 X: WM1, LoC, TaB, RA1, RH1, ER1, TN1
33 same as 32, BH1; <u>bX</u>: In2
34 same as 33, less $\overline{RH1}$; less bX
35 X: In2, LoC, TaB; <u>aX</u>: Cap, $\overline{WM1}$, RA1, ER1, TN1
36 X: LoC, TaB
37 X: LoC, TaB, RA1; <u>R</u>: ML1

38 same as 37; ML1; less <u>R</u>; <u>ADD</u> 1: JKP; <u>Insert</u> <u>43</u>: 1-23: RH1; <u>Insert</u> <u>43</u>:
     1-15: WA1; <u>ADD</u> 85, <u>insert</u> 22: 19b-2<u>10</u>, <u>add</u> <u>255</u>: In2

Scene 49

<u>CUT ALL</u>: Inc, In2, WM1, Cum, ChC, LiL, BT1, SM1, WA1, TaB; <u>CUT ALL BUT</u>
  TRANSFER: Ha1, LoC

1 X: JL1, OA1, JP1, AF1, LK1; <u>MOVE</u> 1-29a to follow <u>46</u>: 39: KyB
2 X: JL1, OA1, JP1, LK1; <u>aX</u>: $\overline{AF1}$
3 same as 2; less <u>aX</u>; <u>cX</u>: $\overline{AF1}$

4 same as 2; less <u>aX</u>

2700	*Eno.* O, bear me witness, night,—	5
2701	*Third Sold.* What man is this?	
2702	*Sec. Sold.* Stand close, and list him.	6
2703	*Eno.* Be witness to me, O thou blessed moon,	7
2704	When men revolted shall upon record	8
2705	Bear hateful memory, poor Enobarbus did	9
2706	Before thy face repent !	
2707	*First Sold.* Enobarbus !	
	Third Sold. Peace ! 10	10
2708	Hark further.	11
2709	*Eno.* O sovereign mistress of true melancholy,	12
2710	The poisonous damp of night disponge upon me,	13
2711	That life, a very rebel to my will,	14
2712	May hang no longer on me: throw my heart	15
2713	Against the flint and hardness of my fault :	
2714	Which, being dried with grief, will break to powder,	16 17
2715	And finish all foul thoughts. O Antony,	18
2716	Nobler than my revolt is infamous,	19
2717	Forgive me in thine own particular ; 20	20
2718	But let the world rank me in register	21
2719	A master-leaver and a fugitive :	22
2720	O Antony ! O Antony ! [*Dies.*	
	Sec. Sold. Let's speak	23
2721	To him.	
2722	*First Sold.* Let's hear him, for the things he speaks	24
2723	May concern Cæsar.	
2724	*Third Sold.* Let's do so. But he sleeps.	25
2725	*First Sold.* Swoons rather ; for so bad a prayer as his	26
2726	Was never yet for sleep.	
2727	*Sec. Sold.* Go we to him.	27
2728	*Third Sold.* Awake, sir, awake ; speak to us.	
2729	*Sec. Sold.* Hear you, sir ?	28
	First Sold. The hand of death hath raught	29
2730-1	him. [*Drums afar off.*] Hark ! the drums	30
2732	Demurely wake the sleepers. Let us bear him 31	31
2733	To the court of guard ; he is of note : our hour	32
2734	Is fully out.	
	Third Sold. Come on, then ;	33
2735	He may recover yet. [*Exeunt with the body.*	34
2735+1	SCENE X. *Between the two camps.*	
2736	*Enter* ANTONY *and* SCARUS, *with their Army.*	

5   same as 4; b<u>X</u>: EdT

6   same as 4, GCa; b<u>X</u>: JKP
7   X: JP1; <u>MOVE</u> 7-1<u>1</u>a to follow <u>4-14</u>: 140: LoC; <u>MOVE</u> 7-23a to follow*
8   X: JP1
9   X: JP1

10 X: GCa, JP1; b<u>X</u>: JL1, EdT, OA1, LK1
11 X: GCa, JL1, Ed<u>T</u>, JP1, LK1; <u>Insert</u> 46: 12-38: JKP
12 X: JKP, EdT
13 X: JKP, EdT
14 X: JKP, EdT
15 X: JKP, EdT; b<u>X</u>: KyB, BA1, IP1, ML1

16 X: JKP, KyB, EdT, BA1, IP1, ML1
17 same as 16
18 X: JKP, EdT; a<u>X</u>: KyB, BA1, IP1, ML1
19 X: EdT, TN1
20 X: EdT
21 X: EdT
22 X: EdT

23 X: GCa, Lac; a<u>X</u>: EdT; b<u>X</u>: JKP, JL1, HIM, KyB, MTh, OA1, RH1, JP1,ML1,
     ER1, LK1; <u>ADD</u> 2: LK1

24 X: GCa, JKP, Lac, JL1, HIM, KyB, MTh, EdT, OA1, RA1, RH1, JP1, ML1,ER1,
     LK1
25 same as 24, less EdT, ML1; a<u>X</u>: EdT, ML1

26 same as 25, EdT, JS1, RH1, ML1; less a<u>X</u>; b<u>X</u>: TN1

27 same as 26, less MTh, RH1; less b<u>X</u>; a<u>X</u>: MTh, RH1, TN1; b<u>X</u>: AF1

28 X: JKP, Lac, JL1, HIM, KyB, OA1, JS1, JP1, AF1, LK1; a<u>X</u>: RA1;b<u>X</u>: EdT
29 X: JKP, JL1, OA1, JP1, LK1; b<u>X</u>: KyB
30 same as 29, KyB; less b<u>X</u>; b<u>X</u>: Lac
31 same as 30, BA1; less b<u>X</u>; a<u>X</u>: Lac
32 same as 31, AF1; less a<u>X</u>; b<u>X</u>: Lac, HIM, EdT

33 same as 32, Lac, EdT; less b<u>X</u>: a<u>X</u>: HIM; b<u>X</u>: ML1, TN1
34 same as 33, ML1, TN1, less <u>Lac</u>; <u>less b</u><u>X</u>

Scene 4-10

<u>ALL CUT</u>: Be1, In2, WM1, Cum, ChC, Lac, Ha1, JL1, HIM, KyB, LiL, MTh, LoC,
   SM1, WA1, OA1, BA1, RH1
**49: 7 <u>4-15</u>: 91: Ha1; <u>MOVE</u> 7-23a to follow <u>4-14</u>: 140: JL1

2737	*Ant.* Their preparation is to-day by sea;	1
2738	We please them not by land.	
2739	*Scar.* For both, my lord.	2
	Ant. I would they 'ld fight i' the fire or i' the	
2740	air;	3
2741	We 'ld fight there too. But this it is; our foot	4
2742	Upon the hills adjoining to the city	5
2743	Shall stay with us: order for sea is given;	6
2744	†They have put forth the haven...	7
2745	Where their appointment we may best discover,	8
2746	And look on their endeavour. [*Exeunt.* 9	9

2746+1   **SCENE XI.** *Another part of the same.*

2747   *Enter* CÆSAR, *and his Army.*

	Cæs. But being charged, we will be still by	
2748	land,	1
2749	Which, as I take 't, we shall; for his best force	2
2750	Is forth to man his galleys. To the vales,	3
2751	And hold our best advantage. [*Exeunt.*	4

2751+1   **SCENE XII.** *Another part of the same.*

2752-3   *Enter* ANTONY *and* SCARUS.

2754	*Ant.* Yet they are not join'd: where yond	
	pine does stand,	1
2755	I shall discover all: I 'll bring thee word	2
2756	Straight, how 'tis like to go. [*Exit.*	
2757	*Scar.* Swallows have built	3
2758	In Cleopatra's sails their nests: the augurers	4
2759	Say they know not, they cannot tell; look grimly,	5
2760	And dare not speak their knowledge. Antony	6
2761	Is valiant, and dejected; and, by starts,	7
2762	His fretted fortunes give him hope, and fear,	8
2763	Of what he has, and has not.	
2763+1	[*Alarum afar off, as at a sea-fight.*	

2764   *Re-enter* ANTONY.

2765	*Ant.* All is lost;	9
2766	This foul Egyptian hath betrayed me: 10	10
2667	My fleet hath yielded to the foe; and yonder	11
2768	They cast their caps up and carouse together	12
	Like friends long lost. Triple-turn'd whore! 'tis	
2769	thou	13
2770	Hast sold me to this novice; and my heart	14
2771	Makes only wars on thee. Bid them all fly;	15

1

2 X: BT1

3 bX : Inc; MOVE 3b-4 to follow 7a: JKP
4 X: Inc, RH1; bX: Cap, SP1, BT1, AF1, ML1, ER1
5 X: Cap, SP1, BT1, RH1, AF1, ML1, ER1
6 X: Cap, Inc, JKP, BT1, IP1, TaB, RH1, AF1, ER1; R: ML1; ADD 1: TN1
7 X: IP1, TaB, RH1, AF1, ER1, TN1; aX: Cap, SP1, ML1; bX: Inc, JKP;*
8 X: JKP, TaB, RH1, AF1, ER1, TN1
9 same as 8

Scene 4-11

ALL CUT: GCa, Bel, Inc, JKP, WM1, SP1, Cum, ChC, Lac, Hal, JL1, HIM, KyB,
  MTh, LoC, BT1, SM1, WA1, OA1, BA1, NM1, TP1, TaB, RA1, JS1, RH1, AF1,
  ER1, TN1
  1 R: ML1
  2
  3
  4 R: ML1

Scene 4-12

1 X: Bel, Inc, JKP, WM1, Cum, ChC, Lac, Hal, JL1, HIM, KyB, LiL, MTh,LoC*
2 same as 1; less aX, bX; aX: SP1, TaB, BH1

3 X: Bel, Cum, Lac, Hal, JL1, HIM, LiL, MTh, SM1, WA1, OA1, BA1; aX: Inc*
4 same as 3, JP1, LK1; less aX, bX, N, MOVE
5 same as 4; bX: WH1
6 same as 4; aX: WM1; bX: TN1
7 X: Bel, Cum, ChC, Lac, Hal, JL1, HIM, KyB, LiL, MTh, LoC, SM1, WA1,OA1*
8 same as 7

9 aX: Bel, Cum, ChC, Lac, Hal, JL1, HIM, KyB, LoC, SM1, WA1, OA1, BA1*
10 bX: KyB
11 X: Cap, Inc, In2, KyB
12 same as 11

13 X: Inc, In2, KyB; aX: Cap; bX: JKP, Hal, JL1, JP1; b: SP1
14 X: Inc, In2, JKP, Hal, JL1, KyB, JP1
15 same as 14, less JKP; aX: JKP

*4-10: 7 ADD 2: SP1; Insert 3b-4, add 3: JKP   *4-12: 1SM1, WA1,
  OA1, BA1, RA1; aX: SP1, BT1, TN1; bX: TaB, BH1   *4-12: 3 JKP, WM1
  ChC, KyB, LoC, RA1; bX: In2, JP1, LiL; N: SP1; MOVE 3b-6 to follow
  37: 7 : ChC, LoC   *4-12: 7 BA1, JP1, LK1,TN1
*4-12: 9 JP1, LK1, TN1; ADD 37: WM1

2772	**For** when I am revenged upon my charm,	16
2773	**I have** done all. Bid them all fly; begone.	17
2773+1	. *[Exit Scarus.*	
2774	**O sun,** thy uprise shall I see no more:	18
2775	**Fortune** and Antony part here; even here	19
2776	**Do we** shake hands. All come to this? The hearts	20
2777	**That** spaniel'd me at heels, to whom I gave 21	21
2778	**Their** wishes, do discandy, melt their sweets	22
2779	**On** blossoming Cæsar; and this pine is bark'd,	23
2780	**That** overtopp'd them all. Betray'd I am:	24
2781	**O** this false soul of Egypt! this grave charm,—	25
2782	**Whose** eye beck'd forth my wars, and call'd them home;	26
2783	**Whose** bosom was my crownet, my chief end,—	27
2784	**Like a** right gipsy, hath, at fast and loose,	28
2785	**Beguiled** me to the very heart of loss.	29
2786	**What,** Eros, Eros!	

2787	*Enter* CLEOPATRA.	
2788	Ah, thou spell! Avaunt! 30	30
2789	*Cleo.* Why is my lord enraged against his love?	31
2790	*Ant.* Vanish, or I shall give thee thy deserving,	32
2791	**And** blemish Cæsar's triumph. Let him take thee,	33
2792	**And** hoist thee up to the shouting plebeians:	34
2793	**Follow** his chariot, like the greatest spot	35
2794	**Of all** thy sex; most monster-like, be shown	36
2795	**For** poor'st diminutives, for doits: and let	37
2796	**Patient** Octavia plough thy visage up	38
	With her prepared nails.	
2797	*[Exit Cleopatra.*	
2798	'Tis well thou'rt gone,	39
2799	**If it** be well to live: but better 'twere 40	40
2800	**Thou** fell'st into my fury, for one death	41
2801	**Might** have prevented many. Eros, ho!	42
2802	**The** shirt of Nessus is upon me: teach me,	43
2803	**Alcides,** thou mine ancestor, thy rage:	44
2804	**Let** me lodge Lichas on the horns o' the moon:	45
2805	**And** with those hands, that grasp'd the heaviest club,	46
2806	**Subdue** my worthiest self. The witch shall die:	47
2807	**To** the young Roman boy she hath sold me, and I fall	48
2808	**Under** this plot; she dies for't. Eros, ho! *[Exit.*	49

2808+1	**SCENE** XIII. *Alexandria. Cleopatra's*
2808+2	*palace.*

16 same as 15; less aX
17 X: Inc, In2, JL1, JP1; aX: KyB

18 X: JP1
19 X: JP1
20 X: JP1; R: In2; aX: Inc; bX: JKP, WM1, ChC, Ha1, JL1, LoC, TaB, RA1*
21 X: Inc, In2, JKP, WM1, ChC, Ha1, JL1, LoC, TaB, RA1, JP1
22 same as 21
23 same as 21; bX: AF1
24 X: inc, In2, TaB, JP1; aX: JKP, WM1, ChC, Ha1, JL1, LoC, RA1, AF1;bX:OA1
25 X: Inc, In2, JKP, TaB, JP1; R: WM1; bX: Cap

26 X: Cap, Inc, In2, OA1, TaB, RH1, JP1, TN1; R: WM1
27 same as 26, BT1, Less RH1; same R
28 X: Cap, Inc, In2, TaB, JP1; R: WM1; bX: ML1
29 same as 28 including R; less bX

30 X: Inc, In2; R: WM1; aX: KyB, TaB, JP1; bX: JKP, Cum
31 X: Inc, In2, JKP, Cum; R: WM1
32 same as 31 including R
33 same as 31 including R
34 same as 31 including R
35 same as 31, JS1; same R; bX: KyB
36 same as 31, KyB; same R; aX: JS1; bX: ChC, LoC, BT1, SM1, WA1, BA1, IP1*
37 X: Cap, Inc, In2, JKP, Cum, ChC, KyB, BT1, ML1; R: WM1; aX: LoC, SM1*
38 X: Inc, In2, JKP, Cum, KyB, BT1, ML1; R: WM1; aX: ChC

39 X: Inc, In2, JKP, Cum, KyB; R: WM1; aX: BT1, ML1; bX: ChC, JL1, LoC,*
40 X: Inc, In2, JKP, Cum, ChC, JL1, KyB, LoC, SM1, WA1, OA1, TN1;R: WM1;bX:*
41 same as 40, Cap, BT1, IP1, GS1, ML1; less R, bX; R: WM1
42 X: Inc, In2, JKP, JL1, KyB, OA1; R: WM1; aX: Cap, Cum, ChC, LoC, BT1, SM1*
43 X: Inc, In2, JL1, OA1, TN1; aX: RH1, BH1; bX: WM1, ChC, KyB
44 X: Inc, In2, WM1, ChC, JL1, KyB, OA1, TN1
45 X: Cap, Inc, In2, WM1, ChC, JL1, KyB, LoC, SM1, WA1, OA1, BH1,AF1;ER1,TN1

46 same as 45
47 X: Inc, In2, OA1; aX: Cap, ChC, JL1, KyB, LoC, SM1, RH1, AF1, ER1,TN1;
      bX: BT1
48 X: Inc, In2, BT1, OA1, RA1
49 X: Inc, In2, OA1; aX: BT1, RA1; Insert 3-13: 1-2: JL1

Scene 4-13

ALL CUT: Be1, Inc

*4-12:20 ADD 128: In2   *4-12:36 ML1   *4-12:37 WA1,
  BA1, IP1   *4-12:39 WA1, OA1, TN1; ADD 1: OA1
*4-12:40 Cap, BT1, IP1, GS1, ML1   *4=12:42 WA1, IP1, GS1, ML1, TN1;
  bX: RH1

2809	*Enter* CLEOPATRA, CHARMIAN, IRAS, *and*	
2809+1	MARDIAN.	
2810	*Cleo.* Help me, my women ! O, he is more mad	1
2811	Than Telamon for his shield ; the boar of Thessaly	2
2812	Was never so emboss'd.	
	Char. To the monument !	3
2813	There lock yourself, and send him word you are	
2814	dead.	4
2815	The soul and body rive not more in parting	5
2816	Than greatness going off.	
2817	*Cleo.* To the monument !	6
2818	Mardian, go tell him I have slain myself ;	7
2819	Say, that the last I spoke was 'Antony,'	8
2820	And word it, prithee, piteously : hence, Mardian,	9
	And bring me how he takes my death. To the	10
2821-2	monument ! [*Exeunt.* 10

| 2822+1 | SCENE XIV. *The same. Another room.* |

| 2823 | *Enter* ANTONY *and* EROS. |

2824	*Ant.* Eros, thou yet behold'st me ?	
2825	*Eros.* Ay, noble lord.	1
	Ant. Sometime we see a cloud that's drag-	
2826	ish ;	2
2827	A vapour sometime like a bear or lion,	3
2828	A tower'd citadel, a pendent rock,	4
2829	A forked mountain, or blue promontory	5
2830	With trees upon't, that nod unto the world,	6
2831	And mock our eyes with air : thou hast seen the	
2832	signs ;	7
2833	They are black vesper's pageants.	
2834	*Eros.* Ay, my lord	8
	Ant. That which is now a horse, even with	
2835	thought	9
2836	The rack dislimns, and makes it indistinct,	10
2837	As water is in water.	
2838	*Eros.* It does, my lord.	11
2839	*Ant.* My good knave Eros, now thy captain	12
2840	Even such a body : here I am Antony :	13
2841	Yet cannot hold this visible shape, my knave	14
2842	I made these wars for Egypt : and the queen—	15
2843	Whose heart I thought I had, for she had mine	16
2844	Which whilst it was mine had annex'd unto't	17
2845	A million more, now lost,—she, Eros, has	18
	Pack'd cards with Cæsar, and false-play'd m

1 R: LoC, SM1; <u>aX</u>: JL1
2 <u>X</u>: ChC, LiL, L̄oC, SM1, WA1, AF1; <u>bX</u>: JKP, WM1, BT1, NM1, IP1, TN1

3 <u>aX</u>: JKP, WM1, ChC, LiL, LoC, BT1, SM1, WA1, NM1, IP1, AF1, TN1

4 X: Lac
5 XL Lac, AF1, ML1, TN1

6 X: Lac; <u>aX</u>: AF1, ML1, TN1
7 <u>aX</u>: JKP, B̄A1
8
9
10 <u>bX</u>: ML1

Scene 4-14

1 X: Inc, In2, OA1

2 same as 1
3 same as 1
4 X: Inc, In2, JKP, OA1, BH1
5 X: Inc, In2, OA1
6 same as 5, BH1

7 same as 6

8 same as 6, BA1; <u>aX</u>: Ha1

9 X: Inc, In2, OA1, BA1
10 same as 9

11 same as 9
12 X: Inc, In2, OA1
13 same as 12
14 same as 12
15 X: Cap, Inc, In2, BT1
16 same as 15, WM1
17 X: Cap, Inc, In2, JKP, WM1, KyB, BT1, SM1, WA1, OA1, BA1, BH1, TN1
18 X: Cap, Inc, In2, BT1, SM1, WA1; <u>aX</u>: JKP, WM1, KyB, OA1, BA1, BH1, TN1

2846	glory	19
2847	Unto an enemy's triumph. z	20
2848	Nay, weep not, gentle Eros; there is left us	21
2849	Ourselves to end ourselves.	
2850	*Enter* MARDIAN.	
	O, thy vile lady!	22
2851	She has robb'd me of my sword.	
2852	*Mar.* No, Antony:	23
2853	My mistress loved thee, and her fortunes mingle	24
2854	With thine entirely.	
2855	*Ant.* Hence, saucy eunuch; peace.	25
2856	She hath betray'd me and shall die the death.	26
2857	*Mar.* Death of one person can be paid but once.	27
2858	And that she has discharged: what thou wouldst	28
2859	Is done unto thy hand: the last she spake	29
2860	Was 'Antony! most noble Antony!' z	30
2861	Then in the midst a tearing groan did break	31
2862	The name of Antony; it was divided	32
2863	Between her heart and lips: she render'd life,	33
2864	Thy name so buried in her.	
2865	*Ant.* Dead, then?	
3866	*Mar.* Dead.	34
2867	*Ant.* Unarm, Eros: the long day's task is done	35
	And we must sleep. [*To Mar.*] That thou o	
2868	part'st hence safe,	36
2869	Does pay thy labour richly; go. [*Exit Mardian*	
2870	Off, pluck off:	37
2871	The seven-fold shield of Ajax cannot keep	38
2872	The battery from my heart. O, cleave, my sides	39
2873	Heart, once be stronger than thy continent, +	40
2874	Crack thy frail case! Apace, Eros, apace.	41
2875	No more a soldier: bruised pieces, go;	42
	You have been nobly borne. From me awhile	43
2876	[*Exit Eros*	
2877	I will o'ertake thee, Cleopatra, and	44
2878	Weep for my pardon. So it must be, for now	45
2879	All length is torture: since the torch is out,	46
2880	Lie down, and stray no farther: now all labour	47
2881	Mars what it does; yea, very force entangles	48
2882	Itself with strength: seal then, and all is done.	49
2883	Eros!—I come, my queen:—Eros!—Stay for me.	50
	Where souls do couch on flowers, we'll hand =	
2884	hand, sl	51
2885	And with our sprightly port make the ghosts gaze:	52

19 X: Cap, Inc, In2, BT1
20 same as 19
21 X: Inc, In2, Cum

22 X: Inc, In2

23 X: Inc, In2, WA1; b$\underline{X}$: WM1
24 X: Inc, In2, WM1, $\overline{BA1}$; b$\underline{X}$: IP1, ML1

25 same as 4; less b$\underline{X}$; a$\underline{X}$: IP1, ML1; b$\underline{X}$: Lac, JL1, ML1
26 X: Inc, In2
27 X: Inc, In2
28 X: Inc, In2; b$\underline{X}$: OA1, BA1, RH1, TN1
29 X: Inc, In2, $\overline{BA1}$; R: ML1; a$\underline{X}$: OA1, RH1, TN1
30 X: Inc, In2, WM1, $\overline{BA1}$
31 X: Inc, In2, WM1, SP1, Cum, Lac, Ha1, HIM, KyB, BT1, SM1, WA1, OA1,*
32 same as 31; b$\underline{X}$: JL1
33 same as 31, $\overline{JL1}$, less BH1, RA1; a$\underline{X}$, J$\underline{KR}$, BT1, RA1; b$\underline{X}$: IP1

34 X: Inc, In2, Cum; a$\underline{X}$: WM1, SP1, Lac, Ha1, JL1, HIM, KyB, SM1, WA1, OA1*
35 X: Inc, In2; a$\underline{X}$: Cum

36 X: Inc, In2; $\underline{R}$: WM1; b$\underline{X}$: KyB, BT1, SM1, RA1, AF1

37 X: Inc, In2, AF1; R: WM1; a$\underline{X}$: KyB, BT1, SM1, RA1
38 X: Inc, In2, JKP, $\overline{OA1}$, AF1
39 same as 38, less AF1; a$\underline{X}$: AF1; b$\underline{X}$: KyB, BT1
40 X: Inc, In2, JKP, WM1, $\overline{KyB}$, BT1, OA1
41 X: Inc, In2, OA1; a$\underline{X}$: JKP, WM1, KyB, BT1; b$\underline{X}$: Cum
42 X: Inc, In2
43 X: Inc, In2; b$\underline{X}$: BT1, OA1

44 X: Inc, In2
45 X: Inc, In2; b$\underline{X}$: KyB, OA1
46 X: Inc, In2, $\overline{KyB}$, OA1; R: JKP; b$\underline{X}$: BA1
47 same as 6, BA1; less R, b$\underline{X}$; b$\underline{X}$ $\overline{JKP}$, WM1, JL1, EdT, BT1, SM1, IP1*
48 X: Inc, In2, JKP, WM1, JL1, $\overline{KyB}$, EdT, BT1, SM1, OA1, BA1, IP1, RA1*
49 same as 48, less WM1, SM1, BA1, IP1; less b$\underline{X}$; a$\underline{X}$: WM1, SM1,OA1,BA1,IP1*
50 X: Inc, In2, JP1; a$\underline{X}$: RH1, ER1; b$\underline{X}$: BT1; c$\underline{X}$: $\overline{ML1}$

51 same as 50; less a$\underline{X}$, b$\underline{X}$, c$\underline{X}$
52 same as 51

*4-14:31 BA1, TaB, RA1, GS1   *4-14:34 BA1, IP1, TaB, GS1
*4-14:47 BA1, IP1, JP1, ER1 $\overline{4-14:48}$ RH1, JP1, ER1; b$\underline{X}$: ML1
*4-14:49 ML1

2886	Dido and her Æneas shall want troops,	53
2887	And all the haunt be ours. Come, Eros, Eros!	54
2888	*Re-enter* EROS.	
2889	*Eros.* What would my lord?	
2890	*Ant.* Since Cleopatra died,	55
2891	I have lived in such dishonour, that the gods	56
2892	Detest my baseness. I, that with my sword	57
2893	Quarter'd the world, and o'er green Neptune's back	58
2894	With ships made cities, condemn myself to lack	59
2895	The courage of a woman; less noble mind 60	60
2896	Than she which by her death our Cæsar tells	61
2897	'I am conqueror of myself.' Thou art sworn, Eros,	62
2898	That, when the exigent should come, which now	63
2899	Is come indeed, when I should see behind me	64
	The inevitable prosecution of	65
2900	Disgrace and horror, that, on my command,	66
2901	Thou then wouldst kill me: do't; the time is come:	67
2902	Thou strikest not me, 'tis Cæsar thou defeat'st.	68
2903	Put colour in thy cheek.	
2904	*Eros.* The gods withhold me!	69
2905	Shall I do that which all the Parthian darts, 70	70
2906	Though enemy, lost aim, and could not?	
2907	*Ant.* Eros,	71
2908	Wouldst thou be window'd in great Rome and see	72
2909	Thy master thus with pleach'd arms, bending down	73
2910	His corrigible neck, his face subdued	74
2911	To penetrative shame, whilst the wheel'd seat	75
2912	Of fortunate Cæsar, drawn before him, branded	76
2913	His baseness that ensued?	
2914	*Eros.* I would not see't.	77
	Ant. Come, then; for with a wound I must be	
2915	cured.	78
2916	Draw that thy honest sword, which thou hast worn	79
2917	Most useful for thy country.	
2918	*Eros.* O, sir, pardon me! 80	80
	Ant. When I did make thee free, sworest thou	
2919	not then	81
2920	To do this when I bade thee? Do it at once;	82
2921	Or thy precedent services are all	83
2922	But accidents unpurposed. Draw, and come.	84
	Eros. Turn from me, then, that noble count-	
2923	enance,	85
2924	Wherein the worship of the whole world lies.	86

53 X: Inc, In2, EdT, JP1
54 X: Inc, In2; aX: EdT, JP1; cX: OA1; ADD 2: JKP; ADD 7: WM1

55 X: Inc, In2, KyB; aX: JKP, WM1; bX: BT1, TN1
56 X: Inc, In2, KyB, B̄T̄1, TN1; bX: L̄oC
57 X: Inc, In2, KyB, LoC, BT1, T̄N̄1; bX: Cap, JP), WM1, ChC, RH), ER1

58 X: Cap, Inc, In2, JKP, WM1, ChC, KyB, LoC, BT1, EH1, ER1, TN1
59 same as 58
60 same as 58; aX: WM1; bX: JL1, EdT, IP1, RA1, ML1
61 same as 58, J̄L̄1, EdT, ĪP̄1, RA1, ML1; less aX, bX
62 X: Inc, In2; aX: Cap, JKP, ChC, JL1, KyB, EdT, LoC, BT1, IP1, RA1, RH1*
63 X: Inc, In2
64 X: Inc, In2; bX: MTh, RA1, BH1
65 X: Inc, In2, B̄T̄1, RA1 , BH1
66 X: Inc, In2; aX: BT1, RA1, BH1
67 XL Inc, In2
68 X: Inc, In2, TN1

69 XL Inc, In2; aX: TN1; bX: AF1
70 X: Inc, In2 B̄T̄1, SM1, W̄Ā1, AF1, ER1, TN1

71 same as 70
72 X: Inc, In2, BT1, SM1, AF1
73 same as 72; cX: IP1
74 same as 72
75 same as 72; bX: KyB, RA1
76 X: Inc, In2, K̄yB, BT1, SM1, RA1, AF1; cX: GS1

77 X: Inc, In2, BT1, SM1, AF1; aX: KyB, RH1

78 X: Bel, Inc, In2, JL1, BT1, RH1, TN1; bX: JKP, IP1
79 same as 78, OA1, Less BT1; less bX; bX: BT1

80 X: Bel, Inc, In2, OA1, RH1; aX: JL1, BT1, TN1

81 same as 80; less aX
82 X: Bel, Inc, Īn̄2, OA1; aX: BT1; bX: JKP, BA1, IP1, TaB
83 X: Bel, Inc, In2, JKP, BT̄1, SM1, W̄Ā1, OA1, BA1, IP1, TaB, RH1,AF1,TN1
84 X: Bel, Inc, In2, SM1, WA1, OA1, TN1; aX: JKP, BT1, BA1, IP1, TaB,
    RH1, AF1
85 X: Inc, In2, WA1, TN1; MOVE 85-87 to follow 92: JKP
86 same as 85; less MOVE

*4-14:62 ML1, ER1, TN1

2925	*Ant.* Lo thee! [*Turning from him.*	87
2926	*Eros.* My sword is drawn.	
2927	*Ant.* Then let it do at once	88
2928	The thing why thou hast drawn it.	
2929	*Eros.* My dear master,	89
2930	My captain, and my emperor, let me say, 90	90
2931	Before I strike this bloody stroke, farewell.	91
2932	*Ant.* 'Tis said, man; and farewell.	92
2933	*Eros.* Farewell, great chief. Shall I strike now?	
2934	*Ant.* Now, Eros.	93
2935	*Eros.* Why, there then: thus I do escape the sorrow	94
2936	Of Antony's death. [*Kills himself.*	
2937	*Ant.* Thrice-nobler than myself!	95
2938	Thou teachest me, O valiant Eros, what	96
2939	I should, and thou couldst not. My queen and Eros	97
2940	Have by their brave instruction got upon me	98
2941	A nobleness in record : but I will be	99
2942	A bridegroom in my death, and run into't 100	100
2943	As to a lover's bed. Come, then; and, Eros,	101
2944	Thy master dies thy scholar: to do thus	102
2944+1	[*Falling on his sword.*	
2945	I learn'd of thee. How! not dead? not dead?	103
2946	The guard, ho! O, dispatch me '	
2947	*Enter* DERCETAS *and* Guard.	
2948	*First Guard.* What's the noise?	104
2949	*Ant.* I have done my work ill, friends: O, make an end	105
2950	Of what I have begun.	
2951	*Sec. Guard.* The star is fall'n.	106
2952	*First Guard.* And time is at his period.	
2953	*All.* Alas, and woe!	107
2954	*Ant.* Let him that loves me strike me dead.	
2955	*First Guard.* Not I.	108
2956	*Sec. Guard.* Nor I. 109	109
2957	*Third Guard.* Nor any one. [*Exeunt Guard.*	110
2958	*Der.* Thy death and fortunes bid thy followers fly.	111
2959	This sword but shown to Cæsar, with this tidings,	112
2960	Shall enter me with him.	113
2961	*Enter* DIOMEDES.	

```
87   X: Inc, In2, TN1

88   X: Inc, In2,JKP, RH1; bX: BT1, TN1

89   X: Inc, In2, TN1; aX: BT1, RH1
90   same as 89; less aX
91   same as 90; B: EdT
92   same as 90; Insert 85-87: JKP

93   X: Inc, In2; aX: TN1

94   X: Inc, In2

95   X: Inc, In2; bX: KyB
96   X: Inc, I2; bX: ChC, LoC

97   X: Inc, In2, ChC, LoC; bX: WM1, KyB, LiL, BT1, SM1, WA1, BA1, RH1
98   X: Cap, Inc, In2, WM1, ChC, LiL, LoC, BT1, SM1, WA1, BA1, RH1;bX:IP1
99   X: Inc, In2, WM1, ChC, LiL, LoC; aX: Cap, KyB, BT1,SM1,WA1,BA1,IPI,*
100  same as 99, BH1; less aX, bX
101  X: Inc, In2; aX: WM1, ChC, LiL, LoC, BH1; bX: KyB, RH1, TN1
102  X: Inc, In2, JKP, RH1, TN1; aX: KyB; bX: WA1

103  X: Inc, In2; aX: JKP, WM1, RH1, TN1; bX: ML1




104  X: Inc, In2; bX: Cum, JL1, KyB, SM1, RA1, AF1, ML1; ADD 1: KyB

105  X: Inc, In2, JKP, WM1, ChC, JL1, KyB, EdT, LoC, SM1, OA1, RA1

106  same as 105; bX: SP1, Cum, Lac, Hal, HIM, LiL, MTh, WA1, ML1, TN1

107  X: Inc, In2, JKP, WM1, SP1, Cum, ChC, KyB, EdT, LoC, SM1, OA1,RA1,
       ML1, TN1; aX: Lac, Hal, JL1, HIM, LiL, MTh, WA1; bX: GS1, RH1,AF1*
108  X: Inc, In2, JKP, WM1, ChC, KyB, EdT, LoC, SM1, RA1, ER1;bX: SP1
109  same as 108, SP1, Cum, Hal; less bX
110  same as 109, TaB, ML1, less Hal; aX: HIM

111  X: Inc, In2, JKP, WM1, ChC, Hal, JL1, KyB, LiL, EdT, LoC, BT1,SM1*
112  same as 111
113  same as 111, less Inc, LiL, ML1; aX: LiL; bX: Inc; ADD 113: Inc
*4-14:99  RH1; bX: BH1              *4-14:107  ER1
*4-14:111 WA1, OA1, BA1, TaB., ML1, ER1
```

2962	*Dio.* Where's Antony?	
2963	*Der.* There, Diomed there.	
	Dio. Lives he?	114
2964	Wilt thou not answer, man? [*Exit Dercetas.*	115
1965	*Ant.* Art thou there, Diomed? Draw thy	
2966	sword, and give me	116
2967	Sufficing strokes for death.	
2968	*Dio.* Most absolute lord,	117
2969	My mistress Cleopatra sent me to thee.	118
2970	*Ant.* When did she send thee?	
2971	*Dio.* Now, my lord.	
2972	*Ant.* Where is she?	119
	Dio. Lock'd in her monument. She had a	
2973	prophesying fear **120**	120
2974	Of what hath come to pass: for when she saw—	121
2975	Which never shall be found—you did suspect	122
2976	She had disposed with Cæsar, and that your rage	123
	Would not be purged, she sent you word she was	
2977	dead;	124
2978	But, fearing since how it might work, hath sent	125
2979	Me to proclaim the truth; and I am come,	126
2980	I dread, too late.	127
	Ant. Too late, good Diomed: call my guard,	
2981	I prithee.	128
2982	*Dio.* What, ho, the emperor's guard! The	
	guard, what, ho!	129
2983	Come, your lord calls! **130**	130
2984	*Enter four or five of the* Guard *of* ANTONY.	
	Ant. Bear me, good friends, where Cleopatra	
2985	bides;	131
2986	'Tis the last service that I shall command you.	132
	First Guard. Woe, woe are we, sir, you may	
2987	not live to wear	133
2988	All your true followers out.	
2989	*All.* Most heavy day!	134
	Ant. Nay, good my fellows, do not please	
2990	sharp fate	135
2991	To grace it with your sorrows: bid that wel- come	136
2992	Which comes to punish us, and we punish it	137
2993	Seeming to bear it lightly. Take me up:	138
2994	I have led you oft: carry me now, good friends,	139
	And have my thanks for all. **140**	140
2995	[*Exeunt, bearing Antony.*	

114 X; Inc, JL1, KyB, WA1, BA1, ER1; bX:In2, JKP, WM1, ChC, Lac, Ha1,HIM*
115 X: Inc, JKP, WM1, ChC, Lac, Ha1, J̄L1, LiL, BT1, SM1, WA1, BA1, TaB,.
      ER1; R: In2; aX: HIM, KyB, MTh, EdT, LoC, TN1
116 X: Inc, H̄al, JL1̄, WA1; R: In2; N: JKP, WM1, LiL, EdT

117 X: Iṅc, WA1; R: In2; aX: Ha1; bX: JKP
118 X: Inc, JKP, W̄M1; N: L̄iL

119 X: WA1; aX: RH1; bX: WM1

120 X: WA1; aX: WM1; bX: Inc, In2, RA1
121 X: ịn2, W̄A1, RA1; aX: Inc
122 X: WA1; aX: Inc, In2̄, JKP, Cum, WM1, RH1
123 X: WA1; aX̄: Inc, In2, WM1; bX: JKP, SP1, Cum, RA1, RH1; ADD 1: Inc

124 X: WA1, RA1; aX: JKP, SP1, Cum, KyB, RH1; bX: Inc, In2; ADD 2:Inc,In2
125 X̣ WA1; aX: ML1̄
126 X:ẉA1
127 X: WA1; bX: ML1, TN1

128 X: WA1, ML1, TN1; bX: WM1, KyB, BT1, SM1, OA1, JP1, ER1;N: WM1, JP1

129 X: WM1, KyB, SM1, WA1, OA1, JP1, ML1, ER1, TN1; aX: BT1; bX: Lac, Ha1*
130 X: In2, WM1, Lac, Ha1, JL1, KyB, BT1, SM1, WA1, J̄P1, ML1, ĒR1; aX:
      Inc, HIM

131 X: WM1, WA1, JP1
132 X: WM1, WA1, JP1, ML1

133 X: WM1, SP1, Cum, ChC, Lac, Ha1, HIM, KyB, MTh, WA1, OA1, BA1, JP1,
      AF1, ML1, ER1, TN1, GS1
134 same as 133, less Ha1, GS1; aX: Ha1, GS1; bX: Inc, In2, LiL, RH1;N:
      JKP
135 X: WM1, SP1, Cum, ChC, KyB, BT1, SM1, WA1, OA1, BA1, RH1, JP1, ML1,
      ER1, TN1; bX: LiL
136 same as 135, L̄iL, EdT; less bX: bX: Inc, In2, JS1; ADD 4: Inc, In2
137 same as 136, JS1, less EdT; less bX, ADD; aX: EdT
138 X: Inc, In2, WM1, BT1, WA1, BA1, J̄P1, ER1; aX: SP1, Cum, ChC, KyB*
139 X: WM1, BT1, WA1, JP1, ER1; bX: AF1; Insert 49: 7-30 and 43: 12-25:LoC
140 XL WM1, LoC, BT1, WA1, JP1, ĀF1, ER1; ADD 48: ChC; Insert 51: 14-67,
      add 2, Inc; Insert 51: 14-67: In2; Insert 46: 16b-49 and 49: 7-
      12a: JL1

*4-14:114 LiL, MTh, EdT, LoC, BT1, SM1; cX: TaB, TN1   *4-14:1:29 JL1,
   HIM; bX: AF1   *4-14:138 LiL, SM1, OA1, JS1, RH1, ML1,
   TN1

2995+1	**SCENE XV.** *The same. A monument.*	
2996	*Enter* CLEOPATRA, *and her maids aloft, with*	
2997	CHARMIAN *and* IRAS.	
2998	*Cleo.* O Charmian, I will never go from hence.	1
2999	*Char.* Be comforted, dear madam.	
3000	*Cleo.* No, I will not:	2
3001	All strange and terrible events are welcome,	3
3002	But comforts we despise; our size of sorrow,	4
3003	Proportion'd to our cause, must be as great	5
3004	As that which makes it.	
3005	*Enter, below,* DIOMEDES.	
3006	How now! is he dead?	6
3007	*Dio.* His death's upon him, but not dead.	/7
3008	Look out o' the other side your monument;	8
3009	His guard have brought him thither.	
3010	*Enter, below,* ANTONY, *borne by the* Guard.	
3011	*Cleo.* O sun,	9
	Burn the great sphere thou movest in! darkling	
3012	stand	10
3013	The varying shore o' the world. O Antony,	11
	Antony, Antony! Help, Charmian, help, Iras,	
3014	help;	12
3015	Help, friends below; let's draw him hither.	
3016	*Ant.* Peace!	13
3017	Not Cæsar's valour hath o'erthrown Antony,	14
3018	But Antony's hath triumph'd on itself.	15
3019	*Cleo.* So it should be, that none but Antony	16
3020-1	Should conquer Antony; but woe 'tis so!	17
3022	*Ant.* I am dying, Egypt, dying; only	18
3023	I here importune death awhile, until	19
3024	Of many thousand kisses the poor last	20
3025	I lay upon thy lips.	
3026	*Cleo.* I dare not, dear,—	21
3027	Dear my lord, pardon,—I dare not,	22
3028	Lest I be taken: not the imperious show	23
3029	Of the full-fortuned Cæsar ever shall	24
	Be brooch'd with me; if knife, drugs, serpents,	
3030	have	25
3031	Edge, sting, or operation, I am safe:	26
3032	Your wife Octavia, with her modest eyes	27
3033	And still conclusion, shall acquire no honour	28
3034	Demuring upon me. But come, come, Antony,—	29

Scene 4-15

ALL CUT: Be1, LiL; SOME USED TO OPE (N: LK1
1   X: Inc, In2, WM1, Ha1, JL1, BT1, TaB; bX: IP1

2   X: In2, Ha1, JL1, BT1, IP1, TaB; bX: Inc, ER1
3   same as 2, ER1
4   same as 3; bX: KyB, BA1
5   same as 3, KyB, BA1, less Ha1; less bX: aX: Ha1

6   X: In2, ChC, JL1, LoC, BT1, IP1, TaB; aX: KyB, BA1, ER1; bX: JKP,EdT*
7   X: In2, ChC, JL1, EdT, LoC, BT1, IP1, TaB
8   X: In2, JKP, ChC, Lac, Ha1, JL1, HIM, KyB, EdT, LoC, BT1, OA1, IP1,
      TaB, RA1, RH1, BH1, TN1

9   X: In2, JKP, Ha1, JL1, IP1, TaB, JP1; R: WM1; aX: ChC, EdT, LoC,BT1;
      bX: OA1; ADD 3: Inc
10 X: Inc, In2, OA1, IP1, TaB; bX: JKP, WM1
11 X: Inc, In2, IP1, TaB; aX: JKP, WM1, OA1

12 X: Inc, In2, Lac, IP1, TaB; R: WM1; bX: ChC, Ha1, JL1, HIM, KyB,MTH,
      EdT, LoC, RA1, ML1, TN1
13 X: Inc, In2, SP1, Cum, ChC, Lac, Ha1, JL1, HIM, KyB, MTh, LoC, IP1*
14 X: Inc, In2, JKP, SP1, KyB, BT1, BA1, IP1, TaB, RH1, ML1, TN1;R:WM1
15 same as 14 including R
16 same as 14 including R
17 same as 14 including R
18 X: SP1; R: Inc, In2; ADD 1: TaB
19 X: NM1, SP1
20 X: WM1, SP1; bX: Ha1, KyB

21 X: SP1, Ha1, KyB; R: GCa; aX: WM1; bX: Inc, In2, Cum, ChC, Lac, JL1*
22 X: Inc, In2, WM1, S P1, Cum, ChC, Lac, Ha1, JL1, KyB, LoC, SM1, WA1,*
23 same as 22; less R; bX: JKP, BT1, BA1, TaB, RH1, ML1,TN1
24 X: Inc, In2, JKP, WM1, SP1, Cum, ChC, Lac, Ha1, JL1, KyB, LoC, BT1,
      SM1, WA1, OA1, BA1, TaB, RA1, RH1, ML1, TN1
25 same as 24, bX: IP1
26 same as 24, IP1
27 same as 26
28 same as 26
29 X: Inc, In2, WM1, SP1, Cum ChC, Lac, Ha1, JL1, KyB, LoC, SM1, WA1,OA1,
      RA1; aX: JKP, BT1, BA1, IP1, TaB, RH1, ML1, TN1

*4-14: 6 ADD 1: JKP   *4-15:13 TaB, RA1, ML1, TN1; R: WM1;
  aX:EdT, JP1; bX: BT1, BA1, RH1; Insert 4-15: 33-40a: SM1; MOVE 13b-21a
to follow 4oa: WA1   *4-15:21 LoC, SM1, WA1, OA1, RH1; ADD
  1: JKP   *4-15:22 OA1, RA1; R: GCa

3035	Help me, my women,—we must draw thee up:	30
3036	Assist, good friends.	31
3037	*Ant.* O, quick, or I am gone.	31
3038	*Cleo.* Here's sport indeed! How heavy weighs	
3039	my lord!	32
3040	Our strength is all gone into heaviness,	33
3041	That makes the weight: had I great Juno's power,	34
3042	The strong-wing'd Mercury should fetch thee up,	35
3043	And set thee by Jove's side. Yet come a little,—	36
3044	Wishers were ever fools,—O, come, come, come:	37
3045	*[They heave Antony aloft to Cleopatra.*	
	And welcome, welcome! die where thou hast	
3046	lived:	38
3047	Quicken with kissing: had my lips that power,	39
3048	Thus would I wear them out.	
3049	*All.* A heavy sight! 40	40
3050	*Ant.* I am dying, Egypt, dying:	41
3051	Give me some wine, and let me speak a little.	42
	Cleo. No, let me speak; and let me rail so	
3052	high,	43
3053	That the false housewife Fortune break her wheel,	44
3054	Provoked by my offence.	
3055	*Ant.* One word, sweet queen:	45
3056	Of Cæsar seek your honour, with your safety. O!	46
3057	*Cleo.* They do not go together.	
3058	*Ant.* Gentle, hear me:	47
3059	None about Cæsar trust but Proculeius.	48
3060	*Cleo.* My resolution and my hands I'll trust;	49
3061	None about Cæsar.	50
3062	*Ant.* The miserable change now at my end	51
3063	Lament nor sorrow at: but please your thoughts	52
3064	In feeding them with those my former fortunes	53
3065	Wherein I lived, the greatest prince o' the world,	54
3066	The noblest; and do now not basely die,	55
3067	Not cowardly put off my helmet to	56
3068	My countryman,—a Roman by a Roman	57
3069	Valiantly vanquish'd. Now my spirit is going:	58
3070	I can no more.	
3071	*Cleo.* Noblest of men, woo't die?	59
3072	Hast thou no care of me? shall I abide	60
3073	In this dull world, which in thy absence is	61
3074	No better than a sty? O, see, my women,	62
3074+1	*[Antony dies*	
3075	The crown o' the earth doth melt. My lord!	63
3076	O, wither'd is the garland of the war,	64

30   same as 29, MTh, less RA1; less <u>aX</u>

31   same as 30, less ChC, LoC; <u>aX</u>: ChC, LoC, JP1, ML1; <u>bX</u>: BA1

32   X: Inc, In2, JKP, WM1, SP1, Cum, ChC, Lac, Ha1, JL1, HIM, KyB, MTh,*
33   same as 32; BT1, IP1, TaB, BH1; less <u>aX</u>, <u>bX</u>, <u>MOVE</u>

34   X: Inc, In2, WM1, SP1, ChC, MTh, EdT, LoC, BT1, OA1, TaB; <u>aX</u>: JKP,Cum*
35   same as 34, JP1, TN1; less <u>aX</u>, bX
36   same as 35, less TN1; <u>R</u>: Ha$\overline{1}$, KyB; <u>aX</u>: TN1; <u>bX</u>: JKP, Lac, IP1, RH1
37   X: SP1, ChC, Lac, Ha1, $\overline{\text{KyB}}$, MTh, Ed$\overline{\text{T}}$, LoC, Ta$\overline{\text{B}}$; <u>aX</u>: Inc, In2, JKP, WM1,
       BT1, OA1, IP1, RA1; <u>bX</u>: JL1, JP1

38   X: WM1, SP1, KyB; <u>aX</u>: In2, EdT, TaB; <u>bX</u>: JKP; <u>ADD</u> 8: Lac
39   X: In2, WM1, JL1, $\overline{\text{KyB}}$; <u>aX</u>: Inc; <u>bX</u>: Ta$\overline{\text{B}}$, RA1, $\overline{\text{ER1}}$

40   X: In2, WM1, JL1; <u>aX</u>: KyB; <u>bX</u>: Inc, JKP, SP1, Cum, Lac, Ha1, HIM, OA1,*
41   X: Inc, In2, WM1, $\overline{\text{TN1}}$
42   X: In2, WM1, KyB, RH1; <u>bX</u>: JL1

43   X: In2, KyB, RH1; <u>aX</u>: Inc; <u>bX</u>: AF1, TN1
44   X: Inc, In2, WM1, $\overline{\text{KyB}}$, RH1, $\overline{\text{AF1}}$, TN1

45   X: WM1, KyB, TN1; <u>aX</u>: Inc, In2, RH1, AF1; <u>bX</u>: BT1; <u>ADD</u> 4: BT1
46   X: WM1, KyB

47   X: KyB; <u>aX</u>: WM1; <u>bX</u>: BT1, OA1, RH1, JP1
48   X: KyB, $\overline{\text{BT1}}$, RH1, $\overline{\text{JP1}}$; <u>bX</u>: JKP
49   X: KyB, BT1, RH1
50   same as 49; <u>ADD</u> 4: JKP
51   X: ML1
52   <u>aX</u>: ML1; <u>bX</u>: RH1
53    $\overline{\text{X}}$: RH1; <u>aX</u>: OA1, ML1
54   X: RH1
55   X: RH1
56   X: RH1; <u>bX</u>: JKP, WM1, Lac
57   <u>aX</u>: JKP, $\overline{\text{WM1}}$, Lac, RH1
58

59   <u>bX</u>: Inc, In2, WM1, ChC, LoC
60    $\overline{\text{X}}$: Inc, In2, WM1, ChC, LoC; <u>bX</u>: JKP
61   same as 60, JKP; less <u>bX</u>
62   X: Inc, In2, ChC, LoC; <u>aX</u>: JKP, WM1; <u>bX</u>: KyB

63   X: ChC, KyB, LoC
64   X: ChC, JL1, KyB, LoC, TaB

*4-15:32 EdT, LoC, OA1, BA1, RA1; <u>aX</u>: TaB; <u>bX</u>: BH1; <u>MOVE</u> 32-40a to follow
  4-15: 13: SM1   *$\overline{\text{4}}$-15:34 Lac, Ha1, $\overline{\text{JL1}}$, HIM, KyB, BA1, IP1,
  $\overline{\text{RA1}}$, BH1; <u>bX</u>: JP1, TN1   *4-15:40 IP1, GS1, RH1, JP1, TaB,
  RA1, ER1; <u>Insert</u> 13b-20a: WA1

3077	The soldier's pole is fall'n : young boys and girls	65
3078	Are level now with men ; the odds is gone,	66
3079	And there is nothing left remarkable	67
3080	Beneath the visiting moon. [*Faints*	
3081	*Char.* O, quietness, lady!	68
3082	*Iras.* She is dead too, our sovereign.	
3083	*Char.* Lady!	
3084	*Iras.* Madam!	69
3085	*Char.* O madam, madam, madam !	
	Iras. Royal Egypt,	70
3086	Empress!	71
3087	*Char.* Peace, peace, Iras!	72
	Cleo. No more, but e'en a woman, and com-	
3088	manded	73
3089	By such poor passion as the maid that milks	74
3090	And does the meanest chares. It were for me	75
3091	To throw my sceptre at the injurious gods ;	76
3092	To tell them that this world did equal theirs	77
3093	Till they had stol'n our jewel. All's but naught:	78
3094	Patience is sottish, and impatience does	79
3095	Become a dog that's mad : then is it sin 80	80
3096	To rush into the secret house of death,	81
3097	Ere death dare come to us? How do you, women!	82
	What, what! good cheer! Why, how now, Char-	
3098	mian !	83
3099	My noble girls! Ah, women, women, look,	84
	Our lamp is spent, it's out! Good sirs, take	
3100	heart :	85
	We'll bury him ; and then, what's brave, what's	
3101	noble,	86
3102	Let's do it after the high Roman fashion,	87
3103	And make death proud to take us. Come, away:	88
3104	This case of that huge spirit now is cold:	89
3105	Ah, women, women ! come : we have no friend	90
3106	But resolution, and the briefest end. 91	91
3107	[*Exeunt ; those above bearing off*	
3107+1	*Antony's body.*	
3107+2	**ACT V.**	
3107+3	SCENE I. *Alexandria. Cæsar's camp.*	
3108	*Enter* CÆSAR, AGRIPPA, DOLABELLA, MECÆ-	
3109	NAS, GALLUS, PROCULEIUS, *and others, his*	
3109+1	*council of war.*	
3110	*Cæs.* Go to him, Dolabella, bid him yield;	1
3111	Being so frustrate, tell him he mocks	2

65 X: WM1, Cum, ChC, JL1, KyB, EdT, LoC, TaB; a̲X̲: JKP; b̲X̲: Inc, In2
66 same as 65; less a̲X̲, b̲X̲; a̲X̲: Inc, In2
67 same as 65, less E̲d̲T̲; less a̲X̲, b̲X̲

68 X: WM1, ChC, JL1, KyB, LoC; a̲X̲: TaB; b̲X̲: JKP, SP1, Cum, Lac, Ha1, HIM,
    MTh; A̲D̲D̲ 5: In2

69 X: In2, JKP, SP1, Cum, ChC, Lac, Ha1, JL1, HIM, KyB, MTh, LoC; R̲: Inc;
    b̲X̲: BT1
70 XL I̲n̲2̲, ChC, HIM, KyB, LoC; R: Inc; a̲X̲: MTh; N̲: WM1
71 X: In2, JKP, ChC, KyB, LoC; R̅: Inc; a̲X̲: HIM
72 same as 71, less JKP; less R̲, a̲X̲; R̲: I̅n̅c; A̲D̲D̲ 1: Tab

73 X: Inc, In2, ChC, KyB, LoC, TaB; b̲X̲: WM1
74 same as 73, WM1, Cum; less b̲X̲
75 X: Inc, In2 ChC, KyB, LoC, T̅aB; a̲X̲: WM1, Cum; b̲X̲: ML1
76 same as 75, ML1; less a̲X̲, b̲X̲
77 same as 76
78 same as 76, less ML1; a̲X̲: ML1; b̲X̲: JKP, SP1, Cum
79 X: Inc, In2, WM1, SP1, Cum, ChC, KyB, LoC, BT1, TaB, JP1; ̸X: JKP
80 same as 79, less JP1; less a̲X̲; a̲X̲: JP1
81 same as 90; less a̲X̲
82 same as 81

83 same as 81
84 X: In2, ChC, KyB, LoC, BT1, TaB, JP1; R̸ Inc; a̲X̲: WM1, SP1, Cum; I̲n̲s̲e̲r̲t̲
    189: Inc
85 X: Inc, Cum, ChC, LoC, BT1 TaB; a̲X̲: In2; b̲X̲: WM1, JL1, HIM, OA1, RA1

86 X: WM1, ChC, JL1, LoC, BT1, TaB
87 same as 86
88 same as 86; b̲X̲: In2, JKP
89 X: In2, JKP, WM1, ChC, JL1, LoC, TaB, ML1; M̲O̲V̲E̲ 89 to follow 84:Inc
90 X: Inc, In2, WM1, ChC, JL1, LoC, TaB; a̲X̲: M̅L̅1
91 same as 90; less a̲X̲; A̲D̲D̲ 41, insert 4̲6̲: 30-39a, and 4̲9̲: 7b-73a: Ha1

Scene 51

C̲U̲T̲ A̲L̲L̲: WM1, ChC, Lac, Ha1, JL1, HIM, KyB, LiL, MTh, EdT, BT1, SM1, WA1,
  OA1, JP1, LK1 C̲U̲T̲ A̲L̲L̲ B̲U̲T̲ T̲R̲A̲N̲S̲F̲E̲R̲: LoC
1 X: Inc, In2; b̲X̲: AF1
2 X: Inc, In2, T̅N1; a̲X̲: AF1; b̲X̲: ML1

3112	The pauses that he makes.	
3113	*Dol.* Cæsar, I shall. [*Exit.*	3
3114	*Enter* DERCETAS, *with the sword of* ANTONY.	
	Ces. Wherefore is that? and what art thou that darest	
3115		4
3116	Appear thus to us?	
3117	*Der.* I am call'd Dercetas:	5
3118	Mark Antony I served, who best was worthy	6
3119	Best to be served: whilst he stood up and spoke,	7
3120	He was my master; and I wore my life	8
3121	To spend upon his haters. If thou please	9
3122	To take me to thee, as I was to him 10	10
	I'll be to Cæsar; if thou pleasest not,	11
3123	I yield thee up my life.	
3124	*Ces.* What is't thou say'st?	12
2125	*Der.* I say, O Cæsar, Antony is dead.	13
	Ces. The breaking of so great a thing should make	
3126		14
3127	A greater crack: †the round world	15
3128	Should have shook lions into civil streets,	16
3129	And citizens to their dens: the death of Antony	17
3130	Is not a single doom; in the name lay	18
3131	A moiety of the world.	
3132	*Der.* He is dead, Cæsar;	19
3133	Not by a public minister of justice, 20	20
3134	Nor by a hired knife; but that self hand,	21
3135	Which writ his honour in the acts it did,	22
3136	Hath, with the courage which the heart did lend it,	23
3137	Splitted the heart. This is his sword;	24
3138	I robb'd his wound of it; behold it stain'd	25
3139	With his most noble blood.	
3140	*Ces.* Look you sad, friends?	26
3141	The gods rebuke me, but it is tidings	27
3142	To wash the eyes of kings.	
3143	*Agr.* And strange it is,	28
3144	That nature must compel us to lament	29
3145	Our most persisted deeds.	
	Mec. His taints and honours 30	30
3146	Waged equal with him.	
3147	*Agr.* A rarer spirit never	31
3148	Did steer humanity: but you, gods, will give us	32
3149	Some faults to make us men. Cæsar is touch'd.	33
	Mec. When such a spacious mirror's set before him,	
3150		34
3151	He needs must see himself.	

3   X: Inc, In2; a̲X̲ ML1, TN1; b̲X̲: JKP

4   X: Inc, In2

5   X: Inc, In2; N: JKP, SP1, BA1
6   X: Inc, In2; b̲X̲: JKP, TN1
7   X: Inc, In2; a̲X̲: JKP, TN1; b̲X̲: RA1
8   X: Inc, In2, R̄A̅1̅; b̲X̲: AF1, M̅L̅1̅, TN1
9   X: Inc, In2, TN1 ; a̲X̲: RA1, AF1, ML1; b̲X̲: ER1
10 X: Inc, In2, ER1, T̅N̅1̅
11 same as 10; b̲X̲: GS1, AF1

12 X: Inc, In2; a̲X̲: GS1, AF1, ER1, TN1
13 X: Inc, In2; M̅O̅V̅E̅ 13-28a to follow 5̲2̲: 340: LoC

14 X: JLP, TN1; M̅O̅V̅E̅ 14-67 to follow 4̲-̲1̲4̲: 140: Inc, In2
15 X: JKP, TN1; R̅:̅ Inc, In2; b̲X̲: RA1, G̅S̅1̅, ML1
16 X: JKP, RA1, G̅S̅1̅, ML1, TN1̅
17 X: JKP, TN1; a̲X̲: RA1, GS1, ML1; b̲X̲: Inc, In2
18 X: JKP, TN1; a̲X̲̲: Inc, In2

19 X: TN1; a̲X̲: JKP; b̲X̲: Inc, In2; N: LoC
20 X: Inc, I̅n̅2̅, SP1, L̅o̅C̅, GS1, A̅F̅1̅,̅ TN1
21 X: In2, LoC, GS1, AF1; a̲X̲: SP1
22 X: In2, LoC, GS1, AF1, T̅N̅1̅
23 same as 22, JKP
24 X: In2, LoC; a̲X̲: JKP, GS1, AF1; b̲X̲: ER1
25 X: In2, LoC, R̅A̅1̅, ER1; a̲X̲: ML1; b̲X̲: TN1

26 X: In2, TN1; a̲X̲: RA1, ER1; b̲X̲: JKP, BA1
27 X: In2, JKP; a̲X̲̲: BA1

28 X: In2, JLP; b̲X̲: BA1, RA1, AF1, ML1
29 X: In2, JKP, B̅A̅1̅, RA1, RH1, ML1

30 same as 29, less JKP; a̲X̲: JKP; b̲X̲: Inc, SP1, Cum, NM1, ER1

31 X: Inc, In2, SP1, Cum, BA1, RH1, ER1; a̲X̲: NM1, RA1, ML1; b̲X̲: GS1
32 same as 31, X̅A1; less a̲X̲, b̲X̲̲; b̲X̲: BH1̅
33 X: Inc, In2, SP1, Cum, B̅A̅1̅, ER̅1̅; a̲X̲: GS1, RH1, BH1; b̲X̲: NM1̲

34 X: Inc, In2, JKP, SP1, Cum, BA1, NM1, RA1, ER1

3152	*Cæs.* O Antony!	35
3153	I have follow'd thee to this; but we do lance	36
3154	Diseases in our bodies: I must perforce	37
3155	Have shown to thee such a declining day,	38
3156	Or look on thine: we could not stall together	39
3157	In the whole world: but yet let me lament, 40	40
2158	With tears as sovereign as the blood of hearts,	41
3159	That thou, my brother, my competitor	42
3160	In top of all design, my mate in empire,	43
3161	Friend and companion in the front of war,	44
3162	The arm of mine own body, and the heart	45
	Where mine his thoughts did kindle,—that our	
363	stars,	46
3164	Unreconciliable, should divide	47
3165	Our equalness to this. Hear me, good friends,—	48
3166	But I will tell you at some meeter season:	49
3169	*Enter an* Egyptian.	
3167	The business of this man looks out of him; 50	50
3168, 70	We'll hear him what he says. Whence are you?	51
	Egyp. A poor Egyptian yet. The queen my	
3171	mistress,	52
3172	Confined in all she has, her monument,	53
3173	Of thy intents desires instruction,	54
3174	That she preparedly may frame herself	55
3175	To the way she's forced to.	
3176	*Cæs.* Bid her have good heart:	56
3177	She soon shall know of us, by some of ours,	57
3178	How honourable and how kindly we	58
	Determine for her; for Cæsar cannot live	59
3179	To be ungentle.	
3180	*Egyp.* So the gods preserve thee! [*Exit.* 60	60
3181	*Cæs.* Come hither, Proculeius. Go and say,	61
3182	We purpose her no shame: give her what comforts	62
3183	The quality of her passion shall require,	63
3184	Lest, in her greatness, by some mortal stroke	64
3185	She do defeat us: for her life in Rome	65
3186	Would be eternal in our triumph: go,	66
3187	And with your speediest bring us what she says,	67
3188	And how you find of her.	
3189	*Pro.* Cæsar, I shall. [*Exit.* 68	
	Cæs. Gallus, go you along. [*Exit Gallus.*]	
	Where's Dolabella,	69
3190-1	To second Proculeius?	
3192	*All.* Dolabella! 70	70
3193	*Cæs.* Let him alone, for I remember now	71

35　aX: Ínc, In2, JKP, SP⌡, Cum, BA1, NM1, RA1, ER1
36　b̄X̄: In2, JKP, RA1, AF1, ML1
37　X̄: RA1, AF1; aX̲: In2, JKP, ML1
38　X: RA1, AF1
39　X: RA1, AF1; bX̲: Inc
40　X: RA1; aX̲: AF1̄, bX̲: Cap, Inc, In2, JKP, GS1, RH1, ML1; ADD̲ i: In2, JKP
41　X: Cap, Īn̄2, JKP, R̄Ā1, GS1, RH1, ML1, TN1̲; R̲: Inc
42　same as 51, ER1, less TN1; same ·R
43　same as 42, including R̲; aX̲: GS1̄
44　same as 42, Inc; less R̲
45　same as 44; bX̲: BA1

46　same as 44; aX̲: BA1
47　same　as 46
48　X: Inc, In2, RA1, RH1, ER1; aX̲: CaP, JKP, ML1; bX̲: BA1, AF1, TN1
49　X: Inc, In2, JKP, BA1, RA1, ḠS̄1, RH1, AF1, ML1, ĒR̄1, TN1

50　same as 49, less ML1
51　X: Inc, In2; aX̲: JL1, BA1, RA1, GS1, RH1, AF1, ML1, ER1, TN1

52　X: Inc, In2; aX̲: RA1, ML1
53　X: Inc, In2
54　X: Inc, In2
55　XL Inc, In2

56　XL Inc, In2
57　X: Inc, In2; bX̲: BA1
58　X: Inc, In2, BA1
59　X: Inc, In2;aX̲: BA1; bX̲: GS1

60　X: Inc, In2; aX̲: GS1
61　R̲: Inc; N: In2̄, Cum
62　b̄X̄: ML1
63　X̄:̄ ML1
64
65
66　bX̲: Inc, In2, AF1, TN1
67　X̄:̄ GS1, AF1, TN1; R̲: Inc , In2

68　X: Inc, In2, AF1; aX̲: GS1, TN1; bX̲: JKP

69　X: Inc, In2, JKP, BA1, NM1, RH1, AF1, ER1; aX̲: RA1; bX̲: GS1

70　same as 69; less aX̲, bX̲; bX̲: GS1, TN1
71　same as 70, GS1, T̄N̄1; less bX̲

3194	How he's employ'd: he shall in time be ready.	72
3195	Go with me to my tent; where you shall see	73
3196	How hardly I was drawn into this war;	74
3197	How calm and gentle I proceeded still	75
3198	In all my writings: go with me, and see	76
3199	What I can show in this. [*Exeunt.*	77

3199+1   **SCENE II.** *Alexandria. A room in the monu-*
3199+2   *ment.*

3200   *Enter* CLEOPATRA, CHARMIAN, *and* IRAS.

3201	*Cleo.* My desolation does begin to make	1
3202	A better life. 'Tis paltry to be Cæsar;	2
3203	Not being Fortune, he's but Fortune's knave,	3
3204	A minister of her will: and it is great	4
3205	To do that thing that ends all other deeds;	5
3206	Which shackles accidents and bolts up change;	6
3207	Which sleeps, and never palates more the dug,	7
3208	The beggar's nurse and Cæsar's.	8

3209   *Enter, to the gates of the monument,* PROCU-
3209+1   LEIUS, GALLUS, *and* Soldiers.

3210	*Pro.* Cæsar sends greeting to the Queen of Egypt;	9
3211	And bids thee study on what fair demands **10**	10
3212	Thou mean'st to have him grant thee.	
3213	*Cleo.* What's thy name?	11
3214	*Pro.* My name is Proculeius.	
3215	*Cleo.* Antony	12
3216	Did tell me of you, bade me trust you; but	13
3217	I do not greatly care to be deceived,	14
3218	That have no use for trusting. If your master	15
3219	Would have a queen his beggar, you must tell him,	16
3220	That majesty, to keep decorum, must	17
3221	No less beg than a kingdom: if he please	18
3222	To give me conquer'd Egypt for my son,	19
3223	He gives me so much of mine own, as I **20**	20
3224	Will kneel to him with thanks.	
3225	*Pro.* Be of good cheer;	21
3226	You're fall'n into a princely hand, fear nothing:	22
3227	Make your full reference freely to my lord,	23
3228	Who is so full of grace, that it flows over	24
3229	On all that need: let me report to him	25
3230	Your sweet dependency: and you shall find	26
3231	A conqueror that will pray in aid for kindness,	27
3232	Where he for grace is kneel'd to.	

72 same as 71
73 X: Inc, In2, IP1, RH1, AF1
74 same as 73, less RH1; R: ML1
75 same as 73
76 same as 73
77 same as 73

Scene 52

1 X: ChC, JL1, LoC, JP1; R: Inc, In2, WM1; MOVE 1-5 to follow 48: BT1
2 same as 1, EdT; same R; less MOVE
3 same as 1, add KyB to R
4 same as 3, including R
5 X: Inc, In2, ChC, JL1, EdT, LoC, JP1; R: WM1
6 X: Inc, In2, ChC, Hal, JL1, EdT, LoC, BT1, OA1, RA1, JP1; R: WM1
7 same as 6, KyB; same R
8 same as 7 including R; ADD 3: JKP

9   X: ChC, JL1, KyB, LoC, TaB; R: WM1; N: Inc, JP1; MOVE 9-10 to follow*
10 same as 9; less R, MOVE; R: WM1, ML1

11 X: ChC, KyB, LoC; R: WM1; aX: JL1, TaB; bX: JKP, RH1; MOVE 11b-13a to
       follow 201: JL1
12 X: JKP, ChC, KyB, LoC, BT1, RH1; R: WM1; bX: JP1; N: Inc, In2, Cum, JP1*
13 same as 12, In2, JP1; less R, bX, N, ADD; R: Inc, WM1; bX: JL1
14 X: Inc, In2, JKP, ChC, JL1, KyB, EdT, LoC, BT1, RH1, JP1; R: WM1
15 X: Inc, In2, WM1, ChC, JL1, KyB, LoC, BT1; R: ML1; aX: JKP, EdT, RH1,*
16 X: Inc, In2, WM1, ChC, JL1, KyB, LiL, LoC, BT1, IP1, ML1, TN1
17 same as 16
18 same as 16, less IP1; aX: IP1; bX: SM1, WA1
19 same as 18, SM1, WA1, less ML1, TN1; less aX, bX
20 same as 19

21 X: Inc, In2, WM1, ChC, JL1, KyB, LoC, BT1; aX: LiL, SM1, WA1; bX: Hal*
22 X: Inc, In2, JKP, WM1, ChC, Hal, JL1, KyB, LoC, BT1, BA1, RA1, TN1;*
23 same as 22, EdT, RH1, AF1, less BA1; less aX, bX
24 same as 23; bX: IP1
25 X: Inc, In2, WM1, ChC, Hal, JL1, KyB, LoC, BT1, IP1, RH1, TN1; aX: JKP*
26 same as 25, SM1, WA1, BA1, ML1, less IP1; less aX, bX; aX: IP1, bX:*
27 same as 26, EdT, AF1; less aX, bX

*51: 9 39: BT1   *51: 12 ADD 1: ER1   *51:15 JP1;
       bX: LiL, TN1   *51:21 ML1, TN1; ADD 1: JKP; "Insert 35".: Lac?
*51:22 aX: ML1; bX: AF1   *51:25 EdT, RA1, AF1; bX: SM1, WA1,
       BA1, ML1   *51:26 EdT, AF1

3233	*Cleo.* Pray you, tell him	28
3234	I am his fortune's vassal, and I send him	29
3235	The greatness he has got. I hourly learn 30	30
3236	A doctrine of obedience; and would gladly	31
3237	Look him i' the face.	
3238	*Pro.* This I'll report, dear lady.	32
3239	Have comfort, for I know your plight is pitied	33
3240	Of him that caused it.	34
3241	*Gal.* You see how easily she may be surprised:	35
3241+1	[*Here Proculeius and two of the Guard*	
+2	*ascend the monument by a ladder placed*	
+3	*against a window, and, having descend-*	
+4	*ed, come behind Cleopatra. Some of*	
+5	*the Guard unbar and open the gates.*	
+6	[*To Proculeius and the Guard*] Guard her till	
3242	Cæsar come. *Exit.*	36
3243	*Iras.* Royal queen !	37
3244	*Char.* O Cleopatra ! thou art taken, queen.	48
3245	*Cleo.* Quick, quick, good hands.	
3245+1	[*Drawing a dagger.*	
3246	*Pro.* Hold, worthy lady, hold :	39
3246+1	[*Seizes and disarms her.*	
3247	Do not yourself such wrong, who are in this 40	40
3248	Relieved, but not betray'd.	
	Cleo. What, of death too,	41
3249	That rids our dogs of languish?	
	Pro. Cleopatra,	42
3250	Do not abuse my master's bounty by	43
3251	The undoing of yourself : let the world see	44
3252	His nobleness well acted, which your death	45
3253	Will never let come forth.	
	Cleo. Where art thou, death ?	46
3254	Come hither, come ! come, come, and take a	47
3255	queen	
3256	Worth many babes and beggars !	
3257	*Pro.* O, temperance, lady !	48
3258	*Cleo.* Sir, I will eat no meat, I 'll not drink, sir ;	49
3259	If idle talk will once be necessary, 50	50
3260	I 'll not sleep neither : this mortal house I 'll ruin,	51
3261	Do Cæsar what he can. Know, sir, that I	52
3262	Will not wait pinion'd at your master's court ;	53
3263	Nor once be chastised with the sober eye	54
3264	Of dull Octavia. Shall they hoist me up	55
3265	And show me to the shouting varletry	56
3266	Of censuring Rome? Rather a ditch in Egypt	57
3267	Be gentle grave unto me ! rather on Nilus' mud	58

28 same as 27, less EdT, SM1, WA1, BA1, AF1; aX: EdT, SM1, WA1, BA1, AF1*
29 same as 28, GS1, JP1, less RH1; less aX, bX
30 same as 29, less TN1; aX: TN1
31 same as 30, less GS1, ML1; less aX; R: ML1; bX: SM1

32 same as 31, less Hal, less R, bX; aX: Hal, SM1, ML1; bX: JKP, BA1
33 X: Inc, In2, JKP, WM1, ChC, JL1, KyB, LoC, BT1, BA1, IP1, JP1, ML1;*
34 same as 33, GCa, less ML1 ; less ADD; aX: ML1; ADD 1: Bel, Cum
35 X: GCa, Inc., In2, JKP, WM1, SP1, Cum, ChC, Hal, JL1, HIM, KyB, EdT,
    LoC, BT1, TaB, RH1, JP1, AF1, ER1; MOVE 35-36 to follow 38: OA1

36 X: GCa, Inc, In2, JKP, WM1, SP1, Cum, KyB, LiL, LoC, WA1, BA1, RH1,JP1*
37 X: Inc, In2, JP1
38 same as 37; Insert 35-36: OA1

39 same as 37, Cum; bX: LiL, Insert 9-11: BT1

40 X: Inc, In2, Cum, LiL, BT1, JP1; bX: WM1, KyB

41 X: Inc, In2, WM1, Cum, KyB, JP1; aX: LiL, BT1; bX: Cap, EdT, IP1, AF1

42 X: Cap, Inc, In2, JKP, WM1, Cum, KyB, EdT, BT1, IP1, AF1, JP1; bX: Lac*
43 X: Cap, Inc, In2, JKP, Cum, Lac, Hal, HIM, KyB, MTh, EdT, BT1, BA1, IP1*
44 same as 43; bX: WM1, SM1, WA1, BA1, GS1, TN1; Insert 36: TN1
45 X: Cap, Inc, In2, JKP, WM1, Cum, Lac, Hal, HIM, KyB, EdT, BT1, BA1, IP1,
    RA1, GS1, JP1, AF1, TN1; aX: MTh
46 X: Cap, Inc, In2, JKP, WM1, Cum, EdT, BA1, IP1, JP1; aX: Lac, HIM, KyB*
47 X: Cap, Inc, In2, Cum, EdT, BA1, IP1, JP1

48 same as 47, less IP1; aX: WM1, IP1; Insert 1-5: BT1
49 same as 48, JL1, less Cap; less aX, Insert
50 X: Inc, In2, JKP, Cum, JL1, EdT, BT1, SM1, WA1, BA1, JP1, ML1, ER1
51 X: Inc, In2, Cum, KyB, EdT, BA1, JP1; aX: JL1, BT1; bX: TN1
52 same as 51, less BA1; less aX, bX; aX: BA1, TN1; bX: JKP, Hal, BT1, RA1
53 X: Inc, In2, JKP, Cum, Hal, EdT, BT1, RA1, JP1
54 same as 53, JL1, less JKP
55 X: Inc, In2, Cum, EdT, JP1; aX: Hal, JL1, BT1, RA1
56 same as 55; less aX
57 same as 56
58 same as 56; bX: ML1

*51:28 bX: JP1   *51:33 ADD 1: GCa   *51:36 ER1;
   MOVE 36 to follow 52: 46: Hal; MOVE 36 to follow 44a: TN1
*51:42 Hal, HIM, MTh, BA1   *51:43 JP1, AF1   *51:46 BT1,
   SM1, WA1, RA1, GS1, AF1, TN1; Insert 36: Hal

3268	**Lay** me stark naked, and let the water-flies	59
3269	**Blow** me into abhorring! rather make **60**	60
3270	**My** country's high pyramides my gibbet,	61
3271	**And** hang me up in chains!	
3272	*Pro.* You do extend	62
3273	**These** thoughts of horror further than you shall	63
3274	**Find** cause in Cæsar.	

3275   *Enter* DOLABELLA.

3276	*Dol.* Proculeius,	64
3277	**What** thou hast done thy master Cæsar knows,	65
3278	**And** he hath sent for thee: for the queen,	66
3279	**I 'll** take her to my guard.	
3280	*Pro.* So, Dolabella,	67
3281	**It** shall content me best: be gentle to her.	68
	[*To Cleo.*] To Cæsar I will speak what you shall	
3282	please,	69
3283	**If** you 'll employ me to him.	
3284	*Cleo.* Say, I would die. **70**	70
3284+1	[*Exeunt Proculeius and Soldiers.*	
3285	*Dol.* Most noble empress, you have heard of me?	71
3286	*Cleo.* I cannot tell.	
3287	*Dol.* Assuredly you know me.	72
	Cleo. No matter, sir, what I have heard or	
3288	known.	73
3289	**You** laugh when boys or women tell their dreams;	74
3290	**Is 't** not your trick?	
3291	*Dol.* I understand not, madam.	75
3292	*Cleo.* I dream'd there was an Emperor Antony:	76
3293	**O,** such another sleep, that I might see	77
3294	**But** such another man!	
3295	*Dol.* If it might please ye,—	78
	Cleo. His face was as the heavens; and	
3296	therein stuck	79
	A sun and moon, which kept their course, and	
3297	lighted	
3298	**The** little O, the earth. **80**	80
3299	*Dol.* Most sovereign creature,—	81
3300	*Cleo.* His legs bestrid the ocean: his rear'd arm	82
3301	**Crested** the world: his voice was propertied	83
3302	**As** all the tuned spheres, and that to friends;	84
3303	**But** when he meant to quail and shake the orb,	85
3304	**He** was as rattling thunder. For his bounty,	86
3305	**There** was no winter in 't; an autumn 'twas	87
3306	**That** grew the more by reaping: his delights	88
3307	**Were** dolphin-like; they show'd his back above	89

```
59    same as 56, ML1
60    same as 59; bX: BA1
61    same as 59, BA1

62    same as 61; bX: JKP, ChC, Ha1, KyB, LoC, BT1, IP1
63    X: Inc, In2, JKP, Cum, ChC, Ha1, KyB, EdT, LoC, BT1, BA1, IP1, JP1,ML1



64    same as 63, less JKP, BA1, IP1, ML1; aX: BA1, IP1, ML1; bX: JL1, LiL*
65    same as 64, JL1, LiL, RH1, LK1; less aX, bX, N
66    same as 65; ADD 1: WM1

67    same as 65; N: JKP
68    same as 65, less LK1; aX: LK1

69    X: Inc, In2, Cum, Ha1, KyB, EdT, LoC, JP1; bX: ML1; N: TaB

70    same as 69, ML1, less KyB, JP1; less bX, N; aX: JP1

71    X: Inc, In2, Ha1, KyB, LiL, EdT, LoC, BT1, TaB; bX: JP1

72    same as 71, JP1; less bX

73    same as 72, less Inc, In2
74    X: SP1, Cum, Lac, Ha1, HIM, KyB, LiL, MTh, EdT, LoC, BT1, TaB, JP1

75    same as 74
76    X: KyB, LiL, EdT, LoC, TaB; R: Ha1
77    same as 76, JKP, Ha1; less R

78    same as 77; bX: Inc, In2, BT1

79    X: Inc, In2, Cum, KyB, LiL, EdT, LoC, BT1, TaB; bX: JKP, WM1

80    same as 79, JKP, WM1; less bX

81    same as 80, less WM1; aX: WM1; bX: SP1
82    same as 81, less JKP
83    same as 82
84    same as 82; bX: JKP, IP1
85    same as 82, IP1
86    same as 82, SP1; aX: IP1
87    same as 86; less aX
88    same as 87; bX: JKP, ChC, JL1, BA1, IP1
89    X: Inc, In2, JKP, SP1, Cum, ChC, JL1, KyB, LiL , EdT, LoC, BT1, BA1,IP1,
      TaB

*51:64 BH1, LK1; N: JKP
```

33-8	The element they lived in : in his livery α	90
3309	Walk'd crowns and crownets; realms and islands were	91
3310	As plates dropp'd from his pocket.	
3311	*Dol.* Cleopatra!	92
3312	*Cleo.* Think you there was, or might be, such a man	93
3313	As this I dream'd of?	
3314	*Dol.* Gentle madam, no.	94
3315	*Cleo.* You lie, up to the hearing of the gods.	95
3316	But, if there be, or ever were, one such,	96
3317	It's past the size of dreaming: nature wants stuff	97
3318	To vie strange forms with fancy; yet, to imagine	98
3319	An Antony, were nature's piece 'gainst fancy,	99
3320	Condemning shadows quite.	
3321	*Dol.* Hear me, good madam. ix	100
3322	Your loss is as yourself, great; and you bear it	101
3323	As answering to the weight : would I might never	102
3324	O'ertake pursued success, but I do feel,	103
3325	By the rebound of yours, a grief that smites	104
3326	My very heart at root.	
3327	*Cleo.* I thank you, sir.	105
3328	Know you what Cæsar means to do with me?	106
3329	*Dol.* I am loath to tell you what I would you knew.	107
3330	*Cleo.* Nay, pray you, sir,—	
3331	*Dol.* Though he be honourable,—	108
3332	*Cleo.* He'll lead me, then, in triumph?	109
	Dol. Madam, he will; I know 't. ir	110
3333	[*Flourish, and shout within,* 'Make way there: Cæsar."	111
3336		
3334	*Enter* CÆSAR, GALLUS, PROCULEIUS, MECE-	
3335	NAS, SELEUCUS, *and others of his Train.*	
3337	*Cæs.* Which is the Queen of Egypt?	112
	Dol. It is the emperor, madam.	113
3338	[*Cleopatra kneels*	
3339	*Cæs.* Arise, you shall not kneel:	114
3340	I pray you, rise; rise, Egypt.	
	Cleo. Sir, the gods	115
3341	Will have it thus; my master and my lord	116
3342	I must obey.	
3343	*Cæs.* Take to you no hard thoughts:	117
3344	The record of what injuries you did us,	118
3345	Though written in our flesh, we shall remember	119
3346	As things but done by chance.	

90 same as 89, less ChC, JL1, BA1, IP1; <u>aX</u>: ChC, JL1, BA1, IP1

91 same as 90; less <u>aX</u>

92 same as 91, less SP1, Cum ; <u>aX</u>: SP1, Cum; <u>bX</u>: Cap, Ha1

93 same as 92, Cap, Ha1, less JKP; less <u>aX</u>, <u>bX</u>; <u>R</u>: WM1

94 same as 93; less <u>R</u>
95 same as 94; <u>ADD 2</u>: JKP
96 same as 94, <u>JKP</u>
97 same as 96, IP1; <u>bX</u>: ChC, JL1, WA1 OA1, BA1, RA1, RH1, JP1
98 X: Cap, Inc, In2, JKP, ChC, Ha1, JL1, KyB, LiL, EdT, LoC, BT1, SM1*
99 same as 98

100 X: Cap, In2, JKP, Ha1, KyB, EdT, BT1, BA1; <u>aX</u>: Inc, ChC, JL1, LiL,LoC*
101 same as 100, WM1; less <u>aX</u>
102 same as 100; less <u>aX</u>; <u>R</u>: ML1; <u>aX</u>: WM1; <u>bX</u>: OA1, TN1
103 same as 100, OA1; <u>less aX</u>; <u>R</u>: ML1; <u>aX</u>: TN1
104 same as 103; less <u>R</u>, <u>aX</u>

105 X: Cap, JKP, Ha1, KyB, BT1, OA1, BA1; <u>aX</u>: EdT
106 X: Cap, JKP, Ha1, KyB

107 same as 106, In2, BT1

108 X: Cap, Inc, JKP, Ha1, KyB; <u>aX</u>: BT1
109 same as 108, less Inc
110 X: Cap, Ha1, KyB; <u>aX</u>: JKP; <u>bX</u>: Inc, In2, Cum, ChC, LoC, BT1, SM1; <u>In-</u>*
111 X: Inc, In2, WM1, <u>ChC</u>, Ha1, <u>KyB</u>, LoC, BT1, SM1, WA1, OA1; <u>bX</u>: JL1

112 X: Inc, In2, WM1, ChC, Lac, Ha1, JL1, HIM, KyB, MTh, LoC, BT1, SM1*
113 same as 112

114 same as 112, less LAC, HIM, MTh

115 same as 114; <u>bX</u>: AF1
116 same as 114, <u>AF1</u>

117 same as 116; <u>bX</u>: GS1
118 same as 116, <u>GS1</u>
119 same as 118

*52:98 WA1, OA1, BA1, IP1, TaB, RA1, RH1, JP1   *52:100 SM1, WA1,
   OA1, IP1, TaB, RA1, RH1, JP1   *52:110 <u>sert</u> 204-207: SM1
*52:112 WA1, OA1

3347	*Cleo.* Sole sir o' the world, 120	120
3348	I cannot project mine own cause so well	121
3349	To make it clear; but do confess I have	122
3350	Been laden with like frailties which before	123
3351	Have often shamed our sex.	
3352	*Cæs.* Cleopatra, know,	124
3353	We will extenuate rather than enforce:	125
3354	If you apply yourself to our intents,	126
	Which towards you are most gentle, you shall	
3355	find	127
3356	A benefit in this change: but if you seek	128
3357	To lay on me a cruelty, by taking	129
3358	Antony's course, you shall bereave yourself 130	130
3359	Of my good purposes, and put your children	313
3360	To that destruction which I'll guard them from,	132
3361	if thereon you rely. I'll take my leave.	133
	Cleo. And may, through all the world: 'tis	
3362	yours; and we,	134
3363	Your scutcheons and your signs of conquest, shall	135
	Hang in what place you please. Here, my good	
3364	lord.	136
3365	*Cæs.* You shall advise me in all for Cleopatra.	137
	Cleo. This is the brief of money, plate, and	
3366	jewels,	138
3367	I am possess'd of: 'tis exactly valued;	139
3368	Not petty things admitted. Where's Seleucus?	14–
3369	*Sel.* Here, madam. 141	141
	Cleo. This is my treasurer: let him speak,	
3370	my lord,	142
3371	Upon his peril, that I have reserved	143
3372	To myself nothing. Speak the truth, Seleucus.	144
	Sel. Madam,	145
3373	I had rather seal my lips, than, to my peril,	146
3374	Speak that which is not.	
3375	*Cleo.* What have I kept back?	147
	Sel. Enough to purchase what you have made	
3376	known.	148
3377	*Cæs.* Nay, blush not, Cleopatra; I approve	149
3378	Your wisdom in the deed.	
3379	*Cleo.* See, Cæsar! O, behold, 150	150
3380	How pomp is follow'd! mine will now be yours;	151
3381	And, should we shift estates, yours would be mine.	152
3382	The ingratitude of this Seleucus does	153
3383	Even make me wild: O slave, of no more trust	154
	Than love that's hired! What, goest thou back?	
3384	thou shalt	155

120 same as 118, SP1, less AF1; <u>aX</u>: AF1; <u>bX</u>: LiL, IP1
121 same as 120, JKP, LiL, IP1
122 same as 121
123 same as 121

124 same as 121; less LiL, IP1, GS1; <u>aX</u>: LiL, IP1, GS1
125 same as 124; IP1
126 same as 124

127 same as 124
128 same as 124
129 same as 124
130 same as 124
131 same as 124
132 same as 124
133 same as 124

134 same as 124, CaP, Cum, JP1
135 same as 134, TN1

136 same as 134; <u>aX</u>: TN1; <u>bX</u>: TaB, RA1, RH1, ML1
137 X: Cap, Inc, $\overline{\text{In}}$2, JKP, $\overline{\text{WM}}$1, SP1, Cum, ChC, Lac, Hal, JL1, HIM, KyB,
    LiL, EdT, LoC, BT1, SM1, WA1, OA1, IP1, TaB, RA1, RH1,JP1,ML1,TN1
138 same as 137, less JKP, IP1
139 same as 138
140 same as 138; <u>bX</u>: JKP, ER1; <u>N</u>: BA1
141 same as 138, $\overline{\text{JKP}}$; less <u>bX</u>, <u>N̄</u>

142 same as 141, AF1
143 same as 141; <u>aX</u>: AF1
144 same as 141, $\overline{\text{NM}}$1; <u>N</u>: BA1
145 same as 144; less <u>N̄</u>
146 same as 145

147 same as 145

148 same as 145
149 same as 145

150 same as 145; <u>bX</u>: GS1, TN1
151 same as 145, $\overline{\text{GS}}$1, TN1; <u>bX</u>: BA1, IP1
152 same as 151, BA1, IP1; $\overline{\text{less}}$ <u>bX</u>
153 same as 152, LiL
154 X: Cap, Inc, In2, JKP, WM1, SP1, Cum, ChC, Hal, JL1, KyB, LiL, EdT,
    LoC, BT1, SM1, WA1, OA1, TaB, RA1, GS1, RH1, JP1, AF1, ML1; <u>aX</u>: BA1*
155 same as 154; less <u>aX</u>

*52:154 IP1, TN1

3385	Go back, I warrant thee; but I'll catch thine eyes,	156
3386	Though they had wings: slave, soulless villain, dog!	157
3387	O rarely base!	
3388	*Cæs.* Good queen, let us entreat you.	158
3389	*Cleo.* O Cæsar, what a wounding shame is this,	159
3390	That thou, vouchsafing here to visit me, 160	160
3391	Doing the honour of thy lordliness	161
3392	To one so meek, that mine own servant should	162
3393	Parcel the sum of my disgraces by	163
3394	Addition of his envy! Say, good Cæsar,	164
3395	That I some lady trifles have reserved,	165
3396	Immoment toys, things of such dignity	166
3397	As we greet modern friends withal: and say,	167
3398	Some nobler token I have kept apart	168
3399	For Livia and Octavia, to induce	169
3400	Their mediation; must I be unfolded 170	170
3401	With one that I have bred? The gods! it smites me	171
3402	Beneath the fall I have. [*To Seleucus*] Prithee, go hence;	172
3403	Or I shall show the cinders of my spirits	173
3404	Through the ashes of my chance: wert thou a man,	174
3405	Thou wouldst have mercy on me.	
3406	*Cæs.* Forbear, Seleucus.	175
3406+1	[*Exit Seleucus.*	
3407	*Cleo.* Be it known, that we, the greatest, are misthought	176
3408	For things that others do ; and, when we fail,	177
3409	We answer others' merits in our name,	178
3410	Are therefore to be pitied.	
3411	*Cæs.* Cleopatra,	179
3412	Not what you have reserved, nor what acknowledged, 180	180
3413	Put we i' the roll of conquest : still be 't yours,	181
3	Bestow it at your pleasure; and believe,	182
3415	Cæsar's no merchant, to make prize with you	183
3416	Of things that merchants sold. Therefore be cheer'd;	184
3417	Make not your thoughts your prisons: no, dear queen ;	185
3418	For we intend so to dispose you as	186
3419	Yourself shall give us counsel. Feed, and sleep:	187
3420	Our care and pity is so much upon you,	188

156 same as 155

157 same as 155, less IP1; aX: IP1

158 same as 157; less aX; bX: TN1
159 same as 157, TN1, less GS1, AF1; less bX
160 same as 159
161 same as 159, less OA1
162 same as 161
163 same as 161; bX: NM1
164 same as 161, NM1, less LiL, TN1;less bX; aX: LiL, TN1; bX: GS1
165 same as 164, GS1; less aX, bX
166 same as 165; bX: TN1
167 same as 165; aX: TN1
168 same as 165, less NM1; aX: NM1
169 same as 168; le s aX
170 same as 169; bX: AF1

171 same as 169; aX: AF1; bX LiL

172 same as 169, less GS1; aX: LiL, GS1; bX: GCa, IP1
173 same as 172, GCa, BA1, IP1, AF1; less aX, bX

174 same as 173, less GCa, AF1; aX: GCa, AF1; bX: TN1

175 same as 174, less IP1; less aX, bX; aX: IP1, TN1; bX: AF1

176 same as 175, LiL, IP1, GS1, BA1, TN1; less TaB; less aX, bX
177 same as 176
178 same as 176

179 X: Cap, Inc, In2, WM1, SP1, Cum, ChC, Ha1, JL1, KyB, EdT, LoC, BT1,
     SM1, WA1, RA1, RH1, JP1, ML1; aX: JKP, LiL, BA1, IP1, GS1, BA1, TN1
180 same as 179; less aX
181 same as 180, OA1
182 same as 181; bX: JKP
183 same as 181, JKP, AF1

184 same as 181, AF1; aX: JKP : bX: WM1

185 same as 184, less RH1, AF1, ML1; less aX; aX: ML1
186 same as 185; less aX
187 same as 186, less WM1, RA1; aX: WM1, AF1
188 same as 187, less JP1; less aX

3421	That we remain your friend; and so, adieu.	189
3422	*Cleo.* My master, and my lord!	
3423	*Cæs.* . Not so. Adieu. 190	190
3424	[*Flourish. Exeunt Cæsar and his train.*	
3425	*Cleo.* He words me, girls, he words me, that I should not	191
3426-7	Be noble to myself: but, hark thee, Charmian.	192
3427+1	[*Whispers Charmian.*	
3428	*Iras.* Finish, good lady; the bright day is done,	193
3429	And we are for the dark.	
3430	*Cleo.* Hie thee again:	194
3431	I have spoke already, and it is provided;	195
3432	Go put it to the haste.	
3433	*Char.* Madam, I will.	196
3434	*Re-enter* DOLABELLA.	
3435	*Dol.* Where is the queen?	
3436	*Char.* Behold, sir. [*Exit.*	
3437	*Cleo.* Dolabella!	197
	Dol. Madam, as thereto sworn by your com-	
3438	mand,	198
3439	Which my love makes religion to obey,	199
3440	I tell you this: Cæsar through Syria 200	200
3441	Intends his journey; and within three days	201
3442	You with your children will he send before:	202
3443	Make your best use of this: I have perform'd	203
3444	Your pleasure and my promise.	
	Cleo. Dolabella,	204
3445	I shall remain your debtor.	
3446	*Dol.* I your servant.	205
3447	Adieu, good queen; I must attend on Cæsar.	206
3448	*Cleo.* Farewell, and thanks. [*Exit Dolabella.*	
3449	Now, Iras, what think'st thou?	207
3450	Thou, an Egyptian puppet, shalt be shown	208
3451	In Rome, as well as I: mechanic slaves	209
3452	With greasy aprons, rules, and hammers, shall	210
3453	Uplift us to the view; in their thick breaths,	211
3454	Rank of gross diet, shall we be enclouded,	212
3455	And forced to drink their vapour.	
3456	*Iras.* The gods forbid!	213
	Cleo. Nay, 'tis most certain, Iras: saucy	
3457	lictors	214
	Will catch at us, like strumpets; and scald	
3458	rhymers	215
3459	Ballad us out o' tune: the quick comedians.	216
3460	Extemporally will stage us, and present	217

189   same as 188, less SP1

190   X: Inc, In2, WM1, ChC, Hal, JL1, KyB, LoC, BT1, SM1, WA1, OA1

191   same as 190
192   X: Inc, In2, WM1, ChC, Hal, KyB, BT1, OA1; aX: JL1, LoC, SM1, WA1;
          bX: JKP, JP1, TN1; ADD 1: JKP:MOVE 192b-196 to· follow 207a: WA1
193   X: Ca1, Inc, In2, JKP, WM1, Hal, JL1, KyB, OA1, IP1; aX: LiL

194   X: Cap, Inc, In2, JKP, WM1, Hal, OA1; aX: JL1, KyB, TN1; bX: JP1
195   same as 194; less aX, bX

196   same as 195, JP1; bX: JL1

197   X: Cap, Inc, JKP, WM1, ChC, Hal, JL1, KyB, LiL, LoC, BT1, SM1, WA1,
          OA1, TaB, ML1; N: EdT, JP1, TN1
198   same as 197, less Inc, JKM; less N; R: Inc
199   same as 198, TN1; less R
200   same as 198, less JL1; TN1;aX: JL1
201   same as 200, less Hal; less aX; Insert 11b-13a: JL1
202   same as 201, JL1, less SM1; less Insert; ADD 6, insert 23b-31: JKP
203   X: Cap, JKP, ChC, JL1, KyB, LiL, LoC, BT1, SM1, WA1, OA1, TaB, JP1,
          ML1; bX: TN1
204   same as 203, less SM1, WA1, OA1; less bX; aX: SM1, WA1, OA1, TN1; bX;
          WM1; MOVE 204b-207a to follow 110: SM1
205   X: Cap, JKP, WM1, KyB, LiL, TaB, JP1, ML1; ADD1: BT1
206   X: Cap, JKP, LiL, TaB, JP1, ML1; aX: KyB; bX: TN1

207   X: Cap, JKP, BT1, JP1; R: Hal; aX: WM1, LiL, TaB, ML1, TN1; bX: JL1:*
208   X: Cap, JKP, JL1, BT1, JP1
209   same .as 208; bX: Inc, In2, KyB, BT1, ML1; ADD 7: Inc
210   X: Cap, Inc, In2, JKP, JL1, KyB, BT1, RH1, JP1, ML1
211   same .as 210; bX: ChC, LiL, LoC, SM1, WA1, OA1, TN1
212   X: Cap, Inc, In2, JKP, ChC, JL1, KyB, LiL, LoC, BT1, SM1, WA1, OA1,
          RH1, JP1, ML1, TN1
213   X: Cap, Inc, In2, JKP, ChC, JL1, LiL, LoC, BT1, RH1, JP1; aX: KyB, SM1
          WA1, OA1, ML1, TN1; bX: WM1; Insert 238-240: WM1
214   same as 213, KyB, less RH1; less aX, bX, Insert; aX: RH1, TN1; bX: SP1,
          Cum, OA1
215   same as 114, SP1, Cum, OA1; less aX, bX; B: EdT
216   X: Cap, Inc, In2, JKP, WM1, ChC, JL1, LoC, BT1, OA1, JP1; aX: KyB
217   same as 216, KyB; less aX; bX: ML1

*52:207 N: Inc; ADD 2: JL1

3461	**Our Alexandrian revels; Antony**	218
3462	**Shall be brought drunken forth, and I shall see**	219
3463	**Some squeaking Cleopatra boy my greatness 220**	220
3464	**I' the posture of a whore.**	
3465	*Iras.* O the good gods!	221
3466	*Clee.* Nay, that's certain.	222
3467	*Iras.* I'll never see't; for, I am sure, my nails	223
3468	**Are stronger than mine eyes.**	
	Clee. Why, that's the way	224
3469	**To fool their preparation, and to conquer**	225
3470	**Their most absurd intents.**	

3471	*Re-enter* CHARMIAN.	

3472	Now, Charmian!	226
3473	**Show me, my women, like a queen: go fetch**	227
3474	**My best attires: I am again for Cydnus,**	228
3475	**To meet Mark Antony: sirrah Iras, go.**	229
3476	**Now, noble Charmian, we'll dispatch indeed; 230**	230
	And, when thou hast done this chare, I'll give	
3477	thee leave	231
3478	**To play till doomsday. Bring our crown and all.**	232
3480	**Wherefore's this noise?**	
3479	[*Exit Iras. A noise within.*	

3481	*Enter a* Guardsman.	

3482	*Guard.* Here is a rural fellow	233
3483	**That will not be denied your highness' presence:**	234
3484	**He brings you figs.**	235
3485	*Cleo.* Let him come in. [*Exit Guardsman.*	
3486	What poor an instrument	236
3487	**May do a noble deed! he brings me liberty.**	237
3488	**My resolution's placed, and I have nothing**	238
3489	**Of woman in me: now from head to foot**	239
3490	**I am marble-constant; now the fleeting moon 240**	240
2391	**No planet is of mine.**	

3492	*Re-enter* Guardsman, *with* Clown *bringing in*	
3492+1	*a basket.*	

3493	*Guard.* This is the man.	241
3494	*Cleo.* Avoid, and leave him.	242
3495	[*Exit Guardsman.*	
3496	**Hast thou the pretty worm of Nilus there,**	243
	That kills and pains not?	244
	Clown. Truly, I have him: but I would not	245

218 same as 216; less aX; bX: SP1, Cum, KyB
219 same as 218, SP1, Cum, KyB; less bX
220 same as 219

221 X: Cap, Inc, In2, JKP, WM1, JL1, KyB, BT1, OA1, JP1; aX: SP1, Cum,ChC*
222 same as 221, BA1; less aX, bX, B; bX: TN1
223 same as 222, TN1, less KyB, OA1; less bX; bX: SP1, Cum

224 same as 223, SP1, Cum; less bX
225 same as 224; bX: KyB, ML1

226 X: Cap, Inc, In2, WM1; aX: JKP, SP1, Cum, JL1, KyB, BT1, BA1, JP1, TN1
227 X: Inc, In2; R: KyB; aX: Cap; b X: ML1
228 X: Inc, In2; R: KyB; aX: ML1
229 X: Inc, In2; bX: JKP, WM1, HIM, KyB, BT1, BH1; cX: SP1
230 X: Inc, In2, JKP, WM1, LiL, BT1; aX: BH1

231 same as 230; less aX
232 X: Inc, In2 JKP; aX: WM1, LiL, BT1

233
234 X: Inc, In2, JKP, LoC, TaB; aX: KyB, TN1; N: SP1
235 same as 233; less aX, N : N: Cum
same as 233; less aX; bX: KyB, RA1

236 X: Inc, In2, LoC, TaB, RA1; aX: JKP, KyB; bX: BT1, BA1, JP1; MOVE *
237 X: Inc, In2, KyB, LoC, BT1, BA1, TaB, RA1, JP1
238 X: Inc, In2, JKP, JL1, KyB, LiL, EdT, LoC, BT1, BA1, TaB, RA1, JP1*
239 same as 238; less MOVE
240 same as 239, less KyB; aX: KyB; bX: WM1, OA1

241 X: Inc, In2, JKP, BA1, TaB, JP1; R: WM1; aX: JL1, LiL, EdT, LoC, BT1⚡
242 same as 241, ML1; less R, aX, bX, B; R: WM1; aX: Ha1

243 X: Inc, In2, JKP, TaB; R: WM1
244 same as 243 uncluding R
245 same as 243 including R ; bX: Cum

*52:221 Lac, HIM, LoC, SM1, WA1; bX: BA1; R: EdT   *52:236 36b-
37 to follow 202: JKP   *52:238 MOVE 238-240a to follow
213: WM1   *52:241 OA1; bX Ha1, OA1, RA1; B: ML1, ER1

3497	Be the party that should desire you to touch him,	246
3498	for his biting is immortal: those that do die of it	247
3499–3500	do seldom or never recover.	248
	Cleo. Rememberest thou any that have died	
3501	on't? 249	249
	Clown. Very many, men and women too. I	250
3502	heard of one of them no longer than yesterday:	251
3503	a very honest woman, but something given to	252
3504	lie: as a woman should not do, but in the way of	253
3505	honesty: how she died of the biting of it, what	254
3506	pain she felt: truly, she makes a very good	255
	report o' the worm; but he that will believe all	256
3507	that they say, shall never be saved by half that	257
3508	they do: but this is most fallible, the worm's an	258
3509	odd worm.	259
2510	*Cleo.* Get thee hence: farewell. 260	260
3511	*Clown.* I wish you all joy of the worm.	261
3511+1	*[Setting down his basket.*	
3512	*Cleo.* Farewell.	262
	Clown. You must think this, look you, that	263
3513–14	the worm will do his kind.	264
3515	*Cleo.* Ay, ay; farewell.	265
	Clown. Look you, the worm is not to be	266
3516	trusted but in the keeping of wise people; for,	267
3517–18	indeed, there is no goodness in the worm.	268
3519	*Cleo.* Take thou no care; it shall be heeded.	269
	Clown. Very good. Give it nothing, I pray	270
3520–1	you, for it is not worth the feeding. 271	271
3522	*Cleo.* Will it eat me?	272
	Clown. You must not think I am so simple	273
3523	but I know the devil himself will not eat a	274
3524	woman: I know that a woman is a dish for the	275
3525	gods, if the devil dress her not. But, truly,	276
3526	these same whoreson devils do the gods great	277
3527	harm in their women; for in every ten that they	278
3528	make, the devils mar five.	279
3529	*Cleo.* Well, get thee gone; farewell. 280	280
	Clown. Yes, forsooth: I wish you joy o' the	281
3530	worm. *[Exit*	282
3530+;	*Re-enter* IRAS *with a robe, crown, &c.*	
	Cleo. Give me my robe, put on my crown;	
3531	I have	283
3532	Immortal longings in me: now no more	284
3533	The juice of Egypt's grape shall moist this lip:	285
3534	Yare, yare, good Iras; quick. Methinks I hear	286

```
246   same as 243, Cum; same R
247   same as 246 including R⁻  ; bX: Hal
248   same as 246, Hal; same R⁻

249   same as 248, BT1, less Cum; same R
250   same as 249 including R; bX: SP1, Cum, RH1
251   X: Cap, Inc, In2, JKP, SP1, Cum, Hal, BT1, TaB, RH1; R: WM1
252   same as 251 including R; bX: LoC
253   X: Cap, Inc, In2, JKP, WM1, SP1,  Cum, ChC, Hal, LiL, BT1, TaB, RH1*
254   same as 253, GS1; less bX
255   same as 254, TN1, less ChC, LoC; aX: ChC
256   same as 255, less TN1; less aX; bX: SM1, WA1, BH1
257   same as 256, SM1, WA1, BH1, less GS1, RH1 less bX; aX: GS1, RH1; cX,TN1
258   same as 257, less BH1, less aX, cX; aX: BH1
259   same as 258; less aX
260   X: Inc, In2, JKP, WM1, SP1, Hal, BT1, TaB
261   same as 260, Cap, Cum

262   X: Cap, Inc, In2, JKP, WM1, SP1, Cum, Hal, JL1, BT1, OA1, TaB, BH1
263   same as 262, Bel, less Cap, JL1
264   same as 263; R: ML1
265   same as 263, WA1
266   same as 265, less RH1
267   same as 266
268   same as 266
269   same as 266
270   same as 266
271   same as 266
272   X: GCa, Cap, Bel, Inc, In2, JKP, WM1, SP1,  Cum, ChC, Hal, LoC, BT1,*
273   same as 272, RH1
274   same as 273; bX: ML1
275   same as 273, ML1
276   same as 275; bX: JL1, SM1, WA1, BA1; B: EdT
277   same as 275 JL1, SM1, WA1, BA1
278   same as 277
279   same as 277
280   X: Bel, Inc, In2, JKP, WM1, OA1,  TaB, RH1, ML1
281   X: Bel, Inc, In2, JKP, WM1, OA1,  TaB; bX: SP1
282   X: Bel, In2, TaB; aX;OA1; ADD 2: JL1


283   X: Inc, In2, KyB; bX: JKP
284   X: Inc, In2, JKP, KyB; bX: WM1, JL1, EdT; Insert 292-293a: JL1
285   X: Inc, In2, JKP, WM1, JL1, KyB, EdT
286   X: KyB; aX: Inc, In2, WM1, EdT

*52:253 bX: GS1                    *52:272  OA1, TaB
```

3535	Antony call; I see him rouse himself	287
3536	To praise my noble act; I hear him mock	288
3537	The luck of Cæsar, which the gods give men 2¾	289
3538	To excuse their after wrath: husband, I come:	290
3539	Now to that name my courage prove my title!	291
3540	I am fire and air; my other elements	292
3541	I give to baser life. So; have you done?	293
3542	Come then, and take the last warmth of my lips	294
3543	Farewell, kind Charmian; Iras, long farewell.	295
3543+1	[*Kisses them. Iras falls and dies.*	
3544	Have I the aspic in my lips? Dost fall?	296
3545	If thou and nature can so gently part,	297
3546	The stroke of death is as a lover's pinch,	298
3547	Which hurts, and is desired. Dost thou lie still!	299
3548	If thus thou vanishest, thou tell'st the world 300	300
3549	It is not worth leave-taking.	301
	Char. Dissolve, thick cloud, and rain; that I	
3550	may say,	302
3551	The gods themselves do weep!	
3552	*Cleo.* This proves me base:	303
3553	If she first meet the curled Antony,	304
3554	He'll make demand of her, and spend that kiss	305
	Which is my heaven to have. Come, thou mor-	
3555	tal wretch,	306
3555+1	[*To an asp, which she applies to her breast.*	
3556	With thy sharp teeth this knot intrinsicate	307
3557	Of life at once untie: poor venomous fool,	308
3558	Be angry, and dispatch. O, couldst thou speak,	309
	That I might hear thee call great Cæsar ass 310	310
3559	Unpolicied!	
3560	*Char.* O eastern star!	
3561	*Cleo.* Peace, peace!	311
3562	Dost thou not see my baby at my breast,	312
3563	That sucks the nurse asleep?	
3564	*Char.* O, break! O, break!	313
	Cleo. As sweet as balm, as soft as air, as	
3565	gentle,—	314
3566	O Antony!—Nay, I will take thee too:	315
3566+1	[*Applying another asp to her arm.*	
3567	What should I stay— [*Dies.*	316
3568	*Char.* In this vile world? So, fare thee well.	317
3569	Now boast thee, death, in thy possession lies	318
3570	A lass unparallel'd. Downy windows, close;	319
3571	And golden Phœbus never be beheld 320	320
3572	Of eyes again so royal! Your crown's awry;	321
3573	I'll mend it, and then play.	322

SS 942c

287 X: KyB
288 X: KyB; bX: JKP, SM1, OA1, RH1
289 X: JKP, K̄yB, BT1, SM1, WA1, OA1, RH1; bX̱; ChC, LoC
290 X: KyB, BT1; aX: JKP, ChC, LoC, SM1, ŌA1; bX̱: înc, In2, WA1, RH1;*
291 X: WM1, KyB
292 X: JKP, WM1, KyB, EdT; MOVE 292-293a to follow 229: JL1
293 X: JKP, WM1, KyB; aX: Ed̄T
294 X: WM1, KyB
295 X: KyB

296 X: Cap, Inc, In2, WM1, ChC, KyB, LoC, TaB; bX: JL1, EdT
297 X: Cap, Inc, In2, WM1, ChC, JL1, MTh, KyB, ĒdT, LoC, TaB; R:JKP
298 same as 297, JKP; less R;
299 same as 298, less WM1, ĒdT; aX: Hɪᴍ, EdT; bX̱: BT1, ML1
300 same as 299, BT1, ML1; less aX̱, bX
301 X: Cap, Inc, In2, WM1, ChC, L̄oC, B̄T1, TaB, ML1; aX: KyB

302 X: Cap, Inc, JKP, WM1, ChC, LiL, LoC; N: In2; MOVE 302-303a to follow
        313: JL1
303 X: Cap, JKP, WM1, ChC, LoC; aX: LiL; bX̱: Inc, In2, JL1, KyB, TaB; *
304 X: Cap, Inc, JKP, WM1, ChC, J̄L1, KyB, L̄oC, TaB; R: In2
305 same as 304, less Cap; R: In2

306 X: Inc; R: In2; aX: JKP, WM1, ChC, JL1, KyB, LoC, TaB

307 X: Inc; R: In2, JKP
308 same as 307 including R; bX: ML1
309 X: Inc; R: In2; bX: W̄M1, LiL, EdT, BT1
310 X: Inc, Īn2, WM1, LiL, EdT, BT1

311 X: Inc, In2; aX: WM1, LiL, EdT, BT1
312 X: Inc, In2; R̄: WM1

313 R: WM1; aX: In2; bX̱: JKP, Lac, Ha1, HIM, LiL, TaB; ADD 1: Inc

314 R: WM1
315 X̄: WM1; bX̱: Inc, In2, JKP, ChC, Ha1, JL1, KyB, LiL, LoC, BT1, SM1,WA1,
        OA1, RH̄1
316 X: In2, JKP, WM1, ChC, JL1, LiL, LoC, SM1, WA1, OA1, RH1; R: Inc; aX:TN1
317 X: In2, JKP, WM1, Cum, ChC, JL1, LiL, MTh, LoC, TaB; R: Inc; aX: BT1*
318 same as 117; same R; less aX; R: Inc
319 same as 117 including R; less aX̱
320 same as 117, Inc; less R, aX
321 same as 320; bX: KyB
322 same as 120, K̄yB

*52:290 ADD 3: Inc, In2   *52:303 ADD 6: Inc
*52:317 SM̄1, WA1, OA1, RA1

3574   *Enter the* Guard, *rushing in.*

3575   *First Guard.* Where is the queen?
3576   *Char.*   Speak softly, wake her not.   323
3577   *First Guard.* Cæsar hath sent—
3578   *Char.*   Too slow a messenger.   324
3578+1   [*Applies an asp.*
3579 O, come apace, dispatch! I partly feel thee.   325
3580   *First Guard.* Approach, ho! All's not well:
3581   Cæsar's beguiled.   326
      Sec. Guard. There's Dolabella sent from
3582   Cæsar: call him.   327
3583   *First Guard.* What work is here! Charmian,
3584   is this well done?   328
      Char. It is well done, and fitting for a
3585   princess   329
3586 Descended of so many royal kings.   330   330
3587 Ah, soldier!   [*Dies.*   331

3588   *Re-enter* DOLABELLA.

3589   *Dol.* How goes it here?
3590   *Sec. Guard.*   All dead.
3591   *Dol.*   Cæsar, thy thoughts   332
3592 Touch their effects in this: thyself art coming   333
3593 To see perform'd the dreaded act which thou   334
3594 So sought'st to hinder.   335
3506   [*Within* 'A way there, a way for Cæsar!'   336

3595   *Re-enter* CÆSAR *and all his train, marching.*

3597   *Dol.* O sir, you are too sure an augurer;   337
3598 That you did fear is done.
3599   *Cæs.*   Bravest at the last,   338
3600 She levell'd at our purposes, and, being royal, 339   339
3601 Took her own way. The manner of their deaths?   340
3602 I do not see them bleed.
3603   *Dol.*   Who was last with them?   341

323   X: ChC, JL1, LiL, MTh, LoC, TaB; bX: Inc, In2

324   X: In2, ChC, Ha1, JL1, LiL, MTh, LoC, TaB

325   X: Inc, In2, WM1, ChC, Ha1, JL1, KyB, LiL, MTh, LoC, BT1, TaB; Page
          lost: AF1
326   X: JKP, ChC, Ha1, JL1, KyB, LiL, MTh, MTh, LoC, BT1, OA1, TaB, ER1;
          aX: Lac, HIM; bX: In2, JP1, TN1; N: SP1
327   X: In2, JKP, WM1, SP1, ChC, KyB, Cum, Lac, Ha1, JL1, HIM, LiL, MTh,
          LoC, BT1, SM1, WA1, OA1, TaB, BH1, ER1, LK1, TN1; B; Inc
328   X: ChC, Ha1, JL1, KyB, LiL, MTh, LoC, OA1, TaB; aX: JKP, WM1, SP1,
          Cum, Lac, HIM, BT1, LK1; N: BT1
329   X: ChC, Ha1, JL1, KyB, LiL, MTh, LoC ; R: In2
330   same as 329, In2; less R
331   X: In2, WM1, ChC, Lac, Ha1, JL1, KyB, LiL, MTh, EdT, LoC. OA1, TaB;
          R: Inc; aX: JKP, Cum

332   same as 131, Inc, HIM, BT1, ML1, ER1; less R, aX; aX: JP1; bX:WA1; *
333   same as 332, WA1, LK1, less RH1, ML1; less aX, bX, abX; aX: RA1,RH1*
334   same as 333, BT1, TN1; less aX, bX
335   same as 334, less WA1; aX: WA1
336   same as 335, BH1, JP1

337   X: WM1, Cum, Lac, Ha1, JL1, HIM, KyB, LiL, MTh, BT1, SM1, TaB, LK1;
          N: SP1; ADD 1: EdT
338   X: JL1, LiL, MTh, OA1, TaB, LK1; aX: Ha1, KyB, BT1, RH1; ADD 1: EdT;*
339   same as 338; less aX, ADD, Insert; bX: TN1
340   X: JL1, LiL, MTh, OA1, TaB, LK1, R: WM1; bX: SP1, Cum, ChC, Lac, Ha1,
          HIM, KyB, EdT, LoC, BT1, SM1, WA1, RA1, GS1, RH1, JP1, ER1, TN1;*
341   X:
          SP1, Cum, ChC, Lac, Ha1, JL1, HIM, KyB, LiL, MTh, EdT, LoC, BT1,
          SM1, WA1, OA1, BA1, TaB, RA1, GS1, RH1, JP1, ER1, LK1, TN1; R: In2,
          WM1; bX: Inc, JKP

*52:332 abX: LK1   *52:333 ML1; bX: BT1, TN1
*52:338 Insert 149b–151a: RH1   *52:340 ADD 10: ChC

3604   *First Guard.* A simple countryman, that
        brought her figs: 342

3605 This was his basket.

3606   *Cæs.*   Poison'd, then.

3607   *First Guard.*   O Cæsar,   343

3608 This Charmian lived but now; she stood and
        spake: 344

3609 I found her trimming up the diadem   345

3610 On her dead mistress; tremblingly she stood   346

3611 And on the sudden dropp'd.

3612   *Cæs.*   O noble weakness!   347

3613 If they had swallow'd poison, 'twould appear   348

3614 By external swelling: but she looks like sleep,   349

3615 As she would catch another Antony   **350**   350

3616 In her strong toil of grace.

3617   *Dol.*   Here, on her breast,   351

3618 There is a vent of blood and something blown: 352

3619 The like is on her arm.   353

3620   *First Guard.* This is an aspic's trail: and
        these fig-leaves   354

3621 Have slime upon them, such as the aspic leaves   355

3622 Upon the caves of Nile.

3623   *Cæs.*   Most probable   356

3624 That so she died; for her physician tells me   357

3625 She hath pursued conclusions infinite   358

3626 Of easy ways to die.   Take up her bed;   359

3627 And bear her women from the monument: **360**   360

3628 She shall be buried by her Antony: 361

3629 No grave upon the earth shall clip in it   362

3630 A pair so famous.   High events as these   363

3631 Strike those that make them; and their story is   364

3632 No less in pity than his glory which   365

3633 Brought them to be lamented.   Our army shall   366

3634 In solemn show attend this funeral;   367

3635 And then to Rome.   Come, Dolabella, see   368

3636 High order in this great solemnity.   [*Exeunt.*   369

SS 943b

342 same as 241, JKP; less R, bX; R: Inc, In2, WM1

343 same as 342, WM1, RH1, less SP1, GS1; less R; R: Inc $\frac{In2}{7}$; aX: SP1, GS1;
     bX: IP1
344 same as 343, In2, SP1, IP1; less R, aX, bX; R: Inc
345 same as 344, Inc; less R
346 same as 345; bX: ML1

347 same as 345, ML1, less JP1; aX: JP1
348 same as 347 GS1, less ML1; less aX
349 X: Inc, In2, WM1, SP1, Cum, ChC, Lac, Ha1, JL1, HIM, KyB, LiL, MTh,*
350 same as 349; less aX, MOVE

351 same as 350, less Inc; aX: Inc; bX: RH1, ML1, ER1, TN1; Insert 138b-* C
352 same as 351, Inc, RH1, ML1, ER1, TN1; less aX,bX, Insert ; bX: JKP
353 same as 352, JKP; less bX

354 same as 353, less Inc, In2, JKP; aX: Inc, In2
355 same as 354; less aX

356 same as 355; bX: GS1
357 same as 355, GS1; bX: IP1
358 same as 357, IP1; less bX
359 same as 358, less EdT, BT1; aX: EdT, BT1; bX: Inc, In2, JKP, BA1
360 same as 359, In2, JKP, BA1;less aX, bX; R: Inc
361 X: JL1, KyB, LiL, MTh, OA1, TaB, LK1
362 X: Inc, In2, JL1, KyB, LiL, MTh, OA1, TaB, LK1
363 same as 362; bX: ChC, Lac, Ha1, HIM, EdT, LoC, BT1, SM1, WA1, BH1
364 X: Inc, In2, ChC, Lac, Ha1, JL1, HIM, KyB, LiL, MTh, EdT, LoC, BT1,SM1*
365 same as 364, TN1, less RH1; less bX
366 X: Inc, In2, JL1, KyB, LiL, MTh, OA1, TaB, LK1; aX: ChC, Lac, Ha1, HIM*
367 same as 366; less aX; aX: ChC
368 X: JL1, KyB, LiL, MTh, OA1,TaB, LK1; bX: ChC, HIM, EdT, LoC, WA1, TN1;*
369 X: ChC, JL1, HIM, KyB, LiL, MTh, EdT, LoC, WA1, OA1, TaB, LK1, TN1;
        ADD 59: Inc, In2

*52:349 EdT, LoC, BT1, SM1, WA1, OA1, BA1, TaB, RA1, LK1; aX: JKP, IP1, GS1,
    RH1, JP1, ER1, TN1; MOVE 349b-351a to follow 338: RH1
*52:251 140a: TN1   *52:164WA1, OA1, TaB, RH1, LK1; bX: TN1
*52:366 EdT, LoC, BT1, SM1, WA1, RH1, TN1   *52:368 N: BT1, JP1

BIBLIOGRAPHY FOR   C Y M B E L I N E

J W1   Mr William Shakespeare, Comedies, Histories and Tragedies.
           London: Jaggard, 1623 (J "The First Folio")
         Kokeritz facsimily. New Haven: Yale U Press, 1954
         No deviation from Globe

C CY1   The Injured Princess, Thomas Durfey. London: Bentley, 1682
         BM 644/b14; Folger PR2734/D'Urfey
         Essentially a new play

J CY2   London: Tonson, Works of Shakespeare 1734
         U Mich RBR uncataloged
         Full text

J CY3   London: Walker, Dramatic Works of William Shakespeare, 1735,
           vol 7
         Folger PR2752/1734-35/Sh Col
         Full text

J CY4   'Charles Marsh.' London: author, 1755
         edition not seen

J CY5   'Charles Marsh.' 1758
         edition not seen

J CY7   'Charles Marsh.' London: author, 1759   ChM
         U Mich RBR PR2806/A22/M56/1759; BM 11763/e19; Nuffield
           50.06/vers 1759 (Ac 13305)

J CY6   'William Hawkins.' London: Rivington, 1759
         U Mich RBR PR822.8/H77/ BM 643/g12; Folger PR2806.1759/
           Copy 1/Sh Col
         Not more than 25% Shakespeare

J CY8   'With alterations by David Garrick. London: n p, 1761   G61
         Folger PR2806/A14/Sh Col
         Portion of the 5th act in italics--cut after first perform-
           ance

J CY9   London: Tonson, 1762
         BM 11763/ppp30; U Mich PR2806/A22/G24/1762a; Nuffield 38
           Coll/3035/3036a/3037; Folger PR1241/Ale/Cage/vol 3; BPL
           S315/1762 (Ac 2773; Cornmarket
         Duplicate of Garrick 1761(J CY8--G61)

J CY10   'Charles Marsh.' London: author, 1762
         Folger PR2806/1762b/Sh Col
         Identical with Marsh, 1759(J CY7--ChM)

J CY8b   'David Garrick.' Dublin: Watts, 1762
         BM 640/h29
         Dyuplicate of Garrickm 1761(J CY8--G61)

S CY44A3 "Mrs Cairn, Stephen Green"(Hand)
        Folger PB CY14; Folger FILM F)/301c.45
        PB in Dublin, Garrick(J CY8b–G61); CUT: 13: 30b–35a; 16:
          4b–9a, 176a, 178b–183a; 36: 12–17a, 53b–55a; ADD: 1 after
          11 4

SS   Dramatic Works of DAVID Garrick
         Harvard U TC)81/Ndo
         Duplicate of 1798

J CY11   'With alterations by David Garrick.' London: Woodfall and
         Rivington, 1767
         Folger PR2806/1767/Copy 1/Sh Col; BM 11783/de24
         Duplicate of Garrick 1671(J CY8––G61)

S CY1   "Thomas Hull"(Hand, S :1767")
         Folger PB CY3
         "Study book"(S) in Woodfall(J CY11–G61); CUT: 14: 105; 24:
          57a, 97b–98a, 131–132, 137b–138a, 146B; 25: 2a, 5b–6a,
          15–16; 33: 21b–26, 47b–49a, 53b–55a, 84b–86a; 36: 82–87a;
          42: 245–246a, 249b, 303b–308; 51: 11b–15, 22b–24a, 29b–
          30; 55: 23–68, 215b–217a, 267–268a; ADD: 1 after 51: 29a

J CY12   'David Garrick.' London: Rivington, 1770
         U Mich RBR PR2806/A22/G24/1770
         Duplicate of Garrick 1761(J CY8-G61)

J CY13   London: Bell, 1774, vol 2 (single play "1773")   Bel
         U Mich RBR Uncataloged

J W59   London: Bell, 'second edition,' 1774
         BM 1609/1349
         Identical with Bell(J CY13––Bel

J Gar 6   Dramatic Works of David Garrick. London: Bald, 1774(J "n p"
         Harvard U, Houghton Library *EC75/01932/1774d; Folger
         microfilm of it
         Duplicate of Garrick 1761(J CY8-G61)

SS CY302 "Excerpt from Garrick Works"(no indication of date)   GaW
         Folger PR2806/A14/Sh Col

SS CY303 London: Oxlade, 1777   Oxl
         BM 11765/a52

J CY14   London: Wenman, 1777, vol 1 $19   Wen
         BM 11770/g1; BM 1474/bb9; Folger PR1241/T38/vol 1/Cage
          (possibly Theatrical Magazine)

J CY15   Henry Brooke, 1778
         Not seen. UCB "from Jaggard"

J CY16   'With alterations.' London, n p, 1780
            J assigns to Warwick; I could not find in Huntington Cat-
            alog; not seen

J CY17   'Garrick.' London: Bathurst, 1784   Bat
            BM 11764/bbb7; BPL S316/1784 (Ac 13419; Nuffield 50.06/ vers
            1781 (Ac 2056)

S CY44C   "Anonymous"(S)
            Nuffield 50.06/vers 1784(Ac 3322)
            PB in Bathurst(J CY17--Bat-; CUT: 11: 1 added after 4, 2
            added after 27, 55R; 14: 75b-76a, 89b-107, 144-149, 161b-
            162a; 16: 39-50a, 68b-74, 85b-93a, 99b-112a, 119b-120a,
            130-135, 152b-153a; 24: 142-143; 25: all; 34: 36b-37a,
            39b-41a, 158b-170; 53: 70b-73a; 55: 61b-62a, 144b-145a,
            213b-214a, 220b-223

SS CY307   Noble Peasant 'Glees, Choruses, etc' London: Robinson, 1786
            Oxford U, Bodlian, Douces/134
            No text

S CY2   "James Bates, Covent Garden, ante 1784"(S)
            Harvard U Widener 13484/22/50
            PB in Rivington(J CY12--G61); CUT: 14: 161b-162a, 163b-166a,
            182-184; 16: 41-43, 65a, 104b, 118-119a, 123b-124, 134-135,
            139b-140; 22: 16b-18a, 22b-23a, 40b-42a; 24: 9-26a, 74b-
            76a, 88b-91a, 95b-98a, 132-133a, 137b-138a; 33: 21b-26,
            40-44a; 36: 36b-37, 69b-71a, 73N; 42: 30N, 31N, 176b-183a;
            44: 3b-7a; 55: 260b

S CY3   "Lumley St George Skeffington, Hackney School, c 1785"(S)
            Folger PB CY10
            PB in Bathurst(J CY17--Bat); CUT: 11: 35a; 14: 21b-23a, 59a,
            60b-61a, 70b-71a, 83b-100, 106b-108, 113b-115, 135-139,
            151b-152a, 155a; 16: 43-55, 76-77a, 79b-86, 104b-113a,
            121-134, 143b-151a, 156-162, 164, 166a, 168R, 180b-181a;
            21: 19B; 22: 11, 19b-21a, 24b-26a, 43b-45a; 23: 17b-18,
            20-28, 31b-32a; 24: 53b-55a, 63b-65a, 71a, 84-85, 135a,
            137b-142a, 150c, 157b-160, 167R, 170-186, 189b, 195-230;
            31: 55; 34: 39b-40a, 42b-44a, 182b-196, 198a; 51: 11b-15,
            26b-27a, 29b-30; 53: 7b-8a, 9a, 11a, 30b-33a, 61-74, 79b-
            82a, 93-106; 54: all; 55: 32b-33a, 44b-46a, 53054a, 64a,
            75b, 162b-164a, 176b-177a, 260-263a, 276-277, 492-494;
            RESTORE: 36: 36-38

J CY18   London: Proprietors, sold by Randall, 1785(J "1788")
            U Mich RBR PR2806/A22/G29/1788; BM 11761/b2
            Duplicate of Garrick 1761(J CY8--G61

S CY4   "William Warren, New Th, Philadelphia"(Hand, S "York, 1788")
            Library Co of Philadelphia, Eng Shak/Cym 1786/Oe2+/11608D
            PB in Bell, 1786; CUT: 11: 18b-19a; 34: 39b-41a; 43: 36-46

SS 943f CYMBELINE Biblio

J CY19 n 1, n p, 1790
   Not seen; UCB gives "from Jaggard"

J CY22 London: Proprietors, n d (J "c1795")   P95
   Folger PR2806/A12/Sh Col

J CY23 London: Barker, 1795   Bar
   BM 643/i4

SS CY304 Dublin: Grueber, 1795
   BM 11765/g28
   Full text

? J Gar7 Dramatic Works of David Garrick, Lndon: n p, 1798
   BM 641/d8; Harvard, Widener
   Duplicate of Garrick 1761,J CY8--G61), but does not men-
    tion cut in 55

J CY25 Kemble, 1800
   Not seen; UCB: "from Jaggard"

J CY26 London: Lowdnes, 1801 (J "n p")   Low
   U Mich, Clements Library C/1801/Sh, "Mrs Siddons' copy';
    U Cambridge, Nn 15.10(837/91), "missing since 1957;"
    Huntington Plays vol 367; U Ill RBR x792.9/Sh 15 cy/No 1

SS 400 "Mrs Sissons"(Clements)
   U Mich , Clements Library c/1801/Sh
   PB in Lowndes(J CY26--Low); 2 short cuts

S CY5 "J Meggett"(S)
   U Ill, RBR x792.9/Sh 15 cy/No 1
   Comments in Lowndes(J CY26--Low); no cuts

S CY6 "George Frederick Cooke, Covent Gardenm 1806"(S)
   Harvard U TC 13484/22/45
   Rolebook in Lowndes(J CY26--Low); no cuts

S CY7 "George Frederick Cooke, 1806"(S)
   Folger PB CY12
   PB in Barker(J CY23--Bar); CUT: 15: 163b-166a; 16: 118;
    24: 69R, 70R; RESTORE: 55: 144b-146a; Cut only in Iach-
   imo scenes

J CY30 London: Roach, 1806   Roa
   Nuffield 50.06/vers 1806 (Ac 1937)

J CY31 'Mrs Inchbald.' London: Longman, n d (J "1808") Inc
   U Mich PR1243/I37/vol 4; BM 1345/al; Folger PR2806/A11/
    Sh Col

J CY32 'Kemble.' London: for Theatre, 1810   JKT
   Folger PR2806/1810/Copy 1/Sh Col; Nuffield 50.06/vers 1810
    Ac 981)

S CY8 "J P Kemble, Covent Garden, 1812"(S)
    Nuffield 50.06/vers 1810 (Ac 981); Folger: micro-
     film of it FILM Acc 479
    PB in Theatre(J CY32--JKT); CUT: 13: 28b-30a; 15:
     57b-60a, 73b-74, 78b-82a, 161b-163a; 16: 62b-63a; 21: 57-
     62; 23: 1 added after 44, 32b-35, 3 added after 35, 99-
     107; 24: 17b-20a, 3 added after 26a, 133b, 150-152; 32:
     49b-55a, 71-73a, 85-98a; 35: 56-65; 34: 15-16, 48b-58a;
     42: 187b-190a; 43: 36-46; 52: 8-10; 53: 78b-83, 409b-
     410a

S CY9 "J P Kemble"(S)
    Garrick Club
    Director's notes in Theatre(J CY32--JKT); no cuts

SS CY401 "J P Kemble," "Mrs Wister"(Hand)
    Folger PB ?; JPKPB
    PB in Theatre(J CY32--JKT); CUT: 24: 5-7a, 17b-20a, 23b-
     25a, 127-128, 133a; 51: 2b-5a, 9-17a, 19b-22a, 26b-29a;
     53: 60-70a, 73b, 78b-83

SS CR413 "J P Kemble"(Folger)
    Folger PB CY18
    Rolebook in Theatre(J CY32--JKT); CUT: 51: 2b-5a, 9b-13a,
     15b-18a, 22b-25; 53: 66-82

J CY33 "John Philip Kemble Select British Theatre. London: Miller,JKM
    1815
    U Mich RBR PR822.08/K31

SS CY414 "F Brown"(Hand)
    Harvard U, Widener 13484/22/55
    Rolebook in Kemble-Miller(J CY33--JKM; no cut

J W173 'Mrs Inchbald.' London: Hurst, 'new edition,' n d (J
    '1816")
    BUS 6557/54/1
    Identical with Inchbald(J CY31--Inc)

J CY35 Oxberry Edition. London: for Proprietors by Simpkin, 1821 Oxb
    BM 11770/f12
    Note by Mrs Cairns: "Identical with Dublin Garrick"(J CY8--
     G61)

J CY36 London: Cumberland, n d (J "1823")
    BM 642/al
    Identical with Cumberland 1829(J CY38--Cum); I have not
     been able to distinguish "1823" from "1829," and assign-
     ments between them are conjectural.

J CY36b London: Dolby, 1823
    Folger PR2806/1823b/Sh Col
    Identical with Cumberland(J CY38--Cum)

J CY37   <u>Oxberry Edition</u>. Boston: Wells, 1823 (J places 1823 in Lon-- USW
               don.)
               Folger PR2806/1823a/Copy 2/Sh Col

J CY38   London: Cumberland, <u>Cumberland's British Theatre</u>, n d (J   Cum
               "1829"), vol 2
               U Mich PR822.08/C97/Vol 2; U Mich RBR PR2806/A22/D18/ n d
               (single, "Davidson" on cover); BM 11768/aa7 "1829;" BPL
               Ac 57436, vol 5 "1831;" Folger PR2806/A2a/Sh Col;

J CY38b   London: Davidson, n d
               Folger PR2806/A2b/Sh Col; U Mich RBR uncataloged
               Identical with Cumberland(J CY38--Cum)

S CY10   "Macready, 1843"(S)   WM1
               Folger PB CY17
               PB in <u>Works</u>

S CY11   "Macready, 1843"(S) "C Kean PB"(Hand)
               Folger PB CY7
               PB in <u>Works</u>; deviations from Macready(S CY10--WM1); CUT:
                 <u>11</u>: 50b-54a, 154-156a, 158b-164, 166-178; <u>12</u>: all; <u>13</u>:
                 28b-30a; <u>14</u>: 75-77a, 147-148a; <u>15</u>: 1-3, 44b-45; <u>16</u>: 41b-
                 43a, 108b-110a, 119b-123a, 129b-130, 147-148a, 150b-152a,
                 153b-155a, 159b-162a; <u>21</u>: 50-51, 57-70; <u>22</u>: 17b-18a; <u>24</u>;
                 88b-91a, 97b-98a, 126b-128; <u>32</u>: 56b-61a; <u>33</u>: 4b-7a, 8-9a;
                 <u>34</u>: 15-16a, 22B, 46b, 48b-51a, 56-58a, 76b-80a, 99, 102-
                 105a, 112b-114a, 177b-182a, 192b-193; <u>35</u>: 151-155a, 159b-
                 167; <u>36</u>: 84b-86; <u>42</u>: 10-14a, 16b-20a, 72b-74a, 167b-169a,
                 189, 196-197a, 234b-240, 253b-254a, 258-275; <u>55</u>: 356b-
                 363a; <u>RESTORE</u> lines cut by Macready <u>23</u>: 15a; <u>34</u>: 51b-
                 54, 106-112a, 173b-175a; <u>36</u>: 34; <u>42</u>: 103

S CY12   "Macready, 1843"(S)
               Folger PB CY8
               Scene maquettes for play "Th Royal, Drury Lane, Season
               1843-44;" no text

S CY13   "Macready 1843"(S)
               Folger PB CY9
               Costume designs for play "Th Royal, Drury Lane, 1843-44;"
               no text

S CY14   "Helen Faucit, c1845"(S)   HnF
               Folger PB CY2
               PB in Knight, 1843

S CY15   "Charles Kean, Princess's Th, London, c 1850"(S) "John Rose,
               Prompter, 1852, Providence, R I"(Hand)
               Harvard U TC TS/2438/300
               PB in <u>Works</u>, no cuts

S CY16 "John Moore, 1850s(S)
    Folfwe PB CY6
    PB in Bell(J CY13--Bel); CUT: 15: 4 added after 29a, 47b-
     48a, 75a, 78b-82a; 14: 20c, 103-105, 130b-132, 161b-162a,
     163b-166a; 21: 3B, 16B, 50-51, 3 added after 56, 57-62;
     23: 1-20, 33b-34a; 24: 148-152; 25: 1-8a, 9-12a, 14b-16;
     33: 21b-26; 34: 48b-59a, 102-118; 42: 9b-14a, 196-197a; 53:
     3 added after 28; 55: 147b-157, 213b-215a, 222-225a, 233a,
     302-305a, 368b-370a; RESTORE: 42: 261, 268-273, 280-281;
     53: 53-55a, 60-62, 63b, 89b-91, 93b-94; ADD: 2 after 25:
     35, 3 after 51: 33

S CY17 "John Moore, 1850s"(S)
    Folger PB CY5
    PB in Wells(J CY37--USW); CUT: 11: 46-47; 21: 16B; 23: 1-20;
     24: 48-49a; 33: 16-21a, 45-73a; 42: 47b-49a; 53: 3 added
     after 28, 84-87a; 55: 301b-305a, 382-387, 391b-395a

SS CY412 "Shakespeare Restoration by F Haywell, " "circa 1852"(Hand)
    Nuffield 50.06/vers 1852 (Ac 7196)
    Marked for Postumous and Pisano; only to extent of restor-
     ations is this a PB; not collated

S CY44A2 "Anonymous"(S)
    Folger PB CY13
    PB in Vicker's Penny Shakespeare(J W536, 1852); CUT: 15:
     5-8, 48b-60, 7 of add after 81; 44: all; 53: all; others
     unclear

J CY40 London: Lacy, n d, vol 64 (J "1865")
    U Mich 822.08/L15/vol 64; BM 2304/f9; Nuffield 50.21/ vers
     1859 (Ac 2548, f96)

J CY40b London and NY: French, n d
    U Mich RBR, uncataloged; Nuffield 50.06/vers 187- (Ac 3010,
     f 97); Nuffield 39/183-/186- (Ac 916); Nuffield O S P
     50.06/vers 187-(Ac 3725, f 103); Nuffield 50.21/vers
     1867 (Ac 2548, f 96); Harvard U, Widener 13484/22/95
    Identixal with Lacy(J CY40--Lac)

S CY40B "John Swinburne PH"(S)
    Harvard U, Widener 13484/22/95
    PB in French-Lacy(J CY40b--Lac)1 CUT: 11: 138-140, 156b, 176b-
     178; 14: 34b-39; 15: 1-3, 75b-85a; 21: 15; 23: 1-18, 28-63;
     24: 60b-61a, 146-1591 34: 84-99a, 132b-135a, 180b-185; 35:
     71-74a, 141b-167; 42: 49-51a, 66-67, 251b-253a, 282-283, 333-
     403; 44: all; 52: 1-7; 55: 25b-34, 100b-110a, 117-119a, 338b-
     352a, 363b-368a, 372b-402a, 421, 475b-482

S CY18 "Samuel Phelps, Sadler's Wells, 1857"(S)
    British Th Museum, stored at V&A, Enthoven Coll, 1976
    PB in Cumberland(J CY38--Cum);CUT: 14: 147-148a, 161b-162a,
     182-184; 15: all; 24: 133a, 146a; 42: 189-190a, 192b-194,
     203b-206a, 213b-215a, 224b-227, 230-233a, 235b-236a, 241-

242a, 246b-249a, 251b-253a, 255-257, 270-283a, 299b-202a,
309-314a, 316b-325, 328bm 330-336, 343b-353a, 363b-365a,
371b-374a, 376b-379a, 380, 384b-386a; 43: 13b-16a, 35b; 52:
8-17, 18; 53: 28b-31, 32b-34a, 36b-37a, 43-50, 51b-65; 54:
all; 55: 180b; ADD 1 after 14: 181, 1 after 23: 14, 3 after
23: 328, 3 after 51: 33, 2 after 52: 7

S CY19   "James Taylor, 1867"(S)
Harvard U TC James Taylor uncataloged
Study book in Cumberland(J CY38--Cum); no cuts

J W809   Charles Kemble's Shakespeare Readings. London: Bell, 1870   KRe
U Mich RBR uncataloged; BM 11764/bbb24, vol 1; BM 11766/
bbb8, 'School Shakespeare'

J CY42   London: Williams, 1872, 'arranged for representation at   Rig
the Queens' Th(George Rignolds as Posthumous)
Folger PB2806/1872/Deck B/Sh Col

S CY20   "Adelaide Neilsen, Daly's Fifth Ave Th, NY, 1877"(S) "John
Moore, Prompter"(Hand)
Harvard U TC 13484/22/81
PB in Davidson(J CY38b--Cum); CUT: 11: 1N, 3N, 76b-79a,
104b-106a, 1 added after 131; 14: 42-45; 15: 51b-60a,
4 of add after 87; 23: 31b-68; 23: 60b-61a, 146b-152;
34: 98b-101a, 182b-187, 196b; 35: 104b-105, 159b-160;
42: 195b, 1 added after 201, 333-336; 43: all; 52: all;
53: 1-65; 55: 7b-10, 379-384, 392-395a; RESTORE: 25:
1-2a, 6b-8, 13-15a, 19b-35; 35: 66-69; 42: 215b-224a,
233b-235a, 236b-240, 242b, 272-275, 283b-290; ADD: 1
after 11: 13, 1 after 25: 35, 3 after 55: 391; MOVE:
23: 1-31a to follow 21: 34; 44: 1-54 to follow 42: 336;
DOES NOT MOVE: 21: 62-70 ro follow 15: 87

J CY49   London: New Shakespeare Society, Trubner, 1883
U Mich RBR PR2888/N53/ser 2/No 11
Collation of 1st, 2nd, 3rd abd 4th Folios by W J Craig

SS CY306   'Mme Helena Modjeska.' Indianapolis: Hasselman Journal Co▯M1
1883
Library of Congress PR2806/A2/N6

S CY21   "Miss Allyn, Stratford-upon-Avon, 1884"(S)
O S D 50.06/vers 187-
Rolebook in French(late Lacy)(J CY40b--Lac); S says "much
cut and rearranged'; I found none

S CY22   "Helena Modjeska, Fourteenth St Th, NY, 1888(S)"Marked
for J Stark as played by Mr Macready at Walnut St Th,
Philadelphia, 1853"(Hand)
Folger PB CY11
Notes in French(J CY40b--Lac); CUT: 15: 72b-75a; 16: 130-
131a; 24: 18b-20a; 55: 382-395a. AT back pp of 42 that
may indicate restorations

J CY54 and J W930 Memorial Theatre Edition, C E Flower. London:French MTh
and Stratfoed-upon-Avon: Boyden, n d (J "1889"
U Mich RBR PR2806/A22/F64; BPL S188/2D (Ac 102487)

J W1070   <u>Henry Irving Shakespeare</u>, Henry Irving and Frank A Marshall HIM
            London: Blackie, 1888
            U Mich 822.8/S53/1888-90/I7

S CY23   "William Seymour, c 1890"(S)   WmS
            Princeton U RBR Seymour Coll, Sox SF2
            PB in French(J CY40b--Lac)

S CY24   "Henry Irving, Lyceum Th, London, 1896"(S)   HIL
            Folger PB CY4
         "Preparation copy"(S) in London: Cassell, 1892

J CY60   'Henry Irving.' London: Chiswick, 1896   HIC
            BM 11664/i20; U Mich TBR PR2806/A22/I72; Nuffield 50.06/
               vers 1896 (Ac 5563, f 119); Nuffield 5006/vers 1896
               (Ac 5294, f 97),
            Proof sheets of full text in preparation for rapidly pre-
            paring a cut version for publication on opening night

S CY25   "Ellen Terry, 1896, Lyceum Th, London"(S)
            Smallhythe
            Rolebook in Hunter ed, Longman-Green 1890; <u>CUT: 32</u>: 58b-60a,
               61b-63a; <u>34</u>: 47-66a, 78b-80a, 82, 86b-98a, <u>102-114</u>, 117-
               143a, 171-175a; <u>37</u>: all; <u>42</u>: 309-312; <u>55</u>: 170-178a, 179B,
               184b-185a, 186a, <u>193b-195a</u>, 199-201, 206b-208a, 230a

S CY26   "Ellen Terry"
            Smallhythe
             Notes in Irving-Chiswick(J CY60--HIC); only 1 lines under-
            lined

S Cy27   "Ellen Terry"(S)
            Smallhythe
             Notes In Irving-Chiswick(J CY60--HIC); a few pencil marks

S CT44A1   "Arnold Daly"(S)
            Folger PB CY1
            BP in Cassell, NY, n d; no cuts

S CY28   "Viola Allen, New Nation Th, Washington, D C, 1906(S)   ViA
            NYPL TC *NCP 330695B
            Typed script

S CY29   "Viola Allen, 1906"(S)
             Folger PB CY/ Folio 1
            Extensive notes "by William Winter, 1905"(Hand); no text

S CY30   "Viola Allen, 1906"(S)
             Folger PB AY-122
            5 pp of notes on direction; no text

S CY31a   "Charles B Hanford, 1910(S)   Han
            Folger PB CY15
            PB in Philadelphia, Alteman, n d

S CY31b   "Hanford"(S)
         Folger PB CY16
         Less developed PB than Hanford(S CY31a--Han); not collated

S CY32   "W Bridges-Adams, 1922"(Hand)   STRATFORD-UPON-AVON BA1
         Nuffield O S 71.21/1922/C (Ac 3685,f89)

J W1070b Henry Irving Shakespeare, Henry Irving and Frank A Marshall.
         London: Gresham , 1922
         BM 11763/t7
         Identical with Irving-Marshall(J W1070--HIM)

SS CY407 "H K Aylift, 1923, Modern Dress"(Hand)
         Birmingham Repertory Th Archives
         PB in Heinemann, 1904; CUT: 15: 25-26a, 33-34a, 42b-44a;
           21: 57-70; 23: 69-80, 121-129a, 132b-136a; 25: 15b-17a;
           32: 1b-6a, 7-9a, 19b-22a, 54b-59a; 33: 82-98; 34: 6b-
           10a, 35b-41a, 60-66a, 86b-98a, 162b-168a; 37: all; 42:
           132b-143a, 176b=181a, 363b-366a; 43: all; 54: 11b-21a,
           24-26a, 30-122, 124-132; 55: 8b-83a, 85b-90a, 162-168a,
           175b-181a, 186b-191a, 202-208, 248b-258a, 282-286a, 291-
           297a, 309b-315a, 327v-333a, 357b-363a, 282-401a, 422b-
           475a

S CY33   "E H Sothern and Julia Marlowe, Jolson Th, NY, 1923"(S)
         MCNY 43/430/632
         "Preparation copu of Julia Marlowe"(S) in full text; Dev-
           iations from S&M(S CY34--SM1 ; CUT: 11 76b-79a, 153b-
           156a, 165-169a; 14: 162; 15: 31b-32, 63b-64a, 96b-98a;
           21: 56, 63-66a; 22: 29; 23: 122b-129a; 24: 6b-10a, 126-
           128a, 142b-143a, 151b-152a; 25: 1-5a, 6b-8, 25-26; 31:
           2b-4a, 6-7a, 50-53a, 54a, 70-77; 32: 2b-5, 8-9a, 13b;
           32:20b-23a, 77-79a; 34: 118b-120a, 155-158a. 188-109a;
           35: 140b-141a; 42: 6, 149b-151a, 190-192, 206b-211a,
           212b-215a, 264-269, 338b-339a, 400b-402a; 55: 124-127,
           181; RESTORE: 12: 1-2, 6b-12, 15, 22, 26-28, 36-37, 39-
           43; 14: 47-49a; 15: 42b-43a; 16: 102b-103; 23: 52b-54a;
           24: 13b-15a, 16; 32: 12-16; 34: 6b-8a, 12b-14a; 35: 19b-
           29a, 56, 77; 36: 6b-8a; 42: 9b-14a, 25-27, 113b-114a,
           116-117a, 326-328, 375-379a; 53: 1-20; 55: 312b-313a;
           MOVE: 25: 9-33a to follow 24: 149a; DOES NOT MOVE 31:
           48-54, 11b-14, 42 to follow 23: 63; 53: 24-27 to fol-
           low 52: 13; 55: 382-398 to follow 55: 485

S CY34   "Sothern and Marlow, 1923"(S)   SM1
         MCNY 43/430/633
         "Preparation book"(S)

S CY35   "Sothern and Morlowe, 1923"(S)
         MCNY 43/430/634
         PB in pencil; deviations from S&M(S CY34--SM1); CUT: 12:
           all; 14: 34b-36a, 83-85; 16: 96b-98a, 151-159a; 21: all;
           31: all except transfers; 32: 2b-6a, 7b-9a, 18b-22a;

34: 188-190a; 41: all; 42: 9b-14a, 190-192, 206b-211a,
212b-215a, 338b-339a, 381, 391b-392a; 41: 9-14a; 53: 85-
88a; 55: 85b-91a, 124b-127a, 382b-389, 394-387a; RESTORE:
32: 59-60a; 34: 6b-8a, 39b-41, 173b-175a, 176b-178a; 42:
109-110, 309-311, 316b-317a, 321-323a, 324b-328; 44: 2-
7a; 53: 79-83; Page missing 33: 61-107

S CY36   "Sothern and Marlowe, 1923"(S)
          NYPL TC *NCP 280791B
          "Preparation copy(S) in Temple; eeviations from S&M(S CY34--
          SM1) CUT: 14: 2-3, 33b-35, 57b-59a, 142-143, 147-148a, 162-
          163, 166b-167; 15: 1b-7a; 21: 2-3a, 11-15a; 22: 29-30;
          23: 108-110, 128b-129a; 24: 6b-10a, 61b-66a, 126-128a,
          142-146, 149b-152; 25: 1-5a, 6b-8; 31: 27; 32: 12-17a,
          77-79a; 34: 87-98a, 116-118a, 122b-123a, 155-156a, 192b-
          193a; 36: 59b-71a; 42: 149b-151s, 206b-211a, 212b-215a;
          54: all; 55: 141-142a, 385-398; RESTORE: 15: 31b-32, 43-
          43a; 16: 43b-46; 34: 6b-8a, 12b-14a, 39b-41, 74-75a, 173b-
          178a, 184-185a; 36: 6b-8a, 21-22a; 42: 9b-14a, 316b-317a,
          325b-328; 53: 70b-73a; 55: 117-118a, 128-129a, 151-152a,
          313b-315a, 318-319a, 326-327a, 328-329a

S CY37   "Sothern and Marlowe, 1923"(S) "M Gilcan"(Hand)
          MCNT 43/430/631A, B, C
          S says "final script. I saw only light plot; no text

SS CY415 "Sothern and Marlowe," "V H Collins, 1119 Rosalind Ave, LA
          Calif"(Hand)
          NYPL TC Restricted Material, 44x220
          Deviations from S&M(S CY34--SM1); CUT: 11: 154-156a; 12: all;
          15: 22b-34a; 21: 1-8, 11-15a, 16-17; 31: 11b-13, 50-51;
          34: 86b-92; 41: all; 53: 79-83; 55: 284b-389, 491b-498;
          RESTORE: 16: 20-21, 102b-103, 107b-110a; 21: 25-27, 66b-
          67a; 22: 12b-14a, 17-18a, 34, 39b-42a; 23: 52b-54a; 24:
          71b-72a; 32: 12-17a; 33: 4b-6, 47b-49a, 56b-58a; 34: 6b-
          8a, 39b-41; 35: 56, 77, 133b-134a, 137, 142b-148, 155b-
          159a; 36: 6b-8a; 42: 9b-19a, 84b-85a, 98-99, 236-238,
          246b-249a, 252-253, 316b-317a, 324b-328, 363b-365a; 55:
          225, 299b-300a; ADD: 13 after 55: 484a; DOES NOT MOVE 31:
          48-54, 11b-14, 42 to follow 23: 63

SS CY409 "B Iden Payne, 1929, Carnegie Tech"(Hand)   IP1
          Carnegie-Mellon U RBR, Payne Coll

SS CY402 "Nugent Monck, Maddewmarket Th (Hand. Production 1923)   NM1
          Nugent Monck Coll Jack Hall
          Memorial PB in Methuen, 2nd ed, 1930

S CY39   "B Iden Payne, 1937"(Hand)   STRATFORD-upon-AVON   IP2
          Nuffield 71.21/1737C (Ac 5329, f 90)and ?8157?)
          2 copies of PB in unidentified full text

S CY40   "Nugent Monck, 1946"(Hand)   STRATFORD–UPON–AVON NM2
             Nuffield O S 71.21/1946C"She (Ac 6309, f87)
             PB in Eversley

SS CY404 "Nugent Monck" (Hand)
             British Drama League
             Deviations from Monck 1946(S CY40––NM2); CUT; 11: 28R; 14:
               170c; 15: 72b–74a; 16: 6b–7a, 33–38, 119b–123a, 132b–135,
               149–155; 25: 32, 35 32: 1–2, 20b–22a; 34: 21b–23a, 141–
               142a; 35: 10–15; 36: 14b–17a, 85–86; 42: 85b–87, 88b,
               334–335; 53: 93b–94a; 55: 288–289; RESTORE: 11: 65b–67,
               86b–88a; 15: 33–42a; 16: 39–42a, 47b–51; 21: 50; 23: 18–
               20, 51b–53a, 64–65a, 73b–75a; 31: 6–8a; 32: 7b–11a, 12–
               13a, 15b–17a, 35b–39, 56; 33: 74–78a, 97=98a, 103b–107a,
               121–122a, 132b=133a, 155–156a, 173b–175a, 176b–178a; 35:
               28–29a, 32b–34a, 104b–105, 118b–122; 41: 13b–14a; 42: 35–
               36, 51–58a, 66b–67a, 147b–149a, 164b–66a, 212b–213a, 252–
               253a; 44: 22b–24a; 54: 210–211a; 55: 2b–14, 199–201a,
               255b–258a, 276b–278a, 299b–301a, 323–324a, 335–336a, 338b–
               347a, 354–360a, 364b–368a, 384b–386, 389–391a; DOES NOT
               MOVE 43: 1–46 to follow 42: 290

S CY41   "Michael Benthall, 1949"(Hand) STRATFORD–UPON–AVON   MB1
             Nuffield O S 71.21/1949C (Ac 6590, f 88)
             PB in unidentified full text

S CY42   "Michael Benthall, 1956"(Hand)   OLD VUC   MB2
             Old Vic Archives
             PB in unidentified full text

SS CY410 "B Iden Payne, 1956"(Hand)   ASHLAND   IP3
             Ore Shakespeare Festival Archives
             PB in unidentified full text

S CY43   "Peter Hall, 1957"(Hand)   STRATFORD–UPON–AVON   PH1
             Nuffield O S 71.21/1957C (Ac 9504)
             PB in unidentified full text

AA CY411 "James Sandoe, 1968"   ASHLAND
             Ore Shakespeaare Festival Archives
             CUT: 15 10b–26a; 16: 3b–9, 38b–50a. 125–135a, 200–204a; 22:
               42b; 23: 31b–35, 141–155a; 24: 70b–76a; 31: 24b–33, 59b–
               62a; 32: 15b–22, 29–43, 59–68a, 80b–82; 34: 35b–41, 60–
               66a, 87b–101a, 154b0168a, 176b–187; 43: 132b–143a, 301–
               307; 43: 36–46; 53: 1–66, 70b–73a' 54: 10–21, 126–133;
               55: 1–19a, 52b–61a, 85b–90a, 153–176a, 221–226, 250b–
               253a, 385–391a, 466–476a

SS CY405 "Jean Gascon, 1970"(Hans)   ONTARIO   JG1
             Stratford Shakespeare Festival Archives
             PB in unidentified full text

SS CY406 "Edited by A J Antoon, 1971" <u>SHAKESPEARE IN THE PARK</u>
           NY Shakespeare Festival Archives   J19
           2 copies of mimeographed script

SS CY403 "Barry Kyle with John Barton and Clifford Williams, 19 74" BK1
           "<u>STRATFORD-UPON-AVON</u>, 1974, Aldwych 1974-75"(Hand)
           Nuffield 71.21/1974/Cym (Ac S1594)
           2 copies of PB in unidentified full text

<u>UNDATED</u>

SS CY408 Anonymous
           U Calif at Davis, RBR
           Unmarked unidentified text

ALPHABETICAL LIST OF SIGLA FOR CYMBELINE

```
BA1  W Bridges-Adams 1922
Bar  London: Barker, 1795
Bat  London: Bathurst, 1784
Bel  London: Bell, 1774
BK1  Barry Kyle and others, 1974
ChM  'Charles Marsh.' London: author, 1759
CKP  Charles Kean PB, 1850
Cum  Loncon: Cumberland, 1823
Dol  London: Dolby, 1823
G61  'David Garrick.' London: n p, n d (J "1761")
Han  Charles B Hanford, 1910
HIC  'Henry Irving.' London: Chiswick, 1896
HIM  Henry Irving-Frank A Marshall, 1888
HIP  Henry Irving PB, 1896
HM1  'Helena Modjeska.' Indianapolis: Hasselman, 1883
HnF  Helen Faucit, c 1845
Inc  'Mrs Inchbald.' London: Longman, 1808
IP1  Ben Iden Payne, 1929
IP2  Ben Iden Payne, 1956
JG1  Jean Garcon, 1970
JKT  'John Philip Kemble.' London: Theatre, 1810
JP1  Joseph Papp,  1971
KRe  Charles Kemble Shakespeare Readings, 1870
Lac  London: Lacy, 1865
Low  London: Lowndes, 1801
MB1  Michael Benthall, 1949
MB2  Michael Benthall, 1956
MTh  Memorial Theatre Edition, 1889
NM1  Nugent Monck, 1923
NM2  Nugent Monck, 1946
Oxb  Oxberry Edition. London: Simpkin, 1821
Ox1  London: Oxlade, 1777
P95  London: Proprietors, c 1795
PH1  Peter Hall, 1957
Rig  'George Rignold.' London: Williams, 1872
Roa  London: Roach, 1806
SM1  Sothern and Marlowe, 1923
USW  Boston: Wells, 1823
ViA  Viola Allen, 1906
Wen  London: Wenman, 1777
WM1  William Charles Macready, 1843
WmS  William Seymour, c 1890
```

CYMBELINE.

DRAMATIS PERSONÆ.

CYMBELINE, king of Britain.

CLOTEN, son to the Queen by a former husband.

POSTHUMUS LEONATUS, a gentleman, husband to Imogen.

BELARIUS, a banished lord, disguised under the name of Morgan.

GUIDERIUS, ARVIRAGUS, sons to Cymbeline, disguised under the names of Polydore and Cadwal, supposed sons to Morgan.

PHILARIO, friend to Posthumus, IACHIMO, friend to Philario, } Italians.

CAIUS LUCIUS, general of the Roman forces.

PISANIO, servant to Posthumus.

CORNELIUS, a physician.

A Roman Captain.

Two British Captains.

A Frenchman, friend to Philario.

Two Lords of Cymbeline's court.

Two Gentlemen of the same.

Two Gaolers.

Queen, wife to Cymbeline.

IMOGEN, daughter to Cymbeline by a former queen.

HELEN, a lady attending on Imogen.

Lords, Ladies, Roman Senators, Tribunes, a Soothsayer, a Dutchman, a Spaniard, Musicians, Officers, Captains, Soldiers, Messengers, and other Attendants.

Apparitions.

SCENE: *Britain; Rome.*

ACT I.

1,+1 **SCENE I.** *Britain. The garden of Cymbeline's palace.*

2 *Enter two* Gentlemen.

3   *First Gent.*   You do not meet a man but
4   frowns: our bloods   1
5–6 No more obey the heavens than our courtiers   2
7 Still seem as does the king.
8   *Sec. Gent.*   But what's the matter?   3
    First Gent.   His daughter, and the heir of 's
9   kingdom, whom   4
10 He purposed to his wife's sole son—a widow   5
11 That late he married—hath referr'd herself   6
12 Unto a poor but worthy gentleman : she's wedded :   7
13 Her husband banish'd : she imprison'd : all   8
14 Is outward sorrow ; though I think the king   9
15 Be touch'd at very heart.
17   *Sec. Gent.*   None but the king? 10   10
    First Gent.   He that hath lost her too; so is
17   the queen,   11
18 That most desired the match : but not a courtier,   12
19 Although they wear their faces to the bent   13
20 Of the king's looks, hath a heart that is not   14
21 Glad at the thing they scowl at.
22   *Sec. Gent.*   And why so?   15
    First Gent.   He that hath miss'd the princess
23   is a thing   16
24 Too bad for bad report: and he that hath her—   17
25 I mean, that married her, alack, good man !   18
26 And therefore banish'd—is a creature such   19
27 As, to seek through the regions of the earth   20   20
28 For one his like, there would be something failing   21
29 In him that should compare.   I do not think   22
30 So fair an outward and such stuff within   23
31 Endows a man but he.
32   *Sec. Gent.*   You speak him far.   24
    First Gent.   I do extend him, sir, within him-
33   self,   25
34 Crush him together rather than unfold   26
35 His measure duly.

Scene 11

ADD 87: ChM
 1 X: ChM, HIP, JP1; N: G61, Bel, Oxl, Bar, Inc, JKT, USW, Cumm WM1, HnF*
 2 X: ChM, HIP, NM1, NM2, JP1

 3 X: ChM; aX: NM1, NM2, JP1; N: Inc, USW, Cum, HnF, HM1, WmA, ViA; ADD
        1: G61, Bel, Wen, Bat, Roa, Cum, Lac, Rig; ADD 3: ,JKT
 4 X: ChM; ADD 1: Oxl, BK1; ADD 4: Low
 5 X: ChM; aX: JG1; bX: Rig; ADD 1: BK1; Insert 16b-17a: JP1
 6 X: ChM; aX: Rig; bX: JG1, BK1; ADD 1: Low
 7 X: ChM; aX: BK1; bX: JP1
 8 X: ChM; R: BK1; aX: JP1
 9 X: ChM

10 X: ChM; bX: KRe, ViA, Han, PH1, JP1, BK1; ADD 1: G61

11 X: ChM, G61, Bel, Oxl, Wen, Bat, Bar, Roa, Inc, JKT, Oxb, Dol, USW,*
12 X: ChM, Bat, Oxb, Dol, USW, ViA, Han, JP1; aX: G61, Bel, Oxl, Bar, Low*
13 X: ChM, Rig, HIP, Han, NM1, NM2, JP1
14 same as 13

15 X: ChM, HIP, NM1, NM2, JP1; aX: Rig, Han

16 X: ChM, HIP; aX: JP1; bX: HIP; ADD 1: WmS, BK1; MOVE 16b-17a to follow*
17 X: ChM, HIP; ADD 1: WmS, BK1
18 X: ChM, WmS, HIP, HIC, PH1, JP1; b X: G61, Oxl, P95, JKT, Rig,NM1,NM2,BK1
19 X: ChM, Bel, Wen, Bat, Bar, HIP, PH1; aX: G61, Oxl, P95, JKT, Rig, WmS*
20 X: ChM, HIP
21 X: ChM, HIP; bX: Wen
22 X: ChM, Wen , HIP; bX: G51, Bel, Oxl, Bat, P95, Bar, Low, Roa, JKT, Oxb*
23 X: ChM, G61, Bel, Oxl, Wen, Bat, P95, Bar, Low, Roa, Inc, JKT, Oxb, Dol,
        USW, Cum, WM1, Lac, Rig, HM1, MTh, WmS, HIP, HIC, ViA, BA1, SM1, NM1*
24 same as 23, CKP, less BK1; less bX; aX: PH1; bX: HnF, KRe, Han

25 same as 23; PH1, JG1, BK1, KRe, Han; less CKP; less aX, bX
26 same as 25
*11: 1 Rig, HM1, WmS, ViA, NM2   *11:11 Cum, WM1, CKP, Lac, KRe, WmS,
    ViA, Han, PH1, JP1, BK1; ADD 1: G6   *11:12 Roa, Inc, JKT,
    Cum, WM1, CKP, Lac, WmS, PH1, BK1, SEE BELOW *11:16 5: JP1
*11:19 NM1, NM2, JP1, BK1   *11:22 Dol, USW, Cum, WM1, Lac, Rig,
    HM1, MTh, WmS, HIC, ViA, BA1, SM1, NM1, NM2, JP1, BK1
*11:23NM2, PH1, BK1; bX: CKP   *11:25 NM2, PH1, JG1, JP1, BK1
*11:12 (CONTINUED); bX: Rig, HIP, NM1, NM2

36	*Sec. Gent.* What's his name and birth?	27
	First Gent. I cannot delve him to the root:	
37	his father	28
38	Was call'd Sicilius, who did join his honour	29
39	Against the Romans with Cassibelan, 30	30
40	But had his titles by Tenantius whom	31
41	He served with glory and admired success,	32
42	So gain'd the sur-addition Leonatus:	33
43	And had, besides this gentleman in question,	34
44	Two other sons, who in the wars o' the time	35
	Died with their swords in hand; for which their	
45	father,	36
46	Then old and fond of issue, took such sorrow	37
47	That he quit being, and his gentle lady,	38
48	Big of this gentleman our theme, deceased	39
49	As he was born. The king he takes the babe 40	40
50	To his protection, calls him Posthumus Leonatus,	41
51	Breeds him and makes him of his bed-chamber,	42
52	Puts to him all the learnings that his time	43
53	Could make him the receiver of; which he took,	44
54	As we do air, fast as 'twas minister'd,	45
55	And in's spring became a harvest, lived in court—	46
56	Which rare it is to do—most praised, most loved	47
57	A sample to the youngest, to the more mature	48
58	A glass that feated them, and to the graver	49
59	A child that guided dotards: to his mistress, 50	50
60	For whom he now is banish'd. her own price	51
61	Proclaims how she esteem'd him and his virtue:	52
62	By her election may be truly read	53
63	What kind of man he is.	
	Sec. Gent. I honour him	54
64	Even out of your report. But, pray you, tell me,	55
65	Is she sole child to the king?	
66	*First Gent.* His only child.	56
67	He had two sons: if this be worth your hearing,	57
68	Mark it: the eldest of them at three years old,	58
	I' the swathing-clothes the other, from their nur-	
69	sery	59
	Were stol'n, and to this hour no guess in know-	
70	ledge 60	60
71	Which way they went.	

27 X: ChM, KRe, HIC, Han, JP1; aX: G61, Bel, Ox1, Wen, Bat, P95, Bar, Low,
    Roa, Inc, JKT, Dol, USW, Cum, WM1, HnF, CKP, Lac, Rig, HM1, MTh, WmS*

28 X: ChM, KRe, HIC, ViA, Han, SM1, MB2, JP1; R: NM2; aX: G61, Bel, Ox1*

29 X: ChM, HnF, KRe, HIP, HIC, ViA, Han, SM1, MB2, JP1; R: Ox1, JG1; aX:*

30 X: ChM, Bat, Bar, HnF, KRe, HIP, HIC, ViA, Han, SM1, MB1, MB2, PH1, JP1*

31 X: ChM, G61, Bel, Ox1, Wen, Bat, Bar, Low, Inc, JKT, Oxb, Dol, Cum, WM1*

32 same as 31, less Bat, Bar, JG1; aX: JG1

33 X: ChM, HnF, KRe, HIP, HIC, ViA, Han, BA1, SM1, NM1, NM2, MB1, MB2, PH1*

34 X: ChM, KRe, HIC, ViA, Han, SM1, NM1, NM2, MB1, MB2, PH1, JP1, BK1; bX:BA1

35 same as 34 including bX

36 same as 35, less NM1, N M2; less bX; bX: NM1, NM2

37 same as 35; less bX

38 same as 35, less PH1, NM1, NM2; aX: NM1, NM2

39 same as 38, less BK1; same ax

40 same as 38; less aX

41 X: ChM, KRe, HIC, ViA, Han, BA1, SM1, MB1, JP1; aX: MB2

42 X: ChM, WM1, HnF, CKP, KRe, HIC, ViA, Han, BA1, SM1, MB1, MB2, JP1

43 X: ChM, KRe, Rig, HIC, ViA, Han, SM1, MB1, MB2, PH1, JP1

44 same as 43; bX: HIP, NM1, BK1

45 X: ChM, KRe, Rig, HIP, HIC, ViA, Han, SM1, NM1, NM2, MB1, MB2, PH1, JP1;*

46 X: ChM, KRe, HIP, HIC, ViA, Han, SM1, NM1, NM2, MB1, MB2, JP1; aX: Rig*

47 X: ChM, WM1, CKP, KRe, HIC, ViA, Han, SM1, MB1, MB2, JP1; aX: HIP

48 X: ChM, WM1, CKP, KRe HIC, ViA, Han, SM1, MB1, MB2, JP1; BK1; R: JG1;*

49 same as 48, HIP, PH1, JG1; less R, bX; aX: BA1, IP1

50 X: ChM, HIC, ViA, Han, SM1, MB1, MB2, JG1, JP1; aX: WM1, CKP, KRe, HIP*

51 X: ChM, G61, Bel, Ox1, Bat, P95, Bar, Low, Roa, Inc, JKT, Oxb, Dol, USW*

52 same as 51; bX: BA1

53 same as 51, BA1, JG1, less Inc, NM2; aX: Inc

54 X: ChM, Cum, Lac, ViA, Han, MB1, MB2, JG1 JP1; aX: G61, Bel, Ox1, Wen, Bat*

55 X: ChM, Cum, Lac, JP1; R: G61, Ox1, Wen, Bat, P95, Oxb; aX: HIP, ViA,
    Han, MB1, MB2, JG1; bX: Bel

56 X: ChM, JP1; aX: Cum, Lac

57 X: ChM; bX: Rig, HIP, PH1, BK1

58 X: ChM, PH1, BK1; aX: Rig, HIP; bX: KRe

59 X: ChM; aX: PH1, BK1

60 X: ChM

*1127 HIP, ViA, BA1, SM1, NM1, JG1; bX: MB2; ADD 2: Bat, Bar, Oxb
*11:28 Wen, Bat, Roa, Inc,,JKT, Oxb, Dol, Cum, WM1, CKP, Lac, Rig, HM1, MTh,
    WmS; ADD 2: G61, Bel, Ox1, Wen, JKT, Oxb, USW   *11:29 WM1; bX:
    Bel, Wen, Bat, Bar, MB1, PH1, BK1; ADD 1: BK1; ADD 2: MB1
*11:30 BK1; R: JKT; bX: HIP, JG1   *11:31 HnF, CKP, Lac, KRe, HM1,
    WmS, HIP, HIC, ViA, Han, BA1, SM1, NM1, IP1, NM2, MB1, MB2, PH1, JG1, JP1,
    BK1; aX: Rig, IP2   *11:33 JP1, BK1   *11:45BK; aX: BA1,
*11:46 BA1, NM1, NM2, PH1, BK1; bX: WM1, CKP   *11:48 bX: HIP, BA1,
    IP1, PH1   *11:50 PH1, BK1; bX: G61, Bel, Ox1, Wen, Bat, P95, Bar,
    Low, Roa, Inc, JKT, Oxb, Dol, USW, Cum, Lac, Rig, HM1, MTh, WmS
*11:51 Cum, Lac, Rig, HM1, MTh, WmS, HIC, ViA, Han, SM1, NM2, MB1, MB2, JP1;
*11:54 P95, Bar, Low, Roa, JKT, Oxb, Dol, USW, Rig, HM1, MTh, WmS, HIC, BA1
    SM1; bX: KRe, HIP; ADD 1: Bel

72	*Sec. Gent.* How long is this ago?	61
73	*First Gent.* Some twenty years.	62
	Sec. Gent. That a king's children should be so	
74	conuey'd,	63
75	So slackly guarded, and the search so slow,	64
76	That could not trace them!	
77	*First Gent.* Howsoe'er 'tis strange,	65
78	Or that the negligence may well be laugh'd at,	66
79	Yet is it true, sir.	
	Sec. Gent. I do well believe you.	67
	First Gent. We must forbear: here comes the	
80	gentleman,	68
81-2	The queen, and princess. *[Exeunt.*	69

Enter the QUEEN, POSTHUMUS, *and* IMOGEN.

Queen. No, be assured you shall not find me,

84	daughter,	**70**	70
85	After the slander of most stepmothers,		71
86	Evil-eyed unto you: you're my prisoner, but		72
87	Your gaoler shall deliver you the keys		73
88	That lock up your restraint. For you, Posthumus,		74
89	So soon as I can win the offended king,		75
90	I will be known your advocate: marry, yet		76
91	The fire of rage is in him, and 'twere good		77
92	You lean'd unto his sentence with what patience		78
93	Your wisdom may inform you.		
94	*Post.* Please your highness,		79
95	I will from hence to-day.		
96	*Queen.* You know the peril. **80**		80
97	I'll fetch a turn about the garden, pitying		81
98	The pangs of barr'd affections, though the king		82
	Hath charged you should not speak together.		83
99	*[Exit.*		
	Imo. O		
100	Dissembling courtesy! How fine this tyrant		84
	Can tickle where she wounds! My dearest hus-		
101	band,		85
102	I something fear my father's wrath: but nothing—		86
103	Always reserved my holy duty—what		87
104	His rage can do on me: you must be gone;		88
105	And I shall here abide the hourly shot		89
106	Of angry eyes, not comforted to live, **90**		90
107	But that there is this jewel in the world		91
108	That I may see again.		
109	*Post.* My queen! my mistress!		92
110	O lady, weep no more, lest I give cause		93

61   X: ChM; bX: KRe, JP1
62   X: ChM, K̄R̄e, JP1; R: IP1, IP2

63   X: ChM, Rig, PH1, JP1
64   same as 63; bX: KRe, HIC

65   X: ChM, Rig, JP1; aX: KRe, HIC, PH1; bX: HM1, BA1, NM1, NM2
66   X: ChM, KRe, Rig, H̄IP, HIC, ViA, HM1, B̄A1, NM1, NM2, JP1, BK1

67   X: ChM, Rig, HM1, BA1, NM1, NM2, JP1; bX: Low, Inc, JKT, Dol, USW,
         Cum, WM1, HnF, CKP, Lac, HM1, WmS
68   X: JG1, JP1; aX: WM1, CKP, HIP; bX: WmS
69   X: JG1, JP1; b̄X̄: WmS

70   X: JG1; MOVE 70-83 to follow 101: WmS
71   X: JG1
72   X: JG1; bX: KRe, PH1, BK1
73   X: KRe, P̄H̄1, JG1, BK1
74   aX: KRe, PH1, JG1, BK1
75
76   bX: KRe, Rig, HIC, PH1, BK1
77   X̄: Rig, HIC, PH1, BK1
78   same as 77; bX: KRe, ViA

79   X: PH1; aX: KRe, Rig, HIC, ViA; abX: BK1

80   ADD 7: ChM; ADD 8: JG1
81   X̄: ChM, KRe, W̄mS, JG1
82   X: ChM, KRe, JG1; aX: WmS; bX: ViA
83   X: ChM, KRe, ViA, J̄Ḡ1; Insert 101b-106a: HIC ; bX: PH1

84   X: ViA, PH1, JG1; MOVE 84-92a to follow 106a: WmS

85   X: ViA; aX: PH1, JG1; bX: Ox1, Oxb
86   X: G61, B̄el, Ox1, Wen, B̄at, Bar, ₵ow, Roa, Inc, JKT, Oxb, Dol, Cum,*
87   same as 86, NM1, NM2; less bX: aX: JG1
88   X: Inc, ViA; aX: G61, Bel, Ōx1, Wen, Bat, Bar, Low, Roa, Inc, JKT, Oxb*
89   X: ViA
90   X: ViA
91   X: ViA

92   X: ViA
93   X: HIC, ViA; bX: BK1

*11:86 WM1, CKP, KRe, Rig, ViA, BK1; bX: NM1, NM2   *11:88 Dol,
    Cum, WM1, CKP, KRe, Rig, NM1, NM2, B̄K1

111	To be suspected of more tenderness	94
112	Than doth become a man. I will remain	95
113	The loyal'st husband that did e'er plight troth:	96
114	My residence in Rome at one Philario's,	97
115	Who to my father was a friend, to me	98
116	Known but by letter: thither write, my queen,	99
117	And with mine eyes I'll drink the words you send,	100
118	Though ink be made of gall.	

119   *Re-enter* QUEEN.

120	*Queen.* Be brief, I pray you: **101**	101
121	If the king come, I shall incur I know not	102
122	How much of his displeasure. [*Aside*] Yet I'll move him	103
123	To walk this way: I never do him wrong,	104
124	But he does buy my injuries, to be friends:	105
125	Pays dear for my offences. [*Exit.*	
126	*Post.* Should we be taking leave	106
127	As long a term as yet we have to live,	107
128	The loathness to depart would grow. Adieu!	108
129	*Imo.* Nay, stay a little:	109
130	Were you but riding forth to air yourself, **110**	110
131	Such parting were too petty. Look here, love;	111
132	This diamond was my mother's: take it, heart;	112
133	But keep it till you woo another wife,	113
134	When Imogen is dead.	
135	*Post.* How, how! another?	114
136	You gentle gods, give me but this I have,	115
137	And sear up my embracements from a next	116
	With bonds of death! [*Putting on the ring.*]	
138	Remain, remain thou here	117
139	While sense can keep it on. And, sweetest, fairest,	118
140	As I my poor self did exchange for you,	119
?141	To your so infinite loss, so in our trifles **120**	120
142	I still win of you: for my sake wear this;	121
143	It is a manacle of love: I'll place it	122
144	Upon this fairest prisoner.	
141+1	[*Putting a bracelet upon her arm.*	
145	*Imo.* O the gods!	123
146	When shall we see again?	

147   *Enter* CYMBELINE *and* Lords.

148	*Post.* Alack, the king!	124
	Cym. Thou basest thing, avoid! hence, from	
149	my sight!	125

```
 94  X: Rig, HIC, ViA, BK1
 95  X: Rig, ViA; aX: HIC, BK1
 96  X: ViA
 97  X: ViA; R: JG1
 98  X: ViA; bX: BK1
 99  X: ViA; aX: ChM, BK1
100  X: ViA


101  aX: ViA; bX: ChM, KRe, HM1; Insert 70-83: WmS; MOVE 101b-106a to fol*
102  X: ChM, KRe, HM1

103  same as 102; bX: HnF
104  X: ChM, HnF, KRe, HM1; bX: WM1, CKP, Lac, Rig, HM1, MTh, WmS, HIP,ViA*
105  X: ChM, WM1,HnF, CKP, Lac, KRe, Rig, HM1, MTh, WmS, HIP, ViA, Han, SM1,
         PH1, BK1
106  X: KRe, ViA; aX: ChM, WM1, HnF, CKP, Lac, Rig, HM1, MTh, WmS, HIP, Han*
107  X: KRe, ViA, JP1
108  X: KRe, ViA; aX: JP1
109
110  X: USW, KRe, HIC, JP1
111  XL KRe, HIC; aX: USW, JP1
112
113

114  bX: PH1, BK1
115  X: PH1, BK1
116  X: PH1, BK1

117  aX: PH1, BK1; b X: JP1

118  aX: JP1; ADD 1: ChM
119  X: JP1; R: ChM
120  X: JP1
121  aX: JP1
222


123  bX: KRe, WmS, Han



124  X: Han; aX: KRe, WmS; bX: JG1

125  X: Han; R: ChM

*11:101 low 83: HIC          *11:104 SM1, PH1, BK1; ADD 20: ViA
*11:106 SM1, PH1, BK1; bX: JP1; Insert 84-92a: WmS
```

150	If after this command thou fraught the court	126
151	With thy unworthiness, thou diest: away!	127
152	Thou'rt poison to my blood.	
153	*Post.* The gods protect you!	128
154	And bless the good remainders of the court!	129
155	I am gone. [*Exit.*	
156	*Imo.* There cannot be a pinch in death 130	130
157	More sharp than this is.	
158	*Cym.* O disloyal thing,	131
159	That shouldst repair my youth, thou heap'st	132
160	A year's age on me.	
161	*Imo.* I beseech you, sir,	133
162	Harm not yourself with your vexation:	134
163	I am senseless of your wrath; a touch more rare	135
164	Subdues all pangs, all fears.	
165	*Cym.* Past grace? obedience?	136
	Imo. Past hope, and in despair; that way, past	
166	grace.	137
167	*Cym.* That mightst have had the sole son of	
168	my queen!	138
169	*Imo.* O blest, that I might not! I chose an eagle,	139
170	And did avoid a puttock. 140	140
	Cym. Thou took'st a beggar; wouldst have	
171	made my throne	141
172	A seat for baseness.	
	Imo. No; I rather added	142
173	A lustre to it.	
174	*Cym.* O thou vile one!	
175	*Imo.* Sir,	143
176	It is your fault that I have loved Posthumus:	144
177	You bred him as my playfellow, and he is	145
178	A man worth any woman, overbuys me	146
179	Almost the sum he pays.	
180	*Cym.* What, art thou mad?	147
	Imo. Almost, sir: heaven restore me! Would	
181	I were	148
182	A neat-herd's daughter, and my Leonatus	149
183	Our neighbour shepherd's son!	
185	*Cym.* Thou foolish thing! 150	150
184	*Re-enter* QUEEN.	
186	They were again together: you have done	151
187	Not after our command. Away with her,	152
188	And pen her up.	
189	*Queen.* Beseech your patience. Peace,	153
190	Dear lady daughter, peace! Sweet sovereign,	154

126 X: Han; R: ChM
127 same as 126 including R

128 X: Han; aX: BK1
129 X: WmS, BK1

130 X: WmS, Han

131 X: Han; aX: WmS; ADD 1: Bel, Ox1, Wen, Bat, Bar, Low, Inc, JKT, Oxb*
132 X: KRe, Han

133 X: KRe, Han; bX: WM1, CKP
134 X: WM1, CKP, KRe, Han; bX: Cum
135 X: Cum, WM1, CKP, KRe; bX: WmS; ADD 1: Bel

136 X: WM1, CKP, KRe, WmS, Han; bX: G61, Bel, Ox1, Wen, Bat, P95, Bar,
        Low, Roa, Inc, JKT, Oxb, Dol, Cum, HnF, Rig
137 X: G61, Bel, Ox1, Wen, Bat, P95, Bar, Low, Roa, Inc, JKT, Oxb, Dol,
        WM1, HnF, CKP, KRe, Rig, WmS, Han
138 X: ChM, WmS, Han
139 same as 138; bX: G61, Bel, Ox1, Wen, Bat, P95, Bar, Low, Inc, JKT, Oxb*
140 X: ChM, G61, Bel, Ox1, Wen, Bat, P95, Bar, Low, Inc, JKT, Oxb, Dol,Cum,
        WM1, HnF, KRe, Rig, WmS, Han; bX: CKP
141 X: ChM, Roa, WM1, CKP, Han, BK1

142 X: ChM, WM1, CKP, BK1; aX: Roa; bX: PH1

143 X: ChM, CKP; aX: WM1, PH1; cX: HnF
144 X: KRe
145 X: KRe
146 X: KRe; bX: JP1, BK1

147 aX: KRe, JP1, BK1

148 bX: KRe
149 X: KRe

150 aX: KRe; bX: ChM, WmS

151 X: ChM, WmS
152 X: ChM; aX: WmS; bX: KRe

153 X: KRe; aX: ChM, ViA
154 X:WM1, KRe, HIC; bX: WmS, BA1

*11:131 Dol, USW, Cum, Rig; Insert 178: G61   *11:139 Dol, Cum,
   WM1, HnF, Rig

	Leave us to ourselves; and make yourself some	
191	comfort	155
192	**Out** of your best advice.	
193	*Cym.* Nay, let her languish	156
194	**A** drop of blood a day; and, being aged,	157
195	**Die** of this folly! [*Exeunt Cymbeline and Lords.*	
197	*Queen.* Fie! you must give way.	158
196	*Enter* PISANIO.	
	Here is your servant. How now, sir! What	
198	news?	159
199	*Pis.* My lord your son drew on my master.	
200	*Queen.* Ha! 160	160
201	**No** harm, I trust, is done?	
202	*Pis.* There might have been,	161
203	**But** that my master rather play'd than fought	162
204	**And** had no help of anger: they were parted	163
205	**By** gentlemen at hand.	
206	*Queen.* I am very glad on't.	164
	Imo. Your son's my father's friend; he takes	
207	his part.	165
208	**To** draw upon an exile! O brave sir!	166
209	**I** would they were in Afric both together;	167
210	**Myself** by with a needle, that I might prick	168
211	**The** goer-back. Why came you from your master?	169
212	*Pis.* On his command: he would not suffer me	170
213	**To** bring him to the haven; left these notes 171	171
214	**Of** what commands I should be subject to,	172
215	**When** 't pleased you to employ me.	
216	*Queen.* This hath been	173
217	**Your** faithful servant: I dare lay mine honour	174
218	**He** will remain so.	
219	*Pis.* I humbly thank your highness.	175
220	*Queen.* Pray, walk awhile.	
221	*Imo.* About some half-hour hence,	176
222	**I** pray you, speak with me: you shall at least	177
223	**Go** see my lord aboard: for this time leave me.	178
224	[*Exeunt.*	
225R,+1	**SCENE II.** *The same. A public place.*	
226	*Enter* CLOTEN *and two* Lords.	
	First Lord. Sir, I would advise you to shift a	1
227	**shirt**; the violence of action hath made you reek	2
228	**as a** sacrifice: where air comes out, air comes in:	3

155 X: G61, WM1, BA1; aX: Bel, Ox1, Wen, Bat, Bar, JKT, Oxb, KRe, WmS, HIC;
    bX: BK1
156 aX: WM1, BA1, BK1; bX: ChM
157 X: ChM, WmS

158 X: ChM; bX: KRe ; ADD 4: Roa; ADD 3, insert 13: 4-37, add 1, insert
    15: 4-87, add 13: Bat; Insert 13: 4b-38 and 15: 4-81, add 11: G61;
    ADD 4, insert 13: 4-39 and 15: 4-87, add 11: Ox1, Bar, Low, Oxb; In-
    sert 13: 1-40 and 15: 1-87, add 11: Dol, USW; Insert 13: 5-45 and*
159 X: G61, Ox1, P95, Roa, Oxb, HnF, KRe, HIC; aX: ChM, G61, Wen, Bat;
    bX: Bel, Inc, JKT; N: Bar, Dol; ADD 4: Inc; ADD 5: Low; Insert 174-*
160 X: Bel, Ox1, P95, Bar, Low, Roa, Inc, Oxb, Dol, HnF, KRe, Rig, HIC;
    R: JKT
161 X: G61, Bel, Ox1, Wen, Bat, Bar, Low, Roa, Inc, Oxb, Dol, HnF, KRe,*
162 same as 161, including R
163 same as 161, including R

164 same as 161, including R; bX: WmS

165 X: G61, Bel, Ox1, Wen, Bat, Bar, Low, Roa, Inc, JKT, Oxb, Dol, WM1, HnF*
166 same as 165, less WM1; bX: JG1
167 X: G61, Bel, Ox1, Wen, Bat, Bar, Low, Roa, Inc, JKT, Oxb, Dol, HnF,*
168 same as 167
169 same as 167, less BA1, NM1, NM2, JG1, PH1; aX: BA1, NM1, NM2, JG1, JP1*
170 same as 169, Cum, PH1, BK1; less aX, bX;; bX: NM1, NM2
171 same as 170; less bX;; bX: ChM; abX, NM1
172 same as 170; less bX; R: ChM; aX: NM1

173 X: G61, Ox1, Wen, Bat, Bar, Low, Roa, Inc, JKT, Oxb, Dol, Cum, KRe, Rig*
174 same as 173, ChM, less KRe; less aX, bX; MOVE 174-175a to follow 159:
    Bar
175 same as 174, Bel; less MOVE; bX: Bel, Bar, KRe; Insert 13: 4b-50a and
    15: 1-87: WmS
176 X: G61, Bel, Ox1, Wen, Bat, Bar, Low, Roa, Inc, JKT, Oxb, Dol, Cum,*
177 same as 176, NM1; less bX; aX: ChM; bX: HIP
178 same as 177, HIP, less G61; less aX, bX ADD 1: BK1; Insert 15: 1-85:
    SM1; MOVE 178 to follow 131: G61

Scene 12

ALL CUT: G61, Bel, Ox1, Wen, Bat, P95, Bar, Low, Roa, Inc, JKT, Oxb, Dol,
Cum, HnF, CKP, KRe, Rig, WmS, HIP, HIC, NM1, NM2; "Scene generally omitted": MTh

 1 X: USW, Lac, HM1, MTh
 2 same as 1; bX: PH1
 3 X: USW, WM1, Lac, HM1, MTh, SM1, PH1, BK1; bX: Han

*11:158 15: 5-104: Rig; Insert 15: 1-87: HIC   *11:159 175a: Bar,
  Lac, Rig; ADD 5, insert 13: 4-37, add 1, insert 15: 4-87; WM1, P95
*11:161 Rig, HIC; R: JKT   *11:165 KRe, Rig, WmS, HIC
*11:167 KRe, Rig, WmS, HIC, BA1, NM1, NM2, JG1, JP1   *11:169 bX:
  Cum, HnF, PH1, BK1; ADD 4: Cum   *11:173 HIC, PH1; aX:
  HnF, WmS, BK1; bX: ChM, Bel   *11:176 HnF, KRe, Rig, WmS, HIC,
  NM2; bX: ChM, HIP, NM1

229	there's none abroad so wholesome as that you	4
230	vent.	5
231	*Clo.* If my shirt were bloody, then to shift it.	6
232	Have I hurt him?	7
	Sec. Lord. [*Aside*] No, 'faith; not so much as	8
233	his patience. **9**	9
	First Lord. Hurt him! his body's a passable	10
234	carcass, if he be not hurt: it is a throughfare for	11
235	steel, if it be not hurt.	12
	Sec. Lord. [*Aside*] His steel was in debt; it	13
236–7	went o' the backside the town.	14
238	*Clo.* The villain would not stand me.	15
	Sec. Lord. [*Aside*] No; but he fled forward	16
239	still, toward your face.	17
	First Lord. Stand you! You have land enough	18
240	of your own: but he added to your having; gave	19
241	you some ground. **20**	20
	Sec. Lord. [*Aside*] As many inches as you	21
242	have oceans. Puppies!	22
243	*Clo.* I would they had not come between us.	23
	Sec. Lord. [*Aside*] So would I, till you had	24
244	measured how long a fool you were upon the	25
245	ground.	26
	Clo. And that she should love this fellow and	27
246–7	refuse me!	28
	Sec. Lord. [*Aside*] If it be a sin to make a	29
248	true election, she is damned.	30
	First Lord. Sir, as I told you always, her	31
249	beauty and her brain go not together: she's a good	32
250–1	sign, but I have seen small reflection of her wit	33
	Sec. Lord. [*Aside*] She shines not upon fools	34
252–3	lest the reflection should hurt her.	35
	Clo. Come, I'll to my chamber. Would there	36
254–5	had been some hurt done!	37
	Sec. Lord. [*Aside*] I wish not so; unless it	38
256–7	had been the fall of an ass, which is no great hurt.	39
258	*Clo.* You'll go with us? *P*	40
259	*First Lord.* I'll attend your lordship.	41
260	*Clo.* Nay, come, let's go together.	42
261	*Sec. Lord.* Well, my lord. [*Exeunt.*	43

262R,+1   **SCENE III.** *A room in Cymbeline's palace.*

263   *Enter* IMOGEN *and* PISANIO.

	Imo. I would thou grew'st unto the shores o'	
264	the haven,	1

```
 4   same as 3, Han,  BA1; less bX
 5   same as 4, JG1, less BK1
 6   X: USW, ViA, Han; aX: Lac, HM1, SM1
 7   X: USW, Han; ADD 1: JP1
 8   X: USW, Han
 9   X: USW; b X: HM1
10   X: HM1, M Th, Han; R: Lac, JP1; bX: ViA
11   X: Lac, HM1, MTh, Han, JP1; aX: ViA; bX: PH1, BK1
12   X: Lac, HM1, MTh, Han, PH1, JP1, BK1
13   X: ChM, WM1, Lac, HM1, MTh, ViA, Han, BA1, SM 1, MB1, MB2,PH1,JP1,BK1
14   same as 13
15   X: HM1
16   X: Lac, HM1, MTh, ViA, Han, BA1, SM1
17   same as 16
18   X: Lac, HM1, MTh, ViA, Han, BA1, SM1, PH1, JG1, JP1, BK1
19   same as 18
20   same as 18
21   X: ChM, WM1, Lac, HM1, MTh, ViA, Han, BA1, SM1, PH1, JG1, JP1, BK1
22   X: ChM, WM1, Han, ViA, PH1, JP1, BK1
23   X: ViA, PH1
24   X: ChM, SM1, MB2, PH1; bX: ViA, JP1
25   X: ChM, ViA, SM1, MB2, PH1, JP1
26   same as 25, less SM1
27
28
29   X: WM1, ViA, Han, BA1, SM1, MB1, MB2
30   same as 29
31   X: Lac, HM1, MTh, ViA, Han, BA1, SM1, PH1
32   same as 31, less ViA; bX: JP1, BK1
33   X: Lac, HM1, MTh, Han, BA1, SM1, PH1, JP1, BK1; Insert 21: 155-156:ViA
34   X: ChM, WM1, Lac, HM1, MTh, ViA, Han, BA1, SM1, MB2, PH1
35   same as 34, BK1, less MB2
36   X: ViA
37   X: ViA
38   X: ChM, ViA, SM1
39   same as 38, MB2
40   X: ViA
41   X: ViA
42   X: USW, ViA
43   X: USW, ViA, Han; aX: BA1; ADD 1: MB1
```

Scene 13

ALL CUT: HIC

```
 1   X: G61, Be1, Ox1, Wen, Bat, P95, Bar, Low, Roa, Inc, JKT, Oxb, Dol, USW,
     Cum, WM1, HnF, CKP, KRe, Rig, WmS, NM1, NM2, JG1; MOVE 1-40 to fol-
     low15: 84a: ViA
```

265   **And** question'dst every sail: if he should write,   2
266   **And** I not have it, 'twere a paper lost,   3
267   **As** offer'd mercy is.   What was the last   4
268   **That** he spake to thee?
269   *Pis.*   It was his queen, his queen.   5
270   *Imo.* **Then waved his handkerchief?**
271   *Pis.*   And kiss'd it, madam   6
272   *Imo.* **Senseless linen! happier therein than I.**   7
273   **And** that was all?
274   *Pis.*   No, madam; for so long   8
275   **As** he could make me with this eye or ear   9
276   **Distinguish** him from others, he did keep   n   10
277   **The** deck, with glove, or hat, or handkerchief,   11
278   **Still** waving, as the fits and stirs of 's mind   12
279   **Could** best express how slow his soul sail'd on,   13
280   **How** swift his ship.
281   *Imo.*   Thou shouldst have made him   14
282   **As** little as a crow, or less, ere left   15
283   **To** after-eye him.
284   *Pis.*   Madam, so I did.   16
    Imo.   I would have broke mine eye-strings
285   crack'd them, but   17
286   **To** look upon him, till the diminution   18
287   **Of** space had pointed him sharp as my needle,   19
288   **Nay,** follow'd him, till he had melted from   r   20
289   **The** smallness of a gnat to air, and then   21
    Have turn'd mine eye and wept. But, good
290   Pisanio,   22
291   **When** shall we hear from him?
292   *Pis.*   Be assured, madam   23
293   **With** his next vantage.   24
294   *Imo.*   I did not take my leave of him, but he   25
295   **Most** pretty things to say: ere I could tell him   26
296   **How** I would think on him at certain hours   27
    Such thoughts and such, or I could make him
297   swear   28
298   **The** shes of Italy should not betray   29
    Mine interest and his honour, or have charged
299   him,   30
300   **At** the sixth hour of morn, at noon, at midnight   31
301   **To** encounter me with orisons, for then   32
302   **I** am in heaven for him; or ere I could   33
303   **Give** him that parting kiss which I had set   34
304   **Betwixt** two charming words, comes in my father   35
305   **And** like the tyrannous breathing of the north   36
306   **Shakes** all our buds from growing.'

```
 2   X: same as 1, less JG1; less MOVE; aX: JG1; bX: BK1
 3   same as 2, BK1, less WM1; less aX, bX
 4   aX: G61, Bel, P95, Bar, Low, Roa, Inc, JKT, Oxb, Dol, USW, Cum, WM1,Han,
        CKP, KRe, Rig, NM1, NM2; MOVE 4b-40 to follow 11: 59: Rig, WmS;MOVE*
 5   R: Bel, Oxl, Bar, JKT, Oxb

 6
 7

 8
 9
10
11
12   bX: BK1
13   X: BK1

14   aX: BK1; bX: BA1
15   X: BA1

16   X: BA1; bX: MB2

17   X: MB2
18   X: MB2; bX: ChM, BA1
19   X: ChM, BA1, MB2
20   X: BA1, MB2
21   X: BA1, MB2

22   aX: BA1, MB2

23
24
25   MOVE 25-37 to follow 40a: BiA
26
27

28   bX: HnF, MB2, PH1
29   X: HnF, HM1, MB2, PH1

30   X: HM1; aX: Han, MB2,  PH1; bX: ViA, BA1, JG1
31   X: BA1, JG1
32   X: BA1, JG1
33   aX: BA1, JG1
34
35
36   ADD 1: USW
```

*12:4 4b-39 to follow 11: 158: G61, Oxl, Bar, Low, Oxb, Dol, USW, BK1;MOVE
   4-37 to follow 11: 159: Wen, Bat, P95

307   *Enter a* Lady.

308   *Lady.*   The queen, madam,   37

309   Desires your highness' company.   38

    Ime. Those things I bid you do, get them

310   dispatch'd.   39

311   I will attend the queen.

312   *Pis.*   Madam, I shall. [*Exeunt.* 40   40

313R,+1   S**CENE** IV. *Rome. Philario's house.*

314   *Enter* P**HILARIO**, I**ACHIMO**, *a* Frenchman, *a*

315   Dutchman, *and a* Spaniard.

    Iack. Believe it, sir, I have seen him in Britain: 1

316   he was then of a crescent note, expected to prove   2

317   so worthy as since he hath been allowed the name   3

318   of; but I could then have looked on him without   4

319   the help of admiration, though the catalogue of   5

320   his endowments had been tabled by his side and   6

321   I to peruse him by items.   7

    Phi. You speak of him when he was less fur-   8

322   nished than now he is with that which makes him   9

323-4   both without and within.   **10**   10

    French. I have seen him in France: we had   11

325   very many there could behold the sun with as   12

326-7   firm eyes as he.   13

    Iack. This matter of marrying his king's   14

328   daughter, wherein he must be weighed rather by   15

329   her value than his own, words him, I doubt not,   16

330-1   a great deal from the matter.   17

332   *French.* And then his banishment.   18

    Iack. Ay, and the approbation of those that   19

333   weep this lamentable divorce under her colours   20

334   are wonderfully to extend him; be it but to for-   21

335   tify her judgement, which else an easy battery   22

336   might lay flat, for taking a beggar without less   23

337   quality. But how comes it he is to sojourn with   24

338   you? How creeps acquaintance?   25

    Phi. His father and I were soldiers together: 26

339   to whom I have been often bound for no less than   27

340   my life. Here comes the Briton: let him be so   28

342   entertained amongst you as suits, with gentlemen   29

343   of your knowing, to a stranger of his quality. 30   30

341   *Enter* P**OSTHUMUS**.

344   I beseech you all, be better known to this gen-   31

345   tleman: whom I commend to you as a noble   32

37 X: USW; bX: G61, P95, Oxb, Dol, Cum, KRe, Rig; N: CKP, Lac; ADD 48,*
38 X: Bel, Oxl, Wen, Bat, P95, Bar, Low, JKT, Oxb, USW, Cum, KRe, Rig; R:
    ChM, G61; aX: Dol; bX: Inc
39 X: ChM, Wen, Bat, JP1; Insert 15: 4-87: Bel, JKT; Insert 15: 3-87, add
    4, insert 21: 62-70: Cum
40 X: ChM, G61, Bel, Oxl, Wen, Bat, P95, Bar, Oxb, Cum, JP1; aX: Low, MB1;
    bX: WmS; ADD 15: Inc; Insert 15: 1-87: KRe; Insert 15: 3-87: Inc,
    JKT; "Scene with Cloten": HnF; Insert 25-37a: ViA

Scene 14

1   X: ChM; bX: KRe, WmS, HIC
2   X: ChM, KRe, WmS, HIC, JP1; bX: ViA, BA1, BK1
3   X: ChM, KRe, WmS, HIC, ViA, BA1, JP1, BK1
4   X: ChM, WmS; aX: KRe, HIC, BA1; bX: NM2
5   X: ChM , WmS, NM2; bX: KRe, ViA, BA1, IP1
6   X: ChM, KRe, WmS, ViA, BA1, IP1, NM2, BK1
7   same as 6, JP1
8   X: ChM, CKP, WmS, NM2
9   same as 8; bX: G61, Bel, Oxl, Wen, Bat, P95, Bar, Low, Inc, JKT, Oxb*
10 X: ChM, G61, Bel, Oxl, Wen, Bat, P95, Bar, Low, Inc, JKT, Oxb, Dol,*
11 X: ChM
12 X: ChM
13 X: ChM, HIP
14 X: ChM, IPJ, MB1
15 X: ChM, WmS, IP1, MB1; b X: ViA
16 X: ChM, WmS, IP1, MB1, JG1; aX: ViA; bX: JP1
17 X: ChM, WmS, IP1, MB1, JP1; aX: JG1
18 X: ChM, IP1, MB1, IP2
19 X: ChM, IP1, MB1, MB2, IP2, PH1, BK1; bX: JP1
20 same as 19, JP1; less bX; bX: ViA
21 X: ChM, ViA, IP1, NM2, MB1, MB2, IP2, PH1, JP1, BK1; bX: KRe, BA1, JG1
22 same as 21, KRe, BA1, JG1; less bX
23 same as 21; aX: KRe, BA1, JG1
24 X: ChM, IP1, JP1; aX: NM2, MB2, IP2, PH1, BK1; bX: KRe, BA1
25 X: ChM , KRe, BA1, JP1
26 X: ChM, JP1; b X: KRe
27 X: ChM, KRe, JP1, BK1
28 X: ChM; aX: JP1; bX: KRe, HIP; abX: BK1
29 X: ChM, KRe, HIP, BK1
30 same as 29

31
32 bX: ChM; ADD 5: ChM

*13:37 insert 15: 1-85a, add 9: ChM   *14: 9 Dol, USW, Cum, WM1,
   KRe, JP1, BK1   *14:10 USW, Cum, WM1, KRe, WmS, NM2, JP1, BK1

346	friend of mine: how worthy he is I will leave to	33
347	appear hereafter, rather than story him in his	34
348	own hearing.	35
	French. Sir, we have known together in Or-	36
349	leans.	37
	Post. Since when I have been debtor to you	38
350	for courtesies, which I will be ever to pay and yet	39
351	pay still. 40	40
	French. Sir, you o'er-rate my poor kindness:	41
352	I was glad I did atone my countryman and you;	42
353	it had been pity you should have been put toge-	43
354	ther with so mortal a purpose as then each bore,	44
355-6	upon importance of so slight and trivial a nature.	45
	Post. By your pardon, sir, I was then a young	46
357	traveller: rather shunned to go even with what	47
358	I heard than in my every action to be guided by	48
359	others' experiences: but upon my mended judge-	49
369	ment—if I offend not to say it is mended—my	50
361	quarrel was not altogether slight. 51	51
	French. 'Faith, yes, to be put to the arbitre-	52
362	ment of swords, and by such two that would by	53
363	all likelihood have confounded one the other, or	54
364	have fallen both.	55
	Iach. Can we, with manners, ask what was	56
365-6	the difference?	57
	French. Safely, I think: 'twas a contention in	58
367	public, which may, without contradiction, suffer	59
368	the report. It was much like an argument that	60
369	fell out last night, where each of us fell in praise	61
370	of our country mistresses: this gentleman at that	62
371	time vouching—and upon warrant of bloody affirm-	63
372	ation—his to be more fair, virtuous, wise, chaste,	64
373	constant-qualified and less attemptable than any	65
374=5	the rarest of our ladies in France. .	66
	Iach. That lady is not now living, or this	67
376-7	gentleman's opinion by this worn out.	68
378	*Post.* She holds her virtue still and I my mind.	69
	Iach. You must not so far prefer her 'fore ours	70
379-80	of Italy. 71	71
	Post. Being so far provoked as I was in France,	72
381	I would abate her nothing, though I profess my-	73
382-3	self her adorer, not her friend.	74
	Iach. As fair and as good—a kind of hand-in-	75
384	hand comparison—had been something too fair	76
385	and too good for any lady in Britain. If she	77
386	went before others I have seen, as that diamond	78

```
33   X: ChM; bX: HIP, HIC, ViA, PH1, JG1, BK1
34   X: ChM, HIP, HIC, ViA, PH1, BK1; bX: BA1
35   X: ChM, HIP, ViA, BA1, JG1, BK1
36   X: BA1, JG1; N: WmS
37
38
39   X: BK1
40   X: BK1
41   X: CKP; bX: WmS
42   X: Rig, WmS; aX: CKP
43   X: Rig, WmS, PH1, BK1
44   same as 43; bX: ViA, JG1
45   same as 44, ViA; less bX; R: JG1; bX: CKP
46   X: CKP, Han, MB1; bX: JP1
47   X: ChM, G61, Bel, Ox1, Wen, Bat, Roa, Inc, JKT, Oxb, Dol, USW, Cum*
48   X: ChM, G61, Bel, Ox1, Wen, Bat, P95, Low, Roa, JKT, Oxb, Dol, USW*
49   X: G61, Han, NM1, NM2, MB1, JP1; aX: ChM, Bel, Ox1, Wen, Bat, P95*
50   X: Ox1, Han, NM1,  NM2, JP1; aX: BA1, JG1; bX: BK1
51   X: Han, NM1, NM2
52   X: Han, NM1, NM2, MB1, MB2, JG1, JP1; bX: Cum
53   X: ChM, Bel, Ox1, Wen, Bat, Bar, Inc, Oxb, Han, BA1, SM1, NM1, NM2*
54   X: ChM, G61, Bel, Ox1, Wen, Bat, P95, Bar, Low,  Roa, Inc, JKT,Oxb*
55   same as 54, less ChM; aX: ChM
56   X: Cum
57   bX: HIP, PH1, JP1, BK1
58   X: KRe, HIP, IP1, PH1, JP1, BK1; bX: HIC, ViA, NM1, NM2, JG1
59   X: KRe, WmS, HIC, BA1, JG1, JP1; aX: HIP, ViA, NM1, IP1, NM2, PH1, BK1
60   X: WmS, JP1; aX: KRe, ViA, BA1
61   aX: WmS, JP1
62   bX: HIP, ViA, BK1
63   aX: BK1; bX: Low, USW, Cum, KRe, HIC, BA1
64   X: Low, USW, Cum; aX: KRe, BA1
65   X: Low, USW, Cum, HIC; aX: BA1; cX: WmS
66   aX: Low, USW, Cum, BA1
67
68
69
70   X: KRe; R: CKP
71   X: KRe
72   X: KRe, MB2, JP1
73   X: KRe,  MB2; aX: JP1; bX: HIP, IP1, IP2, PH1, BK1
74   X: KRe, HIP, IP1, MB2, IP2, PH1, BK1; b X: ChM
75   X: IP1, MB1, MB2, IP2, PH1, JP1; bX: ViA, BK1
76   same as 75; less bX; aX: ViA, BK1; b X: NM1
77   X: IP1, NM2; aX: NM1, MB1, MB2, IP2, PH1, JP1
78   aX: ChM; bX: ChM
```

*14:47 HIC, Han, BA1, SM1, MB1, JP1; R: JG1; bX: P95, Low, WM1, ViA, NM1,
   IP1, NM2, MB2, PH1, BK1   *14:48 Cum, WM1, HIC, Han,
   BA1, SM1, NM1, IP1, NM2, MB1, MB2, PH1, JP1, BK1 ; aX= ViA
*14:49 Low, Roa, Inc, JKT, Oxb, Dol, USW, Cum, WM1, HIC, BA1, SM1, IP1,
   MB2, PH1, BK1   *14:53 MB1, MB2, JG1, JP1; bX: G61,P95,
   Low, Roa, Dol, USW, WM1, HnF, ViA, IP1, PH1   *14:54 Dol, USW,
   Cum, WM1, HnF, HIC, ViA, Han, BA1, SM1, NM1, IP1, NM2, MB1, MB2, PH1,
   JG1, JP1

387 **of yours** outlustres many I have beheld, I could 79
388 **not** but believe she excelled many: but I have 80
389 **not** seen the most precious diamond that is, nor 81
390 **you the lady.** 82
    Post. I praised her as I rated her: so do I 83
391 **my stone.** 84
392   *Iach.* What do you esteem it at? 85
393   *Post.* More than the world enjoys. 86
    Iach. Either your unparagoned **mistress** is 87
394-5 **dead,** or she's outprized by a trifle. 88
    Post. You are mistaken: the one may **be** 89
396 **sold,** or given, if there were wealth enough for 90
397 **the purchase,** or merit for the gift: the other 91
398 **is not a thing** for sale, and only the gift of the 92
399 **gods.** 93
400   *Iach.* Which the gods have given you? 94
401   *Post.* Which, by their graces, I will keep. 95
    Iach. You may wear her in title yours: but, 96
402 **you know,** strange fowl light upon neighbouring 97
403 **ponds.** Your ring may be stolen too: so your 98
404 **brace** of unprizable estimations; the one is but 99
405 **frail** and the other casual; a cunning thief, or a 100
406 **that way** accomplished courtier, would hazard 101
407-8 **the winning** both of first and last. 102
    Post. Your Italy contains none so accom- 103
409 **plished a courtier** to convince the honour of my 104
410 **mistress,** if, in the holding or loss of that, you 105
411 **term her frail.** I do nothing doubt you have 106
412 **store of thieves;** notwithstanding, I fear not my 107
413 **ring.** 108
414   *Phi.* Let us leave here, gentlemen.   **109** 109
    Post. Sir, with all my heart. This worthy 110
415 **signior,** I thank him, makes no stranger of me; 111
416-17 **we are familiar at first.** 112
    Iach. With five times so much conversation, 113
418 **I should get ground** of your fair mistress, make 114
419 **her go back,** even to the yielding, had I admit- 115
420-1 **tance and opportunity** to friend. 116
422   *Post.* No, no. 117
    Iach. I dare thereupon pawn the moiety of 118
423 **my estate** to your ring; which, in my opinion, 119
424 **o'ervalues it** something: but I make my wager 120
425 **rather against** your confidence than her reputa- 121
426 **tion:** and, to bar your offence herein too, I durst 122
427-8 **attempt it** against any lady in the world. 123
    Post. You are a great deal abused in too bold 124

```
79   aX: ChM
80
81
82   X: Low, USW, Cum, Rig
83   same as 82; bX: PH1, BK1
84   X: Low, USW, Cum, WM1, Rig, PH1, BK1
85   X: Cum, ViA, PH1, BK1
86   same as 85
87   X: PH1, BK1
88   X: PH1, BK1
89   X: PH1, BK1
90   X: BA1, PH1, JG1, BK1; bX: IP1
91   X: PH1, BK1; aX: BA1, IP1, JG1
92   aX: PH1, BK1
93
94
95
96   X: JP1; bX: WmS
97   X: WmS, NM1, JP1
98   aX: WM1; bX: ChM, ViA , BA1, JG1, JP1, BK1
99   X: ChM, BA1, JG1, JP1, BK1; aX: ViA
100  X: ChM; aX: BA1, JG1, JP1, BK1
101  X: ChM
102  X: CHM; bX: ViA, BK1
103  X: ChM, WmS, BK1
104  same as 103; bX: BA1, JG1
105  X: ChM, WmS, BA1, JG1, BK1; bX: HIP, IP1, IP2, PH1, JP1
106  X: ChM, HIP; aX: IP1, IP2, PH1, JP1, BK1
107  X: ChM, HIP; aX: JG1
108  X: ChM, WmS, HIP
109  X: WmS, PH1
110  X: WmS; bX: BK1
111  X: WmS, BK1
112  X: WmS, BK1
113  X: WmS, BK1
114  X: WmS; bX: HnF
115  X: WmS; aX: HnF; bX: KRe
116  X: KRe, WmS
117  X: WmS
118  X: JP1
119  X: JP1; bX: IP1, PH1
120  X: PH1, JP1; aX: IP1
121  X: PH1, ,JP1
122  X: PH1, JP1, BK1
123  same as 122
124  X: WmS, HIP, NM1, NM2, JP1, BK1
```

429	a persuasion; and I doubt not you sustain what	125
430-1	you're worthy of by your attempt.	126
432	*Iach.* What's that?	127
	Post. A repulse: though your attempt, as you	128
433-4	call it, deserve more; a punishment too. 129	129
	Phi. Gentlemen, enough of this: it came in	130
435	too suddenly; let it die as it was born, and, I	131
436-7	pray you, be better acquainted.	132
	Iach. Would I had put my estate and my	133
438	neighbour's on the approbation of what I have	134
439	spoke! ·	135
440	*Post.* What lady would you choose to assail?	136
	Iach. Yours; whom in constancy you think	137
441	stands so safe. I will lay you ten thousand ducats	138
442	to your ring, that, commend me to the court	139
443	where your lady is, with no more advantage than	140
444	the opportunity of a second conference, and I	141
445	will bring from thence that honour of hers which	142
446	you imagine so reserved.	143
447	*Post.* I will wage against your gold, gold to	144
448-9	it: my ring I hold dear as my finger; 'tis part of it.	145
	Iach. You are afraid, and therein the wiser.	146
450	If you buy ladies' flesh at a million a dram, you	147
451	cannot preserve it from tainting: but I see you	148
452-3	have some religion in you, that you fear. 149	149
	Post. This is but a custom in your tongue;	150
454-5	you bear a graver purpose, I hope.	151
	Iach. I am the master of my speeches, and	152
456-7	would undergo what's spoken, I swear.	153
	Post. Will you? I shall but lend my diamond	154
458	till your return: let there be covenants drawn	155
459	between's: my mistress exceeds in goodness the	156
460	hugeness of your unworthy thinking: I dare you	157
461-2	to this match: here's my ring.	158
463	*Phi.* I will have it no lay. 159	159
	Iach. By the gods, it is one. If I bring you	160
464	no sufficient testimony that I have enjoyed the	161
465	dearest bodily part of your mistress, my ten thou-	162
466	sand ducats are yours; so is your diamond too:	163
467	if I come off, and leave her in such honour as you	164
468	have trust in, she your jewel, this your jewel, and	165
469	my gold are yours: provided I have your com-	166
470	mendation for my more free entertainment.	167
	Post. I embrace these conditions; let us have	168
471	articles betwixt us. Only, thus far you shall	169
472	answer: if you make your voyage upon her and	170

```
125   X: WmS, HIP, NM1, NM2, JP1; aX: BK1; bX: CKP
126   X: CKP, WmS, HIP, NM1, NM2, JP1
127   X: WmS, HIP, NM1, NM2, JP1; aX: CKP
128   same as 127; less aX; b X: PH1
129   same as 127,  PH1; less aX
130   X: WmS, NM1, NM2; bX: KRe

131   X: KRe, WmS, NM1, NM2
132   same as 131, ViA
133   X: WmS, NM1, NM2, JP1; bX: CKP
134   same as 133; less bX; aX: CKP
135   same as 133, less bX
136
137   X: ViA, Han, BK1
138   aX: ViA, Han, BK1
139   bX: CKP
140   X: CKP; bX: BK1
141   X: CKP; aX: BK1; bX: HIC
142   X: HIC; aX: CKP
143   X: HIC; ADD 3: ChM
144   bX: WM1
145   aX: WM1; bX: BK1
146   X: JP1, BK1; R: Bel, Wen, KRe, SM1; bX: WmS, HIC, IP1
147   X: HnF, WmS, HIC, ViA, NM1, NM2, JP1
148   X: NM1, NM2, JP1; aX: HnF, WmS, HIC, ViA; bX: ChM, BK1
149   X: ChM, NM1, NM2, JP1, BK1
150   X: NM1, NM2, JP1
151   same as 150
152   same as 150
153   same as 150
154   aX: NM1, NM2, JP1; bX: G61, Bel, P95, JKT, KRe
155   X: KRe; aX: G61, Bel, P95; bX: ChM, ViA, PH1, BK1
156   X: KRe, PH1, BK1; aX: ChM, ViA
157   aX: KRe, PH1, BK1
158   bX: PH1, BK1
159   X: CKP
160   X: CKP; bX: NM1, NM2
161   X: NM1, NM2; bX: KRe, WmS, HIC, BA1
162   X: KRe, HIC, NM1, NM2; aX: WmS, BA1; bX: IP1; B: WM1, HnF
163   X: KRe, NM1, IP1, NM2; aX: HIC; bX: Inc, JKT, Dol, WmS, BA1, BK1
164   X: Inc, JKT, Dol,  KRe, WmS, IP1, BK1
165   X: Inc, JKT, Dol, WmS; aX: KRe, IP1, BK1
166   X: WmS, BA1; aX: Inc, JKT; bX: HIC, PH1, BK1
167   X: WmS, HIC, BA1, PH1, BK1
168   bX: HIC, PH1, JP1, BK1
169   X: PH1, JP1, BK1; aX: HIC; b X: HIP
170   X: HIP, HIC; aX: WmS, PH1; bX: HnF
```

473	**give me directly** to understand you have pre-	171
474	**vailed, I** am no further your enemy; she is not	172
475	**worth our** debate: if she remain unseduced, you	173
476	**not making** it appear otherwise, for your ill	174
	opinion and the assault you have made to her	175
477-8	**chastity** you shall answer me with your sword.	176
	Iach. Your hand; a covenant: we will have	177
479	**these things** set down by lawful counsel, and	178
480	**straight away** for Britain, lest the bargain should	179
481	**catch cold** and starve: I will fetch my gold and	180
482-3	**have our** two wagers recorded. **181**	181
484	*Post.* Agreed.	182
	[*Exeunt Posthumus and Iachimo.*	
485	*French.* Will this hold, think you?	183
486	*Phi.* Signior Iachimo will not from it. Pray,	184
487	**let us** follow 'em. [*Exeunt.*	185

488,+1   **SCENE V.** *Britain. A room in Cymbeline's palace.*

489   *Enter* QUEEN, Ladies, *and* CORNELIUS.

490	*Queen.* Whiles yet the dew's on ground, gather	
491	those flowers:	1
492	**Make haste**: who has the note of them?	
493	*First Lady.* I, madam.	2
494	*Queen.* Dispatch. [*Exeunt Ladies.*	3
	Now, master doctor, have you brought those	
495	drugs?	4
	Cor. Pleaseth your highness, ay: here they	
496	are, madam: [*Presenting a small box.*	5
497	**But I** beseech your grace, without offence,—	6
498	**My conscience** bids me ask—wherefore you have	7
	Commanded of me these most poisonous com-	
499	pounds,	8
500	**Which are** the movers of a languishing death;	9
501	**But though** slow, deadly?	
502	*Queen.* I wonder, doctor, **10**	10
503	**Thou ask'st** me such a question. Have I not been	11
504	**Thy pupil** long? Hast thou not learn'd me how	12
505	**To make** perfumes? distil? preserve? yea, so	13
506	**That our** great king himself doth woo me oft	14
507	**For my** confections? Having thus far proceeded,—	15
508	**Unless thou** think'st me devilish—is't not meet	16
509	**That I** did amplify my judgement in	17
510	**Other conclusions?** I will try the forces	18
511	**Of these** thy compounds on such creatures as	19

171 X: HIP; aX: HIC
172 X: HIP; bX: PH1
173 X: HIP, HIC, PH1; bX: WmS
174 X: HIP, BK1; aX: WmS, HIC, PH1
175 X: HIP; aX: BK1
176 X: HIP; abX: KRe
177 X: KRe; aX: ViA
178 X: KRe, BK1; bX: WmS; ADD 2: WmS
179 X: KRe, Wm S; bX: HIC
180 aX: KRe, WmS, HIC; bX: BK1
181 X: BK1
182 X: Dol, Lac, KRe, HM1, ViA, Han

183 same as 182, JKT; ADD 2, insert 31: 1-86: ChM
184 X: ChM, Inc, JKT, Dol, Lac, KRe, HM1, MTh, ViA, Han
185 same as 184

Scene 15

1 X: G61, Bel, Ox1, Wen, Bat, P95, Bar, Low, Roa, Oxb, Dol, USW, Cum,
     WM1, CKP, Rig, ViA; MOVE 1-85a to follow 13: 37: ChM, Inc; MOVE*
2 same as 1, Inc; less MOVEs; aX: BK1
3 same as 1, less Ox1, CKP; less MOVEs; bX HnF; MOVE 3-87 to follow
     11: 159: Ox1
4 aX: Low, Roa; N: Cum; MOVE 4-87 to follow 11: 158: G61, Bel, Dol;
     MOVE 4-87 to follow 13: 40: JKT, Cum; MOVE 4-87 to follow 11:*
5 bX: ChM, G61, Wen, Bat, P95, Low, Roa, Inc, JKT, Dol, USW
6 X: ChM, WM1, CKP; bX: HIP, BA1, PH1, BK1
7 same as 6; less bX; aX: HIP, BA1, PH1, BK1

8 X: WmS, CKP; ADD 3: ChM
9 X: ChM, G61, Bel, Ox1, Wen, Bat, Low, Roa, Inc, JKT, Oxb, Dol, Cum,
     WM1, CKP, ViA, BK1
10 X: ChM, Inc, WM1, CKP; aX: G61, Bel, Ox1, Wen, Bat, Low, Roa, Inc*
11 X: WM1, CKP; aX: Cum
12 X: WM1, CKP; bX: ChM, G61, Bel, Ox1, Wen, Bat, Bar, Roa, Inc, JKT*
13 X: ChM, G61, Bel, Ox1, Wen, Bat, Bar, Low, Roa, Inc, JKT, Oxb, Dol*
14 same as 14, HIP, ViA; less bX
15 same as 14; bX: Lac, HM1, MTh, WmS, PH1
16 X: ChM, G61, Bel, Ox1, Wen, Bat, Bar, Low, Roa, Inc, JKT, Oxb, Dol*
17 same as 16; less aX; aX: BK1
18 X: ChM, WM1, CKP; aX: Bel, Ox1, Wen, Bat, Bar, Low, Roa, Inc, Oxb*
19 X: ChM, Wen, Bat, WM1, CKP; bX: G61, Bel, Ox1, Bar, Low, Inc, JKT,
     Oxb, USW, Cum, Rig

*15: 1 1-87 to follow 11: 158: HIC: MOVE 1-87 to follow 11: 175: WmS, SM;
     MOVE1-87 to follow 13: 40: KRe   *15: 4 159: Wen, Bat, P95,
     Bar, Oxb, USW, Rig   *15:10 JKT, Oxb, Dol, Cum, BK1
*15:12 Oxb, Dol, USW, Cum, Rig; ADD 21: ChM, Low   *15:13 USW,
     Cum, WM1, CKP, Rig; bX: HIP.   *15:16 USW, Cum, WM1, CKP, Lac,
     Rig, HM1, MTh, WmS, ViA, PH1; aX: HIP, BK1   *15:18 Dol, USW,
     Cum, Lac, HM1, MTh, WmS, ViA, PH1; bX: G61, JKT, Rig

512	We count not worth the hanging, but none human,	20
513	To try the vigour of them and apply 21	21
514	Allayments to their act, and by them gather	22
515	Their several virtues and effects.	
516	*Cor.* Your highness	23
517	Shall from this practice but make hard your heart:	24
518	Besides, the seeing these effects will be	25
519	Both noisome and infectious.	
520	*Queen.* O, content thee.	26

521	*Enter* PISANIO.

522	[*Aside*] Here comes a flattering rascal; upon him	27
523	Will I first work: he's for his master,	28
524	And enemy to my son. How now, Pisanio!	29
525	Doctor, your service for this time is ended; 30	30
526	Take your own way.	
527	*Cor.* [*Aside*] I do suspect you, madam;	31
528	But you shall do no harm.	
529	*Queen.* [*To Pisanio*] Hark thee, a word.	32
	Cor. [*Aside*] I do not like her. She doth	
530	think she has	33
531	Strange lingering poisons: I do know her spirit,	34
532	And will not trust one of her malice with	35
533	A drug of such damn'd nature. Those she has	36
534	Will stupify and dull the sense awhile;	37
	Which first, perchance, she'll prove on cats and	
535	dogs,	38
536	Then afterward up higher: but there is	39
537	No danger in what show of death it makes, 40	40
538	More than the locking-up the spirits a time,	41
539	To be more fresh, reviving. She is fool'd	42
540	With a most false effect; and I the truer,	43
541	So to be false with her.	
542	*Queen.* No further service, doctor,	44
543	Until I send for thee.	
544	*Cor.* I humbly take my leave. [*Exit.*	45
545	*Queen.* Weeps she still, say'st thou? Dost	
546	thou think in time	46
547	She will not quench and let instructions enter	47
548	Where folly now possesses? Do thou work:	48
	When thou shalt bring me word she loves my	
549	son,	49
550	I'll tell thee on the instant thou art then 50	50
551	As great as is thy master, greater, for	51
552	His fortunes all lie speechless and his name	52
553	Is at last gasp: return he cannot, nor	53

*1539 Bat, P95, Bar, Low, Inc, JKT, Oxb, Dol, USW, Cum, Lac, Rig, HM1,
   MTh, HIP, ViA, BA1, PH1, JG1, BK1 *15:44 HM1, MTh, WmS, Han
*15:52 bX: MB2

20 X: ChM, G61, Bel, Oxl, Wen, Bat, Bar, Low, Inc, JKT, Oxb, USW, Cum*
21 X: ChM, USW, WM1, CKP, HIP; R: Wen, Bat; aX: G61, Bel, Oxl, Bar, Low*
22 X: ChM, WM1, CKP, PH1, BK1; aX: HIP

23 X: ChM, WM1, CKP; aX: PH1, BK1; bX: G61, Bel, Oxl, Wen, Bat, P95,Bar*
24 X: ChM, G61, Bel, Oxl, Wen, Bat, P95, Bar, Low, Roa, Inc, JKT, Oxb*
25 same as 24, HIP, ViA, PH1, BK1

26 same as 24; aX: HIP, ViA, PH1, BK1

27 X: ChM
28 X: ChM; bX: JG1
29 X: ChM; aX: JG1; bX: Wen, Bat; ADD 3: Bel, Bar, JKT; ADD 4: Oxl,Wen*
30 X: ChM, USW

31 X: ChM, JKT, Dol, CKP, HIC; aX: G61, Bel, Oxl, Wen, Bat, Bar, Roa,
       Inc, Oxb, USW, Cum; bX: WM1, SM1, PH1, BK1
32 X: ChM, HIC, SM1, BK1; aX: JKT, Dol, WM1, CKP, PH1; bX: Low, USW, ViA,
       MB1, MB2; ADD 1: G61; ADD 2: JKT, Dol
33 X: ChM, G61, Bel, Oxl, Wen, Bat, Bar, Low, Roa, Inc, Oxb, Dol, USW*
34 X: ChM, G61, Bel, Wen, Bat, Bar, Roa, HIC, NM1, NM2 aX: Oxl, P95,*
35 X: ChM, Roa, HIP, NM1, NM2
36 X: ChM, HIP, NM1, NM2; aX: Roa; bX: WM1, HnF, CKP, PH1
37 X: ChM, WM1, HnF, CKP, HIP, NM1, NM2, PH1; cX: BA1

38 X: ChM, G61, Bel, Oxl, Wen, Bat, P95, Bar, Low, Inc, JKT, Oxb, Dol,*
39 X: ChM, WM1, HnF , CKP, HIC, SM1, NM1, NM2; aX: G61, Bel, Oxl, Wen,*
40 X: ChM, WM1, HnF, CKP, SM1, NM1, NM2; b X: Bel, Oxl, Wen, Bat,Bar,JKT
41 X: ChM, G61, P95, WM1, HnF, CKP, HIC, SM1, NM1, NM2
42 X: ChM, HIC, SM1; aX: WM1, HnF, CKP, NM1, NM2; bX: HIP, BA1, PH1, JG1,BK1
43 X: ChM, HIP, HIC, BA1, SM1, PH1, JG1, BK1; bX:ViA

44 X: ChM, BK1; aX: HIP, HIC, ViA, BA1, SM1, PH1, JG1; bX: G61, Bel, Oxl,
       Wen, Bat, Bar, Low, Roa, Inc, JKT, Oxb, Dol, USW, Cum, CKP, Lac,Rig*
45 X: ChM, G61, Bel, Oxl, Wen, Bat, Bar, Low, Roa, Inc, JKT, Oxb, Dol,
       USW, Cum, CKP, Lac, Rig, HM1, MTh, WmS; aX: Han
46 aX: WmS; bX: ChM, WM1, CKP; ADD 1: ChM
47 X: ChM, WM1, CKP
48 X: ChM; aX: WM1, CKP

49
50 R: Cum
51 X: ChM; bX: WM1, CKP, Lac, Rig, HM1, MTh, WmS, HIP, ViA, SM1, PH1
52 X: WM1, CKP, Lac, Rig, HM1, MTh, WmS, HIP, HIC, ViA, SM1, PH1, BK1;*
53 same as 52, MB2, less BK1; less bX; aX: BK1; bX: G61, Bel, Oxl, Wen, Bat,
       Bar, Low, Roa, Inc, JKT, Oxb, Dol, USW, Cum, HnF

*15:20 WM1, CKP, Rig   *15:21 Inc, JKT, Oxb, Cum, Rig; bX:PH1, BK1
*15:23 Low, Roa, Inc, JKT, Oxb, Dol, USW, Cum, Rig   *15:24 Dol,
   USW, Cum, WM1, CKP, Rig   *15:29 Oxl, Wen, Bat, Oxb; Insert 75b-78a: G61, Oxl, Roa   *15:33 Cum, NM1, NM2; aX: JKT;
   bX P95, SM1   *15:34 Low, Inc, Oxb, Dol, USW, Cum, SM1; bX:
   HIP   *15:38 USW, Cum, WM1, HnF, CKP, Lac, Rig, HM1, MTh, HIP,
   HIC, ViA, BA1, SM1, NM1, NM2, PH1, JG1, BK1

554	Continue where he is: to shift his being	54
555	Is to exchange one misery with another,	55
556	And every day that comes comes to decay	56
557	A day's work in him. What shalt thou expect,	57
558	To be depender on a thing that leans,	58
559	Who cannot be new built, nor has no friends, 59	59
	So much as but to prop him? [*The Queen drops the*	
560	*box: Pisanio takes it up.*] Thou takest up	60
561	Thou know'st not what; but take it for thy labour:	61
562	It is a thing I made, which hath the king	62
563	Five times redeem'd from death: I do not know	63
564	What is more cordial. Nay, I prithee, take it;	64
565	It is an earnest of a further good	65
566	That I mean to thee. Tell thy mistress how	66
567	The case stands with her; do't as from thyself.	67
568	Think what a chance thou changest on, but think	68
569	Thou hast thy mistress still, to boot, my son,	69
570	Who shall take notice of thee: I'll move the king	70
571	To any shape of thy preferment such 71	71
572	As thou'lt desire; and then myself, I chiefly,	72
573	That set thee on to this desert, am bound	73
574	To load thy merit richly. Call my women:	74
	Think on my words. [*Exit Pisanio.*	
575	A sly and constant knave,	75
576	Not to be shaked; the agent for his master	76
577	And the remembrancer of her to hold	77
578	The hand-fast to her lord. I have given him that	78
579	Which, if he take, shall quite unpeople her	79
580	Of liegers for her sweet, and which she after, 80	80
581	Except she bend her humour, shall be assured	81
582	To taste of too.	
583	*Re-enter* PISANIO *and* Ladies.	
584	So, so: well done, well done:	82
585	The violets, cowslips, and the primroses,	83
586	Bear to my closet. Fare thee well, Pisanio;	84
587	Think on my words. [*Exeunt Queen and Ladies.*	
588	*Pis.* And shall do:	85
589	But when to my good lord I prove untrue,	86
590	I'll choke myself: there's all I'll do for you. [*Exit.*	87
591,+1	SCENE VI. *The same. Another room in the*	
591+2	*palace.*	
592	*Enter* IMOGEN.	
593	*Imo.* A father cruel, and a step-dame false;	1

54 X: G61, Bel, Ox1, Wen, Bat, Bar, Low, Roa, Inc, JKT, Oxb, Dol, USW*
55 same as 54, P95, BA1, IP1, JG1, JP1, BK1; less bX; ADD 4: ChM
56 same as 55, ChM; less ADD
57 X: ChM, WM1, HnF, CKP, LAC, Rig, HM1, MTh, WmS, HIP, HIC, ViA, BA1,SM1*
58 same as 57, less ChM; less aX
59 same as 58

60 X: Rig, HIC; aX: WM1, HnF, CKP, Lac, HM1, MTh, WmS, HIP, ViA, BA1,SM1*
61 aX: Rig
62
63 bX: WM1, CKP, BK1
64 X: HIC; aX: WM1, CKP, BK1
65 X: ChM
66 X: ChM; bX: WM1, CKP, HIP, PH1, JG1, BK1
67 X: ChM, WM1, CKP, HIP, PH1, JG1, BK1; bX: NM1
68 X: ChM, G61, Bel, Ox1, Wen, Bat, Bar, Low, JKT, Oxb, Dol, USW, Cum,WM1*
69 same as 68, BA1, MB2, less Rig; less bX; aX: Rig
70 X: ChM, WM1, HnF, CKP, HIP, PH1, JG1; aX: G61, Ox1, Wen, Bat, Bar,Low*
71 X: ChM, Ox1, WM1, CKP, HIP, PH1, JG1
72 same as 71, BK1; bX: G61, Bel, Wen, Bat, Bar, JKT, Oxb, HIC, ViA,BA1
73 X: ChM, G61, Bel, Ox1, Wen, Bat, Bar, JKT, Oxb, WM1, CKP, HIP, HIC,ViA*
74 X: Bel, Ox1, Wen, Bat, Bar, JKT, Oxb, CKP, HIC, ViA; aX: G61, WM1, HIP,
      SM1, NM1, PH1, JG1; bX: P95, Low, Inc, Dol; ADD 14:Roa,USW, Cum
75 X: P95, Dol, USW; aX: WM1, WmS, HIC, ViA; bX: Bel, Wen, Bar, Low, Inc*
76 X: Bel, Wen, P95, Bar,Low, Inc, JKT, Dol, USW, Cum, CKP, Rig, WmS,BK1*
77 X: ChM, Bel, Wen, P95, Bar, Low, Inc, JKT, Dol, USW, Cum, WM1, CKP, Rig*
78 X: USW, CKP, Rig; aX:WM1, Bel, Wen, P95, Bar, Low, Inc, JKT, Dol, Cum*
79 X: Roa, USW, CKP; bX: ChM; ADD 1: ChM
80 X: ChM, Roa, USW, CKP; bX: WM1
81 X: ChM, Roa, USW, WM1, CKP

82 X: Roa, USW, WM1, CKP; aX: ChM; bX: G61, Bel, Wen, Bat, P95, Bar, Low*
83 X: G61, Bel, Wen, Bat, P95, Bar, Low, Roa, Inc, JKT, Oxb, Dol, USW,Cum*
84 X: Roa, CKP; aX: G61, Bel, Wen, Bat, P95, Bar, Low, Inc, JKT, Oxb, Dol,
      USW, Cum, WM1, Rig, WmS; bX: ViA, Han; Insert 13: 1-40: ViA
85 X: Roa, Han; aX: CKP, ViA; bX: WM1, JG1; ADD 9: ChM; MOVE 86b-87 to*
86 X: ChM, Roa, Han, SM1, JG1
87 same as 86; ADD 11: G61, Bel, Bar, Low, JKT, Dol; ADD 13: Bat; ADD 4,
      insert 21: 62-70: Inc

Scene 16

Records confusing: Han
 1 X: HIC, MB1, MB2

*15:54 Cum, WM1, HnF, CKP, Lac, Rig, HM1, MTh, WmS, HIP, HIC, ViA, SM1,MB2,
   PH1; bX: P95, BA1, IP1, JG1, JP1, BK1   *15:57 MB2, PH1,BK1;
   aX:G61, Bel, Ox1, Wen, Bat, P95, Bar, Low, Roa, Inc, JKT, Oxb, Dol, USW,
   Cum, IP1, JG1, JP1   *15:60 MB2, PH1, BK1   *15:68 HnF,
   CKP, Rig, HIP, HIC, SM1, NM1, IP1, IP2, PH1, JG1, BK1; bX: BA1
*15:70 JKT, Oxb, Dol, USW, Cum, HIC, BA1, SM1, NM1, IP1, MB1, IP2, BK1
*15:73 SM1, NM1, PH1, JG1; aX: BA1   *15:75JKT, Cum, CKP, Rig; Insert
   75b-87: ViA; MOVE 75b-78a to follow 29: G61, Ox1, Bat, Roa, Oxb

594	A foolish suitor to a wedded lady,	2
	That hath her husband banish'd;—O, that hus-	
595	band!	3
596	My supreme crown of grief! and those repeated	4
597	Vexations of it! Had I been thief-stol'n,	5
598	As my two brothers, happy! but most miserable	6
599	Is the desire that's glorious: blest be those,	7
600	How mean soe'er, that have their honest wills,	8
601	Which seasons comfort. Who may this be? Fie!	9

602	*Enter* PISANIO *and* IACHIMO.	
603	*Pis.* Madam, a noble gentleman of Rome, 10	10
604	Comes from my lord with letters.	
605	*Iach.* Change you, madam?	11
606	The worthy Leonatus is in safety	12
607	And greets your highness dearly.	
607+1	[*Presents a letter.*	
608	*Imo.* Thanks, good sir:	13
609	You're kindly welcome.	14
	Iach. [*Aside*] All of her that is out of door	
610	most rich!	15
611	If she be furnish'd with a mind so rare,	16
612	She is alone the Arabian bird. and I	17
613	Have lost the wager. Boldness be my friend!	18
614	Arm me, audacity, from head to foot!	19
615	Or, like the Parthian, I shall flying fight; 20	20
616	Rather, directly fly.	21
617	*Imo.* [*Reads*] 'He is one of the noblest note,	22
618	to whose kindnesses I am most infinitely tied.	23
619	Reflect upon him accordingly, as you value your	24
620	trust— LEONATUS.'	25
621	So far I read aloud:	26
622	But even the very middle of my heart	27
623	Is warm'd by the rest, and takes it thankfully.	28
624	You are as welcome, worthy sir, as I	29
625	Have words to bid you, and shall find it so 30	30
626	In all that I can do.	
627	*Iach.* Thanks, fairest lady.	31
	What, are men mad? Hath nature given them	
628	eyes	32
629	To see this vaulted arch, and the rich crop	33
630	Of sea and land, which can distinguish 'twixt	34
631	The fiery orbs above and the twinn'd stones	35
632	Upon the number'd beach? and can we not	36
633	Partition make with spectacles so precious	37
634	'Twixt fair and foul?	

2 same as 1

3 same as 1
4 same as 1; b$\underline{X}$: WM1 , CKP, KRe, PH1, BK1
5 same as 1; $\underline{aX}$: WM1, CKP, KRe, PH1, BK1
6 same as 1; $\underline{bX}$: KRe, NM1, PH1, JG1, JP1
7 X: HIC, MB1, MB2, PH1, JP1; a$\underline{X}$: KRe, NM1, JG1; b$\underline{X}$: BK1
8 same as 7, BK1; less $\underline{aX}$, b$\underline{X}$
9 X: HIC, MB1, PH1; a$\underline{X}$: $\overline{MB1}$, JP1, BK1; b$\underline{X}$: ChM

10

11 $\underline{cX}$: Wm S
12

13
14

15
16
17
18
19 X: MB1, JG1, JP1
20 X: G61, Bel, Ox1, Wen, Bat, P95, Bar, Low, Roa, Inc, JKT, Oxb, Do1*
21 same as 20, less Cum, CKP, Rig, BA1; a$\underline{X}$: Cum, CKP, BA1
22
23
24 X: BK1
25 X: BK1
26
27 X: KRe
28 X: KRe
29
30

31

32 X: NM1
33 X: NM1; b$\underline{X}$: KRe
34 X: KRe, $\overline{NM1}$
35 XL KRe, NM1
36 X: NM1; a$\underline{X}$: KRe
37 X: NM1; $\underline{bX}$: G61, Bel, Ox1, Wen, Bat, P95, Low, Roa, Inc, JKT, Oxb,
     USW, Cum

*16:20 USW, Cum, WM1, HnF, CKP, KRe, Rig, WmS, HIC, ViA, BA1, SM1, MB2,
  PH1, JG1, JP1

635	*Imo.* What makes your admiration?	38
	Iach. It cannot be i' the eye, for apes and	
336	monkeys	39
637	'Twixt two such shes would chatter this way and	40
	Contemn with mows the other; nor i' the judge-	
638	ment, 41	41
639	For idiots in this case of favour would	42
640	Be wisely definite; nor i' the appetite;	43
641	Sluttery to such neat excellence opposed	44
642	Should make desire vomit emptiness,	45
643	Not so allured to feed.	46
644	*Imo.* What is the matter, trow?	
645	*Iach.* The cloyed will,	47
646	That satiate yet unsatisfied desire, that tub	48
647	Both fill'd and running, ravening first the lamb	49
648	Longs after for the garbage.	
649	*Imo.* What, dear sir, 50	50
650	Thus raps you? Are you well?	51
	Iach. Thanks, madam: well. [*To Pisanio*]	
651	Beseech you, sir, desire	52
652	My man's abode where I did leave him: he	53
653	Is strange and peevish.	
654	*Pis.* I was going, sir,	54
655	To give him welcome. [*Exit.*	55
656	*Imo.* Continues well my lord? His health,	
657	beseech you?	56
658	*Iach.* Well, madam.	57
659	*Imo.* Is he disposed to mirth? I hope he is.	58
	Iach. Exceeding pleasant; none a stranger	
660	there	59
661	So merry and so gamesome: he is call'd 60	60
662	The Briton reveller.	
663	*Imo.* When he was here,	61
664	He did incline to sadness, and oft-times	62
665	Not knowing why.	
666	*Iach.* I never saw him sad.	63
667	There is a Frenchman his companion, one	64
668	An eminent monsieur, that, it seems, much loves	65
669	A Gallian girl at home; he furnaces	66
	The thick sighs from him, whiles the jolly	
670	Briton—	67
	Your lord, I mean—laughs from's free lungs,	
671	cries 'O,	68
	Can my sides hold, to think that man, who	
672	knows	69
673	By history, report, or his own proof, 70	70

38 X: NM1

39 X: KRe, WmS, NM1, NM2, BK1; bX: ChM, HIC, ViA, BA1, SM1
40 X: ChM, KRe, WmS, HIC, ViA, BA1, SM1, NM1, NM2, JG1, BK1

41 X: KRe, WmS, BA1, SM1, NM1, NM2, JG1, BK1; aX: ChM, HIC, ViA; bX: Bel*
42 X: Bel, Ox1, Wen, Bat, Bar, Low, Inc, JKT, Oxb, USW, Cum, WM1, HnF*
43 same as 42, less BA1; aX: BA1; bX: WM1, HIC
44 X: ChM, G61, Bel, Ox1, Wen, Bat, P96, Bar, Low, Roa, Inc, JKT, Oxb,*
45 same as 44; bX: Dol
46 same as 44, Dol, less Wen, Bar, Inc, JKT, Cum; less bX; aX: Wen, Bar,
      Inc, JKT, Cum
47 X: KRe, WmS, ViA, NM1, NM2, MB2, BK1; bX: ChM, Bar, CKP, HIC, BA1
48 X: ChM, G61, Wen, Bat, P95, CKP, KRe, Rig, WmS, HIC, ViA, BA1, NM1,NM2*
49 X: ChM, CKP, KRe, WmS, HIC, ViA , NM1, NM2, MB2, BK1; aX: G61, Bel,
      Wen, Bat, P95, Low, Inc, JKT, Dol, USW, Cum, WM1, HnF, Lac, Rig,HIP*
50 X: ChM, KRe, HIC, NM2; aX: CKP, WmS, ViA, MB2, BK1
51 X: KRe, HIC, NM1, NM2; aX: BA1; bX: WmS

52 X: KRe; aX: WmS, HIC, NM1; bX: ChM, WM1
53 X: ChM, KRe; aX: WM1

54 X: ChM, KRe
55 X: ChM, KRe

56
57
58

59 bX: ChM
60 aX: ChM

61 bX: KRe
62 X: KRe

63 X: KRe; bX: WM1
64 X: WM1, KRe; bX: Ox1, Wen, Bar, Inc, JKT, Dol
65 X: WM1, KRe; aX: Bel, Ox1, Wen, Bar, Inc, JKT, Oxb, Dol, Cum, Rig,WmS
66 X: KRe; aX: WM1; bX: ChM

67 X: KRe; R: ChM

68 X: KRe; aX: ChM

69 X: Kre, NM1, NM2
70 same as 69

*16:41 Ox1, Wen, Bat, Bar , Low, Inc, JKT, Oxb, USW, Cum, WM1, HnF, CKP,
   Rig   *16:42 CKP, KRe, Rig, WmS, BA1, SM1, NM1, NM2, JG1,BK1
*16:44 USW, Cum, WM1, HnF, CKP, KRe, Rig, WmS, HIG, ViA, BA1, SM1, NM1,
   NM2, JG1, BK1   *16:48 MB2, BK1; aX: Bar; bX: Bel, Low, Inc,
   JKT, Dol, USW, Cum, WM1, HnF, BA1   *16:49 BA1, NM1

674	What woman is, yea, what she cannot choose	71
675	But must be, will his free hours languish for.	72
676	Assured bondage?'	
677	*Imo.* Will my lord say so?	73
	Iach. Ay, madam, with his eyes in flood with	
678	laughter:	74
679	It is a recreation to be by	75
	And hear him mock the Frenchman. But, heavens	
680	know,	76
681	Some men are much to blame.	
682	*Imo.* Not he, I hope.	77
683	*Iach.* Not he: but yet heaven's bounty to-	
684	wards him might	78
685	Be used more thankfully. In himself, 'tis much ;	79
686	In you, which I account his beyond all talents, 80	80
687	Whilst I am bound to wonder, I am bound	81
688	To pity too.	
689	*Imo.* What do you pity, sir?	82
690	*Iach.* Two creatures heartily.	
691	*Imo.* Am I one, sir?	83
692	You look on me: what wreck discern you in me	84
693	Deserves your pity?	
694	*Iach.* Lamentable! What,	85
695	To hide me from the radiant sun and solace	86
696	I' the dungeon by a snuff?	
697	*Imo.* I pray you, sir,	87
698	Deliver with more openness your answers	88
699	To my demands: Why do you pity me?	89
700	*Iach.* That others do— 90	90
701	I was about to say—enjoy your——But	91
702	It is an office of the gods to venge it,	92
703	Not mine to speak on 't.	
704	*Imo.* You do seem to know	93
	Something of me, or what concerns me : pray	
705	you,—	94
706	Since doubting things go ill often hurts more	95
707	Than to be sure they do; for certainties	96
708	Either are past remedies, or, timely knowing,	97
709	The remedy then born—discover to me	98
710	What both you spur and stop.	
711	*Iach.* Had I this cheek 99	99
712	To bathe my lips upon: this hand, whose touch,	100
713	Whose every touch, would force the feeler's soul	101
714	To the oath of loyalty; this object, which	102
715	Takes prisoner the wild motion of mine eye,	103
716	Fixing it only here; should I, damn'd then,	104

71 same as 69
72 same as 69; a̲X̲: ChM

73 same as 69

74 same as 69
75 X: KRe

76 X: KRr

77 X: KRe

78 X: KRe
79 X: KRe; b̲X̲: ChM
80 X: KRe; R̲: ChM
81

82

83 X: KRe, WmS
84 X: KRe, WmS; b̲X̲: JP1

85 X: KRe, WmS, JP1; b̲X̲: CKP, MB2, BK1
86 X: CKP, KRe, WmS, M̄B2, JP1, BK1; b̲X̲: IP1

87 X: CKP, KRe, WmS, IP1, JP1, BK1; a̲X̲: MB2
88 X: CKP, WmS, JP1, BK1; a̲X̲: IP1
89 X: CKP, WmS, BK1; a̲X̲: K̄R̄e, JP1
90 X: CKP, KRe
91 X: CKP, KRe
92 X: CKP, KRe

93 X: KRe; a̲X̲: CKP

94 X: KRe
95 X: WM1, KRe; b̲X̲: Rig, BK1
96 X: WM1, KRe, R̄ig; b̲X̲: ChM, G61, Bel, Ox1, Wen, Bat, P95, Bar, Low*
97 X: ChM, G61, Bel, Ōx1, Wen, Bat, P95, Bar, Low, Inc, JKT, Oxb, Dol*
98 X: Oxb, KRe; a̲X̲: ChM, G61, Bel, Ox1, Wen, Bat, P95, Bar, Low, Inc,
     JKT, Dol, U̅S̅W̅, Cum, WM1, HnF, CKP, Rig, WmS, HIC, ViA, BA1, NM2*
99 a̲X̲: Oxb, KRe
100
101
102 b̲X̲: HnF, SM1, PH1, BK1
103 X̅: HnF, KRe, HIC, SM1, PH1, BK1
104 X: KRe, HIC; a̲X̲: HnF, PH1, BK1; b̲X̲: CKP, WmS

*16:96 Inc, JKT, Oxb, Dol, USW, Cum, HnF, CKP, WmS, HIC, ViA, BA1, NM2,
   MB1, MB2, PH1, JG1, JP1   *16:97 USW, Cum, WM1, HnF, CKP,
   KRe, Rig, WmS, HIC, ViA, BA1, NM2, MB1, M̄B2, PH1, JG1, JP1, BK1
*16:98 MB1, MB2, PH1, JG1, JP1, BK1

717	Slaver with lips as common as the stairs	105
718	That mount the Capitol; join gripes with hands	106
719	Made hard with hourly falsehood—falsehood, as	107
720	With labour; then by-peeping in an eye	108
721	Base and unlustrous as the smoky light	109
722	That's fed with stinking tallow; it were fit **110**	110
723	That all the plagues of hell should at one time	111
724	Encounter such revolt.	
725	*Imo.*　　　　　My lord, I fear,	112
726	Has forgot Britain.	
727	*Iach.*　　　　And himself. Not I,	113
728	Inclined to this intelligence, pronounce	114
729	The beggary of his change; but 'tis your graces	115
730	That from my mutest conscience to my tongue	116
731	Charms this report out.	
732	*Imo.*　　　　　Let me hear no more.	117
	Iach. O dearest soul! your cause doth strike	
733	my heart	118
734	With pity, that doth make me sick. A lady	119
735	So fair, and fasten'd to an empery, **120**	120
	Would make the great'st king double,—to be	
736	partner'd	121
737	With tomboys hired with that self-exhibition	122
	Which your own coffers yield! with diseas'd	
738	ventures	123
739	That play with all infirmities for gold	124
	Which rottenness can lend nature! such boil'd	
740	stuff	125
741	As well might poison poison! Be revenged;	126
742	Or she that bore you was no queen, and you	127
743	Recoil from your great stock.	
744	*Imo.*　　　　　　　Revenged!	128
745	How should I be revenged? If this be true,—	129
746	As I have such a heart that both mine ears must	130
747	Must not in haste abuse—if it be true,	131
748	How should I be revenged?	
749	*Iach.*　　　　　　Should he make me	132
750	Live, like Diana's priest, betwixt cold sheets,	133
751	Whiles he is vaulting variable ramps,	134
752	In your despite, upon your purse? Revenge it.	135
753	I dedicate myself to your sweet pleasure,	136
754	More noble than that runagate to your bed,	137
755	And will continue fast to your affection,	138
756	Still close as sure.	
757	*Imo.*　　　　　What, ho, Pisanio!	139
758	*Iach.* Let me my service tender on your lips	140

```
105  X: CKP, WmS
106  aX: CKP, WmS; bX: KRe, JP1, BK1
107  X: KRe, JP1, BK1; bX: Bel, Ox1, Bar, Low, Inc, JKT, Oxb, Dol, CKP*
108  X: Bel, Ox1, Low, JKT, Oxb, Dol, CKP, KRe, HIC, ViA, BA1, SM1, IP1*
109  X: Bel, Ox1, Wen, Bat, Bar, Low, Inc, JKT, Oxb, Dol, Cum, HnF,CKP*
110  X: Bat; R: ChM; aX: Bel, Ox1, Wen, Bar, Low, Inc, JKT, Oxb, Dol,Cum*
111

112

113
114
115
116

117

118  X: Low, Inc, JKT, Dol, USW, Cum, CKP
119  aX: Ox1, Wen, Low, Inc, JKT, Oxb, Dol, USW, Cum, CKP; bX: NM1, MB1*
120  X: NM1, MB1, MB2, BK1

121  same as 120; bX: KRe, WmS
122  X: KRe, WmS, NM1, MB1, MB2, JG1, BK1; R: ChM; bX: JP1

123  X: ChM, KRe, WmS, NM1, MB1, MB2, BK1; aX: JP1; bX: Bel, Ox1, Wen, *
124  X: Bel, Ox1, Wen, Bat, Bar, Low, Inc, JKT, Oxb, Dol, USW, Cum, HnF,
        CKP, LAC, KRe, Rig, HM1, MTh, WmS, HIC, ViA, BA1, SM1, NM1, IP1*
125  same as 124, G61, P95, less BA1; aX: BA1; bX: ChM
126  X: Bat; aX: ChM, G61, Bel, Ox1, Wen, P95, Bar, Low, Inc, JKT, Oxb*
127

128
129  X: BK1; aX: KRe, HIC; bX: WmS, MB1
130  X: KRe, Rig, WmS, HIC, MB1, BK1
131  same as 130

132  X: WmS; aX: MB1; bX: CKP, KRe, HIC, NM1
133  X: CKP, KRe, WmS, HIC, NM1
134  same as 133
135  X: CKP, KRe, HIC, NM1; aX: WmS; cX: JKT, Dol, USW
136
137  X: KRe, HIC
138  X: KRe

139  X: KRe
140

*16:107  HIC, ViA, BA1, SM1, IP1, IP2, JG1              *16:108 IP2, JG1,
    JP1, BK1; R: ChM, G61, P95; bX: Wen, Bat, Bar, Inc, Cum, HnF, PH1
*16:109  KRe, HIC, ViA, BA1, SM1, IP1, IP2, PH1, JG1, JP1, BK1; R: ChM
*16:110  HnF, CKP, KRe, HIC, ViA, BA1, SM1, IP1, IP2, PH1, JG1, JP1, BK1
*16:119  MB2, BK1; cX: Bel, Bar, HnF              *16:123 Bat, Bar, Low, Inc,
    JKT, Oxb, Dol, USW, HnF, CKP, Lac, Rig, HM1,MTh, HIC, ViA, BA1, SM1, IP1
    NM2, PH1        *16:124 NM2, MB1, MB2, PH1, BK1        *16:126 Dol,USW,
    Cum, HnF, CKP, Lac, KRe, Rig, HM1, MTh, WmS, HIC, ViA, SM1, NM1, IP1,NM2,
    MB1, MB2, PH1, BK1
```

	Imo. Away! I do condemn mine ears that	
759	have	141
760	So long attended thee. If thou wert honourable	142
761	Thou wouldst have told this tale for virtue, not	143
762	For such an end thou seek'st,—as base as strange	144
763	Thou wrong'st a gentleman, who is as far	145
764	From thy report as thou from honour, and	146
765	Solicit'st here a lady that disdains	147
766	Thee and the devil alike. What ho, Pisanio!	148
767	The king my father shall be made acquainted	149
768	Of thy assault: if he shall think it fit,	150
769	A saucy stranger in his court to mart	151
770	As in a Romish stew and to expound	152
771	His beastly mind to us, he hath a court	153
772	He little cares for and a daughter who	154
773	He not respects at all. What, ho, Pisanio!	155
774	*Iach.* O happy Leonatus! I may say:	156
775	The credit that thy lady hath of thee	157
776	Deserves thy trust, and thy most perfect goodness	158
777	Her assured credit. Blessed live you long!	159
778	A lady to the worthiest sir that ever	160
779	Country call'd his! and you his mistress, only	161
780	For the most worthiest fit! Give me your pardon	162
781	I have spoke this, to know if your affiance	163
782	Were deeply rooted; and shall make your lord,	164
783	That which he is, new o'er: and he is one	165
784	The truest manner'd; such a holy witch	166
785	That he enchants societies into him;	167
786	Half all men's hearts are his.	
787	*Imo.* You make amends	168
788	*Iach.* He sits 'mongst men like a descended god	169
789	He hath a kind of honour sets him off.	170
790	More than a mortal seeming. Be not angry.	171
791	Most mighty princess, that I have adventured	172
792	To try your taking of a false report; which hath	173
793	Honour'd with confirmation your great judgment	174
794	In the election of a sir so rare,	175
795	Which you know cannot err: the love I bear to	176
796	Made me to fan you thus, but the gods made you	177
797	Unlike all others, chaffless. Pray, your pardon	178
798	*Imo.* All's well, sir: take my power i' the	
799	court for yours.	179
800	*Iach.* My humble thanks. I had almost forgot	180
801	To entreat your grace but in a small request,	181
802	And yet of moment too, for it concerns	182

```
141
142   bX: MB1, MB2
143   X: MB1, MB2
144   X: MB1, MB2; bX: KRe
145   X: KRe
146   X: KRe
147   X: KRe
148   aX: KRe
149   X: NM1, BK1
150   X: NM1, BK1; bX: KRe, JP1
151   X: KRe, NM1, JP1
152   same as 151; bX: Low, Inc, JKT, Dol, USW, Cum, HnF, CKP
153   same as 151; aX: Low, Inc, JKT, Dol, USW, Cum, HnF, CKP; b X: BK1
154   same as 151, BK1
155   X: NM1; aX: KRe, JP1, BK1
156   R: ChM
157   R: ChM
158   R: ChM
159   bX: PH1, BK1; ADD 2: ChM
160   X: ChM, HIC, PH1, BK1
161   same as 160; bX: WmS, JP1
162   X: ChM, HIC; aX: WmS, PH1, JP1, BK1
163   X: ChM, KRe, NM1, NM2
164   X: KRe, NM1, NM2; bX:ChM, JP1
165   X: KRe, NM1, NM2, JP1; aX: ChM; bX: WmS, BA1
166   X: KRe, WmS, BA1, NM1, NM2, JP1
167   same as 166, BK1

168   X: KRe, WmS, NM1, NM2; aX: BA1, JP1
169   X: KRe, NM1, NM2
170   same as 169
171   X: KRe, NM2
172
173   bX: G61, Bel, Ox1, Wen, Bat, Bar,  Low, Inc, JKT, Oxb, Dol, Cum,
          CKP, KRe, Rig, BA1, IP1, PH1, BK1
174   X: G61, Bel, Ox1, Wen, Bat, Bar, Inc, JKT, Oxb, Dol, Cum, CKP, KRe*
175   same as 174, less IP1; aX: IP1
176   aX: G61, Bel, Ox1, Wen, Bat, Bar, Low, Inc, JKT, Oxb, Dol, Cum, CKP*
177   X: HIC; bX: KRe, BK1
178   aX: KRe, HIC, BK1; cX: WmS

179   bX: WmS, JP1
180
181
182   X: KRe
```

*16:174 Rig, BA1, IP1, PH1, BK1   *16:176 KRe, Rig, WmS, BA1, PH1,
   BK1; bX: HIC

803	.. lord; myself and other noble friends	183
804	.. partners in the business.	
805	*Ima.* Pray, what is't?	184
	Iach. Some dozen Romans of us and your	
806	lord—	185
807	The best feather of our wing—have mingled sums	186
808	.. buy a present for the emperor;	187
809	Then I, the factor for the rest, have done	188
810	in France: 'tis plate of rare device, and jewels	189
811	.. rich and exquisite form; their values great;	190
812	.. I am something curious, being strange, 191	191
813	.. have them in safe stowage: may it please you	192
814	to take them in protection?	
815	*Ima.* Willingly;	193
816	.. pawn mine honour for their safety: since	194
817	My lord hath interest in them, I will keep them	195
818	.. my bedchamber.	
819	*Iach.* They are in a trunk,	196
820	.. tended by my men: I will make bold	197
821	To send them to you, only for this night;	198
822	I must aboard to-morrow.	
823	*Ima.* O, no, no.	199
824	*Iach.* Yes, I beseech; or I shall short my word	200
825	By lengthening my return. From Gallia 201	201
826	I cross'd the seas on purpose and on promise	202
827	To see your grace.	
828	*Ima.* I thank you for your pains:	203
829	But not away to-morrow!	
830	*Iach.* O, I must, madam:	204
831	Therefore I shall beseech you, if you please	205
832	To greet your lord with writing, do't to-night:	206
833	I have outstood my time; which is material	207
834	To the tender of our present.	
835	*Ima.* I will write.	208
836	Send your trunk to me; it shall safe be kept, 209	209
	And truly yielded you. You're very welcome.	210
837	[*Exeunt.*	

837+1

ACT II.

838,+1   SCENE I. *Britain. Before Cymbeline's palace.*

839   *Enter* CLOTEN *and two* Lords.

	Clo. Was there ever man had such luck!	1
840	when I kissed the jack, upon an up-cast to be	2
841	hit away! I had a hundred pound on't: and	3

183   X: KRe; bX: BK1

184   X: KRe; aX: BK1

185
186   X: KRe; aX: WmS, BK1
187
188   X: PH1, BK1
189   aX: PH1
190   X: BK1; bX: KRe
191   X: KRe
192   aX: KRe

193
194   X: WmS; bX: HnF
195   X: HnF; aX: WmS

196   R: G61, JKT; aX: HnF
197   X: BK1; b X: WmS
198   X: WmS

199   X: WmS; bX: SM1; ADD 1: ChM
200   X: ChM, KRe, WmS, SM1, JP1, BK1; aX: PH1
201   X: ChM, KRe, PH1, JP1, BK1; aX: WmS, SM1
202   same as 201; less aX

203   same as 202

204   X: ChM, KRe, WmS, PH1; aX: JP1, BK1
205   X: ChM; aX: KRe
206   X: ChM
207   X: ChM, ViA; bX: BA1

208   aX: ChM, ViA, BA1
209   R: G61
210   bX: ChM; ADD 9: ChM

Scene 21

ALL CUT: KRe, HIP, ViA, MB2
  1 X:MB1; bX: WmS, HIC, NM2, PH1, BK1
  2   X: WmS, HIC, ViA, NM1, MB1, MB2, JP1; aX: NM2, PH1, BK1
  3   X: ViA, MB1, MB2, JP1; aX: NM1; bX: WmS; B: HIC

842	——a whoreson jackanapes must take me up for	4
843	swearing: as if I borrowed mine oaths of him	5
844	and might not spend them at my pleasure.	6
	First Lord. What got he by that? You have	7
845-6	broke his pate with your bowl.	8
	Sec. Lord. [*Aside*] If his wit had been like	9
847-8	that broke it, it would have run all out. **10**	10
	Clo. When a gentleman is disposed to swear,	11
849	it is not for any standers-by to curtail his oaths,	12
850	ha!	13
	Sec. Lord. No, my lord; [*Aside*] nor crop	14
851	the ears of them.	15
	Clo. Whoreson dog! I give him satisfaction?	16
852-3	Would he had been one of my rank!	17
854	*Sec. Lord.* [*Aside*] To have smelt like a fool.	18
	Clo. I am not vexed more at any thing in the	19
855	earth: a pox on't! I had rather not be so noble	20
856	as I am; they dare not fight with me, because of	21
857	the queen my mother: every Jack-slave hath his	22
858	bellyful of fighting. and I must go up and down	23
859-60	like a cock that nobody can match.	24
	Sec. Lord. [*Aside*] You are cock and capon	25
861-2	too: and you crow, cock, with your comb on.	26
863	*Clo.* Sayest thou?	27
	Sec. Lord. It is not fit your lordship should	28
864	undertake every companion that you give offence	29
865	to. **30**	30
	Clo. No, I know that: but it is fit I should	31
866-7	commit offence to my inferiors.	32
868	*Sec. Lord.* Ay, it is fit for your lordship only.	33
869	*Clo.* Why, so I say.	34
	First Lord. Did you hear of a stranger that's	35
870-1	come to court to-night?	36
872	*Clo.* A stranger, and I not know on't!	37
	Sec. Lord. [*Aside*] He's a strange fellow him-	38
873	self, and knows it not.	39
	First Lord. There's an Italian come; and,	40
874-5	'tis thought, one of Leonatus' friends. **41**	41
	Clo. Leonatus! a banished rascal; and he's	42
876	another, whatsoever he be. Who told you of	43
877	this stranger?	44
878	*First Lord.* One of your lordship's pages.	45
	Clo. Is it fit I went to look upon him? is there	46
879-80	no derogation in't?	47
881	*Sec. Lord.* You cannot derogate, my lord.	48
882	*Clo.* Not easily, I think. **49**	49

```
 4   X: ViA, MB1, MB2, JP1; aX: WmS; bX: BK1; B: NM1
 5   X: ViA, MB1, MB2, JP1, BK1; bX: PH1
 6   same as 5, PH1; less bX
 7   X: ViA, MB1, MB2, JP1; N: Inc, HnF, Lac, WmS
 8   X: CKP, ViA, MB1, MB2, JP1
 9   X: WM1, CKP, HIC, ViA, BA1, SM1, MB1, MB2, JP1; N: Inc, HnF,Lac,WmS
10   same as 9, less CKP; less N
11   X: HIC, ViA, MB1, MB2, JP1
12   same as 11; bX: CKP; N: CKP
13   same as 11
14   same as 11; bX: WM1, PH1, BK1
15   X: WM1, HIC, ViA, MB1, MB2, PH1, JP1, BK1; bX: BA1, SM1, JG1
16   X: CKP, NM1, N M2, MB1, MB2, JP1; aX: WmS, ViA; B: MTh, HIC, SM1;MOVE*
17   same as 16, less CKP; less aX, B, MOVE; aX: CKP
18   X: G61, Bel, Ox1, Wen, Bat, P95, Bar, Low, Roa, Inc, JKT, Oxb, Do1*
19   X: G61, Bel, Ox1, Wen, Bat, P95, Low, Roa, Inc, JKT, Oxb, Do1, USW,*
20   X: MB1, MB2; aX: WM1, JP1; B: Low, Inc, JKT, Do1, USW, Cum, Lac, MTh*
21   X: CKP, MB1, MB2
22   same as 21; bX: WmS
23   same as 21; aX: Wm S
24   X: MB1, MB2
25   X: ChM, G61, Bel, Ox1, Wen, Bat, P95, Bar, Low, Inc, JKT, Oxb, Do1, USW*
26   same as 25, BA1, BK1, less ViA; less bX
27   X: G61, Bel, Ox1, Wen, P95, Bar, Low, Roa, Inc, JKT, Oxb, Cum, WM1,HnF*
28   X: Ox1, Roa, Oxb, MB1, MB2
29   X: Roa, MB1, MB2
30   same as 29
31   X: MB1, MB2
32   X: CKP, MB1, MB2
33   X: CKP, NM1, NM2, MB1, MB2              : USW, Cum, Wms
34   same as 33; Insert 36-68: Bel, Ox1, Wen, Bat, Bar, Roa, Inc, Oxb, Do1*
35   X: ViA; aX: CKP
36   X: ViA
37   X: Roa, WM1, ViA, PH1
38   X: WM1, WmS, ViA, SM1, NM1, NM2, PH1
39   X: WM1, WmS, HIC, ViA, NM1, NM2, PH1, JG1
40   X: WM1, WmS, ViA; aX: PH1
41   X: WmS, ViA
42   X: Wm S, ViA
43   X: ViA; aX: WmS; bX: BK1
44   X: ViA, BK1
45   X: ViA
46   X: WmS, ViA
47   X: WmS, ViA, JG1
48   X: WmS, ViA; R: JG1
49   X: WmS, ViA; ADD 3: Low
```

*21:16 16b-56 to follow 12: 33: ViA   *21:18 USW, Cum, WM1, HnF,
   HIC, ViA, BA1, SM1, NM1, NM2, MB1, MB2, JP1   *21:19 Cum, WM1,
   HnF, WmS, ViA, MB1, MB2, JP1; aX: Bar   *21:20 WmS, ViA
*21:25 Cum, WM1, HnF, Lac, Rig, HM1, MTh, WmS, HIC, ViA, SM1, NM1, NM2, MB1,
   MB2, PH1; bX: BA1   *21:27 Lac, Rig, HnF, MTh, WmS, HIC, SM1, NM1
   NM2, MB1, MB2   *21:34 USW, Cum, WmS; Insert23: 1-20, 31-35:
   Rig; Insert 23: 40-68: G61; Insert 23: 33-68: Low

Sec. Lord. [*Aside*] You are a fool granted: 50

883 therefore your issues, being foolish, do not dero- 51

884 gate. 52

Clo. Come, I'll go see this Italian: what I 53

885 have lost to-day at bowls I'll win to-night of him. 54

886 Come, go. 55

Sec. Lord. I'll attend your lordship. 56

887 [*Exeunt Cloten and First Lord.*

888 That such a crafty devil as is his mother 57

889 Should yield the world this ass! a woman that 58

890 Bears all down with her brain; and this her son 59

891 Cannot take two from twenty, for his heart, 60 60

892 And leave eighteen. Alas, poor princess, 61

893 Thou divine Imogen, what thou endurest, 62

894 Betwixt a father by thy step-dame govern'd, 63

895 A mother hourly coining plots, a wooer 64

896 More hateful than the foul expulsion is 65

897 Of thy dear husband, than that horrid act 66

Of the divorce he'ld make! The heavens hold

898 firm 67

899 The walls of thy dear honour, keep unshaked 68

900 That temple, thy fair mind, that thou mayst stand, 69

To enjoy thy banish'd lord and this great land! 70

901 [*Exit.* 70

902+1 SCENE II. *Imogen's bedchamber in Cymbe-*

902+2 *line's palace: a trunk in one corner of it.*

903 IMOGEN *in bed, reading; a* Lady *attending.*

904 *Imo.* Who's there? my woman Helen?

905 *Lady.* Please you, madam. 1

906 *Imo.* What hour is it?

907 *Lady.* Almost midnight, madam. 2

908 *Imo.* I have read three hours then: mine eyes

909 are weak: 3

910 Fold down the leaf where I have left: to bed: 4

911 Take not away the taper, leave it burning; 5

912 And if thou canst awake by four o' the clock, 6

913 I prithee, call me. Sleep hath seized me wholly. 7

913+1 [*Exit Lady.*

914 To your protection I commend me, gods. 8

915 From fairies and the tempters of the night 9

916 Guard me, beseech ye. 10 10

917 [*Sleeps. Iachimo comes from the trunk.*

Iach. The crickets sing, and man's o'er-la-

918 bour'd sense. 11

```
50   X: Low, Inc, JKT, Dol, Cum, HnF, WmS,  HIC, ViA, BA1, SM1, NM1, NM2*
51   same as 50, Oxb, less WmS; less bX; R: Wen, JG1; aX: Ox1, WmS;bX:Roa
52   X: Low, Roa, JKT, HnF, ViA, NM1, NM2, PH1, BK1; R: Wen; bX: Bel
53   X: ViA; R: Bel
54   X: Low, ViA; R: Bel, Ox1, Bat, Inc, Oxb, Cum; bX: JKT, USW
55   X: ChM, Bel, Low, USW; R: Ox1, Bat, Inc, Cum; aX: JKT, Oxb; ADD 1:Roa
56   X: ChM, Bel, Inc, USW, Lac, Rig, HM1, JG1, BK1; Insert 23:21-30:WmS

57   X: ChM, Inc, USW, Cum, Rig, HM1, ViA, Han, BA1
58   same as 57; bX: PH1, BK1
59   same as 57, PH1, BK1
60   same as 59
61   same as 57; aX: PH1, BK1
62   same as 57, less Inc; bX: MB1; ADD 3: Inc
63   X: ChM, G61, Bel, Ox1, Wen, Bat, P95, Bar, Low, JKT, Oxb, Dol, USW*
64   same as 63; aX: WmS
65   same as 63
66   same as 63; bX: Inc, WmS, HIC, SM1, JG1, BK1

67   same as 63, Inc, less MB1; aX: WmS, HIC, SM1, JG1, BK1
68   same as 67, less Inc; less aX; aX: Inc
69   same as 68; less aX
70   same as 69
```

Scene 22

```
1    N: ViA

2    R: ChM

3    X: KRe, BK1; R: ChM
4
5    bX: KRe
6    X: KRe
7    aX: KRe

8    MOVE 8 to follow 10: G61, Bel, Ox1, Wen, Bat, Bar, JKT, Oxb
9
10   Insert 8: G61, Bel, Ox1, Wen, Bat, Bar,  Oxb


11

*21:50 MB2, PH1, BK1; bX: Ox1, Oxb                *21:63  Cum, Rig, HM1,
   ViA, Han, BA1, MB1
```

919	**Repairs** itself by rest. Our Tarquin thus	12
920	**Did** softly press the rushes, ere he waken'd	13
921	**The** chastity he wounded. Cytherea,	14
922	**How** bravely thou becomest thy bed, fresh lily,	15
923	**And** whiter than the sheets! That I might touch!	16
924	**But** kiss; one kiss! Rubies unparagon'd,	17
925	**How** dearly they do't! 'Tis her breathing that	18
926	**Perfumes** the chamber thus: the flame o' the taper	19
927	**Bows** toward her, and would under-peep her lids,	20
928	**To** see the enclosed lights, now canopied 21	21
929	**Under** these windows, white and azure laced	22
930	**With** blue of heaven's own tinct. But my design,	23
931	**To** note the chamber: I will write all down:	24
932	**Such** and such pictures; there the window; such	25
933	**The** adornment of her bed: the arras: figures,	26
934	**Why,** such and such; and the contents o' the story.	27
935	**Ah,** but some natural notes about her body,	28
936	**Above** ten thousand meaner moveables	29
937	**Would** testify, to enrich mine inventory. 30	30
938	**O** sleep, thou ape of death, lie dull upon her!	31
939	**And** be her sense but as a monument,	32
940	**Thus** in a chapel lying! Come off, come off:	33
940+1	*[Taking off her bracelet.*	
941	**As** slippery as the Gordian knot was hard!	34
942	**'Tis** mine; and this will witness outwardly,	35
943	**As** strongly as the conscience does within,	36
944	**To** the madding of her lord. On her left breast	37
945	**A** mole cinque-spotted, like the crimson drops	38
946	**I'** the bottom of a cowslip: here's a voucher,	39
947	**Stronger** than ever law could make: this secret	40
948	**Will** force him think I have pick'd the lock and ta'en 41	41
949	**The** treasure of her honour. No more. To what end?	42
950	**Why** should I write this down, that's riveted,	43
951	**Screw'd** to my memory? She hath been reading late	44
952	**The** tale of Tereus; here the leaf's turn'd down	45
953	**Where** Philomel gave up. I have enough:	46
954	**To** the trunk again, and shut the spring of it.	47
955	**Swift,** swift, you dragons of the night, that dawning	48
956	**May** bare the raven's eye! I lodge in fear;	49
957	**Though** this a heavenly angel, hell is here. 50	50

```
12  bX: SM1, NM1, NM2
13  X: SM1, NM1, NM2
14  aX: SM1, NM1, NM2
15
16  bX: WmS
17  X: WmS, SM1; bX: Bel, Oxl, Bar, Low, Inc, JKT, Oxb, Dol, USW, Cum,*
18  X: WmS; R: ChM; aX: Bel, Oxl, Bar, Low, Inc, JKT, Oxb, Dol, USW, Cum,
       KRe, Rig, ViA, Han, SM1
19  R: ChM; aX: WmS
20
21  X: NM1; b X: KRe, NM2
22  X: KRe, NM1, NM2
23  aX: KRe, NM1, NM2
24
25  aX: HIC
26

27  X: ChM; bX: KRe
28  X: CKP, ViA; bX: KRe
29  X: CKP, ViA, BK1
30  X: CKP, ViA
31
32
33  aX: ViA

34  X: KRe, SM1, NM2, MB1
35
36  X: KRe, BK1
37  bX: HnF, CKP
38  X: HnF, CKP
39  X: HnF; aX: CKP; bX: HIC, SM1
40  X: HnF, HIC, SM1; bX: Bel, Oxl, Wen, Bat, Bar, Low, Inc, Oxb, Dol,
       USW, Cum, WM1, CKP, KRe, Rig
41  X: Bel, Oxl, Wen, Bat, Bar, Low, Inc, JKT, Oxb, Dol, USW, Cum, WM1,
       HnF, CKP, KRe, Rig, HIC, SM1
42  X: HnF; aX: Bel, Oxl, Wen, Bat, Bar, Low, Inc, Oxb, Dol, USW, ,WM1*
43  X: ChM, HnF, KRe

44  X: KRe; aX: ChM, HnF; bX: IP2
45  X: KRe, IP2
46  X: KRe; aX: IP2; bX: JKT
47  bX: KRe

48  X: KRe
49  aX: KRe
50
```

*22:17 KRe, Rig, ViA, Han   *22:42 CKP, KRe, Rig, SM1; bX:
    ChM, JKT, Cum; abX: HIC

958   One, two, three: time, time!   [*Clock strikes.*   51

959   [*Goes into the trunk.   The scene closes.*

960,+1   **SCENE III.** *An ante-chamber adjoining Imo-
                       gen's apartments.*

961   *Enter* CLOTEN *and* Lords.

        First Lord. Your lordship is the most patient   1
962   man in loss, the most coldest that ever turned up   2
963   ace.   3
964   *Clo.* It would make any man cold to lose.   4
        First Lord. But not every man patient after   5
965   the noble temper of your lordship. You are   6
966-7   most hot and furious when you win.   7
           Clo. Winning will put any man into courage.   8
968   If I could get this foolish Imogen, I should have   9
969-70 gold enough. It's almost morning, is't not?   10   10
971   *First Lord.* Day, my lord.   11
           Clo. I would this music would come: I am   12
972   advised to give her music o' mornings; they say   13
973   it will penetrate.   14

974   *Enter* Musicians.

        Come on; tune: if you can penetrate her with   15
975   your fingering, so; we'll try with tongue too: if   16
976   none will do, let her remain; but I'll never give   17
977   o'er. First, a very excellent good-conceited thing; 18
978   after, a wonderful sweet air, with admirable rich   19
979-80 words to it: and then let her consider.   20   20

981   .   SONG.   21
982   Hark, hark! the lark at heaven's gate sings,   22
983   And Phœbus 'gins arise,   23
984   His steeds to water at those springs   24
985   On chaliced flowers that lies;   25
        And winking Mary-buds begin   26
986   To ope their golden eyes: 27
        With every thing that pretty is,   28
987   My lady sweet, arise: 29
988   Arise, arise.   30   30

           Clo. So, get you gone. If this penetrate, I 31
989   will consider your music the better: if it do not   32
990   it is a vice in her ears, which horse-hairs and   33
991   calves'-guts, nor the voice of unpaved eunuch to   34

51   X: ChM, ViA, Han; <u>Insert 23</u>: 24-28,   <u>24</u>: 1-154: Rig

Scene 23

ALL CUT BUT TRANSFER: ChM
1 X:CKP, HIP; <u>N</u>: HnF, ViA; <u>MOVE</u> 1-20 to follow <u>21</u>: 34: Rig; <u>bX</u>: KRe
2   X: CKP, <u>KRe</u>, HIP; <u>bX</u>: <u>ViA</u>
3   X: CKP, HIP, ViA
4   X: CKP, HIP, JP1
5   X: WM1, CKP, HIP, PH1, JP1, BK1
6   X: WM1, CKP, HIP, JP1; <u>aX</u>: PH1, BK1
7   same as 6; less <u>aX</u>
8   X: WM1, CKP, <u>HIP</u>
9   X: CKP, HIP
10 X: CKP, HIP; <u>bX</u>: Rig
11 X: CKP, HIP; <u>R</u>: G61, Rig; <u>aX</u>: JG1
12 X: CKP, NM1, <u>NM2</u>; <u>R</u>: Ox1; <u>ADD</u> 1: Oxb
13 X: CKP; <u>bX</u>: WM1, <u>BA1</u>
14 X: WM1, <u>CKP</u>, BA1; <u>ADD</u> 2: G61, Bel, Ox1, Bar, Low, Roa, Inc, Oxb,Dol,
      USW, Cum

15 X: WM1, CKP, Han; <u>R</u>: Wen; <u>bX</u>: G61, Bel, Ox1, Bat, Bar, Low, Roa, Inc*
16 X: G61, Bel, Ox1, Bar, Low, Roa, Inc, Oxb, Dol, USW, Cum, WM1, CKP*
17 same as 16, IP1, PH1; less R, <u>aX</u>, bX; R: Bat, JKT; <u>aX</u>: Wen, BK1
18 X: WM1, CKP, HM1, NM2, IP2, <u>PH1</u>, JG1, BK1; <u>aX</u>: Bel, Ox1, Bat, Bar,*
19 X: CKP, HM1, NM2; <u>aX</u>: WM1, IP2, PH1
20 same as 19; less <u>aX</u>; <u>bX</u>: WM1, Rig

21 X: CKP, HM1, HIP; <u>MOVE</u> 21-30 to follow <u>24</u>: 56: WmS; <u>MOVE</u> 21-30 to*
22 same as 21; less <u>MOVE</u>s
23 same as 22
24 same as 22
25 same as 22
26 same as 22
27 same as 22
28 same as 22
29 same as 22
30 same as 22
31 same as 22; <u>aX</u>: PH1; <u>bX</u>: WM1, HnF; <u>MOVE</u> 31-35 to follow 68:BK1;*
32 X: WM1, HnF, <u>CKP</u>, HM1; <u>bX</u>: KRe, HIP, HIC, BA1, SM1, MB1
33 X: WM1, HnF, KRe, HM1, <u>HIP</u>, HIC, BA1, SM1, MB1; <u>bX</u>: Lac, WmS, IP1*
34 X: WM1, HnF, KRe, HM1, HIP, HIC, BA1, SM1, IP1, <u>NM2</u>, MB1, IP2; <u>aX</u>
      Lac, WmS; <u>bX</u>: NM1

*23:15 JKT, Oxb, Dol, USW, Cum, Lac, KRe, WmS, HIC, BA1, SM1, IP2
*23:16 KRe, HM1, HIC, BA1, SM1, IP2; <u>R</u>: Wen, Bat, JKT; <u>aX</u>: Lac, Wm S,BK1;
  <u>bX</u>: PH1   *23:18 Low, Inc, JKT, Oxb, USW, <u>KRe</u>, HIC, BA1, SM1, IP1
*23:21 follow <u>22</u>: 51: Rig   *23:31 <u>MOVE</u> 31-35 to follow
  <u>21</u>:34: Rig   *23:33 NM2, IP2

992	boot, can never amend. [*Exeunt Musician*	35
994	*Sec. Lord.* Here comes the king.	36
	Clo. I am glad I was up so late; for that's the	37
995	reason I was up so early: he cannot choose but	38
996	take this service I have done fatherly.	39

Enter CYMBELINE *and* QUEEN.

997	Good morrow to your majesty and to my gracious	40
998	mother. 4	41
	Cym. Attend you here the door of our stern	
999	daughter?	42
1000	Will she not forth?	43
	Clo. I have assailed her with music, but she	44
1001-2	vouchsafes no notice.	45
1003	*Cym.* The exile of her minion is too new;	46
1004	She hath not yet forgot him: some more time	47
1005	Must wear the print of his remembrance out,	48
1006	And then she's yours.	
1007	*Queen.* - You are most bound to the king,	49
1008	Who lets go by no vantages that may 5	50
1009	Prefer you to his daughter. Frame yourself	51
1010	To orderly soliciting, and be friended	52
1011	With aptness of the season; make denials	53
1012	Increase your services; so seem as if	54
1013	You were inspired to do those duties which	55
1014	You tender to her; that you in all obey her,	56
1015	Save when command to your dismission tends,	57
1016	And therein you are senseless.	
1017	*Clo.* Senseless! not so	58

1017+1	*Enter a* Messenger.	
	Mess. So like you, sir, ambassadors from	
1018	Rome;	59
1019	The one is Caius Lucius.	
1020	*Cym.* A worthy fellow, 6	60
1021	Albeit he comes on angry purpose now;	61
1022	But that's no fault of his: we must receive him	62
1023	According to the honour of his sender;	63
1024	And towards himself, his goodness forespent on us,	64
1025	We must extend our notice. Our dear son,	65
	When you have given good morning to your	
1026	mistress,	66
1027	Attend the queen and us; we shall have need	67
1028	To employ you towards this Roman. Come, our	
1029	queen. [*Exeunt all but Cloten*	68
1030	*Clo.* If she be up, I'll speak with her; if not,	69

*23:64 Cum, WM1, HnF, KRe, Rig, WmS, HIP, ViA, IP1, NM2, IP2, PH1, JG1,
    JP1, BK1; <u>a</u>X: Bat; <u>b</u>X: HIC

35 same as 34; less aX, bX, ADD 3: Inc, Cum; ADD 4: Wen, Low, Roa, JKT
36 X: G61, Rig, HM1, HIP; MOVE 36-68 to follow 21: 34: Wen, Bar, Roa*
37 X: G61, Bel, Oxl, Wen, Bat, Bar, Low, Roa, JKT, Oxb, Dol, USW, Cum*
38 same as 37; less aX; bX: WM1, KRe, HIC, BA1, SM1, PH1, BK1
39 X: G61, Low, Roa, Dol, USW, WM1, HnF, Rig, HIP, PH1; R: Bel, Bat; aX:
    Oxl, Wen, Bar, JKT, Oxb, Cum, KRe, HIC, BA1, SM1, JG1, BK1

40 X: Rig, HIP; R: Low, USW; cX: HIC; MOVE 40-68 to follow 21: 32:G61
41 X: Rig, HIP, JG1

42 X: Rig, HIP; ADD 1: Cum
43 X: Rig, HIP
44 X: Rig, HIP; R: G61, Oxl, Roa, Oxb, Cum; aX: Wen, Bat; Tr: Low,Dol,USW
45 X: Rig, HIP; R: G61, Roa, Oxb, CKP; ADD 1: Dol; ADD 2: Wen, Bat
46 X: CKP, Rig, HIP
47 same as 46
48 same as 46

49 same as 46
50 X: WM1, CKP, Rig, HIP
51 same as 50; bX: G61, Bel, Oxl, Wen, Bat, P95, Bar, Low, Roa, Inc, JKT*
52 X: G61, Bel, Oxl, Wen, Bat, P95, Bar, Low, Roa, Inc, JKT, Oxb, Dol*
53 same as 52, HIC, SM1, less CKP, IP1, NM2; less bX; aX: CKP, IP1,NM2,IP2
54 same as 53, less KRe, HIC, BA1, SM1; less aX; aX: KRe, HIC, BA1, SM1*
55 same as 54, ViA, PH1, BK1; less aX, bX
56 same as 55
57 same as 55, less ViA

58 same as 57, less HnF, Rig; aX: HnF

59 X: CKP, KRe, Rig, HIP; N: Inc, WmS

60 X: KRe, Rig, HIP; aX: CKP
61 same as 60; less aX
62 same as 61; bX: G61, Bel, Oxl, Wen, Bat, Bar, Low, Roa, Inc, JKT,Oxb*
63 X: G61, Bel, Oxl, Wen, Bat,P95, Bar, Low, Roa, Inc, JKT, Oxb, Dol,USW*
64 X: G61, Bel, Oxl, Wen, P95, Bar, Low, Roa, Inc, JKT, Oxb, Dol, USW*
65 X: Rig, HIP; aX: G61, Bel, Oxl, Wen, P95, Bar, Low, Roa, Inc, JKT, Oxb,
    Dol, USW, Cum, WM1, HnF, WmS, ViA, IP1, NM2, IP2, PH1, JG1,JP1,BK1
66 X: CKP, KRe, Rig, HIP
67 same as 66; bX: WmS

68 same as 66; aX: WmS; bX: Wen, Inc, Cum; ADD 1: G61, Bel, Oxl, Wen, Bat*
69 X: CKP, Rig, WmS; ADD 3: Dol, USW

*23:36 Inc, JKT, Oxb, Dol, USW, Cum, WmS; MOVE 36-68 to follow 21: 32: Bel,
    Oxl, Wen, Low   *23:37 HnF, Rig, HIP, JG1; aX: WmS
*23:51 Oxb, Dol, USW, Cum, HnF, KRe, WmS, BA1, IP1, NN2, MB1, MB2
*23:52 USW, Cum, WM1, HnF, CKP, KRe, Rig, WmS, HIP, BA1, IP1, NM2, MB1,
    MB2; bX: HIC, IP2, BK1   *23:54 bX: ViA, PH1, BK1
*23:62 Dol, USW, Cum, WmS   *23:63 KRe, Rig, WmS, HIP, ViA, JP1;
    Insert 31: 48-54, 11-14, 42: HIC

	Let her lie still and dream. [*Knocks*] By your	
1031	leave, ho! **70**	70
1032	I know her women are about her: what	71
1033	If I do line one of their hands? 'Tis gold	72
	Which buys admittance; oft it doth; yea, and	
1034	makes	73
1035	Diana's rangers false themselves, yield up	74
	Their deer to the stand o' the stealer; and 'tis	
1036	gold	75
	Which makes the true man kill'd and saves the	
1037	thief;	76
	Nay, sometime hangs both thief and true man:	
1038	what	77
1039	Can it not do and undo? I will make	78
1040	One of her women lawyer to me, for	79
1041	I yet not understand the case myself. **80**	80
1042	[*Knocks*] By your leave.	81

1043	*Enter a* Lady.	
1044	*Lady.* Who's there that knocks?	
1045	*Clo.* A gentleman.	
1046	*Lady.* No more?	82
1047	*Clo.* Yes, and a gentlewoman's son.	
1048	*Lady.* That's more	83
1049	Than some, whose tailors are as dear as yours,	84
	Can justly boast of. What's your lordship's	
1050	pleasure?	85
1051	*Clo.* Your lady's person: is she ready?	
	Lady. **Ay,**	86
1052	To keep her chamber.	
1053	*Clo.* There is gold for you;	87
1054	Sell me your good report.	88
	Lady. How! my good name? or to report of	
1055	you	89
1056	What I shall think is good?—The princess! **90**	90

1057	*Enter* IMOGEN.	
	Clo. Good morrow, fairest: sister, your sweet	
1058	hand. [*Exit Lady.*	91
	Imo. Good morrow, sir. You lay out too	
1059	much pains	92
1060	For purchasing but trouble: the thanks I give	93
1061	Is telling you that I am poor of thanks	94
1062	And scarce can spare them.	
1063	*Clo.* Still, I swear I love you.	95
	Imo. If you but said so, 'twere as deep with	

70   same as 69; less ADB; bX: HIC, SM1, PH1, JG1
71   X: WM1, CKP, KRe, Rig, WmS, HIP, HIC, SM1, MB1, MB2, PH1, BK1
72   same as 71

73   same .as 71; bX: HnF, ViA, Han, IP1, NM2, IP2, JG1; Insert 31: 48-*
74   X: WM1, HnF, CKP, KRe, Rig, WmS, HIP, HIC, ViA, Han, BA1, SM1, NM1,
        IP1, NM2, MB1, MB2, IP2, PH1, JG1, BK1; bX: SM1
75   X: WM1, HnF, CKP, KRe, Rig, WmS, HIP, HIC, ViA, SM1, MB1, MB2, PH1,
        JG1, BK1; aX: Han, BA1, IP1, NM2, IP2
76   X: WM1, HnF, CKP, KRe, Rig, WmS, HIP, HIC, ViA, SM1, MB1, MB2, PH1, JG1,
        BK1
77   same as 76, less CKP
78   X: WM1, KRe, Rig, WmS, HIP, HIC, SM1, MB1, MB2, JG1, BK1; aX: ViA, PH1;*
79   X: WM1, HnF, CKP, KRe, Rig, WmS, HIP, HIC, SM1, MB1, MB2, JG1, BK1
80   same as 79
81   X: WM1, CKP, KRe, Rig, WmS, HIP, HIC, SM1, MB1, MB2, BK1

82   same as 81, less WmS, KRe; bX: KRe, HIP

83   same as 82, KRe, HIC; less bX; bX: WM1, HnF, PH1
84   X: WM1, HnF, CKP, KRe, Rig, WmS, HIP, HIC, SM1, MB1, MB2, PH1, BK1

85   X: WM1, CKP, Rig, WmS, HIC, SM1, MB1, MB2, PH1, BK1; aX: HnF, KRe, HIP;
        N: USW
86   same as 85, less CKP; less aX, N; bX: KRe

87   same as 86, KRe, less PH1; less bX; aX: PH1
88   same as 87; less aX; bX: CKP

89   same as 87, CKP, JP1; less aX
90   X: WM1, Rog, WmS, HIC, SM1, MB1, MB2, BK1; aX: CKP, KRe, JP1

91   X: CKP, Rig, WmS; bX: KRe, HIC

92   same as 91; less bX
93   same as 92; bX: G61, Bel, Ox1, Wen, Bat, Bar, Low, Roa, Inc, JKT, Oxb*
94   X: G61, Bel, Ox1, Wen, Bat, Bar, Low, Roa, Inc, JKT, Oxb, Dol, USW, Cum,
        WM1, HnF, Rig, WmS, BK1
95   X: Rig, WmS; aX: G61, Bel, Ox1, Wen, Bat, Bar, Low, Roa, Inc, JKT, Oxb,
        Dol, USW, Cum, WM1, HnF, BK1; bX: CKP

*23:73 54, 11b-14, 42: SM1   *23:78 bX: HnF, CKP
*23:93 Dol, USW, Cum, WM1, HnF, KRe, BK1

1064	me:	96
1065	If you swear still, your recompense is still	97
1066	That I regard it not.	
1067	*Clo.* This is no answer.	98
	Imo. But that you shall not say I yield being	
1068	silent,	99
1069	I would not speak. I pray you, spare me: 'faith,	100
1070	I shall unfold equal discourtesy **101**	101
1071	To your best kindness: one of your great knowing	102
1072	Should learn, being taught, forbearance.	103
	Clo. To leave you in your madness, 'twere	
1073	my sin:	104
1074	I will not.	105
1075	*Imo.* Fools are not mad folks.	
1076	*Clo.* Do you call me fool?	106
1077	*Imo.* As I am mad, I do:	107
1078	If you'll be patient, I'll no more be mad:	108
1079	That cures us both. I am much sorry, sir,	109
1080	You put me to forget a lady's manners, **110**	110
1081	By being so verbal: and learn now, for all,	111
1082	That I, which know my heart, do here pronounce,	112
1083	By the very truth of it, I care not for you,	113
1084	And am so near the lack of charity—	114
1085	To accuse myself—I hate you; which I had rather	115
1086	You felt than make't my boast.	
1087	*Clo.* You sin against	116
1088	Obedience, which you owe your father. For	117
1089	The contract you pretend with that base wretch,	118
1090	One bred of alms and foster'd with cold dishes,	119
1091	With scraps o' the court, it is no contract, none:	120
1092	And though it be allow'd in meaner parties— **121**	121
1093	Yet who than he more mean?—to knit their souls,	122
1094	On whom there is no more dependency	123
1095	But brats and beggary, in self-figured knot;	124
1096	Yet you are curb'd from that enlargement by	125
1097	The consequence o' the crown, and must not soil	126
1098	The precious note of it with a base slave,	127
1099	A hilding for a livery, a squire's cloth,	128
1100	A pantler, not so eminent.	
1101	*Imo.* Profane fellow!	129
1102	Wert thou the son of Jupiter and no more **130**	130
1103	But what thou art besides, thou wert too base	131
1104	To be his groom: thou wert dignified enough,	132
1105	Even to the point of envy, if 'twere made	133
1106	Comparative for your virtues, to be styled	134
1107	The under-hangman of his kingdom, and hated	135

```
 96  X: WM1, CKP, KRe,  Rig,  WmS, MB1, MB2, JP1, BK1
 97  same as 96, PH1, less KRe; bX: KRe

 98  X: WM1, CKP, KRe, Rig, WmS, MB1, MB2, JP1; aX: PH1

 99  same as 98, PH1, less WM1; less aX
100  X: G61, Low, KRe, Rig, WmS, MB1, MB2, PH1, JP1; bX: HnF
101  X: WM1, HnF, KRe, Rig, WmS, BA1, MB1, MB2, PH1, JP1, BK1
102  X: WM1, KRe, Rig, WmS, BA1, MB1, MB2, JP1; aX: HnF, PH1, BK1;bX:IP1
103  same as 102, IP1; less aX, bX

104  X: KRe,  Rig, WmS, IP1, MB1, MB2
105  same as 104


106  same as 105, CKP
107  same as 105
108  X: KRe, Rig, WmS, HIC, MB1, MB2; aX: IP1
109  X: CKP, KRe, Rig, WmS, HIC; aX: MB1, MB2
110  same as 109; less aX
111  X: G61, Bel, Ox1, Wen, Bat, Bar, Inc, JKT, Oxb, Dol, USW, WM1, HnF*
112  X: CKP, Rig,  WmS, BK1; R: Ox1
113  X: Rig, HM1, WmS; aX: BK1
114  X: G61, Bel, Ox1, Wen, Bat, Bar, Low, Roa, Inc,  JKT, Oxb, Dol, USW*
115  same as 114, less ViA, Han; aX: ViA, Han; bX: IP1, IP2

116  X: G61, Bel, Ox1, Wen, Bat, Bar, Low, Roa, Inc, JKT, Oxb, Dol, USW*
117  same as 116, less CKP; less aX, MOVE ; bX: CKP
118  X: CKP, Rig
119  X: WM1, CKP, Rig, ViA, IP1, IP2, BK1; bX: KRe
120  X: WM1, CKP, Rig, ViA, IP1; aX: KRe, IP2, PH1, BK1
121  X: G61, Bel, Ox1, Wen, Bat, P95, Bar, Low, Roa, Inc, JKT, Oxb, Dol,*
122  same as 21,  Rig, MB1, MB2; aX: IP1; bX: HIC
123  same as 122, WM1, HIC, Han, BA1; less aX. bX
124  same as 123, less CKP, Han; aX: CKP, Han
125  G61, Bel, Ox1, Wen, Bat, P95, Bar, Low, Roa, Inc, JKT, Oxb, Dol, USW*
126  same as 125; less bX
127  same as 126, less JP1; aX: JP1; bX: CKP
128  same as 127, IP2; less aX, bX; bX: ViA


129  X: CKP, KRe, Rig, BA1; aX: G61, Bel, Ox1, Wen, Bat, P95, Low, Roa,Inc*
130  X: CKP, Rig
131  X: Rig; aX: CKP
132  X: Rig; bX: G61, Bel, Ox1, Wen, Bat, P95, Bar, Low, Roa, Inc, JKT, Oxb
133  X: G61, Bel, Ox1, Wen, Bat, P95, Bar, Low, Roa, Inc, JKT, Oxb, Dol,Cum*
134  same as 133; aX: HIC, ViA, IP1, IP2
135  same as 133
```

*23:111 CKP, Rig, WmS; aX: KRe, HIC; bX: BK1   *23:114 Cum, WM1,
   HnF, CKP, Lac, KRe, Rig, HM1, MTh, WmS, ViA, Han
*23:116 Cum, WM1, CKP, Rig; aX:HnF, KRe, HM1, MTh, WmS, IP1, IP2; MOVE 16b-
   152a to follow 32: 23: WmS   *23:21 USW, Cum, WM1, HnF, CKP, Rig,
   WmS, ViA, BA1, JG, JP1, BK1   *23:25 Cum, WM1,HnF, KRe, Rig,
   WmS, HIC, BA1, JP1; bX: BK1   *23:29 JKT, Oxb, Dol, USW, Cum,WM1,
   HnF, WmS, HIC, ViA   *23:133 WM, HnF, KRe, Rig, WmS, BA1, NM1,
  NM2, MB1, MB2, PH1, JG1, JP1, BK1; bX: HIC, ViA, IP1, IP2

1108   For being preferr'd so well.
1109   *Clo.*   The south-fog rot him !   136
       Imo. He never can meet more mischance than
1110   come   137
1111   To be but named of thee. His meanest garment,   138
1112   That ever hath but clipp'd his body, is dearer   139
1113   In my respect than all the hairs above thee, 140   140
       Were they all made such men. How now, Pi-
1114   sanio !   141
1115   *Enter* PISANIO.

1116   *Clo.* 'His garment !' Now the devil—   142
       Imo. To Dorothy my woman hie thee pre-
1117   sently—   143
1118   *Clo.* 'His garment !'
1119   *Imo.*   I am sprited with a fool,   144
1120   Frighted, and anger'd worse : go bid my woman   145
1121   Search for a jewel that too casually   146
1122   Hath left mine arm : it was thy master's :'shrew me,   147
1123   If I would lose it for a revenue   148
1124   Of any king's in Europe. I do think   149
1125   I saw't this morning : confident I am   **150**   150
1126   Last night 'twas on mine arm ; I kiss'd it :   151
1127   I hope it be not gone to tell my lord   152
1128   That I kiss aught but he.
1129   *Pis.*   'Twill not be lost.   153
1130   *Imo.* I hope so : go and search.
1130+1   [*Exit Pisanio.*
1131   *Clo.*   You have abused me :   154
1132   'His meanest garment !'
1133   *Imo.*   Ay, I said so, sir :   155
1134   If you will make't an action, call witness to't.   156
1135   *Clo.* I will inform your father.
1136   *Imo.*   Your mother too :   157
1137   She's my good lady, and will conceive, I hope,   158
1138   But the worst of me. So, I leave you, sir,   159
1139   To the worst of discontent.   [*Exit.*
1140   *Clo.*   I 'll be revenged : **160**   160
1141   'His meanest garment !' Well.   [*Exit.*   161

1142,+1   **SCENE IV.** *Rome. Philario's house.*

1143   *Enter* POSTHUMUS *and* PHILARIO.

1144   *Post.* Fear it not, sir : I would I were so sure   1
1145   To win the king as I am bold her honour   2
1146   Will remain hers.
1147   *Phi.*   What means do you make to him ?   3

136 X: Rig, PH1; aX: G61, Bel, Oxl, Wen, Bat, P95, Bar, Low, Roa, Inc, JKT,
        Oxb, Dol, Cum, WM1, HnF, KRe, WmS, BA1, NM1, NM2, MB1, MB2,JG1,JP1,BK1
137 X: Rig, PH1
138 X: Rig; aX: PH1; N: CKP
139 X: Rig; aX: NM1
140 X: Rig; R: G61, Wen, Bat; bX: Oxb

141 X: Rig; R: Wen, Bat, Oxb; bX: Oxl; N: Inc, JKT, Dol, Cum

142 X: Rig

143 X: Rig; N: Oxl, Low, Inc, JKT, Dol, Cum, WM1

144 X: Rig; bX: KRe
145 X: KRe, Rig; MOVE 145-154a to follow 32: 23: ChM
146 X: Rig; bX: KRe
147 X: CKP, Rig; aX: KRe
148 X: KRe, Rig; aX: CKP
149 X: KRe, Rig
150 X: KRe, Rig; bX: BK1
151 X: CKP, Rig, BK1
152 X: G61, Bel, Oxl, Wen, Bat, P95, Low, Roa, Inc, JKT, Oxb, Dol, USW,
        Cum, WM1, Rig, BK1; bX: KRe, WmS
153 X: Rig, WmS, BK1; aX: G61, Bel, Oxl, Wen, Bat, P95, Low, Roa, Inc,
        JKT, Oxb, Dol, USW, Cum, WM1, KRe

154 X: Rig, WmS , BK1

155 X: Rig, WmS; aX: BK1; bX: G61, Bel, Oxl, Wen, Bat, P95, Low, Roa,Inc*
156 X: G61, Bel, Oxl, Wen, Bat, P95, Low, Roa, Inc, JKT, Oxb, Dol, USW,
        Cum, WM1, HnF, KRe, Rig, WmS, PH1
157 X: HnF, Rig, WmS; bX: KRe
158 X: HnF, KRe, Rig, WmS, JP1
159 X: KRe, Rig, WmS, JP1; aX: HnF

160 X: Rig, Wm S; aX: KRe, JP1
161 X: Rig, WmS

Scene 24

1 X: JP1; MOVE 1-154 to follow 22: 54: Rig
2 X: JP1

3 X: Rig; bX: ChM, HIP

*23:155 JKT, Oxb, Dol, USW, Cum, WM1

1148	*Post.* Not any, but abide the change of time,	4
1149	Quake in the present winter's state and wish	5
1150	That warmer days would come: in these sear'd hopes,	6
1151	I barely gratify your love; they failing,	7
1152	I must die much your debtor.	8
1153	*Phi.* Your very goodness and your company	9
1154	O'erpays all I can do. By this, your king 10	10
1155	Hath heard of great Augustus: Caius Lucius	11
1156	Will do's commission throughly : and I think	12
1157	He'll grant the tribute, send the arrearages,	13
1158	Or look upon our Romans, whose remembrance	14
1159	Is yet fresh in their grief.	
1160	*Post.* I do believe,	15
1161	Statist though I am none, nor like to be,	16
1162	That this will prove a war; and you shall hear	17
1163	The legions now in Gallia sooner landed	18
1164	In our not-fearing Britain than have tidings	19
1165	Of any penny tribute paid. Our countrymen 20	20
1166	Are men more order'd than when Julius Cæsar	21
1167	Smiled at their lack of skill, but found their courage	22
1168	Worthy his frowning at: their discipline,	23
1169	Now mingled with their courages,will make known	24
1170	To their approvers they are people such	25
	That mend upon the world.	
1171	*Enter* IACHIMO.	
1172	*Phi.* See! Iachimo!	26
	Post. The swiftest harts have posted you by land;	
1173		27
1174	And winds of all the corners kiss'd your sails,	28
1175	To make your vessel nimble.	
1176	*Phi.* Welcome, sir.	29
1177	*Post.* I hope the briefness of your answer made	30
1178	The speediness of your return.	
1179	*Iach.* Your lady 31	31
1180	Is one of the fairest that I have look'd upon.	32
	Post. And therewithal the best; or let her beauty	
1181		33
1182	Look through a casement to allure false hearts	34
1183	And be false with them.	
1184	*Iach.* Here are letters for you.	35
1185	*Post.* Their tenour good, I trust.	
1186	*Iach.* 'Tis very like.	36
1187	*Phi.* Was Caius Lucius in the Britain court	37
1188	When you were there?	

4 X: HIP, JP1
5 X: KRe, HIP, JP1

6 same as 5; b̲X̲ HIC, PH1, BK1
7 X: KRe, HIP, HIC, PH1, JP1, BK1
8 same as 7
9 same as 7
10 X: ChM, KRe, JP1; a̲X̲: HIC, PH1, BK1; b̲X̲: WmS, Han, MB1, MB2
11 X: ChM, KRe, WmS, Han, MB1, MB2, JP1
12 same as 11; b̲X̲: HnF
13 X: ChM, HnF, KRe, WmS, Han, MB1, MB2, JP1; R: Inc, Cum; b̲X̲: WM1, CKP*
14 X: ChM, Cum, WM1, HnF, CKP, KRe, Rig, WmS, HIC, Han, SM1, MB1, MB2,
      PH1, JP1, BK1
15 X: ChM, HnF, KRe, WmS, Han, MB1, MB2, JP1; a̲X̲: WM1, CKP, Rig, HIC,SM1*
16 X: ChM, HnF, KRe, WmS, HIC, ViA, Han, SM1, MB1, MB2, PH1, JP1, BK1
17 X: ChM, HnF, KRe, WmS, Han, MB1, MB2, JP1; R: JKT; b̲X̲: G61, Bel, Ox1,*
18 X: ChM, Bel, Ox1, Wen, Bat, Bar, Low, JKT, USW, WM1, HnF, CKP, KRe*
19 same as 18, Oxb, less Ox1; less R; R: G61; a̲X̲: Ox1
20 X: ChM, G61, HnF, KRe, WmS, Han, MB1, MB2, JP1; a̲X̲: Wen, Bat, Bar, Low*
21 same as 20, HIC, SM1, less G61; less a̲X̲, b̲X̲, c̲X̲
22 same as 21; b̲X̲: PH1
23 same as 21, PH1; a̲X̲: Roa; b̲X̲: ViA, BA1, JG1, BK1
24 same as 23, ViA, BA1,JG1, BK1; less a̲X̲, b̲X̲
25 same as 24, less JG1

26 X: ChM, KRe; a̲X̲: HnF, WmS, HIC, ViA, Han, BA1, SM1, MB1, MB2, PH1, JP1;
      ADD 3: G61, Bel, Ox1, Wen, Bat, Bar, Low, Roa, Inc, JKT, Oxb, Dol*
27 X: ChM, ViA, JP1
28 same as 27

29 X: ChM; a̲X̲: ViA, JP1; N̲: JP1
30 X: ChM, WmS

31 a̲X̲: ChM, WmS
32

33 b̲X̲: KRe, WmS, PH1, BK1
34 X̲: KRe, WmS, PH1, BK1

35 a̲X̲: KRe, WmS, PH1, BK1

36 X: KRe
37 X: ChM

*24:13 Rig, HIC, SM1, PH1, BK1   *24:15 PH1, BK1
*24:17 Wen, Bat, Bar, Low, Roa, Oxb, USW, WM1, CKP, ViA, PH1, BK1; ADD 3:
   Low; ADD 5: Rig   *24:18 WmS, ViA, Han, MB1, MB2, PH1, JP1,BK1
*24:20 JKP, Oxb, USW, ViA, PH1, BK1; b̲X̲: HIC, SM1; c̲X̲: Bel
*24:26 USW, Cum

1189	*Iach.* He was expected then,	38
1190	But not approach'd.	
1191	*Post.* All is well yet.	39
1192	Sparkles this stone as it was wont? or is't not 40	40
1193	Too dull for your good wearing?	
1194	*Iach.* If I had lost it,	41
1195	I should have lost the worth of it in gold.	42
1196	I'll make a journey twice as far, to enjoy	43
1197	A second night of such sweet shortness which	44
1198	Was mine in Britain, for the ring is won.	45
1199	*Post.* The stone's too hard to come by.	
1200	*Iach.* Not a whit,	46
1201	Your lady being so easy.	
1202	*Post.* Make not, sir,	47
1203	Your loss your sport: I hope you know that we	48
2104	Must not continue friends.	
2105	*Iach.* Good sir, we must,	49
1206	If you keep covenant. Had I not brought 50	50
1207	The knowledge of your mistress home. I grant	51
1208	We were to question further: but I now	52
1209	Profess myself the winner of her honour,	53
1210	Together with your ring; and not the wronger	54
1211	Of her or you. having proceeded but	55
1212	By both your wills.	
1213	*Post.* If you can make't apparent	56
1214	That you have tasted her in bed, my hand	57
1215	And ring is yours; if not, the foul opinion	58
1216	You had of her pure honour gains or loses	59
1217	Your sword or mine, or masterless leaves both 60	60
1218	To who shall find them.	
1219	*Iach.* Sir, my circumstances,	61
1220	Being so near the truth as I will make them,	62
1221	Must first induce you to believe: whose strength	63
1222	I will confirm with oath; which, I doubt not,	64
1223	You'll give me leave to spare, when you shall find	65
1224	You need it not.	
1225	*Post.* Proceed.	
1226	*Iach.* First, her bedchamber,—	66
1227	Where, I confess, I slept not, but profess	67
1228	Had that was well worth watching—it was hang'd	68
1229	With tapestry of silk and silver; the story	69
1230	Proud Cleopatra, when she met her Roman, 70	70
1231	And Cydnus swell'd above the banks, or for	71
1232	The press of boats or pride: a piece of work	72
1233	So bravely done, so rich, that it did strive	73
1234	In workmanship and value: which I wonder'd	74

38   X: ChM; <u>R</u>: Ox1, Low, Inc; <u>bX</u>: JKT, Dol, USW, Cum

39   X: ChM; <u>R</u>: Ox1, Inc, JKT, Cum; <u>aX</u>: Low, Dol, USW
40

41   X: KRe
42   X: KRe
43   X: KRe, HIC, SM1; <u>R</u>: ChM
44   X: ChM, KRe, HIC, $\overline{\text{SM1}}$
45   X: ChM, KRe; <u>aX</u>: HIC, SM1

46   <u>aX</u>: KRe

47
48

49
50   X: JP1; <u>bX</u>: KRe, WmS
51   X: KRe, $\overline{\text{WmS}}$, JP1
52   X: JP1; <u>R</u>: KRe; <u>aX</u>: WmS
53   <u>bX</u>: HIC
54   $\overline{\text{aX}}$: HIC; <u>b X</u>: MB2, JP1, BK1
55   $\overline{\text{X}}$: MB2, JP$\overline{\text{1}}$, BK1

56   X: BK1; <u>aX</u>: MB2, JP1; <u>bX</u>: NM1, NM2, PH1
57   X: HIC, $\overline{\text{NM1}}$, NM2, BK1; <u>aX</u>: WM1, HnF, ViA, SM1
58   X: NM1, NM2, BK1; <u>bX</u>: $\overline{\text{PH1}}$
59   X: NM1, NM2, PH1, $\overline{\text{BK1}}$; B: WmS
60   same as 59; less <u>B</u>; <u>bX</u>: $\overline{\text{KRe}}$, JP1

61   X: KRe, NM1, NM2, JP1, BK1; <u>aX</u>: PH1; <u>bX</u>: HIC
62   same as 61, HIC; less <u>aX</u>, <u>bX</u>
63   same as 62; <u>bX</u>: PH1
64   same as 62, $\overline{\text{PH1}}$; less <u>bX</u>
65   same as 64

66   <u>aX</u>: KRe, HIC, NM1, NM2, PH1, JP1, BK1
67   $\overline{\text{X}}$: HnF, KRe, HIC, SM1; <u>bX</u>: WM1, CKP, Rig
68   <u>aX</u>: WM1, HnF, CKP, KRe, $\overline{\text{Rig}}$, HIC, SM1; <u>ADD</u> 1: KRe
69   $\overline{\text{R}}$: G61, Bel, Wen, Bat, P95, Bar, Oxb
70   $\overline{\text{X}}$: G61, Bel, Wen, Bat, P95, Bar, Roa, Oxb
71   X: G61, Bel, Ox1, Wen, P95, Bar, Low, Roa, Inc, JKT, Oxb, Dol, USW*
72   X: KRe, BK1; <u>aX</u>: G61, Bel, Ox1, Wen, P95, Bar, Low, Roa, Inc, JKT, Oxb*
73   X: BK1
74   X: BK1; <u>bX</u>: G61, Bel, Ox1, Wen, Bat, P95, Bar, Low, Inc, JKT, Oxb, Dol,
       USW, Cum, WM1, CKP, KRe, Rig, WmS, HIC, ViA, BA1, PJ1

*24:71 Cum, HnF, KRe, Rig, WmS, ViA, BA1, JP1, BK1; <u>aX</u>: Bat; <u>bX</u>: HIC, SM1
*24:72 Dol, USW, Cum, HnF, WmS, HIC, ViA, BA1, SM1, $\overline{\text{JP1}}$

1235	Could be so rarely and exactly wrought,	75
1236	Since the true life on't was—	
1237	*Post.* This is true:	76
1238	And this you might have heard of here, by me,	77
1239	Or by some other.	
1240	*Iach.* More particulars	78
1241	Must justify my knowledge.	
1242	*Post.* So they must,	79
1243	Or do your honour injury.	
1244	*Iach.* The chimney	80
1245	Is south the chamber, and the chimney-piece	81
1246	Chaste Dian bathing: never saw I figures	82
1247	So likely to report themselves: the cutter	83
1248	Was as another nature, dumb; outwent her,	84
1249	Motion and breath left out.	
1250	*Post.* This is a thing	85
1251	Which you might from relation likewise reap,	86
1252	Being, as it is, much spoke of.	
1253	*Iach.* The roof o' the chamber	87
1254	With golden cherubins is fretted: her andirons—	88
1255	I had forgot them—were two winking Cupids	89
1256	Of silver, each on one foot standing, nicely	90
1257	Depending on their brands.	
1258	*Post.* This is her honour!	91
1259	Let it be granted you have seen all this—and praise	92
1260	Be given to your remembrance—the description	93
1261	Of what is in her chamber nothing saves	94
1262	The wager you have laid.	
1263	*Iach.* Then, if you can,	95
1263+1	[*Showing the bracelet.*	
1264	Be pale: I beg but leave to air this jewel: see!	96
1265	And now 'tis up again: it must be married	97
1266	To that your diamond; I'll keep them.	
1267	*Post.* Jove!	98
1268	Once more let me behold it: is it that	99
1269	Which I left with her?	
1270	*Iach.* Sir—I thank her—that: 100	100
1271	She stripp'd it from her arm: I see her yet;	101
1272	Her pretty action did outsell her gift,	102
1273	And yet enrich'd it too: she gave it me, and said	103
1274	She prized it once.	
1275	*Post.* May be she pluck'd it off	104
1276	To send it me.	
1277	*Iach.* She writes so to you, doth she?	105
	Post. O, no- no, no! 'tis true. Here, take this	
1278	too; [*Gives the ring.* 106	106

75 X: ChM, G61, Bel, Ox1, Wen, Bat, P95, Bar, Low, Roa, Inc, JKT, Oxb,
     Dol, USW, Cum, WM1, CKP, KRe, Rig, WmS, HIC, ViA, BA1, SM1,PH1,BK1
76 aX: ChM, G61, Bel, Ox1, Wen, Bat, P95, Bar, Low, Roa, Inc, JKT, Oxb,*
77

78 bX: KRe, WmS

79 X: KRe, WmS

80 aX: WmS; bX: KRe
81 aX: KRe
82 bX: HnF, BK1
83 X: HnF, BK1; bX: KRe, ViA, BA1, MB2, JP1
84 X: HnF, KRe, ViA, BA1, MB2 , JP1, BK1

85 X: HnF, BK1; aX: KRe, ViA, BA1, MB2, JP1
86 X: HnF, BK1

87 X: Lac, WmS; R: KRe; aX: HnF, Rig; bX: Roa, HM1, MTh
88 X: Lac, HM1, MTh, WmS; bX: G61, Bel, Ox1, Wen, Bat, P95, Bar, Low,*
89 X: G61, Bel, Ox1, Wen, Bat, P95, Bar, Low, Roa, Inc, JKT, Oxb, Dol,*
90 same as 89

91 X: Ox1, HnF, Lac, WmS; R: G61, P95; aX: Bel,Wen, Bat, Bar, Low, Roa,*
92 X: WmS; aX: Ox1; bX: HnF
93 X: HnF, WmS; R: G61, P95
94 X: WmS

95 aX: Rig, WmS

96
97 X: KRe, WmS; bX: Bel, Ox1, Bat, Bar, Low, Inc, JKT, Oxb, Dol, USW, Cum,
     Rig
98 X: Bel, Ox1, Bar, Low, Inc, Oxb, Dol, USW, Cum, Rig, WmS; aX: KRe;cX:Roa
99

100
101
102
103

104 bX: KRe; cX: P95; ADD 2: Bar

105

106 bX: WmS; MOVE 106b-108a to follow 113: ViA

*24:76 Dol, USW, Cum, WM1, CKP, KRe, Rig, WmS, HIC, ViA, BA1, SM1, PH1,BK1
*24:88 Roa, Inc, JKT, Oxb, Dol, USW, Cum, HnF, KRe   * 24:89 USW,
   Cum, HnF, Lac, KRe, HM1, MTh, WmS   *24:91 Inc, JKT, Oxb, Dol,
   USW, Cum, KRe, HM1, MTh

1279	It is a basilisk unto mine eye,	107
1280	Kills me to look on't. Let there be no honour	108
	Where there is beauty; truth, where semblance;	
1281	love, 109	109
1282	Where there's another man: the vows of women	110
1283	Of no more bondage be, to where they are made,	111
1284	Than they are to their virtues; which is nothing.	112
1285	O, above measure false!	
1286	*Phi.* Have patience, sir,	113
1287	And take your ring again; 'tis not yet won:	114
1288	It may be probable she lost it; or	115
1289	Who knows if one of her women, being corrupted,	116
1290	Hath stol'n it from her?	
1291	*Post.* Very true;	117
1292	And so, I hope, he came by 't. Back my ring:	118
1293	Render to me some corporal sign about her,	119
1294	More evident than this; for this was stolen. 120	120
1295	*Iach.* By Jupiter, I had it from her arm.	121
	Post. Hark you, he swears; by Jupiter he	
1296	swears.	122
1297	'Tis true:—nay, keep the ring—'tis true: I am sure	123
1298	She would not lose it: her attendants are	124
	All sworn and honourable:—they induced to steal	
1299	it!	125
1300	And by a stranger!—No, he hath enjoy'd her:	126
1301	The cognizance of her incontinency	127
	Is this: she hath bought the name of whore thus	
1302	dearly.	128
1303	There, take thy hire; and all the fiends of hell	129
1304	Divide themselves between you!	
1305	*Phi.* Sir, be patient: 130	130
1306	This is not strong enough to be believed	131
1307	Of one persuaded well of—	
1308	*Post.* Never talk on't;	132
1309	She hath been colted by him.	
1310	*Iach.* If you seek	133
1311	For further satisfying, under her breast—	134
1312	Worthy the pressing—lies a mole, right proud	135
1313	Of that most delicate lodging: by my life,	136
1314	I kiss'd it; and it gave me present hunger	137
1315	To feed again, though full. You do remember	138
1316	This stain upon her?	
1317	*Post.* Ay, and it doth confirm	139
1318	Another stain, as big as hell can hold, 140	140
1319	Were there no more but it.	
1320	*Iach.* Will you hear more?	141

107
108 X: KRe; b̲X̲: WmS̡Han, PH1

109 X: KRe,̡WmS, Han, PH1
110 X: KRe, Han, PH1; a̲X̲: WmS; b̲X̲: HnF, ViA, BK1
111 X: HnF, KRe, ViA, H̄an, PH1, BK1; b̲X̲: ChM
112 same as 11; less b̲X̲

113 a̲X̲: HnF, Han, PH1, BK1; Insert 106b-108a: ViA
114 X̄: KRe, PH1, BK1
115 X: PH1, BK1
116

117 R̲: KRe; b̲X̲: BK1
118 X̄: KRe; a̲X̲: BK1; b̲ X: WmS
119
120
121

122
123 X: KRe, WmS; b̲X̲: BK1
124 X: KRe, WmS, B̄K̄1̄

125 same as 24; a̲X̲: G61, Bel, Wen, Bat, Bar, Oxb; c̲X̲: P95
126 X: KRe, WmS, H̄IC, BK1; b̲X̲: HnF, NM1, NM2
127 X: HnF, KRe, WmS, HIC, N̄M̄1, NM2, PH1, JG1, BK1

128 same as 127; b̲X̲: MTh, ViA, SM1; A̲D̲D̲ 1: ViA
129 X: WmS, PH1

130 X: PH1; a̲X̲: WmS; b̲X̲: KRe
131 X: KRe

132 X: KRe; b̲X̲: HnF, WmS, HIC, ViA, BA1, PH1

133 X: HnF; R̲: ChM; a̲X̲: WM1, KRe, WmS, HIC, ViA, BA1, SM1, NM1, PH1
134 X: HnF
135 X: HnF; a̲b̲X̲: WmS
136 X: HnF, W̄m̄S̄; b̲X̲: Dol, USW, Lac, KRe, Rig, HM1, MTh, HIC, ViA,NM1*
137 X: Dol, USW, H̄nF, KRe, Rig, HM1, MTh, WmS, HIC, ViA, SM1, NM1, NM2;*
138 X: HnF; a̲X̲: Bel, Ox1,Wen, Bat, Bar, Low, Inc, JKT, Oxb, Dol, USW,Cum,
        WM1, KRe, Rig, HM1, MTh, WmS, HIC, ViA, SM1, NM1, NM2
139 X: HnF; b̲X̲: KRe, JP1
140 X: HnF, K̄R̄e, JP1

141 X: ChM, HnF, KRe, JP1; b̲X̲: WmS

*24:136 NM1, NM2   *24:37 b̲X̲: Bel, Ox1, Wen, Bat, Bar, Low,
   Inc, JKT, Oxb, Cum, WM1, Lac

1321	*Post.* Spare your arithmetic: never count the	142
	turns;	
1322	Once, and a million!	
1323	*Iach.* I'll be sworn—	
1324	*Post.* No swearing.	143
1325	If you will swear you have not done't, you lie;	144
1326	And I will kill thee, if thou dost deny	145
1327	Thou 'st made me cuckold.	
1328	*Iach.* I'll deny nothing.	146
	Post. O, that I had her here, to tear her limb-	
1329	meal!	147
1330	I will go there and do't, i' the court, before	148
1331	Her father. I 'll do something— [*Exit.*	
1332	*Phi.* Quite besides	149
1333	The government of patience! You have won: 150	150
1334	Let's follow him, and pervert the present wrath	151
1335	He hath against himself.	
1336	*Iach.* With all my heart. [*Exeunt.*	152

1336+1 SCENE V. *Another room in Philario's house.*

1337 *Enter* POSTHUMUS.

1338	*Post.* Is there no way for men to be but women	1
1339	Must be half-workers? We are all bastards;	2
1340	And that most venerable man which I	3
1341	Did call my father, was I know not where	4
3142	When I was stamp'd; some coiner with his tools	5
1343	Made me a counterfeit: yet my mother seem'd	6
1344	The Dian of that time: so doth my wife	7
1345	The nonpareil of this. O, vengeance, vengeance!	8
1346	Me of my lawful pleasure she restrain'd	9
1347	And pray'd me oft forbearance: did it with 10	10
1348	A pudency so rosy the sweet view on't	11
1349	Might well have warm'd old Saturn; that I	
1350	thought her	12
1351	As chaste as unsunn'd snow. O, all the devils!	13
1352	This yellow Iachimo, in an hour,—was't not?—	14
1353	Or less,—at first?—perchance he spoke not, but,	15
1354	Like a full-acorn'd boar, a German one,	16
1355	Cried 'O!' and mounted; found no opposition	17
1356	But what he look'd for should oppose and she	18
1357	Should from encounter guard. Could I find out	19
	The woman's part in me! For there's no	
1358	motion 20	20
1359	That tends to vice in man, but I affirm	21
1360	It is the woman's part: be it lying, note it,	22

142 X: ChM, HnF, KRe, WmS, HIC

143 X: ChM, HIC; aX: HnF, KRe, WmS
144 X: ChM, HnF, KRe, HIC
145 X: ChM, HnF, KRe, HIC, NM1, NM2; R: G61; bX: WM1, Han

146 X: ChM, HnF, KRe, HIC, NM1; R: G61; aX: WM1, MTh, WmS, ViA, Han, NM2;
       B: CKP, Rig
147 X: Han; MOVE 147-152a to follow 25: 32a: ViA
148 X: Han

149 X: Han; bX: Inc, Dol, Cum, CKP, Lac, KRe, HM1, WmS; Insert 25: 20-*
150 X: Inc, Dol, Cum, CKP, Lac, KRe, HM1, WmS, Han
151 same as 150

152 same as 150; bX: ViA

                        Scene 25

ALL CUT: Ox1, Low, Inc, JKT, USW, Cum, WM1, HnF, CKP, HM1, WmS, HIP, WM1;
ALL CUT EXCEPT TRANSFER: KRe. "Frequently omitted": MTh

  1 X: HIC; R: Wen, Bat, Oxb; bX: Bar
  2 X: HIC; R: Wen, Bat, Oxb; aX: Bel, Bar; bX: Lac, Rig, ViA; ADD 1:Bel,Han
  3 X: Lac, Rig, MTh, HIC, ViA, Han
  4 same as 3
  5 same as 3; bX: ChM, SM1
  6 X: HIC, ViA; aX: ChM, Lac, Rig, MTh, Han, SM1
  7 X: HIC, ViA
  8 X: HIC, ViA; bX:NM2
  9 X: Lac, Rig, MTh, HIC, ViA, Han, NM2
 10 same as 9; bX: IP2
 11 same as 9, IP2; bX: IP1

 12 X: HIC, NM2; aX: Lac, Rig, MTh, ViA, Han, IP1, IP2
 13 X: HIC, NM2; bX: ViA
 14 X: HIC, ViA, NM2; bX BA1
 15 X: HIC, ViA, BA1, NM2; bX: Lac, Rig, MTh, Han, SM1
 16 X: ChM, Lac, Rig, MTh, HIC, ViA, Han, BA1, SM1, IP1, NM2; bX: JG1
 17 X: ChM, Lac, Rig, MTh, HIC, ViA, Han, BA1, NM2; R: Bel, Wen, Bat, Bar*
 18 X: ChM, Wen, Bat, Oxb, Lac, Rig, MTh, HIC, ViA, Han, BA1, SM1, NM2*
 19 X: MTh, HIC; R: Bel, Bar; aX: ChM, Wen, Bat, Oxb, Lac, Rig, ViA, Han,
       BA1, SM1, NM2, BK1
 20 X: Bel; aX: HIC; MOVE 20-25 to follow 24:149a: KRe, HIC
 21 X: Bel
 22 aX: Han, JG1

*24:149 35: KRe, HIC   *25:17 Oxb; aX: SM1; bX: BK1; ADD 1:G61
*25:18 BK1; R: Bel, Bar

1361   The woman's; flattering, hers; deceiving, hers;   23
              Lust and rank thoughts, hers, hers; revenges,
1362   hers;   24
1363   Ambitions, covetings, change of prides, disdain,   25
1364   Nice longing, slanders, mutability,   26
              All faults that may be named, nay, that hell
1365   knows,   27
              Why, hers, in part or all; but rather, all;   28
1366   For even to vice   29
1367   They are not constant, but are changing still 30   30
1368   One vice, but of a minute old, for one   31
1369   Not half so old as that.   I'll write against them,   32
1370   Detest them, curse them: yet 'tis greater skill   33
1371   In a true hate, to pray they have their will: 34
              The very devils cannot plague them better.   35
1372   *[Exit.*

1372+1   # ACT III.

1373,+1   SCENE I. *Britain.   A hall in Cymbeline's*
1373+2   *palace.*

1374   *Enter in state,* CYMBELINE, QUEEN, CLOTEN,
1375   *and* Lords *at one door, and at another,* CAIUS
1376   LUCIUS *and* Attendants.

           Cym.   Now say, what would Augustus Cæsar
1377   with us?   1
           Luc.   When Julius Cæsar, whose remem-
1378   brance yet   2
1379   Lives in men's eyes and will to ears and tongues   3
1380   Be theme and hearing ever, was in this Britain   4
1381   And conquer'd it, Cassibelan, thine uncle,—   5
1382   Famous in Cæsar's praises, no whit less   6
1383   Than in his feats deserving it—for him   7
1384   And his succession granted Rome a tribute,   8
              Yearly three thousand pounds, which by thee
1385   lately   9
1386   Is left untender'd.
1387   *Queen.*   And, to kill the marvel,   10   10
1388   Shall be so ever.
1389   *Clo.*   There be many Cæsars,   11
1390   Ere such another Julius. Britain is   12
1391   A world by itself; and we will nothing pay   13
1392   For wearing our own noses.
1383   *Queen.*   That opportunity   14
1394   Which then they had to take from 's, to resume   15

23 X: Han, JG1

24 X: HIC, Han, JG1
25 X: HIC, ViA, Han, SM1, PH1, JG1, BK1
26 same as 25

27 X: Han
28 X: Han, SM1; bX: BK1; cX: ViA
29 X: Han, SM1, B̄K1; bX: H̄IC
30 X: HIC, Han, SM1, B̄K1
31 X: HIC, Han, SM1; aX: BK1
32 R: ChM; aX: HIC, Han, SM1; bX: ViA; ADD 2, insert 24: 147-152a: ViA
33 X̄: ViA; R̄: ChM; bX: SM1
34 X: ViA, S̄M1; R: C̄hM
35 X: ViA, SM1; ADD 2: BK1

Scene 31

ALL CUT: KRe, WmS, HIP; ALL CUT EXCEPT TRANSFERS: HIP
 1 MOVE 1-86 to follow 34: 196: ViA, Han; MOVE 1-86 to follow 182: ChM

 2 bX: G61, Bel, Ox1, Wen, Bat, Bar, Low, Roa, Inc, JKT, Oxb, Dol, USW*
 3 X: G61, Bel, Ox1, Wen, Bat, Bar, Low, Roa, Inc, JKT, Oxb, Dol, USW*
 4 aX: G61, Bel, Ox1, Wen, Bat, Bar, Low, Roa, Inc, JKT, Oxb, Dol, USW*
 5 aX: G61, Bel, Wen, Bat, Bar; bX: PH1
 6 X: G61, Bel, Wen, Bat, Bar, JKT, ViA, SM1, NM2, MB2, PH1, JP1, BK1*
 7 X: WM1, NM2, BK1; aX: ChM, G61, Bel, Wen, Bat, Bar, JKT, ViA, SM1*
 8 aX: NM1, NM2

 9

10

11 MOVE 11b-14a to follow 33: 62: HIC, SM1
12
13

14 bX: G61, Bel, Ox1, Wen, Bat, P95, Bar, Low, Roa, Inc, JKT, Dol, USW*
15 X: G61, Bel, Ox1, Wen, Bat, P95, Bar, Low, Roa, Inc, JKT, Dol, USW,
       Cum, WM1, HnF, CKP, Rig, PH1, JP1, BK1; bX: Oxb, ViA

*31: 2 Cum, WM1, CKP, Rig, ViA, SM1, MB2, JP1, BK1   *31: 3 Cum,
    WM1, CKP, Rig, ViA, SM1, MB2, JP1, BK1; bX: NM1   *31: 4 Cum,WM1,
    CKP, Rig, ViA, SM1, MB2, JP1, BK1   *31: 6 bX: ChM
*31: 7 MB2, PH1, JP1   *31:14 Cum, WM1, HnF, CKP, Rig, PH1,JP1,
    BK1

1395	We have again. Remember, sir, my liege,	16
1396	The kings your ancestors, together with	17
1397	The natural bravery of your isle, which stands	18
1398	As Neptune's park, ribbed and paled in	19
1399	With rocks unscaleable and roaring waters, 20	20
1400	With sands that will not bear your enemies' boats,	21
1401	But suck them up to the topmast. A kind of conquest	22
1402	Cæsar made here; but made not here his brag	23
1403	Of 'Came' and 'saw' and 'overcame:' with shame—	24
1404	The first that ever touch'd him—he was carried	25
1405	From off our coast, twice beaten; and his shipping—	26
1406	Poor ignorant baubles!—on our terrible seas,	27
1407	Like egg-shells moved upon their surges, crack'd	28
1408	As easily 'gainst our rocks: for joy whereof	29
1409	The famed Cassibelan, who was once at point—	30
1410	O giglot fortune!—to master Cæsar's sword, 31	31
1411	Made Lud's town with rejoicing fires bright	32
1412	And Britons strut with courage.	33
	Clo. Come, there's no more tribute to be	34
1413	paid: our kingdom is stronger than it was at	35
1414	that time: and, as I said, there is no moe such	36
1415	Cæsars: other of them may have crook'd noses,	37
1416	but to owe such straight arms, none.	38
1417	*Cym.* Son, let your mother end. 39	39
	Clo. We have yet many among us can gripe	40
1418	as hard as Cassibelan: I do not say I am one;	41
1419	but I have a hand. Why tribute? why should	42
1420	we pay tribute? If Cæsar can hide the sun from	43
1421	us with a blanket, or put the moon in his pocket,	44
1422	we will pay him tribute for light; else, sir, no	45
1423	more tribute, pray you now.	46
1424	*Cym.* You must know,	47
1425	Till the injurious Romans did extort	48
1426	This tribute from us, we were free: Cæsar's ambition,	49
1427	Which swell'd so much that it did almost stretch 50	50
1428	The sides o' the world, against all colour here	51
1429	Did put the yoke upon 's; which to shake off	52
1430	Becomes a warlike people, whom we reckon	53
	Ourselves to be.	
	Clo. and Lords. We do.	

```
16  same as 15, Oxb, ViA, less PH1, JG1, BK1; less bX; aX: JP1, BK1;bXSM1,PH1
17  same as 16, SM1, PH1; less aX, bX
18  same as 18
19  same as 17
20  same as 17; bX: NM1, NM2

21  same as 17, NM1, NM2

22  X: G61, Bel, Ox1, Wen, Bat, P95, Bar, Low, Roa, Inc, JKT, Oxb, Dol,USW*
23  same as 22; less aX

24  same as 23
25  same as 23; aX: SM1

26  same as 23; bX: Lac, MTh, HIM, ViA, Han, NM1, NM2, BK1
27  X: G61, Bel, Ox1, Wen, Bat, P95, Bar, Low, Roa, Inc, JKT, Oxb, Dol,  USW*
28  same as 27 including R
29  same as 27, less Lac, MTh, HIM, Han; R: ChM; aX: Lac,MThHIM,Han;bX:IP1
30  same as 29, IP1, less HM1, BK1; same R; bX SM1
31  same as 30, ChM, SM1; less R, bX
32  same as 31, less ChM, SM1, NM1, NM2
33  same as 32, Han
34  X: G61, Bel, Ox1, Wen, Bat, P95, Bar, Low, Roa, Inc, JKT, Oxb, Dol,USW*
35  same as 34
36  same as 24; bX: BK1
37  same as 34, BK1; less bX
38  same as 37
39  same as 37, ViA, less BK1
40  same  as 39, BK1, less Han
41  same as 40, less G61, CKP; aX: G61, CKP
42  X: HM1; aX: Bel, Ox1, Wen, Bat, P95, Bar, Low, Roa, Inc, JKT, Oxb, Dol*
43  X: HM1; aX: BK1; ADD 1: ViA
44  X: HM1
45  X: HM1; bX: Bel, Ox1, Wen, Bat, Bar, Low, Inc, JKT, Oxb, Dol
46  X: Bel, Ox1, Bar, Low, Cum ; aX: Bat, HM1; bX: ChM, G61, P95, Roa, Dol,*
47  X: ChM, ViA; bX: Dol, HM1
48  X: Dol, CKP, HM1,  ViA; MOVE 48-54a to follow 23: 63: HIC, SM1

49  X: Dol, CKP, HM1; aX: ViA; bX: G61, Bel, Ox1, Wen, Bat, P95, Bar, Low,
      Roa, Inc, JKT, Oxb, USW, Cum, Rig
50  X: G61, Bel, Ox1, Wen, Bat, P95, Bar, Low, Roa, Inc, JKT, Oxb, Dol,USW*
51  same as 50
52  X: G61, Bel, Ox1, Wen, Bat, P95, Bar, Low, Roa, Inc, JKT, Oxb, Dol,USW*
53  same as 52, CKP; less bX; bX: ChM; ADD 2: ViA

*31:22 HnF, CKP, Rig; aX: ViA, SM1, NM1, NM2, PH1          *31:27 Cum, WM1,
   HnF, CKP, Lac, Rig, HM1, MTh, HIM, ViA, Han, NM1, NM2, BK1; R: ChM
*31:34 Cum, WM1, HnF, CKP, Lac, Rig, HM1, MTh, HIM, Han, NM1, NM2, PH1
*31:42 USW, Cum, WM1, HnF, Lac, Rig, MTh, HIM, ViA, NM1, NM2, PH1,bX: BK1;
   MOVE  42b to follow 23: 63: HIC, SM1            *31:46 USW, ViA
*31:50 Cum, WM1, Lac, Rig, HM1, MTh, HIM, ViA, NM1, NM2
*31:52 Cum, Rig; bX: CKP
```

1431	*Cym.* Say, then, to Cæsar,	54
1432	Our ancestor was that Mulmutius which	55
1433	Ordain'd our laws, whose use the sword of Cæsar	56
	Hath too much mangled; whose repair and	
1434	franchise	57
1435	Shall, by the power we hold, be our good deed,	58
	Though Rome be therefore angry: Mulmutius	
1436	made our laws,	59
1437	Who was the first of Britain which did put 60	60
1438	His brows within a golden crown and call'd	61
1439	Himself a king.	
1440	*Luc.* I am sorry, Cymbeline,	62
1441	That I am to pronounce Augustus Cæsar—	63
1442	Cæsar, that hath more kings his servants than	64
1443	Thyself domestic officers—thine enemy:	65
1444	Receive it from me, then: war and confusion	66
1445	In Cæsar's name pronounce I 'gainst thee: look	67
1446	For fury not to be resisted. Thus defied,	68
1447	I thank thee for myself.	
1448	*Cym.* Thou art welcome, Caius.	69
1449	Thy Cæsar knighted me; my youth I spent 70	70
1450	Much under him; of him I gather'd honour;	71
1451	Which he to seek of me again, perforce,	72
1452	Behoves me keep at utterance. I am perfect	73
1453	That the Pannonians and Dalmatians for	74
1454	Their liberties are now in arms; a precedent	75
1455	Which not to read would show the Britons cold:	76
1456	So Cæsar shall not find them.	
1457	*Luc.* Let proof speak.	77
	Clo. His majesty bids you welcome. Make	78
1458	pastime with us a day or two, or longer: if you	79
1459	seek us afterwards in other terms, you shall find	80
1460	us in our salt-water girdle: if you beat us out	81
1461	of it, it is yours; if you fall in the adventure,	82
1462	our crows shall fare the better for you; and	83
1463	there's an end.	84
1464	*Luc.* So, sir.	85
	Cym. I know your master's pleasure and he	
1465	mine:	86
1466	All the remain is 'Welcome!' [*Exeunt.*	87
1467,+1	SCENE II. *Another room in the palace.*	
1468	*Enter* PISANIO, *with a letter.*	
	Pis. How! of adultery? Wherefore write	
1469	you not	1

54 X: USW, CKP; aX: ChM, G61, Bel, Ox1, Wen, Bat, P95, Bar, Low, Roa,X
55 X: USW, WM1, CKP, BA1, IP1, MB1, MB2, IP2, PH1, JP1; bX; NM2
56 same as 55, NM2; less bX'bX: BK1

57 same as 56, less USW; less bX; aX: USW, BK1
58 same as 57, less NM2; less aX; aX: NM2

59 same as 58; less aX; bX: G61, Bel, Ox1, Wen, Bat, P95, Bar, Low, Roa*
60 X: G61, Bel, Ox1, Wen, Bat, P95, Bar, Low, Roa, Inc, JKT, Oxb, Dol*
61 same as 60, less G61; less aX; aX: G61

62 X: HnF, CKP; aX:Bel, Wen, Bat, P95, Bar, Dol, USW, Cum, WM1, Lac, Rig,*
63 X: HnF; aX: CKP
64 X: G61, Bel, P95, Low, Inc, JKT, Dol, USW, Cum, WM1, HnF, Rig, SM1;*
65 X: Bel, Wen, Bat, HnF, Rig; R: G61, Ox1, P95, Bar, Low, JKT, Oxb, USW*
66 X: Oxb, HnF; aX: G61, Bel, Ox1, Wen, Bat, P95, Bar
67 X: HnF; aX: Oxb
68 X: HnF, CKP; MOVE 68-69 to follow 73a: JP1

69 X: HnF, CKP, Han; bX: Lac, HM1, MTh, HIM
70 X: G61, Bel, Ox1, Wen, Bat, P95, Bar, Low, Roa, Inc, JKT, Oxb, Dol*
71 same as 70
72 same as 70, NM1, NM2, JG1; R: ChM
73 same as 73, less JG1; same R; aX: JG1; bX: IP1, PH1, JP1, BK1; Insert*
74 same as 73, IP1, PH1, JP1, BK1; same R; less aX, bX, Insert
75 same as 74; same R' ADD 1: ChM
76 same as 75, less CKP; less R, ADD

77 X: G61, Bel, Ox1, Wen, Bat, P95, Bar, Low, Roa, Inc, JKT, Dol, USW*
78
79 X: JP1
80 aX: JP1
81
82
83
84 ADD 4: ViA; ADD 6, insert 35: 1-19: JP1
85 X: ChM, ViA, Han, JP1

86 X: Han, JP1; ADD 2: ViA
87 X: ChM, ViA, Han, JP1; Insert 35: 1-28: ChM; Insert 36: 21-22a: MB1
    MB2

Scene 32

 1 X: NM1; bX: KRe; B: KRe, HIC
*31:54 Inc, JKT, Oxb, Dol, Cum, Rig,MTh; bX:WM1,BA1,IP1,MB1,MB2,IP2,PH1,JP1
*31:59 Inc, JKT, Oxb, Dol, USW, Cum, HnF, Lac, Rig, MTh, HIM, ViA, SM1,
    NM1, JG1, BK1   *31:60 USW, Cum, WM1, HnF, Lac, Rig, HM1,
    MTh, HIM, ViA, BA1, SM1, IP1, MB1, MB2, IP2, PH1, JG1, JP1, BK1 ;aX:ChM
*31:62 HM1, MTh, HIM, ViA, BA1, SM1, NM1, IP1, MB1, MB2, IP2, PH1, JG1,
    JP1, BK1 ; aX:Ba Od *31:64 R: Wen, Bat, Bar   *31:65 Cum; aX: Inc,
    Dol, WM1, SM1   *31:70 USW, Cum, WM1, HnF, CKP, Lac, Rig, HM1,
    MTh, HIM, ViA, Han   *31:73 68b-69, add 3: JP1
*33:77 Cum, WM1, HnF, Rig, HM1, HIM, ViA, Han, NM1, JP1; aX Oxb, Lac, MTh,
    IP1, NM2, PH1, BK1

1470	What monster's her accuser? Leonatus!	2
1471	O master! what a strange infection	3
1472	Is fall'n into thy ear! What false Italian,	4
1473	As poisonous-tongued as handed, hath prevail'd	5
1474	On thy too ready hearing? Disloyal! No:	6
1475	She's punish'd for her truth, and undergoes.	7
1476	More goddess-like than wife-like, such assaults	8
1477	As would take in some virtue. O my master!	9
1478	Thy mind to her is now as low as were .10	10
1479	Thy fortunes. How! that I should murder her!	11
1480	Upon the love and truth and vows which I	12
1481	Have made to thy command? I, her? her blood!	13
1482	If it be so to do good service, never	14
1483	Let me be counted serviceable. How look I,	15
1484	That I should seem to lack humanity	16
	So much as this fact comes to? [Reading] 'Do't:	
1485	the letter .	17
1486	That I have sent her, by her own command	18
1487	Shall give thee opportunity.' O damn'd paper!	19
	Black as the ink that's on thee! Senseless	
1488	bauble, 20	20
1489	Art thou a feodary for this act, and look'st	21
1490	So virgin-like without? Lo, here she comes.	22
1492	I am ignorant in what I am commanded.	23
1491	*Enter* ISOGEN.	
1493	*Imo.* How now, Pisanio!	24
1494	*Pis.* Madam, here is a letter from my lord.	25
	Imo. Who? thy lord? that is my lord,	
1495	Leonatus!	26
1496	O, learn'd indeed were that astronomer	27
1497	That knew the stars as I his characters;	28
1498	He'ld lay the future open. You good gods,	29
1499	Let what is here contain'd relish of love, 30	30
1500	Of my lord's health, of his content, yet not	31
1501	That we two are asunder; let that grieve him:	32
	Some griefs are med'cinable; that is one of	
1502	them,	33
1503	For it doth physic love: of his content,	34
1504	All but in that! Good wax, thy leave. Blest be	35
	You bees that make these locks of counsel!	
1505	Lovers	36
1506	And men in dangerous bonds pray not alike:	37
1507	Though forfeiters you cast in prison, yet	38
	You clasp young Cupid's tables. Good news,	
1508	gods! 39	39

*32:35 BK1; bX: HIC, NM1, NM2
HnF, Rig, IP1, PH1, JP1, BK1
CKP, KRe, Rig, WmS, HIC, ViA, BA1, IP1,
JP1, BK1
*32:36 Inc, Dol, USW, Cum,
*32:37 USW, Cum, WM1, HnF,
NM2, MB1, MB2, IP2, PH1, JG1

2 X: KRe, NM1; bX: HIC, BK1
3 X: KRe, HIC, BK1
4 X: KRe, BK1; aX: HIC; bX: ChM, PH1, JG1
5 X: KRe, PH1, JG1, BK1; aX: ChM, WmS; bX: MB2; Insert 34: 22b-32: MB2
6 X: KRe, JG1, BK1; aX: PH1
7 X: MB2, JG1, BK1; bX: WM1, CKP, HIC, NM1, NM2, PH1
8 X: WM1, CKP, HIC, NM1, NM2, MB2, PH1, JG1, JP1, BK1
9 X: WM1, NM1, NM2, MB2, JG1, JP1; aX: CKP, HIC, PH1, BK1
10 X: WM1, CKP, KRe, HIP, NM1, NM2, MB2, JG1
11 X: KRe; aX: WM1, CKP, HIP, NM1, NM2, MB2, JG1; Insert 34: 23b-32:MB1
12 X: KRe, ViA, SM1, NM1, NM2
13 X: KRe, SM1; aX: ViA, NM1, NM2; bX: HIC;Insert 23: 116b-152a: WmS
14 X: WM1, CKP, HIP, HIC, SM1, JG1
15 X: HIC, SM1, JG1; aX: WM1, CKP, HIP; bX: BA1, NM1, NM2, IP2, JP1,BK1
16 X: HIC, BA1, SM1, NM1, NM2, IP2, JG1, JP1, BK1

17 aX: HIC, BA1, SM1, NM1, NM1, IP2, JG1, JP1, BK1
18
19 bX: HIP, JG1

20 X: HIP; bX: G61, Bel, Ox1, Wen, Bat, Bar, Low, Roa, Inc, JKT, Oxb, Dol*
21 X: G61, Bel, Ox1, Wen, Bat, Bar, Low, Roa, Inc, JKT, Oxb, Dol, USW,*
22 X: HnF, MB2, JG1, BK1; aX: G61, Bel, Ox1, Wen, Bat, Bar, Low, Roa, Inc*
23 X: HnF, KRe, MB2, JG1, BA1; R: ChM; Insert 23: 116b-153a: WmS

24
25

26 aX: KRe
27 X: Ox1, USW, WM1, CKP, KRe, MB1, MB2, JP1
28 same as 27
29 X: MB1, MB2; aX: Ox1, USW, WM1, CKP, KRe, JP1; bX: BA1
30 X: KRe, BA1, MB1, MB2
31 same as 30; bX: G61, Bel, Wen, Bat, Bar, Low, Roa, Inc, JKT, Oxb, Dol*
32 X: G61, Bel, Ox1, Wen , Bat, P95, Bar, Low, Roa, Inc, JKT, Oxb, Dol,
     USW, Cum, WM1, CKP, KRe, Rig, WmS, BA1, MB1, MB2; bX: NM1, NM2,JG1,BK1
33 same as 32, ViA, NM1, NM2, PH1, JG1, BK1; less bX; bX: ChM
34 X: ChM, G61, Bel, Ox1, Wen, Bat. P95, Bar, Low, Roa, Inc, JKT, Oxb,Dol*
35 X: WM1, CKP, KRe, WmS, BA1, IP2; aX: ChM, G61, Bel, Ox1, Wen, Bat,P95,
     Bar, Low, Roa, Inc, JKT, Oxb, Dol, USW, Cum, Rig, MB1, MB2, PH1, JG1*
36 X: WM1, CKP, KRe, WmS, HIC, BA1, NM2, MB1, IP2; aX: NM1; bX: P95, Low*
37 X: ChM, G61, Bel, Ox1, Wen, Bat, P95, Bar, Low, Roa, Inc,JKT, Oxb, Dol*
38 same as 37

39 X: ChM, HnF, KRe, BA1, NM2; aX: G61, Bel, Ox1, Wen, Bat, P95, Bar, Low,
     R oa, Inc, JKT, Oxb, Dol, USW, Cum, WM1, CKP, Rig, WmS, HIC, ViA, IP1,
     MB1, MB2, IP2, PH1, JG1, JP1, BK1

*32:20 USW, Cum, WM1, HnF, CKP, KRe, Rig, ViA, BA1, NM1, MB2, IP2, PH1, JG1,
     JP1, BK1   *32:21 Cum, WM1, HnF, CKP, KRe, Rig, HIP, ViA,
     BA1, NM1, MB2, IP2, PH1, JG1, JP1, BK1   *32:22 JKT, Oxb,Dol,
     UWS, Cum, WM1, CKP, KRe, Rig, HIP, ViA, BA1, NM1, IP2, PH1, JP1
 *32:31 USW, Cum, WM1, CKP, Rig, WmS   *32:34 USW, Cum, WM1, CKP,
     KReRig, BA1MB1, MB2, PH1, JG1, BK1; aX:WmS, ViA, NM1, NM2; bX: IP2

	[*Reads*] 'Justice, and your father's wrath,	40
1509	should he take me in his dominion, could not	41
1510	be so cruel to me, as you, O the dearest of	42
	creatures, would even renew me with your eyes.	43
1511	Take notice that I am in Cambria, at Milford-	44
1512	Haven: what your own love will out of this	45
1513	advise you, follow. So he wishes you all hap-	46
	piness, that remains loyal to his vow, and your,	47
1514	increasing in love,	48
1515	LEONATUS POSTHUMUS.'	49
1516	O, for a horse with wings! Hear'st thou, Pisanio?	50
1517	He is at Milford-Haven: read, and tell me 51	51
1518	How far 'tis thither. If one of mean affairs	52
1519	May plod it in a week, why may not I	53
1520	Glide thither in a day? Then, true Pisanio,—	54
	Who long'st, like me, to see thy lord; who	
1521	long'st,—	55
1522	O, let me bate,—but not like me—yet long'st,	56
1523	But in a fainter kind:—O, not like me:	57
	For mine's beyond beyond—say, and speak	
1524	thick;	58
1525	Love's counsellor should fill the bores of hearing.	59
1526	To the smothering of the sense—how far it is 60	60
1527	To this same blessed Milford: and by the way	61
1528	Tell me how Wales was made so happy as	62
1529	To inherit such a haven: but first of all,	63
1530	How we may steal from hence, and for the gap	64
	That we shall make in time, from our hence-	
1531	going	65
	And our return, to excuse: but first, how get	
1532	hence:	66
1533	Why should excuse be born or e'er begot?	67
1534	We'll talk of that hereafter. Prithee, speak,	68
1535	How many score of miles may we well ride	69
1536	Twixt hour and hour?	
1537	*Pis.* One score 'twixt sun and sun,	70
	Madam, 's enough for you: [*Aside*] and too much	
1538	too. 71	71
	Imo. Why, one that rode to's execution,	
1539	man,	72
	Could never go so slow: I have heard of riding	
1540	wagers,	73
1541	Where horses have been nimbler than the sands	74
	That run i' the clock's behalf. But this is	
1542	foolery:	75
1543	Go bid my woman feign a sickness: say	76

*32:75 Dol, USW, Cum, Rig, ViA, BA1; bX: Oxb, PH1, BK1

40   X: IP1, IP2, BK1; b̲X̲: KRe
41   same as 40; less b̲X̲; a̲X̲; KRe
42   X: IP1, BK1; a̲X̲: I̅P̅2
43   X: IP1; a̲X̲: B̅K̅1̅; b̲X̲: IP2
44
45
46
47
48
49   a̲X̲: ChM; b̲X̲: JG1
50   a̲X̲: WmS; b̲X̲: CKP
51   X̅: CKP; b̲X̲: KRe
52   X: Inc, K̅R̅e; a̲X̲: CKP; b̲X̲: WM1
53   X: WM1, KRe; b̲X̲: Bat
54   X: Bat, Bar, I̅n̅c, Oxb, Cum, KRe, WmS; a̲X̲: WM1

55   X: G61, Bel, Oxl, Wen, Bat, P95, Bar, Low, Roa, Inc, JKT, Oxb, Dol,*
56   same as 55, NM1, NM2, JG1, less BA1; less b̲X̲; a̲X̲: ViA; b̲X̲: CKP; abX:Han
57   same as 56, CKP, ViA, Han, less NM1, NM2, J̅G̅1̅; less a̲X̲, b̲X̲, abX; b̲X̲:
       HIC, BA1
58   same as 57, HIC, BA1, less CKP; less b̲X̲; a̲X̲: CKP; b̲X̲:ChM, HnF, NM1,*
59   X: ChM, G61, Bel, Oxl, Wen, Bat, P95, Low, Roa, Inc, JKT, Oxb, Dol,USW*
60   X: CKP; a̲X̲: ChM, Bel, Oxl, Wen, Bat, Bar, Low, Roa, Inc, JKT, Oxb,Dol*
61   X: CKP, B̅A̅1; b̲X̲: G61, Bel, Oxl, Wen, Bar, P95, Bar, Low, Roa, Inc, JKT*
62   X: G61, Bel, O̅xl, Wen, Bat, P95, Bar, Low, Roa, Inc, JKT, Oxb, Dol,*
63   same as 62, less P95, Rig, HIC; a̲X̲: P95, Rig, HIC; b̲X̲: JG1
64   X: WM1, CKP, KRe, WmS, BA1, JG1; b̲X̲: H61, Bel, Oxl, Wen, Bat, P95,Bar,
       Low, Roa, Inc, JKT, Oxb, Dol, USW, Cum, HnF, Rig, ViA·
65   X: G61, Bel, Oxl, Wen, Bat, P95, Bar, Low, Roa, Inc, JKT, Oxb, Dol,
       USW, Cum, WM1, HnF, CKP, KRe, Rig, WmS, ViA, BA1, JG1
66   same as 65, less P95, Rig, JG1; a̲X̲: CKP, P95, JG1; b̲X̲: ChM
67   same as 66, ChM, Han, BK1; less a̲X̲, bX
68   X: BK1; a̲X̲: ChM, G61, Bel, Oxl, W̅en, B̅at, P95, Bar, Low, Roa, Inc, JKT*
69

70

71   b̲X̲: CKP

72   X: CKP, KRe

73   X: CKP, KRe; b̲X̲: G61, Bel, Oxl, Wen, Bat, Bar, Low, Inc, JKT, Oxb, Dol*
74   X: G61, Bel, O̅xl, Wen, Bat, Bar, Low, Inc, JKT, Oxb, Dol, USW, Cum,WM1,
       HnF, KRe, Rig, ViA, Han, BA1, PH1, BK1
75   X: WM1, HnF, KRe, Han; a̲X̲: G61, Bel, Oxl, Wen, Bat,Bar, Low, Inc, JKT*
76   b̲X̲: KRe

*32:55 USW, Cum, KRe, Rig, Wm S, BA1; bX:Han, JG1   *32:58IP1, IP2,
   PH1, BK1   *32:59 HnF, KRe, Rig, WmS, HIC, V̅iA, Han, SM1,
   NM1, IP1, NM2, IP2, PH1, JG̅1̅, BK1; a̲X̲: Bar, BA1; b̲X̲: CKP
*32:60 USW, Cum, HnF, KRe, WmS, HIC, V̅iA, Han, SM1, N̅M1, IP1, NM2, IP2, PH1
   JG1, BK1; b̲X̲: BA1   *32:61 Oxb, Dol, USW, Cum , WM1, Rig, WmS,
   HIC   *32:62 USW, Cum, W̅M̅1, CKP, KRe, Rig, WmS, HIC, BA1
*32:68 Oxb, Dol, USW, Cum, WM1, HnF, KRe, Rig, WmS, HIC, ViA, Han, BA1
*32:73 USW, Cum, WM1, HnF, Rig, ViA, Han, BA1, PH1, BK1

	She'll home to her father: and provide me pre-	
1544	sently	77
1545	A riding-suit, no costlier than would fit	78
1546	A franklin's housewife.	
1547	*Pis.* Madam, you're best consider.	79
1548	*Imo.* I see before me, man : nor here, nor here,	80
1549	Nor what ensues, but have a fog in them, 81	81
1550	That I cannot look through. Away, I prithee ;	82
1551	Do as I bid thee : there's no more to say :	83
1552	Accessible is none but Milford way. (*Exeunt.*	84

| 1553,+1 | Scene III.   *Wales: a mountainous country* |
| 1553+2 | *with a cave.* |

| 1554 | *Enter, from the cave,* Belarius ; Guiderius, |
| 1554+1 | *and* Arviragus *following.* |

1555	*Bel.* A goodly day not to keep house, with such	1
	Whose roof's as low as ours ! Stoop, boys ; this	
1556	gate	2
	Instructs you how to adore the heavens and bows	
1557	you	3
1558	To a morning's holy office : the gates of monarchs	4
1559	Are arch'd so high that giants may jet through	5
1560	And keep their impious turbans on, without	6
1561	Good morrow to the sun. Hail, thou fair heaven !	7
1562	We house i' the rock, yet use thee not so hardly	8
1563	As prouder livers do.	
1564	*Gui.* Hail, heaven !	
1565	*Arv.* Hail, heaven !	9
	Bel. Now for our mountain sport : up to yond	
1566	hill ; 10	10
	Your legs are young ; I 'll tread these flats. Con-	
1567	sider,	11
1568	When you above perceive me like a crow,	12
1569	That it is place which lessens and sets off :	13
	And you may then revolve what tales I have	
1570	told you	14
1571	Of courts, of princes, of the tricks in war :	15
1572	This service is not service, so being done,	16
1573	But being so allow'd : to apprehend thus,	17
1574	Draws us a profit from all things we see ;	18
1575	And often, to our comfort, shall we find	19
1576	The sharded beetle in a safer hold **20**	20
1577	Than is the full-wing'd eagle. O, this life	21
1578	Is nobler than attending for a check,	22
1579	Richer than doing nothing for a bauble,	23
1580	Prouder than rustling in unpaid-for silk :	24

77 X: KRe, HIC
78 X: CKP, HIC

79 X: CKP; aX: HIC
80 X: WM1, K̄Re, BA1; R̲: ChM; aX: CKP
81 same as 80 including R̲; less aX
82 X: KRe; R̲: ChM; aX: W̄M1, BA1
83 R̲: ChM
84 R̲: ChM; ADD 1: ChM; Insert 34: 1-196: Han

Scene 33

1 X: PH1; bX: ChM; MOVE 1-98 to follow 35: 167: ViA

2 X: PH1; aX: ChM; bX: MB2

3 X: MB2, PH1
4 X: MB2, PH1; bX: KRe, HIP, HIC, ViA, BA1, SM1
5 X: KRe, HIP, H̄ĪC, ViA, BA1, SM1, MB2, PH1
6 same as 5
7 aX: KRe, HIP, HIC, ViA, BA1, MB2
8 X̄: HIC, ViA, SM1, PH1, JP1, BK1

9 aX: HIC, ViA, SM1, PH1, JP1, BK1

10

11 bX: WmS, NM1, NM2
12 X̄: HIP. NM1, NM2
13 same as 12

14 X: KRe, HIP, NM1, NM2, BK1
15 same as 14
16 X: WM1, HnF, CKP, Lac, KRe, Rig, MTh, HIM, WmS, HIP, ViA, SM1, NM1*
17 same as 16, HM1, BA1, less SM1, PH1, JG1, JP1; less bX; aX:SM1,PH1,JG1,JP1
18 same as 17; less aX
19 X: WM1, HnF, CKP, H̄IP, BA1, NM1, NM2, MB1, MB2
20 same as 19
21 X: WM1, CKP; aX: HnF, HIP, BA1, NM1, MB1, MB2; bX: Ox1, Inc, JKT, Oxb*
22 X: Ox1, Inc, J̄KT, Oxb, Dol, USW, Cum, WM1, CKP, L̄ac, KRe, Rig, HM1, MTh*
23 same as 22, less JG1
24 same as 23

*33:16 NM2, MB1, MB2, PH1, JG1, JP1, BK1; bX̲: BA1   *33:21Dol,
    USW, Cum, Lac, KRe, Rig, HM1, MTh, HIM, WmS, HIC, ViA
*32:22 HIM, WmS, HIC, ViA, SM1, JG1

1581	Such gain the cap of him that makes 'em fine,	25
1582	Yet keeps his book uncross'd: no life to ours.	26
	Gui. Out of your proof you speak: we, poor	
1583	unfledged,	27
	Have never wing'd from view o' the nest, nor	
1584	know not	28
1585	What air's from home. Haply this life is best,	29
1586	If quiet life be best; sweeter to you 30	30
1587	That have a sharper known; well corresponding	31
1588	With your stiff age: but unto us it is	32
1589	A cell of ignorance; travelling a-bed;	33
1590	A prison for a debtor, that not dares	34
1591	To stride a limit.	
1592	*Arv.* What should we speak of	35
1593	When we are old as you? when we shall hear	36
1594	The rain and wind beat dark December, how,	37
1595	In this our pinching cave, shall we discourse	38
1596	The freezing hours away? We have seen nothing:	39
1597	We are beastly, subtle as the fox for prey, 40	40
1598	Like warlike as the wolf for what we eat:	41
1599	Our valour is to chase what flies: our cage	42
1600	We make a quire, as doth the prison'd bird,	43
1601	And sing our bondage freely.	
1602	*Bel.* How you speak!	44
1603	Did you but know the city's usuries	45
1604	And felt them knowingly; the art o' the court,	46
1605	As hard to leave as keep: whose top to climb	47
1606	Is certain falling, or so slippery that	48
1607	The fear's as bad as falling: the toil o' the war,	49
1608	A pain that only seems to seek out danger 50	50
	I' the name of fame and honour; which dies i' the	
1609	search,	51
1610	And hath as oft a slanderous epitaph	52
1611	As record of fair act: nay, many times,	53
1612	Doth ill deserve by doing well; what's worse,	54
1613	Must court'sy at the censure:—O boys, this story	55
1614	The world may read in me: my body's mark'd	56
1615	With Roman swords, and my report was once	57
1616	First with the best of note: Cymbeline loved me,	58
1617	And when a soldier was the theme, my name	59
1618	Was not far off: then was I as a tree 60	60
	Whose boughs did bend with fruit: but in one	
1619	night,	61
1620	A storm or robbery, call it what you will,	62
1621	Shook down my mellow hangings, nay, my leaves,	63
1622	And left me bare to weather.	

25 X: ChM, Ox1, Inc, JKT, Oxb, Do1, USW, Cum, WM1, HnF, CKP, Lac, KRe*
26 same as 25, less Do1, HnF, KRe, HIP, IP1, JP1; aX: Do1, HnF, KRe, HIP,
   IP1, JP1
27 bX: KRe

28 X: KRe; bX: Wen, Bat
29 aX: Wen, Bat, KRe; bX: WM1, CKP, HIP
30 X: WM1, CKP, HIP; bX: KRe, ViA, NM1, NM2
31 X: WM1, CKP, KRe, HIP, ViA, NM1, NM2
32 X: WM1, C KP, HIP, NM1, NM2; aX: KRe, ViA
33 same as 32; less aX; bX: Bel, Wen, Bat, Bar, HnF, HIC, ViA, Han, BA1*
34 X: WM1, HnF, CKP, HIP, HIC, ViA, Han, BA1, SM1, NM1, NM2, PH1; bX: BK1

35 aX: WM1, HnF, CKP, HIP, HIC, ViA, Han, BA1, SM1, NM1, NM2, PH1, BK1
36 bX: WM1, CKP, KRe, HIP
37 X: WM1, CKP, KRe, HIP
38 same as 37
39 X: CKP; aX: WM1, CKP, HIP; bX: NM1, NM2
40 X: G61, Bel, Ox1, Wen, Bat, P95, Bar, Low, Roa, Inc, JKT, Oxb, Do1*
41 same as 40, Rig, BK1
42 X: G61, Bel, Ox1, Wen, Bat, P95, Bar, Low, Roa, Inc, JKT, Oxb, Do1*
43 same as 42; less aX

44 X: WM1, CKP; R: ChM; aX: G61, Bel, Ox1, Wen, Bat, P95, Bar, Low, Roa*
45 X: Bel, Ox1, Wen, Bat, Bar, Oxb, WM1, CKP
46 X: Bel, Ox1, Wen, Bat, Bar, Oxb , KRe, JP1; aX: WM1, CKP; bX: BK1
47 X: Bel, Ox1, Wen, Bat, Bar, Oxb, KRe, JP1, BK1; bX: WM1, CKP, BA1, SM1
48 X: Bel, Ox1, Wen, Bat, Bar, Oxb, WM1, CKP, KRe, HIC, BA1, SM1, JP1, BK1
49 X: Bel, Ox1, Wen, Bat, Bar, Oxb, KRe, HIP, HIC, JP1, BK1; aX: WM1, CKP*
50 X: Bel, Ox1, Wen, Bat, Bar, Oxb, HnF, HIP, NM1, NM1, MB1, MB2, PH1, JP1,
   BK1
51 same as 50, ViA; bX: KRe
52 same as 50, KRe
53 same as 52, less Oxb; bX: WM1, CKP, ViA, BA1, SM1
54 X: ChM, Bel, Wen, Bat, Bar, WM1, HnF, CKP, KRe, HIP, HIC, ViA, BA1, SM1*
55 X: ChM, Bel, Wen, Bat, Bar, HIC, JP1; aX: WM1, HnF, CKP, KRe, Rig, HIP*
56 X: Bel, Wen, Bat, Bar; bX: HnF, HIP, HIC, SM1
57 X: Bel, Wen, Bat, Bar, HnF, HIP, HIC, SM1, JG1; bX: BA1
58 X: Bel, Wen, Bat, Bar; aX: HnF, HIP, HIC, BA1, SM1, JG1
59 same as 58; less aX
60 same as 59; bX: HIP, ViA

61 X: Bel, Wen, Bat, Bar, HIP, ViA
62 same as 61
63 same as 61

*33:25 Rig, HM1, MTh, HIM, WmS, HIP, HIC, BA1, SM1, IP1, IP2, PH1, JG1, JP1,
   BK1   *33:33 SM1, PH1   *33:40 USW, Cum, WM1,
   HnF, CKP, KRe, HIP, HIC, ViA, SM1, NM1, NM2   *32:42 USW, Cum, WM1,
   CKP, KRe, Rig, ViA; aX: NM1, NM2   *33:44 Inc, JKT, Oxb, Do1, USW,
   Cum, Rig, ViA   *33:49 BA1, SM1; bX: HnF, NM1, NM2, MB1, MB2, PH1
*33:54 NM1, NM2, MB1, MB2, PH1, JG1, JP1, BK1; bX: Rig   *33:55 ViA,
   BA1, SM1, NM1, NM2, MB1, MB2, PH1, JG1 BK1

1623	*Gui.* Uncertain favour!	64
	Bel. My fault being nothing—as I have told	
1624	you oft—	65
1625	But that two villains, whose false oaths prevail'd	66
1626	Before my perfect honour, swore to Cymbeline	67
1627	I was confederate with the Romans: so	68
1628	Follow'd my banishment, and this twenty years	69
	This rock and these demesnes have been my	
1629	world; 70	70
1630	Where I have lived at honest freedom, paid	71
1631	More pious debts to heaven than in all	72
	The fore-end of my time. But up to the moun-	
1632	tains!	73
1633	This is not hunters' language: he that strikes	74
1634	The venison first shall be the lord o' the feast;	75
1635	To him the other two shall minister;	76
1636	And we will fear no poison, which attends	77
1637	In place of greater state. I'll meet you in the	78
1638	valleys. [*Exeunt Guiderius and Arviragus.*	
1639	How hard it is to hide the sparks of nature!	79
1640	These boys know little they are sons to the king:	80
1641	Nor Cymbeline dreams that they are alive. 81	81
1642	They think they are mine; and though train'd up	
1643	thus meanly	82
	I' the cave wherein they bow, their thoughts do hit	
1644	do hit	83
1645	The roofs of palaces, and nature prompts them	84
1646	In simple and low things to prince it much	85
1647	Beyond the trick of others. This Polydore,	86
1648	The heir of Cymbeline and Britain, who	87
1649	The king his father call'd Guiderius,—Jove!	88
1650	When on my three-foot stool I sit and tell	89
1651	The warlike feats I have done, his spirits fly out	90
1652	Into my story: say 'Thus mine enemy fell, 91	91
1653	And thus I set my foot on's neck:' even then	92
1654	The princely blood flows in his cheek, he sweats,	93
	Strains his young nerves and puts himself in	
1655	posture	94
1656	That acts my words. The younger brother, Cadwal,	95
1657	Once Arviragus, in as like a figure,	96
1658	Strikes life into my speech and shows much more	97
1659	His own conceiving.—Hark, the game is roused!—	98
1660	O Cymbeline! heaven and my conscience knows	99
1661	Thou didst unjustly banish me: whereon, 100	100
1662	At three and two years old, I stole these babes;	101
1663	Thinking to bar thee of succession, as	102

```
64   same as 61

65   same as 61
66   same as 61, less HIP; bX: KRe, BA1, BK1
67   same as 66; less bX; aX: KRe, BA1, BK1
68   same as 67; less aX
69   same as 67; bX: WM1, CKP

70   X: Bel, Wen, Bat, Bar, WM1, CKP, ViA; cX: KRe
71   X: Bel, Wen, Bat, Bar, WM1, CKP, KRe, Rig, ViA, BA1, PH1, BK1; bX:HIP
72   same as 71, HIP; less bX

73   X: PH1; aX: Bel, Wen, Bat, Bar, WM1, CKP, KRe, Rig, HIP, ViA, BA1, BK1
74   X: NM1, NM2
75   X: NM1, NM2
76   X: KRe, HIC, ViA, SM1, NM1, NM2, PH1, JG1, BK1
77   X: WM1, CKP, KRe, Rig, HIP, HIC, ViA, SM1, NM1, NM2, PH1, JG1, BK1
78   aX: WM1, CKP, KRe, Rig, HIP, HIC, ViA, SM1, NM1, NM2, PH1, JG1, BK1;
       ADD2: ChM
79
80
81   X: KRe, IP1, PH1, BK1

82   X: PH1; bX: KRe, HIP, NM1, NM2

83   X: KRe, HIP, ViA, NM1, NM2, PH1
84   X: HIP, NM1, NM2, PH1; bX: HIC, BA1, SM1, IP1 ; aX: KRe, ViA
85   X: KRe, HIP, HIC, BA1, SM1, IP1, NM2, PH1; ax: NM1
86   X: KRe, SM1, PH1; aX: HIP, HIC, BA1, IP1, NM2; bX: MB1, MB2
87   X: KRe, HIC, SM1, MB1, MB2, PH1
88   X: KRe, ViA, SM1, MB1, MB2, PH1; bX: HIP, BK1
89   X: KRe, HIP, SM1, MB1, MB2, PH1, BK1
90   same as 89; bX: NM2
91   same as 90, NM1, NM2; less bX; bX: HIC, Rig, ViA
92   X: KRe, HIP, HIC, ViA, SM1, NM1, MB1, MB2, PH1, BK1; aX: NM2
93   same as 92, less NM1; less aX

94   same as 93
95   X: KRe, SM1, MB1, MB2, PH1; aX: HIP, HIC, ViA, BK1; bX: BA1
96   X: KRe, BA1, SM1, MB1, MB2, PH1; aX: ViA; bX: BK1; N: Bel, Wen, Bar
97   X: KRe, BA1, SM1, NM2, MB1, MB2, PH1, JP1, BK1; bX: NM1
98   X: PH1; aX: KRe, BA1, SM1, NM1, NM2, MB1, MB2, BK1
99   X: KRe, ViA, SM1
100  same as 99
101  same as 99
102  same as 99; R: Wen
```

1664	**Thou** reft'st me of my lands. Euriphile,	103
	Thou wast their nurse; they took thee for their	104
1665	mother,	
1666	**And** every day do honour to her grave:	105
1667	**Myself,** Belarius, that am Morgan call'd,	106
	They take for natural father. The game is up.	107
1668	[*Exit.*	

1669,+1   **SCENE IV.** *Country near Milford-Haven.*

1670   *Enter* PISANIO *and* IMOGEN.

	Imo. Thou told'st me, when we came from	
1671	horse, the place	1
1672	**Was** near at hand: ne'er long'd my mother so	2
1673	**To see** me first, as I have now. Pisanio! man!	3
1674	**Where** is Posthumus? What is in thy mind,	4
	That makes thee stare thus? Wherefore breaks	
1675	that sigh	5
1676	**From** the inward of thee? One, but painted thus,	6
1677	**Would** be interpreted a thing perplex'd	7
1678	**Beyond** self-explication: put thyself	8
1679	**Into** a haviour of less fear, ere wildness	9
1680	**Vanquish** my staider senses. What's the matter?	10
1681	**Why** tender'st thou that paper to me, with ::	11
1682	**A look** untender? If't be summer news,	12
1683	**Smile** to't before; if winterly, thou need'st	13
	But keep that countenance still. My husband	
1684	hand!	14
1685	**That** drug-damn'd Italy hath out-craftied him.	15
	And he's at some hard point. Speak, man: thy	
1686	tongue	16
1687	**May** take off some extremity, which to read	17
1688	**Would** be even mortal to me.	
1689	*Pis.* Please you, read:	18
1690	**And** you shall find me, wretched man, a thing	19
1691	**The** most disdain'd of fortune. ::	20
1692	*Imo.* [*Reads*] 'Thy mistress, Pisanio, has	21
1693	played the strumpet in my bed; the testimonies	22
1694	whereof lie bleeding in me. I speak not out of	23
1695	weak surmises, but from proof as strong as my	24
	grief and as certain as I expect my revenge.	25
1696	That part thou, Pisanio, must act for me, if thy	26
1697	faith be not tainted with the breach of hers. Let	27
1698	thine own hands take away her life: I shall give	28
	thee opportunity at Milford-Haven. She hath	29
1699	my letter for the purpose: where, if thou fear'st	30

*34: 9(Continued) IP1, NM2, MB2, PH1, JP1, BK1   *34:10 Oxb, Dol,USW,
   Cum, WM1, HnF, CKP, Rig, ViA, BA1, NM2, MB2, PH1, JP1, BK1
 *31:11 WM1, CKP, KRe, Rig   *34:12 JKT, Oxb, Dol, USW, Cum, Rig
 *34:23follow 32: 11a: MB1

103   same as 102 including R̲; b̲X̲: ChM, HIP, HIC, NM1, NM2, MB1, MB2, PH1,
      JP1
104   X: ChM, KRe, HIP, HIC, ViA, SM1, NM1, NM2, MB1, MB2, PH1, JP1
105   same as 104
106   X: ChM, KRe, HIP, HIC, ViA, SM1, NM1, NM2; b̲X̲: MB1, MB2
107   C: ChM, KRe, HIP, ViA, SM1; a̲X̲: HIC, NM1, NM̲2̲; Insert 3̲5̲: 1-65:
      G61, Bel, Ox1, Wen, Bat, Bar, Low, Roa, Oxb, JP1̲; Insert 3̲5̲: 1-78:
      USW; Insert 3̲5̲: 1-167: HnF

Scen e 34

1   MOVE 1-196 to follow 3̲2̲: 89: Han; MOVE 1-196 to follow 3̲5̲: 65:Inc*
2   R̲: Wen, Bat; b̲X̲: G61, Bel, Ox1, Bar, Low, Roa, Inc, JKT, Oxb, Dol*
3   X: G61, Roa, Oxb, HnF; R̲: Bel, Wen, Bat, Bar, KRe; a̲X̲: Ox1, Low, Inc*
4   R̲: Wen, Bat; ADD 1: G61

5   X: KRe, HIC, NM1, NM2; b̲X̲: G61, Bel, Ox1, Wen, Bat, Bar, Roa, Inc*
6   X: Ox1, Oxb, Dol, WM1, KRe, Rig, HIC, BA1, NM1, NM2, BK1; a̲X̲: G61*
7   X: Ox1, Oxb, WM1, CKP, KRe, Rig, HIC, ViA, BA1, SM1, NM1, IP1,NM2*
8   same as 7, less SM1, JG1; a̲X̲: SM1, JG1; b̲X̲: G61, Bel, Wen, Bat,Bar*
9   X: G61, Bel, Ox1, Wen, Bat, Bar, Roa, Inc, JKT, Oxb, Dol, USW, Cum*
10   X: KRe, HIC, NM1; a̲X̲: G61, Bel, Ox1, Wen, Bat, Bar, Roa, Inc, JKT*
11   X: ViA; b̲X̲: G61, Bel, Ox1, Wen, Bar, Inc, Oxb, Dol, USW, Cum, WM1*
12   X: WM1, CKP, KRe, ViA; a̲X̲: G61, Bel, Ox1, Wen, Bat, Bar, Roa, Inc*
13   X: WM1, CKP, KRe, HIC, ViA, BA1, SM1, JP1

14   X: KRe; a̲X̲: WM1, CKP, HIC, ViA, BA1, SM1, JP1
15   X: ChM, Ox1, Oxb, USW, KRe, MB2, BK1

16   X: BK1; a̲X̲: ChM, Ox1, Oxb, USW, KRe, MB2; b̲X̲: PH1, JG1
17   X: PH1, JG1, BK1

18   a̲X̲: PH1, JG1, BK1
19   X̲: BA1, BK1
20   X: BA1, BK1
21   b̲X̲: MTh; MOVE 21-23a to follow 3̲1̲: 87: MB1, MB2
22   a̲X̲: MTh, HIM; b̲X̲: WM1, BK1
23   a̲X̲: NM1; b̲X̲: BK̲1̲; MOVE 23b-32 to follow 3̲2̲: 68: MB2; MOVE 23b-32 to*
24   X̲: BK1
25   a̲X̲: BK1; b̲X̲: WmS
26   X̲: WmS; b̲X̲: BK1
27   a̲X̲: WmS, BK1
28
29   b̲X̲: BK1
30   X̲: BK1; b̲X̲: WmS

*34: 1 JKT, Cum   *34: 2 USW, Cum, WM1, CKP, KRe, Rig, BA1,
  NM1, NM2, MB2, BK1   *34: 3 JKT, Dol, USW, Cum, WM1, CKP,
  Rig, BA1, NM1, NM2, MB2, BK1   *34: 5 JKT, Oxb, Dol, USW, Cum,
  WM1, HnF, Rig, WmS, BA1, BK1   *34: 6 Bel, Wen, Bat, Bar, Roa,
  Inc, JKT, USW, Cum, WmS; b̲X̲: CKP, ViA, SM1, MB2, PH1, JG1, JP1
*34: 7 MB2, PH1, JG1, JP1, BK1   *34: 8 Roa, Inc, JKT, Dol, USW,
  Cum, HnF   *34: 9 WM1, HnF, CKP, KRe, Rig, HIC, ViA, BA1, NM1*

1700	strike and to make me certain it is done, thou r.	31
1701	the pandar to her dishonour and equally to ≈	32
1702	disloyal.'	33
	Pis. What shall I need to draw my sword!	
1703	the paper	34
1704	Hath cut her throat already. No, 'tis slander.	35
	Whose edge is sharper than the sword, whose	
1705	tongue	36
1706	Outvenoms all the worms of Nile, whose breath	37
1707	Rides on the posting winds and doth belie	38
	All corners of the world: kings, queens and	
1708	states,	39
1709	Maids, matrons, nay, the secrets of the grave ≈	40
	This viperous slander enters. What cheer.	
1710	madam?	41
1711	*Imo.* False to his bed! What is it to be false!	42
1712	To lie in watch there and to think on him?	43
	To weep 'twixt clock and clock? if sleep charge	
1713	nature,	44
1714	To break it with a fearful dream of him	45
	And cry myself awake? that's false to's bed	
1715	is it?	46
1716	*Pis.* Alas, good lady!	47
1717	*Imo.* I false! Thy conscience witness: Iachimo	48
1718	Thou didst accuse him of incontinency;	49
1719	Thou then look'dst like a villain; now methinks	50
1720	Thy favour's good enough. Some jay of Italy	51
	†Whose mother was her painting, hath betray'd	
1721	him:	52
1722	Poor I am stale, a garment out of fashion;	53
1723	And, for I am richer than to hang by the walls,	54
1724	I must be ripp'd:—to pieces with me!—O,	55
	Men's vows are women's traitors! All good	
1725	seeming,	56
1726	By thy revolt, O husband, shall be thought	57
1727	Put on for villany; not born where't grows,	58
1728	But worn a bait for ladies.	
	Pis. Good madam, hear me	59
	Imo. True honest men being heard, like false	
1730	Æneas,	60
	Were in his time thought false, and Sinon's	
1731	weeping	61
1732	Did scandal many a holy tear, took pity	62
	From most true wretchedness: so thou, Posthu-	
1733	mus,	63
1734	Wilt lay the leaven on all proper men:	64

```
31   X: BK1; aX: WmS
32   X: BK1
33   X: BK1

34   bX: MB1
35   X: MB1; bX: KRe, MB2, PH1, BK1

36   X: KRe, ViA, MB1, MB2, PH1, BK1; bX: JP1
37   X: KRe, MB1, MB2, PH1, JP1, BK1; aX: ViA; bX: CKP
38   X: CKP, KRe, MB1, MB2, PH1, JP1, BK1

39   X: KRe, MB1, MB2, PH1, JP1, BK1; aX: CKP; bX: Ox1, Wen, Bar, Low,Inc*
40   X: Ox1, Wen, Bat, Low, Inc, JKT, Oxb, Dol, USW, Cum, WM1, HnF, KRe,
        Rig, HIC, ViA, BA1, SM1, MB1, MB2, PH1, JG1, JP1, BK1
41   X: Rig, SM1; aX: Ox1, Wen, Bat, Bar, Low, Inc, JKT, Oxb, Dol, USW,*
42   R: Rig; B: NM1
43

44
45

46
47   MOVE 47 to follow 41: HnF
48   X: KRe, HIC; bX: Ox1, Oxb, USW, NM1, JG1; cX: HnF
49   X: Ox1, Oxb, USW, KRe, HIC, NM1, JG1; bX: CKP, NM2
50   X: Ox1, Oxb, USW, CKP, KRe, HIC, NM1, NM2
51   X: Ox1, Oxb, USW, CKP, KRe, HIC; aX: NM1, NM2; bX: WM1, MB1, MB2, BK1

52   X: Ox1, P95, Oxb, USW, WM1, CKP, KRe, HIC, MB1, MB2, BK1; R: G61, Wen*
53   X: Ox1, Oxb, USW, WM1, KRe, HIC, IP1, MB1, MB2; aX: CKP
54   X: G61, Bel, Ox1, Wen, Bat, P95, Bar, Low, Inc, JKT, Oxb, Dol, USW*
55   X: Ox1, Oxb, USW, WM1, KRe, MB2; aX: WmS, HIC, IP1, MB1; bX: IP2

56   X: Ox1, Oxb, USW, HnF, KRe, HIC, NM1, NM2, MB1, MB2, IP2; bX: CKP,MTh*
57   X: Ox1, Oxb, USW, HnF, Lac, KRe, Rig, HM1, MTh, HIM, WmS, HIC, ViA,Han*
58   same as 57; less aX; bX: G61, Bel, Wen, Bat, P95, Bar, Low, Roa,Inc,
        JKT, Dol, Cum, WM1, MB1
59   X: HnF, CKP, Lac, Rig, HM1, MTh, HIM, WmS, HIC, BA1, NM1, NM2, JG1; aX:
        G61, Bel, Ox1, Wen, Bat, P95, Bar, Low, Roa, Inc, JKT, Oxb, Dol, USW*
60   X: G61, Bel, Ox1, Wen, Bat, P95, Bar, Low, Roa, Inc, JKT, Oxb, Dol,
        USW, Cum, WM1, HnF, CKP, Lac, KRe, Rig, HM1, MTh, HIM, WmS, HIC, ViA*
61   same as 60; bX: IP1
62   same as 60, IP1

63   same as 60; aX: IP1
64   same as 60, less CKP;          aX: CKP
```

*34:39 JKT, Oxb, Dol, USW, Cum, WM1, HnF, Rig, HIC, ViA, BA1, SM1, JG1
*34:41 Cum, WM1, HnF, KRe, ViA, BA1, MB1, MB2, PH1, JG1, JP1; BK1; Insert
    47: HnF   *34:52 Bat; aX: WmS, SM1   *34:54Cum, WM1,
  HnF, KRe, WmS, HIC, IP1, MB1, MB2   *34:56 HIM, WmS, ViA, BA1,
  PH1, JG1, JP1, BK1   *34:57 BA1, NM1, NM2, MB2, IP2, PH1, JG1
  JP1, BK1;aX: ChM   *34:59 Cum, WM1, KRe, ViA, Han, MB1, MB2, IP2, PH1
  JP1, BK1   *34:60 Han, BA1, NM1, NM2, MB1, MB2, IP2, PH1, JG1,
  JP1, BK1

1735	Goodly and gallant shall be false and perjured	65
1736	From thy great fail. Come, fellow, be thou honest:	66
	Do thou thy master's bidding: when thou see'st	
1737	him,	67
1738	A little witness my obedience: look!	68
1739	I draw the sword myself: take it, and hit	69
1740	The innocent mansion of my love, my heart: 70	70
1741	Fear not; 'tis empty of all things but grief:	71
1742	Thy master is not there, who was indeed	72
1743	The riches of it: do his bidding: strike	73
1744	Thou mayst be valiant in a better cause;	74
1745	But now thou seem'st a coward.	
1746	*Pis.* Hence, vile instrument!	75
1747	Thou shalt not damn my hand.	
1748	*Imo.* Why, I must die;	76
1749	And if I do not by thy hand, thou art	77
1750	No servant of thy master's. Against self-slaughter	78
1751	There is a prohibition so divine	79
	That cravens my weak hand. Come, here's my	
1752	heart. 80	80
1753	Something's afore't. Soft, soft! we'll no defence;	81
1754	Obedient as the scabbard. What is here?	82
1755	The scriptures of the loyal Leonatus,	83
1756	All turn'd to heresy? Away, away,	84
1757	Corrupters of my faith! you shall no more	85
1758	Be stomachers to my heart. Thus may poor fools	86
	Believe false teachers: though those that are be-	
1759	tray'd	87
1760	Do feel the treason sharply, yet the traitor	88
	Stands in worse case of woe.	89
1761	And thou, Posthumus, thou that didst set up 90	90
1762	My disobedience 'gainst the king my father	91
1763	And make me put into contempt the suits	92
1764	Of princely fellows, shalt hereafter find	93
1765	It is no act of common passage, but	94
1766	A strain of rareness: and I grieve myself	95
1767	To think, when thou shalt be disedged by her	96
1768	That now thou tirest on, how thy memory	97
1769	Will then be pang'd by me. Prithee, dispatch:	98
1770	The lamb entreats the butcher: where's thy knife?	99
1771	Thou art too slow to do thy master's bidding, 100	100
1772	When I desire it too.	
1773	*Pis.* O gracious lady,	101
1774	Since I received command to do this business	102
1775	I have not slept one wink.	
1776	*Imo.* Do't, and to bed then.	103

65 same as 60
66 X: KRe; aX: G61, Bel, Oxl, Wen, Bat, P96, Bar, Low, Roa, Inc, JKT, Oxb,
       Dol, USW, Cum, WM1, Lac, Rig, HM1, MTh, HIM, WmS, HIC, ViA, Han, BA1*
67 aX: KRe; abX: BK1
68 aX: HIC, BK1
69
70
71
72 X: ViA
73 aX: ViA; bX: PH1, BK1
74 X: HnF, WmS, SM1, MB1, PH1, BK1

75 aX: HnF, WmS, SM1, MB1, PH1, BK1

76 bX: Oxl, Oxb, USW
77 X: Oxl, Oxb, USW, KRe, HIC
78 same as 77
79 same as 77, CKP

80 X: CKP, KRe; aX: Oxl, Oxb, USW, HIC
81 X: ChM, CKP, NM1, JP1, BK1; aX: KRe, PH1; bX: WM1, NM2
82 X: ChM, CKP, HIC, ViA, JP1, BK1; aX: G61, Bel, Oxl, Wen, Bat, Bar, Low,
83 X: ChM, CKP, JP1, BK1
84 same as 83; bX: NM1, NM2
85 X: ChM, CKP, NM1, NM2, JP1, BK1; bX: KRe, ViA, IP1
86 X: ChM, CKP, KRe, ViA, IP1, JP1, B K1; aX: NM1, NM2; bX: G61, Bel, Oxl,
       Wen, Bat, P95, Bar, Roa, Inc, JKT, Oxb, Dol, USW, Cum, WM1, Rig, WmS*
87 X: ChM, G61, Bel, Oxl, Wen, Bat, P95, Bar, Low, Roa, Inc, JKT, Oxb, Dol*
88 same as 87
89 same as 87; aX: BK1; bX: PH1
90 same as 87, HnF, PH1
91 same as 90, less HnF
92 same as 91
93 same as 91
94 same as 91, less PH1
95 same as 94; aX: PH1; bX: JG1
96 same as 94, JG1, less CKP; aX: CKP
97 same as 96; less aX
98 X: Bel, Bat, Roa; aX: ChM, G61, Oxl, Wen, Bat, P95, Low, Inc, JKT, Oxb,*
99 X: Oxl, Oxb, USW, KRe, WmS, HIC; aX: Bel, Bar, Roa, SM1; bX: ChM, MB2*
100 X: PH1, BK1

101 aX: PH1, BK1; bX: WmS
102 X: Oxl, Oxb, USW, WmS, MB2

103 same as 102; bX: ViA, MB1

*34:66 NM1, NM2, MB1, MB2, IP2, PH1, JG1, JP1, BK1   *34:86 HIC,
   BA1, MB1, MB2, IP2   *34:87 USW, Cum, WM1, CKP, KRe, Rig, WmS, HIC,
   ViA, BA1, IP1, MB1, MB2, IP2, JP1   *34:98 Dol, USW, Cum, WM1,
   KRe, Rig, WmS, HIC, ViA, BA1, IP1, MB1, MB2, IP2, JG1, JP1
*34:99 PH1, BK1

1777	*Pis.* I'll wake mine eye-balls blind first.	
1778	*Imo.* Wherefore then	104
1779	Didst undertake it? Why hast thou abused	105
1780	So many miles with a pretence? this place?	106
1781	Mine action and thine own? our horses' labour?	107
1782	The time inviting thee? the perturb'd court,	108
1783	For my being absent? whereunto I never	109
1784	Purpose return. Why hast thou gone so far. 110	110
1785	To be unbent when thou hast ta'en thy stand,	111
1786	The elected deer before thee?	
1787	*Pis.* But to win time	112
1788	To lose so bad employment; in the which	113
1789	I have consider'd of a course. Good lady,	114
1790	Hear me with patience.	
1791	*Imo.* Talk thy tongue weary; speak:	115
1792	I have heard I am a strumpet; and mine ear,	116
1793	Therein false struck, can take no greater wound,	117
1794	Nor tent to bottom that. But speak.	
1795	*Pis.* Then, madam,	118
1796	I thought you would not back again.	
1797	*Imo.* Most like;	119
1798	Bringing me here to kill me.	
1799	*Pis.* Not so, neither: 120	120
1800	But if I were as wise as honest, then	121
1801	My purpose would prove well. It cannot be	122
1802	But that my master is abused:	123
1803	Some villain, ay, and singular in his art,	124
1804	Hath done you both this cursed injury.	125
1805	*Imo.* Some Roman courtezan.	
1806	*Pis.* No, on my life.126	
1807	I'll give but notice you are dead and send him	127
1808	Some bloody sign of it; for 'tis commanded	128
1809	I should do so: you shall be miss'd at court,	129
1810	And that will well confirm it.	
1811	*Imo.* Why, good fellow, 130130	
1812	What shall I do the while? where bide? how live?131	
1813	Or in my life what comfort, when I am	132
1814	Dead to my husband?	
1815	*Pis.* If you'll back to the court—133	
1816	*Imo.* No court, no father; nor no more ado	134
1817	†With that harsh, noble, simple nothing,	135
1818	That Cloten, whose love-suit hath been to me	136
1819	As fearful as a siege.	
1820	*Pis.* If not at court,	137
1821	Then not in Britain must you bide.	
1822	*Imo.* Where then?	138

*34:118 Rig, MB2, PH1; cX: KRe, NM2; abX: IP2   *34:134 Inc, JKT,
Oxb, Dol, USW, Cum, WM1, HnF, KRe, Rig   *34:135 USW, Cum,WM1,
HnF, KRe, Rig, WmS, HIC

104 X: Ox1, Oxb, USW, CKP, WmS, MB1, MB2; R: Wen; bX: HIC
105 X: Ox1, Roa, Oxb, USW, HnF, CKP, WmS, HIC, MB1, MB2; bX: G61, Bel,*
106 X: G61, Bel, Ox1, Wen, Bat, P95, Bar, Low, Roa, Inc, JKT, Oxb, Dol*
107 same as 106, IP2, PH1; less bX; bX: BA1, BK1
108 same as 107, BA1, BK1; less bX
109 same as 108
110 X: Ox1, Oxb, USW, W, Lac, Rog, HM1, MTh, HIM, WmS, HIC, ViA, BA1,NM1*
111 same as 110; less aX

112 X: Ox1, Oxb, USW, WmS, HIC, MB1, MB2; aX: WM1, Lac, Rig, HM1, MTh,*
113 same as 112, KRe; less aX; bX: CKP, BK1
114 X: Ox1, Oxb, USW, CKP, KRe, HIC, MB1; aX: WmS, HIC; bX: WM1

115 X: Ox1, Oxb, USW, CKP; bX: WM1
116 X: Ox1, Oxb, USW, WM1, HnF, CKP, WmS, HIC, NM1, NM2; bX: HnF
117 same as 116; less bX; aX: BK1

118 X: Ox1, Oxb, USW, WM1, HnF, CKP, NM2, BA1, BK1; aX: HIC, NM1; bX:
        ChM, G61, Bel, Wen, Bat, P95, Bar, Low, Roa, Inc, JKT, Dol, Cum,*
119 X: ChM, G61, Bel, Ox1, Wen, Bat, P95, Bar, Low, Roa, Inc, JKT, Oxb,
        Dol, USW, Cum, WM1, HnF, CKP, KRe, Rig, WmS, BA1, MB2, IP1, PH1,BK1
120 same as 119, less CKP; aX: CKP
121 same as 120, HIC, NM1, NM2, JP1; less aX
122 X: WmS, HIC; aX: ChM, G61, Bel, Ox1, Wen, Bat, P95, Bar, Low, Roa*
123 X: WmS; aX: HIC
124 X: WmS; aX: KRe, BK1
125 X: WmS

126 X: KRe, ViA, MB1, MB2; aX: WmS
127 X: HIC
128 X: HIC; bX: BK1
129 X: HIC; aX: BK1; bX: KRe, ViA

130 X: CKP, KRe, HIC, ViA; bX: WmS
131 X: WmS, HIC, ViA; aX: CKP; bX: KRe
132 X: WM1, KRe, WmS, HIC, ViA, NM1, NM2; bX: CKP

133 X: CKP, WmS, HIC; aX: WM1, ViA, NM1, NM2
134 same as 133; less aX; bX: G61, Bel, Ox1, Wen, Bat, P95, Bar, Low, Roa*
135 X: G61, Bel, Ox1, Wen, Bat, P95, Bar, Low, Roa, Inc, JKT, Oxb, Dol*
136 same as 135; less aX; bX: ViA

137 X: KRe, WmS, HIC; aX: G61, Bel, Ox1, Wen, Bat, P95, Bar, Low, Roa,
        Inc, JKT, Oxb, Dol, USW, Cum, WM1, HnF, Rig, ViA; bX: CKP
138 X: CKP, KRe, WmS, HIC; bX: Bel, Bar, Rig; N: Ox1, Wen, Inc,Dol, USW

*34:105 Wen, Bat, P95, Bar, Low, Inc, JKT, Dol, Cum, WM1, Lac, KRe, Rig,
    HM1, MTh, HIM, ViA, NM1, NM2   *34:106 USW, Cum, WM1, HnF,CKP,
    Lac, KRe, Rig, HM1, MTh, HIM, WmS, HIC, ViA, NM1, NM2, MB1, MB2; bX:
    IP1, PH1   *34:110 NM2, MB1, MB2, PH1; aX: G61, Bel,
    Wen, Bat, P95, Bar, Low, Roa, Inc, JKT, Oxb, Dol, Cum, HnF, CKP, KRe,
    IP2   *34:112 HIM, ViA, BA1, NM1, NM2, PH1, BK1

1823	Hath Britain all the sun that shines? Day, night,	139
1824	Are they not but in Britain? I' the world's volume	140
1825	Our Britain seems as of it, but not in't: 141	141
1826	In a great pool a swan's nest: prithee, think	142
1827	There's livers out of Britain.	
1828	*Pis.* I am most glad	143
1829	You think of other place. The ambassador,	144
1830	Lucius the Roman, comes to Milford-Haven	145
1831	To-morrow: now, if you could wear a mind	146
1832	Dark as your fortune is, and but disguise	147
1833	That which, to appear itself, must not yet be	148
1834	But by self-danger, you should tread a course	149
1835	†Pretty and full of view; yea, haply, near 150	150
1836	The residence of Posthumus; so nigh at least	151
1837	That though his actions were not visible, yet	152
1838	Report should render him hourly to your ear	153
1839	As truly as he moves.	
1840	*Imo.* O, for such means!	154
1841	Though peril to my modesty, not death on't,	155
1842	I would adventure.	
1843	*Pis.* Well, then, here's the point:	156
1844	You must forget to be a woman; change	157
1845	Command into obedience: fear and niceness—	158
1846	The handmaids of all women, or, more truly,	159
1847	Woman its pretty self—into a waggish courage:	160
1848	Ready in gibes, quick-answer'd, saucy and 161	161
1849	As quarrelous as the weasel; nay, you must	162
1850	Forget that rarest treasure of your cheek,	163
1851	Exposing it—but, O, the harder heart!	164
1852	Alack, no remedy!—to the greedy touch	165
1853	Of common-kissing Titan, and forget	166
1854	Your laboursome and dainty trims, wherein	167
1855	You made great Juno angry.	
1856	*Imo.* Nay, be brief:	168
1857	I see into thy end, and am almost	169
1858	A man already.	
1859	*Pis.* First, make yourself but like one. 170	170
1860	Fore-thinking this, I have already fit—	171
1861	'Tis in my cloak-bag—doublet, hat, hose, all	172
1862	That answer to them: would you in their serving,	173
1863	And with what imitation you can borrow	174
1864	From youth of such a season, 'fore noble Lucius	175
1865	Present yourself, desire his service, tell him	176
	Wherein you're happy,—which you'll make him	
1866	know,	177
1867	If that his head have ear in music,—doubtless	178

*34:158 Cum, WM1, HnF, Lac, KRe, Rig, HM1, MTh, HIM, WmS, ViA, Han, SM1, NM1, IP1, NM2, IP2   *34:159 HnF, CKP, Lac, KRe, Rig, HM1, MTh, HIM, WmS, ViA, Han, SM1, NM1, IP1, NM2, MB1, MB2, IP2, JG1; bX: BK1   *34:162 MB2, PH1, JG1, JP1   *34:168 HnF, CKP, Rig, WmS, JP1; aX: Lac, KRe, HM1, MTh, HIM, HIC, BA1, SM1, NM1, NM2,MB2, IP2, PH1, JG1   *34:173 ViA, BA1, SM1, IP1, NM2, MB1, MB2,IP2, PH1, JP1,BK1   *34:174 IP2, PH1, JP1, BK1   *34:175 MB2,IP2, PH1, JP1,BK1   *34:177 bX: Han

139 X: CKP, KRe, WmS, HIC; bX: G61, Bel, Oxl, Wen, Bat, P95, Bar, Low,*
140 X: G61, Bel, Oxl, Wen, Bat, P95, Bar, Low, Roa, Inc, JKT, Oxb, Dol*
141 X: ChM, G61, Bel, Oxl , Wen, Bat, P95, Bar, Low, Roa, Inc, JKT,Oxb*
142 X: G61, Bel, Wen, Bat, P95, Bar, Roa, KRe, WmS, HIC, ViA, Han, BA1,
      JP1; aX: ChM, Oxl, Low, Inc, JKT, Oxb, Dol, USW, Cum, WM1, HnF,Rig*
143 X: KRe, WmS, HIC; aX: G61, P95, Bar, ViA, Han, BA1; bX: BK1
144 X: KRe; aX: WmS, HIC, JP1, BK1
145 X: KRe; bX: CKP
146 X: CKP, KRe; bX: ViA, BA1, MB2, IP2, JG1; MOVE 146b-148 to follow*
147 X: G61, P95, KRe; R: MB2; aX: CKP, ViA, BA1, JG1; bX: ChM, Bel, Oxl,*
148 X: ChM, G61, Bel, Oxl, Wen, Bat, P95, Bar, Low, Inc, JKT, Oxb, Dol*
149 X: ChM, KRe, JP1; aX: G61, Bel, Oxl, Wen, Bat, P95, Bar, Low, Inc*
150 X: KRe; aX: ChM, IP2, JP1
151 X: KRe; aX: IP2; bX: ViA, PH1, BK1
152 X: KRe, ViA, PH1, BK1
153 same as 152

154 X: KRe; aX: ViA, PH1, BK1; Insert 146b-148: JP1
155 X: KRe, HIC, NM1, NM2, BK1

156 aX: KRe, HIC, NM1, NM2; bX: CKP
157 X: CKP
158 X: CKP; bX: Bel, Oxl, Wen, Bat, Bar, Low, Inc, JKT, Oxb , Dol, USW*
159 X: Bel, Oxl, Wen, Bat, Bar, Low, Inc, JKT, Oxb, Dol, USW, Cum, WM1*
160 same as 159, less MB1, MB2, JG1, BK1; less bX;aX:MB1, MB2, JG1,BK1
161 same as 160, less ChM, MB1; less aX; bX: BA1
162 same as 161, BA1, less IP1, MB1; less bXaX: IP1, MB1,PH1, HIC; bX:*
163 same as 162, MB2, PH1, JG1, JP1, less ChM; less aX, bX; bX: BK1
164 same as 163 BK1; less bX; bX: IP1
165 same as 164; less bX; aX: IP1
166 same as 165, less ViA; lessaX; aX: ViA
167 same as 166, less Han, BK1; less aX; aX: Han

168 X: Bel, Oxl, Wen, Bat, Bar, Low, Inc, JKT, Oxb, Dol, USW, Cum, WM1*
169 same as 168, less CKP, JP1; less aX: aX: JP1

170 same as 169; less aX
171 X: HIC; bX: CKP
172 X: CKP, Lac, HM1, HIM, WmS, HIC; R: Rig
173 X: WmS, HIC, JG1; R: Lac; aX: CKP, Rig, HM1, HIM; bX: ChM, WM1,KRe*
174 X: ChM, WM1, KRe, WmS, HIC, ViA, BA1, SM1, NM1, IP1, NM2, MB1,MB2*
175 X: KRe; aX: ChM, WM1, WmS, HIC, ViA, BA1, SM1, NM1, IP1, NM2, MB1*
176 X: KRe; bX: ChM, HIC, ViA, BA1, SM1, NM1, NM2, MB2, PH1, JG1,JP1,BK1

177 X: KRe, HIC, ViA, BA1, SM1, NM1, IP1, NM2, MB2, PH1, JP1, BK1;aX: JG1*
178 X: KRe; aX: HIC, ViA, Han, BA1, SM1, NM1, IP1, NM2, MB2, PH1,JG1,JB1,
      BK1

*34:139 Roa, Inc, JKT, Oxb, Dol, USW, Cum, WM1, Rig, NM1, NM2
*34:;40 USW, Cum, WM1, KRe, Rig, WmS, HIC, NM1, NM2; aX: CKP; bX: ChM,HnF,
   Rig, ViA, Han, BA1, JP1   *34:141 Dol, USW, Cum, WM1, HnF,
   KRe, Rig, WmS, HIC, ViA, Han, BA1, NM1, NM2, JP1   *34:142 NM1
   MB2, JP1   *34:146 154: JP1   *34:147 Wen, Bat, Bar,
   Low, Inc, JKT, Oxb, Dol, USW, Cum, WM1, HnF, NM1, IP1, NM2, IP2, PH1,BK1
*34:148 USW, Cum, WM1, HnF, KRe, NM1, IP1, NM2, MB2, PH1, BK1
*34:149 JKT, Oxb, Dol, USW, Cum, WM1, HnF, NM1, IP1, NM2, MB2, PH1, BK1

1868	With joy he will embrace you, for he's honour- able	179
1869	And doubling that, most holy. Your means abroad, **180**	180
1870	You have me, rich: and I will never fail	181
1871	Beginning nor supplyment.	
1872	*Imo.* Thou art all the comfort	182
1873	The gods will diet me with. Prithee, away:	183
1874	There's more to be consider'd; but we'll even	184
1875	All that good time will give us: this attempt	185
1876	I am soldier to, and will abide it with	186
1877	A prince's courage. Away, I prithee.	187
	Pis. Well, madam, we must take a short fare-	
1878	well,	188
1879	Lest, being miss'd, I be suspected of	189
1880	Your carriage from the court. My noble mistress,	190
1881	Here is a box; I had it from the queen: **191**	191
1882	What's in't is precious: if you are sick at sea,	192
1883	Or stomach-qualm'd at land, a dram of this	193
1884	Will drive away distemper. To some shade,	194
1885	And fit you to your manhood. May the gods	195
1886	Direct you to the best!	196
1887	*Imo.* Amen: I thank thee. [*Exeunt, severally.*	197

1888,+1	**Scene V.** *A room in Cymbeline's palace.*	
1889	*Enter* Cymbeline, Queen, Cloten, Lucius,	
1890	Lords, *and* Attendants.	
1891	**Cym.** Thus far; and so farewell.	
1892	**Luc.** Thanks, royal sir.	1
1893	My emperor hath wrote, I must from hence;	2
1894	And am right sorry that I must report ye	3
1895	My master's enemy.	
1896	**Cym.** Our subjects, sir,	4
1897	Will not endure his yoke; and for ourself	5
1898	To show less sovereignty than they, must needs	6
1899	Appear unkinglike.	
1900	**Luc.** So, sir: I desire of you	7
1901	A conduct over-land to Milford-Haven.	8
	Madam, all joy befal your grace!	
1902	**Queen.** And you!	9
	Cym. My lords, you are appointed for that	
1903	office; **10**	10
1904	The due of honour in no point omit.	11
1905	So farewell, noble Lucius.	
1906	**Luc.** Your hand, my lord.	12

*35: 1 MOVE 1–167 to follow 33: 107: HnF, HM1; MOVE 1–65 to follow 33:
117: G61, Bel, Wen, Bat, Bar, Low, Roa, Dol; MOVE 1–78 to follow 31:
107: USW; MOVE 1–28 to follow 31: 87: ChM; MOVE 1–19 to follow 31:
84: JP1   *35: 2 CKP, Lac, Rig, HM1, MTh, HIM, WmS, HIP,ViA,
IP2, JP1, BK1   *35: 4 Oxb, Dol, USW, Cum, KRe
*35: 5Cum , WM1, CKP, Lac, KRe, Rig, HM1, MTh, HIM, WmS, HIP, ViA, JP1
*35: 7 Oxb, Wen, Bat, P95, Bar, Low, Roa, Inc, JKT, Oxb, Dol, USW,Cum,KRe

179 X: KRe; bX: ViA

180 X: KRe; aX: ViA, JP1; bX: HIC, BA1, IP1, PH1, BK1
181 X: KRe, HIC , BA1, IP1, PH1, BK1; bX: CKP

182 X: CKP, KRe, PH1, BK1; aX: HIC, BA1, IP1; MOVE 182b–187 to follow 96:*
183 X: KRe, PB1, BK1; bX: ChM, G61, Bel, Ox1, Wen, Bat, P95, Bar, Low*
184 X: ChM, G61, Bel, Ox1, Wen, Bat, P95, Bar, Low, Roa, Inc, JKT, Oxb*
185 X: Roa, KRe; aX: ChM, G61, Bel, Ox1, Wen, Bat, P95, Bar, Low, Inc, JKT*
186 X: KRe; aX: JP1
187 R : KRe; bX: Ox1, Low, Inc, JKT, Oxb, Dol, USW, Cum, WM1, HnF, HIC, SM1

188 X: HnF, BA1, IP2
189 X: HnF, BA1; R: ChM; aX: IP2
190 X: ChM; aX: HnF, BA1
191 X: ChM; R: G61, Bel, Wen, Bat, P95, Bar
192 bX: ChM, HIC, ViA, BA1; ADD 1: ChM, BK1
193 X: ChM; aX: HIC, ViA, BA1, BK1
194 bX : HnF, HIC
195 X: HnF; aX: HIC; bX: WmS; Insert 182b–187, add 1: WmS
196 X: WmS; aX: HnF; bX: ChM; ADD 15: ChM; Insert 31: 1–86: ViA
197

Scene 35

1 X: WM1, HnF, CKP, Lac, Rig, MTh, HIM, WmS, HIP, ViA, Han; bX: JP1;*
2 X: G61, Bel, Ox1, Wen, Bat, Bar, Roa, Inc, JKT, Oxb, Dol, USW, Cum, WM1*
3 X: WM1, CKP, Lac, Rig, HM1, MTh, HIM, WmS, HIP, ViA, JP1

4 same as 3; bX: G61, Bel, Ox1, Wen, Bat, P95, Bar, Low, Roa, Inc, JKT*
5 X: G61, Bel, Ox1, Wen, Bat, P95, Bar, Low, Roa, Inc, JKT, Oxb, Dol, USW*
6 same as 5

7 X: WM1, CKP, Lac, Rig, HM1, MTh, HIM, WmS, HIP, ViA, JP1; aX: G61, Bel*
8 same as 7, Bar; less aX; ADD 7: ChM

9 X: ChM, G61, Bel, Ox1, Wen, Bat, P95, Bar, Low, Roa, Inc, JKT, Oxb, Dol,
     USW, Cum, WM1, CKP, Lac, KRe, Rig, HM1, MTh, HIM, WmS, HIP, ViA, JP1
10 X: ChM, WM1, CKP, Lac, Rig, HM1, MTh, HIM, WmS, HIP, ViA, NM1, JP1
11 same as 10, BK1

12 same as 10, Han, less ChM; aX: ChM, PH1; bX: KRe

*34:182 WmS   *34:183 Inc, JKT, Oxb, Dol, USW, Cum, WM1, HnF,
   Lac, Rig, HM1, MTh, HIM, WmS, HIC, ViA, NM1, NM2, MB1, MB2
*34:184 Dol, USW, Cum, WM1, HnF, Lac, KRe, Rig, HM1, MTh, HIM, WmS, HIC, ViA,
   SM1, NM1, NM2, MB1, MB2, IP2, PH1, BK1; bX: BA1   *34:185 Oxb,
   Dol, USW, Cum, WM1, HnF, Lac, Rig, HM1, MTh, HIM, WmS, HIC, ViA, BA1, SM1,
   NM1, NM2, MB1, MB2, IP2, PH1, BK1

1907	*Clo.* Receive it friendly; but from this time forth	13
1908	I wear it as your enemy.	
1909	*Luc.* Sir, the event	14
1910	Is yet to name the winner: fare you well.	15
1911	*Cym.* Leave not the worthy Lucius, good my lords,	16
	Till he have cross'd the Severn. Happiness!	17
1912	[*Exeunt Lucius and Lords.*	
1913	*Queen.* He goes hence frowning: but it honours us	18
1914	That we have given him cause.	
1915	*Clo.* 'Tis all the better;	19
1916	Your valiant Britons have their wishes in it. 20	20
1917	*Cym.* Lucius hath wrote already to the emperor	21
1918	How it goes here. It fits us therefore ripely	22
1919	Our chariots and our horsemen be in readiness:	23
1920	The powers that he already hath in Gallia	24
1921	Will soon be drawn to head, from whence he moves	25
1922	His war for Britain.	
1923	*Queen.* 'Tis not sleepy business;	26
1924	But must be look'd to speedily and strongly.	27
1925	*Cym.* Our expectation that it would be thus	28
1926	Hath made us forward. But, my gentle queen,	29
1927	Where is our daughter? She hath not appear'd	30
1928	Before the Roman, nor to us hath tender'd 31	31
1929	The duty of the day: she looks us like	32
1930	A thing more made of malice than of duty:	33
1931	We have noted it. Call her before us; for	34
1932	We have been too slight in sufferance.	
1932+1	[*Exit an Attendant.*	
1933	*Queen.* Royal sir,	35
1934	Since the exile of Posthumus, most retired	36
1935	Hath her life been; the cure whereof, my lord,	37
1936	'Tis time must do. Beseech your majesty,	38
1937	Forbear sharp speeches to her: she's a lady	39
1938	So tender of rebukes that words are strokes 40	40
1939	And strokes death to her.	
1940	*Re-enter* Attendant.	
1941	*Cym.* Where is she, sir? How	41
1942	Can her contempt be answer'd?	
1943	*Atten.* Please you, sir,	42
1944	Her chambers are all lock'd; and there's no answer	43
1945	That will be given to the loudest noise we make	44

13   same as 12, KRe; less aX, bX

14   same as 12; less aX, bX; aX: KRe
15   same as 14, less JP1; less aX; aX: JP1, R:C/.+

16   X: G61, Bel, Ox1, Wen, Bat, Bar, Low, Roa, Inc, JKT, Oxb, Dol, USW*
17   same as 16, less JP1; less R; aX: JP1

18   X: WM1, HnF, CKP, Lac, Rig, HM1, MTh, HIM, Wm S, HIP, Via

19   same as 18; bX: Roa, HIC, SM1, NM1, NM2, MB1, PH1, BK1
20   X: Roa, WM1, HnF, CKP, Lac, KRe, Rig, HM1, MTh, HIM, WmS, HIP, HIC,*
21   X: G61, Bel, Ox1, Wen, Bat, P95, Bar, Low, Roa, Inc, JKT, Oxb, Dol,*
22   same as 21, less PH1, BK1; aX: PH1, BK1
23   same as 22; less aX
24   same as 23, HnF

25   same as 24; bX: BK1

26   X: WM1, CKP, Lac, KRe, Rig, HM1, MTh, HIM, WmS, HIP, HIC, ViA, Han*
27   same as 26; less aX
28   same as 27, NM1, NM2, less Han; aX: Han; ADD 2: ChM
29   X: ChM, WM1, CKP, Lac, KRe, Rig, HM1, MTh, HIM, WmS, HIP, HIC, NM1;*
30   X: ChM, WM1, CKP, Lac, Rig, HM1, MTh, HIM, Wm S
31   same as 30; bX: KRe
32   X: ChM, WM1, CKP, Lac, KRe, Rig, HM1, MTh, HIM, WmS; bX: HnF, ViA,NM2
33   X: ChM, WM1, HnF, CKP, Lac, KRe, Rig, HM1, MTh, HIM, WmS, ViA, NM1*
34   X: ChM, WM1, CKP, Lac, KRe, Rig, HM1, MTh, HIM, WmS; aX: HnF,ViA,NM1,
       NM2; bX: HIC, SM1, BK1

35   X: ChM, WM1, CKP, Lac, KRe, Rig, HM1, MTh, HIM, WmS, HIC, BK1; aX:HnF*
36   same as 35, SM1; less aX, bX
37   same as 36
38   same as 36
39   same as 36; bX: Bel, Ox1, Wen, Bat, Bar, Low, Inc, JKT, Oxb, USW, Cum
40   X: ChM, Bel, Ox1, Wen, Bat, Bar, Low, Inc, JKT, Oxb, Dol, USW, Cum,
       WM1, CKP, Lac, KRe, Rig, HM1, MTh, HIM, WmS, HIC, SM1, BK1

41   X: ChM, WmS, BK1; aX: Bel, Ox1, Wen, Bat, Bar, Low, Inc, JKT, Oxb, Dol,
       USW, Cum, WM1, CKP, Lac, KRe, Rig, HM1, MTh, HIM, HIC, SM1
42   X: ChM, WmS; aX: BK1; N: Ox1
43   X: ChM, WmS; N: Oxb
44   X: ChM, WmS

*35:16 Cum, WM1, CKP, Lac, KRe, Rig, HM1, MTh, HIM, WmS, HIP, ViA,JP1BK1;
    R: NM2   *35:20 ViA, SM1, NM1, NM2, MB1, PH1, JP1, BK1
*35:21USW, Cum, WM1, CKP, Lac, KRe, Rig, HM1, MTh, HIM, WmS, HIP, HIC, ViA,
    Han, SM1, NM1, NM2, MB1, PH1, JP1, BK1   *35:26 SM1, MB1,
    JP1; aX: G61, Bel, Ox1, Wen, Bat, P95, Bar, Low, Roa, Inc, JKT, Oxb,Dol,
    USW, Cum, HnF, NM1, NM2, BK1   *35:29 aX: ViA, SM1, NM2, MB1,JP1
*35:33 NM2; bX: HIC   *35:35 bX: PH1

1946	*Queen.* My lord, when last I went to visit her,	45
1947	She pray'd me to excuse her keeping close,	46
1948	Whereto constrain'd by her infirmity,	47
1949	She should that duty leave unpaid to you,	48
1950	Which daily she was bound to proffer: this	49
1951	She wish'd me to make known; but our great court ⁵⁰	50
1952	Made me to blame in memory.	
1953	*Cym.* Her doors lock'd!	51
1954	Not seen of late? Grant, heavens, that which I fear	52
1955	Prove false! [*Exit*	
1956	*Queen.* Son, I say, follow the king.	53
1957	*Clo.* That man of hers, Pisanio, her old servant	54
1958	I have not seen these two days.	
1959	*Queen.* Go, look after. [*Exit Cloten.*	55
1960	Pisanio, thou that stand'st so for Posthumus!	56
1961	He hath a drug of mine: I pray his absence	57
1962	Proceed by swallowing that, for he believes	58
1963	It is a thing most precious. But for her,	59
1964	Where is she gone? Haply, despair hath seized her, ⁶⁰	60
1965	Or, wing'd with fervour of her love, she's flown	61
1966	To her desired Posthumus: gone she is	62
1967	To death or to dishonour: and my end	63
1968	Can make good use of either: she being down,	64
1969	I have the placing of the British crown.	65
1970	*Re-enter* CLOTEN.	
1971	How now, my son!	
1972	*Clo.* 'Tis certain she is fled.	66
1973	Go in and cheer the king: he rages; none	67
1974	Dare come about him.	
1975	*Queen.* [*Aside*] All the better: may	68
1976	This night forestall him of the coming day! [*Exit*	69
1977	*Clo.* I love and hate her: for she's fair and royal, ⁷⁰	70
1978	And that she hath all courtly parts more exquisite	71
1979	Than lady, ladies, woman; from every one	72
1980	The best she hath, and she, of all compounded,	73
1981	Outsells them all; I love her therefore: but	74
1982	Disdaining me and throwing favours on	75
1983	The low Posthumus slanders so her judgement	76
1984	That what's else rare is choked; and in that point	77
1985	I will conclude to hate her, nay, indeed,	78
	To be revenged upon her. For when fools ⁷⁹	79
1986	Shall—	

CONTINUATIONS FROM G961b

*35:148 G61, CKP, KRe cX: Bel, Ox1, Wen, Bat, Bar, Low, Inc, JKT, Oxb,
   Cum, Rig, BK1; abX: Dol   *35:149 P95, Low, USW
*35:156 USW, Cum, WM1, KRe, Rig, HIP, SM1, NM1, IP1, MB2, JG1, BK1

45   X: ChM, KRe, WmS, HIC, SM1, MB1, MB2, PH1
46   same as 45
47   X: ChM, WM1,   CKP, KRe, WmS, HIC, ViA, SM1, MB1, MB2, PH1, BK1
48   same as 47
49   same as 47; bX: JG1

50   same as 47, JG1, less ViA, BK1; aX: ViA

51   X: ChM, WmS; aX: WM1, CKP, KRe, HIC, SM1, MB1, MB2, PH1, JG1
52   X: ChM, WmS

53   X: ChM, WmS; bX: KRe
54   X: ChM, KRe, WmS

55   same as 54
56   X: ChM, Ox1, Oxb, USW, KRe, WmS, HIC, SM1; bX: ViA
57   X: ChM, Ox1, Oxb, USW, KRe, WmS
58   same as 57
59   same as 57

60   same as 57; bX: WM1, CKP
61   X: ChM, Ox1, Oxb, USW, WM1, CKP, KRe, WmS
62   same as61
63   same as 61
64   same as 61, less KRe; aX: KRe
65   same as 64; less aX; Insert 34: 1-196: Inc, JKT, Cum

66
    X: ChM, G61, Bel, Ox1, Wen, Bat, Bar, Low, Roa, Inc, JKT, Oxb, Dol*
67   same as 66, KRe

68   same as 67
69   same as 67

70   X: G61, Rig, MB2; MOVE 70-80 to follow 36: 95: ChM
71   X: G61, Bel, Ox1, Wen, Bat, Bar, Low, Roa, Inc, JKT, Oxb, USW, Cum,WM1*
72   same as 71; Dol, BK1; R: P95; bX: KRe
73   same as 72, less G61; less R, bX; aX: KRe; bX: BA1
74   X: WmS, SM1, MB2; aX: Bel, Ox1, Wen, Bat, Bar, Low, Roa, Inc, JKT, Oxb*
75   X: WmS, MB2
76   X: WmS, MB2
77   X: G61, Bel, Ox1, Wen, Bat, Bar, Low, Inc, JKT, Oxb, Dol, USW, Cum,KRe*
78   X: CKP, MB2   ; bX: G61, Bel, Wen, Bat, Bar, Roa, Cum, ViA
79   X: G61, Bel, Wen, Bat, Bar, Roa, Cum, MB2, JP1; aX: CKP, ViA; bX: Ox1,
      Low, Inc, JKT, Oxb, Dol,   USW, WM1, KRe, Rig, WmS, HIC,   SM1, BK1

*35:66   USW, Cum, WmS   *35:71 CKP, Rig, Wm S, ViA, SM1, MB2
*35:74 Dol, USW, Cum, WM1, CKP, Rig, ViA, BA1, BK1   *35:77 WmS,HIC,
    BA1, SM1, MB2; bX: CKP

1987	*Enter* PISANIO.	
1988	Who is here? What, are you packing, sirrah?	80
1989	Come hither: ah, you precious pandar! Villain,	81
1990	Where is thy lady? In a word: or else	82
1991	Thou art straightway with the fiends.	
1992	*Pis.* O, good my lord!	83
1993	*Clo.* Where is thy lady? or, by Jupiter,—	84
1994	I will not ask again. Close villain,	85
1995	I'll have this secret from thy heart, or rip	86
1996	Thy heart to find it. Is she with Posthumus?	87
1997	From whose so many weights of baseness cannot	88
1998	A dram of worth be drawn.	
1999	*Pis.* Alas, my lord, 89	89
2000	How can she be with him? When was she miss'd?	90
2001	He is in Rome.	
2002	*Clo.* Where is she, sir? Come nearer;	91
2003	No further halting: satisfy me home	92
2004	What is become of her.	93
2005	*Pis.* O, my all-worthy lord!	
2006	*Clo.* All-worthy villain!	94
2007	Discover where thy mistress is at once,	95
2008	At the next word: no more of 'worthy lord!'	96
2009	Speak, or thy silence on the instant is	97
2010	Thy condemnation and thy death.	
2011	*Pis.* Then, sir,	98
2012	This paper is the history of my knowledge 99	99
2013	Touching her flight. [*Presenting a letter.*	
2014	*Clo.* Let's see't. I will pursue her	100
2015	Even to Augustus' throne.	
2016	*Pis.* [*Aside*] Or this, or perish.	101
2017	She's far enough; and what he learns by this	102
2018	May prove his travel, not her danger.	
2019	*Clo.* Hum!	103
	Pis. [*Aside*] I'll write to my lord she's dead.	
2020	O Imogen,	104
2021	Safe mayst thou wander, safe return again!	105
2022	*Clo.* Sirrah, is this letter true?	106
2023	*Pis.* Sir, as I think.	107
	Clo. It is Posthumus' hand; I know't. Sir-	108
2024	rah, if thou wouldst not be a villain, but do me	109
2025	true service, undergo those employments wherein	110
2026	I should have cause to use thee with a serious	111
2027	industry, that is, what villany soe'er I bid thee	112
2028	do, to perform it directly and truly, I would	113
	think thee an honest man: thou shouldst neither	114

80 X: Bar, WM1; aX: Bel, BK1; bX, G61, Ox1, P95, Roa, Inc, JKT, Cum,KRe*
81 X: ChM, Wen, Bat ; aX: G61, Bel, Ox1, P95, Bar, Low, Roa, Inc, JKT*
82 X: ChM; bX: HnF, WmS

83 X: ChM, Han; aX: WmS; bX: KRe, HIC
84 X: ChM, KRe; bX: BK1
85 X: ChM, KRe, HIC, SM1, BK1; bX: HnF, HIP
86 X: ChM, HnF, KRe, HIP, HIC, SM1, BK1
87 X: ChM, KRe, HIC, SM1; aX: HnF, HIP, BK1
88 X: ChM, G61, Bel, Ox1, Wen, P95, Bar, Low, Roa, Inc, JKT, Oxb, Dol,
        USW, Cum, WM1, HnF, CKP, Lac, KRe, Rig, HM1, MTh, HIM, WmS, HIC,ViA*
89 X: ChM, KRe, WmS, HIC, SM1, MB1, BK1; aX: G61, Bel, Ox1, Wen, P95,*
90 X: ChM, KRe, WmS, HIC, SM1; bX: WM1, CKP, BK1

91 X: ChM, KRe, HIC, SM1; aX: Bel, Bar, Roa, WmS; bX: P95, Rig; cX: BK1;*
92 X: ChM, Bel, Bar, Roa, WM1, CKP, KRe, HIP, HIC, BA1, SM1, NM1, NM2,*
93 X: ChM, KRe, HIC, BA1, SM1, NM2; aX: NM1

94 X: ChM, PH1
95 ChM, G61, Bel, Ox1, Wen, Bat, P95, Bar, Low, Roa, Inc, JKT, Oxb, Dol*
96 same as 95, WmS; bX: HnF, HIP
97 X: ChM, HnF, PH1

98 X: ChM; aX: HnF, PH1; bX: BK1
99 X: ChM

100 X: ChM; bX: KRe, WmS

101 X: ChM, KRe, NM1; bX: WmS, NM1, NM2, BK1; N: HIC
102 X: ChM, KRe, NM1, NM2; aX: BK1

103 X: ChM, KRe, NM1; aX: NM2; bX: Bel, Bar, Low

104 X: ChM, Bel, Wen, Bar, KRe, BK1; aX: WmS; bX: NM2
105 X: ChM, Bel, Wen, Bar, KRe, NM2, BK1
106 X: ChM, KRe
107 X: ChM, KRe
108 X: ChM, SM1; bX: WmS
109 X: ChM, SM1, MB1; bX: CKP, HIC
110 X: ChM, G61, Bel, Ox1, Wen, Bat, Bar, Inc, JKT, Oxb, Cum, CKP, KRe,HIP*
111 X: ChM, G61, Bel, Ox1, Wen, Bat, P95, Bar, Low, Inc, JKT, Oxb, Cum, WM1*
112 X: ChM, HIP, HIC, SM1, MB2; aX: G61, P95, Low, WM1, HnF, Rig,ViA, PH1*
113 X: ChM, KRe, HIP, HIC, SM1, MB2; bX: CKP, PH1
114 X: ChM, CKP, HIP, HIC, SM1, MB2; aX: KRe, PH1; bX: WM1, BK1

*35:80 WmS, HIC, SM1; abX: Dol   *35:81 Oxb, Dol, USW, Cum, WM1,
    WmS   *35:88 BA1, SM1, NM1, NM2, PH1, JG1, JP1, BK1
*35:89 Bar, Low, Roa, Inc, JKT, Oxb, Dol, USW, Cum, WM1, HnF, CKP, Lac, Rig,
    HM1, MTh, HIM, ViA, BA1, NM1, NM2, JG1   *35:91 abX: G61, Ox1,
    Wen, Bat, Low, Inc, JKT, Oxb, Dol, USW, Cum, WM1, CKP, HIP
*35:92 BK1; aX: G61, Ox1, Wen, Bat, P95, Low, Inc, JKT, Oxb, Dol, USW, Cum,
    Rig   *35:95 USW, Cum, KRe, Rig, MB2, PH1   *35:110 HIC,
    BA1, SM1, MB2, JG1; bX: P95, Low, WM1, HnF, Rig, ViA, PH1, BK1
*35:111 HnF, KRe, Rig, HIP, HIC, ViA, BA1, SM1, MB2, PH1, JG1, BK1;aX:CKP
*35:112 BK1; bX: KRe

2029	want my means for thy relief nor my voice for thy	115
2030-1	preferment.	116
2032	*Pis.* Well, my good lord.	117
	Clo. Wilt thou serve me? for since patiently	118
2033	and constantly thou hast stuck to the bare fortune	119
2034	of that beggar Posthumus, thou canst not, in the	120
2035	course of gratitude, but be a diligent follower of	121
2036-7	mine: wilt thou serve me?	122
2038	*Pis.* Sir, I will.	123
	Clo. Give me thy hand; here's my purse.	124
2039	Hast any of thy late master's garments in thy	125
2040	possession?	126
2041	*Pis.* I have, my lord, at my lodging, the same	127
	suit he wore when he took leave of my lady and	128
2042-3	mistress. **129**	129
	Clo. The first service thou dost me, fetch that	130
2044-5	suit hither: let it be thy first service; go.	131
2046	*Pis.* I shall, my lord. [*Exit.*	132
	Clo. Meet thee at Milford-Haven!—I forgot	133
2047	to ask him one thing; I'll remember't anon:—	134
2048	even there, thou villain Posthumus, will I kill	135
2049	thee. I would these garments were come. She	136
2050	said upon a time—the bitterness of it I now belch	137
2051	from my heart—that she held the very garment	138
2052	of Posthumus in more respect than my noble and	139
2053	natural person, together with the adornment of	140
	my qualities. With that suit upon my back, will	141
2054	I ravish her: first kill him, and in her eyes; there	142
2055	shall she see my valour, which will then be a tor-	143
2056	ment to her contempt. He on the ground, my	144
2057	speech of insultment ended on his dead body, and	145
2058	when my lust hath dined,—which, as I say, to	146
2059	vex her I will execute in the clothes that she so	147
	praised,—to the court I'll knock her back, foot	148
2060	her home again. She hath despised me rejoic-	149
2061-2	ingly, and I'll be merry in my revenge. **150**	150
2063	*Re-enter* PISANIO, *with the clothes.*	
2064	Be those the garments?	151
2065	*Pis.* Ay, my noble lord.	152
	Clo. How long is't since she went to Milford-	
2066	Haven?	153
2067	*Pis.* She can scarce be there yet.	154
	Clo. Bring this apparel to my chamber: that	155
2068	is the second thing that I have commanded thee:	156
2069	the third is, that thou wilt be a voluntary mute to	157

*35:141(Continued) Oxb, Lac, MTh,   *35:142 HIC, JG1;abX: KRe;
B: Low, USW, HM1, SM1; ADD 1: Roa   *35:143 Wm1, HnF, KRe,
Rig͵ViA, SM1, NM1, NM2, JG1; bX: BK1   *35:144 JG1; aX: Ox1,
Low, Inc, JKT, Oxb, Dol, USW, Cum, WM1, KRe, Rig, SM1, NM1,BK1; bX:
HIP   *35:145 Bar, JG1; bX: USW, KRe; B: Bel, Ox1, Wen,Bat,
Bar, Inc, Oxb, USW; N: Cum   *35:146 Ox1, Bat, P95, Oxb,
Dol, Cum, Rig, WmS, ViA   *35:147 HIP, HIC, SM1, NM1, NM2;
aX: Bel, Ox1, Wen, Bar, Inc, Oxb, Cum, KRe, ViA   SEE ⌐960c

```
115  X: ChM, WM1, HIP, HIC, SM1, MB2, BK1
116  same as 115; bX: CKP
117  X: ChM, CKP, WmS, HIP, HIC, SM1, MB2; bX: KRe
118  X: ChM, G61, Bel, Wen, Bat, P95, Bar, Roa, CKP, KRe, Rig, SM1, NM1*
119  X: ChM, G61, Bel, Oxl, Wen, Bat, P95, Bar, Low, Roa, Inc, JKT, Oxb*
120  same as 119, less CHP
121  same as 120
122  same as 120, less Oxb, SM1, MTh; aX: Oxb, MTh
123  X: ChM, Bel, Wen, Bat, P95, Bar, Roa, MB2
124  X: ChM, MB2; aX: HnF, KRe, ViA
125  X: ChM,
126  X: ChM; cX: WmS, BA1
127  X: ChM; aX: ViA; cX: BK1
128  X: ChM; bX: CKP
129  X: ChM; aX: CKP
130  X: ChM; aX: KRe, MB2, BK1
131  X: ChM; bX: G61, Bel, P95, Bar, CKP, NM2, MB2, BK1
132  X: ChM; aX: CKP
133  X: ChM, NM2; bX: G61, Bel, Oxl, Wen, Bat, P95, Bar, Low, Roa, Inc,*
134  X: ChM, G61, P95, Low, Roa, Dol, USW, WM1, Rig, NM2; aX: Bel, Oxl*
135  X: ChM, NM1, NM2; bX: Bel, Wen, Bat, Bar, KRe, HIC, JG1; B: CKP
136  X: ChM, NM1, NM2; aX: Bel, Wen, Bat, Bar, KRe, JG1; bX: G61, P95,Roa*
137  X: ChM, Bel, Oxl, Wen, Bat, Bar, Oxb, KRe, WmS, HIC, SM1, NM1, NM2;*
138  X: ChM, WmS, NM1, NM2; aX: G61, P95, Roa, JKT, Dol, USW, WM1,HnF, Rig
139  X: ChM, CKP, WmS, NM1, NM2; bX: JKT
140  X: ChM, Bel, Oxl, Wen, Bat, Bar, Inc, Oxb, Cum, CKP, KRe, WmS, NM1*
141  X: ChM, NM1, NM2; aX: G61, P95, Low, JKT, Dol, USW, WM1, BK1; bX:Cum*
142  X: ChM, Bel, Wen, Bat, Bar, JKT, HnF, Rig, NM1, NM2; aX: WM1, ViA*
143  X: ChM, G61, Bel, Oxl, Wen, Bat, P95Low, Roa, Inc, Oxb, Dol, USW,Cum*
144  X: ChM, G61, Bel, Wen, Bat, P95, Bar, Roa, HnF, HIC, ViA, SM1, NM1,*
145  X: ChM, P95, Roa, HnF, Rig, HIP, HIC, NM2; aX: G61, Bel, Wen, Bat,*
146  X: ChM, Wen, Roa, WM1, HnF, KRe, HIP, HIC, SM1, NM1, NM2; bX: G61,Bel*
147  X: ChM, G61, Bat, P95, Low, Roa, JKT, Dol, USW, WM1, HnF, Rig, WmS*
148  X: ChM, Roa, HnF, HIP, HIC, SM1, NM1, NM2; aX: P95, USW, WM1, WmS;bX:*
149  X: ChM, G61, Roa, JKT, Dol, CKP, Rig, HIP, HIC, NM1, NM2; aX: HnF; bX:*
150  X: ChM, G61, Bel, Oxl, Wen, Bat, P95, Bar, Low, Roa, Inc, JKT, Oxb,Dol,
       USW, Cum CKP, Rig, HIP, NM1, NM2

151  same as 150, less HIP
152  same as 151, KRe, less CKP

153  same as 152
154  same as 152; aX: CKP
155  same as 152, less BK1;bX: SM1, JG1
156  X: ChM, G61, Bel, Oxl, Wen, Bat, P95, Bar, Low, Roa, Inc, JKT, Oxb,Dol*
157  same as 156, NM2, less NM1, BK1; aX: BK1

*35:118MB2; bX: Oxl, Low, Inc, JKT, Oxb, Dol, USW, Cum, WM1, Lac, HM1,MTh,
   HIM, WmS, HIC, ViA, NM2, JG1, BK1          *35:119 Dol, USW, Cum, WM1,CKP,
   Lac, KRe, Rig, HM1, MTh, HIM, WmS, HIC, ViA, SM1, NM1, NM2, MB2, JG1,BK1
*35:133 Inc, JKT, Oxb, Dol, USW, Cum, WM1, KRe, Rig, NM2, SM1
*35:134 Wen, Bat, Bar, Inc, JKT, Oxb, Cum, KRe, WmS, SM1; bX: CKP
*35:136 HnF, WmS; abX: HIC            *35:137 aX: CKP; bX: G61, P95, Roa,
   JKT, Dol, USW, WM1, Rig        *35:140 NM2; aX: JKT; bX: G61, P95, Low
   Dol, USW, WM1, BK1    *35:141  HnF, KRe, HIC; B:Bel,Oxl,Wen,Bat,Bar,Inc*
```

2070	**my** design. Be but duteous, and true prefer-	158
2071	ment shall tender itself to thee. My revenge is	159
2072	**now at** Milford: would I had wings to follow it!	160
2073	**Come,** and be true. [*Exit.*	161
	Pis. Thou bid'st me to my loss: for true to	
2074	thee	162
2075	Were to prove false, which I will never be,	163
2076	To him that is most true. To Milford go,	164
	And find not her whom thou pursuest. Flow,	
2077	flow,	165
	You heavenly blessings, on her! This fool's	
2078	speed	166
	Be cross'd with slowness; labour be his meed!	167
2079	[*Exit.*	

2080R,+**SCENE VI.** *Wales. Before the cave of Belarius.*

2081   *Enter* IMOGEN, *in boy's clothes.*

2082	*Imo.* I see a man's life is a tedious one:	1
2083	I have tired myself, and for two nights together	2
	Have made the ground my bed. I should be	
2084	sick,	3
2085	But that my resolution helps me. Milford,	4
2086	When from the mountain-top Pisanio show'd thee,	5
2087	Thou wast within a ken: O Jove! I think	6
2088	Foundations fly the wretched; such, I mean,	7
	Where they should be relieved. Two beggars	
2089	told me	8
2090	I could not miss my way: will poor folks lie,	9
2091	That have afflictions on them, knowing 'tis 10	10
2092	A punishment or trial? Yes; no wonder,	11
	When rich ones scarce tell true. To lapse in	
2093	fulness	12
2094	Is sorer than to lie for need, and falsehood	13
2095	Is worse in kings than beggars. My dear lord!	14
	Thou art one o' the false ones. Now I think on	
2096	thee,	15
2097	My hunger's gone: but even before, I was	16
2098	At point to sink for food. But what is this?	17
2099	Here is a path to't: 'tis some savage hold:	18
2100	I were best not call; I dare not call: yet famine,	19
2101	Ere clean it o'erthrow nature, makes it valiant. 20	20
2102	Plenty and peace breeds cowards: hardness ever	21
2103	Of hardiness is mother. Ho! who's here?	22
2104	If any thing that's civil, speak; if savage,	23

*36:13 HIC, ViA, BA1, NM1, NM2, MB1, MB2, IP2, PH1, JG1, BK1; aX: IP1
*36:17 MB2, BK1   *36:21 PH1, JG1, BK1   *36:22 PH1, JG1,BK1

158 same as 157, less IP1, NM2; less aX; aX: IP1, NM2; bX: HIC, ViA, BA1*
159 X: ChM, Low, KRe, Rig; aX: G61, Bel, Ox1, Wen, Bat, P95, Bar, Roa,*
160 X: ChM, KRe, Rig; aX: Low, JG1; bX: Bel, Ox1, Wen, Bat, Bar, Inc, Cum
161 X: ChM , G61, Bel, Ox1, Wen, Bat, P95, Bar, Low, Roa, Inc, JKT, Oxb,
    Dol, USW, Cum, KRe, Rig, MB2; ADD 1: PH1
162 X: ChM, G61, Bel, Ox1, Wen, Bat, P95, Bar, Low, Roa, Inc, JKT, Oxb*
163 same as 162
164 same as 162, less SM1, NM1, NM2, MB2, JG1; aX: SM1, NM1, NM2, MB2, JG1;
    bX: HIC, PH1, BK1
165 X: ChM, G61, Bel, Ox1, Wen, Bat, P95, Bar, Low, Roa, Inc, JKT, Oxb,
    Dol USW, Cum, KRe, Rig, HIC, BA1, PH1, BK1
166 same as 165; bX: WmS
167 same as 165, WmS; Insert 33: 1-98: ViA

Scene 36

1
2 bX: ChM

3 bX: BK1
4 aX: BK1; bX: MB1, MB2, JP1; cX: ChM
5 X: MB1, MB2, JP1; bX: Oxb
6 X: Oxb, MB1, MB2, JP1; bX: Ox1, Low, Inc, JKT, Dol, USW, Cum, WM1HnF*
7 X: Ox1, Low, Inc, JKT, Dol, USW, Cum, WM1, HnF, CKP, Rig, HIC, ViA,
    BA1, SM1, NM1, NM2, MB1, MB2, JG1, JP1, BK1; aX: Oxb; bX: IP1, PH1
8 X: NM1, NM2, MB1, MB2; aX: Ox1, Low, Inc, JKT, Dol, USW, Cum, WM1,HnF*
9 X: KRe, NM1, NM2, MB1, MB2
10 X: KRe, ViA, NM1, NM2, MB1, MB2; bX: G61, Bel, Ox1, Wen, Bat, P95*
11 X: Ox1, Low, JKT, Oxb, USW, KRe, NM1, NM2, MB1, MB2; aX: G61, Bel, Wen,
    Bat, P95, Bar, PH1, JG1
12 same as 12; less aX; bX: Inc, Dol, Cum, WM1, HnF, CKP, Rig, WmS, HIC*
13 X: Ox1, Low, Inc, JKT, Oxb, Dol, USW, Cum, WM1, HnF, CKP, KRe, Rig,WmS*
14 X: Ox1, Low, JKT, Oxb, USW, WM1, CKP, KRe, NM1, NM2, MB1, MB2; aX: Inc,
    Dol, Cum, HnF, Rog, WmS, HIC, ViA, BA1, IP2, PH1, JG1, BK1
15 same as 14; less aX·bX: BK1
16 same as 15, BK1; less bX
17 X: USW, NM1; aX: Ox1, Low, JKT, Oxb, Dol, WM1, CKP, KRe, Rig, NM2, MB1*
18 X: NM1; aX: Inc, USW, Cum
19 X: NM1, NM2
20 X: NM1, NM2; R: JG1
21 X: Ox1, Low, JKT, Oxb, USW, HnF, KRe, HIC, ViA, Han, SM1, NM1, NM2,*
22 X: KRe, HIC; aX: Ox1, Low, JKT, Oxb, USW, HnF, ViA, Han, SM1, NM1, NM2*
23 X: WM1, CKP, KRe; bX: G61, Bel, Ox1, Bat, Bar, Low, Inc, JKT, Oxb,Dol,
    USW, Cum, Wm S

*35:158 JG1; bX: IP2, BK1   *35:159 Inc, JKT, Oxb, Dol, USW, Cum,
  WM1, HIP, HIC, BA1, SM1, MB2, IP2, BK1   *35:162 Dol, USW, Cum,
  KRe, Rig, BA1, SM1, NM1, NM2, MB2, JG1   *36: 6 CKP, Rig, HIC,
  ViA, BA1, SM1, NM1, NM2, JG1, BK1   *36: 8 CKP, Rig, HIC,ViA,
  BA1, SM1; bX: KRe, JG1, JP1, BK1   *36:10 Bar, Low, JKT, Oxb,USW,
  PH1, JG1   *36:12 ViA, BA1, IP1, IP2, PH1, JG1, BK1

Take or lend. Ho! No answer? Then I'll
2105 · enter. 24
2106 **Best** draw my sword; and if mine enemy 25
But fear the sword like me, he'll scarcely look
2107 on't. 26
2108 **Such** a foe, good heavens! [*Exit, to the cave.* 27
(2109)
2110 *Enter* BELARIUS, GUIDERIUS, *and* ARVIRAGUS.

Bel. You, Polydore, have proved best wood-
2111 man and 28
2112 **Are** master of the feast: Cadwal and I 29
2113 **Will** play the cook and servant; 'tis our match: 30
2114 **The** sweat of industry would dry and die, 31 31
2115 **But** for the end it works to. Come; our stomachs 32
2116 **Will** make what's homely savoury: weariness 33
2117 **Can** snore upon the flint, when resty sloth 34
2118 **Finds** the down pillow hard. Now peace be here, 35
2119 **Poor** house, that keep'st thyself!
2120 *Gui.* I am throughly weary. 36

Arv. I am weak with toil, yet strong in appe-
2121 tite. 37
Gui. There is cold meat i' the cave; we'll
2122 browse on that, 38
2123 **Whilst** what we have kill'd be cook'd. 39
2124 *Bel.* [*Looking into the cave*] Stay; come not in. 40
2125 **But** that it eats our victuals, I should think 41 41
2126 **Here** were a fairy.
2127 *Gui.* What's the matter, sir? 42
2128 *Bel.* By·Jupiter, an angel! or, if not, 43
2129 **An** earthly paragon! Behold divineness 44
2130 **No** elder than a boy! 45

2131 *Re-enter* IMOGEN.

2132 *Imo.* Good masters, harm me not: 46
2133 **Before** I enter'd here, I call'd; and thought 47
To have begg'd or bought what I have took: good
2134 troth, 48
I have stol'n nought, nor would not, though I
2135 had found 49
Gold strew'd i' the floor. Here's money for my
2136 meat: 50 50
2137 **I** would have left it on the board so soon 51
2138 **As** I had made my meal, and parted 52
2139 **With** prayers for the provider.
2140 *Gui.* Money, youth? 53
2141 *Arv.* All gold and silver rather turn to dirt! 54

24 aX: G61, Bel, Oxl, Bat, Bar, Low, Inc, JKT, Oxb, Dol, USW, Cum, WM1*
25 aX: Wen

26
27 R: P95; Insert 41: 1-25a: WmS

28 aX: MB1; N: MB2
29 bX: MB1, MB2
30 bX: G61, Oxl, Wen, Bat, P95, Low, Inc, JKT, Oxb, Dol, USW, Cum, WM1*
31 X: ChM, G61, Bel, Oxl, Wen, Bat, P95, Bar, Low, Inc, JKT, Oxb, Dol*
32 X: ChM, Bel, Bar, KRe, MTh, ViA, MB1, MB2, PH1, JP1; aX: G61, Oxl*
33 X: ChM, KRe, MTh, ViA, MB1, MB2, PH1, JP1; bX: HnF, HIC, BA1, SM1,*
34 X: WM1, HnF, KRe, MTh, HIC, ViA, BA1, SM1, MB1, MB2, PH1, JG1,JP1,BK1
35 X: MB1, MB2, BK1; aX: HnF, KRe, MTh, HIC, ViA, SM1, PH1; bX: Bel,HIP,
      JG1, JP1
36 X: Bel, BK1; aX: HIP, MB1, MB2; bX: G61, Wen, Bat, P95, Bar,Roa,KRe

37 X: G61, Wen, Bat, P95, Bar, Roa, KRe

38 X KRe; bX: ChM
39 X: ChM, KRe; bX: WmS
40 aX: KRe, WmS
41

42 X: JG1
43 aX: JG1; bX: BK1
44 aX: BK1; bX: HIC
45 aX: HIC

46
47 X: BK1; bX: KRe

48 X: BK1; aX: KRe

49 bX: BK1

50 aX: BK1
51 X: BK1
52 X: BK1

53 X: CKP; aX: BK1
54 X: WM1, CKP, BK1; N: HnF

*36:24 CKP, KRe, WmS, JG1; bX: Wen, Dol   *36:30 CKP, KRe, MTh,
   HIP, BA1, MB1, PH1, JG1, JP1, BK1   *36:31 USW, Cum, WM1,HnF,
   CKP, KRe, MTh, HIP, HIC, ViA, BA1, SM1, MB1, MB2, PH1, JG1, JP1, BK1
36:32 Wen, Bat, P95, Low, Inc, JKT, Oxb, Dol, USW, Cum, WM1, HnF, CKP, HIP,
   HIC, BA1, SM1, JG1, BK1   *36:33 JG1, BK1

2142	**As 'tis no better reckon'd, but of those**	55
2143	**Who worship dirty gods.**	
2144	*Imo.* I see you're angry:	56
2145	**Know, if you kill me for my fault, I should**	57
2146	**Have died had I not made it.**	
2147	*Bel.* **Whither bound?**	58
2148	*Imo.* **To Milford-Haven.**	59
2149	*Bel.* **What's your name?** **6o**	60
2150	*Imo.* **Fidele, sir. I have a kinsman who**	61
2151	**Is bound for Italy; he embark'd at Milford:**	62
2152	**To whom being going, almost spent with hunger,**	63
2153	**I am fall'n in this offence.**	
2154	*Bel.* **Prithee, fair youth,**	64
2155	**Think us no churls, nor measure our good minds**	65
2156	**By this rude place we live in. Well encounter'd!**	66
2157	**'Tis almost night: you shall have better cheer**	67
2158	**Ere you depart; and thanks to stay and eat it.**	68
2159	**Boys, bid him welcome.**	
2160	*Gui.* **Were you a woman, youth,**	69
	I should woo hard but be your groom. In	
2161	**honesty,** **70**	70
2162	**I bid for you as I'ld buy.**	
2163	*Aro.* **I'll make't my comfort**	71
2164	**He is a man; I'll love him as my brother:**	72
2165	**And such a welcome as I'ld give to him**	73
2166	**After long absence, such is yours: most welcome!**	74
2167	**Be sprightly, for you fall 'mongst friends.**	
2168	*Imo.* **'Mongst friends,**	75
	If brothers. [*Aside*] Would it had been so, that	
2169	**they**	76
2170	**Had been my father's sons! then had my prize**	77
2171	**Been less, and so more equal ballasting**	78
2172	**To thee, Posthumus.**	
2173	*Bel.* **He wrings at some distress.**	79
2174	*Gui.* **Would I could free't!**	
2175	*Aro.* **Or I, whate'er it be, &o**	80
2176	**What pain it cost, what danger. Gods!**	
2177	*Bel.* **Hark, boys.**	81
2177+1	**[***Whispering.***	
2178	*Imo.* **Great men,**	82
2179	**That had a court no bigger than this cave,**	83
2180	**That did attend themselves and had the virtue**	84
2181	**Which their own conscience seal'd them—laying by**	85
2182	**That nothing-gift of differing multitudes—**	86
	Could not out-peer these twain. Pardon me,	
2183	**gods!**	87

55 X: WM1, BK1; aX: CKP; bX: KRe

56 X: NM1; aX: KRe, BK1
57 aX: WM1

58
59
60
61 bX: HIC, BK1
62 X: HIC, BKk
63 X: HIC, BK1

64 aX: HIC, BK1
65 bX : KRe
66 X: KRe
67 X: BK1; aX: KRe
68 X: BK1; bX: CKP

69 X: CKP; bX: G61, Bel, Ox1, Wen, Bat, P95, Bar, Low, Roa, Inc, JKT,
        Oxb, Dol, USW, Cum, Lac, KRe, Rig, HM1, HIM, HIC, MB1, MB2
70 X: G61, Bel, Ox1, Wen, Bat, P95, Bar, Low, Roa, Inc, JKT, Oxb, Dol,
        USW, Cum, Lac, KRe, Rig, HM1, HIM, WmS, HIP, MB1, MB2; aX: CKP;bX:*
71 X: G61, Bel, Ox1, Wen, Bat, P95, Bar, Low, Roa, Inc, JKT, Oxb, Dol*
72 X: ViA, MB1, MB2; aX: G61, Bel, Ox1, Wen, Bat, P95, Bar, Low, Roa,Inc*
73 X: KRe, ViA, MB1, MB2, PH1; N: G61, USW, CKP, HM1
74 X: KRe, MB1, MB2, PH1; N: Bel, Ox1, Wen, Bat, P95, Bar, Low, Inc, JKT,
        Oxb, Dol, Cum, Lac, Rig

75 X: MB1, MB2

76 X: MB1, MB2; bX: CKP
77 X: CKP, MB1, MB2; bX: WM1, KRe, ViA, BA1, PH1, JP1, BK1
78 X: WM1, CKP, KRe, ViA, BA1, MB1, MB2, PH1, JP1, BK1; bX: G61

79 same as 78, less ViA, BA1; less bX; aX: G61, ViA, BA1

80 X: WM1, KRe, MB1, MB2, PH1, JP1, BK1; aX: CKP

81 X: ChM, KRe, MB1, MB2, PH1, JP1, BK1; aX: WM1; bX: USW; B: Ox1, Wen, Bat,
        Low, Roa, Oxb
82 same as 81; less aX, bX, B
83 same as 82, ViA
84 X: CKP, KRe, HIC, ViA, BA1, MB1, MB2, PH1, JG1, JP1, BK1
85 same as 84, NM1; bX: Ox1, JKT, Oxb, USW, HnF, Han
86 X: Ox1, JKT, Oxb, USW, HnF, KRe, HIC, ViA, Han, BA1, NM1, MB1, MB2, PH1,
        JG1, JP1, BK1; aX: CKP
87 X: KRe, MB1, MB2, JP1, BK1; aX: PH1

*36:70 HnF, ViA   *36:71 USW, Cum, Lac, Rig, HM1, HIM, HIC, MB1,MB2,
    BK1; aX: HnF, CKP, ViA, JG1; bX: KRe, WmS   *36:72 JKT, Oxb,
    Dol, USW, Cum, Lac, KRe, Rig, HM1, WmS, HIC

2184	I'ld change my sex to be companion with them,	88
2185	Since Leonatus's false.	
2186	*Bel.* It shall be so.	89
	Boys, we'll go dress our hunt. Fair youth,	
2187	come in:	90
2188	Discourse is heavy, fasting; when we have supp'd,	91
2189	We'll mannerly demand thee of thy story,	92
2190	So far as thou wilt speak it.	
2191	*Gui.* Pray, draw near.	93
2192	*Arv.* The night to the owl and morn to the	94
2193	lark less welcome.	95
2194	*Imo.* Thanks, sir.	96
2195	*Arv.* I pray, draw near. [*Exeunt.*	97

2196,+1	SCENE VII. *Rome. A public place.*	
2197	*Enter two* Senators *and* Tribunes.	
	First Sen. This is the tenour of the emperor's	
2198	writ:	1
2199	That since the common men are now in action	2
2200	'Gainst the Pannonians and Dalmatians,	3
2201	And that the legions now in Gallia are	4
2202	Full weak to undertake our wars against	5
2203	The fall'n-off Britons, that we do incite	6
2204	The gentry to this business. He creates	7
2205	Lucius proconsul: and to you the tribunes,	8
2206	For this immediate levy, he commends	9
2207	His absolute commission. Long live Cæsar! 10	10
2208	*First Tri.* Is Lucius general of the forces?	
2209	*Sec. Sen.* Ay.	11
2210	*First Tri.* Remaining now in Gallia?	
2211	*First Sen.* With those legions	12
2212	Which I have spoke of, whereunto your levy	13
2213	Must be supplyant: the words of your commission	14
2214	Will tie you to the numbers and the time	15
2215	Of their dispatch.	
	First Tri. We will discharge our duty.	16
2216	[*Exeunt.*	

2216+1	ACT IV.	
2217,+1	SCENE I. *Wales: near the cave of Belarius.*	
2218	*Enter* CLOTEN.	
	Clo. I am near to the place where they should	1
2219	meet, if Pisanio have mapped it truly. How	2

88 X: KRe, MB1, MB2, JP1 , BK1

89 X: KRe, MB1, MB2, BK1; aX: JP1; bX: HIP, PH1; N: Bel, Wen, Bat, Bar

90 X: WmS, HIP; aX: MB2, PH1, BK1
91 X: WmS, HIP; aX: MB2; bX: KRe
92 X: KRe, WmS, HIP

93 X: WmS, HIP; aX: KRe
94 X: HIP, ViA, Han
95 X: ChM, KRe, WmS, HIP, ViA, Han, NM2; MOVE 75-80 to follow 36: 95: ChM
96 same as 95, less NM2; less MOVE; Insert 43: 1--46: G61; Insert 43:*
97

Scene 37

ALL CUT: ChM, G61, Bel, Ox1, Wen, Bat, P95, Bar, Low, Roa, Inc, JKT, Oxb,
  Dol, USW, Cum, WM1, HnF, CKP, Lac, KRe, Rig, HM1, MTh, HIM, WmS, HIP,HIC,
  ViA, Han, SM1, NM1, MB1, MB2, PH1, JG1, BK1
 1 X: JP1
 2 X: JP1
 3 X: JP1
 4 X: JP1
 5 X: JP1
 6 X: JP1
 7 X: JP1
 8 X: JP1
 9 X: JP1
10 aX : JP1

11 X: JP1

12 X: JP1
13 X: JP1
14 X: JP1
15 X: JP1

16 X: JP1

Scene 41

 1 X: MB2; MOVE 1-25a to follow 36: 27: WmS
 2 X: MB2; aX: ChM

*36:96 1-54: P95, Low

2220	his garments serve me! Why should his mistress,	3
2221	who was made by him that made the tailor, not	4
2222	be fit too? the rather—saving reverence of the	5
2223	word—for 'tis said a woman's fitness comes by fits.	6
2224	Therein I must play the workman. I dare speak	7
2225	it to myself—for it is not vain-glory for a man and	8
2226	his glass to confer in his own chamber—I mean,	9
	the lines of my body are as well drawn as his; no	10
2227	less young, more strong, not beneath him in for-	11
2228	mes, beyond him in the advantage of the time,	12
2229	above him in birth, alike conversant in general	13
2230	services, and more remarkable in single opposi-	14
2231	tions: yet this imperceiverant thing loves him in	15
2232	my despite. What mortality is! Posthumus, thy	16
2233	head, which now is growing upon thy shoulders,	17
2234	shall within this hour be off; thy mistress en-	18
	forced; thy garments cut to pieces before thy	19
2235	face: and all this done, spurn her home to her	20
2236	father; who may haply be a little angry for my so	21
22	rough usage; but my mother, having power of	22
238	his testiness, shall turn all into my commenda-	23
2239	tions. My horse is tied up safe: out, sword, and	24
2240	to a sore purpose! Fortune, put them into my	25
	hand! This is the very description of their meet-	26
2241	ing-place; and the fellow dares not deceive me.	27
2242	*[Exit.*	

2243,+1   **SCENE II.** *Before the cave of Belarius.*

2244	*Enter, from the cave,* BELARIUS, GUIDERIUS,	
2245	ARVIRAGUS, *and* IMOGEN.	
	Bel. [*To Imogen*] You are not well: remain	
2246	here in the cave;	1
2247	We'll come to you after hunting.	
2248	*Arv.* [*To Imogen*] Brother, stay here:	2
2249	Are we not brothers?	
2250	*Imo.* So man and man should be;	3
2251	But clay and clay differs in dignity,	4
2252	Whose dust is both alike. I am very sick.	5
2253	*Gui.* Go you to hunting; I'll abide with him.	6
2254	*Imo.* So sick I am not, yet I am not well;	7
2255	But not so citizen a wanton as	8
2256	To seem to die ere sick: so please you, leave me:	9
	Stick to your journal course: the breach of	
2257	custom **10**	10
2258	Is breach of all. I am ill, but your being by me	11

3   X: CKP, MB2; bX: G61, Bel, Oxl, Wen, Bat, P95, Bar, Low, Roa, Inc*
4   X: G61, Bel, Oxl, Wen, Bat, P95, Bar, Low, Roa, Inc, JKT, Oxb, Dol*
5   same as 4, ChM, JG1, less MB2, BK1; less aX;MBX, BK1
6   same as 5, MB2; less aX
7   same as 6, IP2, PH1, less HM1, NM1, NM2, MB1, MB2; aX: HM1, NM1, NM2*
8   same as 7, less BA1, JG1; less aX; aX: BA1, JG1; bX: BK1
9   same as 8, less HIC, PH1; less aX; aX: HIC, BK1
10 same as 9, less ChM, SM1, IP1, IP2; less aX; bX JG1
11 same as 10; less bX; aX: JG1; bX: MB2
12 same as 11, ChM, MB2; less aX, bX; bX: JG1, BK1
13 same as 12, less ChM, MB2; less bX; aX: JG1; bX: ChM, BA1, SM1, NM2*
14 same as 13, ChM, HIC, SM1, IP1, PH1, BK1, less CKP; less aX, bX; aX:*
15 X: G61, Bel, Oxl, Wen, Bat, P95, Low, Roa, Inc, JKT, Oxb, Dol, USW*
16 X: KRe; aX: G61, Bel, Oxl, Wen, Bat, P95, Low, Roa, Inc, JKT, Oxb,Dol*
17 X: KRe
18 X: KRe; cX: HIC; bX: MTh, ViA, NM1, NM2; cX: HIC
19 X: KRe, MTh, ViA; aX: NM2; bX: HIP
20 X: KRe, MTh, HIP, ViA; bX: ChM, HIC, SM1
21 X: ChM, KRe, MTh, HIP, HIC, ViA, SM1; bX: Han
22 X: ChM, KRe, MTh, HIP, HIC, ViA, Han, SM1
23 same as 22, less HIC, SM1; aX: HIC, SM1
24 X: KRe, MTh; aX: ViA, Han, BK1
25 X: MTh; aX: KRe; bX: WmS
26 X: MTh, WmS; bX:BK1
27 X: MTh, WmS, BK1

Scene 42

1

2 aX: ChM; bX: HIC

3 X: HIC, PH1; bX: HnF, BK1
4 X: HIC, ViA, BA1, PH1, BK1
5 X: HIC, BA1; aX: ViA, PH1, BK1
6 X: ChM
7 X: ChM, KRe, MB1, MB2; bX: BA1
8 X: ChM, G61, Bel, Oxl, Wen, Bat, P95, Bar, Low, Roa, Inc, JKT, Oxb*
9 X: Oxl, Oxb, WM1, MB1, BK1; aX: ChM, G61, Bel, Wen, Bat, P95, Bar, Low,
    Roa, Inc, JKT, Dol, USW, Cum, HnF, CKP, KRe, Rig, Wm S, ViA, MB2,IP2
10 X: Oxl, Oxb, USW, KRe, HIC, ViA, SM1, JP1; bX: BA1, IP2, PH1, BK1;R:JG1
11 X: Oxl, Oxb, USW, KRe, ViA, BA1, SM1, MB1, JG1; aX: HIC, IP2, PH1, JP1,
    BK1; bX: MB1

**41: 3 JKT, Oxb, Dol, USW, Cum, WM1, KRe, Rig, WmS, HIP, HIC, BA1, SM1,NM1,
   NM2, MB1   *41: 4 USW, Cum, WM1, CKP, KRe, Rig, WmS, HIP,HIC,
   BA1, SM1, NM1, IP1, NM2, MB1, BK1; bX: ChM   *41: 7 NM2, MB1,
   MB2   *41:13 IP2, PH1, BK1   *41:14 ChM, BA1,NM2
*41:15 Cum, WM1, KRe, Rig, WmS, HIP; aX: ChM, Bar   *41:16 USW, Cum,
   WM1, Rig, WmS, HIP   *42: 8 Dol, USW, Cum, WM1, HnF, CKP,
   KRe, Rig, WmS, ViA, BA1, MB1, MB2, BK1; R: GJ1

2259   Cannot amend me: society is no comfort   12
2260   To one not sociable: I am not very sick,   13
2261   Since I can reason of it. Pray you, trust me here: 14
2262   I'll rob none but myself; and let me die,   15
2263   Stealing so poorly.
2264   *Gui.*   I love thee; I have spoke it: 16
2265   How much the quantity, the weight as much,   17
2266   As I do love my father.
2267   *Bel.*   What! how! how!   18
2268   *Arv.* If it be sin to say so, sir, I yoke me   19
2269   In my good brother's fault: I know not why   20   20
2270   I love this youth; and I have heard you say,   21
2271   Love's reason's without reason: the bier at door,   22
2272   And a demand who is't shall die, I'ld say   23
2273   'My father, not this youth.'
2274   *Bel.*   [*Aside*] O noble strain!   24
2275   O worthiness of nature! breed of greatness!   25
2276   Cowards father cowards and base things sire base: 26
2277   Nature hath meal and bran, contempt and grace.   27
2278   I'm not their father; yet who this should be,   28
2279   Doth miracle itself, loved before me.   29
2280   'Tis the ninth hour o' the morn.
2281   *Arv.*   Brother, farewell. 30   30
2282   *Imo.* I wish ye sport.
2283   *Arv.*   You health. So please you, sir.   31
2284   *Imo.* [*Aside*] These are kind creatures. Gods,
2285   what lies I have heard!   32
2286   Our courtiers say all's savage but at court: 33
2287   Experience, O, thou disprovest report!   34
2288   The imperious seas breed monsters, for the dish   35
2289   Poor tributary rivers as sweet fish.   36
2290   I am sick still; heart-sick. Pisanio,   37
2291   I'll now taste of thy drug.   [*Swallows some.*
2292   *Gui.*   I could not stir him: 38
2293   He said he was gentle, but unfortunate;   39
2294   Dishonestly afflicted, but yet honest.   40   40
2295   *Arv.* Thus did he answer me: yet said, here-
       after
2296   I might know more.   41
2297   *Bel.*   To the field, to the field!   42
2298   We'll leave you for this time: go in and rest.   43
2299   *Arv.* We'll not be long away.
2300   *Bel.*   Pray, be not sick,   44
2301   For you must be our housewife.
2302   *Imo.*   Well or ill,   45
2303a   I am bound to you.

12 X: Ox1, Oxb, USW, KRe, BA1, SM1, MB1; a̲X̲ ViA, JG1; b̲X̲: HIC, PH1, BK1
13 X: Ox1,Oxb, USW, SM1, MB1, BK1; a̲X̲: KRe, HIC, BA1, PH1, BK1; b̲X̲:ChM,MB2
14 X: Rig, MB2; a̲X̲: ChM, Ox1, Oxb, U̅S̅W̅, SM1, MB1; b̲X̲: PH1, JG1
15 X: G61, Bel, O̅x̅1, Wen, Bat, P95, Bar, Low, Roa, I̅n̅c̅, JKT, Oxb, Dol,USW,
     Cum, WM1, HnF, CKP, KRe, Rig, WmS, MB1, PH1, JG1, BK1; b̲X̲: Lac, HM1*
16 X: G61, Bel, Ox1, Wen, Bat, P95, Bar, Low, Roa, Inc, JKT, Oxb, Dol,*
17 same as 16, BA1, NM1, NM2; less a̲X̲, b̲X̲; b̲X̲: ChM, HIC

18 same as 17, ChM, HIC, less BA1; less b̲X̲
19 same as 18
20 same as 18; b̲X̲: WM1, CKP
21 same as 18, W̅M̅1, CKP, less ChM; a̲X̲: ChM
22 same as 21, less WM1; less a̲X̲; b̲X̲: ChM, BA1, IP1, IP2, NM1, PH1, BK1
23 X: ChM, G61, Bel, Ox1, Wen, Bat, P95, Bar, Low, Roa, Inc, JKT, Oxb,Dol,
     USW, Cum, CKP, Lac, KRe, Rig, HM1, MTh, HIM, WmS, HIC, ViA, BA1,NM1*
24 same as 23, less ChM, IP1, IP2; a̲X̲: ChM, IP1, IP2; b̲X̲: JP1
25 same as 24, HIP, SM1, MB1; less a̲X̲, b̲X̲
26 same as 25, ChM, MB2, JG1, JP1
27 same as 26, IP2, less HIP
28 same as 27, less SM1, IP2, JG1
29 same as 28, less JP1

30 X: ChM, Low, KRe; a̲X̲: G61, Bel, Ox1, Wen, Bat, P95, Bar, Roa, Inc, JKT,
     Oxb, Dol, USW, Cum, CKP, Lac, Rig, HM1, MTh, HIM, WmS, HIC, ViA,BA1*
31 X: ChM, KRe; b̲X̲: CKP

32 b̲X̲: KRe, WmS; M̲O̲V̲E̲ 32-38a to follow 46: JP1
33 X̲:̲ KRe, WmS
34 X: G61, Bel, Ox1, Wen, Bat, P95, Bar, Low, Roa, Inc, JKT, Oxb, Dol,USW*
35 X: ChM, G61, Bel, Ox1, Wen, Bat, P95, Bar, Low, Roa, Inc, JKT, Oxb, Dol*
36 same as 35, NM1
37 X: NM1

38 b̲X̲: Lac, KRe, Rig, HM1, MTh, HIM, WmS, HIC, ViA, SM1, MB1, MB2, JP1, BK1
39 X̲:̲ Lac, KRe, Rig, HM1, MTh, HIM, WmS, HIC, ViA, SM1, MB1, MB2, JP1, BK1*
40 same as 39, PH1; less b̲X̲

41 X: Lac, KRe, Rig, MTh, HIM, WmS, HIC, ViA, SM1, MB2, JP1, BK1;a̲X̲:HM1, MB1,
     PH1
42 X: BK1; R̲: ChM; a̲X̲: Lac, KRe, Rig, MTh, HIM, WmS, HIC,Via,SM1,MB1,MB2,JP1
43 X: ChM; a̲X̲: BK1

44 a̲X̲: ChM, Han

45 b̲X̲: Bel, WmS

*42:15 MTh, HIM, HIC, ViA, BA1   *42:16 USW, Cum, Lac, KRe, Rig, HM1,
  MTh, HIM, WmS, ViA; a̲X̲: WM1, HnF, CKP, H̅I̅C̅, BA1, MB2, PH1, JG1, BK1;b̲X̲:NM1,NM2
42:23 IP1, NM2, IP2, PH̅1̅, BK1   *42:30 MB1, PH1
*42:34 Cum, CKP, KRe, Rig, WmS, ViA, PH1   *42:35 USW, Cum, HnF, CKP,
  Lac, KRe, Rig, HM1, HIM, WmS, HIC, ViA, BA1, SM1, IP1, NM2, MB1, MB2,IP2,
  PH1, JG1, BK1   *42:39 b̲X̲: PH1

2304	*Bel.* And shalt be ever.	46
2303b	[*Exit Imogen, to the cave.*	
	This youth, howe'er distress'd, appears he hath	
2305	had	47
2306	Good ancestors.	
2307	*Arv.* How angel-like he sings!	48
2308	*Gui.* But his neat cookery! he cut our roots	
2309	In characters,	49
3210	And sauced our broths, as Juno had been sick 50	50
2311	And he her dieter.	
2312	*Arv.* Nobly he yokes	51
2313	A smiling with a sigh, as if the sigh	52
2314	Was that it was, for not being such a smile:	53
2315	The smile mocking the sigh, that it would fly	54
2316	From so divine a temple, to commix	55
2317	With winds that sailors rail at.	
2318	*Gui.* I do note	56
2319	That grief and patience, rooted in him both,	57
2320	Mingle their spurs together.	
2321	*Arv.* Grow, patience!	58
2322	And let the stinking elder, grief, untwine	59
2323	His perishing root with the increasing vine! 60	60
	Bel. It is great morning. Come, away!—	
2324	Who's there?	61
2325	*Enter* CLOTEN.	
2326	*Clo.* I cannot find those runagates; that villain	62
2327	Hath mock'd me. I am faint.	
2328	*Bel.* 'Those runagates!'	63
2329	Means he not us? I partly know him: 'tis	64
2330	Cloten, the son o' the queen. I fear some ambush.	65
2331	I saw him not these many years, and yet	66
2332	I know 'tis he. We are held as outlaws: hence!	67
	Gui. He is but one: you and my brother	
2333	search	68
2334	What companies are near: pray you, away;	69
2335	Let me alone with him.	
2335+1	[*Exeunt Belarius and Arviragus.*	
2336	*Clo.* Soft! What are you 70	70
2337	That fly me thus? some villain mountaineers?	71
2338	I have heard of such. What slave art thou?	
2339	*Gui.* A thing	72
2340	More slavish did I ne'er than answering	73
2341	A slave without a knock.	
2342	*Clo.* Thou art a robber,	74
2343	A law-breaker, a villain: yield thee, thief.	75

*42:56(continued)Oxb, Dol, USW, WM1, HnF, CKP, MB1, JP1   *42:58 NM2,
   MB2, PH1, JG1, BK1; bX: ChM, Bel, Ox1, Bar, Low, Inc, JKT, Oxb, Dol,USW,
   Cum, Wm1, HnC, CKP, JP1   *42:59 Lac, KRe, Rig, HM1, MTh, HIM,
   WmS, HIP, HIC, ViA, Han, BA1, SM1, NM1, NM2, MB2, PH1, JG1, JP1, BK1
*42:66 USW, Cum, KRe, Rig, WmS, BK1; bX: NM2   *42:72 KRe, PH1,
   BK1   *42:74 KRe, PH1, BK1

46 bX: G61, Ox1, Wen, Bat, P95, Bar, Low, Roa, Inc, JKT, Oxb, Dol, USW,
    Cum, MB2; Insert 32-38a: JP1

47 X: MB2, JG1

48 X: MB2; R: Inc; aX: JG1; bX: ChM, WmS, ViA, Han; ADD 1: ViA

49 X: ChM, G61, Bel, Ox1, Wen, Bat, P95, Bar, Low, Roa, Inc, JKT, Oxb,Dol*
50 same as 49

51 X: G61, Bel, Wen, Bat, Bar, KRe, Rig, MTh, WmS, HIP, ViA, Han, MB2; aX:*
52 X: G61, Bel, Wen, Bat, Bar, Lac, KRe, Rig, HM1, MTh, HIM, WmS, HIP,HIC*
53 X: ChM, G61, Bel, Ox1, Wen, Bat, P95, Bar, Low, Roa, Inc, JKT, Oxb,Dol*
54 same as 53, less CKP
55 same as 54, JG1

56 X: ChM, Cum, Lac, KRe, Rig, HM1, MTh, HIM, WmS, HIP, HIC, ViA, Han,BA1*
57 X: Lac, KRe, Rig, HM1, MTh, HIM, WmS, HIP, HIC, ViA, Han, BA1, SM1, NM1,
    NM2, MB1, PH1, JG1, BK1
58 X: Lac, KRe, Rig, HM1, MTh, HIM, WmS, HIP, HIC, ViA, Han, BA1, SM1, NM1*
59 X: ChM, Bel, Ox1, Bar, Low, Inc, JKT, Oxb, Dol, USW, Cum, WM1, HnF, CKP*
60 same as 59

61 X: Han; aX: ChM, Rig, HIP, ViA; ADD 1: Oxb, Inc, JKT, Oxb, Dol, Cum

62

63 cX: Bel, Ox1, Wen, Bat, Bar, Inc, JKT, Oxb, Cum, Rig, WmS, ViA
64
65
66 X: ChM, G61, Bel, Ox1, Wen, Bat, P95, Bar, Low, Roa, Inc, JKT, Oxb, Dol*
67 same as 66, less ChM; less bX; aX: ChM, NM2

68
69

70
71

72 bX: G61, Bel, Ox1, Wen, Bat, Bar, Low, Roa, Inc, JKT, Oxb, Dol, USW, Cum*
73 X: G61, Bel, Ox1, Wen, Bat, Bar, Low, Roa, Inc, JKT, Oxb, Dol, USW,Cum,
    KRe, PH1, BK1
74 aX: G61, Bel, Ox1, Wen, Bat, Bar, Low, Roa, Inc, JKT, Oxb, Dol, USW,Cum*
75 X: PH1, BK1

*42:49 USW, Cum, WM1, CKP, KRe, Rig, MTh, WmS, HIP, ViA, Han, MB2, JP1
*42:51 aX: ChM, Ox1, P95, Low, Roa, Inc, JKT, Oxb, Dol, USW, Cum, WM1, CKP,
    JP1; bX: Lac, HM1, HIM, HIC, BA1, SM1, NM1, NM2, MB1, PH1
*42:52 ViA, Han, BA1, SM1, NM1, NM2, MB1, MB2, PH1; bX: ChM, Ox1, P95, Low,
    Roa, Inc, JKT, Oxb, Dol, USW, Cum, WM1, HnF, CKP, JP1, BK1
42:53 USW, Cum, WM1, HnF, CKP, Lac, KRe, Rig, HM1, MTh, HIM, WmS, HIP, HIC,
    ViA, Han, BA1, SM1, NM1, NM2, MB1, MB2, PH1, JP1, BK1   *42:56 SM1,NM1,
    NM2, MB1, JG1; aX: G61, Bel, Ox1, Wen, Bat, P95, Bar, Low, Roa, Inc, JKT*

	Gui. To who? to thee? What art thou?	
2344	Have not I	76
2345	An arm as big as thine? a heart as big?	77
2346	Thy words, I grant, are bigger, for I wear not	78
2347	My dagger in my mouth. Say what thou art,	79
2348	Why I should yield to thee?	
2349	*Clo.* Thou villain base, 80	80
2350	Know'st me not by my clothes?	
2351	*Gui.* No, nor thy tailor, rascal,	81
2352	Who is thy grandfather: he made those clothes,	82
2353	Which, as it seems, make thee.	
2354	*Clo.* Thou precious varlet,	83
2355	My tailor made them not.	
2356	*Gui.* Hence, then, and thank	84
2357	The man that gave them thee. Thou art some fool :	85
2358	I am loath to beat thee.	
2359	*Clo.* Thou injurious thief,	86
2360	Hear but my name, and tremble.	
2361	*Gui.* What's thy name?	87
2362	*Clo.* Cloten, thou villain.	88
2363	*Gui.* Cloten, thou double villain, be thy name,	89
2364	I cannot tremble at it: were it Toad, or Adder, Spider, **90**	90
2365	'Twould move me sooner.	
2366	*Clo.* To thy further fear,	91
2367	Nay, to thy mere confusion, thou shalt know	92
2368	I am son to the queen.	
2369	*Gui.* I am sorry for 't ; not seeming	93
2370	So worthy as thy birth.	
2371	*Clo.* Art not afeard ?	94
	Gui. Those that I reverence those I fear, the	
2372	wise :	95
2373	At fools I laugh, not fear them.	
2374	*Clo.* Die the death :	96
2375	When I have slain thee with my proper hand,	97
2376	I 'll follow those that even now fled hence,	98
2377	And on the gates of Lud's-town set your heads:	99
2378	Yield, rustic mountaineer. [*Exeunt, fighting.* **100**	100
2379	*Re-enter* BELARIUS *and* ARVIRAGUS.	
2380	*Bel.* No companies abroad ?	101
	Arv. None in the world: you did mistake	
2381	him, sure.	102
2382	*Bel.* I cannot tell: long is it since I saw him,	103
2383	But time hath nothing blurr'd those lines of favour	104

CONTINUATIONS FROM G966b

*41:324 ViA, BA1, SM1; ADD 4: Low, USW˜   *42:325 WM1, CKP, KRe,HM1,
WmS, HIC, SM1, MB2, JG1, BK1; aX: G61, P95, Cum, Lac, Rig, HIM, Han,
BA1, PH1; bX: NM1, NM2   *41:329 317a, 313-314, 320c, 321b,
329: HIC   *42:330 WM1, HnF, CKP, KRe, Rig, ViA, BA1, SM1, IP1;
R: JKT, Do1, USW   *41:333 Do1, USW, Cum, WM1, CKP, Rig, WmS,
JP1; R: HM1, ViA; aX: MB2   *41:336 aX: G61, Bel, Ox1, Wen,Bat,
P95, Bar, Roa, Oxb, WM1, BK1

```
 76
 77
 78   X: BK1
 79   X: BK1

 80   bX: ChM, KRe

 81   X: ChM, KRe; bX: Bat, PH1
 82   X: ChM, KRe, ViA, PH1, JP1, BK1; aX: G61 ,Bel, Wen, Bat, P95,Bar,Roa,
         HIP
 83   X: ChM, KRe, PH1, JP1, BK1; aX: ViA; bX: G61, Bel, Ox1, Wen, Bat, P95,
         Bar, Low, Roa, Inc, JKT, Oxb, Dol, USW, Cum, WM1, CKP, KRe, Rig,WmS*
 84   X: ChM,G61, Bel, Ox1, Wen, Bat, P95, Bar, Low, Roa, Inc, JKT, Oxb,Dol,
         USW, Cum, WM1, CKP, KRe, Rig, WmS, HIC, PH1, JP1; bX: SM1
 85   same as 84, SM1, less PH1, JP1; less bX; aX: PH1, JP1

 86   X: ChM, JKT, SM1; aX: G61, Bel, Ox1, Wen, Bat, P95, Bar, Roa, Inc, Oxb,
         Dol, USW, Cum, WM1, CKP, KRe, Rig, WmS, HIC
 87   aX : JKT, SM1
 88
 89   bX: ViA

 90   aX: ViA; bX: NM1, NM2

 91   aX: NM1, NM2
 92   R: ChM

 93   bX: WmS

 94   X: WmS; R: ChM; bX: NM1, NM2

 95   X: WmS, NM1, NM2

 96   X: WmS; R: ChM; aX: NM1, NM2
 97   X: WmS; bX: ChM
 98   X: WmS, SM1, bX: ChM
 99   X: ChM, WmS, SM1
100   X: WmS


101   X: KRe

102   X: KRe
103   X: G61, Bel, Ox1, Wen, Bat, Bar, Low, Inc, JKT, Oxb, Dol, USW, Cum, WM1*
104   X: KRe, PH1, BK1; R: G61

*42:83 HIC              *42:103 CKP, Rig; aX: KRe
```

2384	**Which** then he wore; the snatches in his voice,	105
2385	**And** burst of speaking, were as his: I am absolute	106
2386	**'Twas** very Cloten.	
2387	*Arv.* In this place we left them:	107
2388	I wish my brother make good time with him,	108
2389	You say he is so fell.	
2390	*Bel.* Being scarce made up,	109
2391	I mean, to man, he had not apprehension 110	110
2392	Of roaring terrors: for the effect of judgement	111
2393,5	Is oft the cause of fear. But, see, thy brother.	112
2394	*Re-enter* GUIDERIUS, *with* CLOTEN's *head.*	
2396	*Gui.* This Cloten was a fool, an empty purse;	113
2397	There was no money in't: not Hercules	114
	Could have knock'd out his brains, for he had	
2398	none:	115
2399	Yet I not doing this, the fool had borne	116
2400	My head as I do his.	
2401	*Bel.* What hast thou done?	117
	Gui. I am perfect what: cut off one Cloten's	
2402	head,	118
2403	Son to the queen, after his own report:	119
2404	Who call'd me traitor, mountaineer, and swore 120	120
2405	With his own single hand he 'ld take us in,	121
	Displace our heads where—thank the gods!—they	
2406	grow,	122
2407	And set them on Lud's-town.	
2408	*Bel.* We are all undone	123
	Gui. Why, worthy father, what have we to	
2409	lose,	124
2410	But that he swore to take, our lives? The law	125
2411	Protects not us: then why should we be tender	126
2412	To let an arrogant piece of flesh threat us,	127
2413	Play judge and executioner all himself,	128
2414	For we do fear the law? What company	129
2415	Discover you abroad?	
2416	*Bel.* No single soul 130	130
2417	Can we set eye on: but in all safe reason	131
	He must have some attendants. Though his	
2418	humour	132
2419	Was nothing but mutation, ay, and that	133
2420	From one bad thing to worse; not frenzy, not	134
2421	Absolute madness could so far have raved	135
2422	To bring him here alone; although perhaps	136
2423	It may be heard at court that such as we	137
2424	Cave here, hunt here, are outlaws, and in time	138

*42:134 USW, Cum, HnF, Lac, KRe, Rig, HM1, MTh, HIM, WmS, HIP, HIC, ViA,
     BA1, SM1, MB1, PH1, JG1, JP1, BK1; R: ChM; aX: WM1, CKP, NM1, NM2, IP2
*42:135 USW, Cum, HnF, Lac, KRe, Rig, HM1, MTh, HIM, WmS, HIP, HIC, ViA,
     BA1, SM1, MB1, MB2, PH1, JG1, JP1, BK1

105 X: PH1, BK1; aX: KRe
106 X: PH1, BK1

107 X: PH1; aX: BK1; bX: HnF, KRe, MTh, ViA, MB1, MB2
108 X: G61, Bel, Ox1, Wen, Bat, P96, Bar, Low, Roa, Inc, JKT, Oxb, Dol,
    USW, Cum, WM1, HnF, CKP, Lac, KRe, Rig, HM1, MTh, HIM, WmS, HIC,ViA*
109 same as 108, less JKT, Oxb, HIC; same R; bX: JKT, BA1, IP1,PH1,JG1,BK1
110 same as 109, ChM, JKT, BA1, IP1, PH1, JG1, BK1; less R, bX
111 same as 110, HIC
112 X: JKT, KRe, BA1, IP1, MB1, MB2, BK1; aX ChM, G61, Bel, Ox1, Wen,Bat,
    P95, Bar, Low, Roa, Inc, Oxb, Dol, USW, Cum, WM1,HnF, CKP, Lac,Rig,
    HM1, MTh, HIM, WmS, HIC, ViA, SM1, PH1, JG1
113 bX: ChM, G61, Bel, Ox1, Wen, Bat, P95, Bar, Low, Roa, Inc, JKT, Oxb*
114 aX : ChM, G61, Bel, Ox1, Wen, Bat, P95, Bar, Low, Roa, Inc, JKT, Oxb,
    Dol, USW, WM1, CKP, KRe, Rig, SM1, PH1; bX: BK1
115 X: BK1
116 X: ChM, G61, Bel, Ox1, Wen, Bat, P95, Bar, Low, Roa, Inc, JKT, Oxb,
    USW, Cum, WM1, HnF, CKP, KRe, Rig, HIC, ViA, SM1, IP1, PH1, BK1;bX:IP2
117 X: PH1; aX: ChM, G61, Bel, Ox1, Wen, Bat, P95, Bar, Low, Roa, Inc,JKT,
    Oxb, USW, Cum, WM1, HnF, CKP, KRe, Rig, HIC, ViA, SM1, IP1,IP2, BK1
118 aX: ChM, G61, Bel, Ox1, Wen, Bat, P95, Bar, Low, Roa, Inc, JKT, Oxb*
119 aX: PH1; bX: BK1
120 X: G61, Bel, Wen, Bat, P95, Bar, Roa, HIC, NM1, BK1; aX: ViA
121 same as 120, SM1, NM2; less aX

122 same as 121, ViA

123 X: HIC, SM1; aX: G61, Bel, Wen, Bat, P95, Bar, Roa, ViA, NM1, NM2, BK1;
    bX: KRe
124 X: KRe, HIC, SM1
125 X: KRe, HIP, HIC, SM1; bX: WmS, PH1, BK1
126 X: KRe, WmS, HIP, HIC, SM1, PH1, BK1
127 same as 126
128 ChM, HnF, KRe, WmS, HIP, HIC, PH1, BK1
129 X: KRe, WmS, HIP, HIC, ViA, SM1, PH1, BK1; aX: ChM, HnF; bX: Lac,Rig,
    HM1, MTh, HIM
130 X: Lac, KRe, Rig, HM1, MTh, HIM, WmS, HIP, HIC, ViA, SM1, PH1
131 same as 130; bX: JP1

132 same as 131, JP1; bX: ChM, G61, Bel, Ox1, Wen, Bat, P95, Bar, Low,Roa*
133 X: G61, Bel, Wen, Bat, P95, Bar, Low, Roa, Inc, JKT, Dol, USW, CumWM1*
134 X: G61, Bel, Ox1, Wen, Bat, P95, Bar, Low, Roa, Inc, JKT, Oxb, Dol*
135 X: ChM, G61, Bel, Ox1, Wen, Bat, P95, Bar, Low, Roa, Inc, JKT, Oxb,Dol*
136 same as 135; less PH1, JG1, JP1; aX: PH1, JG1, JP1;bX:WM1,CKP,NM1,NM2
137 same as 136, WM1, CKP, NM1; NM2; less aX, bX
138 same as 137; bX: PH1, JG1

*42:108 SM1, MB1, MB2; R: ChM   *42:113 Cum, WM1, KRe, Rig,SM1,
  PH1   *42:118 Dol, USW, Cum, WM1, HnF, CKP, KRe, Rig, HIC,
  IP1, PH1   *42:132 Inc, JKT, Oxb, Dol, USW, Cum, WM1, HnF,
  CKP, BA1, NM1, NM2, MB1, MB2, IP2, JG1, BK1   *42:133 HnF, CKP,
  Lac, KRe, Rig, HM1, MTh, HIM, WmS, HIP, HIC, ViA, BA1, SM1, NM1, NM2,MB1,
  MB2, IP2, PH1, JG1, JP1, BK1 ; R: ChM, Oxb, Ox1

	May make some stronger head; the which is	
2425	hearing—	139
2426	As it is like him—might break out, and swear is	140
2427	He'ld fetch us in; yet is't not probabie	141
2428	To come alone, either he so undertaking,	142
	Or they so suffering: then on good ground we	
2429	fear,	143
2430	If we do fear this body hath a tail	144
2431	More perilous than the head.	
2432	*Arv.* Let ordinance	145
2433	Come as the gods foresay it: howsoe'er,	146
2434	My brother hath done well.	
2435	*Bel.* I had no mind	147
2436	To hunt this day: the boy Fidele's sickness	148
2437	Did make my way long forth.	
2438	*Gui.* With his own swo	149
	Which he did wave against my throat, I ha	
2439	ta'en ه	150
2440	His head from him: I'll throw't into the creek	151
2441	Behind our rock; and let it to the sea,	152
2442	And tell the fishes he's the queen's son, Cloten:	153
2443	That's all I reck. [*Exi*	
2444	*Bel.* I fear 'twill be revenged:	154
	Would, Polydore, thou hadst not done't! thy	
2445	valour	155
2446	Becomes thee well enough.	
2447	*Arv.* Would I had done't	156
2448	So the revenge alone pursued me! Polydore,	157
2449	I love thee brotherly, but envy much	158
	Thou hast robb'd me of this deed: I would re	
2450	venges,	159
	That possible strength might meet, would seek	
2451	us through ه	160
2452	And put us to our answer.	
2453	*Bel.* Well, 'tis done:	161
2454	We'll hunt no more to-day, nor seek for dange	162
2455	Where there's no profit. I prithee, to our roc	163
2456	You and Fidele play the cooks: I'll stay	164
2457	Till hasty Polydore return, and bring him	165
2458	To dinner presently.	
2459	*Arv.* Poor sick Fidele!	166
2460	I'll willingly to him: to gain his colour	167
2461	I'ld let a parish of such Clotens blood,	168
2462	And praise myself for charity. [*Exi*	
2463	*Bel.* O thou goddess, n	169
2464	Thou divine Nature, how thyself thou blazon's	170

*42:161 Low, Roa, Inc, JKT, Oxb, Dol, USW, Cum, WM1, HnF, CKP, Lac, Rig, HM1, MTh, HIM, WmS, BA1, SM1, IP1, MB1, MB2, IP2, PH1, JP1, BK1

139 same as 137, PH1, JG1
140 same as 139
141 X: ChM, Ox1, Oxb, WM1, HnF, CKP, Lac, KRe, Rig, HM1, MTh, HIM, WmS*
142 same as 141, IP2; less aX; bX: G61, Bel, Wen, Bat, P95, Bar, Low, Roa,
        Inc, JKT, Dol, USW, Cum, JG1, JP1
143 X: ChM, G61, Bel, Ox1, Wen, Bat, P95, Bar, Low, Roa, Inc, JKT, Oxb, Dol*
144 same as 143, less JG1; less aX

145 same as 144, less P95, Roa, BA1, MB1, MB2, JP1; aX: P95, Roa, BA1*
146 same as 145, less Bel, BK1; less aX; bX; aX: Bel, Wen, PH1, BK1

147 X: G61, WM1, CKP, Lac, Rig, HM1, MTh, HIM, WmS, HIP, HIC, SM1; aX: Ox1*
148 X: ChM, G61, WM1, CKP, Lac, Rig, HM1, MTh, HIM, WmS, HIP, HIC, ViA,
        SM1, NM1, NM2, MB1, MB2, PH1, JG1, BK1
149 X: HIC, ViA; aX: ChM, G61, WM1, CKP, Lac, Rig, HM1, MTh, HIM, WmS, HIP,
        SM1, NM2, MB1, MB2, PH1, JG1, BK1
150 X: HIC, MB2; R: ChM
151 aX : HIC; bX: KRe
152 aX : KRe
153

154 aX : ViA; bX: MB1

155 X: NM1; bX: ViA, PH1; N: MB1

156 X: ViA, NM1; aX: PH1; bX: NM2
157 X: G61, Bel, Ox1, Wen, Bat, P95, Bar, Low, Roa, Inc, JKT, Oxb, Dol*
158 same as 157, HnF, SM1, MB1, MB2, PH1, BK1; less bX

159 same as 158, less PH1; bX: ChM, Lac, HM1, MTh, HIM, WmS, BA1, IP1, IP2
        PH1
160 same as 159, ChM, Lac, HM1, MTh, HIM, WmS, BA1, IP1, IP2; less bX

161 X: KRe, HIC, ViA, NM1, NM2; aX: ChM, G61, Bel, Ox1, Wen, Bat, p95, Bar*
162 R : ChM; bX: HnF, KRe, HIP, BK1
163 R : ChM, BK1; aX: HnF, KRe, HIP; bX: Ox1, JKT, Oxb, USW
164 X: ChM; bX: NM2
165 X: ChM, NM2; bX: BK1

166 aX: ChM, NM2, BK1; bX: KRe
167 X: KRe; R: ChM; aX: Bel, Wen, Bat, Bar; bX: WmS, BK1
168 X: KRe, NM2, BK1; R: ChM; ADD 2: ChM

169 X: KRe; aX: ChM, NM2, BK1
170 X: KRe

*42:141 HIP, HIC, ViA, BA1, SM1, NM1, NM2, MB1, MB2, PH1, BK1; aX: G61, Bel,
    Wen, Bat, P95, Bar, Low, Roa, JKT, Dol, USW, JG1; bX: IP2; R: Inc, Cum
*42:143 USW, Cum, WM1, HnF, CKP, Lac, KRe, Rig, HM1, MTh, HIM, WmS, HIP, HIC,
    ViA, BA1, SM1, MB2; aX: NM1, NM2, MB1, IP2, PH1, JG1, JP1, BK1
*42:145 MB2, JP1; bX: PH1   *42:147 Bar, Low, Inc, JKT, Oxb; bX:
    ChM, Dol, USW, Cum, HnF, KRe, ViA, NM1   *42:157 USW, Cum, WM1,
    CKP, KRe, Rig, ViA, NM1, NM2, JP1; bX: HnF, SM1, HIC, MB1, MB2, BK1

2465	In these two princely boys! They are as gentle	171
2466	As zephyrs blowing below the violet,	172
2467	Not wagging his sweet head; and yet as rough,	173
2468	Their royal blood enchafed, as the rudest wind,	174
2469	That by the top doth take the mountain pine,	175
2470	And make him stoop to the vale. 'Tis wonder	176
2471	That an invisible instinct should frame them	177
2472	To royalty unlearn'd, honour untaught,	178
2473	Civility not seen from other, valour	179
2474	That wildly grows in them, but yields a crop 180	180
2475	As if it had been sow'd. Yet still it's strange	181
2476	What Cloten's being here to us portends,	182
2477	Or what his death will bring us.	
2478	*Re-enter* GUIDERIUS.	
2479	*Gui.* Where's my brother?	183
2480	I have sent Cloten's clotpoll down the stream,	184
2481	In embassy to his mother: his body's hostage	185
2482	For his return. [*Solemn music.*	
2483	*Bel.* My ingenious instrument!	186
2484	Hark, Polydore, it sounds! But what occasion	187
2485	Hath Cadwal now to give it motion? Hark!	188
2486	*Gui.* Is he at home?	
2487	*Bel.* He went hence even now.	189
2488	*Gui.* What does he mean? since death of my	
2489	dear'st mother 190	190
2490	It did not speak before. All solemn things	191
2491	Should answer solemn accidents. The matter?	192
2492	Triumphs for nothing and lamenting toys	193
2493	Is jollity for apes and grief for boys.	194
2494	Is Cadwal mad?	
2495	*Bel.* Look, here he comes,	195
2496	And brings the dire occasion in his arms	196
2497	Of what we blame him for.	
2498	*Re-enter* ARVIRAGUS, *with* IMOGEN, *as dead,*	
2499	*bearing her in his arms.*	
2500	*Arv.* The bird is dead	197
2501	That we have made so much on. I had rather	198
2502	Have skipp'd from sixteen years of age to sixty,	199
2503	To have turn'd my leaping-time into a crutch, 200	200
2504	Than have seen this.	
2505	*Gui.* O sweetest, fairest lily!	201
2506	My brother wears thee not the one half so well	202
2507	As when thou grew'st thyself.	
2508	*Bel.* O melancholy!	203

*42:195 P95, Bar, Low, Roa, Inc, JKR, Oxb, Dol, USW, Cum, WM1, CKP, KRe, HIC, BA1, SM1, NM1, NM2; bX: Lac, MTh, HIM, BK1   *42:197 HIM, WmS, NM1, IP1, NM2, MB2, PH1, BK1

171 X: KRe; bX: SM1, NM2
172 X: KRe, S̄M̄1, NM2
173 same as 172
174 same as 172
175 same as 172
176 same as 172; bX: HnF, HIP, HIC, ViA, BA1, NM1, IP1, MB1, MB2, PH1,*
177 X: HnF, KRe, H̄ĪP, HIC, ViA, BA1, SM1, NM1, IP1, NM2, MB1, MB2, PH1*
178 same as 177, b X: BK1
179 same as 177, B̄K̄1; bX: IP2
180 same as 179, IP2; l̄ess bX
181 X: HnF, KRe, HIP, HIC, V̄iA, SM1, BK1; aX, BA1, NM11 IP1, NM2, MB1,MB2*
182 same as 181; less aX; ADD 2: NM2

183 aX : HnF, KRe, HIP, HIC, ViA, SM1, BK1; bX: NM2, JG1
184 X: NM2
185 X: NM2; bX: MB1; abX: BK1

186 X: NM2, MB1; bX: HIP, NM1, MB2, PH1; cX: BK1
187 X: NM1, NM2, M̄B1, MB2, PH1
188 same as 187, USW; bX: Ox1

189 X: Ox1, Oxb, Lac, KRe, Rig, HIM, WmS, NM1, NM2, MB1, MB2, PH1, BK1; aX:
    USW, HM1
190 X: HIC, NM1, NM2, MB1, MB2, PH1; aX: Ox1, Oxb, Rig; bX: JG1
191 same as 190; less aX, bX; bX: WM1, H̄nF, CKP, BA1, BK̄1
192 X: WM1, HnF, CKP, W̄mS, HIC, BA1, NM1, NM2, MB1, MB2, PH1, BK1; bX: G61*
193 X: ChM, G61, Bel, Ox1, Wen, Bat, P95, Bar, Low, Roa, Inc, JKT, Ōxb*
194 same as 193

195 X: HnF, Rig, WmS, IP1, MB1, MB2, PH1; aX: ChM, G61, Bel, Ox1, Wen, Bat*
196 X: Ox1, Low, Inc, JKT, Oxb, Dol, USW, C̄um, HnF, Lac, KRe, Rig, HM1, MTh
       HIM, WmS, WM1, IP1, NM2, MB1, MB2, PH1, BK1

197 aX : Ox1, Low, Inc, JKT, Oxb, Dol, USW, Cum, HnF, Lac, KRe, Rig, HM1,MTh*
198 bX: KRe, HIP, ViA, NM1, NM2, MB2, BK1
199 X: KRe, HIP, ViA, NM1, NM2, MB2, BK1
200 X: G61, Bel, Ox1, Wen, Bat, Bar, Inc, JKT, Oxb, Dol, USW, Cum, WM1,HnF,
    CKP, KRe, HIP, ViA, BA1, NM1, NM2, MB2, BK1
201 X: ViA; aX: KRe, HIP, NM1, NM2, MB2, BK1; bX: HnF, HIC; ADD 1:Low,Inc,JKT
202 X: Bel, Ōx1, Wen, Bat, P95, Bar, Low, Roa, Īnc, JKT, Oxb, Dol, USW, WM1,
    HnF, CKP, Lac, Rig, HM1, MTh, HIM, WmS, ViA, SM1; R: G61, Cum, HIC
203 X: Bat, P95, Roa, Inc, JKT, Dol, USW, WM1, HnF, CKP, L̄ac, Rig, HM1, MTh,
    HIM, WmS, HIC, ViA; R: G61, Cum; aX: Oxb, SM1; bX: Bel, Wen, Bar,KRe,
    BA1, NM1, IP1, NM2, ĪP2, PH1, JG1, BK1; MOVE 203b-208 to follow 251:
    G61, Ox1, Low, Oxb

*42:176 JG1, JP1   *42:177 JG1, JP1   *42:181 IP2, PH1,
  JG1, JP1   *42:192 Bel, Ox1, Wen, Bat, P95, Bar, Low, Roa, Inc,
  JKT, Oxb, Dol, USW, Cum, Lac, KRe, Rig, HM1, HIM, HIP, JG1
*42:193 Dol, USW, Cum, Wml, HnF, CKP, Lac, KRe, Rig, HM1, HIM, WmS, HIP,HIC,
  ViA, BA1, SM1, NM1, IP1, NM2, MB1, MB2, IP2, PH1, JG1, BK1

2509	Who ever yet could sound thy bottom? find	204
2510	The ooze, to show what coast thy sluggish crare	205
2511	Might easiliest harbour in? Thou blessed thing!	206
	Jove knows what man thou mightst have made:	
2512	but I,	207
2513	Thou diedst, a most rare boy, of melancholy.	208
2514	How found you him?	
2515	*Arv.* Stark, as you see: 209	209
2516	Thus smiling, as some fly had tickled slumber.	210
	Not as death's dart, being laugh'd at: his right	
2517	cheek	211
2518	Reposing on a cushion.	
2519	*Gui.* Where?	
2520	*Arv.* O' the floor:	212
2521	His arms thus leagued: I thought he slept, and put	213
	My clouted brogues from off my feet, whose rude-	
2522	ness	214
2523	Answer'd my steps too loud.	
2524	*Gui.* Why, he but sleeps:	215
2525	If he be gone, he'll make his grave a bed:	216
2526	With female fairies will his tomb be haunted,	217
2527	And worms will not come to thee.	
2528	*Arv.* With fairest flowers	218
2529	Whilst summer lasts and I live here, Fidele, 21ö	219
2530	I'll sweeten thy sad grave: thou shalt not lack	220
2531	The flower that's like thy face, pale primrose, nor	221
2532	The azured harebell, like thy veins, no, nor	222
2533	The leaf of eglantine, whom not to slander,	223
2534	Out-sweeten'd not thy breath: the ruddock would,	224
2535	With charitable bill,—O bill, sore-shaming	225
2536	Those rich-left heirs that let their fathers lie	226
2537	Without a monument!—bring thee all this:	227
	Yea, and furr'd moss besides, when flowers are	
2538	none,	
2539		228
2539	To winter-ground thy corse.	
2540	*Gui.* Prithee, have done:	229
2541	And do not play in wench-like words with that	230
2542	Which is so serious. Let us bury him, 231	231
2543	And not protract with admiration what	232
2544	Is now due debt. To the grave!	
2545	*Arv.* Say, where shall's lay him?	233
2546	*Gui.* By good Euriphile, our mother.	
2547	*Arv.* Be't so:	234
2548	And let us, Polydore, though now our voices	235
	Have got the mannish crack, sing him to the	
2549	ground.	236

*42:229 Cum, WM1, HnF, CKP, HIC, BK1; aX: Lac, Rig, HM1, HIM, WmS, ViA,
  Han, SM1, IP1, JP1   *42:131 Cum, Rig; aX: WM1, HnF, CKP, KRe, WmS,
  HIc, ViA

204 X: Bel, Wen, Bat, P95, Bar, Roa, Inc, JKT, Dol, USW, Cum, WM1, HnF*
205 same as 204, HIP; less bX
206 X: Bel, Wen, Bat, P95 Bar, Roa, Inc, JKT, Dol, USW, Cum, HnF, CKP,Lac,
       Rig, HM1, MTh, HIM, WmS, HIC, MB1, MB2, BK1; aX: WM1, KRe, HIP,ViA*
207 same as 206, WM1, ViA, PH1, JG1, less HnF, MB1, MB2; less aX
208 same as 207, HIP, less ViA, PH1, JG1

209 X: Bat, Oxb, HIC; aX: Roa, Dol, USW; bX: Oxl, Wen, P95, Low, Inc,JKT*
210 X: Dol, USW, HIC, ViA; aX: Bar, Inc, JKT; bX: G61, Bat

211 X: HnF, HIC, ViA, BK1; bX: SM1, IP2, JP1

212 X: HIC, IP2, BK1; aX: HnF, ViA, SM1, JP1; bX: KRe, NM2
213 X: KRe, HIC, IP2; aX: Bel, Bar, NM2; bX: Oxl, Low, Inc, JKT, Oxb, Dol,
       USW, Cum, WM1, HnF, CKP, Lac, Rig, HM1, HIM, WmS, ViA, Han
214 X: Oxl, Inc, JKT, Dol, USW, Cum, WM1, HnF, CKP, Lac, KRe, Rig, HM1,HIM ,
       WmS, HIC, ViA, Han, IP2, BK1
215 X: Oxl, Roa, Inc, JKT, Oxb, Dol, USW, Cum, HnF, IP2, BK1; aX: WM1, CKP*
216 X: Bel, Oxl, Wen, Bat, Bar, Low, Inc, JKT, Oxb, Dol, USW, Cum, HnF,Han*
217 same as 216, less BK1

218 same as 217, less Han, IP2; aX: Han, IP2
219 same as 218; less aX
220 same as 219, Cum; bX: G61, P95, Roa
221 same as 220, G61, P95, Roa
222 same as 221; bX: BK1
223 same as 221, BK1; bX: ViA, JP1
224   same as 223, ViA, JP1; bX: WM1, CKP, Lac, Rig, HM1, HIM, WmS, HIC*
225 same as 224, IP1, less HM1; less bX; bX: ChM, KRe, BA1, NM2, IP2,PH1,JG1
226 X: ChM, G61, Bel, Oxl, Wen, Bat, P95, Bar, Low, Roa, Inc, JKT, Oxb,Dol*
227 same as 266, less ChM, BA1, NM1, NM2, IP2, PH1, JG1; less aX; aX: ChM,
       BA1, NM1, NM2, IP2, PH1, JG1
228 same as 227; less aX

229 X: G61, Bel, Oxl, Wen, Bat, P95, Bar, Low, Roa, Inc, JKT, Oxb, Dol,USW*
230 same as 229, KRe, Rig, WmS, ViA
231 X: G61, Bel, Oxl, Wen, Bat, P95, Bar, Low, Roa, Inc, JKT, Oxb, Dol,USW*
232 same as 231, KRe, PH1, BK1; less aX

233 same as 232, less Rig; aX: Rig; bX: WM1, CKP, HIC, NM1, NM2, MB2,JP1

234 same as 233, HIC, WM1, NM2, MB2, less BK1; less aX, bX; aX: WM1, CKP, JP1
235 same as 234, ChM, less HIC, PH1; less aX; bX: WM1, HnF, CKP, KRe, Rig,
       HIC, ViA
236 same as 235, SM1, BK1;less bX; bX: WM1, HnF, CKP, KRe, Rig, HIC, ViA

*42:204 CKP, Lac, KRe, Rig, HM1, MTh, HIM, WmS, HIC, ViA, BA1, SM1, NM1,IP1,
   NM2, MB1, MB2, IP2, PH1, JG1, JP1, BK1; bX: HIP ;B.B./   *42:206 BA1,SM1,
   NM1, IP1, NM2, IP2, PH1, JG1, JP1   *42:209 Cum, ViA, BK1
*42:215 Lac, KRe, Rig, HM1, HIM; bX: G61, Bel, Wen, Bat, Bar, Low, WmS, HIC,
   ViA, Han   *42:216 IP2, BK1   *42:224 Han, SM1, NM1
*42:226 USW, Cum, WM1, HnF, CKP, Lac, Rig, HM1, HIM, WmS, HIC, ViA, Han, BA1,
   SM1, NM1, IP1, NM2, IP2, PH1, JG1, JP1, BK1; aX: KRe

2550	**As** once our mother: use like note and words,	237
2551	Save that Euriphile must be Fidele.	238
1552	*Gui.* Cadwal,	239
1553	I cannot sing: I'll weep, and word it with thee:	240
1554	For notes of sorrow out of tune are worse **241**	241
2555	Than priests and fanes that lie.	
2556	*Arv.* We'll speak it, then.	242
	Bel. Great griefs, I see, medicine the less;	
2557	for Cloten	243
2558	Is quite forgot. He was a queen's son, boys;	244
2559	And though he came our enemy, remember	245
	He was paid for that: though mean and mighty,	
2560	rotting	246
2561	Together, have one dust, yet reverence,	247
2562	That angel of the world, doth make distinction	248
	Of place 'tween high and low. Our foe was	
2563	princely:	249
2564	And though you took his life, as being our foe,	250
2565	Yet bury him as a prince.	
2566	*Gui.* Pray you, fetch him hither. **251**	251
2567	Thersites' body is as good as Ajax',	252
2568	When neither are alive.	
2569	*Arv.* If you'll go fetch him,	253
2570	We'll say our song the whilst. Brother, begin.	254
2570+1	[*Exit Belarius.*	
	Gui. Nay, Cadwal, we must lay his head to	
2571	the east:	255
2572	My father hath a reason for't.	
2573	*Arv.* 'Tis true.	256
2574	*Gui.* Come on then, and remove him.	
2575	*Arv.* So. Begin.	257

2576	**SONG.**	

2577	*Gui.* **Fear no more the heat o' the sun,**	258
2578	**Nor the furious winter's rages;**	259
2579	**Thou thy worldly task hast done, 260**	260
2580	**Home art gone, and ta'en thy wages:**	261
2581	**Golden lads and girls all must,**	262
2582	**As chimney-sweepers, come to dust.**	263

2583	*Arv.* **Fear no more the frown o' the great;**	264
2584	**Thou art past the tyrant's stroke;**	265
2585	**Care no more to clothe and eat:**	266
2586	**To thee the reed is as the oak:**	267
2587	**The sceptre, learning, physic, must**	268
2588	**All follow this, and come to dust.**	269

*42:251 Do1, Cum, KReRig, WmS; cX: WM1; ADD 7: Roa;; ADD 10: Bat, Inc, USW;
ADD 11: Cum; ADD: 12: JKT, Do1; ADD 12, insert 203b-208, add 4: Ox1,Low,
Oxb; ADD 4, insert 203b-208 G61   *42:252 Bar; bX: Wen; ADD 10:Wen
*42:253 SM1, NM1, MB2, IP2; R: Bel, Bar; aX: WM1, HnF, CKP, KRe, Rig, HIP,
NM2, MB1, JP1   *42:255 R: Bel, Bar   *42:260 Insert 43:
1-54: Low, Do1, USW   *42:261 Inc, JKT, Oxb   *42:262 Ox1,
Bar, Inc, JKT, Oxb   *42:263 Insert 44: 1-55:Inc
*42: 264 USW, Cum, HM1

237 same as 236, HIC, PH1, JP1; less aX; bX: MTh, ViA, IP1, IP2, JG1
238 same as 237, WM1, CKP, MTh, ViA, IP1, IP2, JG1; less BX; aX: JP1
239 X: ChM, G61, Bel, Ox1, Wen, Bat, P95, Bar, Low, Roa, Inc, JKT, Oxb*
240 same as 239, WM1, less BK1; aX: BK1
241 X: ChM, G61, Bel, Ox1, Wen, Bat, P95, Bar, Low, Roa, Inc, JKT, Oxb,
        Dol, USW, Cum, HnF, CKP, Rig, WmS, ViA, NM1, NM2, MB1, MB2, PH1*
242 X: ChM, G61, Bel, Ox1, Wen, Bat, P95, Bar, Low, Roa, Inc, JKT, Oxb,
        Dol, USW, Cum, CKP, KRe, WmS, MB1, MB2, JP1; aX: HnF, Rig, ViA*
243 X: MB2, JP1
244 X: MB2, JP1; bX: MB1
245 X: KRe, ViA, BA1, MB1, MB2, JP1, BK1

246 same as 245; bX: G61, Bel, Ox1, Wen, Bat, P95, Bar, Low, Roa, Inc,JKT*
247 X: G61, Bel, Ox1, Wen, Bat, P95, Bar, Low, Roa, Inc, JKT, Oxb, Dol*
248 same as 247

249 X: KRe, BA1, NM1, NM2, MB2, JG1, JP1; aX: G61, Bel, Ox1, Wen, Bat,*
250 X: NM1, NM2, MB1, JP1

251 X: MB2, PH1; R: CKP; bX: G61, Bel, Ox1, Bat, Bar, Roa, Inc, JKT,Oxb*
252 X: G61, Ox1, Bat, Low, Roa, Inc, JKT, Oxb, Dol, USW, Cum, WM1, HnF,
        CKP, KRe, Rig, WmS, HIP, SM1, NM1, NM2, MB1, MB2, IP2, JP1; R: Bel*
253 X: G61, Ox1, Wen, Bat, Low, Roa, Inc, JKT, Oxb, Dol, USW, Cum, WmS*
254 same as 253, ChM, less WmS, SM1, NM1, IP2; less R, aX; R: Bel,Bar;
        aX: WmS; bX: WM1, CKP

255 X: G61, Ox1, Wen, Bat, Low, Roa, Inc, JKT, Oxb, Dol, USW, Cum, WM1,
        HnF, CKP, Lac, Rig, MTh, HIM, WmS, ViA, Han, BA1, NM1, NM2,MB1, MB2:*
256 same as 255, HM1, PH1; same R; aX: NM2

257 X: ChM, G61, Ox1, Wen, Bat, Low, Inc, JKT, Oxb, Dol, USW, Lac, Rig,
        HM1, MTh, HIM, ViA, BA1, NM2, MB1, MB2; less R, aX; R: Bel, Bar,Cum;
        aX: Roa, WM1, HnF, CKP, WmS, Han, NM1; ADD 3: Bel, Bar
258 X: ChM, Oxb, HM1; R: Cum; N: Inc
259 X: ChM, HM1; R: Cum
260 X: ChM, Cum, HM1; ADD 3: Dol; ADD 3, insert 43: 1-46: Wen, Bat, Roa;*
261 X: ChM, Wen, Bat, Low, Roa, Dol, USW, Cum, HM1; R: G61, Bel, Ox1, Bar*
262 X: ChM, Wen, Bat, Low, Roa, Dol, USW, Cum, KRe, HM1, ViA; R: G61, Bel*
263 X: ChM, Wen, Bat, Low, Roa, Dol, USW, Cum, KRe, HM1, ViA; R: G61, Bel,
        Ox1, Bar, Inc, JKT, Oxb; Insert 43: 1-46: Bel, Ox1, Bar, Inc,JKT;*
264 X: ChM, G61, Bel, Ox1, Wen, Bat, Bar, Low, Roa, Inc, JKT, Oxb, Dol*
265 same as 264
266 same as 264
267 same as 264
268 same as 264, KRe
269 same as 268

*42:239 Dol, USW, Cum, NM1, NM2, MB1, MB2, JP1, BK1   *42:241 aX:WM1
*42:242 NM1, NM2, JG1   *42:246 Oxb, Dol, USW, Cum, WM1, HnF, CKP,
   Lac, Rig, HM1, MTh, HIM, WmS, HIP, HIC, SM1, IP1, IP2, PH1, JG1
*42:246 USW, Cum, WM1, HnF, CKP, KRe, Rig, HM1, MTh, HIM, WmS, HIP, HIC, ViA,.
   BA1, SM1, IP1, MB1, MB2, IP2, PH1, JG1, JP1, BK1   *42:249 P95,Bar,
   Low, Roa, Inc, JKT, Oxb, Dol, USW, Cum, WM1, HnF, CKP, Lac, Rig, HM1, MTh,
   HIM, WmS, HIP, HIC, ViA, SM1, IP1, MB1, IP2, PH1, BK1

2589	*Gui.* Fear no more the lightning-flash, **270**	270
2590	*Arv.* Nor the all-dreaded thunder-stone;	271
2591	*Gui.* Fear not slander, censure rash;	272
2592	*Arv.* Thou hast finish'd joy and moan:	273
2593	*Both.* All lovers young, all lovers must	274
2594	Consign to thee, and come to dust.	275
2595	*Gui.* No exorciser harm thee!	276
2596	*Arv.* Nor no witchcraft charm thee!	277
2597	*Gui.* Ghost unlaid forbear thee!	278
2598	*Arv.* Nothing ill come near thee!	279
2599	*Both.* Quiet consummation have; **280**	280
2600	And renowned be thy grave!	281
2601	*Re-enter* BELARIUS, *with the body of* CLOTEN.	
2602	*Gui.* We have done our obsequies: come, lay	
2603	him down.	282
	Bel. Here's a few flowers; but 'bout midnight,	
2604	more:	283
2605	The herbs that have on them cold dew o' the night	284
2606	Are strewings fitt'st for graves. Upon their faces.	285
2607	You were as flowers, now wither'd: even so	286
2608	These herblets shall, which we upon you strew.	287
2609	Come on, away: apart upon our knees.	288
2610	The ground that gave them first has them again:	289
2611	Their pleasures here are past. so is their pain. 290	290
2611+1	[*Exeunt Belarius, Guiderius, and Arviragus.*	
2612	*Imo.* [*Awaking*] Yes, sir, to Milford-Haven;	
2613	which is the way?—	291
	I thank you.—By yond bush?—Pray, how far	
2614	thither?	292
2615	'Ods pittikins! can it be six mile yet?—	293
	I have gone all night. 'Faith, I'll lie down and	
2616	sleep.	294
2617	But, soft! no bedfellow!—O gods and goddesses!	295
2617+1	[*Seeing the body of Cloten.*	
2618	These flowers are like the pleasures of the world:	296
2619	This bloody man, the care on 't. I hope I dream;	297
2620	For so I thought I was a cave-keeper,	298
2621	And cook to honest creatures: but 'tis not so;	299
2622	'Twas but a bolt of nothing. shot at nothing. 300	300
2623	Which the brain makes of fumes: our very eyes	301
	Are sometimes like our judgements, blind. Good	
2624	faith,	302
2625	I tremble still with fear: but if there be	303

*42:300 Cum, WM1, HnF, CKP, KRe, Rig, WmS, HIC, ViA, BA1, NM1, NM2, MB1,MB2,
  PH1, BK1   *42:302 aX: G61, Ox1, P95, Low, Inc, JKT, Oxb,Dol,
  USW, Cum, Rig, ViA, MB2, PH1, JG1, BK1

```
270    same as 268, HIC, ViA, Han, SM1, less KRe
271    same as 270
272    same as 270
273    same as 270
274    same as 270, KRe
275    same as 274

276    X: ChM, G61, Bel, Oxl, Wen, Bat, Bar, Low, Roa, Inc, JKT, Oxb, Dol*
277    same as 276
278    same as 276
279    same as 276
280    same as 276
281    same as 276, HIC, ViA, Han, SM1


282    X: ChM , G61, Bel, Oxl, Wen, Bat, Bar, Low, Roa, Inc, JKT, Oxb, Dol,
          USW, Cum, Rig, WmS, ViA, SM1; aX: WM1, CKP
283    X: G61, Bel, Oxl, Wen, Bat, Bar, Low, Roa, Inc, JKT, Oxb, Dol, USW*
284    same as 283, WM1, CKP, HIP, JG1, less MB2; less aX, bX, ADD
285    same as 283, less MB2; less aX, bX, ADD; R: IP2; aX: WM1, CKP, HIP*
286    X: G61, Bel, Oxl, Wen, Bat, Bar, Low, Roa, Inc, JKT, Oxb, Dol,USW*
287    same as 286, HM1; less R, bX
288    X: G61, Bel, Oxl, Wen, Bat, Bar, Low, Roa, Inc, JKT, Oxb, Dol, USW*
289    X: G61, Bel, Oxl, Wen, Bat, Bar,  Low, Roa, Inc, JKT, Oxb, Dol, USW*
290    same as 289, less HnF; Insert 43: 1-46: NM2


291    bX: IP2; MOVE 291-403 to follow 43: 46: ChM

292    aX : IP2
293    X: ChM; aX: ViA

294    bX : ChM
295    aX : ChM; bX: NM1, NM2

296    X: NM1, NM2
297    X: KRe, NM1, NM2
298    same as 297; R: Wen, Bat
299    same as 297; bX: G61, Bel, Oxl, Wen, Bat, P95, Bar, Low, Inc, JKT*
300    X: G61, Bel, Oxl, Wen, Bat, P95, Bar, Low, Inc, JKT, Oxb, Dol, USW*
301    same as 300, less WmS; aX: WmS; bX: JG1

302    X: Bel, Wen, Bat, Bar, WM1, HnF, CKP, KRe, HIC, BA1, NM1, NM2, MB1;*
303    X: WM1, CKP, KRe, BA1, NM1, NM2, MB1

*42:276  USW, Cum, WM1, HnF, CKP, Lac, Rig, HM1, MTh, HIM, WmS, HIC, ViA,
    Han, SM1                  *42:283 Cum, KRe, MB2; aX: ChM, Rig, ViA;
    bX: HIP, JG1; ADD 1: ChM              *42:285 JG1; bX: Lac, Rig,
  MTh, HIM, WmS, HIC, ViA, SM1, NM1            *42:286 Cum,  Lac, KRe,
    Rig, MTh, HIM, WmS, HIC, ViA, SM1, NM1, PH1, JG1, BK1; R: IP2; bX:HM1
*42:288 Cum, WmS, NM1, PH1, BK1; bX: JG1              *42:289 Cum, HnF
*42:299 Oxb, Dol, USW, Cum, WM1, CKP, Rig
```

2626	Yet left in heaven as small a drop of pity	304
2627	As a wren's eye, fear'd gods, a part of it!	305
2628	The dream's here still: even when I wake, it is	306
2629	Without me, as within me: not imagined, felt.	307
2630	A headless man! The garments of Posthumus!	308
2631	I know the shape of 's leg: this is his hand;	309
2632	His foot Mercurial; his Martial thigh; 310	310
2633	The brawns of Hercules: but his Jovial face—	311
2634	Murder in heaven?—How!—'Tis gone. Pisanio,	312
2635	All curses madded Hecuba gave the Greeks,	313
2636	And mine to boot, be darted on thee! Thou,	314
2637	Conspired with that irregulous devil, Cloten,	315
2638	Hast here cut off my lord. To write and read	316
2639	Be henceforth treacherous! Damn'd Pisanio	317
2640	Hath with his forged letters,—damn'd Pisanio—	318
2641	From this most bravest vessel of the world	319
2642	Struck the main-top! O Posthumus! alas, 320	320
	Where is thy head? where's that? Ay me!	
2643	where's that?	321
2644	Pisanio might have kill'd thee at the heart,	322
	And left this head on. How should this be?	
2645	Pisanio?	323
2646	'Tis he and Cloten: malice and lucre in them	324
	Have laid this woe here. O, 'tis pregnant, preg-	
2647	nant!	325
2648	The drug he gave me, which he said was precious	326
2649	And cordial to me, have I not found it	327
2650	Murderous to the senses? That confirms it home:	328
2651	This is Pisanio's deed, and Cloten's: O!	329
2652	Give colour to my pale cheek with thy blood,	330
2653	That we the horrider may seem to those	331
2654	Which chance to find us: O, my lord, my lord!	332
2654+1	[Falls on the body.	
2655	Enter LUCIUS, a Captain and other Officers, and	
2655+1	a Soothsayer.	
2656	Cap. To them the legions garrison'd in Gallia	333
2657	After your will, have cross'd the sea, attending	334
2658	You here at Milford-Haven with your ships:	335
2659	They are in readiness.	
2660	Luc. But what from Rome?	336
2661	Cap. The senate hath stirr'd up the confiners	337
2662	And gentlemen of Italy, most willing spirits,	338
2663	That promise noble service: and they come	339
2664	Under the conduct of bold Iachimo, 340	340

*42:316JKT, Oxb, Dol, Cum, WM1, CKP, Rig, Wm S, HIC, Han, SM1, MB1, MB2,
PH1, BK1   *42:317 WM1, CKP, KRe, Rig, WmS, JG1; R: Bel, Bar; aX:
Ox1, HIC, Han, SM1, MB1, PH1, BK1   *42:318 Dol, USW, Cum, WM1, CKP,
KRe, Rig, Wm S, JG1, BK1; aX: HIC   *42:321 Dol, USW, Cun, WM1,
CKP, Lac, KRe, Rig, MTh, HIM, WmS, ViA, Han, BA1, SM1, NM1, IP1,NM2,
MB1, MB2, JG1   *42:323 WmS, HIC, ViA, Han, BA1, MB1, JG1; aX.
G61, Wen, P95, Low, Roa, USW, Cum, WM1, CKP, KRe, SM1, NM1, NM2,BK1 ;bX:PH1
          SEE G964a

304 same as 303
305 same as 303
306 X: KRe, NM1, IP1, NM2, MB1; bX: MB1
307 same as 306, MB2; less bX
308 aX : ˙P1, MB1, MB2; ADD 1: ChM, Cum
309 X: ChM,Low, Inc, JKT, Cum, WM1, HnF, CKP, Lac, KRe, Rig, HM1, MTh,HIM*
310 X: ChM, G61, Ox1, Wen, Bat, P95, Low, Roa, Inc, JKT, Oxb, Dol, USW,*
311 same as 310, less Han; same R; aX: Han, PH1
312 X: ChM, Bat, Low, Inc, JKT, Oxb, Dol, USW, Cum, KRe, Rig, HIC; R: Bel*
313 X: ChM, G61, Bel, Wen, Bat, P95, Bar, Low, Roa, Inc, JKT, Dol, USW*
314 X: Low, Roa, Inc, JKT, Dol, USW, KRe, WmS, ViA, NM1; aX: ChM, G61,*
315 X: Low, Roa, JKT, Dol, USW, KRe, HIC; aX:NM2; cX: WmS
316 X: Low, USW, KRe, JG1; bX: ChM, G61, Bel, Ox1, Wen, Bat, Bar,Roa,Inc*
317 X: ChM, G61, Wen, Bat, P95, Low, Roa, Inc, JKT, Oxb, Dol, USW, Cum*
318 X: ChM, G61, Bel, Ox1, Wen, Bat, P95, Bar, Low, Roa, Inc, JKT, Oxb*
319 same as 218, JG1, less BK1; less aX
320 same as 319, less HIC; aX: HIC; bX: Lac, HM1, MTh, HIM, ViA, Han,
     NM1, NM2, MB1, MB2
321 X: ChM, G61, Bel, Ox1, Wen, Bat, P95, Bar, Low, Roa, Inc, JKT, Oxb*
322 same as 121, HM1, HIC, BK1, less BA1, IP1

323 X: ChM, Bel, Ox1, Bat, Bar, JKT, Oxb, Dol,   Rig, HM1, MTh, HIM*
324 same as 123, Oxb, PH1, BK1, less Dol, MTh, ViA,BA1; less aX, bX; aX:
     MTh; bX: G61, Wen, P95, Low, Roa, Dol, USW, WM1, CKP, Lac, KRe*
325 X: ChM, Bel,Ox1, Wen, Bat, Bar, Low, Roa, Inc, JKT, Oxb, Dol,USW*
326 X: ChM, KRe, HIC, SM1, MB2, BK1; bX: PH1
327 same as 362, PH1; less bX
328 same as 362; less bX; aX: PH1
329 X: ChM, ViA, MB2, BK1; bX: BA1; ADD 2: Low, Inc, Cum; Insert 316a,*.
330 X: ChM, G61, Bel, Ox1, Wen, Bat, P95, Bar, Low, Roa, Inc, Oxb, Cum,*
331 same as 330, WmS; same R
332 X: ChM, SM1; R: JKT; aX: G61, Bel, Ox1, Wen, Bat, P95, Bar, Low, Roa,
     Inc, Oxb, Dol, USW, Cum, WM1, HnF, CKP, KRe, Rig, WmS, ViA, BA1,IP1;
     Insert 44: 1-52: WmS

333 X: ChM, G61, Bel, Ox1, Wen, Bat, P95, Bar, Low, Roa, Inc, JKT, Oxb*
334 same as 133, NM1; less R, aX; bX: KRe
335 same as 334, KRe; less bX; bX: BK1

336 X: ChM, Low, Inc, JKT, Dol, USW, Cum, CKP, KRe, Rig, WmS, JP1; aX:*
337 X: ChM, KRe, WmS, JP1; N: Ox1, Oxb
338 same as 337; less N; bX: HIC, PH1, BK1
339 X: ChM, KRe, PH1, JP1, BK1; aX: WmS, HIC
340 X: ChM, KRe, JP1

*42: 309 WmS, HIC; R: Ox1, Wen, Bat, Roa, Oxb, Dol, USW, ViA, Han, BA1,
    SM1, IP1; bX: Bel, Bar   *42:310 Cum, WM1, HnF, CKP, Lac,
    KRe, Rig, HM1, MTh, HIM, WmS, HIC, ViA, Han, BA1, SM1, NM1, IP1, MB2;
    R: Bel, Bar   *42:312 R: Bel, Bar; aX: Wen; bX: G61, P95,
CKP, IP1; cX: Roa, WM1, BA1, NM2; ADD 1: Roa   *42:313 Cum, WM1,CKP,
    KRe, Rig, WmS, ViA, NM1; bX: JG1; MOVE 313-314 to follow 329: Ox1,Oxb,
    HIC   *42:314 Bel, Wen, Bat, P95, Bar,Cum, WM1, CKP, Rig,JG1

2665	Syenna's brother.	
2666	*Luc.*　　　　　When expect you them?	341
2667	*Cap.*　With the next benefit o' the wind.	
2668	*Luc.*　　　　　　　This forwardness	342
	Makes our hopes fair.　Command our present	
2669	numbers	343
2670	Be muster'd; bid the captains look to't.　Now, sir,	344
	What have you dream'd of late of this war's pur-	
2671	pose?	345
	Sooth.　Last night the very gods show'd me a	
2672	vision—	346
2673	I fast and pray'd for their intelligence—thus:	347
2674	I saw Jove's bird, the Roman eagle, wing'd	348
2675	From the spongy south to this part of the west,	349
2676	There vanish'd in the sunbeams: which portends—	350
2677	Unless my sins abuse my divination—	351
2678	Success to the Roman host.	
2679	*Luc.*　　　　　　　Dream often so,	352
2680	And never false.　Soft, ho! what trunk is here	353
2681	Without his top?　The ruin speaks that sometime	354
2682	It was a worthy building.　How! a page!	355
2683	Or dead, or sleeping on him?　But dead rather;	356
2684	For nature doth abhor to make his bed	357
2685	With the defunct, or sleep upon the dead.	358
2686	Let's see the boy's face.	
2687	*Cap.*　　　　　　He's alive, my lord.	359
	Luc.　He'll then instruct us of this body.	
2688	Young one,　　　　　　　　300	360
2689	Inform us of thy fortunes, for it seems	361
690	They crave to be demanded.　Who is this	362
2691	Thou makest thy bloody pillow?　Or who was he	363
2692	That, otherwise than noble nature did,	364
	Hath alter'd that good picture?　What's thy in-	
2693	terest	365
2694	In this sad wreck?　How came it?　Who is it?	366
2695	What art thou?	
2696	*Imo.*　　　　　I am nothing: or if not,	367
2697	Nothing to be were better.　This was my master,	368
2698	A very valiant Briton and a good,	369
2699	That here by mountaineers lies slain.　Alas! 370	370
2700	There is no more such masters: I may wander	371
2701	From east to occident, cry out for service,	372
2702	Try many, all good, serve truly, never	373
2703	Find such another master.	
2704	*Luc.*　　　　　　'Lack, good youth!	374
2705	Thou movest no less with thy complaining than	375

*42:365 aX: Oxb, Low, Inc, JKT, Dol, USW, Cum, WM1, HnF, CKP, Rig, WmS, HIP, H̄IC̄, ViA, SM1, NM1, IP1, NM2, PH1, JG1　　　*42:371 USW, WM1, HnF, CKP, Rig　　　*42:372 WM1, HnF, CKP, KRe, Rig, WmS
*42:374 JKT, Dol, USW, WM1, HnF, CKP, Rig; bX: HIP, HIC, ViA, Han, SM1

341 X: ChM, WmS, JP1; aX: KRe, MB2

342 same as 341; less aX

343 X: ChM, WmS, JP1; bX: G61, Bel, Wen, Bat, P95, Bar, Low, Roa, Inc,JKT*
344 X: ChM, G61, Bel, Wen, Bat, P95, Bar, Low, Roa, Inc, JKT, Oxb, Dol,
        USW, Cum, WM1, HnF, CKP, Lac, KRe, Rig, HM1, MTh, HIM, WmS, HIP,NM1*
345 X: ChM, G61, Bel, Wen, Bat, P95, Bar, Low, Roa, Inc, JKT, Dol, USW,
        Cum, WM1, HnF, CKP, Lac, KRe, Rig, HM1, MTh, HIM, WmS, HIP, HIC, ViA*
346 same as 345; less aX
347 same as 346,BA1
348 same as 346
349 same as 346
350 same as 346; bX: BK1
351 same as 346, BA1, BK1; bX: Oxb

352 same as 351, Oxb, less HnF, WmS, HIP, BA1, BK1less bX; aX: HnF, WmS*
353 X: Oxb; aX: ChM, G61, Bel, Wen, Bat, P95, Low, Roa, Inc, JKT, Dol*
354 X: KRe, MB2; aX: Oxb, HIC, SM1, PH1, BK1; bX: ChM, WmS, JG1
355 X: KRe; R: ChM; aX: WmS, MB2, JG1
356 X: KRe, HM1; bX: HIC, ViA, BA1, SM1, PH1, JG1, BK1
357 X: Oxb, KRe, WmS, HIC, ViA, BA1, SM1, PH1, JG1, BK1
358 same as 357; bX: ChM

359 R : KRe; aX: ChM, Oxb, PH1, BK1

360 X: ChM, Oxb
361 X: ChM; aX: WmS; bX: HnF, KRe, PH1, BK1
362 X: ChM; aX: HnF, KRe, PH1, BK1; bX: WmS
363 X: ChM; aX: WmS; bX: G61, Bel, Ox1, Wen, Bat, P95, Bar, Low, Roa, Inc*
364 X: ChM, G61, Bel, Ox1, Wen, Bat, P95, Bar, Low, Roa, Inc, JKT, Dol,
        USW, Cum, WM1, HnF, CKP, KRe, Rig, HIP, HIC, ViA, BA1, SM1, NM1,IP1*
365 X: ChM, G61, Bel, Wen, Bat, P95, Bar, Roa, Oxb, KRe, BA1, MB1,MB2,BK1;*
366 X: ChM, Bel, Bat, P95, Bar, KRe, MB1, MB2, BK1; R: G61; aX: Wen, Roa,
        Oxb, WmS; bX: PH1, JG1; abX: BA1
367 X: IP2; bX: BK1
368 aX : BK1; ADD 2: ChM
369 X: KRe
370 bX : KRe
371 X: KRe; bX: G61, Bel, Ox1, Wen, Bat, P95, Bar, Low, Roa, Inc, JKT,Dol*
372 X: G61, Bel, Ox1, Wen, Bat, P95, Bar, Low, Roa, Inc, JKT, Dol, USW,Cum*
373 same as 272

374 X: Inc, Cum, KRe, WmS; aX: G61, Bel, Ox1, Wen, Bat, P95, Bar, Low, Roa*
375 X: Lac, Cum, KRe, WmS, HIP, HIC, ViA, Han, SM1, PH1

*42:343 Oxb, Dol, USW, Cum, WM1, HnF, CKP, Lac, KRe, Rig, HM1, MTh, HIM,HIP,
    NM1, IP1, NM2   *42:344 IP1, NM2, JP1, BK1; bX: ViA, Han, MB1,
    MB2, IP2, PH1, JG1   *42:345 Han, SM1, NM1, IP1, NM2, MB1, MB2,IP2,
  PH1, JG1, JP1, BK1;aX:Oxb   *42:352 HIP, Han, BK1   *42:353 USW,
    Cum, WM1, HnF, CKP, Lac, KRe, Rig, HM1, MTh, HIM, WmS, HIP, HIC, ViA,BA1,
  SM1, NM1, IP1, NM2, MB1, MB2, IP2, PH1, JG1, JP1   *42:363 JKT,
    Dol, USW, Cum, WM1, HnF, Rig, HIP, HIC, ViA, BA1, SM1, IP1, NM2, MB1,MB2,
    PH1, JG1   *42:364 NM2, MB1, MB2, PH1, JG1; bX: Oxb, WmS

2706	Thy master in bleeding: say his name, good friend.	376
2707	*Imo.* Richard du Champ. [*Aside*] If I do lie and do	377
2708	No harm by it, though the gods hear, I hope	378
2709	They'll pardon it.—Say you, sir?	
2710	*Luc.* **Thy name?**	
2711	*Imo.* **Fidele, sir.**	379
2712	*Luc.* Thou dost approve thyself the very same:	380
2713	Thy name well fits thy faith, thy faith thy name.	381
2714	Wilt take thy chance with me? I will not say	382
2715	Thou shalt be so well master'd, but, be sure,	383
2716	No less beloved. The Roman emperor's letters,	384
2717	Sent by a consul to me, should not sooner	385
2718	Than thine own worth prefer thee: go with me.	386
2719	*Imo.* I'll follow, sir. But first, an't please the gods,	387
2720	I'll hide my master from the flies, as deep	388
2721	As these poor pickaxes can dig; and when	389
2722	With wild wood-leaves and weeds I ha' strew'd his grave, **390**	390
2723	And on it said a century of prayers,	391
2724	Such as I can, twice o'er, I'll weep and sigh;	392
2725	And leaving so his service, follow you,	393
2726	So please you entertain me.	
2727	*Luc.* Ay, good youth;	394
	And rather father thee than master thee.	395
2728	My friends,	396
2829	The boy hath taught us manly duties: let us	397
2730	Find out the prettiest daisied plot we can,	398
2731	And make him with our pikes and partisans	399
2732	A grave: come, arm him. Boy, he is preferr'd	400
2733	By thee to us, and he shall be interr'd **401**	401
2734	As soldiers can. Be cheerful; wipe thine eyes:	402
	Some falls are means the happier to arise.	403
2735	[*Exeunt.*	

2736,+1	SCENE III. *A room in Cymbeline's palace.*

2737	*Enter* CYMBELINE, Lords, PISANIO, *and*
2737+1	Attendants.

2738	*Cym.* Again; and bring me word how 'tis with her. [*Exit an Attendant.*	1
2739	A fever with the absence of her son,	2
	A madness, of which her life's in danger. Hea-	

*42: 1 111: P95; <u>MOVE</u> 1-46 to follow36: 97: G61, Low; <u>MOVE</u> 1-46 to fol-
low42: 240: Bel, Wen, Bar, Roa, JKT, Oxb, Dol; <u>MOVE</u> 1-46 to follow
42: 213: Ox1; <u>MOVE</u> 1-46 to follow42: 160: Bel, <u>Inc</u>, KRe, HM 1, HIM,
WmS, HIP, HIC, <u>ViA</u>, Han, SM1, NM1; <u>MOVE</u> 1-46 to follow 42: 281: NM2;
"Now generally omitted:" MTh

376 same as 375; R: Wen; aX: HIP; bX: Low, Roa, USW, WM1, HnF, CKP, Lac,
       Rig, HM1, MTh, HIM, IP1, IP2
377 X: ChM, H61, Bel, Oxl, Wen, Bat, P95, Bar, Low, Roa, Inc, Dol, USW*
378 same as 377, JKT, BA1, JG1; less bX

379 X: G61, P95, JKT; aX: ChM, Bel, Oxl, Wen, Bat, Bar, Low, Roa, Inc,Dol*
380 X: ChM, G61, Bel, Oxl, Wen, Bat, Bar, Low, Roa, JKT, Dol, USW, Cum*
381 X: HM1, WmS; aX: KRe; bX: G61, Roa, Dol, WM1, CKP
382 bX: USW
383 aX : Dol,   USW; ADD 1: ViA
384 bX : G61, Bel, Oxl, Wen, Bat, P95, Bar, Roa, JKT, Dol, USW, Cum,WM1*
385 X: G61, Bel, Oxl, Wen, Bat, P95, Bar, Low, Roa, JKT, Dol, USW, Cum,*
386 X; Cum, Lac, KRe, HIP, ViA, NM1; aX: G61, Bel, Oxl, Wen, Bat, P95,
       Bar, Low, Roa, JKT, Dol, USW, WM1, HnF, CKP, Rig, HM1, MTh, HIM,*
387 aX:Cum, Lac, KRe; bX: ViA
388
389

390
391 X: G61, KRe
392 X: KRe; bX: BK1
393 X: KRe; aX: BK1; ADD 1: ViA

394 X: ChM, ViA; bX: MTh, WmS
395 X: KRe, MTh, WmS, ViA, BK1
396 X: KRe, MTh, ViA
397 same as 296, MB2; bX: ChM, WmS
398 X: ChM, KRe, MTh, WmS, ViA, MB2
399 X: KRe, MTh, WmS, ViA, MB2; ADD 7: ChM
400 X: ChM, KRe, MTh, WmS, ViA; aX: MB2; bX: HIC, Han, IP2, BK1
401 X: ChM, KRe, MTh, WmS, HIC, ViA, Han, BK1; aX: IP2
402 X: ChM, MTh, ViA, Han; aX: KRe, WmS, HIC, B K1
403 X: ChM, Oxb, Cum, MTh, ViA; ADD 1: G61, Wen, Bat, Dol, JKT

<u>Scene 43</u>

ALL CUT: WM1, HnF, CKP, Lac, Rig
  1 abX: BK1; MOVE 1-54 to follow 42: 364: USW; MOVE 1-32 to follow 37:*
  2

*42:377 Cum, WM1, HnF, CKP, Lac, KRe, Rig, HM1, MTh, HIM, WmS, HIC, ViA,
     Han, SM1,IP1, MB1, MB2, IP2, PH1, BK1; bX: BA1, JG1, BK1
*42:379 USW, Cum, HnF, CKP, Lac, KRe, Rig, HM1, MTh, HIM, WmS, HIC,ViA,
    Han, BA1, SM1, IP1, MB1, MB2, IP2, PH1, JG1, BK1   *42:380 WM1,
    CKP, Rig, HM1, WmS, BK1   *42:384 HnF, CKP, Lac, KRe, Rig,
    HM1, MTh, HIM, WmS, HIP, HIC, ViA, SM1, NM1, NM2, MB2, JG1
*42:385 WM1, HnF, CKP, KRe, Rig, HM1, MTh, HIM, WmS, HIP, HIC, ViA, SM1,
    NM1, NM2, MB2, JG1   *43:386 WMS, HIC, SM1, NM2, MB2,BK1

2740	vens,	3
2741	How deeply you at once do touch me! Imogen,	4
2742	The great part of my comfort, gone; my queen	5
2743	Upon a desperate bed, and in a time	6
2744	When fearful wars point at me; her son gone,	7
2745	So needful for this present: it strikes me, past	8
2746	The hope of comfort. But for thee, fellow,	9
2747	Who needs must know of her departure and 10	10
2748	Dost seem so ignorant, we'll enforce it from thee	11
2749	By a sharp torture.	
2750	*Pis.* Sir, my life is yours:	12
2751	I humbly set it at your will; but, for my mistress,	13
2752	I nothing know where she remains, why gone,	14
2753	Nor when she purposes return. Beseech your highness,	15
2754	Hold me your loyal servant.	
2755	*First Lord.* Good my liege,	16
2756	The day that she was missing he was here:	17
2757	I dare be bound he's true and shall perform	18
2758	All parts of his subjection loyally. For Cloten,	19
2759	There wants no diligence in seeking him, 20	20
2760	And will, no doubt, be found.	
2761	*Cym.* The time is troublesome.	21
	[*To Pisanio*] We'll slip you for a season; but our jealousy	22
2762		
2763	Does yet depend.	
2764	*First Lord.* So please your majesty,	23
2765	The Roman legions, all from Gallia drawn,	24
2766	Are landed on your coast, with a supply	25
2767	Of Roman gentlemen, by the senate sent.	26
	Cym. Now for the counsel of my son and queen!	27
2768		
2769	I am amazed with matter.	
2770	*First Lord.* Good my liege,	28
2771	Your preparation can affront no less	29
	Than what you hear of: come more, for more you're ready: 30	30
2772		
2773	The want is but to put those powers in motion	31
2774	That long to move.	
2775	*Cym.* I thank you. Let's withdraw;	32
2776	And meet the time as it seeks us. We fear not	33
2777	What can from Italy annoy us; but	34
	We grieve at chances here. Away!	35
2778	[*Exeunt all but Pisanio.*	
2779	*Pis.* I heard no letter from my master since	36
2780	I wrote him Imogen was slain: 'tis strange:	37

3
4 X: Bel, Wen, Bat, Bar
5
6 <u>ADD</u> 7: ChM
7 <u>X</u>: ChM; b<u>X</u>: MB2
8 X: ChM; a<u>X</u>: MB2; b<u>X</u>: PH1, BK1
9 X: ChM, <u>PH</u>1, BK1
10 same as 9
11 same as 9

12 X: PH1, BK1; aX: ChM; b X: P95
13 X: P95, PH1, <u>BK</u>1; <u>R</u>: G<u>61</u>; b<u>X</u>: Ox1, Wen, Bat, Low, Roa, Inc, JKT, Oxb*
14 X: G61, Bel, Ox1, <u>W</u>en, Bat, P95, Bar, Low, Roa, Inc, JKT, Oxb, Dol,
       USW, Cum, PH1, BK1
15 same as 14

16 X: PH1, BK1; a<u>X</u>: G61, Bel, Ox1, Wen, Bat, P95, Bar, Low, Roa, Inc;b<u>X</u>:*
17 X: ChM, <u>NM</u>2, PH1, BK1
18 same as 17
19 same as 17
20 same as 17

21 X: PH1, BK1; a<u>X</u>: ChM, Bat, NM2

22 X: PH1, BK1

23 a<u>X</u> : ChM, PH1, BK1
24
25 b<u>X</u>: G61, Bel, Ox1, Wen, Bat, Bar, Low, Roa, JKT, Oxb, Dol, USW,Cum,JP1
26 <u>X</u>: G61, Bel, Ox1, Wen, Bat, Bar, Low, Roa, JKT, Dol, USW, Cum; <u>R</u>: P95

27 X: Low, NM2

28 X: Ox1, Low, Inc, JKT, Oxb, Dol, USW, Cum, NM2; b<u>X</u>: G61, Bel, Wen, Bat*
29 X: G61; Bel; Ox1; Wen, Bat, P95, Bar, Low, Roa, Inc, JKT, Oxb,Dol,
       USW, Cum, BA1, NM2, PH1, JP1, BK1
30 same as 29
31 same as 29, less Oxb; a<u>X</u>: Oxb

32 a<u>X</u> : G61, Bel, Ox1, Wen, Bat, P95, Bar, Low, Roa, Inc, JKT, Dol, USW,Cum*
33 <u>X</u>: P95; a<u>X</u>: JG1
34 X: P95
35 X: P95; <u>Insert</u> <u>55</u>: 25-36, <u>add</u> 30: ChM

36 X:ChM, P95, MB1, MB2, PH1
37 same as 36

*43:13 Dol, USW, Cum; ab<u>X</u>: Bel, Bar   *43:16 BA1, NM2; <u>N</u>: Ox1,
   JKT, Oxb, Dol, USW, <u>Cum</u>   *43:28 P95, <u>Bar</u>, Roa, B A1, PH1,
  JP1, BK1   *43:32 BA1, <u>NM</u>2, PH1, JP1, BK1

2781	Nor hear I from my mistress, who did promise	38
2782	To yield me often tidings; neither know I	39
2783	What is betid to Cloten; but remain 40	40
2784	Perplex'd in all. The heavens still must work.	41
2785	Wherein I am false I am honest; not true, to be true.	42
2786	These present wars shall find I love my country,	43
2787	Even to the note o' the king, or I 'll fall in them.	44
2788	All other doubts, by time let them be clear'd:	45
	Fortune brings in some boats that are not steer'd.	46
2789	[*Exit.*	

2790,+1 SCENE IV. *Wales: before the cave of Belarius.*

2791 *Enter* BELARIUS, GUIDERIUS, *and* ARVIRAGUS.

2792	*Gui.* The noise is round about us.	
2793	*Bel.* Let us from it.	1
2794	*Arv.* What pleasure, sir, find we in life, to lock it	2
2795	From action and adventure?	
2796	*Gui.* Nay, what hope	3
2797	Have we in hiding us? This way, the Romans	4
2798	Must or for Britons slay us, or receive us	5
2799	For barbarous and unnatural revolts	6
2800	During their use, and slay us after.	
2801	*Bel.* Sons,	7
2802	We 'll higher to the mountains; there secure us.	8
2803	To the king's party there 's no going: newness	9
2804	Of Cloten's death—we being not known, not muster'd 10	10
2805	Among the bands—may drive us to a render	11
2806	Where we have lived, and so extort from 's that	12
2807	Which we have done, whose answer would be death	13
2808	Drawn on with torture.	
2809	*Gui.* This is, sir, a doubt	14
2810	In such a time nothing becoming you,	15
2811	Nor satisfying us.	
2812	*Arv.* It is not likely	16
2813	That when they hear the Roman horses neigh.	17
2814	Behold their quarter'd fires, have both their eyes	18
2815	And ears so cloy'd importantly as now,	19
2816	That they will waste their time upon our note, 20	20
2817	To know from whence we are.	
2818	*Bel.* O, I am known	21

```
38    same as 36
39    same as 36
40    same as 36
41    same as 36

42    X: ChM, P95, BA1, NM2, MB1, MB2, PH1, BK1; bX: JG1
43    same as 42, JG1, less BA1; less bX
44    same as 43, BA1
45    X: ChM, P95, MB2, JG1
46    same as 45; Insert 41: 291-403: ChM
```

<u>Scene 44</u>

ALL <u>CUT</u>: HnF, KRe, MTh, HIP

```
 1    N: WM1; ADD 30: ChM; MOVE 1-52 to follow 42: 332: WmS; MOVE 1-54
         to follow 42: 263: Inc
 2    X: ChM, G61, Bel, Ox1, Wen, Bat, Bar, Low , Roa, Inc, JKT, Oxb,Dol,
         USW, Cum, WM1, CKP, Lac, Rig, HM1, HIM, Wm S, HIC, ViA,Han,SM1,PH1
 3    same as 2; bX: BK1
 4    same as 2, BK1; bX: NM1, NM2, MB2
 5    same as 4, NM1, NM2, less PH1; less bX
 6    same as 5

 7    same as 5, less WM1, SM1, NM1, NM2, BK1; aX: WM1, SM1, NM1, NM2, BK1;*
 8    X: ChM, MB1, MB2
 9    same as 8, WmS; bX: BK1

10    X: ChM, WmS, MB1, MB2, BK1; aX: NM2; bX: BA1, NM1, IP1, PH1, JG1
11    same as 10; less aX, bX; aX: BA1, NM1, IP1, PH1, JG1; bX: NM2
12    X: ChM, WmS, NM2, MB1, MB2, BK1; bX: NM1

13    same as 12, NM1; less bX

14    same as 13; bX: HIC, ViA, SM1, IP1, PH1
15    X: ChM, WmS, HIC, ViA, SM1, NM1, IP1, NM2, MB1, MB2, PH1, BK1

16    X: ChM, HIC, ViA, SM1, NM1, NM2, MB1, MB2; aX: WmS, IP1, PH1, BK1;bX:Han
17    X: ChM, WmS, HIC, ViA, Han, SM1, NM1, NM2, MB1, MB2
18    same as 17, BA1, PH1, BK1; bX: JG1
19    same as 18, JG1; less bX
20    X: ChM, HIC, ViA, Han, SM1, NM1,NM2, MB1, MB2, BK1

21    X: HIC, ViA, Han, SM1, MB1, BK1; aX: ChM, NM1, NM2, MB2, JG1

*44: 7 bX: P95, MB1
```

2819	**Of** many in the army: many years,	22
2820	**Though** Cloten then but young, you see, not wore him	23
2821	**From** my remembrance. And, besides, the king	24
2822	**Hath** not deserved my service nor your loves;	25
2823	**Who** find in my exile the want of breeding,	26
2824	**The** certainty of this hard life: aye hopeless	27
2825	**To** have the courtesy your cradle promised,	28
2826	**But** to be still hot summer's tanlings and	29
2827	**The** shrinking slaves of winter.	
2828	*Gui.* Than be so 30	30
2829	**Better** to cease to be. Pray, sir, to the army:	31
2830	**I** and my brother are not known; yourself	32
2831	**So** out of thought, and thereto so o'ergrown,	33
2832	**Cannot** be question'd.	
2833	*Arv.* By this sun that shines,	34
2834	**I'll** thither: what thing is it that I never	35
2835	**Did** see man die! scarce ever look'd on blood,	36
2836	**But** that of coward hares, hot goats, and venison!	37
2837	**Never** bestrid a horse, save one that had	38
2838	**A** rider like myself, who ne'er wore rowel	39
2839	**Nor** iron on his heel! I am ashamed **40**	40
2840	**To** look upon the holy sun, to have	41
2841	**The** benefit of his blest beams, remaining	42
2842	**So** long a poor unknown.	
2843	*Gui.* By heavens, I'll go:	43
2844	**If** you will bless me, sir, and give me leave,	44
2845	**I'll** take the better care, but if you will not,	45
2846	**The** hazard therefore due fall on me by	46
2847	**The** hands of Romans!	
2848	*Arv.* So say I: amen.	47
2849	*Bel.* No reason I, since of your lives you set	48
2850	**So** slight a valuation, should reserve	49
	My crack'd one to more care. Have with you,	
2851	boys! **50**	50
2852	**If** in your country wars you chance to die,	51
2853	**That** is my bed too, lads, and there I'll lie:	52
	Lead, lead. [*Aside*] The time seems long; their	
2854	blood thinks scorn,	53
	Till it fly out and show them princes born.	54
2855	*[Exeunt.*	

2855+1	# ACT V.
2856,+1	**Scene I.** *Britain. The Roman camp.*
2857	*Enter* Posthumus, *with a bloody handkerchief.*

*44:40(continued) Rig, HM1, HIM, HIC, ViA, ŞM1, NM1, NM2, PH1, JP1
*44:53 Cum, CKP, Lac, Rig, HM1, HIM, WmS, HI, ViA, MB2, BK1

22   same as 21, NM2; less aX, bX; bX: ChM, G61, Bel, Ox1, Wen, Bat, P95,
        Bar, Low, Inc, JKT, Oxb, Dol, USW, Cum, WM1, CKP, NM1, NM2, PH1, JG1, JP1

23   X: ChM, Bel, Ox1, Wen, Bat, P95, Bar, Low, Inc, JKT, Oxb, Dol, USW*

24   X: Rig, HIC, ViA, Han, SM1, MB1, JP1, BK1; aX: ChM, G61, Bel, Ox1, Wen*

25   same as 24, IP1, MB2; less aX, bX; bX: BA1, PH1

26   X: G61, Bel, Ox1, Wen, Bat, P95, Bar, Low, Roa, Inc, JKT, Oxb, Dol, USW*

27   same as 26, BK1, less CKP; less bX; R: ChM

28   same as 27, including R

29   same as 27, less JG1; less R; R: ChM, JG1

30   same as 29, less BA1, IP1; less R; R: ChM; aX: BA1, IP1

31   X: Roa, Han, BK1; aX: G61, Ox1, Wen, Bat, P95, Bar, Low, Roa, Inc, JKT*

32   X: Han, BK1

33   X: Han, BA1, BK1

34   X: BK1; aX: Han; bX: ChM

35   X: BK1; bX: ChM, Lac, Rig, HM1, HIM, WmS, HIC, ViA, Han, SM1, NM2

36   X: ChM, Lac, Rig, HM1, HIM, WmS, HIC, ViA, Han, SM1, NM1, NM2, BK1

37   same as 36, BA1

38   X: ChM, G61, Bel, Ox1, Wen, Bar, Low, Roa, Inc, JKT, Oxb, Dol, USW, Cum*

39   same as 38, P95, Bar, Low, WM1, CKP; less bX; aX: HM1; bX: PH1

40   X: ChM, WmS, BK1; aX: G61, Bel, Ox1, Wen, Bat, P95, Bar, Low, Roa, Inc*

41   X: ChM, Rig, BK1; aX: Lac, HM1, HIM, WmS

42   X: ChM, BK1

43   aX: ChM; bX: JP1

44

45

46   ADD 6: ChM

47   X: ChM

48   X: ChM, MB1, PH1, BK1

49   same as 48

50   X: ChM; aX: MB1, PH1

51   X: ChM

52   X: ChM

53   X: ChM, G61, Bel, Ox1, Wen, P95, Bar, Low, Roa, Inc, JKT, Oxb, Dol, USW*

54   same as 53, Bat, WM1, SM1, MB1, PH1; less bX: Insert 52: 11-18: NM1

Scene 51

*44:23 Cum, WM1, CKP, Rig, HIC, ViA, Han, BA1, SM1, NM2, MB1, PH1, JG1, JP1
  BK1; R: G61   *44:24 Bat, P95, Bar, Low, Inc, JKT, Oxb, Dol,
  USW, Cum, WM1, CKP, BA1, NM2, PH1, JG1; bX: IP1, MB2   *44:26 Cum,
  WM1, CKP, Lac, Rig, HM1, HIM, WmS, HIC, ViA, Han, BA1, SM1, NM1, IP1, NM2,
  MB1, MB2, PH1, JG1, JP1; bX: ChM, BK1   *44:31 Oxb, Dol, USW, Cum
  WM1, CKP, Lac, HM1, HIM, WmS, HIC, SM1, MB1, MB2, PH1, JP1 , same R.
*44:38 Lac, Rig, HM1, HIM, WmS, HIC, ViA, Han, SM1, NM1, NM2, JP1, BK1; bX:
  P95, WM1, CKP   *44:40 JKT, Oxb, Dol, USW, Cum, WM1, CKP, Lac*

2858 *Post.* Yea, bloody cloth, I'll keep thee, for I
wish'd   1

2859 Thou shouldst be colour'd thus. You married ones,   2

2860 If each of you should take this course, how many   3

2861 Must murder wives much better than themselves   4

2862 For wrying but a little! O Pisanio!   5

2863 Every good servant does not all commands: 6

2864 No bond but to do just ones. Gods! if you   7

2865 Should have ta'en vengeance on my faults, I never   8

2866 Had lived to put on this: so had you saved   9

2867 The noble Imogen to repent, and struck   10   10
Me, wretch more worth your vengeance. But,

2868 alack,   11

You snatch some hence for little faults; that's

2869 love,   12

2870 To have them fall no more: you some permit   13

2871 †To second ills with ills, each elder worse,   14

2872 And make them dread it, to the doers' thrift.   15

2873 But Imogen is your own: do your best wills,   16

2874 And make me blest to obey! I am brought hither   17

2875 Among the Italian gentry, and to fight   18

2876 Against my lady's kingdom: 'tis enough   19

2877 That, Britain, I have kill'd thy mistress: peace!   20
I'll give no wound to thee. Therefore, good

2878 heavens,

2879 Hear patiently my purpose: I'll disrobe me   22

2880 Of these Italian weeds and suit myself   23

2881 As does a Briton peasant: so I'll fight   24

2882 Against the part I come with; so I'll die   25

2883 For thee, O Imogen, even for whom my life   26

2884 Is every breath a death; and thus, unknown,   27

2885 Pitied nor hated, to the face of peril   28

2886 Myself I'll dedicate. Let me make men know   29

2887 More valour in me than my habits show.   30   30

2888 Gods, put the strength o' the Leonati in me!   31

2889 To shame the guise o' the world, I will begin   32

2890 The fashion, less without and more within. [*Exit*   33

2891,+1 SCENE II. *Field of battle between the British*

2891+2 *and Roman camps.*

2892 *Enter, from one side,* LUCIUS, IACHIMO, *and*

2893 *the* Roman Army: *from the other side, the*

2894 British Army: LEONATUS POSTHUMUS *fol-*

2895 *lowing, like a poor soldier. They march over*

"51 and 52 are sometimes, but rarely represented": MTh
1 X: HIC, ViA, PH1; bX: MB1; MOVE 1-9a to follow 25a: JG1; MOVE 1-33*
2 same as 2, less bX, MOVES; aX: MB2; bX: HnF, HIP, BA1
3 X: HnF, HIP, HIC, ViA, BA1, PH1
4 same as 3, KRe
5 X: KRe, HIP, BA1, PH1; aX: HnF, HIC, ViA; bX: BK1
6 X: HIP, BA1, PH1, BK1; aX: KRe
7 X: PH1, BK1; aX: HIP, BA1; b X: MB2
8 X: MB2, PH1; bX: KRe
9 X: MB2, PH1; b X: KRe, ViA, JG1
10 X: KRe, ViA, MB2, PH1, JG1

11 same as 10; bX: Ox1, Wen, Bat, Low, Inc, Oxb, Cum, WM1, HnF, CKP, HIP
     HIC, Han, NM1,NM2; ADD 40:BK1
12 X: Bel, Ox1, Wen, Bat, Bar, Low, Inc, JKT, Oxb, Dol, USW, Cum, WM1, HnF*
13 same as 12
14 same as 12
15 same as 12, ChM, BA1, IP1
16 X: HnF, KRe, HIC, ViA, Han, NM1, NM2, MB2, PH1, JG1, BK1
17 X: BK1; R: KRe; aX: HnF, HIC, ViA, Han, NM1, NM2, MB2, PH1, JG1; bX: *
18 X: ChM, BK1
19 X: ChM, BK1
20 X: BK1

21 X: BK1; bX: ChM, WmS, HIC, ViA, PH1
22 X: ChM, BK1; R: Ox1, Wen, Bat, Inc, JKT, Oxb, Dol, KRe, WmS; aX: ViA*
23 X: ChM, Bel, KRe, Rig, HIC, NM2, BK1; R: Ox1, Wen, Bat, Bar, Inc, JKT*
24 X: ChM, BK1; R: Ox1, Wen, Bat, JKT, Oxb, Dol, Cum, KRe; aX: Inc, Rig*
25 X: ChM, BK1; aX: Cum, WmS; Insert 1-9a: JG1
26 X: BK1
27 X: BK1; bX: ChM, KRe, HIC; ADD 9: ChM
28 X: ChM, KRe, HIC, BK1
29 same as 28; R: Wen; bX: Bel, Bat, Bar, Low, Inc, Cum, Rig, HIP, Han,BA1*
30 X: ChM, Low, Inc, Cum, KRe, Rig, HIP, HIC, Han, BA1, SM1, NM1, NM2, MB2*
31 X: ChM, KRe, HIP, HIC, Han, SM1, NM1, NM2, MB2, IP2, BK1; ADD 2: JG1
32 X: ChM, Ox1, JKT, Oxb, Dol, USW, CKP, KRe, HIP. HIC, Han, SM1, NM1,NM2*
33 same as 32; ADD 1: G61; ADD 2: Ox1, Rig; ADD 3:Wen, Bat, Low, Roa,Inc,
     Dol, USW; ADD 13: Bel, Bar, JKT; Insert 52: 11: ViA

Scene 52

*51: 1 to follow 42: 332: WmS   *51:12 CKP, KRe, Rig, HIP,
   HIC, ViA, Han, NM1, NM2, MB1, PH1, JG1, BK1   *51:17 ChM;ADD
   1: ChM   *51:22 PH1; bX: Bel, Bar, USW, Rig, NM2, IP2
*51:23 Oxb, Dol, USW, Cum, WmS; aX: IP2; ADD 1: Bar   *51:24 WmS, NM2
*51:29 SM1, NM1, NM2, MB2   *51:30 BK1; R: Bel, Wen, Bat, Bar
*51:32 MB2, PH1, JG1, BK1

2896	*and go out. Then enter again, in skirmish,*	
2897	IACHIMO *and* POSTHUMUS: *he vanquisheth*	
2897+1	*and disarmeth* IACHIMO, *and then leaves him.*	
	Iach. The heaviness and guilt within my	
2898	bosom	1
2899	Takes off my manhood: I have belied a lady,	2
2900	The princess of this country, and the air on't	3
2901	Revengingly enfeebles me : or could this carl,	4
2902	A very drudge of nature's, have subdued me	5
	In my profession? Knighthoods and honours,	
2903	borne	6
2904	As I wear mine, are titles but of scorn.	7
2905	If that thy gentry, Britain, go before	8
2906	This lout as he exceeds our lords, the odds	9
	Is that we scarce are men and you are gods. · 10	10
2907	[*Exit.*	
2908	*The battle continues; the* Britons *fly;* CYMBE-	
2909	LINE *is taken: then enter, to his rescue,*	
2910	BELARIUS, GUIDERIUS, *and* ARVIRAGUS.	
	Bel. Stand, stand! We have the advantage	
2911	of the ground :	11
2912	The lane is guarded: nothing routs us but	12
2913	The villany of our fears.	
2914	*Gui.* }	13
	Arv. } Stand, stand, and fight!	
2915	*Re-enter* POSTHUMUS, *and seconds the* Britons:	
2916	*they rescue* CYMBELINE, *and exeunt. Then*	
2917	*re-enter* LUCIUS, *and* IACHIMO, *with* IMOGEN.	
	Luc. Away, boy, from the troops, and save	
2918	thyself:	14
2919	For friends kill friends, and the disorder's such	15
2920	As war were hoodwink'd.	
2921	*Iach.* 'Tis their fresh supplies.	16
2922	*Luc.* It is a day turn'd strangely: or betimes	17
2923	Let's re-inforce, or fly. [*Exeunt.*	18
2924,+1	SCENE III. *Another part of the field.*	
2925	*Enter* POSTHUMUS *and a* British Lord.	
	Lord. Camest thou from where they made	
2926	the stand?	
2927	*Post.* I did:	1
2928	Though you, it seems, come from the fliers.	
2929	*Lord.* I did.	2

CONTINUATIONS FROM G969a

*53:32 Do1, USW, Cum, WM1, NM1, IP1, NM2, IP2, BK1MOVE 32-53a to follow
81: Bat, JP1   *53:33 Cum, WM1, HnF, CKP, Rig, HM1, HIM, HIC,
ViA, Han, BA1, SM1, NM1, IP1, NM2, IP2, PH1, JG1, JP1   *53:34 lnc,
JKT, Do1, USW, Cum, WM1, BA1, IP1, IP2; bX: BK1

ALL CUT: Bel, Bar, KRe, WmS, NM2; <u>SEE NOTE TO 51</u>: MTh, BK1
1   X: NM1; <u>MOVE</u> 1-10 to follow 13: Han
2   X: NM1bX: M̲B̲1
3   X: NM1, MB1
4   X: NM1, MB1
5   X: NM1, MB1

6   X: NM1; <u>aX</u>: ViA, MB1; <u>bX</u>: MB2
7   X: NM1, M̲B̲2; <u>ADD</u> 2: Low, Roa
8   X: Low, Roa, L̄ac, HIM, HIC, ViA, SM1, NM1, MB2, PH1; <u>R</u>: ChM, G61,Ox1*
9   same as 9, including <u>R</u>
10 X: ChM, G61, Ox1, Bat̄, Low, Roa, Inc, JKT, Oxb, Dol, USW, Cum, CKP,
      Lac, HIM, HIC, ViA, SM1 , NM1, MB2, PH1; <u>R</u>: Wen

11 same as 10, Wen, WM1, HnF, Rig, BA1, less ViA, SM1, NM1, MB2, PH1; <u>MOVE</u>:*
12 same as 11; less <u>MOVE</u>; aX: HIC

13 same as 12, less Wen, Bat; less <u>aX</u>; <u>aX</u>: Wen, Bat; <u>bX</u>: MB2; <u>ADD</u> 1: Wen,
      Bat; <u>Insert</u> 1-10: Han; <u>Insert</u> 53: 24-27: SM1

14 same as 13, Wen, Bat, HIC, Han; less <u>aX</u>, <u>bX</u>, <u>ADD</u>, <u>Inserts</u>
15 same as 14

16 same as 14, less G61, Roa,Oxb; <u>aX</u>: G61, Roa; <u>bX</u>: PH1
17 X: ChM, Ox1, Wen, Bat, JKT, USW, WM1, HnF, CKP, Lac, Rig, HIM, HIC,ViA*
18 X: ChM, G61, Ox1, Wen, Bat, Low, Roa, Inc, JKT, Oxb, Dol, USW,WM1,HnF,
      CKP, Lac, Rig, HIM, HIC, ViA, Han, BA1, PH1; <u>aX</u>: Cum, JP1; <u>ADD</u> 1:
      P95, JG1

Scene 53

ALL CUT: KRe, MTh, WmS,HIP, MB2
1   X: CKP, Lac, Rig, HM1, HIM, HIC, ViA, Han, SM1, MB1, PH1, JG1, JP1; <u>N</u>:
      ChM, Bel, Ox1, Wen, Bar
2   same as 1; less <u>N</u>; <u>N</u>: G61, Ox1, Bat, Low, JKT

*52: 8 Wen, Bat, Inc, JKT, Oxb, Dol, USW, Cum, CKP; <u>ADD</u> 1: ChM
*52:11 11-18 to follow 44: 54: NM1; <u>MOVE</u> 11 to follow 51: 33: ViA
*52:17 Han, BA1; <u>bX</u>: G61, Low, Roa, Inc, Oxb, Dol, Cum, PH1, JP1

2930	*Post.* No blame be to you, sir; for all was lost,	3
2831	But that the heavens fought: the king himself	4
2932	Of his wings destitute, the army broken,	5
2933	And but the backs of Britons seen, all flying	6
2934	Through a strait lane; the enemy full-hearted,	7
2935	Lolling the tongue with slaughtering, having work	8
2936	More plentiful than tools to do't, struck down 9	9
2937	Some mortally, some slightly touch'd, some falling	10
	Merely through fear; that the strait pass was	
2938	damm'd	11
2939	With dead men hurt behind, and cowards living	12
2940	To die with lengthen'd shame.	
2941	*Lord.* Where was this lane?	13
	Post. Close by the battle, ditch'd, and wall'd	
2942	with turf;	14
2943	Which gave advantage to an ancient soldier,	15
2944	An honest one, I warrant; who deserved	16
2945	So long a breeding as his white beard came to,	17
2946	In doing this for's country: athwart the lane,	18
2947	He, with two striplings—lads more like to run 19	19
2948	The country base than to commit such slaughter;	20
2949	With faces fit for masks, or rather fairer	21
2950	Than those for preservation cased, or shame,—	22
2951	Made good the passage: cried to those that fled,	23
2952	'Our Britain's harts die flying, not our men:	24
2953	To darkness fleet souls that fly backwards. Stand;	25
2954	Or we are Romans and will give you that	26
	Like beasts which you shun beastly, and may	
2955	save,	27
	But to look back in frown: stand, stand.' These	
2956	three,	28
2957	Three thousand confident, in act as many—	29
2958	For three performers are the file when all 30	30
	The rest do nothing—with this word 'Stand,	
2959	stand,'	31
2960	Accommodated by the place, more charming	32
	With their own nobleness, which could have	
2961	turn'd	33
2962	A distaff to a lance, gilded pale looks,	34
	Part shame, part spirit renew'd; that some,	
2963	turn'd coward	35
2964	But by example—O, a sin in war,	36
2965	Damn'd in the first beginners!—gan to look	37
2966	The way that they did, and to grin like lions	38
2967	Upon the pikes o' the hunters. Then began	39
2968	A stop i' the chaser, a retire, anon 40	40

*53:23 R: G61, Oxl, Wen, Bat, Inc, Oxb, Cum, Lac; aX: ChM; bX: Low
*53:24 Lac, Rig, HM1, HIM, HIC, ViA, Han, NM1, NM2, MB1, IP2, PH1, JG1,
   JP1; MOVE 24-28a to follow 52: 13: SM1   *53:28 Roa, SM1,
   BK1; ADD 1: Low; ADD 3: Roa, Dol; Insert 86-87a: Wen, Oxb
*53:29 BA1, SM1, NM2, PH1, JG1, JP1; BK1; R: G61, Bel, Oxl, Wen, Bar,
   Inc, JKT, Oxb, USW, Cum; bX: WM1, IP1, IP2; MOVE 29-53a to follow
   81: WM1, MB1   *53:31 Bar, Inc, JKT, Oxb, USW, Cum, PH1
JP1; aX: BA1, NM2, IP2; ADD 1: Bel, Bar   SEE G968c

3   same as 1; less N̲; N̲: Wen, Bat
4   same as 1; less N̄; b̲X̲: BA1, IP2, BK1
5   same as 1, BA1; less N̲; a̲X̲: IP2, BK1
6   same as 5; less a̲X̲
7   same as 5; b̲X̲: NM̄1̄, NM2, BK1
8   same as 5, Īn̄c̄, Cum, NM1, NM2; less a̲X̲; b̲X̲: Oxl, Wen, Bat, JKT, Oxb*
9   X: G61, Bel, Bar, Dol, Cum, CKP, Lac, Ri̲g̲, HM1, HIM, HIC, ViA, Han*
10   X: CKP, Lac, Rig, HM1, HIM, HIC, ViA, Han, BA1, SM1, NM1, MB1,IP2,
      PH1, JG1, JP1, BK1
11   same as 10, less NM1, IP2; a̲X̲: NM1, IP2; b̲X̲: ChM
12   same as 11, ChM; less a̲X̲, b̲X̲; a̲X̲: ChM; b̲X̲: IP2

13   same as 12, less USW, BK1; less a̲X̲, b̲X̲; a̲X̲: IP2, BK1

14   same as 13; less a̲X̲
15   same as 14, less B̄Ā1̄; aX: BA1
16   same as 15, BK1; less a̲X̲; b̲X̲: G61, Bel, Oxl, Wen, Bat, P95, Bar, Low*
17   X: G61, Bel, Oxl, Wen, Bat, P95, Bar, Low, Roa, Inc, JKT, Oxb, Dol*
18   X: Inc, Cum, CKP, Lac, Rig, HM1, HIM, HIC, ViA, Han, SM1, MB1, PH1*
19   same as 18, less Inc, Cum; less a̲X̲; b̲X̲: BA1
20   same as 20, BA1; less b̲X̲; a̲X̲: BK̄1̄
21   X: G61, Bel, Oxl, Wen, Bat Bar, Low, Roa, Inc, JKT, Oxb, Dol, Cum,WM1*
22   same as 21; ChM; less bX
23   X: HnF, CKP, Rig, HM1, H̄IM, HIC, ViA, Han, SM1, MB1, IP2, PH1,JG1,JP1;*
24   X: G61, Bel, Oxl, Wen, Bat, Bar, Low, Roa, JKT, Oxb, USW, WM1, HnF,CKP*
25   sam?as 24, Inc, Cum, IP1, less Bat; less MO̲V̲E̲; a̲X̲: Bat
26   X: ChM, Inc, Cum, HnF, CKP, Lac, Rig, HM1, H̄IM̄, H̄IC̄, ViA, Han, BA1,IP1,
      MB1, IP2, PH1, JG1, JP1; R: NM2
27   same as 26, less Inc, Cum; l̄ess R̲; a̲X̲: BK1; b̲X̲: WM1, WmS

28   same as 27, NM2, less ChM, IP2; less a̲X̲, b̲X̲; a̲X̲: WM1, IP2; b̲X̲: G61,Low*
29   X: ChM, Bat, P95, Low, Roa, HnF, CKP, Lac, Rig, HM1, HIM, HIC, ViA,Han*
30   same as 29, Wen, WM1, IP1, MB1, IP2, less PH1, JP1, BK1 less R̲, b̲X̲, MO̲V̲E̲;
      R̲: G61, Bel, Oxl, Bar, Inc, JKT, Oxb, USW, Cum, PH1, JP1;a̲X̲:BK1
31   same as 30, BK1, less ChM, BA1, NM2, IP2; less R̲, a̲X̲; R̲: G61, Bel, Oxl*
32   X: P95, Low, HnF, CKP, Lac, Rig, HM1, HIM, HIC, Vi̲A̲, Han, BA1, SM1, MB1,
      PH1, JG1, JP1; R: Oxl, Oxb; b̲X̲: G61, Bel, Wen, Bat, Bar, Inc, JKT*
33   X: G61, Bel, Oxl, Wen, Bat, P9̄5̄, Bar, Low, Roa, Inc, JKT, Oxb, Dol, USW*
34   X: Oxl, P95, Roa, Oxb, HnF, CKP, Lac, Rig, HM1, HIM, HIC, ViA, Han,SM1,
      NM1, NM2, MB1, PH1, JG1, JP1; R: ChM; a̲X̲: G61, Bel, Wen, Bat, Bar, Low*
35   same as 34, less Oxl, Ria, Oxb; l̄ess R̲, a̲X̲, b̲X̲; R: ChM; a̲X̲: IP1
36   same as 35; less R̲, a̲X̲; R̲: ChM; a̲X̲: BK̄1̄; b̲X̲: G61, Bel, Ox1̄, Wen,B̲at,Bar
37   same as 35;less R̲, a̲X̲; a̲X̲: G61, Bē1̄, Oxl, B̄at, Bar, Low, Roa, USW,Cum,WM1
38   same as 35,ChM; l̄ess R̲, a̲X̲; b̲X̲: IP2
39   same as 38, BK1, less ChM̄, NM2̲; less b̲X̲; a̲X̲: ChM, NM2, IP2; b̲X̲: BA1
40   same as 39, BA1, less NM1; less a̲X̲, b̲X̲

*53: 8 WM1, IP2   *53: 9 BA1, SM1, NM1, MB1, IP2, PH1, JG1,
   JP1, BK1; a̲X̲: Oxl, Wen, Bat, Low, Inc, JKT, Oxb, WM1, NM2
*53:16 JKT, Oxb, Dol, USW, WM1, BA1, NM1, IP1, NM2, IP2   *53:17 USW,Cum
   WM1, CKP, Lac, Rig, HM1, HIM, HIC, ViA, Han, BA1, SM1, NM1, IP1̄, NM2,MB1,
   IP2, PH1, JG1, JP1, BK1   *53:18 JG1, JP1; a̲X̲: G61, Bel, Oxl,
   Wen, Bat, P95, Bar, Low, Roa, JKT, Oxb̄, Dol, USW, WM1, B̄A1, NM1, IP1,NM2,
   IP2, BK1   *53:21 CKP, Lac, Rig, HM1, HIM, HIC, ViA, Han, BA1, SM1,NM1,
   IP1, NM2, MB1, IP2, PH1, JG1, JP1, BK1; b̲X̲: ChM

2969	A rout, confusion thick ; forthwith they fly	41
	Chickens, the way which they stoop'd eagles ;	
2970	slaves,	42
	The strides they victors made: and now our	
2971	cowards,	43
2972	Like fragments in hard voyages, became	44
	The life o' the need : having found the back-door	
2973	open	45
	Of the unguarded hearts, heavens, how they	
1974	wound !	46
2975	Some slain before : some dying ; some their friends	47
2976	O'er-borne i' the former wave : ten, chased by one,	48
2977	Are now each one the slaughter-man of twenty :	49
2978	Those that would die or ere resist are grown 50	50
2979	The mortal bugs o' the field.	
2980	*Lord.* This was strange chance :	51
2981	A narrow lane, an old man, and two boys.	52
2982	*Post.* Nay, do not wonder at it : you are made	53
2983	Rather to wonder at the things you hear	54
2984	Than to work any. Will you rhyme upon't,	55
2985	And vent it for a mockery? Here is one :	56
2986	'Two boys, an old man twice a boy, a lane,	57
2987	Preserved the Britons. was the Romans' bane.'	58
2988	*Lord.* Nay, be not angry, sir.	
2989	*Post.* 'Lack, to what end?	59
2990	Who dares not stand his foe, I'll be his friend ; 60	60
2991	For if he'll do as he is made to do,	61
2992	I know he'll quickly fly my friendship too.	62
2293	You have put me into rhyme.	
2994	*Lord.* Farewell ; you're angry.	63
	Post. Still going? [*Exit Lord.*] This is a	
2995	lord ! O noble misery,	64
2996	To be i' the field, and ask 'what news?' of me !	65
2997	To-day how many would have given their honours	66
2998	To have saved their carcases ! took heel to do't,	67
2999	And yet died too ! I, in mine own woe charm'd,	68
3000	Could not find death where I did hear him groan,	69
	Nor feel him where he struck : being an ugly	
3001	monster, 70	70
3002	'Tis strange he hides him in fresh cups, soft beds,	71
3003	Sweet words : or hath more ministers than we	72
	That draw his knives i' the war. Well, I will	
3004	find him :	73
3005	For being now a favourer to the Briton,	74
3006	No more a Briton, I have resumed again	75
3007	The part I came in : fight I will no more.	76

*53:55 G61, P95, WM1, BA1   *53:56 Cum, WM1, HnF, CKP, Lac,Rig,
  HM1, HIM, HIC, ViA, Han, BA1, SM1, MB1, PH1, JG1, JP1, BK1
*53:61Cum, WM1, HnF, ViA, Han, BA1, SM1, ĮP1, MB1, IP2, PH1, JG1, JPĮ; R:
  ChM   *53:70 PH1, JG1, BK1   *53:71 IP1, NM2, MB1,
  IP2, PH1, JG1; b̄X: BK1   *53:73 SM1, IP1, IP2, PH1, JG1
*53:74 HIC, ViA, Han, BA1, NM1, IP1, NM2, MB1, IP2, PH1

41　X: P95, HnF, CKP, Lac, Rig, HM1, HIM, HIC, ViA, Han, BA1, SM1, MB1,
　　　　PH1, JG1, JP1, BK1; R: Ox1, Oxb; bX: ChM, G61, Bel, Wen, Bat, Bar*
42　X: P95, Low, Roa, Oxb, WM1, HnF, CKP, Lac, Rig, HM1, HIM, HIC, ViA,Han,
　　　　BA1, IP1; R: G61, Bel, Ox1, Wen, Bat, Bar, Inc, JKT, Dol, USW,Cum*
43　X: G61, Bel, Ox1, Wen, Bat, P95, Bar, Low, Roa, Inc, Oxb, Dol,Cum,WM1*
44　same as 43, JKT, NM1; less R, bX; R: USW

45　same as 44, including R; bX: NM2

46　same as 44, NM2; same R
47　same as 46, USW; less R; bX: ChM
48　same as 47, less BA1, NM1; less bX; aX: BA1, NM1
49　same as 48; less aX
50　same as 49, BA1, less NM2, BK1

51　X: ChM, USW, HnF, CKP, Lac, Rig, HM1, HIM, HIC, ViA, Han, BA1, SM1*
52　same as 51; less aX; R: G61, Ox1, Wen, Bat, Inc, JKT, Oxb, Dol, Cum;aX:*
53　same as 51; IP1, IP2; less R, aX, ADDs; bX: G61, Bel, Ox1, Wen, Bat*
54　X: ChM, Wen, Bat, Low, Roa, Inc, Oxb, Dol, USW, Cum, HnF, CKP, Lac,*
55　same as 54, BK1; less R; R: Bel, Ox1, Bar, Inc, JKT; aX: IP1, IP2; bX:*
56　X: ChM, Bel, Ox1, Wen, Bat, P95, Bar, Low, Roa, Inc, JKT, Oxb, Dol,USW*
57　same as 56, G61, less BK1; less R; aX: BK1
58　same as 57, less Cum; less aX; aX: ChM; bX: BK1

59　same as 58, BK1; less aX, bX; R: ChM
60　same as 58, less aX; bX: ChM
61　X: G61, Bel, Ox1, Wen, Bat, P95, Bar, Low, Roa, Inc, JKT, Oxb, Dol,USW*
62　same as 61, including R

63　same as 62, ChM, BK1, less P95, WM1, BA1, IP1, IP2; less R; aX: P95, WM1,
　　　　BA1
64　same as 63; less aX; aX: P95, WM1; bX: IP2
65　same as 63, IP2; less aX, bX
66　X: ChM, HnF, Han, MB1, JG1, JP1, BK1; MOVE 66-78 to follow 87: Bat, SM1
67　X: ChM, HnF, Han, MB1, JG1, JP1; aX: BK1
68　X: ChM, HnF, Han, MB1, JG1, BK1; R: PH1; aX: JP1; bX: NM1, NM2
69　X: ChM, Han, NM1, NM2, MB1

70　same as 69; bX: Ox1, Low, Inc, JKT, Dol, USW, Cum, HIC, ViA, BA1, SM1,IP2*
71　X: ChM, Ox1, Low, Inc, JKT, Dol, USW, Cum, HIC, ViA, Han, BA1, SM1, NM1*
72　same as 71; less bX; aX: BK1

73　X: ChM, Cum, Han, NM1, NM2, MB1; aX: Ox1, Low, JKT, Dol, USW, HIC, ViA,*
74　X: ChM, G61, Bel, Ox1, Wen, Bat, Low, Roa, Inc, JKT, Oxb, Dol, USW, Cum*
75　X: Han, BA1, NM1, NM2; aX: HIC, ViA
76　X: Han; aX: BA1, NM1, NM2, PH1

*53:41 Low, Roa, Inc, JKT, Dol, USW, Cum, WM1, IP1, IP2; ADD 1: Low, Roa
*53:42 SM1, MB1, IP2, PH1, JG1, JP1, BK1; aX: ChM　　　　　　*53:43 HnF,CKP,
　　Lac, Rig, HM1, HIM, HIC, ViA, Han, BA1, SM1, IP1, MB1, IP2, PH1, JG1, JP1;
　　R:JKT, USW; bX: NM1　　　　　　*53:51 MB1, HIM, JG1, JP1; aX: G61, Bel,Ox1,
　　Wen, Bat, P95, Bar, Roa, Inc, JKT, Oxb, Dol, Cum, WM1, IP1, IP2, BK1
*53:52 Bel, Bar; ADD 1: P95, Bar; ADD 2: Cum　　　　*53:53 Bar, Low, Roa,
　　Inc, JKT, Oxb, Dol, Cum, BK1; ADD 1: Roa　　　　*53:54 Rig, HM1, HIM,HIC,
　　ViA, Han, SM1, IP1, MB1, IP2, PH1, JG1, JP1; R: Bel, Ox1, Bar, JKT

3008	But yield me to the veriest hind that shall	77
3009	Once touch my shoulder. Great the slaughter is	78
3010	Here made by the Roman: great the answer be	79
3011	Britons must take. For me, my ransom's death;	80
3012	On either side I come to spend my breath; 81	81
3013	Which neither here I'll keep nor bear again,	82
2014	But end it by some means for Imogen.	83

3015   *Enter two* British Captains *and* Soldiers.

First Cap.   Great Jupiter be praised!   Lucius
3016   is taken.   84
3017   'Tis thought the old man and his sons were angels.   85
       Sec. Cap.   There was a fourth man, in a silly
3018   habit,   86
3019   That gave the affront with them.
3020   *First Cap.*   So 'tis reported: 87
       But none of 'em can be found.   Stand!   who's
3021   there?   88
3022   *Post.*   A Roman,   89
3023   Who had not now been drooping here, if seconds
3024   Had answer'd him.   90
3025   *Sec. Cap.*   Lay hands on him: a dog!   91   91
3026   A leg of Rome shall not return to tell   92
       What crows have peck'd them here.   He brags
3027   his service   93
3028   As if he were of note: bring him to the king.   94

3029   *Enter* CYMBELINE, BELARIUS, GUIDERIUS, AR-
3030   VIRAGUS, PISANIO, Soldiers, Attendants, *and*
3031   Roman Captives.   *The* Captains *present* POST-
3031+1   HUMUS *to* CYMBELINE, *who delivers him over*
3031+2   *to a* Gaoler: *then exeunt omnes.*

3032,+1   SCENE IV.   *A British prison.*

3033   *Enter* POSTHUMUS *and two* Gaolers.

3034   *First Gaol.*   You shall not now be stol'n, you
3035   have locks upon you;   1
3036   So graze as you find pasture.
3037   *Sec. Gaol.*   Ay, or a stomach.   2
3037+1   [*Exeunt Gaolers.*
       Post.   Most welcome, bondage! for thou art
3038   a way,   3
3039   I think, to liberty: yet am I better   4
       Than one that's sick o' the gout; since he had
3040   rather   5

77   X: Han
78   X: Han; bX: Low, HIC, ViA, BA1, PH1, JG1; ADD 9: JKT
79   X: Bel, Ox1, Wen, Bar, Low, Roa, Inc, JKT, Oxb, Dol, USW, Cum, HIC,ViA*
80   X: ChM, Bel, Wen, Bar, Roa, Inc, JKT, Oxb, Dol, USW,HIC, ViA, Han*
81   X: ChM,CKP, Lac, Rig, HM1, HIM, HIC, ViA, Han, SM1, IP1, BK1; R: Ox1; aX⚹
82   same as 81, Roa, IP2, less ChM, IP1; less R, aX; bX, ADD, Insert;aX:ChM
83   same as 82, ChM, JKT; less aX; R: Ox1, Oxb

84   X: G61, Bel, Bat, Bar, Roa, Inc, JKT, CKP, Lac, Rig, HM1, HIM, BA1
85   same as 84

86   X: G61, Bel, Bar, Roa, Inc, JKT, ViA, BA1, NM2; R: Ox1; B: Bat, PH1;
       MOVE 86-87 to follow 28: Wen, Oxb
87   same as 86, HnF; less R, B, MOVE; R: Ox1; aX: PH1; bX: Wen, Low; ADD
       9: ChM, Oxb, USW, Cum; Insert 66-78: SM1; Insert 66-83:Bat, SM1
88   X: ChM, G61, Bel, Wen, Bar, Roa, Inc, JKT, Oxb, HnF; aX: Oxb, Low,USW*
89   same as 88, less ChM; less aX; aX: ChM

90   same as 89, PH1, BK1, less HnF; less aX; aX: HnF; bX: CKP, Rig
91   same as 90, CKP, Rig, less PH1, BK1; less aX, bX; aX: PH1, BK1
92   same as 91, ViA, BK1

93   G61, Bel, Wen, Bat, Bar, Roa, Inc, JKT, Oxb, ViA; aX: CKP, Rig,HIC,BK1*
94   same as 93; less aX, bX; aX: ChM; bX: MB1, JG1, BK1; Insert 54: 152-
       183: JP1

Scene 54

ALL CUT : Cum, G61, Bel, Ox1, Wen, Bat, Bar, Low, Roa, Inc, JKT, Oxb, Dol,
    USW, Cum, HnF, CKP, Lac, KRe, Rig, HM1, MTh, HIM, WmS, HIP, HIC, ViA,
    Han, BA1, IP1, MB2
 1   X: WM1, SM1, PH1, BK1

 2   X: WM1, SM1, PH1

 3
 4   bX: WM1, SM1, IP2, PH1, JP1, BK1

 5   X: WM1, SM1, MB1, MB2, PH1, JP1, BK1

*53:79 Han, BA1, SM1, PH1, JG1; bX: ChM   *53:80 SM1; R: Cum; aX:
   Low, BA1, PH1, JG1; bX: Ox1, BK1   *53:81 JKT; bX: Bel, Wen, Bat,
   Bar, Roa, HM1; ADD 2: Bar   ; ADD 4: Roa; Insert 32-53a: Bat; Insert 29-
   53a, add 2:Wen   *53:88 Cum, BA1, NM2   *53:93 bX: ChM,
   PH1

3041	**Groan** so in perpetuity than be cured	6
3042	**By** the sure physician, death, who is the key	7
3043	**To** unbar these locks. My conscience, thou **art** fetter'd	8
3044	**More** than my shanks and wrists: you good gods, give me	9
3045	**The** penitent instrument to pick that bolt, 10	10
3046	**Then,** free for ever! Is't enough I am sorry?	11
3047	**So** children temporal fathers do appease;	12
3048	**Gods** are more full of mercy. Must I repent?	13
3049	**I** cannot do it better than in gyves,	14
3050	**Desired** more than constrain'd: to satisfy,	15
3051	**If** of my freedom 'tis the main part, take	16
3052	**No** stricter render of me than my all.	17
3053	**I** know you are more clement than vile men,	18
3054	**Who** of their broken debtors take a third,	19
3055	**A** sixth, a tenth, letting them thrive again 20	20
3056	**On** their abatement: that's not my desire:	21
3057	**For** Imogen's dear life take mine; and though	22
3058	**'Tis** not so dear, yet 'tis a life; you coin'd it:	23
3059	**'Tween** man and man they weigh not every stamp;	24
3060	**Though** light, take pieces for the figure's sake:	25
3061	**You** rather mine, being yours: and so, great powers,	26
3062	**If** you will take this audit, take this life,	27
3063	**And** cancel these cold bonds. O Imogen!	28
3064	**I'll** speak to thee in silence. *[Sleeps.*	29

3065	*Solemn music. Enter, as in an apparition,*	
3066	SICILIUS LEONATUS, *father to Posthumus, an*	
3067	*old man, attired like a warrior; leading in*	
3068	*his hand an ancient matron, his wife, and*	
3069	*mother to Posthumus, with music before them:*	
3070	*then, after other music, follow the two young*	
3071	LEONATI, *brothers to Posthumus, with wounds*	
3071+1	*as they died in the wars. They circle* POST-	
3071+2	HUMUS *round, as he lies sleeping.*	

3072	*Sici.* No more, thou thunder-master, show 30	30
3073	Thy spite on mortal flies:	31
	With Mars fall out, with Juno chide,	32
3074	That thy adulteries	33
3075	Rates and revenges.	34
3076	Hath my poor boy done aught but well,	35
3077	Whose face I never saw?	36
3078	I died whilst in the womb he stay'd	37

```
6   same as 5
7   same as 5

8   X: WM1, SM1, MB1, IP1, JP1; aX: PH1, BK1

9   X: WM1, SM1, MB1, IP2; aX: JP1
10  same as 9, JP1; less aX
11  X: WM1, SM1, MB1; aX: IP2, JP1
12  X: WM1, SM1, MB1, JG1
13  X: SM1, JG1; aX: MB1; bX: WM1, IP2
14  X: WM1, SM1, IP2, JG1
15  same as 4, PH1; bX: MB1, JP1, BK1
16  X: WM1, SM1, MB1, IP2, PH1, JG1, JP1, BK1
17  same as 16
18  same as 16, less JG1
19  same as 18
20  same as 18
21  same as 18
22  X: NM1, MB1; bX: WM1, IP2, PH1, JG1, BK1
23  X: WM1, NM1, MB1, IP2, PH1, JG1, BK1; bX: SM1
24  same as 23, SM1, JP1; less bX
25  same as 24


26  same as 24 less JP1; aX: JP1
27  X: WM1, SM1, MB1, PH1, JG1, BK1
28  aX: SM1, MB1, IP2, PH1; bX: WM1
29  X: WM1, SM1




30  X: P95, WM1, SM1, NM1, NM2, MB1, IP2, PH1; bX: JP1
31  same as 30, JP1, BK1
32  same as 31
33  same as 31
34  same as 31
35  X: P95, WM1, SM1, NM1, NM2, MB1, IP2; bX: JP1
36  same as 35, JP1; less bX
37  same as 36
```

3079	Attending nature's law:	38
3080	Whose father then, as men report	39
3081	Thou orphans' father art, 40	40
3082	Thou shouldst have been, and shielded him	41
3083	From this earth-vexing smart.	42
3084	*Moth.* Lucina lent not me her aid,	43
3085	But took me in my throes:	44
3086	That from me was Posthumus ript,	45
3087	Came crying 'mongst his foes,	46
3088	A thing of pity!	47
3089	*Sici.* Great nature, like his ancestry,	48
3090	Moulded the stuff so fair,	49
3091	That he deserved the praise o' the world,	50
3092	As great Sicilius' heir. 51	51
3093	*First Bro.* When once he was mature for man,	52
3094	In Britain where was he	53
3095	That could stand up his parallel:	54
3096	Or fruitful object be	55
3097	In eye of Imogen, that best	56
3098	Could deem his dignity?	57
3099	*Moth.* With marriage wherefore was he mock'd	58
3100	To be exiled, and thrown	59
3101	From Leonati seat, and cast &	60
3102	From her his dearest one,	61
3103	Sweet Imogen?	62
	Sici. Why did you suffer Iachimo,	63
3104	Slight thing of Italy,	64
	To taint his nobler heart and brain	65
3105	With needless jealousy:	66
	And to become the geck and scorn	67
3106	O' th' other's villany?	68
3107	*Sec. Bro.* For this from stiller seats we came,	69
3108	Our parents and us twain,	70
3109	That striking in our country's cause	71
3110	Fell bravely and were slain,	72
	Our fealty and Tenantius' right	73
3111	With honour to maintain.	74
3112	*First Bro.* Like hardiment Posthumus hath	75
3113	To Cymbeline perform'd:	76
	Then, Jupiter, thou king of gods,	77
3114	Why hast thou thus adjourn'd	78

```
38    same as 36
39    X: P95, WM1,   SM1, NM1, NM2, IP2, PH1,   JG1, JP1, BK1
40    same as 39,   :
41    same as 39, MB1
42    same as 41

43    X: P95, WM1, SM1, NM1, NM2, MB1, IP2, JP1; MOVE 43-47 to follow 51:PH1
44    same as 43; less MOVE
45    same as 44
46    same as 44
47    same as 44,  less JP1

48    same as 44
49    same as 48, JP1
50      same as 44   less JP1; aX : JP1
51    same as 44, less JP1; aX: JP1: Insert 43-47: PH1

52    X: P95, WM1, SM1, NM1, NM2, MB1, IP2, OH1, JP1, BK1
53    same as 52
54    same as 52
55    same as 52
56    same as 52
57    same as 52
58    X: P95, WM1, SM1, NM1, NM2, MB1, IP2;   R:JP1
59    same as 58 including R
60    same as 58 ; less R

61    same as 60; aX: JP1
62    same as 61, including aX

63    same as 61  including aX; MOVE 63-66 to follow 80: PH1
64    same as 61, JP1; less aX
56    same as 61; aX: JP1
66    same as 61, JP1
67    X: P95, WM1, SM1, NM1, NM2, MB1, IP2, BK1
68    same as 67

69    same as 67, JP1
70    same as 69
71    same as 69
72    same as 69
73    same as 69
74    same as 69

75    same as 69, less BK1
76    same as 75
77    same as 75, less JP1
78    same as 77; bX: JP1
```

	The graces for his merits due,	79
3115	Being all to dolours turn'd? &c	80
3116	*Sici.* Thy crystal window ope; look out;	81
3117	No longer exercise	82
	Upon a valiant race thy harsh	83
3118	And potent injuries.	84
3119	*Moth.* Since, Jupiter, our son is good,	85
3120	Take off his miseries.	86
3121	*Sici.* Peep through thy marble mansion; help;	87
3122	Or we poor ghosts will cry	88
	To the shining synod of the rest	89
3123	Against thy deity. *go*	90
3124	*Both Bro.* Help, Jupiter; or we appeal,	91
3125	And from thy justice fly.	92
3126	JUPITER *descends in thunder and lightning.*	
3127	*sitting upon an eagle: he throws a thunder-*	
3128	*bolt. The Ghosts fall on their knees.*	
3129	*Jup.* No more, you petty spirits of region low,	93
	Offend our hearing; hush! How dare you	
3130	ghosts	94
3131	Accuse the thunderer, whose bolt, you know,	95
3132	Sky-planted batters all rebelling coasts?	96
3133	Poor shadows of Elysium, hence, and rest	97
3134	· Upon your never-withering banks of flowers:	98
3135	Be not with mortal accidents opprest;	99
3136	No care of yours it is; you know 'tis ours. *100* 100	
3137	Whom best I love I cross: to make my gift,	101
3138	The more delay'd, delighted. Be content;	102
3139	Your low-laid son our godhead will uplift:	103
3140	His comforts thrive, his trials well are spent.	104
3141	Our Jovial star reign'd at his birth, and in	105
3142	Our temple was he married. Rise, and fade.	106
3143	He shall be lord of lady Imogen,	107
3144	And happier much by his affliction made.	108
3145	This tablet lay upon his breast, wherein	109
3146	Our pleasure his full fortune doth confine: *110* 110	
3147	And so, away: no further with your din	111
3148	Express impatience, lest you stir up mine.	112
	Mount, eagle, to my palace crystalline.	113
3149	[*Ascends.*	
3150	*Sici.* He came in thunder; his celestial breath 114	
3151	Was sulphurous to smell: the holy eagle	115

```
79    same as 75
80    same as 75; Insert 63-66: PH1

81    same as 75, BK1
82    same as 81
83    same as 81
84    same as 81

85    same as 81
86    same as 81, less JP1
87    same as 81, less BK1
88    same as 87, less JP1
89    same as 87
90    same as 87

91    same as 87, less JP1; bX: JP1
92    same as 91; less bX; aX: JP1


93    same as 91; less bX

94    same as 93
95    same as 93
96    same as 93
97    same as 93
98    same as 93
99    same as 93
100   same as 93
101   same as 93
102   same as 93
103   same as 93
104   same as 93
105   same as 93, PH1, B K1
106   same as 105
107   same as 105, less BK1
108   same as 107
109   same as 107, JG1
110   same as 109
111   same as 107
112   same as 107
113   same as 107

114   X: P95, WM1, SM1, NM1, NM2, MB1, IP2, PH1, BK1; R: JP1
115   same as 114, including R
```

3152	Stoop'd, as to foot us: his ascension is	116
3153	More sweet than our blest fields: his royal bird	117
3154	Prunes the immortal wing and cloys his beak,	118
3155	As when his god is pleased.	
3156	*All.* Thanks, Jupiter!	119
	Sici. The marble pavement closes, he is	
3157	enter'd **120**	120
3158	His radiant roof. Away! and, to be blest,	121
	Let us with care perform his great behest.	122
3159	[*The Ghosts vanish.*	
	Post. [*Waking*] Sleep, thou hast been a grand-	
3160	sire, and begot	123
3161	A father to me; and thou hast created	124
3162	A mother and two brothers: but, O scorn!	125
	Gone! they went hence so soon as they were	
3163	born:	126
3164	And so I am awake. Poor wretches that depend	127
3165	On greatness' favour dream as I have done,	128
3166	Wake and find nothing. But, alas, I swerve:	129
3167	Many dream not to find, neither deserve, **130**	130
3168	And yet are steep'd in favours; so am I,	131
3169	That have this golden chance and know not why.	132
	What fairies haunt this ground? A book? O	
3170	rare one!	133
3171	Be not, as is our fangled world, a garment	134
3172	Nobler than that it covers: let thy effects	135
3173	So follow, to be most unlike our courtiers,	136
3174	As good as promise.	137
3175	[*Reads*] ' When as a lion's whelp shall, to himself	138
3176	unknown, without seeking find, and be embraced	139
3177	by a piece of tender air; and when from a stately	140
3178	cedar shall be lopped branches, which, being	141
	dead many years, shall after revive, be jointed	142
3179	to the old stock and freshly grow; then shall	143
3180	Posthumus end his miseries, Britain be fortunate	144
3181-2	and flourish in peace and plenty.'	145
3183	'Tis still a dream, or else such stuff as madmen	146
3184	Tongue and brain not; either both or nothing;	147
3185	Or senseless speaking or a speaking such	148
3186	As sense cannot untie. Be what it is,	149
3187	The action of my life is like it, which **150**	150
3188	I'll keep, if but for sympathy.	151
3189	*Re-enter* Gaolers.	
	First Gaol. Come, sir, are you ready for	152
3190	death?	153

```
116   same as 114 including R
117   same as 114 including R̄; bX: JG1
118   same as 114, JG1, JP1; less R


119   X: P95, WM1, SM1 , NM1, NM2, MB1, IP2; aX: PH1, JG1, JP1, BK1


120   same as 119, JP1; less aX; aX: BK1
121   sam' as 120; less aX
122   same as 121



123   same as 121, PH1, less JP1
124   same as {23, BK1; R: JP1
125   X: P95, WM1, SM1, N̄M1, NM2, MB1, IP2; aX: PH1, BK1


126   same as 125; less aX
127   same as 126; bX: P̄H̄1, BK1
128   same as 126, P̄H̄1, BK1
129   same as 126, PH1; aX: BK1
130   same as 126
131   same as 126
132   same as 126; bX: PH1


133   same as 126, JG1; aX: PH1; bX: JP1; ADD 22: JP1
134   X: P95, WM1, SM1, N̄M1, NM2, M̄B1, IP2, PH1, JG1, JP1, BK1
135   same as 134
136   same as 134
137   same as 134
138   same as 134, less BK1
139   same as 138
140   same as 138
141   same as 138
142   same as 138
143   same as 138
144   same as 138
145   same as 138
146   same as 138, less PH1
147   same as 146; bX: PH1, BK1
148   same as 146, P̄H̄1; aX: BK1
149   same as 148, less aX·bX: BK1
150   same as 148, BK1; less aX
151   same as 150


152   X: P95, WM1,  SM1, MB1; MOVE 152-183 t.o follow 53: 94: JP1
153   same as 152; less MOVE
```

3191	*Post.* Over-roasted rather; ready long ago.	154
	First Gaol. Hanging is the word, sir: if you	155
3192-3	be ready for that, you are well cooked.	156
	Post. So, if I prove a good repast to the	157
3194-5	spectators, the dish pays the shot.	158
	First Gaol. A heavy reckoning for you, sir.	159
3196	But the comfort is, you shall be called to no	160
3197	more payments, fear no more tavern-bills: which	161
3198	are often the sadness of parting, as the procuring	162
3199	of mirth: you come in faint for want of meat,	163
3200	depart reeling with too much drink: sorry that	164
	you have paid too much, and sorry that you are	165
3201	paid too much; purse and brain both empty:	166
3202	the brain the heavier for being too light, the	167
3203	purse too light, being drawn of heaviness: of	168
3204	this contradiction you shall now be quit. O,	169
3205	the charity of a penny cord! it sums up thou-	170
3206	sands in a trice: you have no true debitor and	171
	creditor but it: of what's past, is, and to come,	172
3207	the discharge: your neck, sir, is pen, book and	173
3208-9	counters; so the acquittance follows.	174
	Post. I am merrier to die than thou art	175
3210	to live.	176
	First Gaol. Indeed, sir, he that sleeps feels	177
3211	not the tooth-ache: but a man that were to sleep	178
3212	your sleep, and a hangman to help him to bed,	179
3213	I think he would change places with his officer:	180
3214	for, look you, sir, you know not which way you	181
3215	shall go.	182
3216	*Post.* Yes, indeed do I, fellow.	183
	First Gaol. Your death has eyes in 's head	184
3217	then; I have not seen him so pictured: you	185
3218	must either be directed by some that take upon	186
3219	them to know, or do take upon yourself that	187
3220	which I am sure you do not know, or jump the	188
	after inquiry on your own peril: and how you	189
3221	shall speed in your journey's end, I think you'll	190
3222-3	never return to tell one. **191**	191
	Post. I tell thee, fellow, there are none want	192
3224	eyes to direct them the way I am going, but such	193
3225-6	as wink and will not use them.	194
	First Gaol. What an infinite mock is this,	195
3227	that a man should have the best use of eyes to	196
3228	see the way of blindness! I am sure hanging's	197
3229	the way of winking.	198

```
154    same as 153
155    same as 153
156    same as 153
157    same as 153
158    same as 153, BK1
159    same as 153
160    same as 153
161    same as 153
162    same as 153
163    same as 153
164    same as 153
165    same as 153; bX: JG1
166    same as 152, J̄Ḡ1; bX: PH1, BK1
167    X: P95, WM1, SM1, M̄B̄1, PH1, BK1; aX: JG1
168    same as 167; less aX; bX: JG1
169    same as 168, including b̄X̄
170    X: P95, WM1, SM1, MB1, J̄Ḡ1; bX: IP2
171    X: P95, WM1, SM1, MB1; aX: IP2, JG1; bX: PH1, BK1
172    X: P95, WM1, SM1, MB1, P̄H̄1, BK1
173    same as 172
174    same as 172
175    X: P95, Wm1,   SM1, MB1
176    same as 175
177    same as 175
178    same as 175
179    same as 175
180    same as 175
181    same as 175
182    same as 175
183    same as 175
184    same as 175, JP1
185    same as 184
186    same as 184; bX: IP2, BK1
187    same as 184, B̄K̄1; aX: IP2
188    same as 187; less a̅X̅; bX: JG1
189    same as 187; less a̅X̅; aX: JG1
190    same as 187; less a̅X̅
191    same as 190
192    same as 190, PH1
193    same as 192; bX: IP2
194    same as 192, Ī P̄2
195    X: P95, Wm1, SM1, MB1, PH1, JP1, BK1
196    same as 195
197    same as 195; bX: IP2
198    same as 195, Ī P̄2
```

3230   *Enter a* Messenger.

Mess.. Knock off his manacles; bring your   199
3231-2 prisoner to the king.   **200**   200
Post. Thou bring'st good news; I am called   201
3233-4 to be made free.   202
3235 *First Gaol.* I'll be hang'd then.   203
Post. Thou shalt be then freer than a gaoler;   204
3236-7 no bolts for the dead.   205
3237+1   *[Exeunt all but the First Gaoler.*
First Gaol. Unless a man would marry a   206
3238 gallows and beget young gibbets, I never saw   207
3239 one so prone. Yet, on my conscience, there are   208
3240 verier knaves desire to live, for all he be a   209
3241 Roman: and there be some of them too that die   210
against their wills; so should I, if I were one.   211
3242 I would we were all of one mind, and one mind   212
3243 good: O, there were desolation of gaolers and   213
3244 gallowses! I speak against my present profit,   214
3245-6 but my wish hath a preferment in 't.   *[Exit.*   215

32447,+1   **SCENE V.** *Cymbeline's tent.*

3248 *Enter* CYMBELINE, BELARIUS, GUIDERIUS, AR-
3249   VIRAGUS, PISANIO, Lords, Officers, *and* At-
3249+1   tendants.

Cym. Stand by my side, you whom the gods
3250   have made   1
3251 Preservers of my throne. Woe is my heart   2
3252 That the poor soldier that so richly fought,   3
Whose rags shamed gilded arms, whose naked
3253   breast   4
3254 Stepp'd before targes of proof, cannot be found: 5
3255 He shall be happy that can find him, if   6
3256 Our grace can make him so.
Bel.   I never saw   7
3257
3258 Such noble fury in so poor a thing;   8
3259 Such precious deeds in one that promised nought   9
3269 But beggary and poor looks.
3261 *Cym.*   No tidings of him? 10   10
Pis. He hath been search'd among the dead
3262   and living,   11
3263 But no trace of him.
3264 *Cym.*   To my grief, I am   12
The heir of his reward; [*To Belarius, Guiderius,*
3265   *and Arviragus*] which I will add   13
3266 To you, the liver, heart and brain of Britain,   14

199 X: P95, WM1, SM1, MB1, JP1; aX: PJ1
200 same as 199; less aX
201 X: P95, WM1, SM1, MB1; aX: JP1
202 same as 201; less aX
203 same as 202
204 same as 202
205 same as 202

206 same as 202, JP1
207 same as 206
208 same as 206; bX: PH1, BK1
209 same as 206, PH1, BK1
210 same as 209
211 same as 209; bX: IP2
212 same as 209
213 same as 209
214 same as 209
215 same as 209

Scene 55

1 X: PH1, BK1; R: JG1
2 X: PH1, BK1; bX: HIC, ViA, Han, BA1, SM1, NM2, JG1
3 X: HIC, ViA, Han, BA1, SM1, NM2, PH1, JG1, BK1; bX: HIP

4 X: KRe, HIP,   HIC, ViA, Han, BA1, SM1, NM2, PH1, JG1, BK1
5 same as 4, less KRe; aX: KRe
6 same as 4

7 same as 4; bX: Lac, Rig, HM1, MTh, HIM, WmS, NM1, MB1, MB2
8 X: Lac, KRe, Rig, HM1, MTh, HIM, WmS, HIC, ViA, Han, BA1, SM1, NM1*
9 X: G61, Bel, Ox1, Wen, Bat, P95, Bar, Low, Roa, Inc, JKT, Oxb, Dol,
     USW, Cum, WM1, CKP, Lac, KRe, Rig, HM1, MTh, HIM, WmS, HIC, ViA*
10 X: Lac, KRe, Rig, HM1, HIM, WmS, HIC, ViA, Han, BA1, SM1, NM2, PH1
     JG1, BK1; aX: G61, Bel, Ox1, Wen, Bat, P95, Bar, Low, Roa, Inc*
11 X: ChM, Inc, KRe, HIC, ViA, Han, BA1, SM1, NM2, PH1, JG1, BK1

12 X: HIC, ViA, Han, BA1, SM1, NM2, PH1, JG1, BK1; aX: ChM, Inc, KRe

13 same as 12; less aX; b X: IP1
14 X: HIC, ViA, Han, BA1, IP1, NM2, PH1, JG1; aX: SM1

*55: 8NM2, MB1, MB2, PH1, JG1, BK1   *55:10 JKT, Oxb, Dol, USW,
   Cum, WM1, CKP, MTh, NM1, MB1, NM2

3267	**By whom I grant she lives.** 'Tis now the time	15
3268	**To ask of whence you are.** Report it.	
3269	*Bel.* Sir,	16
3270	**In Cambria are we born,** and gentlemen:	17
3271	**Further to boast were neither true nor modest,**	18
3272	**Unless I add,** 'we are honest.	
3273	*Cym.* Bow your knees.	19
3274	**Arise my knights o' the battle:** I create you **20**	20
3275	**Companions to our person** and will fit you	21
3276	**With dignities becoming your estates.**	22

3277   *Enter* CORNELIUS *and* Ladies.

3278	**There's business in these faces.** Why so sadly	23
3279	**Greet you our victory?** you look like Romans,	24
3280	**And not o' the court of Britain.**	
3281	*Cor.* Hail, great king!	25
3282	**To sour your happiness,** I must report	26
3283	**The queen is dead.**	
3284	*Cym.* Who worse than a physician	27
3285	**Would this report become?** But I consider,	28
3286	**By medicine life may be prolong'd,** yet death	29
3287	**Will seize the doctor too.** How ended she? **30**	30
3288	*Cor.* With horror, madly dying, like her life,	31
3289	**Which, being cruel to the world,** concluded	32
3290	**Most cruel to herself.** What she confess'd	33
3291	**I will report,** so please you: these her women	34
3292	**Can trip me,** if I err; who with wet cheeks	35
3293	**Were present when she finish'd.**	
3294	*Cym.* Prithee, say.	36
	Cor. First, she confess'd she never loved you,	
3295	only	37
3286	**Affected greatness got by you,** not you:	38
3297	**Married your royalty,** was wife to your place;	39
3298	**Abhorr'd your person.**	
3299	*Cym.* She alone knew this; **40**	40
3300	**And, but she spoke it dying,** I would not	41
3301	**Believe her lips in opening it.** Proceed.	42
	Cor. Your daughter, whom she bore in hand	
3303	to love	43
3303	**With such integrity,** she did confess	44
3304	**Was as a scorpion to her sight;** whose life,	45
3305	**But that her flight prevented it,** she had	46
3306	**Ta'en off by poison.**	
3307	*Cym.* O most delicate fiend!	47
3308	**Who is't can read a woman?** Is there more?	48

*55:34 HnF, CKP, Lac, KRe, Rig, HM1, MTh, HIM, HIP, HIC, ViA, SM1, NM1;
bX: WmS, BA1

15   X: PH1; <u>aX</u>: HIC, ViA, Han, BA1, IP1, JG1; <u>bX</u>: BK1

16   X: PH1, BK1
17   X: PH1, BK1
18   X: KRe, HIP, PH1, BK1

19   X: PH1; <u>aX</u>: KRe, HIP, BK1
20
21
22

23   X: Bel, Ox1, Wen, Bat, Bar, Low, Inc, JKT, Oxb, Dol, USW, Cum, WM1*
24   same as 23,   BA1; less <u>bX</u>; <u>bX</u>: ViA, JG1, BK1

25   same as 24, less HM1, MTh, HIM, WmS, BK1; <u>aX</u>: Lac, HM1, MTh, HIM, WmS*
26   same as 25; less <u>aX</u>, <u>N</u>, <u>MOVE</u>

27   same as 26, JG1; bX: G61, P95, Roa, Lac, HM¡ MTh, HIM, WmS, ViA, MB2;*
28   X: G61, Bel, Ox1, Wen, Bat, Bar, Low, Roa, Inc, JKT, Oxb, Dol, USW*
29   same as 28, P95, BA1, NM1, MB1, PH1, BK1; less <u>bX</u>
30   X: Bel, Ox1, Wen, Bat, Bar, Low, Inc, JKT, Oxb, Dol, USW, Cum, WM1*
31   same as 30; less <u>aX</u>; R: USW
32   same as 31; less <u>R</u>; <u>bX</u>: BK1
33   same as 31; less <u>R</u>; <u>bX</u>: Lac, HM1, MTh, HIM, ViA, NM1
34   X: Bel, Ox1, Wen, Bat, Bar, Low, Inc, JKT, Oxb, Dol, USW, Cum, WM1*
35   same as 34, Wm S, BA1, PH1; less <u>bX</u>, <u>cX</u>

36   same as 35, less BA1, NM1, PH1; <u>aX</u>: BA1, NM1; <u>bX</u>: Han; <u>cX</u>: BK1

37   same as 36, ChM, Han; less <u>aX</u>, <u>bX</u>, <u>cX</u>
38   same as 37
39   same as 37, BA1, BK1

40   same as 37; <u>bX</u>: BK1
41   same as 37, <u>PH1</u>, BK1
42   same as 37, PH1; <u>aX</u>: BK1

43   same as 42, less PH1; <u>bX</u>: BK1
44   same as 43, BA1, BK1
45   same as 43
46   same as 43

47   same as 43, less Han; <u>aX</u>: Han; <u>bX</u>: NM2
48   same as 47, NM2; <u>aX</u>: <u>JG1</u>

*55:23 HnF, C KP, Lac, KRe, Rig, HM1, MTh, HIM, WmS, HIP, HIC, SM1; bX:
    BA1; "Omit 23-68 after first performance": G61   *55:25 <u>ViA</u>,
    BA1, JG1, BK1; N: JG1; <u>MOVE</u> 25-36 to follow 43: 22: ChM
*55:27 <u>ADD</u> 1: Roa   *55:28 Cum, WM1, HnF, CKP, Lac, KRe,
    Rig, <u>HM1</u>, MTh, HIM, WmS, HIP, <u>HIC</u>, ViA, SM1, MB2, JG1; R: P95; bX: BA1,
    IP1, NM2, MB1, PH1, BK1   *55:30 HnF, CKP, <u>KRe</u>, Rig, <u>HIP</u>, HIC
    SM1; <u>aX</u>: G61, P95, Roa, Lac, HM1, MTh, <u>HIM</u>, WmS, ViA, BA1, IP1, NM2,
    MB1, <u>MB2</u>, PH1, JG1, BK1

Cor. More, sir, and worse. She did confess
3309   she had   49
3310 **For** you a mortal mineral ; which, being took, 50   50
3311 **Should** by the minute feed on life and lingering   51
    By inches waste you: in which time she pur-
3312   posed,   52
3313 **By** watching, weeping, tendance, kissing, to   53
3314 **O'ercome** you with her show, and in time,   54
3315 **When** she had fitted you with her craft, to work   55
3316 **Her** son into the adoption of the crown: 56
3317 **But,** failing of her end by his strange absence,   57
3318 **Grew** shameless-desperate ; open'd, in despite   58
3319 **Of** heaven and men, her purposes : repented   59
3320 **The** evils she hatch'd were not effected ; so   60   60
3321 **Despairing** died.
3322   *Cym.*   Heard you all this, her women?   61
3323   *First Lady.* We did, so please your highness.
3324   *Cym.*   Mine eyes   62
3325 **Were** not in fault, for she was beautiful ;   63
3326 **Mine** ears, that heard her flattery ; nor my heart,   64
    That thought her like her seeming ; it had been
3327   vicious   65
3328 **To** have mistrusted her : yet, O my daughter!   66
3329 **That** it was folly in me, thou mayst say,   67
3330 **And** prove it in thy feeling. Heaven mend all!   68

3331 *Enter* LUCIUS, IACHIMO, *the* Soothsayer, *and*
3332   *other* Roman Prisoners, *guarded;* POSTHUM-
3332+1   *behind, and* IMOGEN.

3333 **Thou** comest not, Caius, now for tribute ; that   69
3334 **The** Britons have razed out, though with the loss   70
    Of many a bold one ; whose kinsmen have made
3335   suit   71
    That their good souls may be appeased with
3336   slaughter   72
3337 **Of** you their captives, which ourself have granted: 73
3338 **So** think of your estate.   74
3339   *Luc.* Consider, sir, the chance of war : the day   75
3340 **Was** yours by accident ; had it gone with us,   76
    We should not, when the blood was cool, have
3341   threaten'd   77
3342 **Our** prisoners with the sword. But since the gods   78
3343 **Will** have it thus, that nothing but our lives   79
3344 **May** be call'd ransom, let it come : sufficeth   80
3345 **A** Roman with a Roman's heart can suffer :   81
3346 **Augustus** lives to think on't : and so much   82

```
49    same as 48,less ViA; less aX; aX: ViA
50    same as 49; less aX
51    same as 50

52    same as 50; bX: ViA, MB1, MB2, BK1
53    same as 50, ViA, BK1
54    same as 53, MB1, MB2, JG1; R: P95; aX: BK1
55    same as 54, G61, less BA1, JG1; less R, aX; aX: P95, BK1
56    same as 55, less G61; less aX
57    same as 56, BA1, PH1, BK1
58    same as 57; bX: JG1
59    same as 57; R: JG1; aX: ViA
60    same as 59, JG1; less R, aX

61    X: ChM, Bel, Ox1, Wen, Bat, Bar, Low, Inc, JKT, Oxb, Dol, USW, Cum,WM1,
         HnF, CKP, Lac, KRe, Rig, MTh, HIM, WmS, HIP, HIC, Han, SM1, JG1;aX*
62    same as 61, less Han, JG1; less aX, bX; aX: Han, JG1
63    same as 62, less ViA; less aX; cX: PH1, ADD 1: ViA
64    same as 63, ViA, NM1; less cX, ADD

65    same as 64; bX: HnF, BA1, Wen, Bat, BK1
66    same as 66, Han, BA1; less bX; aX: BK1
67    same as 66; less aX
68    same as 67, less BA1; aX: BA1




69    N: KRe
70    X: JP1

71    X: JP1; bX: ChM, NM1, NM2

72    X: ChM, NM1, NM2, JP1
73    same as 72; bX: HIC
74    same as 72
75    X: ChM, HIP
76    X: ChM, HIP; bX: ViA, JP1

77    X: HIP, ViA, JP1
78    aX : HIP, ViA, JP1; bX: KRe, WmS, NM1, NM2, PH1
79    X: KRe, WmS, NM1, NM2, PH1, BK1
80    X: KRe, WmS, NM1, NM2; aX: PH1, BK1; bX: HIC, SM1, MB2, JG1, JP1
81    X: KRe, WmS, HIC, SM1, NM1, NM2, MB2, JG1, JP1
82    same as 81, ViA; bX: ChM

*55:61 BA1, NM2, MB2; bX: ViA, PH1, BK1
```

3347	For my peculiar care. This one thing only	83
3348	I will entreat; my boy, a Briton born,	84
3349	Let him be ransom'd : never master had	85
3350	A page so kind, so duteous. diligent,	86
3351	So tender over his occasions, true,	87
3352	So feat, so nurse-like : let his virtue join	88
	With my request, which I'll make bold y⨯	
3253	highness	89
3354	Cannot deny; he hath done no Briton harm. ⨯	90
3355	Though he have served a Roman : save him, ⨯.	91
3356	And spare no·blood beside.	
3357	*Cym.* I have surely seen h⨯:	92
3358	His favour is familiar to me. Boy,	93
3359	Thou hast look'd thyself into my grace,	94
3360	†And art mine own. I know not why, wheref⨯	95
3361	To say 'live, boy:' ne'er thank thy master; L⨯.	96
3362	And ask of Cymbeline what boon thou wilt,	97
3363	Fitting my bounty and thy state, I'll give it;	98
3364	Yea, though thou do demand a prisoner,	99
3365	The noblest ta'en.	
3366	*Imo.* I humbly thank your highness. ⨯	100
3367	*Luc.* I do not bid thee beg my life, good ⨯:	101
3368	And yet I know thou wilt.	
3369	*Imo.* No, no : alack,	102
3370	There's other work in hand : I see a thing	103
3371	Bitter to me as death : your life, good master,	104
3372	Must shuffle for itself.	
3373	*Luc.* The boy disdains me,	105
3374	He leaves me, scorns me : briefly die their j⨯⨯	106
3375	That place them on the truth of girls and boys.	107
3376	Why stands he so perplex'd?	
3377	*Cym.* What wouldst thou. b⨯!	108
3378	I love thee more and more : think more and m⨯⨯	109
	What's best to ask. Know'st him thou look's	
3379	on? speak,	110
3380	Wilt have him live? Is he thy kin? thy friend?	111
3381	*Imo.* He is a Roman ; no more kin to me	112
	Than I to your highness; who, being born y⨯⨯	
3382	vassal.	113
3383	Am something nearer.	
3384	*Cym.* Wherefore eyest him so?	114
3385	*Imo.* I'll tell you, sir, in private, if you pl⨯⨯	115
3386	To give me hearing.	
3387	*Cym.* Ay, with all my heart,	116
3388	And lend my best attention. What's thy nam⨯	117
3389	*Imo.* Fidele, sir.	

*55:110 Dol, USW, Cum, KRe, Rig, HIC, BAl, IPl, NM2, PHl, JG1

83   aX : ChM, KRe, WmS, HIC, ViA, SM1, NM1, NM2, MB2, JG1, JP1
84
85   bX : Bel, Wen, Bat, Bar, KRe, WmS, HIC, MB1, MB2
86   X: Bel, Wen, Bat, Bar, KRe, WmS, HIC, MB1, MB2; bX: BA1, NM1,NM2,PH1
87   X: Bel, Ox1, Wen, Bat, Bar, Low, Inc, JKT, Oxb, Dol, USW, Cum, WM1*
88   same as 87, ChM, G61, less BA1; less R, bX; aX: ViA, BA1

89   same as 88; less aX; bX: BA1, IP1
90   X: KRe, JG1; aX: ChM, G61, Bel, Ox1, Wen, Bat, Bar, Low, Inc, JKT*
91   X: B K1; aX: WmS, ViA, JG1

92   aX : ChM, KRe, BK1; MOVE 92b-270 to follow 368a: ChM
93   Insert 120-129: MB1
94   aX: Bel
95   R: JG1; aX: G61, Bel, Wen, Bat, P95, Bar; bX: KRe, BA1, NM2
96   X: IP1; R: JG1; aX: KRe, BA1
97
98   X: ViA, BA1; aX: HIC, JG1; bX: BK1
99   X: G61, Bel, Wen, Bat, P95, Bar, Roa, ViA, BK1

100   X: G61, Bel, Wen, Bat, P95, Bar, Roa, Oxb, Dol, Rig, HIC, ViA; aX:HIC*
101   X: G61, Bel, Ox1, Wen, Bat, P95, Bar, Roa, Inc, JKT, Oxb, Dol,USW,Cum,
        WM1, HnF, CKP, KRe, Rig, Wm S
102   same as 101
103   same as 101
104   same as 101, ChM; bX: HIC, ViA, BA1, MB1, MB2

105   same as 104, BA1, less ChM; less bX; aX: HIC, ViA, MB1, MB2; bX: Lac*
106   X: ChM, G61, Bel, Ox1, Wen, Bat, P95, Bar, Low, Roa, Inc, JKT, Oxb,Dol*
107   same as 106, SM1, MB2, PH1, BK1, less ViA; less aX, bX, aX: ViA

108   X: G61, Bel, Ox1, Wen, Bat, P95, Bar, Low, Roa, Inc, JKT, Oxb, Dol,USW*
109   X: G61, Bel, Ox1, Wen, Bat, P95, Bar, Low, Roa, Inc, JKT, Oxb,Dol,USW*

110   X: BK1; aX: G61, Bel, Ox1, Wen, Bat, P95, Bar, Low, Roa, Inc, JKT, Oxb*
111   X: JG1, BK1; bX: MB2, PH1
112   X: MB2, JG1, BK1; bX: PH1

113   X: MB2, PH1, JG1, BK1; bX:HIC, BA1

114   X: MB2, JG1; aX: HIC, BA1, PH1, BK1
115   X: NM1, NM2, MB2, JG1

116   same as 115; bX: WmS, BK1
117   X: Ox1, Low, Inc, JKT, Oxb, Dol, USW, Cum, WM1, CKP, Rig, WmS, BA1,SM1,
        NM1, NM2, MB2, JG1; aX: BK1; bX: KRe

*55:87 HnF, CKP, KRe, Rig, WmS, HIC, BA1, NM1, NM2, MB1, MB2, PH1, JG1, BK1;
   R: ChM; bX: G61, ViA   *55:90 Oxb, USW, Cum, WM1, HnF, CKP, Rig,
WmS, HIC, BA1, NM1, IP1, NM2, MB1, MB2, PH1, BK1; bX: ViA
*55:100 BK1; bX: Ox1, Low, Inc, JKT, USW, Cum, SM1, KRe   *55:105 HM1,
   HIM, NM2   *55:106 USW, Cum, WM1, HnF, CKP, KRe, Rig, HIM, WmS,
   HIC, ViA, BA1, NM1, NM2; aX: ViA; bX: SM1, MB2, PH1   *55:108 Cum,KRe,
   Rig; aX: Lac, HM1, HIM, WmS, HIC, BA1, NM1, NM2, PH1, JG1   *55:109 Cum,
   KRe, Rig, BA1, NM1, IP1, NM2, PH1, JG1; bX: HIC, BK1

3390	*Cym.*　　Thou'rt my good youth, my page;	118
3391	I'll be thy master: walk with me; speak freely.	119
3391+1	[*Cymbeline and Imogen converse apart.*	
3392	*Bel.* Is not this boy revived from death?	
3393	*Arv.*　　　　　One sand another 120	120
3394	Not more resembles that sweet rosy lad	121
3395	Who died, and was Fidele. What think you?	122
3396	*Gui.* The same dead thing alive.	123
	Bel. Peace, peace! see further; he eyes us	
3397	not; forbear;	124
3398	Creatures may be alike: were't he, I am sure	125
3399	He would have spoke to us.	
3400	*Gui.*　　　　　But we saw him dead.	126
3401	*Bel.* Be silent; let's see further.	
3402	*Pis.*　　　　[*Aside*] It is my mistress:	127
3403	Since she is living, let the time run on	128
3	To good or bad.	
	[*Cymbeline and Imogen come forward.*	
	Cym.　　　Come, stand thou by our side:	;29
	Make thy demand aloud. [*To Iachimo*]　Sir,	
4 c	step you forth;　　　　　　130	130
3 07	Give answer to this boy, and do it freely;	131
3408	Or, by our greatness and the grace of it,	132
3409	Which is our honour, bitter torture shall	133
	Winnow the truth from falsehood. On, speak to	
3410	him.	134
3411	*Imo.* My boon is, that this gentleman may render	135
3412	Of whom he had this ring.	
3413	*Post.*　　　[*Aside*] What's that to him?	136
3414	*Cym.* That diamond upon your finger, say	137
3415	How came it yours?	138
	Iach. Thou'lt torture me to leave unspoken	
3416	that	139
3417	Which, to be spoke, would torture thee.	
3418	*Cym.*　　　　　How! me? 140	140
3419	*Iach.* I am glad to be constrain'd to utter that	141
3420	Which torments me to conceal. By villany	142
3421	I got this ring: 'twas Leonatus' jewel;	143
	Whom thou didst banish; and—which more may grieve thee,	
3422		144
3423	As it doth me—a nobler sir ne'er lived	145
	Twixt sky and ground. Wilt thou hear more,	
3424	my lord?	146
3425	*Cym.* All that belongs to this.	
3426	*Iach.*　　　　That paragon, thy daughter,—	147

118   same as 117, ChM, KRe, less SM1; less aX, bX; aX: SM1; bX: BK1

119   X: ChM, BA1, NM1, NM2, MB2, JG1, BK1; aX: Ox1, Low, Inc, JKT, Oxb, Dol, USW, Cum, WM1, CKP, KRe, Rig; cX: ViA

120   X: NM1, JG1; bX: HIC, BA1, PH1, BK1; MOVE 120-129 to follow 93:MB1

121   X: HIC, BA1, NM1, PH1, JG1, BK1

122   X: HIC, BA1, NM1, JG1; aX: PH1, BK1; bX: G61, Bel, P95, ViA, NM2

123   X: KRe, BA1, NM1, NM2, JG1; bX: ChM

124   X: HnF, Lac, KRe, Rig, HM1, MTh, HIM, WmS, HIC, ViA, BA1, NM1, NM2*

125   X: G61, Bel, Ox1, Wen, Bat, P95, Bar, Low, Roa, Inc, JKT, Oxb, Dol, USW, Cum, WM1, HnF, CKP, Lac, KRe, Rig, HM1, MTh, HIM, WmS, HIC, ViA*

126   same as 125, less ViA; aX: ViA; bX: ChM

127   X: Lac, KRe, Rig, HM1, MTh, HIM, WmS, HIC, ViA, NM1, JG1; aX:ChM,G61*

128   X : KRe, Rig, HM1, MTh, HIM, WmS, HIC, ViA, SM1, NM1, NM2,JG1,BK1

129   X: NM1, JG1, BK1; aX: Lac, KRe, Rig, HM1, MTh, HIM, WmS, HIC, ViA, SM1, NM2

130   X: NM1, NM2, MB2, JG1; aX: BK1

131   same as 130; less aX

132   X: KRe, HIC, ViA, NM1, NM2, MB2, PH1, JG1, BK1; bX: Low, Inc, JKT*

133   same as 132, Low, BA1; less bX; aX: Inc, JKT, Dol, USW, Cum, WM1,HnF, CKP, Lac, HM1, HIM, WmS

134   X: KRe, HIC, NM1, NM2, MB2, PH1, JG1, BK1; aX: ViA

135   aX : PH1

136   bX: WmS, ViA, JG1

137   aX : ViA; ADD 30: BK1

138   X: BK1

139   X: ChM, KRe, IP1, JG1, BK1

140   X: ChM, KRe, JG1, BK1; aX: IP1; bX: BA1

141   X: KRe, HIC, ViA, BA1, BK1

142   X: BK1; aX: HIC, ViA, BA1

143   X: BK1

144   X: BK1; aX: HIC; bX: Bel, Wen, Bat, Bar, KRe, ViA, BA1, JG1

145   X: Bel, Wen, Bat, Bar, BK1; aX: KRe, HIC, ViA, BA1, JG1

146   X: NM2, BK1; aX: Bel, Wen, Bat, Bar; bX: KRe, MB1, PH1

147   X: MB1, BK1; aX: KRe, NM2, PH1; bX: MB2

*55:124 PH1, JG1, BK1; bX: G61, Bel, Ox1, Wen, Bat, P95, Bar, Low, Roa, Inc, JKT, Oxb, Dol ,Cum, WM1, CKP, MB1   *55:125 BA1, NM1, NM2, MB1, PH1, JG1, BK1   *55:127 Bel, Ox1, Wen, Bat, P95, Bar, Low, Roa, Inc, JKT, Oxb, Dol, USW, Cum, WM1, CKP, BA1, BK1

*55:132 Dol, USW, Cum, WM1, HnF, CKP, Lac, HM1, HIM, WmS, BA1

3427	For whom my heart drops blood, and my false spirits	148
3428	Quail to remember— Give me leave: I faint.	149
	Cym. My daughter! what of her? Renew	
3429	thy strength: 150	150
3430	I had rather thou shouldst live while nature will	151
3431	Than die ere I hear more : strive, man, and speak.	152
3432	Iach. Upon a time,—unhappy was the clock	153
	That struck the hour!—it was in Rome,—ac-	
3433	cursed	154
3434	The mansion where!—'twas at a feast,—O, would	155
3435	Our viands had been poison'd, or at least	156
	These which I heaved to head!—the good Post-	
3436	humus—	157
3437	What should I say? he was too good to be	158
3438	Where ill men were; and was the best of all	159
3439	Amongst the rarest of good ones,—sitting sadly,	160
3440	Hearing us praise our loves of Italy 161	161
3441	For beauty that made barren the swell'd boast	162
3442	Of him that best could speak, for feature, laming	163
3443	The shrine of Venus, or straight-pight Minerva,	164
3444	Postures beyond brief nature, for condition,	165
3445	A shop of all the qualities that man	166
3446	Loves woman for, besides that hook of wiving,	167
3447	Fairness which strikes the eye—	
	Cym. I stand on fire:	168
3448	Come to the matter.	
3449	Iach. All too soon I shall,	169
	Unless thou wouldst grieve quickly. This Post-	
3450	humus, 170	170
3451	Most like a noble lord in love and one	171
3452	That had a royal lover, took his hint ;	172
3453	And, not dispraising whom we praised,—therein	173
3454	He was as calm as virtue—he began	174
	His mistress' picture ; which by his tongue being	
3455	made,	175
3456	And then a mind put in't, either our brags	176
3457	Were crack'd of kitchen-trulls, or his description	177
3458	Proved us unspeaking sots.	
3459	Cym. Nay, nay, to the purpose.	178
3460	Iach. Your daughter's chastity—there it begins.	179
3461	He spake of her, as Dian had hot dreams, 180	180
3462	And she alone were cold: whereat I, wretch,	181
3463	Made scruple of his praise; and wager'd with him	182
3464	Pieces of gold 'gainst this which then he wore	183
3465	Upon his honour'd finger, to attain	184

148 X: MB1, MB2, BK1
149 same as 148; bX: JG1

150 same as 148; bX: HIC, BA1, JG1
151 X: CKP, KRe, WmS, HIC, ViA, BA1, SM1, MB1, MB2, PH1, JG1, BK1
152 X: MB1, MB2, PH1, BK1; aX: CKP, KRe, WmS, HIC, ViA, BA1; bX: Oxb, Low;
153 X: MB1, MB2, BK1; bX: ChM, WmS, NM2, PH1

154 X: ChM, NM2, MB1, MB2, BK1; aX: PH1; bX: WmS
155 same as 154; less aX, bX; aX: WmS; bX: Rig, HIC, ViA, BA1
156 X: ChM, Rig, HIC, BA1, SM1, NM2, MB1, MB2, PH1, BK1; bX: WmS, JG1;
    cX: ViA
157 X: Rig, NM1, NM2, MB1, MB2, BK1; aX: ChM, WmS, HIC, ViA, BA1, SM1,*
158 X: ChM, G61, Bel, Oxl, Wen, Bat, Bar, Low, Roa, Inc, Oxb, Dol, USW*
159 same as 158, JKT; less R, aX; bX: SM1
160 same as 159, less BA1, JG1; less bX; aX: BA1, SM1, JG1
161 same as 160, WM1, MTh, less ChM, NM1, PH1; less aX
162 same as 161, SM1, JP1
163 same as 162; bX: HIC, BA1, NM1, PH1, JG1
164 same as 163, HIC, BA1, NM1, PH1, JG1; less bX; bX: IP1
165 same as 164; less bX; aX: IP1; bX: ChM
166 same as 165, ChM; less aX, bX
167 same as 166, less BA1; aX: BA1

168 X: G61, Oxl, Low, Roa, Inc, JKT, Oxb, Dol, USW, Cum, WM1, HnF, CKP,
    Lac, KRe, Rig, HM1, MTh, HIM, WmS, HIC, ViA, Han, MB1, MB2, PH1,JP1*
169 X: JKT, Dol, WM1, HnF, CKP, MTh, Wm S, ViA, NM2, MB1, MB2, PH1, BK1;
    bX: G61, Bel, Oxl, Wen, Bat, Bar, Low, Roa, Inc, Oxb, USW, Cum, Lac*
170 X: G61, Bel, Oxl, Wen, Bat, Bar, Low, Roa, Inc, JKT, Oxb, Dol, USW*
171 same as 170, less NM2, JG1; less aX; aX: NM2
172 same as 171; less aX
173 same as 172, IP1; bX: BA1, NM1
174 same as 173, ChM, less IP1; less bX; aX: BA1, NM1, IP1, JG1

175 same as 174, less ChM; less aX; bX: ChM, BA1, PH1, JG1, JP1
176 same as 175, ChM, BA1, PH1, JG1, JP1; less bX; bX: IP1
177 same as 176; less bX; aX: IP1

178 X: G61, Bel, Oxl, Bat, Bar, Low, Roa, Inc, JKT, Oxb, Dol, USW, Cum,*
179 X: BA1, NM2, BK1; bX: KRe, NM1
180 X: KRe, ViA, BA1, NM2, BK1; aX: NM2; bX: WmS, HIC
181 X: KRe, BK1; aX: WmS, HIC, ViA, BA1, NM1; bX: PH1
182 XL: PH1, BK1; aX: KRe, ViA
183 X: BK1
184 X: PH1, BK1; bX: HIC, BA1, SM1, JG1

*55:152 Oxb , Dol, USW, SM1, JG1   *55:157 PH1, JG1
*55:158 Cum, HnF, CKP, Lac, KRe, Rig, HM1, HIM, WmS, ViA, Han, BA1, NM1,MB1,
    MB2, PH1, JG1, BK1; R: JKT; aX: NM2   *55:168 BK1; aX: ChM, Bel,
    Wen, Bat, Bar, SM1, NM1, JG1 .   *55:169 Rig, HM1, HIM, Han
*55:1 70 Cum, WM1, HnF, CKP, Lac, KRe, Rig, HM1, MTh, HIM, WmS, HIC, ViA,
    Han, SM1, NM2, MB1, MB2, JG1, BK1; aX: PH1   *55:178 CKP, Lac,KRe,
    Rig, HM1, HIM, WmS, HIC, Han, BA1, SM1, MB2, BK1; aX: ChM, WM1, HnF,
    ViA, MB1, MB2, PH1, JG1, JP1

3466	In suit the place of 's bed and win this ring	185
3467	By hers and mine adultery. He, true knight,	186
3468	No lesser of her honour confident	187
3469	Than I did truly find her, stakes this ring;	188
3470	And would so, had it been a carbuncle 189	189
3471	Of Phœbus' wheel, and might so safely, had it	190
3472	Been all the worth of 's car. Away to Britain	191
3473	Post I in this design: well may you, sir,	192
3474	Remember me at court; where I was taught	193
3475	Of your chaste daughter the wide difference	194
3476	'Twixt amorous and villanous. Being thus quench'd	195
3477	Of hope, not longing, mine Italian brain	196
3478	'Gan in your duller Britain operate	197
3479	Most vilely: for my vantage, excellent:	198
3480	And, to be brief, my practice so prevail'd,	199
3481	That I return'd with simular proof enough 200	200
3482	To make the noble Leonatus mad,	201
3483	By wounding his belief in her renown	202
3484	With tokens thus, and thus: averring notes	203
3485	Of chamber-hanging, pictures, this her bracelet,—	204
3486	O cunning, how I got it!—nay, some marks	205
3487	Of secret on her person, that he could not	206
3488	But think her bond of chastity quite crack'd,	207
3489	I having ta'en the forfeit. Whereupon—	208
3490	Methinks, I see him now—	
3491	*Post.* [*Advancing*] Ay, so thou dost,	209
3492	Italian fiend! Ay me, most credulous fool, 210	210
3493	Egregious murderer, thief, any thing	211
3494	That 's due to all the villains past, in being,	212
3495	To come! O, give me cord, or knife, or poison,	123
3496	Some upright justicer! Thou, king, send out	124
3497	For torturers ingenious: it is I	125
3498	That all the abhorred things o' the earth amend	216
3499	By being worse than they. I am Posthumus,	217
3500	That kill'd thy daughter:—villain-like. I lie—	218
3501	That caused a lesser villain than myself,	219
3502	A sacrilegious thief, to do 't: the temple 220	220
3503	Of virtue was she; yea, and she herself.	221
3504	Spit, and throw stones, cast mire upon me, set	222
3505	The dogs o' the street to bay me: every villain	223
3506	Be call'd Posthumus Leonatus: and	224
3507	Be villany less than 'twas! O Imogen!	225
3508	My queen, my life, my wife! O Imogen,	226
3509	Imogen, Imogen!	
3510	*Imo.* Peace, my lord; hear, hear—	227

*55:203 JKT, Oxb, Do1, Cum, WM1, HnF, CKP, Lac, Rig, HM1, MTh, HIM, WmS,
ViA   *55:204 Cum, WM1, HnF, CKP, Lac, KRe, Rig, HM1, MTh,
HIM, WmS, PH1, JG1, BK1; aX: JKT   *55:215 WM1, HnF, CKP, Rig,
HIP, ViA, NM1   *55:216 HIP, ViA, BA1, NM1, PH1, JG1, BK1
*55:217 Rig, WmS, HIP, ViA, BA1, PJ1, JG1, BK1
*55:206 Bat, Low Roa, Inc, Oxb, Do1, USW, Cum, WM1, HnF, CKP, Lac, H41,

HIM, WmS, ViA; bX: HIC, BA1

185 X: SM1, BK1; aX: HIC, BA1, PH1, JG1; cX: NM1
186 X: ViA, BK1; aX: HIC, SM1, NM1; bX: G61, Bel, Ox1, Wen, Bat, Bar*
187 X: G61, Bel, Ox1, Wen, Bat, Bar, Low, Roa, Inc, JKT, Oxb, Dol,USW*
188 same as 187, less NM1
189 X: ChM, G61, Bel, Ox1, Wen, Bat, Bar, Low, Roa, Inc, JKT, Oxb,Dol*
190 same as 189
191 X: ChM, KRe, MB2, BK1; aX: G61, Bel, Ox1, Wen, Bat, Bar, Low, Roa*
192 X: ChM, KRe, MB2, BK1; bX: ViA, PH1
193 same as 192; less bX; aX: ViA, PH1; bX: HIC, JP1
194 X: ChM, KRe, HIC, MB2, JP1, BK1; bX: NM1, NM2

195 same as 194; less bX; aX: HIC, MB2; bX: G61, Bel, Ox1, Wen, Bat,Bar*
196 X: ChM, G61, Bel, Ox1, Wen, Bat, Bar, Low, Roa, Inc, JKT, Oxb,Dol*
197 same as 196, less NM1, NM2; aX: NM1, NM2
198 same as 197, HIC, SM1, PH1; less aX; bX: BA1
199 X: HIC, ViA, SM1, BK1; aX: WmS, BA1
200 X: HIC, SM1, BK1
201 X: BK1.
202 X: KRe, ViA, MB1, PH1, BK1; bX: JG1
203 X: KRe, PH1, JG1, BK1; R: ChM; bX: G61, Ox1, Wen, Bat, Low, Roa,Inc*
204 X: ChM, G61, Bel, Ox1, Wen, Bat, Bar, Low, Roa, Inc, Oxb, Dol,USW*
205 same as 204; less aX; aX: SM1
206 X: ChM, Bel, Bar, KRe, Rig, MTh, PH1, JG1, BK1; aX: G61, Ox1, Wen✶
207 X: ChM, Rig, HIC, BA1, SM1, PH1, JG1, BK1; aX: MTh
208 X: BK1; aX: Rig, HIC, ViA, BA1, SM1, JG1

209 X: BK1
210 X: BK1; bX:WmS, BA1, NM1, PH1, JG1
211 X: WmS, BA1, NM1, PH1, JG1, BK1; bX: ViA
212 same as 211, ViA; less bX
213 X: WmS, ViA, PH1; aX: BA1, NM1, NM2, JG1, BK1
214 X: WmS, PH1, BK1; aX: ViA, NM1; bX: BA1, JG1
215 X: WmS, BA1, PH1, JG1, BK1; bX: Bel, Wen, Bat, Bar, Inc, JKT, Cum*
216 X: Bel, Wen, Bat, Bar, Inc, JKT, Dol, Cum, WM1, HnF, CKP, Rig, WmS*
217 X: NM1; aX: Bel, Wen, Bat, Bar, Inc, JKT, Dol, Cum, WM1, HnF, CKP*
218 R: Wen; aX: NM1; bX: Dol, Cum, WmS, Rig, BK1; ADD 1: Bel,Bat,Bar,Inc,JKT
219 X: Inc, Dol, Cum, Rig, WmS, BK1
220 X: BK1; aX: Inc, Dol, Cum, Rig, WmS, ViA
221 X: HIC, BK1; bX: ViA
222 X: ChM, HIP, HIC, ViA, PH1, BK1
223 same as 222, HnF
224 same as 223
225 X: ChM, HIC, SM1, PH1, BK1; aX: HnF, HIP, ViA
226

227 aX : ChM

*55:186 Roa, Inc, JKT, Oxb, Dol, USW, Cum, WM1, CKP, Rig, BA1, JG1
*55:187CKP, Rig, ViA, BA1, NM1, JG1, BK1   *55:189 USW, Cum, WM1,
   HnF, CKP, Lac, KRe, Rig, HM1, MTh, HIM, WmS, ViA, BA1, SM1, NM1, MB1,MB2,
   PH1, JG1, BK1   *55:191 Inc, JKT, Oxb, Dol, USW, Cum, WM1,HnF,
   CKP, Lac, Rig, HM1, MTh, HIM, Wm S, ViA, BA1, SM1, NM1, MB1, PH1, JG1
*55:195 Low, Roa, Inc, JKT, Oxb, Dol, USW, Cum, WM1, HnF, CKP, Lac, Rig, HM1,
   MTH, HIM, WmS   *55:196 USW, Cum, WM1, HnF, CKP, Lac, KRe, Rig,
   HM1, MTh, HIM, WmS, ViA, NM1, NM2, JP1, BK1

3511 *Post.* Shall's have a play of this? Thou scorn- 228
    ful page,

3512 There be thy part.   [*Striking her: she falls.*

3513   *Pis.*   O, gentlemen, help!   229 229

3514 Mine and your mistress! O, my lord Posthumus! 230

3515 You ne'er kill'd Imogen till now. Help, help! 231

3516 Mine honour'd lady!

3517   *Cym.*   Does the world go round? 232

3518   *Post.* How come these staggers on me?

3519   *Pis.*   Wake, my mistress! 233

    Cym. If this be so, the gods do mean to

3520   strike me 234

3521 To death with mortal joy.

3522   *Pis.*   How fares my mistress? 235

3523   *Imo.* O, get thee from my sight: 236

3524 Thou gavest me poison: dangerous fellow, hence! 237

3525 Breathe not where princes are.

3526   *Cym.*   The tune of Imogen! 238

    Pis. Lady, 239

3527 The gods throw stones of sulphur on me, if 240 240

3528 That box I gave you was not thought by me 241

3529 A precious thing: I had it from the queen. 242

3530   *Cym.* New matter still?

3531   *Imo.*   It poison'd me.

3532   *Cor.*   O gods! 243

3533 I left out one thing which the queen confess'd, 244

3534 Which must approve thee honest: ' If Pisanio 245

3535 Have' said she 'given his mistress that confection 246

3536 Which I gave him for cordial, she is served 247

3537 As I would serve a rat.'

3538   *Cym.*   What's this, Cornelius? 248

3539   *Cor.* The queen, sir, very oft importuned me 249

3540 To temper poisons for her, still pretending 250 250

3541 The satisfaction of her knowledge only 251

3542 In killing creatures vile, as cats and dogs, 252

3543 Of no esteem: I, dreading that her purpose 253

3544 Was of more danger, did compound for her 254

3545 A certain stuff, which, being ta'en, would cease 255

3546 The present power of life, but in short time 256

3547 All offices of nature should again 257

3548 Do their due functions. Have you ta'en of it? 258

3549   *Imo.* Most like I did, for I was dead.

    Bel.   My boys, 259

3550 There was our error.

3551   *Gui.*   This is, sure, Fidele. 260 260

    Imo. Why did you throw your wedded lady

228 R: G61; aX: Bel, Ox1, Wen, Bat, Bar, Low, Roa, Inc, JKT, Oxb, Dol,USW,
     Cum, WM1, HnF, CKP, KRe, Rig, WmS ; ADD 1: Low, Oxb

229 R: Inc, Cum; aX: G61, Ox1, Low, Oxb; bX: WmS, HIC, PH1, BK1;ADD 1:ViA
230 aX: WmS, HIC, PH1, JG1, BK1; bX: Cum
231 X: NM1, NM2; aX: Cum

232 X: NM2; aX: NM1; bX: Cum, Low, Inc, JKT, Oxb, Dol, USW, Cum, HnF, CKP,
     Rig, WmS, ViA, MB1, JG1
233 X: KRe, HIC, BA1, MB2, JG1; aX: HnF, ViA, NM2, BK1; bX: ChM, Rig,PH1

234 X: KRe, HIC, BA1, MB2, PH1; R: ChM; aX: NM2

235 X: KRe, HIC, BA1; R: ChM; aX: MB2; bX: G61, Bel, Ox1, Wen, Bat,P95*
236 X: G61, Bel, Ox1, Wen, Bat, P95, Bar, Low, Roa, Inc, JKT, Oxb, Dol*
237 same as 236, HIM; less R; R: ChM; bX: BK1

238 same as 237, less NM2; less R, bX; R: ChM; aX: NM2, BK1; ADD 2: ChM
239 same as 238; less R, aX, ADD; bX: ChM
240 same as 238, BK1; less R, aX,ADD; R: ChM
241 same as 240, including R
242 same as 240 including R

243 same as 240 including R;; aX: PH1, JG1, BK1
244 same as 240, JG1; same R; less aX
245 same as 244, including R; bX: HIP, PH1
246 same as 244,PH1, HIP; same R
247 same as 246, ChM, NM2; less R

248 same as 247, NM1, less HIP, NM2, PH1, JG1; aX: HIP, NM2, PH1, JG1
249 same as 248, MB2, NM1; less aX
250 same as 249,   PH1, JG1, BK1; bX: NM1, NM2, MB1
251 same as 250, NM1, MB1, MB2; less bX; bX: HIP
252 same as 251, HIP, less NM2; less bX; aX: NM2
253 same as 252, less HIP, NM1, MB1, MB2, JG1; less aX; aX: HIP,NM1,MB1*
254 same as 253; less aX; aX: NM1, MB1, PH1, JG1
255 same as 253, less SM1, BK1; less aX; bX: NM1
256 same as 253; less aX
257 same as 253, NM2; less aX
258 same as 257, less NM1, NM2; aX: NM1, NM2

259 same as 258; less aX

260 same as 258, less SM1;aX: SM1; bX: MB1, JG1
*55:235 Bar, Low, Roa, Inc, JKT, Oxb, Dol, USW, Cum, Rig, NM2
*55:236 USW, Cum, WM1, HnF, CKP, Lac, KRe, Rig, HM1, MTh, WmS, HIC, ViA,
     BA1, SM1, NM2; R:ChM   *55:253 MB2, JG1

3552	from you?	261
3553	Think that you are upon a rock ; and now	262
3554	Throw me again. [*Embracing him.*	
3555	*Post.* Hang there like fruit, my soul,	263
3556	Till the tree die!	
3557	*Cym.* How now, my flesh, my child!	264
3558	What, makest thou me a dullard in this act?	265
3559	Wilt thou not speak to me?	
3560	*Imo.* [*Kneeling*] Your blessing, sir.	266
	Bel. [*To Guiderius and Arviragus*] Though	
3561	you did love this youth, I blame ye not;	267
3562	You had a motive for't	
3563	*Cym.* My tears that fall	268
3564	Prove holy water on thee! Imogen,	269
3565	Thy mother's dead.	
3566	*Imo.* I am sorry for't, my lord. 270	270
	Cym. O, she was naught; and long of her it	
3567	was	271
3568	That we meet here so strangely: but her son	272
3569	Is gone, we know not how nor where.	
3570	*Pis.* My lord,	273
	Now fear is from me, I'll speak troth. Lord	
3571	Cloten.	274
3572	Upon my lady's missing, came to me	275
	With his sword drawn; foam'd at the mouth, and	
3573	swore,	276
3574	If I discover'd not which way she was gone,	277
3575	It was my instant death. By accident,	278
3576	I had a feigned letter of my master's	279
3577	Then in my pocket; which directed him ᴫᴸ	280
3578	To seek her on the mountains near to Milford;	281
3579	Where, in a frenzy, in my master's garments,	282
3580	Which he enforced from me, away he posts	283
3581	With unchaste purpose and with oath to violate	284
3582	My lady's honour: what became of him	285
3583	I further know not.	
	Gui. Let me end the story:	286
3584	I slew him there.	
3585	*Cym.* Marry, the gods forfend!	287
3586	I would not thy good deeds should from my lips	288
3587	Pluck a hard sentence: prithee, valiant youth,	289
3588	Deny't again.	
3589	*Gui.* I have spoke it, and I did it. ᴫᴸ	290
3590	*Cym.* He was a prince.	291
3591	*Gui.* A most incivil one: the wrongs he did me	292
3592	Were nothing prince-like; for he did provoke me	293

261 MOVE 261b-266 to follow 273a: SM1
262 X: JP1

263 aX: JP1

264 R: G61, Inc, Dol, Cum; bX: Bel, Wen, Bat, P95, Bar, Low, JKT, USW*
265 X: Low, Roa, Oxb, USW, Cum, Rig, ViA, BA1; R: G61, Bel, Oxl. Wen,Bat,
     P95, Bar, Inc, JKT, Dol, KRe, WmS, HIC, BK1
266 R: Inc, Cum; aX: G61, Bel, Oxl, Wen, Bat, P95, Bar, Low, Roa, JKT,Oxb,
     Dol, USW, Rig
267 X: ChM, HnF, Lac, HM1, MTh, HIM, WmS, HIC, Han, BA1, SM1, NM2, MB1,
     JG1
268 X: HM1, HIM, WmS, HIP; aX: ChM, HnF, Lac, MTh, HIC, Han, BA1, SM1*
269 X: Inc, Cum, HIP; aX: Low, JKT, Oxb, Dol, Rig, HIM, WmS; bX: ChM

270 X: HIP; R: ChM; aX: BK1; bX: KRe, WmS, BA1, NM2

271 X: HIP, HIC, BA1, NM1, NM2, MB1, MB2; R: ChM, WmS; bX: KRe
272 X: HIP; R: ChM; aX: KRe, WmS, HIC, BA1, NM1, NM2, MB1, MB2

273 X: HIP; R: ChM; bX: G61, Bel, Oxl, Wen, Bat, Bar, Low, Roa, Inc,JKT,
     Oxb, Dol, USW, Cum, WM1, HnF, CKP, Lac, Rig, HM1, MTh, HIM, WmS*
274 X: G61, Bel, Oxl, Wen, Bat, Bar, Low, Roa, Inc, JKT, Oxb, Dol, USW,*
275 same as 274; less R, aX; R: ChM

276 same as 275; same R; aX: BK1; bX: NM2
277 same as 275, NM2; same R
278 same as 277,less MB1; same R; aX: MB1; bX: JG1
279 same as 278, JG1; same R; less aX, bX
280 same as 278; same R; aX: JG1, BK1
281 same as 278; same R; bX: BK1
282 same as 278, NM2, JG1, BK1; less bX; same R
283 same as 282, ChM, NM1; less R; aX: NM2
284 X: ChM, G61, Bel, Oxl, Wen, Bat, P95, Bar, Low, Roa, Inc, JKT, Oxb,Dol*
285 same as 284, less P95, NM1, NM2, JG1, BK1; less bX; aX: P95, NM1, NM2,
     JG1; bX: BK1
286 C: ChM, HIP, HIC, SM1; aX: G61, Bel, Oxl, Wen, Bat, Ba r, Low, Roa, Inc,
     JKT, Oxb, Dol,USW, Cum, WM1, HnF, CKP, Lac, KRe,Rig, HM1, MTh,HIM*
287 X: HIP; R: Oxl; aX: ChM, Oxb, SM1; bX: BA1
288 X: HnF, Lac, KRe, Rig, HM1, HIM, WmS, HIP, HIC, ViA, BA1, SM1, NM1
289 same as 288, less ViA; aX: ViA, BA1

290 X: Lac, Rig, HM1, HIM, WmS, HIP, HIC
291 X: HIP; aX: HnF, HIM; bX: SM1
292 X: HIP, SM1; bX: KRe, HIC
293 X: KRe, HIP, HIC, SM1; R: ChM; bX: ViA, BA1, NM1, NM2

*55:264 Rig, WmS;ADD 1: Roa   *55:268 NM2; bX: Low, Inc, JKT,
   Oxb, Dol, Cum, Rig, MB1, JG1   *55:273 HIC, ViA, Han, SM1, NM1,
   NM2, MB2   *55:274 Cum, WM1, HnF, CKP, Lac, Rig, HM1, MTh, HIM,
   WmS, HIP, HIC, ViA, Han, SM1, SEE BELOW   *55:284 Dol, USW, Cum, WM1,
   HnF, CKP, Lac, Rig, HM1, MTh, HIM, WmS, HIP, HIC, ViA, Han, SM1, SM1,NM2,
   MB2, JG1, BK1; bX: KRe, BA1   *55:286 WmS, ViA, Han, BA1,MB2,
   BK1   *55:274(continued)MB2; R: ChM; aX: NM1, NM2, BK1

3593	With language that would make me spurn the sea.	294
3594	If it could so roar to me : I cut off's head ;	295
3595	And am right glad he is not standing here	296
3596	To tell this tale of mine.	
3597	*Cym.* I am sorry for thee:	297
	By thine own tongue thou art condemn'd, and	
3598	must	298
3599	Endure our law : thou'rt dead.	
	Imo. That headless man	299
3600	I thought had been my lord.	
3601	*Cym.* Bind the offender, 300	300
3602	And take him from our presence.	
3603	*Bel.* Stay, sir king:	301
3604	This man is better than the man he slew,	302
3605	As well descended as thyself : and hath	303
3606	More of thee merited than a band of Clotens	034
	Had ever scar for. [*To the Guard*] Let his arms	
3607	alone ;	305
3608	They were not born for bondage.	
3609	*Cym.* Why, old soldier,	306
3610	Wilt thou undo the worth thou art unpaid for,	307
3611	By tasting of our wrath? How of descent	308
3612	As good as we?	
3613	*Arv.* In that he spake too far.	309
3614	*Cym.* And thou shalt die for't.	
3615	*Bel.* We will die all three: 310	310
3616	But I will prove that two on's are as good	311
3617	As I have given out him. My sons. I must,	312
3618	For mine own part, unfold a dangerous speech,	313
3619	Though, haply, well for you.	
3620	*Arv.* Your danger's ours.	314
3621	*Gui.* And our good his.	
3622	*Bel.* Have at it then, by leave.	315
3623	Thou hadst, great king, a subject who	316
3624	Was call'd Belarius.	
	Cym. What of him? he is	317
3625	A banish'd traitor.	
3626	*Bel.* He it is that hath	318
3627	Assumed this age : indeed a banish'd man :	319
3628	I know not how a traitor.	
3629	*Cym.* Take him hence: 320	320
3630	The whole world shall not save him.	
3631	*Bel.* Not too hot:	321
3632	First pay me for the nursing of thy sons;	322
3633	And let it be confiscate all, so soon	323
3634	As I have received it.	

CONTINUATIONS FROM G975b

*55:388 Do1, USW, Cum, WM1, HnF, CKP, Lac, KRe, Rig, HM1, MTh, HIM, WmS, HIP, HIC, ViA, BA1, NM1, NM2, MB1, MB2, PH1, JG1   *55:391 WmS, HIP, HIC, BA1, IP1, MB1, MB2; aX: Ox1, Low, Inc, JKT, Oxb, Do1, USW, Cum, WM1, HnF, CKP, SM1, NM2, JG1   *55:396 IP1, NM2, PH1

294 X: WmS, HIP, HIC, ViA, BA1, SM1, NM1, NM2, BK1; R: ChM; aX: KRe
295 X: HIP, HIC, SM1; aX: WmS, ViA, BA1, NM1, NM2, BK1
296 X: ChM, HIP, HIC, SM1, BK1

297 X: HIP, BK1; aX: ChM, HIC, SM1; bX: G61, Bel, Wen, Bat, Bar, Roa

298 X: G61, Bel, Wen, Bat, Bar, Roa, HIP

299 same as 298; bX: ChM, Ox1, Low, Inc, JKT, Oxb, Dol, USW, HIC, BA1,
      SM1, NM1, NM2, JG1, BK1 '
300 X: HIP, HIC, NM1, NM2, BK1; aX: ChM, G61, Bel, Ox1, Wen, Bat, Bar,
      Low, Roa, Inc, JKT, Oxb, Dol, USW, Cum, WM1, HnF, CKP, Lac, Rig⸸
301 X: HIP; aX: HIC, ViA, Han, NM1, NM2, BK1
302 X: HIP
303 X: HIP; bX: BA1, MB2, JG1, JP1, BK1
304 X: HIP, BA1, MB2, JG1, JP1, BK1; bX: ChM

305 X: HIP, ViA. BK1; aX: ChM, BA1, MB2, JG1, JP1; bX: NM2, PH1

306 X: HIP, PH1; aX: ViA, NM1, NM2, BK1; bX: HIC, BA1, SM1
307 X: HIP, HIC, BA1, SM1, PH1, JG1
308 X: HIP, HIC, BA1, SM1; aX: ChM; bX: NM1, NM2

309 X: P95, HIP, HIC, BA1, SM1, NM1, NM2; bX: G61, Bel, Ox1, Wen, Bat, Bar,
      Low, Roa, Inc, JKT, Oxb, Dol, USW, Cum, WM1, HnF, CKP, Lac, KRe*
310 X: G61, Bel, Ox1, Wen, Bat, P95, Bar, Low, Roa, Inc, JKT, Oxb, Dol*
311 same as 310
312 same as 310, less HIP, HIC, BA1, SM1, MB2; aX: HIP, HIC, BA1, SM1, MB2*
313 same as 312, PH1, BK1; less aX, bX; bX: BA1, SM1

314 same as 313, BA1, SM1; less bX; bX: MB2

315 same as 314, MB2, less BA1, SM1, PH1; less bX; aX: SM1, PH1; bX: BK1
316 same as 315, less MB2; less aX, bX; aX: MB2

317 same as 316. less aX; bX: ChM

318 same as 316, less aX; bX: HIC, SM1
319 same as 316; less aX; aX: HIC, SM1

320 same as 316; less aX; bX: BA1, SM1

321 same as 316; less aX ; aX: NM2
322 same as 316; less aX
323 same as 322, HIC, NM2, JG1, JP1, BK1

*55:300 HM1, HIM, WmS, BA1, SM1, JG1, ViA, HM1   *55:309 Rig, HM1,
  MTh, HIM, WmS, ViA, Han, MB2   55:310 USW, Cum, WM1, HnC, CKP,
  KRe, Rig, HM1, MTh, HIM, WmS, HIP, HIC, ViA, Han, BA1, SM1, NM1, NM2,
  MB2   855:312 bX: PH1, BK1

3635	*Cym.* Nursing of my sons!	324
	Bel. I am too blunt and saucy: here's my	325
3636	knee:	
3637	Ere I arise, I will prefer my sons:	326
3638	Then spare not the old father. Mighty sir,	327
3639	These two young gentlemen, that call me father	328
3640	And think they are my sons, are none of mine:	329
3641	They are the issue of your loins, my liege, 330	330
3642	And blood of your begetting.	
3643	*Cym.* How! my issue!	331
	Bel. So sure as you your father's. I, old	
3644	Morgan,	332
3645	Am that Belarius whom you sometime banish'd:	333
	Your pleasure was my mere offence, my punish-	
3646	ment	334
3647	Itself, and all my treason: that I suffer'd	335
3648	Was all the harm I did. These gentle princes—	336
3649	For such and so they are—these twenty years	337
3650	Have I train'd up: those arts they have as I	338
3651	Could put into them: my breeding was, sir, as 339	339
3652	Your highness knows. Their nurse, Euriphile,	340
3653	Whom for the theft I wedded, stole these children	341
3654	Upon my banishment: I moved her to't,	342
3655	Having received the punishment before,	343
3656	For that which I did then: beaten for loyalty	344
3657	Excited me to treason: their dear loss,	345
3658	The more of you 'twas felt, the more it shaped	346
3659	Unto my end of stealing them. But, gracious sir,	347
3660	Here are your sons again: and I must lose	348
3661	Two of the sweet'st companions in the world.	349
3662	The benediction of these covering heavens 350	350
3663	Fall on their heads like dew! for they are worthy	351
3664	To inlay heaven with stars.	
3665	*Cym.* Thou weep'st, and speak'st.	352
3666	The service that you three have done is more	353
3667	Unlike than this thou tell'st. I lost my children:	354
3668	If these be they, I know not how to wish	355
3669	A pair of worthier sons.	
3679	*Bel.* Be pleased awhile.	356
3671	This gentleman, whom I call Polydore,	357
3672	Most worthy prince, as yours, is true Guiderius:	358
3673	This gentleman, my Cadwal, Arviragus, 359	359
3674	Your younger princely son: he, sir, was lapp'd	360
3675	In a most curious mantle, wrought by the hand	361
3676	Of his queen mother, which for more probation	362
3677	I can with ease produce.	

*55::347 Roa, Inc, JKT, Oxb, Dol, USW, Cum, WM1, HnF, CKP, Lac, KRe, Rig, HM1, MTh, HIM, HIP, ViA, BA1, SM1, IP1, NM2, MB1, MB2, PH1, JG1, JP1
*55:352 HIM, HIC, SM1, IP1, PH1, BK1   *55:353 HM1, MTh, HIM, HIC, ViA, Han, BA1, SM1, IP1, PH1, BK1   *55:354 HnF, Lac, Rig, HM1, MTh, HIM, HIC, ViA, Han, IP1, PH1; bX: NM1, NM2
*55:356 Inc, JKT, Oxb, Dol, USW, Cum, HnF, Lac, Rig, HM1, MTh, HIM, HIC, ViA, HnFMB1, MB2   *55:357 USW, Cum, HnF, Lac, KRe, Rig, HM1,   MTh, HIM, HIC, ViA, Han, SM1, NM1, NM2, MB1, MB2

324   same as 323, less NM1, NM2, JG1, JP1, BK1; aX: NM1, NM2, JG1,JP1,BK1

325   X: Inc, Dol, HnF, BA1

326   X: G61, Bel, Ox1, Wen, Bat, Bar, Low, Roa, JKT, Oxb, USW, Cum,WM1*

327   X: KRe, HIM, HIC, BA1; aX: G61, Bel, Ox1, Wen, Bat, Bar, Low,Roa,JKT*

328   bX: HIC, DM1

329   aX: ViA, SM1, BK1

330

331   aX: MTh, ViA; bX: WmS

332   X: WmS; bX: KRe, HIP, BA1, MB1, MB2, BK1

333   X: KRe, WmS, HIP, BA1, BK1

334   X: KRe, WmS, HIP, HIC, ViA, BA1, SM1, IP1, MB1, PH1, JG1, JP1, BK1*

335   same as 334, NM2, MB2; same R; less bX; bX: G61

336   X: Bel, Bat, WmS, HIC, SM1; R: ChM; aX: G61, Wen, Bat, HnF, KRe,HIP*

337   X: WmS, HIC, SM1; R: ChM; aX: ViA, PH1

338   X: ChM, WmS, HIC, SM1; bX: BA1, IP1, NM2, MB1, MB2, PH1

339   X: ChM, WmS, HIC, BA1, SM1, IP1, NM2, MB1, MB2, PH1, BK1; bX: G61*

340   X: ChM, G61, Bel, Ox1, Wen, Bat, Bar, Low, Roa, Inc, JKT, Oxb, Cum*

341   same as 340, Dol, USW, HM1, Han, JP1; less aX, bX

342   same as 241, MB1; bX: HIP, BA1, JG1

343   same as 342, HIP, BA1, JG1, BK1; less bX

344   same as 343, less MB1; bX: IP1,

345   same as 344, IP1, less ChM.; less bX;bX: ChM

346   s ame as 345, Han; less bX;R: ChM

347   X: HIC, BK1; R: ChM, WmS, Han; aX: G61, Bel, Ox1, Wen , Bat, Bar,Low*

348   X: ChM, WmS, Han; aX: BK1

349   same as 348; less aX

350   XL WmS, HIP, ViA, Han, BA1, NM1, NM2; bX: HnF

351   X: HnF, HIP, ViA, Han, BA1, NM1, NM2

352   X: HnF, ViA, Han, BA1, NM1, NM2; aX: HIP; bX: Lac, KRe, Rig, HM1,MTh*

353   X: Ox1, Low, Inc, JKT, Oxb, Dol, USW, Cum, WM1, HnF, Lac, KRe, Rig*

354   X: KRe, BA1, SM1, BK1; aX: Ox1, Low, Inc, JKT, Oxb, Dol, USW, Cum,WM1*

355   X: KRe, JKT, SM1, NM1, NM2

356   X: KRe, BA1,, SM1, NM2; bX:G61, Bel, Ox1, Wen, Bat, P95, Bar, Low, Roa*

357   X: G61, Bel, Ox1, Wen, Bat, P95, Bar, Low, Roa, Inc, JKT, Oxb, Dol*

358   same as 257, NM2; aX: ChM

359   same as 358; less aX

360   same as 358, less Han; less aX; aX: ChM, Han; bX: HIP, BA1, IP1,JG1,BK1

361   same as 360, HIP, BA1, BK1; less aX ,bX

362   same as 361

*55:326 HnF, CKP, Lac, KRe, Rig, HM1, HIM, WmS, HIC, ViA, BA1, SM1, MB1,MB2, PH1; aX: Inc, Dol   *55:327 Oxb, USW, Cum, WM1, HnF, CKP, Lac, Rig,HM1, WmS, VIA, BA1, SM1, MB1, MB2, PH1, JG1   *55:334 R: ChM,HnF; bX: MB2   55:336 ViA, BA1, IP1, NM2, MB1, MB2, PH1, JG1,JP1,BK1 *55:339 Bel, Ox1, Wen, Bat, Bar, Low, Roa, Inc, JKT, Oxb, Dol, USW, Cum,WM1, HnF, CKP, Lac, KRe, Rig, HM1, MTh, HIM, ViA   *55:340 WM1, HnF, CKP, Lac, KRe, Rig, MTh, HIM, WmS, HIC, ViA, SM1, NM2, MB1, MB2, PH1; aX: BA1, IP1, BK1; bX: Dol, USW, HM1, Han, JP1

3678	*Cym.* Guiderius had	363
3679	Upon his neck a mole, a sanguine star;	364
3680	It was a mark of wonder. .	
3681	*Bel.* This is he;	365
3682	Who hath upon him still that natural stamp:	366
3683	It was wise nature's end i .e donation,	367
3684	To be his evidence now.	
3685	*Cym.* O, what, am I	368
3686	A mother to the birth of three? Ne'er mother 369	369
3687	Rejoiced deliverance more. Blest pray you be,	370
3688	That, after this strange starting from your orbs,	371
3689	You may reign in them now! O Imogen,	372
3690	Thou hast lost by this a kingdom.	
3691	*Imo.* No, my lord:	373
3692	I have got two worlds by't. O my gentle brothers,	374
3693	Have we thus met? O, never say hereafter	375
3694	But I am truest speaker: you call'd me brother,	376
3695	When I was but your sister; I you brothers,	377
3696	When ye were so indeed.	
3697	*Cym.* Did you e'er meet?	378
3698	*Aro.* Ay, my good lord.	
3699	*Gui.* And at first meeting loved;	379
3700	Continued so, until we thought he died. 380	380
3701	*Cor.* By the queen's dram she swallow'd	
3702	*Cym.* O rare instinct!	381
	When shall I hear all through? This fierce	
3703	abridgement	382
3704	Hath to it circumstantial branches, which	383
	Distinction should be rich in. Where? how lived	
3705	you?	384
3706	And when came you to serve our Roman captive?	385
	How parted with your brothers? how first met	
3707	them?	386
	Why fled you from the court? and whither?	
3708	These,	387
3709	And your three motives to the battle, with	388
3710	I know not how much more, should be demanded;	389
3711	And all the other by-dependencies, 390	390
	From chance to chance: but nor the time nor	
3712	place	391
3713	Will serve our long inter'gatories. See,	392
3714	Posthumus anchors upon Imogen,	393
3715	And she, like harmless lightning, throws her eye	394
3716	On him, her brothers, me, her master, hitting	395
3717	Each object with a joy: the counterchange	396
3718	Is severally in all. Let's quit this ground,	397

*55:380 HIC, BA1, SM1, NM1, IP1, NM2, MB1, MB2, BK1   *55:381 HnF, CKP,
Lac, Rig, HM1, HIM, BM1, NM2, MB2, JG1, BK1   *55:382 WmS, HIP,
HIC, PH1; bX:ChM, Ox1, Low, Inc, JKT, Oxb, USW, Cum, WM1, HnF, CKP,BA1,
NM1, IP1, NM2, MB1, MB2, JG1, BK1; ADD 26: ChM, Dol; MOVE 382-396 to
follow483: SM1   *55:383 HIC, ViA, BA1, SM1, NM1, IP1, NM2,
MB1, MB2, PH1, JG1, BK1; bX: Oxb, BK1   *55:384 MTh, HIM,
WmS, HIP, HIC, ViA, BA1, NM2, MB1, MB2, PH1; aX: Ox1, Low, Inc, JKT,
Oxb, Dol , USW, Cum, WM1, CKP, SM1, NM1, IP1, JG1, BK1 SEE G974c

363 X: HnF, KRe, MTh, WmS, HIP, HIC, ViA, SM1, IP1, NM2, MB1, MB2, JG1;*
364 same as 363; less aX

365 same as 364
366 same as 364
367 same as 364, BK1

368 X: HnF, KRe, MTh, WmS, HIP, HIC, ViA, NM2; aX: SM1, IP1, MB1, MB2*
369 X: ChM, Ox1, Low, Inc, JKT, Oxb, Dol, USW, Cum, WM1, HnF, CKP, Lac*
370 X: ChM, HnF, WmS, HIC, NM1, NM2; aX: Ox1, Low, Inc, JKT, Oxb, Dol*
371 X: ChM, HnF, BA1, SM1, NM1, IP1, NM2, BK1
372 X: ChM, HnF; aX: HIC, BA1, SM1, NM1, IP1, NM2, BK1

373 aX: ChM
374
375 bX: BK1
376 aX: OkI
377

378 X: ubxLac, KRe, Rig, HM1, MTh, HIP, HIC

379 X: Lac, KRe, Rig, HM1, MTh, HIM, WmS, HIP, HIC; bX: BA1
380 X: G61, Bel, Ox1, Wen, Bat, P95, Bar, Low, Roa, Inc, JKT, Oxb, Dol,
      USW, Cum, WM,1, HnF, CPK, Lac, KRe, Rig, HM1, MTh, HIM, WmS, HIP*
381 X: G61, Bel, Wen, Bat, P95, Bar, Roa, KRe, MTh, WmS, HIP, BA1, NM1,
      IP1, MB1, PH1; aX: ChM, Ox1, Low, Inc, JKT, Oxb, Dol, USW, Cum,WM1*
382 X: G61, Bel, Wen, Bat, P95, Bar, Roa, KRe, Rig, HM1, MTh, HIM, WmS*
383 X: ChM, G61, Bel, Ox1, Wen, Bat, P95, Bar, Low, Roa, Inc, JKT, Oxb,
      Dol, USW, Cum, WM1, HnF, CKP, Lac, KRe, Rig, HM1, MTh, HIM, WmS,HIP*
384 X: ChM, G61, Bel, Wen, Bat, P95, Bar, Roa, HnF, Lac, KRe, Rig, HM1*
385 same as 384; less aX

386 same as 485, IP1, BK1; bX: JG1

387 same as 485, NM1, JG1; bX Low, USW, WM1, CKP
388 X: ChM, G61, Bel, Ox1, Wen, Bat, P95, Bar, Low, Roa, Inc, JKT, Oxb*
389 same as 388, less Wm1, PH1
390 same as 389, SM1, IP1, NM2, BK1

391 X: ChM, G61, Bel, Wen, Bat, P95, Bar, Roa, Lac, KRe, Rig, HM1, MTh, HIM*
392 same as 391; less aX; bX: JP1
393 same as 391, JP1, less IP1; less aX
394 same as 393
395 same as 393, HnF; bX: Ox1, Low, Inc, JKT, Oxb, Dol, USW, Cum
396 same as 395, Low, Inc, JKT, Oxb, Dol, USW, BK1; less bX; bX: WM1,CKP*
397 X: ChM, G61, Bel, Wen, Bat, P95, Bar, Low, Roa, Inc, JKT, Oxb, Dol,USW,
      Cum, HnF, Rig, HM1, MTh, HIM, WmS, HIP, HIC, ViA, PH1, JP1; aX: WM1;
      CKP, KRe, BA1, IP1, NM2, MB1, MB2, BK1

*55:363aX: G61, Bel, Ox1, Wen, Bat, ,P95, Bar, Low, Roa, Inc, JKT, Oxb, Dol,
   USW, Cum, Lac, Rig, HM1,MTh,HIM,,HIP,NM1,BK1   *55:368 JG1; bX: ChM,Ox1,
   Low, Inc, JKT, Oxb, Dol, USW, Cum, WM1, CKP, Lac, Rig, HM1, HIM, BA1;
   ADD 34, insert 192b-269a: ChM, NM1   *55:369 KRe, Rig, HM1, MTh,
   HIM, WmS, HIP, HIC, ViA, BA1, NM1, MB2   *55:370 USW, Cum, WM1,
   CKP, Lac, KRe, Rig, HM1, MTh, HIM, HIP, ViA, BA1, BK1 ; bX: SM1, IP1

3719	And smoke the temple with our sacrifices.	398
3720	[To Belarius] Thou art my brother; so we'll hold thee ever.	399
3721	Imo. You are my father too, and did relieve me, **400**	400
3722	To see this gracious season.	
3723	Cym. All o'erjoy'd,	401
3724	Save these in bonds: let them be joyful too,	402
3725	For they shall taste our comfort.	
3726	Imo. My good master, I will yet do you service.	403
3727	Luc. Happy be you!	404
3728	Cym. The forlorn soldier, that so nobly fought,	405
3729	He would have well becomed this place, and graced	406
3730	The thankings of a king.	
3731	Post. I am, sir,	407
3732	The soldier that did company these three	408
3733	In poor beseeming; 'twas a fitment for	409
3734	The purpose I then follow'd. That I was he, **410**	410
3735	Speak, Iachimo: I had you down and might	411
3736	Have made you finish.	
3737	Iach. [Kneeling] I am down again:	412
3738	But now my heavy conscience sinks my knee,	413
3739	As then your force did. Take that life, beseech you,	414
3740	Which I so often owe: but your ring first;	415
3741	And here the bracelet of the truest princess	416
3742	That ever swore her faith.	
3743	Post. Kneel not to me:	417
3744	The power that I have on you is to spare you;	418
3745	The malice towards you to forgive you: live,	419
3746	And deal with others better.	
3747	Cym. Nobly doom'd! **420**	420
3748	We'll learn our freeness of a son-in-law;	421
3749	Pardon's the word to all.	
3750	Arv. You holp us, sir,	422
3751	As you did mean indeed to be our brother;	423
3752	Joy'd are we that you are.	424
3753	Post. Your servant, princes. Good my lord of Rome,	425
3754	Call forth your soothsayer: as I slept, methought	426
3755	Great Jupiter, upon his eagle back'd,	427
3756	Appear'd to me, with other spritely shows	428
3757	Of mine own kindred: when I waked, I found	429
3758	This label on my bosom; whose containing **430**	430

398   same as 397, WM1, CKP, Lac, KRe; less <u>a</u>X

399   X: ChM, G61, Bel, Wen, Bat, P95, Bar, Low, Roa, Inc, JKT, Oxb, Dol,
        USW, HnF, KRe, PH1
400   same as 399, WM1, CKP, BA1, NM1, NM2; <u>b</u>X: BK1

401   X: ChM, HnF, KRe, NM1, NM2; <u>a</u>X: G61, Bel, Ox1, Wen, Bat, P95, Bar,*
402   X: ChM, HnF, KRe, BA1, NM1, NM2

403   same as 402; <u>b</u>X: Bel, Ox1, Wen, Bat, Bar, Low, Inc, JKT, Oxb, Dol,
        USW, Cum, Lac, Rig, HM1, MTh, HIM, WmS
404   X: ChM, Bel, Ox1, Wen, Bat, Bar, Low, Inc, JKT, Oxb, Dol, USW, Cum*
405   X: ChM, HnF, NM1, NM2

406   same as 405

407   same as 405; <u>b</u>X: BA1
408   X: ChM, HnF, <u>BA1</u>, NM1, NM2, BK1
409   X: ChM, HnF, KRe, ViA, BA1, NM1, NM2, BK1
410   X: ChM, HnF, KRe, NM1, NM2, BK1; <u>a</u>X: ViA, BA1
411   X: ChM, HnF, NM1, NM2, BK1

412   same as 411, less BK1; <u>a</u>X: BK1; <u>b</u>X: WmS, BA1; <u>ADD</u> 18: BK1
413   X: ChM, HnF, WmS, BA1, <u>NM1</u>, NM2

414   X: ChM, HnF, WmS; <u>a</u>X: BA1, NM1, NM2; <u>b</u>X: Bel, Ox1, Wen, Bat, Bar, Low*
415   X: ChM, HnF, WmS; <u>a</u>X: Bel, Wen, Bat, Bar, Low, Inc, Cum; <u>b</u>X CKP
416   X: ChM, HnF, WmS, <u>ViA</u>

417   X: HnF, WmS; <u>a</u>X: ChM, CKP; <u>ADD</u> 2: Bel, Wen, Bat, Bar, Dol, Inc, Cum*
418   X: HnF, WmS, <u>Cum</u>
419   X: ChM, HnF, WmS

420   X: HnF, WmS; <u>b</u>X: HIP; <u>ADD</u> 15: ChM
421   X: ChM, HnF, <u>KRe</u>, WmS, <u>HIP</u>

422   X: ChM, HnF, HIP; <u>b</u>X G61, Bel, Ox1, Wen, Bat, P95, Bar, Low, Roa, Inc*
423   X: <u>BLOCK (See below)</u> IP1, NM2, MB2, PH1, BK1; R: JP1
424   same as 423 including <u>R</u>

425   same as 423, CKP; same <u>R</u>; <u>b</u>X: JG1
426   same as 425, JG1, less <u>PH1</u>, BK1; same <u>R</u>; less <u>b</u>X; <u>b</u>X: MB1
427   same as 426; same <u>R</u>; less <u>b</u>X
428   same as 427 including <u>R</u>; <u>b</u>X: <u>MB1</u>, PH1
429   same as 427, MB1, PH1, <u>JP1</u>, BK1; less R, <u>b</u>X
430   same as 429, less MB1, PH1; <u>a</u>X: MB1, PH1

*55:401 Low, Roa, Inc, JKT, Oxb, Dol, USW, Cum, WM1, CKP, PH1, BK1
*55:404 HnF, Lac, KRe, Rig, HM1, MTh, HIM, WmS, BA1, NM1, NM2; <u>b</u>X: HIC
*55:414 Inc, Cum; <u>MOVE</u> 414b-415a to follow 417: JKT, Oxb, Dol, <u>USW</u>,Rig
*55:417 <u>Inser</u>414b-415a: JKT, Oxb, Dol, USW, Rig   *55:422 JKT, Oxb, Dol,
    USW, Cum, WM1, CKP, Lac, KRe, Rig, HM1, MTh, HIM, WmS, HIC, ViA,Han,
   BA1, SM1, NM1, IP1, NM2, MB2, JP1, BK1
<u>BLOCK</u>, 423-475: G61, Bel, Ox1, Wen, Bat, P95, Bar, Low, Roa, Inc, JKT, Oxb,
    DolUSW, Cum, WM1, HnF, CKP, Lac, KRe, Rig, HM1, MTh, HIM, WmS, HIP, HIC,
   ViA, Han, BA1, SM1, NM1

3759	Is so from sense in hardness, that I can	431
3760	Make no collection of it: let him show	432
3761	His skill in the construction.	
3762	*Luc.* Philarmonus!	433
3763	*Sooth.* Here, my good lord.	
3764	*Luc.* Read, and declare the meaning.	434
3765	*Sooth.* [*Reads*] 'When as a lion's whelp shall,	435
3766	to himself unknown, without seeking find, and be	436
3767	embraced by a piece of tender air; and when	437
3768	from a stately cedar shall be lopped branches,	438
	which, being dead many years, shall after revive,	439
3769	be jointed to the old stock, and freshly grow;	440
3770	then shall Posthumus end his miseries, Britain be	441
3771-2	fortunate and flourish in peace and plenty.'	442
3773	Thou, Leonatus, art the lion's whelp;	443
3774	The fit and apt construction of thy name,	444
3775	Being Leo-natus, doth import so much.	445
	[*To Cymbeline*] The piece of tender air, thy	
3776	virtuous daughter,	446
3777	Which we call 'mollis aer;' and 'mollis aer'	447
3778	We term it 'mulier:' which 'mulier' I divine	448
3779	Is this most constant wife; who, even now,	449
3780	Answering the letter of the oracle, 450	450
3781	Unknown to you, unsought, were clipp'd about	451
3782	With this most tender air.	
3783	*Cym.* This hath some seeming.	452
3784	*Sooth.* The lofty cedar, royal Cymbeline,	453
3785	Personates thee: and thy lopp'd branches point	454
3786	Thy two sons forth; who, by Belarius stol'n,	455
3787	For many years thought dead, are now revived,	456
3788	To the majestic cedar join'd, whose issue	457
3789	Promises Britain peace and plenty.	
3790	*Cym.* Well:	458
3791	My peace we will begin. And, Caius Lucius,	459
3792	Although the victor, we submit to Cæsar,	460
3793	And to the Roman empire; promising	461
3794	To pay our wonted tribute, from the which	462
3795	We were dissuaded by our wicked queen;	463
3796	Whom heavens, in justice, both on her and hers,	464
3797	Have laid most heavy hand.	465
	Sooth. The fingers of the powers above do	
3798	tune	466
3799	The harmony of this peace. The vision	467
3800	Which I made known to Lucius, ere the stroke	468
3801	Of this yet scarce-cold battle, at this instant	469
3802	Is full accomplish'd; for the Roman eagle,	470

```
431   same as 430, less BK1; less aX
432   same as 431; aX: BK1; bX: PH1

433   same as 432, PH1; less aX, bX;bX: MB1

434   same as 432; less aX, bX
435   same as 434
436   same as 434
437   same as 434
438   same as 434
439   same as 434
440   same as 434
441   sane as 434
442   same as 434
443   same as 434
444   same as 434, MB1, PH1, BK!
445   same as 444

446   same as 444, less PH1, BK1
447   same as 445
448   same as 446
449   sam´e as 446
450   same as 446
451   same as 446

452   same as 446
453   same as 445, less MB1
454   same as 453
455   same as 453
456   same as 453
457   same as 453

458   same as 453
459   same as 453, less IP1, NM2, MB1; aX: NM1, IP1, MB1
460   same az 459; less aX
461   same as 460; bX: NM1
462   same as 460, NM1; bX: NM2
463   same as 462, NM2
464   same as 463, BK1
465   same as 464

466   same as 464, MB1,  less JG1, BK1
467   same as 466, JG1; bX: IP1, PH1
468   same as 467, IP1, PH1, BK1
469   same as 468
470   same as 468, less BK1
```

3803	From south to west on wing soaring aloft,	471
3804	Lessen'd herself, and in the beams o' the sun	472
3805	So vanish'd: which foreshow'd our princely eagle	473
3806	The imperial Cæsar, should again unite	474
3807	His favour with the radiant Cymbeline,	475
3808	Which shines here in the west.	
3809	*Cym.* Laud we the gods:	476
	And let our crooked smokes climb to the	477
3810	nostrils	478
3811	From our blest altars. Publish we this peace	479
3812	To all our subjects. Set we forward: let	480
3813	A Roman and a British ensign wave	481
3814	Friendly together: so through Lud's-town march:	482
3815	And in the temple of great Jupiter	483
3816	Our peace we'll ratify; seal it with feasts.	484
3817	Set on there! Never was a war did cease,	485
3818	Ere bloody hands were wash'd, with such a peace

[Exeunt

471   same as 470
472   same as 470
473   same as 470   ; R: BK1
474   same as 470, less $\overline{NM2}$
475   same as 474, less CUSW, CKP; aX: USW, CKP

476   X: ChM, HnF, Rig, WmS , HIP, ViA, Han, NM1; aX: G61, Bel, Ox1, Wen*
477   same as 476; less aX; bX: CKP
478   X: ChM, WmS, ViA, $\overline{NM1}$; aX: HnF, CKP, Rig, HIP, Han; bX: Ox1, Low,Inc*
479   X: ChM, KRe, WmS, HIC, $\overline{ViA}$; aX: Low, Inc, JKT, Oxb, $\overline{Dol}$, USW, Cum,WM1*
480   X: ChM
481   X: ChM, KRe, WmS, ViA; bX: HnF, HIP
482   X: ChM, Ox1, Low, Inc, $\overline{JKT}$, Oxb, Dol, USW, Cum, HnF, KRe, HIP, ViA*
483   same as 482; bX: Lac, Rig, HM1, HIM, WmS
484   X: ChM, WmS, $\overline{HIC}$, ViA; aX: Lac, KRe, Rig, HM1, HIM, JG1; bX: HnF,SM1
485   X: ChM, WmS, HIC, ViA, $\overline{Han}$, SM1; Insert 368-370, add 4, 382-398:SM1

*55:476 Bat, P95, Bar, Low, Roa, Inc, JKT, Oxb, Dol, Cum, WM1, Lac, KRe,
    HM1, MTh, HIM, HIC, BA1, SM1, IP1, MB1, MB2, JG1, JP1
*55:478 JKT, Oxb, Dol, USW, Cum, WM1, KRe, HIC, BA;   *55:479 KRe,
    WmS, ViA, BA1, NM1   *55:482 BA1, NM1, NM2

BIBLIOGRAPHY FOR   P E R I C L E S

J PE1   The Painfull Adventures of Pericles, Prince of Tyre . . .
        John Gower.(J "by George Wilkins.") London: T P for But-
        ter, 1608
        Microfilm: STC 19628(Reel 8560); reprinted, Oldenberg:
        Stalling, 1857 (see J PE22)
        Not Shakespeare's text, but a passage from it was inserted
        in the Ontario production, 1973

J PE2   The late, and much admired Play, called Pericles, Prince
        of Tyre. London: Gosson, 1609
        Microfilm: STC 22335 (Reel 1007); facsimilies: Shakespeare
        Quarto Facsimilies. London: Praetorius, 1886; Shakes-
        peare Quartos. London: Shakespeare Association, Sidg-
        wick, 1950; BM c12k5
        CUT: 31: 51: 35N, 36N; MOVE: 31: 53b to follow 31: 55a

J PE2b The late, and much admired Play, called Pericles, Prince
        of Tyre. London: Gosson, 1609 (J "numerous small Tex-
        tual variations")
        Shakespeare Quarto Facsimilies. London: Praetorius, 1866;
        BM C34/k36
        Otherwise full text

J PE3   The late, and much admired Play, Called Pericles, Prince
        of Tyre. London, n p(J "Simon Stafford"), 1611
        Microfilm: STC 22336 (Reel 1007)
        Full text

J PE4   The late, and much admired Play called Pericles, Prince
        of Tyre. Printed for T P(J "Thomas Pavier by Isaac Jag-
        gard"), 1619 (bound with The Whole Contention)
        BM C34/k38; Folger 26101/Copy 1/York, House of
        Full text

J PE5 or 6 The late, and much admired Play, called Pericles, Prince
        of Tyre. London: printed by I N for R B (J "Richard
        Badger"), 1630 (J "set twice from different fonts")
        Microfilm: STC 22338(Reel 1219)
        Slight editorial changes

J PE7   The late, and much admired Play, called Pericles, Prince
        of Tyre. London: Cotes, 1635
        Microfilm: STC 12339(Reel 1156, Huntington)

J W4   One leaf of Third Folio, 1663
        Folger Fragment of 3rd Folio; shelved in Proclamation
        Case, Vault 4
        No marks

J W5   <u>The late, and much admired Play called Pericles, Prince</u>
        <u>of Tyre</u>. London: for P ₵(J "Philip Chetwynde"".1664
        U Mich, RBR, Third Folio(usual full title)
        The first folio to include <u>PE</u>. Divergence from Globe: <u>CUT</u>:
        11: 56N; 51: 8, 252b; 53: 16a

J PE9   London: Tonson, <u>Works of Shakespeare</u>, 1735(single play
        '1734')
        U Mich RBR Tonson, 1735
        Full text

J PE10 and W20 London: Walker, <u>Dramatic Works of William Shakespeare</u>,
        1734
        BM 11763/w37; Folger PR2752/1734-35/Copy 1, vol 3

J PE12 <u>Marina</u>, Mr Lillo. London: Gray, 1738
        U Mich RBR PR3541/L5/M3
        Essentially new play, but uses lines from 42 and 46

J OE14 London: Cawthorne, 1796
        BUS
        'Omissions marked by inverted commas, playhouse additions
        in italics;' collation only for these;I find no notes

J PE15 London: Cawthorne, <u>Bell's British Theatre</u>, incorporating
        Cawthorne' text, 1797 (single play '1796')
        BM 2304/c
        Identical with Carthorne (J PE14)

J PE17 'edited by Aex Chalmers.' London: Rivington, n d (J "c1811")
        Nuffield 50.26/vers 1805
        Notes missing

J PE19 <u>Marina, or the foster child</u>, William Kirkland, 1820
        BUS G4014/53 (Ac 151473)
        'Advertisement . . . 1300 of 2000 lines are original . . .
        change of fable'; not collated

S PE1   "Samuel Phelps, Sadler's Wells, 1854"(S)
        Folger PB PE1
        PB in <u>Works</u>; I have no notes

S PE2   "Phelps"(S)
        Folger PB PE2
        PB in unidentified full text; "expansion of S PE1"(S);no notes

S PE3   "Phelps"(S)   SP1
        Nuffield 50.26/vers 1805 (Creswick)
        PB in unidentified text

SS PE400 "Phelps"(Folger)   SP2
          Folger PR2752/1843-45/v 33/Sh Col
          Workbook in progress, in Cabinet Ed #3, Knight, 1845

J PE22   The painfull adventures of Pericles, 1608 'by George Wil-
              kins; Prof Tycho Mommsen, preface and introduction by
              J P Collier. Oldenberg: Stalling, 1857 (J "n p")
          U Mich RBR PR2878/P4/W68/1857; Folger PR3190/W6/P5/1857
          Prose narration(see J PE1)

J PE28   Strange and worthy accidents in the birth and life of
              Marina, Rev O F Fleay. London: New Shakespeare Society,
              n n d(J '1874")
          U Mich PR2888/A53/Ser 1/Nos 1, 2; U Mich PR2888/L8
          Long argument that Shakespeare wrote only Marina scenes,
          others added Gower elements and brothel scenes; extracts
          the Shakespeare almost verbatim. Uses: 31, 32, 33, 34,
          41, 43 to 53; CUTS: 31: 4R; 41: 15R; 53: 85-102

J PE31   'The First Quarto.' Shakespeare Quarto Facsimilies, #22.
              London: Praetorius, 1886
          U Mich, RBR
          See J PE2

J PE32   'The Second Quarto. London: Gosson, 1609.' Shakespeare
              Quarto Facsimilies #18. London: Praetorius, 1886
          U Mich RBR
          See J PE2b

J W1070   Henry Irving Shakespeare, Henry Irving and Frank A Marshall HIM
              London: Blackie, 1888
          U Mich 822.8/S53/1888-1890/I7

J PE34   Memorial Theatre Edition, C E Flower. 'Asked Mr Cheswick   MTh
              to arrange an acting version based on that of Sadler's
              Wells.' Stratford-upon-Avon: Boyden for Memorial The-
              atre, and London: French, n d (J "1890")
          U Mich RBR, uncataloged, filed at 1894; Nuffield 50.26/
              vers 1891 (Ac 480)

J PE39   Marina, a dramatic romance. Being the Shakespeare portion
              of 'Pericles,' S Wellwood. London: Richards, 1902
          BM 11764/f13; Folger PR2830/A3/W4
          USES: 31: 1-8; 32: 1-41; 33: 1-41; 34: 1-8; 4 PRO; 41: 1-
              103; 43: 1-51; 51: 1-265; 52: 1-84

SS PR300 'Algernon Charles Swinburne.' London: privately printed,1914
          Folger PR2830/S8/Sh Col
          A prose essay; no text

SS PE401 "Nugent Monck, Maddenmarket Th"(Hand. Production 1929)   NM1
          Nugent Monck Coll, Jack Hall
          Memorial PB in Methuen, 2nd ed, 1930

SS PE301   'First Quarto, London: Gosson, 1609.' Shakespeare Quartos
             #3. London: Shakespeare Association, Sidgwick, 1940
             U Mich 822.8/S53/1939/#5
             See J PE2

S PE4   "Nugent Monck, 1947, Paul Scofield."(Hand) STRATFORD-UPON-
             Nuffield O S 71.21/1947/She PE (Ac 6383,f 87)   AVON
             PB in Dent; duplicate of Monck(SS PE401--NM1)

SS PE402   'Nugent Monck, 1951 Prompt"(Hand. Production 1951)   NM2
             British Drama League
             PB in New Temple

SS PE03   "Nugent Monck #2, Cut Copy"(Hand)
             British Drama League
             PB in New Temple; deviations from Monck(SS PR402--NM2);
               CUT: 21 all; RESTORE: 45: all; 52: 13-14

SS PE408   "Douglas Seale, 1954"(Hand)   DS1
             Birmingham Repertory Th Archives
             PB in Temple

SS PE407   "Robert B Loper, 1957"(Hand)   ASHLAND
             Ore Shakespeare Festival Archives
             PB in unidentified full text; CUT: 23: 40-44; 44: 5-9a,
               21b-45

S PE5   "Tony Robertson , 1958"(Hand)   STRATFORD-UPON-AVON TR1
             Nuffield O S 71.21/1858P (Ac 9677)

SS PE409   "Nagle Jackson, 1967"(Hand)   ASHLAND
             Ore Shakespeare Festival Archives
             PB in unidentified full text; CUT: 12: 35-37, 40-46, 49-
               51a, 52a, 74; 21: 120-121, 133b-135, 166-169; 23: 26R,
               27-28; 44: 38b-43; 46: 108b-122; ADD: 155 after 46: 108a

SS PE404   "Terry Hands and Buzz Goodbody, 1969"(Hand) STRATFORD-   TH1
             Nuffield 71.21/1969P (Ac S749i)   UPON-AVON
             PB in Dent

SS PE411   "Tony Robertson   Prospect Th Co, 1973, Derek Jacobi"   TR2
             Barbara Montagna from 'Robertson script
             A story told in a male brothel

SS PE405   'Jean Gascon, 1973, Nicholas Pennell"(Hand) ONTARIO   JG1
             Stratford Shakespeare Festival Archives
             Passage inserted revised from Wilkins(J PE1)

SS PE412   "Jean Gascon, 1974"(Hand)   ONTARIO
             Stratford Shakespeare Festival Archives
             Deviations from Gascon(SS PE405--JG1); CUT: 1PRO: 10R,
               move 101b-103 to follow 106; 12: 9-10; 13: all; 21: 1

added aftee 172; <u>24</u>: all; <u>25</u>: 79b; <u>32</u>: 67b-78a; <u>51</u>: 28R;
<u>RESTORE</u>: 1PRO: 5-$\overline{10}$; <u>11</u>: 1$\overline{5}$-46, 77; $\overline{12}$: 1a, 40-4$\overline{1}$, 44-45,
$\overline{48}$-50a, 5$\overline{3}$-56a, 60a, $\overline{73}$-74, 81-82, 8$\overline{4}$-87, 90, 94-95a, 99-
100, 122-124; <u>32</u>: 90-91a; <u>ADD</u>: 2 after <u>23</u>: 10, 1 after<u>45</u>:
1, 2 after <u>46</u>: $\overline{1}$65

SS PE406   "Edward Berkeley, 1974"(Hand)   <u>SHAKESPEARE IN THE PARK</u>   EdB
NY Shakespeare Festival Archives
Xeroxed scripts

<u>UNDATED</u>

SS PE410   "Scenarius"(Hand)
Players PB312
Script in German; not collated

ALPHABETICAL LIST OF SIGLA FOR P E R I C L E S

DS1 Douglas Seale, 1954
EdB Edward Berkeley, 1974
HIM Henry Irving-Frank A Marshall, 1888
JG1 Jean Gascon, 1973
MTh Memorial Theatre Edition, 1890
NM1 Nugent Monck, 1929
NM2 Nugent Monck, 1951
SP1 Samuel Phelps, 1854
SP2 Samuel Phelps, 1954
TH1 Terry Hands, 1959
TR1 Tony Robertson, 1958
TR2 Tony Robertson, 1973

PERICLES.

DRAMATIS PERSONÆ.

ANTIOCHUS, king of Antioch.
PERICLES, prince of Tyre.
HELICANUS, } two lords of Tyre.
ESCANES,
SIMONIDES, king of Pentapolis.
CLEON, governor of Tarsus.
LYSIMACHUS, governor of Mytilene.
CERIMON, a lord of Ephesus.
THALIARD, a lord of Antioch.
PHILEMON, servant to Cerimon.
LEONINE, servant to Dionyza.
Marshal.
A Pandar.
BOULT, his servant.
The Daughter of Antiochus.
DIONYZA, wife to Cleon.
THAISA, daughter to Simonides.
MARINA, daughter to Pericles and Thaisa.
LYCHORIDA, nurse to Marina.
A Bawd.

Lords, Knights, Gentlemen, Sailors, Pirates, Fishermen, and Messengers.

DIANA.

GOWER, as Chorus.

SCENE: *Dispersedly in various countries.*

ACT I.

Enter GOWER.

Before the palace of Antioch.

To sing a song that old was sung,	1
From ashes ancient Gower is come ;	2
Assuming man's infirmities,	3
To glad your ear, and please your eyes.	4
It hath been sung at festivals,	5
On ember-eves and holy-ales:	6
And lords and ladies in their lives	7
Have read it for restoratives:	8
The purchase is to make men glorious;	9
Et bonum quo antiquius, eo melius.	10
If you, born in these latter times,	11
When wit's more ripe, accept my rhymes,	12
And that to hear an old man sing	13
May to your wishes pleasure bring,	14
I life would wish, and that I might	15
Waste it for you, like taper-light.	16
This Antioch, then, Antiochus the Great	17
Built up, this city, for his chiefest seat:	18
The fairest in all Syria,	19
I tell you what mine authors say:	20
This king unto him took a fere,	21
Who died and left a female heir,	22
So buxom, blithe, and full of face,	23
As heaven had lent her all his grace;	24
With whom the father liking took,	25
And her to incest did provoke:	26
Bad child; worse father! to entice his own	27
To evil should be done by none:	28
But custom what they did begin	29
Was with long use account no sin.	30
The beauty of this sinful dame	31
Made many princes thither frame,	32
To seek her as a bed-fellow,	33
In marriage-pleasures play-fellow:	34
Which to prevent he made a law,	35
To keep her still, and men in awe,	36
That whoso ask'd her for his wife,	37
His riddle told not, lost his life:	38

P E R I C L E S

ACT 1 PROLOG

ALL CUT: SP1, SP2, MTh. INSERT 46: 185-191: TR2; ADD 19: TR1

```
 1
 2
 3
 4
 5     X: JG1
 6     X: JG1
 7     X: NM1, NM2, JG1
 8     same as 7
 9     same as 7, TR2; ADD 7: TH1
10     same as 9; less ADD
11
12
13
14
15
16
17     X: HIM, NM1, NM2
18     same as 17
19     same as 17
20     same as 17, TR2
21     same as 17
22     same as 17
23     same as 17
24     same as 17
25     same as 17
26     same as 17
27     same as 17
28     same as 17
29     same as 17, EdB
30     same as 29
31     same as 17
32     same as 17
33     same as 17
34     same as 17
35     same as 17
36     same as 17
37     same as 17
38     same as 17
```

So for her many a wight did die, 39
As yon grim looks do testify. **40** 40
What now ensues, to the judgement of your eye 41
I give, my cause who best can justify. [*Exit.* 42

SCENE I. *Antioch. A room in the palace.*

Enter ANTIOCHUS, PRINCE PERICLES, *and
followers.*

Ant. Young prince of Tyre, you have at large
received 1
The danger of the task you undertake. 2
Per. I have, Antiochus, and, with a soul 3
Embolden'd with the glory of her praise, 4
Think death no hazard in this enterprise. 5
Ant. Bring in our daughter, clothed like a
bride, 6
For the embracements even of Jove himself; 7
At whose conception, till Lucina reign'd, 8
Nature this dowry gave, to glad her presence, 9
The senate-house of planets all did sit, **10** 10
To knit in her their best perfections. 11

Music. Enter the Daughter of Antiochus.

Per. See where she comes, apparell'd like the
spring, 12
Graces her subjects, and her thoughts the king 13
Of every virtue gives renown to men! 14
Her face the book of praises, where is read 15
Nothing but curious pleasures, as from thence 16
Sorrow were ever razed, and testy wrath 17
Could never be her mild companion. 18
You gods that made me man, and sway in love, 19
That have inflamed desire in my breast **20** 20
To taste the fruit of yon celestial tree, 21
Or die in the adventure, be my helps, 22
As I am son and servant to your will, 23
To compass such a boundless happiness! 24
Ant. Prince Pericles,— 25
Per. That would be son to great Antiochus. 26
Ant. Before thee stands this fair Hesperides, 27
With golden fruit, but dangerous to be touch'd: 28
For death-like dragons here affright thee hard: 29

```
39    same as17
40    same as 17
41    same as 17
42    same as 17
```

Scene 1

ALL CUT: NM1

```
 1
 2
 3
 4
 5


 6    R: SP1; aX: SP2
 7    X̄: HIM, N̄M2
 8    X: HIM, TR1, JG1, EdB; bX: NM2
 9    same as 8 including bX
10    same as 9, less bX
11    same as 10


12    X: SP1, HIM; bX: TR
13    X: SP1, HIM
14    X: SP1, HIM, MTh
15    X: SP1, SP2, HIM,  MTh, TR1, TH1, JG1
16    same as 15, less TH1
17    same as 16
18    same as 16
19    X: NM1, NM2
20    X: NM1, NM2
21    X: NM1, NM2
22    X: NM1, NM2
23    X: HIM, NM2, TR1
24    same as 23
25
26    X: TR1
27
28
29
```

Her face, like heaven, enticeth thee to view   30   30
Her countless glory, which desert must gain: 31
And which, without desert, because thine eye   32
Presumes to reach, all thy whole heap must die.   33
You sometimes famous princes, like thyself,   34
Drawn by report, adventurous by desire,   35
Tell thee, with speechless tongues and semblance
    pale,   36
That without covering, save yon field of stars,   37
Here they stand martyrs, slain in Cupid's wars;   38
And with dead cheeks advise thee to desist   39
For going on death's net, whom none resist.   40   40
   Per. Antiochus, I thank thee, who hath taught   41
My frail mortality to know itself,   42
And by those fearful objects to prepare   43
This body, like to them, to what I must: 44
For death remember'd should be like a mirror,   45
Who tells us life 's but breath, to trust it error.   46
I 'll make my will then, and, as sick men do   47
Who know the world, see heaven, but, feeling woe,   48
Gripe not at earthly joys as erst they did;   49
So I bequeath a happy peace to you   50   50
And all good men, as every prince should do;   51
My riches to the earth from whence they came;   52
But my unspotted fire of love to you.   53
                 [To the daughter of Antiochus.
Thus ready for the way of life or death,   54
I wait the sharpest blow, Antiochus.   55
   Ant. Scorning advice, read the conclusion,
    then: 56
Which read and not expounded, 'tis decreed,   57
As these before thee thou thyself shalt bleed.   58
   Daugh. Of all say'd yet, mayst thou prove
    prosperous!   59
Of all say'd yet, I wish thee happiness!   60   60
   Per. Like a bold champion, I assume the lists,   61
Nor ask advice of any other thought   62
But faithfulness and courage.   63
             He reads the riddle.
   I am no viper, yet I feed   64
   On mother's flesh which did me breed.   65
   I sought a husband, in which labour   66
   I found that kindness in a father: 67
   He's father, son, and husband mild;   68
   I mother, wife, and yet his child.   69
   How they may be, and yet in two,   70   70

```
30  X: TH1, TR2, JG1
31  same as 30
32  X: TR1, TH1, TR2, JG1; ADD 1: NM2
33  X: NM2, TR1, TH1, TR2, JG1
34  R: SP1, SP2
35

36  X: TR2
37  X: SP1, SP2, TR2, JG1
38  X: TR2; aX: SP1, SP2
39  aX: SP1, SP2, NM2, TR1, TH1
40
41
42
43  X: SP2
44  X: SP2
45  X: TR1, TH1, JG1
46  same as 45
47  same as 45; bX: TR1
48  X: NM2, TR1, TH1, TR2, JG1
49  same as 48
50  X: TH1, TR2, JG1
51  X: NM2, TR1, TH1, TR2, JG1
52  X: TH1, TR2, JG1
53  same as 52

54  X: TH1
55  X: TH1

56  R: SP2
57  X: TR2
58  X: TH2

59  X: SP1, SP2, MTh, TH1, TR2
60  same as 59
61  X: TR2
62  X: TR2
63  X: TR2; R: JG1

64  X: SP1, SP2, MTh
65  same as 66
66  same as 66
67  same as 66
68  same as 66
69  same as 66
70  same as 66
```

As you will live, resolve it you. 71
Sharp physic is the last: but, O you powers 72
That give heaven countless eyes to view men's
acts, 73
Why cloud they not their sights perpetually, 74
If this be true, which makes me pale to read it? 75
Fair glass of light, I loved you, and could still, 76
  [*Takes hold of the hand of the Princess.*
Were not this glorious casket stored with ill: 77
But I must tell you, now my thoughts revolt; 78
For he's no man on whom perfections wait 79
That, knowing sin within, will touch the gate. So 80
You are a fair viol, and your sense the strings; 81
Who, finger'd to make man his lawful music, 82
Would draw heaven down, and all the gods, to
hearken: 83
But being play'd upon before your time, 84
Hell only danceth at so harsh a chime. 85
Good sooth, I care not for you. 86
 Ant. Prince Pericles, touch not, upon thy life, 87
For that's an article within our law, 88
As dangerous as the rest. Your time's expired: 89
Either expound now, or receive your sentence. 90
 Per. Great king, 91
Few love to hear the sins they love to act: 92
'Twould braid yourself too near for me to tell it 93
Who has a book of all that monarchs do, 94
He's more secure to keep it shut than shown: 95
For vice repeated is like the wandering wind, 96
Blows dust in others' eyes, to spread itself; 97
And yet the end of all is bought thus dear, 98
The breath is gone, and the sore eyes see clear 99
To stop the air would hurt them. The blind mole
casts 100
Copp'd hills towards heaven, to tell the earth is
throng'd 101
By man's oppression; and the poor worm doth
die for't. 102
Kings are earth's gods; in vice their law's their
will; 103
And if Jove stray, who dares say Jove doth ill! 104
It is enough you know: and it is fit, 105
What being more known grows worse, to smother it. 106
All love the womb that their first being bred. 107
Then give my tongue like leave to love my head 108

```
71    same as 66
72    aX: SP1, MTh, TH1, JG1

73    X: NM2
74    X: NM2
75
76    X: SP1, SP2

77    X: SP1, SP2, MTh
78    X: SP1, SP2, MTh, TR1, JG1, EdB
79    same as 78
80    same as 78
81    X: SP1, SP2, HIM, MTh, TR1, JG1
82    same as 81

83    szme as 81
84    same as 81
85    same as 81; ADD 6:TH1
86    X: SP1, SP2, HIM, MTh, TR1, TH1
87    X: MTh, TR1; bX: SP1, SP2, NM2, DS1
88    X: SP1, SP2, MTh, NM2, DS1, TH1
89    aX: SP1, SP2, MTh, NM2, DS1
90
91
92
93
94    X: TH1, EdB
95    X: TH1, EdB
96    X: SP1,  SP2, MTh, TH1, JG1
97    same as 96
98    same as 96, EdB
99    same as 98, NM2

100   same as 99, less EdB; aX: EdB

101   same as 100; less aX

102   same as 101

103   X: SP1, MTh, NM2
104   same as 103
105   X: NM2, EdB; bX: TH1

106   X: TR1, EdB
107   X: TR1
108   X: TR1
```

Ant. [*Aside*] Heaven, that I had thy ha.
he has found the meaning: 109
But I will gloze with him.—Young prince of Ty.   110
Though by the tenour of our strict edict,   111
Your exposition misinterpreting,   112
We might proceed to cancel of your days;   113
Yet hope, succeeding from so fair a tree   114
As your fair self, doth tune us otherwise: 115
Forty days longer we do respite you: 116
If by which time our secret be undone,   117
This mercy shows we'll joy in such a son: 118
And until then your entertain shall be   119
As doth befit our honour and your worth.   120

[*Exeunt all but Peri...*

Per. How courtesy would seem to cover si   121
When what is done is like an hypocrite.   122
The which is good in nothing but in sight!   123
If it be true that I interpret false,   124
Then were it certain you were not so bad   125
As with foul incest to abuse your soul;   126
Where now you're both a father and a son.   127
By your untimely claspings with your child,   128
Which pleasure fits an husband, not a father;   129
And she an eater of her mother's flesh,   130
By the defiling of her parent's bed;   131
And both like serpents are, who though they fe.   132
On sweetest flowers, yet they poison breed.   133
Antioch, farewell! for wisdom sees, those men   134
Blush not in actions blacker than the night.   135
Will shun no course to keep them from the li=   136
One sin, I know, another doth provoke: 137
Murder's as near to lust as flame to smoke: 138
Poison and treason are the hands of sin,   139
Ay, and the targets, to put off the shame: 140
Then, lest my life be cropp'd to keep you clear.   141
By flight I'll shun the danger which I fear. [*Ex*   142

Re-enter ANTIOCHUS.

Ant. He hath found the meaning, for wh=
we mean   143
To have his head.   144
He must not live to trumpet forth my infamy,   145
Nor tell the world Antiochus doth sin   146
In such a loathed manner;   147
And therefore instantly this prince must die: 148

109 b<u>X</u>: TH1
110 a<u>X</u>: SP2, TH1
111
112
113
114
115
116
117
118
119 X: TH1
120 X: TH1

121 X: JG1
122 X: NM2, JG1
123 X: SP1, NM2, TR1, JG1
124 X: SP1, HIM, NM2
125 X: SP1, HIM
126 X: SP1, HIM
127 X: SP1, SP2, NM1, NM2, JG1
128 same as 127, TR1, less NM2
129 same as 127, TR1
130 X: SP1, SP2, HIM, JG1
131 same as 130, NM2
132 same as 130, TR1
133 same as 132
134 b<u>X</u>: NM2, EdB
135 <u>X</u>: NM2, EdB
136 X: NM2, EdB
137 X: HIM, TH1
138 X: HIM, TR1
139 X: HIM, NM2, TR1, JG1
140 same as 139
141 X: HIM
142 X: HIM

143
144 X: TR2; <u>ADD</u> 2: SP2
145 X: HIM
146 X: SP1, SP2, HIM
147 same as 146
148 X: HIM

For by his fall my honour must keep high.   149
Who attends us there?

Enter THALIARD.

Thal.   Doth your highness call? 150   150
Ant. Thaliard,   151
You are of our chamber, and our mind partakes   152
Her private actions to your secrecy;   153
And for your faithfulness we will advance you.   154
Thaliard, behold, here's poison, and here's gold: 155
We hate the prince of Tyre, and thou must kill
    him: 156
It fits thee not to ask the reason why,   157
Because we bid it.   Say, is it done?
Thal.   My lord,   158
'Tis done.   159
Ant. Enough.   160   160

Enter a Messenger.

Let your breath cool yourself. telling your haste. 161
    Mess. My lord, prince Pericles is fled. [*Exit.*
Ant.   As thou   162
Wilt live, fly after: and like an arrow shot   163
From a well-experienced archer hits the mark   164
His eye doth level at, so thou ne'er return   165
Unless thou say 'Prince Pericles is dead.'   166
    Thal. My lord,   167
If I can get him within my pistol's length,   168
I'll make him sure enough: so, farewell to your
    highness.   169
    Ant. Thaliard, adieu! [*Exit Thal.*] Till
    Pericles be dead,   170   170
My heart can lend no succour to my head. [*Exit.* 171

SCENE II.   *Tyre.   A room in the palace.*

Enter PERICLES.

Per. [*To Lords without*] Let none disturb   1
    us.—Why should this change of thoughts,   2
The sad companion, dull-eyed melancholy,   3
Be my so used a guest as not an hour,   4
In the day's glorious walk, or peaceful night,
The tomb where grief should sleep, can breed
    me quiet?   5
Here pleasures court mine eyes, and mine eyes
    shun them,   6

149 X: HIM, TR1

150 X: SP1
151
152
153
154
155 X: SP1, SP2, NM2

156
157

158
159
160 X: TH1

161 X: SP1, SP2, TR1, TH1

162 X: SP1
163
164
165 bX: HIM
166 X̄: HIM
167 X: HIM, JG1
168 X: HIM

169 X: HIM

170 aX: HIM
171 Insert PRO 2: 1-8: TR1; Insert PRO 2: 1-4: TH1; Insert 13: 1-10: TR2

                    Scene 12

ALL CUT: NM1, NM2
  1 aX: JG1, EdB
  2
  3
  4

  5 X: TR1; aX: SP2

  6

And danger, which I fear'd, is at Antioch,   7

Whose aim seems far too short to hit me here: 8

Yet neither pleasure's art can joy my spirits,   9

Nor yet the other's distance comfort me.   **10**   10

Then it is thus: the passions of the mind,   11

That have their first conception by mis-dread,   12

Have after-nourishment and life by care: 13

And what was first but fear what might be done,   14

Grows elder now and cares it be not done.   15

And so with me: the great Antiochus,   16

'Gainst whom I am too little to contend,   17

Since he's so great can make his will his act,   18

Will think me speaking, though I swear to silence: 19

Nor boots it me to say I honour him,   **20**   20

If he suspect I may dishonour him: 21

And what may make him blush in being known,   22

He'll stop the course by which it might be known;   23

With hostile forces he'll o'erspread the land,   24

And with the ostent of war will look so huge,   25

Amazement shall drive courage from the state;   26

Our men be vanquish'd ere they do resist,   27

And subjects punish'd that ne'er thought offence: 28

Which care of them, not pity of myself,   29

Who am no more but as the tops of trees,   30 $

Which fence the roots they grow by and defend

    them,   **30**   31 $

Makes both my body pine and soul to languish,   32

And punish that before that he would punish.   33

Enter HELICANUS, *with other* Lords.

First Lord. Joy and all comfort in your sacred

    breast!   34

  Sec. Lord. And keep your mind, till you

    return to us,   35

Peaceful and comfortable!   36

  Hel. Peace, peace, and give experience

    tongue.   37

They do abuse the king that flatter him: 38

For flattery is the bellows blows up sin: 39

The thing the which is flatter'd, but a spark,   **40**   40

To which that blast gives heat and stronger

    glowing;   41

Whereas reproof, obedient and in order,   42

Fits kings, as they are men, for they may err.   43

When Signior Sooth here does proclaim a peace,   44

He flatters you, makes war upon your life.   45

$ I believe "30" should be one lines earlier

```
 7
 8   X: TR1; ADD 1:0: JG1
 9   X: JG1
10   X: JG1
11   X: SP1, SP2, JG1, EdB; bX: MTh, TR1, TR2
12   X: SP1,  SP2, MTh, Th1, TR2, JG1, EdB
13   same as 12
14   same as 12
15   same as 12
16   X: SP1, SP2, DS1, JG1; aX: MTh, TR1, TR2, EdB
17   same as 16; less aX
18   sameas 17
19   same as 17
20   X: SP1, SP2, DS1, TR1, TH1, JG1
21   same as 20
22   same as 20
23   X: SP1, SP2, DS1, TH1, JG1
24   same as 23, less TH1
25   same as 24
26   same as 24
27   same as 24
28   same as 24
29   same as 24, DS1, TR1
30   X: SP1, SP2, HIM, DS1, TR1, TH1, JG1, EdB

31   same as 30, less EdB; aX: EdB
32   X: SP1, HIM, DS1, TR1, JG1
33   same as 32; ADD 1: TH1



34   X: SP1, DS1, TH1, JG1, EdB

35   same as 34, less SP1
36   same as 34

37   X: TH1, EdB; R: JG1
38   X: TH1, EdB
39   X: TH1, EdB
40   X: TH1, JG1, EdB; R: SP1

41   X: SP1, TH1, JG1, EdB
42   X: TH1, EdB
43   X: TH1, EdB
44   X: SP1, MTh, TR1, TH1, JG1, EdB
45   same as 44, DS1
```

Prince, pardon me, or strike me, if you please; 46
I cannot be much lower than my knees. 47

   Per. All leave us else; but let your cares
o'erlook 48
What shipping and what lading's in our haven, 49
And then return to us. [*Exeunt Lords.*] Heli-
canus, thou 50
Hast moved us: what seest thou in our looks? 51

   Hel. An angry brow, dread lord. 52

   Per. If there be such a dart in princes' frowns, 53
How durst thy tongue move anger to our face? 54

   Hel. How dare the plants look up to heaven,
from whence 55
They have their nourishment? 56

   Per.   Thou know'st I have power
To take thy life from thee. 57

   Hel. [*Kneeling*] I have ground the axe myself; 58
Do you but strike the blow.

   Per.   Rise, prithee, rise. 59
Sit down: thou art no flatterer: 60
I thank thee for it; and heaven forbid 61
That kings should let their ears hear their faults
hid!
Fit counsellor and servant for a prince, 6?
Who by thy wisdom makest a prince thy servant, (
What wouldst thou have me do?

   Hel.   To bear with patience 65
Such griefs as you yourself do lay upon yourself. 66

   Per. Thou speak'st like a physician, Helicanus, 67
That minister'st a potion unto me 68
That thou wouldst tremble to receive thyself. 69
Attend me, then: I went to Antioch, 70
Where as thou know'st, against the face of death, 71
I sought the purchase of a glorious beauty, 72
From whence an issue I might propagate, 73
†Are arms to princes, and bring joys to subjects. 74
Her face was to mine eye beyond all wonder; 75
The rest—hark in thine ear—as black as incest: 76
Which by my knowledge found, the sinful father 77
Seem'd not to strike, but smooth: but thou
know'st this, 78
'Tis time to fear when tyrants seem to kiss. 79
Which fear so grew in me, I hither fled, 80
Under the covering of a careful night, 81
Who seem'd my good protector; and, being here, 82

```
46   X: DS1, TH1, EdB
47   same as 46, TR1

48   X: DS1, TH1, JG1, EdB
49   same as 48

50   X: DS1, TH1; aX: JG1, EdB
51   X: DS1, TR1, T̄H̄1̄
52   X: DS1, TH1
53   X: DS1, TH1, JG1, EdB
54   same as 53

55   same as 53

56   X: DS1, TH1, EdB; aX: JG1
57   same as 56; less aX̄

58   same as 57

59   same as 57; bX: TR1
60   X: DS1, TH1; R̄: SP1; aX: SP2, JG1
61   X: DS1, TR1, T̄H̄1̄; bX: S̄P̄2̄

62   X: SP2, DS1, TR1, TH1
63   X: SP2, TR1, TH1
64   same as 63

65   X: TH1
66   X: TH1
67   X: HIM, TH1
68   X: HIM, TH1
69   X: HIM, TH1
70   X: HIM, TH1, EdB
71   same as 70
72   X: HIM, TH1
73   X: SP1, HIM, TH1, TR2, JG1
74   same as 73, DS1
75   X: HIM, TH1
76   X: HIM, TH1
77   X: HIM, TH1

78   X: HIM, TH1
79   X: HIM, TH1
80   X: HIM, TH1, TR2
81   same as 80, JG1
82   same as 81
```

Bethought me what was past, what might succeed. 83
I knew him tyrannous; and tyrants' fears 84
Decrease not, but grow faster than the years: 85
And should he doubt it, as no doubt he doth, 86
That I should open to the listening air 87
How many worthy princes' bloods were shed, 88
To keep his bed of blackness unlaid ope, 89   89
To lop that doubt, he'll fill this land with arms, 90
And make pretence of wrong that I have done him; 91
When all, for mine, if I may call offence, 92
Must feel war's blow, who spares not innocence: 93
Which love to all, of which thyself art one, 94
Who now reprovest me for it,—
  Hel.   Alas, sir! 95
  Per. Drew sleep out of mine eyes, blood
    from my cheeks, 96
Musings into my mind, with thousand doubts 97
How I might stop this tempest ere it came; 98
And finding little comfort to relieve them, 99
I thought it princely charity to grieve them. 100   100
  Hel. Well, my lord, since you have given me
    leave to speak, 101
Freely will I speak. Antiochus you fear, 102
And justly too, I think, you fear the tyrant, 103
Who either by public war or private treason 104
Will take away your life. 105
Therefore, my lord, go travel for a while, 106
Till that his rage and anger be forgot, 107
Or till the Destinies do cut his thread of life. 108
Your rule direct to any; if to me, 109   109
Day serves not light more faithful than I'll be. 110
  Per. I do not doubt thy faith; 111
But should he wrong my liberties in my absence? 112
  Hel. We'll mingle our bloods together in the
    earth, 113
From whence we had our being and our birth. 114
  Per. Tyre, I now look from thee then, and to
    Tarsus 115
Intend my travel, where I'll hear from thee; 116
And by whose letters I'll dispose myself. 117
The care I had and have of subjects' good 118
On thee I lay, whose wisdom's strength can
    bear it. 119   119
I'll take thy word for faith, not ask thine oath: 120
Who shuns not to break one will sure crack both: 121
But in our orbs we'll live so round and safe, 122

83	X: HIM, TH1, TR2
84	X: HIM, TH1, TR2, JG1; b$\underline{X}$: TR1
85	X: HIM, TR1, TH1, TR2, $\overline{JG1}$
86	X: HIM, TH1, TR2, JG1
87	same as 86
88	X: HIM, TH1, TR2
89	same as 88
90	same as 88, JG1
91	same as 88
92	same as 88, TR1; R: JG1
93	same as 92; less $\overline{R}$
94	same as 92, including $\underline{R}$
95	X: HIM, TH1, TR2; $\underline{R}$: JG1; $\underline{aX}$: TR1
96	X: HIM, TR1, TH1, TR2; $\underline{bX}$: JG1
97	same as 96; less $\underline{bX}$
98	same as 97
99	X: SP1, HIM, MTh, TR1, TH1, TR2, JG1
100	same as 99
101	X: HIM, TR1
102	R: TH1; $\underline{aX}$: TR1
103	$\overline{ADD}$ 2: $\overline{TH1}$
104	$\overline{X}$: TH1
105	$\underline{aX}$: TH1
106	
107	
108	
109	X: TH1
110	X: TH1
1112	X: TH1
112	X: TH1
113	X: TH1
114	X: TH1; $\underline{bX}$: TR1
115	
116	
117	X: DS1; $\underline{Insert}$ $\underline{PRO}$ 2: 5-8: TH1
118	X: TH1
119	X: TH1
120	X: TH1, TR2
121	X: TR1, TH1, TR2
122	X: SP1, MTh, DS1, TH1, JG1

That time of both this truth shall ne'er convince, 123
Thou show'dst a subject's shine, I a true prince. 124
[Exeunt.

SCENE III. *Tyre. An ante-chamber in the palace.*

Enter THALIARD.

Thal. So, this is Tyre, and this the court. 1
Here must I kill King Pericles; and if I do it 2
not, I am sure to be hanged at home: 'tis dan- 3
gerous. Well, I perceive he was a wise fellow, 4
and had good discretion, that, being bid to ask 5
what he would of the king, desired he might 6
know none of his secrets: now do I see he had 7
some reason for't; for if a king bid a man be a 8
villain, he's bound by the indenture of his oath 9
to be one. Hush! here come the lords of Tyre. 10

Enter HELICANUS *and* ESCANES, *with other*
Lords *of Tyre.*

Hel. You shall not need, my fellow peers of
Tyre. 11
Further to question me of your king's departure: 12
His seal'd commission, left in trust with me, 13
Doth speak sufficiently he's gone to travel. 14
Thal. [*Aside*] How! the king gone! 15
Hel. If further yet you will be satisfied, 16
Why, as it were unlicensed of your loves, 17
He would depart, I'll give some light unto you. 18
Being at Antioch——
Thal. [*Aside*] What from Antioch? 19
Hel. Royal Antiochus—on what cause I know
not— 20
Took some displeasure at him; at least he judged
so: 21
And doubting lest that he had err'd or sinn'd, 22
To show his sorrow, he'ld correct himself; 23
So puts himself unto the shipman's toil, 24
With whom each minute threatens life or death. 25
Thal. [*Aside*] Well, I perceive 26
I shall not be hang'd now, although I would; 27
But since he's gone,† the king's seas must please: 28
He 'scaped the land, to perish at the sea. 29
I'll present myself. Peace to the lords of Tyre! 30
Hel. Lord Thaliard from Antiochus is we-

123   same as 122
124   same as 122; <u>ADD</u> 1: SP2

<u>Scene 13</u>

<u>ALL CUT</u>:NM1, NM2, TH1, EdB
 1   <u>MOVE</u> 1--10 to follow <u>11</u>: 171: TR1
 2
 3   b<u>X</u>: TR2, JG1
 4   <u>X</u>: TR2, JG1
 5   X: TR2, JG1
 6   X: TR2, JG1
 7   X: TR2, JG1
 8   X: TR2, JG1
 9   X: TR2, JG1
10   X: TR2, JG1

11   X: TR2, JG1
12   X: TR2, JG1
13   X: DS1, TR2, JG1
14   same as 13
15   X: TR2, JG1
16   X: TR2, JG1
17   X: TR2, JG1
18   X: TR2, JG1

19   X: TR2 a<u>X</u>: JG1

20   X: TR2

21   X: TR2
22   X: TR2
23   X: TR2
24   X: TR2
25   X: TR2; <u>ADD</u> 1: JG1
26   X: TR2, <u>JG1</u>
27   X: TR2, JG1; b<u>X</u>: DS1
28   X: DS1, TR2, <u>JG1</u>
29   X: TR2, JG1
30   a<u>X</u>: TR2, JG1

come.   *?*   31

Thal.   From him I come   32
With message unto princely Pericles: 33
But since my landing I have understood   34
Your lord has betook himself to unknown travel 35
My message must return from whence it came   36

Hel.   We have no reason to desire it,   37
Commended to our master, not to us: 38
Yet, ere you shall depart, this we desire,   39
As friends to Antioch, we may feast in Tyre. *?* 40

                                 [*Exeunt*

SCENE IV.   *Tarsus. A room in the Governor's
                house.*

Enter CLEON, *the governor of Tarsus, with*
         DIONYZA, *and others.*

Cle.   My Dionyza, shall we rest us here,   1
And by relating tales of others' griefs,   2
See if 'twill teach us to forget our own?   3

Dio.   That were to blow at fire in hope to
       quench it: 4
For who digs hills because they do aspire   5
Throws down one mountain to cast up a higher. 6
O my distressed lord, even such our griefs are: 7
Here they're but felt, and seen with mischief's
       eyes,   8
But like to groves, being topp'd, they higher rise

Cle.   O Dionyza,   9
Who wanteth food, and will not say he wants it 10
Or can conceal his hunger till he famish?   11
Our tongues and sorrows do sound deep   12
Our woes into the air: our eyes do weep,   13
Till tongues fetch breath that may proclaim them 14
       louder: 15
That, if heaven slumber while their creatures
       want,   16
They may awake their helps to comfort them. 17
I'll then discourse our woes, felt several years 18
And wanting breath to speak help me with tears 19

Dio.   I'll do my best, sir.   *?* 20

Cle.   This Tarsus, o'er which I have the
       government,   21
A city on whom plenty held full hand,   22
For riches strew'd herself even in the streets: 23

```
31
32  X: JG1
33  X: JG1
34  X: JG1
35  X: JG1
36  X: JG1
37  X: JG1
38  X: JG1
39  X: JG1
40  X: JG1; ADD 10: SP1
```

Scene 14

```
ALL CUT: NM1, NM2
 1  X: TR1, TH1, TR2
 2  same as 1
 3  same as 1

 4  same as1
 5  same as 1, JG1
 6  same as 5
 7  X: SP1, SP2, MTh, TR1, TH1,  TR2; bX: JG1

 8  same as 7, JG1; less bX
 9  same as 8
10  X: TR1, TH1, TR2
11  same as 10
12  same as 10
13  X: DS1, TR1, TH1,  TR2, JG1
14  same as 13

15  same as 13

16  same as 13
17  same as 13
18  X: TR1, TH1, TR2
19  same as 18
20  same as 18, DS1

21
22
23
```

Whose towers bore heads so high they kiss'd the
    clouds,   24
And strangers ne'er beheld but wonder'd at;   25
Whose men and dames so jetted and adorn'd,   26
Like one another's glass to trim them by: 27
Their tables were stored full, to glad the sight,   28
And not so much to feed on as delight;   29
All poverty was scorn'd, and pride so great,   30   30
The name of help grew odious to repeat.   31
  Dio. O, 'tis too true.   32
  Cle. But see what heaven can do! By this
    our change,   33
These mouths, who but of late, earth, sea, and air,   34
Were all too little to content and please,   35
Although they gave their creatures in abundance,   36
As houses are defiled for want of use,   37
They are now starved for want of exercise: 38
Those palates who, not yet two summers younger,   39
Must have inventions to delight the taste,   40   40
Would now be glad of bread, and beg for it: 41
Those mothers who, to nousle up their babes,   42
Thought nought too curious, are ready now   43
To eat those little darlings whom they loved.   44
So sharp are hunger's teeth, that man and wife   45
Draw lots who first shall die to lengthen life: 46
Here stands a lord, and there a lady weeping;   47
Here many sink, yet those which see them fall   48
Have scarce strength left to give them burial.   49
Is not this true?   50   50
  Dio. Our cheeks and hollow eyes do witness it.   51
  Cle. O, let those cities that of plenty's cup   52
And her prosperities so largely taste,   53
With their superfluous riots, hear these tears!   54
The misery of Tarsus may be theirs.   55

Enter a Lord.

  Lord. Where's the lord governor?   56
  Cle. Here.   57
Speak out thy sorrows which thou bring'st in
    haste,   58
For comfort is too far for us to expect.   59
  Lord. We have descried, upon our neighbour-
    ing shore,   60   60
A portly sail of ships make hitherward.   61
  Cle. I thought as much.   62

```
24
25
26   X: DS1, TR2, JG1
27   same as 26
28   X: DS1, TR2
29   X: DS1, GR2
30   X: DS1, TR1, TH1, TR2
31   same as 30
32   X: DS1, TH1, TR2

33   bX: EdB
34   X̄: JG1, EdB
35   X: JG1, EdB
36   X: TH1, TR2, JG1, EdB
37   X: SP2, TR1, TH1, TR2, JG1, EdB
38   X: TR2, JG1, EdB
39   X: TH1, TR2, EdB
40   same as 39
41   X: TH1, EdB
42   X: HIM, EdB
43   X: HIM, EdB; aX: TR2
44   X: EdB
45   X: EdB
46   X: EdB
47   X: TR1, TH1, TR2, JG1, EdB
48   X: TR1, TH1, JG1, EdB
49   same as 48
50   X: DS1, TH1, EdB; ADD 1: TR2
51   X: DS1, TH1
52   X: TR2
53   X: TR2
54   X: TR2
55   X: TR2



56
57

58
59   X: TR2

60
61
62   X: TR1, TH1,  TR2
```

One sorrow never comes but brings an heir,   63
That may succeed as his inheritor;   64
And so in ours: some neighbouring nation,   65
Taking advantage of our misery,   66
Hath stuff'd these hollow vessels with their power,   67
To beat us down, the which are down already;   68
And make a conquest of unhappy me,   69
Whereas no glory's got to overcome.   **70**   70
   Lord. That's the least fear; for, by the sem-
     blance   71
Of their white flags display'd, they bring us peace,   72
And come to us as favourers, not as foes.   73
   Cle. Thou speak'st like him's untutor'd to
     repeat: 74
Who makes the fairest show means most deceit.   75
But bring they what they will and what they can,   76
What need we fear?   77
The ground's the lowest, and we are half way
     there.   78
Go tell their general we attend him here,   79
To know for what he comes, and whence he comes,   80
And what he craves.   **81**   81
   Lord. I go, my lord.   *[Exit.*   82
   Cle. Welcome is peace, if he on peace consist: 83
If wars, we are unable to resist.   84

     Enter PERICLES *with* Attendants.

   Per. Lord governor, for so we hear you are,   85
Let not our ships and number of our men   86
Be like a beacon fired to amaze your eyes.   87
We have heard your miseries as far as Tyre,   88
And seen the desolation of your streets: 89
Nor come we to add sorrow to your tears,   **90**   90
But to relieve them of their heavy load;   91
And these our ships, you happily may think   92
Are like the Trojan horse was stuff'd within   93
With bloody veins, expecting overthrow,   94
Are stored with corn to make your needy bread,   95
And give them life whom hunger starved half
     dead.   96
   All. The gods of Greece protect you!   97
And we'll pray for you.
   Per.   Arise, I pray you, rise: 98
We do not look for reverence, but for love,   99
And harbourage for ourself, our ships, and men.   100
   Cle. The which when any shall not gratify, **101**   101

```
63   X: TR2
64   X: TR2
65   X: TR2
66   X: TR2
67   X: TR2
68   X: TR2
69   X: DS1, TR1, TR2, JG1
70   X: DS1, TR1, TR2

71   X: TR2, JG1, bX: TH1
72   R: TH1
73

74   X: SP1, SP2, TR1
75   X: TR1
76
77

78
79
80
81
82
83
84   ADD 4: MTh

85   bX: JG1
86
87
88
89   X: SP2
90
91
92   bX: SP1, MTh, TH1, JG1
93   X: SP1, MTh, TH1
94   same as 93
95

96   X: TR1
97   X: DS1, EdB

98   aX: DS1
99
100  X: SP1, SP2
101  X: SP2
```

Or pay you with unthankfulness in thought,   102
Be it our wives, our children, or ourselves,   103
The curse of heaven and men succeed their evils!   104
Till when,—the which I hope shall ne'er be
    seen,—   105
Your grace is welcome to our town and us.   106
   Per. Which welcome we'll accept; feast here
    awhile,   107
Until our stars that frown lend us a smile.   108
                                  [*Exeunt.*

ACT II.

Enter GOWER.

   Gow. Here have you seen a mighty king   1
His child, I wis, to incest bring: 2
A better prince and benign lord,   3
That will prove awful both in deed and word.   4
Be quiet then as men should be,   5
Till he hath pass'd necessity.   6
I'll show you those in troubles reign,   7
Losing a mite, a mountain gain.   8
The good in conversation,   9
To whom I give my benison,   **10**   10
Is still at Tarsus, where each man   11
Thinks all is writ he speken can;   12
And, to remember what he does,   13
Build his statue to make him glorious: 14
But tidings to the contrary   15
Are brought your eyes; what need speak I?   16

DUMB SHOW.

Enter at one door PERICLES *talking with*
CLEON; *all the train with them. Enter at*
another door a Gentleman, *with a letter to*
PERICLES; PERICLES *shows the letter to*
CLEON; *gives the* Messenger *a reward, and*
knights him. Exit PERICLES *at one door, and*
CLEON *at another.*

Good Helicane, that stay'd at home,   17
Not to eat honey like a drone   18
From others' labours; for though he strive   19
To killen bad, keep good alive;   **20**   20
And to fulfil his prince' desire,   21
Sends word of all that haps in Tyre: 22

102
103
104

105   X: SP2
106   X: SP2; <u>ADD</u> 10: MTh; <u>ADD</u> 15: SP1

107   X: SP1, MTh
108   X: SP1, MTh

2 PRØLOG

<u>ALL CUT</u>: SP1, SP2, NM1, MTh
1   X: HIM;; <u>MOVE</u> 1-4 to follow <u>11</u>: 171: TH1; <u>MOVE</u> 1-8 to follow <u>11</u>:*
2   X: HIM; <u>ADD</u> 2: NM2
3   X: HIM, <u>NM2</u>; <u>R</u>: EdB
4   X: HIM, NM2
5   X: HIM, NM2, EdB; <u>MOVE</u> 5-8 to follow <u>12</u>: 117: TH1
6   same as 5; less <u>MOVE</u>
7   X: HIM, NM2
8   X: HIM, NM2
9   X: HIM, NM2, DS1, TR1
10   X: HIM, NM2, DS1, TR1, TR2, EdB
11   X: HIM, NM2, DS1, TR1; <u>bX</u>: EdB
12   X: HIM, NM2, DS1, TR1, <u>EdB</u>
13   same as 12
14   same as 12
15   same as 12, TH1
16   same as 15; <u>bX</u>: JG1

17   X: NM 2, TH1
18   X: NM2, TH1
19   X: NM2, TH1; <u>bX</u>: TR1
20   X: NM2, TR1, <u>TH1</u>
21   X: NM2, TH1
22   X: NM2, TH1

How Thaliard came full bent with sin   23
And had intent to murder him;   24
And that in Tarsus was not best   25
Longer for him to make his rest.   26
He, doing so, put forth to seas,   27
Where when men been, there's seldom ease: 28
For now the wind begins to blow;   29
Thunder above and deeps below   30   30
Make such unquiet, that the ship   31
Should house him safe is wreck'd and split;   32
And he, good prince, having all lost,   33
By waves from coast to coast is tost: 34
All perishen of man, of pelf,   35
Ne aught escapen but himself;   36
Till fortune, tired with doing bad,   37
Threw him ashore, to give him glad: ·   38
And here he comes.   What shall be next,   39
Pardon old Gower,—this longs the text.   40   40

[Exit.

SCENE I.   *Pentapolis.   An open place by the
sea-side.*

Enter PERICLES, *wet.*

Per. Yet cease your ire, you angry stars of
  heaven!   1
Wind, rain, and thunder, remember, earthly man 2
Is but a substance that must yield to you;   3
And I, as fits my nature, do obey you: 4
Alas, the sea hath cast me on the rocks,   5
Wash'd me from shore to shore, and left me
  breath   6
Nothing to think on but ensuing death: 7
Let it suffice the greatness of your powers   8
To have bereft a prince of all his fortunes; 9 9
And having thrown him from your watery grave, 10
Here to have death in peace is all he'll crave. 11

Enter three Fishermen.

First Fish. What, ho, Pilch!   12
Sec. Fish. Ha, come and bring away the nets! 13
First Fish. What, Patch-breech, I say!   14
Third Fish. What say you, master?   15
First Fish. Look how thou stirrest now! come 16
away, or I'll fetch thee with a wanion.   17
  Third Fish. 'Faith, master, I am thinking of 18

102
103
104

105   X: SP2
106   X: SP2; <u>ADD</u> 10: MTh; <u>ADD</u> 15: SP1

107   X: SP1, MTh
108   X: SP1, MTh

2 PRØLOG

<u>ALL CUT</u>: SP1, SP2, NM1, MTh
1   X: HIM;; <u>MOVE</u> 1-4 to follow <u>11</u>: 171: TH1; <u>MOVE</u> 1-8 to follow <u>11</u>:*
2   X: HIM; <u>ADD 2</u>: NM2
3   X: HIM, <u>NM2</u>; <u>R</u>: EdB
4   X: HIM, NM2
5   X: HIM, NM2, EdB; <u>MOVE</u> 5-8 to follow <u>12</u>: 117: TH1
6   same as 5; less <u>MOVE</u>
7   X: HIM, NM2
8   X: HIM, NM2
9   X: HIM, NM2, DS1, TR1
10 X: HIM, NM2, DS1, TR1, TR2, EdB
11 X: HIM, NM2, DS1, TR1; <u>bX</u>: EdB
12 X: HIM, NM2, DS1, TR1, <u>EdB</u>
13 same as 12
14 same as 12
15 same as 12, TH1
16 sameas 15; <u>bX</u>: JG1

17 X: NM 2, TH1
18 X: NM2, TH1
19 X: NM2, TH1; <u>bX</u>: TR1
20 X: NM2, TR1, <u>TH1</u>
21 X: NM2, TH1
22 X: NM2, TH1

How Thaliard came full bent with sin 23
And had intent to murder him; 24
And that in Tarsus was not best 25
Longer for him to make his rest. 26
He, doing so, put forth to seas, 27
Where when men been, there's seldom ease: 28
For now the wind begins to blow; 29
Thunder above and deeps below   30   30
Make such unquiet, that the ship 31
Should house him safe is wreck'd and split; 32
And he, good prince, having all lost, 33
By waves from coast to coast is tost: 34
All perishen of man, of pelf, 35
Ne aught escapen but himself; 36
Till fortune, tired with doing bad, 37
Threw him ashore, to give him glad: · 38
And here he comes.   What shall be next, 39
Pardon old Gower,—this longs the text.   40   40

                            [Exit.

SCENE I. *Pentapolis.*   *An open place by the*
                sea-side.

Enter PERICLES, *wet.*

Per.   Yet cease your ire, you angry stars of
      beaven! 1
Wind, rain, and thunder, remember, earthly man 2
Is but a substance that must yield to you; 3
And I, as fits my nature, do obey you: 4
Alas, the sea hath cast me on the rocks, 5
Wash'd me from shore to shore, and left me
      breath 6
Nothing to think on but ensuing death: 7
Let it suffice the greatness of your powers 8
To have bereft a prince of all his fortunes;   9   9
And having thrown him from your watery grave, 10
Here to have death in peace is all he'll crave. 11

Enter three Fishermen.

First Fish.   What, ho, Pilch! 12
Sec. Fish.   Ha, come and bring away the nets! 13
First Fish.   What, Patch-breech, I say! 14
Third Fish.   What say you, master? 15
First Fish.   Look how thou stirrest now! come 16
away, or I'll fetch thee with a wanion. 17
   Third Fish.   'Faith, master, I am thinking of 18

```
23  X: NM2
24
25  X: NM2
26  X: NM2
27  R: DS1
28  R̄: NM2, DS1; aX: EdB
29
30
31
32  R: NM2; ADD 4: TR2
33  X̄: TH1
34  X: TH1
35  X: EdB
36  X: EdB
37  XL NM2, EdB
38  X: NM2, EdB
39  X: NM2, EdB; bX: TH1, TR2
40  X: NM2, TR1, TR̄2, EdB
```

<u>Scene 21</u>

```
 1  X: TR2, EdB
 2  X: TR2, EdB
 3  X: TR2, EdB
 4  X: TR1, TR2, EdB
 5  X: TR1, TH1, JG1, EdB

 6  same as 5
 7  same as 5
 8  X: EdB
 9  X: EdB
10  X: TR1, EdB
11  X: EdB


12  X: SP1
13  X: SP2
14  X: SP1, SP2
15  X: SP1
16  X: SP1, SP2
17  X: SP1, SP2
18  X: SP1, SP2
```

the poor men that were cast away before us even now. 20 19

20

First Fish. Alas, poor souls, it grieved my heart to hear what pitiful cries they made to us to help them, when, well-a-day, we could scarce help ourselves. 21

22

23

24

Third Fish. Nay, master, said not I as much when I saw the porpus how he bounced and tumbled? they say they're half fish, half flesh: a plague on them, they ne'er come but I look to be washed. Master, I marvel how the fishes live in the sea. 30 25

26

27

28

29

30

First Fish. Why, as men do a-land; the great ones eat up the little ones: I can compare our rich misers to nothing so fitly as to a whale: a' plays and tumbles, driving the poor fry before him, and at last devours them all at a mouthful: such whales have I heard on o' the land, who never leave gaping till they've swallowed the whole parish, church, steeple, bells, and all. 31

32

33

34

35

36

37

38

Per. [*Aside*] A pretty moral. 39 39

Third Fish. But, master, if I had been the sexton, I would have been that day in the belfry. 40

41

Sec. Fish. Why, man? 42

Third Fish. Because he should have swallowed me too: and when I had been in his belly, I would have kept such a jangling of the bells, that he should never have left, till he cast bells, steeple, church, and parish, up again. But if the good King Simonides were of my mind,— 43

44

45

46

47

48

Per. [*Aside*] Simonides! 49 49

Third Fish. We would purge the land of these drones, that rob the bee of her honey. 50

51

Per. [*Aside*] How from the finny subject of the sea 52

These fishers tell the infirmities of men; 53

And from their watery empire recollect 54

All that may men approve or men detect! 55

Peace be at your labour, honest fishermen. 56

Sec. Fish. Honest! good fellow, what's that! If it be a day fits you, †search out of the calendar, and nobody look after it. 57

58

59

Per. May see the sea hath cast upon your coast. 60 60

Sec. Fish. What a drunken knave was the sea to cast thee in our way! 61

62

```
19   X:  SP1,   SP2
20   X:  SP1,  SP2
21   X:  SP2
22   X:  SP2
23   X:  SP2
24   X:  SP2
25   X:  SP2
26   X:  SP2
27   X:  SP2
28   X:  SP2
29   X:  SP2;  MOVE 29b–47a to follow 83: EdB
30   X:  SP2
31   X:  SP2
32   X:  SP2
33   X:  SP2
34   X:  SP2
35   X:  SP2
36   X:  SP2
37   X:  SP2
38   X:  SP2
39   X:  SP1, SP2, DS1, TR1, TH1, TR2, JG1
40   X:  SP2
41   X:  SP2
42   X:  SP2
43   X:  SP2
44   X:  SP2
45   X:  SP2
46   X:  SP2
47   X:  SP2; bX:  TH1, EdB
48   X:  SP2, T̄H̄1, EdB
49   X:  SP1, SP2, TR1, TH1, TR2, JG1, EdB
50   X:  SP2, TH1, EdB; bX: TR1
51   X:  SP2, TR1, TH1, ĒdB; Insert 119–121: SP1

52   X:  SP2, MTh, TR1, EdB; MOVE 52–59 to follow 118: SP1
53   same as 52; less MOVE
54   same as 53
55   same as 53
56   X:  SP2, TR1
57   X:  SP2, TR1; R: JG1; bX: DS1
58   X:  SP2, DS1, T̄R̄1, TH1, EdB; bX: JG1
59   same as 58, JG1; less bX

60   X:  SP2,, DS1; aX: TR1, TH1
61   X:  SP2
62   X:  SP2; ADD SONG: TR2
```

Per. A man whom both the waters and the
    wind,   63
In that vast tennis-court, have made the ball   64
For them to play upon, entreats you pity him;   65
He asks of you, that never used to beg.   66
    First Fish. No, friend, cannot you beg? Here's   67
them in our country of Greece gets more with   68
begging than we can do with working.   69
    Sec. Fish. Canst thou catch any fishes, then?   70
    Per. I never practised it.   71   71
    Sec. Fish. Nay, then thou wilt starve, sure;   72
for here's nothing to be got now-a-days, unless   73
thou canst fish for't.   74
    Per. What I have been I have forgot to know;   75
But what I am, want teaches me to think on: 76
A man throng'd up with cold: my veins are chill,   77
And have no more of life than may suffice   78
To give my tongue that heat to ask your help;   79
Which if you shall refuse, when I am dead, 80   80
For that I am a man, pray see me buried.   81
    First Fish. Die quoth-a? Now gods forbid!   82
I have a gown here; come, put it on; keep thee   83
warm. Now, afore me, a handsome fellow! Come,   84
thou shalt go home, and we'll have flesh for   85
holidays, fish for fasting-days, and moreo'er pud-   86
dings and flap-jacks, and thou shalt be welcome.   87
    Per. I thank you, sir.   88
    Sec. Fish. Hark you, my friend; you said you   89
could not beg.   90   90
    Per. I did but crave.   91
    Sec. Fish. But crave! Then I'll turn craver   92
too, and so I shall 'scape whipping.   93
    Per. Why, are all your beggars whipped,   94
    then?   94
    Sec. Fish. O, not all, my friend, not all; for   95
if all your beggars were whipped, I would wish   96
no better office than to be beadle. But, master,   97
I'll go draw up the net.   98
             [Exit with Third Fisherman.
    Per. [*Aside*] How well this honest mirth   99
    becomes their labour!   100
    First Fish. Hark you, sir, do you know where
ye are?   101   101
    Per. Not well.   102
    First Fish. Why, I'll tell you: this is called   103
Pentapolis, and our king the good Simonides.   104

```
 63   X: SP2
 64   X: SP2
 65   X: SP2
 66   X: SP2
 67   X: SP2, TR1
 68   X: SP2, TR1; cX: DS1, TH1
 69   X: SP2, TR1
 70   X: SP2, TR1
 71   X: SP2, TR1
 72   X: SP2, TR1
 73   X: SP2, TR1
 74   X: SP2, TR1
 75   X: SP2
 76   X: SP2
 77   X: SP2
 78   X: SP2
 79   X: SP2
 80   X: SP2
 81   X: SP2, TR1
 82   X: SP2; bX: SP1, DS1, EdB
 83   X: SP1, S̄P2, DS1; bX: EdB; Insert 29b-47a: EdB
 84   X: SP2, EdB; aX: S̄P1, DS1
 85   X: SP 2, EdB; b̄X: JG1
 86   X: SP2, JG1, ĒdB
 87   X: SP2, EdB; aX: JG1
 88   X: SP2, EdB
 89   X: SP2, TR1, EdB
 90   X: SP1, SP2, NTh, TR1, JG1, EdB
 91   same as 90
 92   same as 90, TR2
 93   same as 92

 94   same as 92
 95   same as 92
 96   same as 92
 97   X: SP2, MTh, TR1; aX: SP1, TR2, JG1, EdB
 98   X: SP2, TR1

 99   X: SP2, TR1, TH1, TR2, JG1; MOVE 99 to follow 110: SP1
100   X: SP2, TH1

101   X: SP2, TR1
102   X: SP2
103   X: SP2
104   X: SP2
```

Per. The good King Simonides, do you call
him? 105
106

First Fish. Ay, sir; and he deserves so to be
called for his peaceable reign and good government. 107
108

Per. He is a happy king, since he gains from
his subjects the name of good by his government.
How far is his court distant from this shore? 111 109
110
111

First Fish. Marry, sir, half a day's journey:
and I'll tell you, he hath a fair daughter, and to-
morrow is her birth-day: and there are princes
and knights come from all parts of the world to
just and tourney for her love. 112
113
114
115
116

Per. Were my fortunes equal to my desires,
I could wish to make one there. 117
118

First Fish. O, sir, things must be as they
may; and what a man cannot get, he may law-
fully deal for—† his wife's soul. 121 119
120
121

Re-enter Second *and* Third Fishermen, *drawing
up a net.*

Sec. Fish. Help, master, help! here's a fish
hangs in the net, like a poor man's right in the
law; 'twill hardly come out. Ha! bots on't, 'tis
come at last, and 'tis turned to a rusty armour. 122
123
124
125

Per. An armour, friends! I pray you, let me
see it. 126

Thanks, fortune, yet, that, after all my crosses,
Thou givest me somewhat to repair myself;
And though it was mine own, part of my heritage,
Which my dead father did bequeath to me. 130
With this strict charge, even as he left his life,
'Keep it, my Pericles; it hath been a shield
Twixt me and death;'—and pointed to this
brace:—
'For that it saved me, keep it; in like necessity—
The which the gods protect thee from!—may
defend thee.'
It kept where I kept. I so dearly loved it:
Till the rough seas, that spare not any man,
Took it in rage, though calm'd have given't again:
I thank thee for't: my shipwreck now's no ill,
Since I have here my father's gift in's will. 140 127
128
129
130
131
132
133
134
135
136
137
138
139
140

First Fish. What mean you, sir? 141

Per. To beg of you, kind friends, this coat of
worth,
For it was sometime target to a king: 142
143

```
105  X: SP2
106  X: SP2
107  X: SP2
108  X: SP2
109  X: SP2
110  X: SP2
111  X: SP2
112  X: SP2
113  X: SP2
114  X: SP2
115  X: SP2
116  X: SP2
117  X: SP2
118  X: SP2; Insert 57-59, 99: SP1
119  X: SP2, MTh, TH1; bX: TR1, TR2, JG1; MOVE 119-121 to follow 51: SP1
120  X: SP2, MTh, TR1, TH1, TR2, JG1
121  same as 120


122  X: SP2
123  X: SP2
124  X: SP2; b X: TR2
125  X: SP2, TR2

126  X: SP2
127  X: SP2
128  X: SP2
129  X: SP2
130  X: SP2
131  X: SP2, EdB; bX: SP1
132  X: SP2, EdB

133  X: SP2, EdB; bX: SP1, TR1
134  X: SP2, TR1, EdB

135  same as 134
136  X: SP2, TR1
137  X: SP2, TR1, TR2
138  same as 137
139  X: SP2; bX: TR1
140  X: SP2, TR1
141  X: SP2

142  X: SP2
143  X: SP2
```

I know it by this mark.   He loved me dearly,   144
And for his sake I wish the having of it: 145
And that you'ld guide me to your sovereign's
    court,   146
Where with it I may appear a gentleman: 147
And if that ever my low fortune's better,   148
I'll pay your bounties: till then rest your debtor.   149
   First Fish. Why, wilt thou tourney for the lady?   150
   Per.   I'll show the virtue I have borne in arms.   151
   First Fish.   Why, do 'e take it, and the gods   152
give thee good on't!   153
   Sec. Fish.   Ay, but hark you, my friend: 'twas   154
we that made up this garment through the rough   55
seams of the waters: there are certain condole-   156
ments, certain vails. I hope, sir, if you thrive,   157
you'll remember from whence you had it.   158
   Per.   Believe 't, I will.   159
By your furtherance I am clothed in steel;   160   160
And, spite of all the rapture of the sea,   161
This jewel holds his building on my arm: 162
Unto thy value I will mount myself   163
Upon a courser, whose delightful steps   164
Shall make the gazer joy to see him tread.   165
Only, my friend, I yet am unprovided   166
Of a pair of bases.   167
   Sec. Fish. We'll sure provide: thou shalt   168
have my best gown to make thee a pair; and I'll   169
bring thee to the court myself.   170   170
   Per.   Then honour be but a goal to my will,   171
This day I'll rise, or else add ill to ill. [*Exeunt.*   172

SCENE II. *The same. A public way or plat-*
form leading to the lists. A pavilion by the
side of it for the reception of the King, Princess,
Lords, &c.

Enter SIMONIDES, THISA, Lords, *and* Attendants.

   Sim. Are the knights ready to begin the
    triumph?   1
   First Lord. They are, my liege;   2
And stay your coming to present themselves.   3
   Sim. Return them, we are ready; and our
    daughter,   4
In honour of whose birth these triumphs are,   5
Sits here, like beauty's child, whom nature gat   6

144 X: SP2
145 X: SP2

146 X: SP2
147 X: SP2
148 X: SP2, TR1, JG1
149 same as 148
150 X: SP2
151 X: SP2
152 X: SP2
153 X: SP2
154 X: SP2; b̲X̲: TR2
155 X: SP2, T̅R̅2
156 X: SP2, TR2
157 X: SP2, TR2
158 X: SP2, TR2
159 X: SP2, TR2
160 X: SP2, TH1
161 X: SP2
162 X: SP2, DS1
163 X: SP2, DS1, JG1
164 same as 163
165 same as 163
166 X: SP1, SP2, DS1, TR1, JG1; b̲X̲: TH1
167 same as 166, TH1; less b̲X̲
168 X: SP1, SP2, DS1, TR1, J̅G̅1; b̲X̲: TH1
169 X: SP2, DS1, JG1; a̲X̲: SP1, T̅R̅1, TH1
170 same as 169; less a̲X̲
171 X: SP2
172 X: SP2; A̲D̲D̲ 1: DS1, JG1; A̲D̲D̲ 2: SP1

Scene 22

A̲L̲L̲ C̲U̲T̲: SP2
  1 X: DS1
  2 X: DS1
  3 X: DS1; R̲: SP1

  4
  5
  6 b̲X̲: TH1

For men to see, and seeing wonder at. 7

[Exit a Lord.

Thai. It pleaseth you, my royal father, to
express 8

My commendations great, whose merit's less. 9

Sim. It's fit it should be so; for princes are 10 10

A model, which heaven makes like to itself: 11

As jewels lose their glory if neglected, 12

So princes their renowns if not respected. 13

'Tis now your honour, daughter, to explain 14

The labour of each knight in his device. 15

Thai. Which, to preserve mine honour, I'll
perform. 16

Enter a Knight: *he passes over, and his* Squire
presents his shield to the Princess.

Sim. Who is the first that doth prefer himself? 17

Thai. A knight of Sparta, my renowned father; 18

And the device he bears upon his shield 19

Is a black Ethiope reaching at the sun; 20 20

The word, 'Lux tua vita mihi'. 21

Sim. He loves you well that holds his life of you. 22

[The Second Knight passes over.

Who is the second that presents himself? 23

Thai. A prince of Macedon, my royal father; 24

And the device he bears upon his shield 25

Is an arm'd knight that's conquer'd by a lady; 26

The motto thus, in Spanish, 'Piu por dulzura
que por fuerza.' 27

[The Third Knight passes over.

Sim. And what's the third?

Thai.   The third of Antioch; 28

And his device, a wreath of chivalry; 29

The word, 'Me pompæ provexit apex.' 30 30

[The Fourth Knight passes over.

Sim. What is the fourth? 31

Thai. A burning torch that's turned upside
down; 32

The word, 'Quod me alit, me extinguit.' 33

Sim. Which shows that beauty hath his power
and will, 34

Which can as well inflame as it can kill. 35

[The Fifth Knight passes over.

Thai. The fifth, an hand environed with clouds, 36

Holding out gold that's by the touchstone tried; 37

The motto thus, 'Sic spectanda fides.' 38

7

8
9
10
11
12
13 ADD 6: SP1
14 X: SP1, DS1
15 X: SP1, DS1

16 X: SP1, DS1

17 X: SP1, DS1; R: TH1
18 X: SP1, DS1, TH1
19 X: SP1, DS1
20 X: SP1, DS1
21 X: SP1, DS1
22 X: SP1, DS1

23 X: SP1, DS1; ADD 1: TR1
24 X: SP1, DS1, TH1
25 X: SP1, DS1, TR2
26 X: SP1, DS1, JG1·

27 same as 26; bX: TH1, TR2; ADD 2: TH1

28 same as 26; ADD 1: TR1
29 ·same as 26
30 X: SP1, DS1, TR2, JG1; ADD 1: TH1

31 same as 26; ADD 1: TR1

32 X: SP1, DS1, TR1
33 same as 32, TR2

34 same as 32
35 same   as 32; ADD 2: JG1

36 same as 32
37 same as 32
38 same as 32. TR2; ADD 2: JG1; ADD 4: TH1

[The Sixth Knight, Pericles, passes over.
Sim. And what's   .   39
The sixth and last, the which the knight himself   40
With such a graceful courtesy deliver'd?   41   41
   Thai. He seems to be a stranger; but his
     present is   42
A wither'd branch, that's only green at top;   43
The motto, 'In hac spe vivo'.   44
   Sim. A pretty moral;   45
From the dejected state wherein he is,   46
He hopes by you his fortunes yet may flourish.   47
   First Lord. He had need mean better than
   his outward show   48
Can any way speak in his just commend;   49
For by his rusty outside he appears   50   50
To have practised more the whipstock than the
   lance.   51
   Sec. Lord. He well may be a stranger, for he
   comes   52
To an honour'd triumph strangely furnished.   53
   Third Lord. And on set purpose let his
   armour rust   54
Until this day, to scour it in the dust.   55
   Sim. Opinion's but a fool, that makes us scan   56
The outward habit by the inward man.   57
But stay, the knights are coming: we will with-
   draw   58
Into the gallery.   *[Exeunt.*   59
   [Great shouts within, and all cry 'The mean
       knight!'

     SCENE III. *The same. A hall of state: a*
          banquet prepared.

Enter SIMONIDES, THAISA, Lords, Attendants,
     and Knights, *from tilting.*

   Sim. Knights,   1
To say you're welcome were superfluous.   2
To place upon the volume of your deeds,   3
As in a title-page, your worth in arms,   4
Were more than you expect, or more than's fit,   5
Since every worth in show commends itself.   6
Prepare for mirth, for mirth becomes a feast: 7
You are princes and my guests.   8
   Thai. But you, my knight and guest;   9
To whom this wreath of victory I give,   10   10

39 X: SP1, DS1
40 X: SP1, DS1
41 X: SP1, DS1, TR2

42 X: SP1, DS1
43 X: DS1
44 X: DS1, TR2; <u>R</u>: JG1; <u>bX</u>: SP1; <u>ADD</u> 1: TH1
45 X: DS1, TR2
46 X: DS1
47 X: DS1; <u>ADD</u> 3: JG1

48 X: DS1, JG1, EdB
49 same as 48
50 X: DS1, TR2, JG1, EdB

51 same as 50

52 X: DS1, JG1, EdB
53 same as 52

54 X: SP1, DS1, TR1, TR2, JG1, EdB
55 same as 54
56 X: DS1, JG1, EdB
57 same as 56; <u>ADD</u> 3: TR1

58 X: DS1, TR1, JG1, EdB; <u>aX</u>: SP1; <u>bX</u>: TH1, TR2, EdB
59 X: DS1, TR1, TH1, TR2, $\overline{\text{JG1}}$, EdB

Scene 23

1   X: SP2, EdB; <u>MOVE</u> 1-8 to follow
2   X: SP2
3   X: SP2
4   X: SP2
5   X: SP2
6   X: SP2
7   X: SP2
8   X: SP2
9   X: SP2
10 X: SP2

And crown you king of this day's happiness. 11
   Per. 'Tis more by fortune, lady, than by merit. 12
   Sim. Call it by what you will, the day is yours; 13
And here, I hope, is none that envies it. 14
In framing an artist, art hath thus decreed, 15
To make some good, but others to exceed: 16
And you are her labour'd scholar. Come, queen
    o' the feast,— 17
For, daughter, so you are,—here take your place: 18
Marshal the rest, as they deserve their grace. 19
   Knights. We are honour'd much by good
    Simonides. **20** 20
   Sim. Your presence glads our days: honour
   we love; 21
For who hates honour hates the gods above. 22
   Marshal. Sir, yonder is your place.
   Per.   Some other is more fit. 23
   First Knight. Contend not, sir; for we are
   gentlemen 24
That neither in our hearts nor outward eyes 25
Envy the great nor do the low despise. 26
   Per. You are right courteous knights.
   Sim.   Sit, sir, sit. 27
   Per. By Jove, I wonder, that is king of
   thoughts, 28
These cates resist me, she but thought upon. 29
   Thai. By Juno, that is queen of marriage, 30
All viands that I eat do seem unsavoury, 31
Wishing him my meat. Sure, he's a gallant gen-
   tleman. 32
   Sim. He's but a country gentleman; 33
Has done no more than other knights have done: 34
Has broken a staff or so; so let it pass. 35
   Thai. To me he seems like diamond to glass. 36
   Per. Yon king's to me like to my father's
   picture, 37
Which tells me in that glory once he was; 38
Had princes sit, like stars, about his throne, 39
And he the sun, for them to reverence; 40
None that beheld him, but, like lesser lights, 41
Did vail their crowns to his supremacy: 42
Where now his son's like a glow-worm in the
   night, 43
The which hath fire in darkness, none in light: 44
Whereby I see that Time's the king of men, 45
He's both their parent, and he is their grave, 46

```
11   X: SP2
12   X: SP2
13   X: SP2; ADD 4: DS1
14   X: SP2
15   X: SP1, SP2, DS1, TR1; MOVE 15-17a to follow 27: TH1
16   same as 15; less MOVE

17   X: SP2; aX: SP1, DS1, TH1; MOVE 17b-19 to follow 27: TH1
18   X: SP2
19   X: SP2, DS1

20   X: SP1, SP2; MOVE 2-22 to follow 27: TH1

21   X: SP1, SP2
22   X: SP1, SP2

23

24   bX: TR1
25   X: TR1
26   X: TR1

27   bX: TH1; Insert 1-17a, 1-9, 20-23, 17b-19: TH1

28   X: SP1, SP2, MTh; cX: TH1
29   same as 28; less cX; R: TH1
30   same as 28; less cX
31   same as 30

32   aX: SP1, SP2, MTh
33   X: SP2
34
35
36

37
38
39
40
41   X: SP2, TR2
42   X: SP2, TR2

43   X: EdB
44   X: EdB
45   X: SP1, SP2, MTh, EdB
46   same as 45
```

And gives them what he will, not what they crave. 47

 Sim. What, are you merry, knights? 48

 Knights. Who can be other in this royal presence?
              49

 Sim. Here, with a cup that's stored unto the brim,—   50   50

As you do love, fill to your mistress' lips,— 51

We drink this health to you.

 Knights.   We thank your grace. 52

 Sim. Yet pause awhile: 53

Yon knight doth sit too melancholy, 54

As if the entertainment in our court 55

Had not a show might countervail his worth. 56

Note it not you, Thaisa?

 Thai.   What is it 57

To me, my father?

 Sim.   O, attend, my daughter: 58

Princes in this should live like gods above, 59

Who freely give to every one that comes & 60

To honour them: 61

And princes not doing so are like to gnats, 62

Which make a sound, but kill'd are wonder'd at. 63

Therefore to make his entrance more sweet, 64

Here, say we drink this standing-bowl of wine to him. 65

 Thai. Alas, my father, it befits not me 66

Unto a stranger knight to be so bold: 67

He may my proffer take for an offence, 68

Since men take women's gifts for impudence. 69

 Sim. How!   70 70

Do as I bid you, or you'll move me else. 71

 Thai. [*Aside*] Now, by the gods, he could not please me better. 72

 Sim. And furthermore tell him, we desire to know of him, 73

Of whence he is, his name and parentage. 74

 Thai. The king my father, sir, has drunk to you. 75

 Per. I thank him. 76

 Thai. Wishing it so much blood unto your life. 77

 Per. I thank both him and you, and pledge him freely. 78

 Thai. And further he desires to know of you, 79

Of whence you are, your name and parentage. 80 80

 Per. A gentleman of Tyre; my name, Pericles: 81

My education been in arts and arms; 82

```
47   same as 45, TR1
48   X: SP1, SP2, MTh, TR1, TH1

49   same as 48

50   same as 48, less TH1
51   same as 50, JG1

52   same as 50; bX: TH1
53   same as 50, TH1
54   X: SP1
55
56

57

58
59
60
61
62   X: SP1, SP2, MTh, TR1
63   same as 62
64

65   ADD 1: JG1
66
67
68   X: TR1
69   X: TR1
70   ·
71

72

73
74
75
76
77

78
79
80

81
82
```

Who, looking for adventures in the world, 83
Was by the rough seas reft of ships and men, 84
And after shipwreck driven upon this shore. 85
 Thai. He thanks your grace; names himself
  Pericles, 86
A gentleman of Tyre, 87
Who only by misfortune of the seas 88
Bereft of ships and men, cast on this shore. 89
 Sim. Now, by the gods, I pity his misfortune, 90
And will awake him from his melancholy.   91 91
Come, gentlemen, we sit too long on trifles, 92
And waste the time, which looks for other revels. 93
Even in your armours, as you are address'd, 94
Will very well become a soldier's dance. 95
I will not have excuse, with saying this 96
Loud music is too harsh for ladies' heads, 97
Since they love men in arms as well as beds. 98
     [The Knights dance.
So, this was well ask'd, 'twas so well perform'd. 99
Come, sir;   100 100
Here is a lady that wants breathing too: 101
And I have heard, you knights of Tyre 102
Are excellent in making ladies trip; 103
And that their measures are as excellent. 104
 Per. In those that practise them they are, my
  lord.
                   105
 Sim. O, that's as much as you would be denied
Of your fair courtesy.   106
    [The Knights and Ladies dance.
    Unclasp, unclasp: 107
Thanks, gentlemen, to all; all have done well, 108
[To Per.] But you the best. Pages and lights, to
  conduct 109
These knights unto their several lodgings! *[To*
  Per.] Yours, sir,   110 110
We have given order to be next our own. 111
 Per. I am at your grace's pleasure. 112
 Sim. Princes, it is too late to talk of love; 113
And that's the mark I know you level at: 114
Therefore each one betake him to his rest; 115
To-morrow all for speeding do their best. 116
           [Exeunt.

SCENE IV.   *Tyre. A room in the Governor's
  house.*

```
83
84
85

86    X: SP2
87    X: SP2
88    X: SP2
89    X: SP2; R: JG1
90
91
92    bX: EdB
93    X: EdB
94    X: EdB; R: JG1
95    X: SP2, EdB; R: JG1
96    X: SP2, HIM, NM1, NM2, JG1
97    same as 96, TR1
98    X: SP1, SP2, HIM, MTh, NM1, NM2, JG1; aX: TR1

99    X: SP1, SP2, MTh, DS1, TR1, EdB
100   X: SP1, HIM, MTh
101   same as 100
102   same as 100
103   same as 100
104   same as 100

105   same as 100
106   same as 100; R: JG1


107   aX: SP1, HIM, MTh
108   Insert PRO 3: 1-7: TR1

109   bX: TR2

110   X: TR2
111   MOVE 111 to follow 116: TH1
112   X: TH1, TR2
113   X: TR2
114   X: TR2
115   X: TR2
116   X: TR2; ADD 1, insert  101, add 17 and song: TH1
```

Enter HELICANUS *and* ESCANES.

Hel. No, Escanes, know this of me,   1
Antiochus from incest lived not free: 2
For which, the most high gods not minding longer   3
To withhold the vengeance that they had in store,   4
Due to this heinous capital offence,   5
Even in the height and pride of all his glory,   6
When he was seated in a chariot   7
Of an inestimable value, and his daughter with him,   8
A fire from heaven came and shrivell'd up   9
Their bodies, even to loathing: for they so stunk,   10
That all those eyes adored them ere their fall 11   11
Scorn now their hand should give them burial.   12
 Esca. 'Twas very strange.
 Hel.   And yet but justice; for though   13
This king were great, his greatness was no guard   14
To bar heaven's shaft, but sin had his reward.   15
 Esca. 'Tis very true.   16

Enter two or three Lords.

 First Lord. See, not a man in private confer-
ence   17
Or council has respect with him but he.   18
  Sec. Lord. It shall no longer grieve without
reproof.   19
  Third Lord. And cursed be he that will not
second it.   20   20
  First Lord. Follow me, then. Lord Helicane,
a word.   21
  Hel. With me? and welcome: happy day, my
lords.   22
  First Lord. Know that our griefs are risen to
the top,   23
And now at length they overflow their banks.   24
  Hel. Your griefs! for what? wrong not your
prince you love.   25
  First Lord. Wrong not yourself, then, noble
Helicane;   26
But if the prince do live, let us salute him,   27
Or know what ground's made happy by his breath.   28
If in the world he live, we'll seek him out: 29
If in his grave he rest, we'll find him there; 30   30
And be resolved he lives to govern us,   31
Or dead, give's cause to mourn his funeral,   32
And leave us to our free election.   33
  Sec. Lord. Whose death indeed's the strongest

S cene 24

ALL CUT: SP2, NM1, NM2, DS1, TR1, TH1, TR2, EdB

```
 1   X: HIM, MTh, JG1
 2   same as 1
 3   same as 1
 4   same as 1
 5   same as 1
 6   same as 1
 7   same as 1
 8   same as 1
 9   same as 1
10   same as 1
11   same as 1
12   same as 1

13   X: HIM, MTh
14   X: HIM, MTh
15   X: HIM, MTh
16   X: HIM, MTh; ADD 6: JG1


17   X: HIM, MTh
18   X: HIM, MTh

19   X: HIM, MTh

20   X: HIM, MTh

21   X: HIM; aX: MTh

22   X: HIM

23   X: JG1
24   X: JG1

25   X: JG1

26   X: JG1
27
28
29
30   ADD 2: JG1
31   X: JG1
32   X: JG1
33   R: JG1
```

in our censure: 34
And knowing this kingdom is without a head,— 35
Like goodly buildings left without a roof 36
Soon fall to ruin,—your noble self, 37
That best know how to rule and how to reign, 38
We thus submit unto,—our sovereign. 39
   All. Live, noble Helicane!   40   40
   Hel. For honour's cause, forbear your suf-
frages: 41
If that you love Prince Pericles, forbear. 42
Take I your wish, I leap into the seas, 43
Where's hourly trouble for a minute's ease. 44
A twelvemonth longer, let me entreat you to 45
Forbear the absence of your king: 46
If in which time expired, he not return, 47
I shall with aged patience bear your yoke. 48
But if I cannot win you to this love, 49
Go search like nobles, like noble subjects,   50   50
And in your search spend your adventurous worth; 51
Whom if you find, and win unto return, 52
You shall like diamonds sit about his crown. 53
   First Lord. To wisdom he's a fool that will
not yield: 5 4
And since Lord Helicane enjoineth us, 55
We with our travels will endeavour us. 56
   Hel. Then you love us, we you, and we'll clasp
hands: 57
When peers thus knit, a kingdom ever stands. 58
                           [*Exeunt.*

SCENE V. *Pentapolis. A room in the palace.*

Enter SIMONIDES, *reading a letter, at one door:
the* Knights *meet him.*

   First Knight. Good morrow to the good Si-
monides. 1
   Sim. Knights, from my daughter this I let
you know, 2
That for this twelvemonth she'll not undertake 3
A married life. 4
Her reason to herself is only known, 5
Which yet from her by no means can I get. 6
   Sec. Knight. May we not get access to her,
my lord? 7
   Sim. 'Faith, by no means; she hath so strictly
tied 8

34   X: JG1
35   R: JG1
36   $\overline{X}$: JG1
37   $\underline{aX}$: JG1
38   $\overline{\underline{bX}}$: JG1
39
40

41
42
43
44
45
46
47
48
49
50
51
52
53

54
55
56

57
58   ADD 4: SP1

Scene 25

1   X: SP1, MTh, DS1, TR1, TH1, TR2

2   X: SP1, MTh, DS1, TR1
3   same as 2
4   same as 2
5   same as 2
6   same as 2

7   same as 2

8   same as 2; bX: TH1

Her to her chamber, that 'tis impossible.   9
One twelve moons more she'll wear Diana's
   livery;   10   10
This by the eye of Cynthia hath she vow'd,   11
And on her virgin honour will not break it.   12
   Third Knight. Loath to bid farewell, we take
   our leaves.   [*Exeunt Knights.*   13
   Sim. So,   14
They are well dispatch'd; now to my daughter's
   letter: 15
She tells me here, she'll wed the stranger knight, 16
Or never more to view nor day nor light.   17
'Tis well, mistress; your choice agrees with mine: 18
I like that well: nay, how absolute she's in't,   19
Not minding whether I dislike or no!   20   20
Well, I do commend her choice;   21
And will no longer have it be delay'd.   22
Soft! here he comes: I must dissemble it.   23

Enter PERICLES.

   Per. All fortune to the good Simonides!   24
   Sim. To you as much, sir! I am beholding
   to you   25
For your sweet music this last night: I do   26
Protest my ears were never better fed   27
With such delightful pleasing harmony.   28
   Per. It is your grace's pleasure to commend;   29
Not my desert.
   Sim.   Sir, you are music's master.   30   30
   Per. The worst of all her scholars, my good
   lord.   31
   Sim. Let me ask you one thing: 32
What do you think of my daughter, sir?   33
   Per. A most virtuous princess.   34
   Sim. And she is fair too, is she not?   35
   Per. As a fair day in summer, wondrous fair.   36
   Sim. Sir, my daughter thinks very well of you; 37
Ay, so well, that you must be her master,   38
And she will be your scholar: therefore look to it. 39
   Per. I am unworthy for her schoolmaster. 40   40
   Sim. She thinks not so; peruse this writing
   else.   41
   Per. [*Aside*] What's here?   42
A letter, that she loves the knight of Tyre!   43
'Tis the king's subtilty to have my life.   44

9   same as 2, TH1; less b<u>X</u>

10 same as 2
11 same as 2
12 same as 2

13 X: SP1, DS1, TR1
14 same as 14

15 X: TR2; <u>aX</u>: SP1, SP1, DS1, TR1
16 X: TR2
17 X: TR1, TR2
18 X: TR2
19 X: TR2; <u>aX</u>: TR1
20 X: TR2
21 X: TR1, TR2
22 X: TR1, TR2
23 X: TR2

24 X: TR2

25 <u>aX</u>: TR2
26
27
28
29

30

31
32
33
34
35
36
37
38 X: TR1
39 X: TR1
40 X: TR1

41 <u>aX</u>: TR1
42
43
44 <u>bX</u>: TR1

O, seek not to entrap me, gracious lord, 45
A stranger and distressed gentleman, 46
That never aim'd so high to love your daughter, 47
But bent all offices to honour her. 48
   Sim. Thou hast bewitch'd my daughter, and
     thou art 49
A villain. **50** 50
   Per. By the gods, I have not: 51
Never did thought of mine levy offence; 52
Nor never did my actions yet commence 53
A deed might gain her love or your displeasure. 54
   Sim. Traitor, thou liest.
   Per.   Traitor!
   Sim.   Ay, traitor. 55
   Per. Even in his throat—unless it be the king— 56
That calls me traitor, I return the lie. 57
   Sim. [*Aside*] Now, by the gods, I do applaud
     his courage. 58
   Per. My actions are as noble as my thoughts, 59
That never relish'd of a base descent. **60** 60
I came unto your court for honour's cause, 61
And not to be a rebel to her state; 62
And he that otherwise accounts of me, 63
This sword shall prove he's honour's enemy. 64
   Sim. No? 65
Here comes my daughter, she can witness it. 66

     Enter THAISA.

   Per. Then, as you are as virtuous as fair, 67
Resolve your angry father, if my tongue 68
Did e'er solicit, or my hand subscribe 69
To any syllable that made love to you. 70
   Thai. Why, sir, say if you had, 71
Who takes offence at that would make me glad? 72
   Sim. Yea, mistress, are you so peremptory? 73
[*Aside*] I am glad on't with all my heart.— 74
I'll tame you; I'll bring you in subjection. 75
Will you, not having my consent, 76
Bestow your love and your affections 77
Upon a stranger? [*Aside*] who, for aught I know, 78
May be, nor can I think the contrary, 79
As great in blood as I myself.— 80
Therefore hear you, mistress; either frame 81
Your will to mine,—and you, sir, hear you, 82
Either be ruled by me, or I will make you— 83
Man and wife: 84

```
45
46   X: TR1
47
48

49
50
51
52   X: TR1
53   X: TR1
54   X: TR1

55
56   bX: TR1
57

58   X: TR1; aX: TH1
59   X: TR1
60   X: TR1
61
62   X: TR1
63   X: TR1, TR2
64   X: TR1, TR2
65   X: TR1
66   X: TR1

67
68   bX: TR1
69   aX: TR1
70
71
72
73
74
75
76
77
78   R: SP1; bX: NM2
79   X̄: SP1, N̄M2; aX: TR1; bX: TH1
80   X: NM2
81   aX: NM2
82
83
84
```

Nay, come, your hands and lips must seal it too: 85
And being join'd, I 'll thus your hopes destroy;   86
And for a further grief,—God give you joy!—   87
What, are you both pleased?
  Thai.   Yes, if you love me, sir.   88
  Per.   Even as my life my blood that fosters it.   89
  Sim.   What, are you both agreed?   90
  Both.   Yes, if it please your majesty.   91
  Sim.   It pleaseth me so well, that I will see
    you wed: 92
And then with what haste you can get you to
    bed.   *[Exeunt.*   93

ACT III.

Enter GOWER.

Gow.   Now sleep yslaked hath the rout: 1
No din but snores the house about,   2
Made louder by the o'er-fed breast   3
Of this most pompous marriage-feast.   4
The cat, with eyne of burning coal,   5
Now couches fore the mouse's hole: 6
And crickets sing at the oven's mouth,   7
E'er the blither for their drouth.   8
Hymen hath brought the bride to bed,   9
Where, by the loss of maidenhead,   12   10
A babe is moulded.   Be attent,   11
And time that is so briefly spent   12
With your fine fancies quaintly eche: 13
What's dumb in show I 'll plain with speech.   14

DUMB SHOW.

Enter, PERICLES *and* SIMONIDES, *at one door,
with* Attendants: *a* Messenger *meets them,
kneels, and gives* PERICLES *a letter:* PERICLES
shows it SIMONIDES; *the* Lords *kneel to him.
Then enter* THAISA *with child, with* LYCHO-
RIDA *a nurse. The* KING *shows her the letter:
she rejoices: she and* PERICLES *take leave of
her father, and depart with* LYCHORIDA *and
their* Attendants. *Then exeunt* SIMONIDES
and the rest.

By many a dern and painful perch   15
Of Pericles the careful search,   16

```
85
86   X: TR1, JG1
87   aX: TR1, JG1

88
89
90   X: HIM
91   X: HIM

92   X: HIM; ADD 42: NM2; ADD 54: SP1

93   X: SP1, HIN, NM1, NM2
```

3 PROLOG

```
ALL CUT: SP1, SP2, MTh
  1   X: HIM; MOVE 1-8 to follow 23: 116: TR1
  2   X: HIM
  3   X: HIM
  4   X: HIM
  5   X: HIM
  6   X: HIM
  7   X: HIM, EdB
  8   X: HIM, EdB
  9   X: HIM
 10   X: HIM, NM1, NM2
 11   same as 10; bX: DS1; ADD 1: DS1; ADD 4: TH1
 12   X: HIM, NM1, NM2, DS1
 13   same as 12
 14   same as 12; ADD 1: TR1




 15   X: NM1, NM2, DS1, TR1
 16   same as 15
```

By the four opposing coigns   17
Which the world together joins,   18
Is made with all due diligence   19
That horse and sail and high expense   20 20
Can stead the quest.   At last from Tyre,   21
Fame answering the most strange inquire,   22
To the court of King Simonides   23
Are letters brought, the tenour these: 24
Antiochus and his daughter dead;   25
The men of Tyrus on the head   26
Of Helicanus would set on   27
The crown of Tyre, but he will none: 28
The mutiny he there hastes t' oppress;   29
Says to 'em, if King Pericles   30 30
Come not home in twice six moons,   31
He, obedient to their dooms,   32
Will take the crown.   The sum of this,   33
Brought hither to Pentapolis,   34
Y-ravished the regions round,   35
And every one with claps can sound,   36
'Our heir-apparent is a king!   37
Who dream'd, who thought of such a thing?'   38
Brief, he must hence depart to Tyre: 39
His queen with child makes her desire—   40 40
Which who shall cross?—along to go: 41
Omit we all their dole and woe: 42
Lychorida, her nurse, she takes,   43
And so to sea.   Their vessel shakes   44
On Neptune's billow; half the flood   45
Hath their keel cut: but fortune's mood   46
Varies again; the grisled north   47
Disgorges such a tempest forth,   48
That, as a duck for life that dives,   49
So up and down the poor ship drives: 50 50
The lady shrieks, and well-a-near   51
Does fall in travail with her fear: 52
And what ensues in this fell storm   53
Shall for itself itself perform.   54
I nill relate, action may   55
Conveniently the rest convey: 56
Which might not what by me is told.   57
In your imagination hold   58
This stage the ship, upon whose deck   59 59
The sea-tost Pericles appears to speak. [*Exit.*   60

```
17   same as 15, TH1
18   same as 17
19   same as 15
20   same as 15
21   X: NM1, NM2, DS1; aX: TR1
22   X: NM1, NM2, TR1, EdB
23   X: EdB
24
25   X: NM1, NM2; ADD 6: TH1
26   X: TH1
27   X: TH1
28   X: TH1
29   X: TR1, TH1
30   X: TH1
31   X: TH1
32   X: TH1
33   aX: TH1; bX: NM1, NM2, DS1
34   X: NM1, NM2, DS1
35   same as 34
36   same as 34
37   same as 34
38   same as 34
39   aX: DS1
40
41
42   X: TR2
43
44
45
46
47
48
49   X: NM1, NM2
50   X: NM1, NM2
51
52
53
54
55   X: DS1
56   X: DS1
57   X: DS1
58   X: DS1
59   X: NM1, NM2
60   X: NM1, NM2
```

SCENE I.

Enter PERICLES, *on shipboard.*

Per. Thou god of this great vast, rebuke
these surges,   1
Which wash both heaven and hell; and thou,
that hast   2
Upon the winds command, bind them in brass,   3
Having call'd them from the deep! O, still   4
Thy deafening, dreadful thunders; gently quench   5
Thy nimble, sulphurous flashes! O, how, Ly-
chorida,   6
How does my queen? Thou stormest venom-
ously: 7
Wilt thou spit all thyself? The seaman's whistle   8
Is as a whisper in the ears of death,   9
Unheard. Lychorida!—Lucina, O   10   10
Divinest patroness, and midwife gentle   11
To those that cry by night, convey thy deity   12
Aboard our dancing boat; make swift the pangs   13
Of my queen's travails!

Enter LYCHORIDA, *with an Infant.*

Now, Lychorida!   14

Lyc. Here is a thing too young for such
a place,   15
Who, if it had conceit, would die, as I   16
Am like to do: take in your arms this piece   17
Of your dead queen.
Per.   How, how, Lychorida!   18
Lyc. Patience, good sir; do not assist the
storm.   19
Here's all that is left living of your queen,   20   20
A little daughter: for the sake of it,   21
Be manly, and take comfort.
Per.   O you gods!   22
Why do you make us love your goodly gifts,   23
And snatch them straight away? We here below 24
Recall not what we give, and therein may   25
Use honour with you.
Lyc.   Patience, good sir,   26
Even for this charge.
Per.   Now, mild may be thy life! 27
For a more blustrous birth had never babe: 28
Quiet and gentle thy conditions! for   29
Thou art the rudeliest welcome to this world 30 30

Scene 31

1

2
3
4
5

6

7
8
9
10   cX: JG1
11
12
13

14

15
16
17

18

19   MOVE 19b to follow 26: TH1
20
21

22
23
24   bX: SP1, MTh, TR1, TH1
25   X: SP1, MTh, TR1, TH1

26   aX: SP1, MTh, TR1, TH1; Insert 19b: TH1

27
28
29
30

That ever was prince's child.   Happy what
    follows!   31
Thou hast as chiding a nativity   32
As fire, air, water, earth, and heaven can make,   33
To herald thee from the womb: even at the first   34
Thy loss is more than can thy portage quit,   35
With all thou canst find here.   Now, the good
    gods   36
Throw their best eyes upon't!   37

Enter two Sailors.

  First Sail. What courage, sir? God save you!   38
  Per. Courage enough: I do not fear the flaw;   39
It hath done to me the worst. Yet, for the love 40   40
Of this poor infant, this fresh-new sea-farer,   41
I would it would be quiet.   42
  First Sail. Slack the bolins there! Thou wilt   43
not, wilt thou? Blow, and split thyself.   44
  Sec. Sail. But sea-room, an the brine and   45
cloudy billow kiss the moon, I care not.   46
  First Sail. Sir, your queen must overboard: 47
the sea works high, the wind is loud, and will not   48
lie till the ship be cleared of the dead.   49
  Per. That's your superstition.   50   50
  First Sail. Pardon us, sir: with us at sea it   51
hath been still observed: and we are strong in   52
custom. Therefore briefly yield her; for she   53
must overboard straight.   54
  Per. As you think meet. Most wretched
    queen!   55
  Lyc. Here she lies, sir.   56
  Per. A terrible childbed hast thou had, my
    dear;   57
No light, no fire: the unfriendly elements   58
Forgot thee utterly: nor have I time   59
To give thee hallow'd to thy grave, but straight 60   60
Must cast thee, scarcely coffin'd, in the ooze;   61
Where, for a monument upon thy bones,   62
And e'er-remaining lamps, the belching whale   63
And humming water must o'erwhelm thy corpse,   64
Lying with simple shells.   O Lychorida,   65
Bid Nestor bring me spices, ink and paper,   66
My casket and my jewels: and bid Nicander   67
Bring me the satin coffer: lay the babe   68
Upon the pillow: hie thee, whiles I say   69
A priestly farewell to her: suddenly, woman. 70   70
                    [*Exit Lychorida.*

31 bX: SP1, MTh, TR1
32 X̄: SP1, MTh, TR1
33 same as 32
34 same as 32
35 same as 32

36 same as 32
37 same as 32

38 ADD 1: TR1
39
40
41
42 ADD 1: TR1
43 b̄X̄: TR1
44 X̄: TR1
45 X: TR1
46 X: TR1; Insert 65b-70: TH1
47 MOVE 47a to follow 53: JG1
48
49
50 ADD 1: TR1
51
52
53 bX: TH1; Insert 47a: JG1
54 X̄: TH1; bX̄: JG1

55 X: TR1; aX: JG1; Insert 71-82: TH1
56 X: SP1, N̄M1, NM2, D̄S1, TR1, TH1

57 MOVE 57-65a to follow 85: TR1
58
59
60
61
62 bX: MTh
63 āX̄: MTh
64
65 bX: NM1, NM2; MOVE 65b-70 to follow 46: TH1; MOVE 65b-70a to follow*
66
67
68 aX: TR2; bX: NM1, NM2
69 āX̄: NM1, N̄M2
70 b̄X̄: NM1, TR1

*31:65 84: TR1

Sec. Sail. Sir, we have a chest beneath the 71
hatches, caulked and bitumed ready. 72
Per. I thank thee. Mariner, say what coast
is this?
73
Sec. Sail. We are near Tarsus. 74
Per. Thither, gentle mariner. 75
Alter thy course for Tyre. When canst thou
reach it?
76
Sec. Sail. By break of day, if the wind cease. 77
Per. O, make for Tarsus! 78
There will I visit Cleon, for the babe 79
Cannot hold out to Tyrus: there I 'll leave it 80 80 q
At careful nursing. Go thy ways, good mariner: 81
I 'll bring the body presently. [*Exeunt.* 82

SCENE II. *Ephesus. A room in Cerimon's
house.*

Enter CERIMON, *with a Servant, and some
Persons who have been shipwrecked.*

Cer. Philemon, ho! 1

Enter PHILEMON.

Phil. Doth my lord call? 2
Cer. Get fire and meat for these poor men: 3
'T has been a turbulent and stormy night. 4
Serv. I have been in many; but such a night
as this,
5
Till now, I ne'er endured. 6
Cer. Your master will be dead ere you return; 7
There's nothing can be minister'd to nature 8
That can recover him. [*To Philemon*] Give this
to the 'pothecary,
9
And tell me how it works.
[*Exeunt all but Cerimon.*

Enter two Gentlemen.

First Gent. Good morrow. 10 10
Sec. Gent. Good morrow to your lordship. 11
Cer. Gentlemen,
Why do you stir so early?
12
First Gent. Sir, 13
Our lodgings, standing bleak upon the sea, 14
Shook as the earth did quake; 15
The very principals did seem to rend, 16

71 <u>MOVE</u> 71-82 to follow 55: TH1
72

73
74
75

76
77
78
79
80
81 bX: TH
82 X: TR1 ; <u>Insert</u> 65b-70a, 57-65a: TR1

<u>Scene 32</u>

1   X: SP1, JG1; <u>bX</u>: TR1

2   X: SP1, TH1, JG1; <u>abX</u>: TH1
3   X: SP1, JG1
4   X: JG1

5   X: JG1
6   X: JG1
7   X: SP1, MTh, NM1, NM2, TR1, TR2, JG1, EdB
8   same as 7, less EdB

9   X: SP1, NM1, NM2, TR1, JG1; <u>aX</u>: MTh, TR2, JG1

10 X: SP1, NM1; <u>aX</u>: NM2, TR1

11 X: NM1; <u>bX</u>: SP1
12 X: NM1
13
14
15
16

And all-to topple: pure surprise and fear 17
Made me to quit the house. 18
   Sec. Gent.   That is the cause we trouble you
     so early; 19
'Tis not our husbandry.
   Cer.   O, you say well.   **20** 20
   First Gent.   But I much marvel that your
     lordship, having 21
Rich tire about you, should at these early hours 22
Shake off the golden slumber of repose. 23
'Tis most strange, 24
Nature should be so conversant with pain, 25
Being thereto not compell'd.
   Cer.   I hold it ever, 26
Virtue and cunning were endowments greater 27
Than nobleness and riches: careless heirs 28
May the two latter darken and expend; 29
But immortality attends the former,   **30** 30
Making a man a god. 'Tis known, I ever 31
Have studied physic, through which secret art, 32
By turning o'er authorities, I have, 33
Together with my practice, made familiar 34
To me and to my aid the blest infusions 35
That dwell in vegetives, in metals, stones; 36
And I can speak of the disturbances 37
That nature works, and of her cures; which doth
     give me 38
A more content in course of true delight 39
Than to be thirsty after tottering honour,   *f* 40
Or tie my treasure up in silken bags, 41
To please the fool and death. 42
   Sec. Gent.   Your honour has through Ephesus
     pour'd forth 43
Your charity, and hundreds call themselves 44
Your creatures, who by you have been restored: 45
And not your knowledge, your personal pain,
     but even 46
Your purse, still open, hath built Lord Cerimon 47
Such strong renown as time shall ne'er decay. 48

   Enter two or three Servants *with a chest.*

   First Serv.   So; lift there.
   Cer.   What is that?
   First Serv.   Sir, even now 49
Did the sea toss upon our shore this chest: 5 50

17
18

19

20 R: SP1

21
22
23
24 X: TH1
25 X: TH1; R: JG1

26 aX: TH1
27
28
29 aX: SP1
30
31 bX: SP1, NM1, NM2, TH1; ADD 3: SP1
32 X: NM1, NM2, TH1; bX: SP1
33 X: SP1, NM1, NM2, TH1; aX: JG1
34 X: NM1, NM2, TH1; aX: JG1
35 same as 34, including aX
36 same as 34; less aX; bX: SP1; ADD 1: SP1
37 X: SP1, TH1

38 X: SP1, TH1
39 X: SP1, TH1
40 X: SP1, TH1
41 X: SP1, TH1, TR2
42 same as 41

43 X: SP1
44
45

46 X: TH1, TR2
47 X: TH1, TR2
48 X: TH1, TR2

49
50

'Tis of some wreck.

Cer.   Set 't down, let's look upon't   §1

Sec. Gent. 'Tis like a coffin, sir.

Cer.   Whate'er it be,   §2

'Tis wondrous heavy. Wrench it open straight: §3

If the sea's stomach be o'ercharged with gold,   §4

†'Tis a good constraint of fortune it belches upon us   §5

Sec. Gent. 'Tis so, my lord.   §6

Cer.   How close 'tis caulk'd and bitumed!   §7

Did the sea cast it up?

First Serv. I never saw so huge a billow, sir,   §8

As toss'd it upon shore.

Cer.   Wrench it open;   59

Soft! it smells most sweetly in my sense.   6c   60

Sec. Gent. A delicate odour.   61

Cer. As ever hit my nostril. So, up with it   62

O you most potent gods! what's here? a corse!   63

First Gent. Most strange!   64

Cer. Shrouded in cloth of state; balm'd and

entreasured   65

With full bags of spices! A passport too!   66

Apollo, perfect me in the characters!   67

         [*Reads from a scroll*

' Here I give to understand,   68

If e'er this coffin drive a-land,   69

I, King Pericles, have lost   ?   70 ¶

This queen, worth all our mundane cost.   71

Who finds her, give her burying;   72

She was the daughter of a king: 73

Besides this treasure for a fee,   74

The gods requite his charity!'   75

If thou livest, Pericles, thou hast a heart   76

That even cracks for woe! This chanced to

night.   77

Sec. Gent. Most likely, sir.

Cer.   Nay, certainly to-night;   78

For look how fresh she looks! They were too

rough   79   79

That threw her in the sea. Make a fire within: 80

Fetch hither all my boxes in my closet.   81

         [*Exit a Servant*

Death may usurp on nature many hours,   82

And yet the fire of life kindle again   83

The o'erpress'd spirits. †I heard of an Egyptian   84

That had nine hours lien dead,   85

Who was by good appliance recovered.   86

§1   cX: NM1, TH1

§2   aX: NM2; bX: MTh
§3   X̄: MTh; aX̄: NM2; bX: TH1
§4   X: MTh
§5   X: MTh
§6   X: MTh
§7   X: MTh, JG1

§8   X: MTh, JG1; bX: SP1

59   X: SP1, JG1; aX: MTh, NM2
60   aX: SP1; bX: N̄M̄1
61   X̄: NM1, NM2
62   X: NM1, NM2
63   X: NM1; aX: NM2
64

65
66   R: TH1, JG1; ADD 3: SP1
67   X̄: SP1

68   X: SP1
69   X: SP1
70   X: SP1
71   ADD 1: TR2
72
73
74
75
76

77

78

79
80
81

82
83
84   bX: JG1; ADD 2: JG1
85   X̄: JG1
86   X: JG1

Re-enter a Servant, *with boxes, napkins,
and fire.*

Well said, well said ; the fire and cloths.   87
The rough and woeful music that we have,   88
Cause it to sound, beseech you.   89
The viol once more: how thou stirr'st, thou
   block !   90   90
The music there !—I pray you, give her air.   91
Gentlemen,   93
This queen will live: nature awakes; a warmth   93
Breathes out of her: she hath not been entranced   94
Above five hours: see how she gins to blow   95
Into life's flower again !
   First Gent.   The heavens,   96
Through you, increase our wonder and set up   97
Your fame for ever.
   Cer.   She is alive; behold,   98
Her eyelids, cases to those heavenly jewels   99
Which Pericles hath lost,   100   100
Begin to part their fringes of bright gold: 101
The diamonds of a most praised water   102
Do appear, to make the world twice rich.   Live,   103
And make us weep to hear your fate, fair creature,   104
Rare as you seem to be.   [*She moves.*
   Thai.   O dear Diana,   105
Where am I? Where's my lord? What world
   is this?   106
   Sec. Gent. Is not this strange?
   First Gent.   Most rare.
   Cer.   Hush, my gentle neighbours!   107
Lend me your hands; to the next chamber bear
   her.   108
Get linen: now this matter must be look'd to,   109
For her relapse is mortal. Come, come;   110   110
And Æsculapius guide us !   111
     [*Exeunt, carrying her away.*

SCENE III. *Tarsus. A room in Cleon's house.*

Enter PERICLES, CLEON, DIONYZA, *and* LYCHO-
   RIDA *with* MARINA *in her arms.*

   Per. Most honour'd Cleon, I must needs be
   gone;   ;
My twelve months are expired, and Tyrus stands   2
In a litigious peace. You, and your lady,   3

```
87   R:  TR1
88
89   aX: TR1

90   X: TR1, JG1;  bX: TH1
91   aX: TR1, TH1, JG1
92
93   bX: TH1
94   X: TH1
95   X: TH1

96   X: TH1
97   X: TH1

98   aX: TH1, JG1
99
100
101
102
103
104

105  bX: DS1

106  X: DS1; Insert 34: 1-18: SP1; Insert 34: 1-11: TH1

107  bX: TR2, EdB; Insert 34: 5-11: TR2

108  aX: TR1; bX: NM1, JG1
109
110  bX: DS1
111  X: DS1, EdB; Insert 34: 1-18: MTh, DS1
```

Scene 33

```
ALL CUT: SP2
  1
  2  X: NM1, NM2, TH1
  3  X: TH1; aX: NM1, NM2
```

Take from my heart all thankfulness! The gods   4
Make up the rest upon you!   5
   Cle. Your shafts of fortune, though they hurt
    you mortally,   6
Yet glance full wanderingly on us.
   Dion.   O your sweet queen!   7
That the strict fates had pleased you had brought
    her hither,   8
To have bless'd mine eyes with her!
   Per.   We cannot but obey   9
The powers above us. Could I rage and roar 10   10
As doth the sea she lies in, yet the end   11
Must be as 'tis. My gentle babe Marina, whom,   12
For she was born at sea, I have named so, here   13
I charge your charity withal, leaving her   14
The infant of your care: beseeching you   15
To give her princely training, that she may be   16
Manner'd as she is born.
   Cle.   Fear not, my lord, but think   17
Your grace, that fed my country with your corn,   18
For which the people's prayers still fall upon you,   19
Must in your child be thought on. If neglection   20
Should therein make me vile. the common body,   21
By you relieved, would force me to my duty: 22
But if to that my nature need a spur,   23
The gods revenge it upon me and mine,   24
To the end of generation!
   Per.   I believe you: 25
Your honour and your goodness teach me to't,   26
Without your vows. Till she be married, madam,   27
By bright Diana, whom we honour, all   28
Unscissar'd shall this hair of mine remain,   29
Though I show ill in't. So I take my leave. **30** 30
Good madam, make me blessed in your care   31
In bringing up my child.
   Dion.   I have one myself,   32
Who shall not be more dear to my respect   33
Than yours, my lord.
   Per.   Madam, my thanks and prayers.   34
   Cle. We'll bring your grace e'en to the edge
    o' the shore,   35
Then give you up to the mask'd Neptune and   36
The gentlest winds of heaven.
   Per.   I will embrace   37
Your offer. Come, dearest madam. O, no tears,   38
Lychorida, no tears: 39

```
 4
 5

 6   X: TR1

 7   aX: TR1

 8

 9
10
11
12
13
14
15   bX: TR2
16   X: TR2

17   X: TR2; bX: NM1, NM2
18   X: NM1, NM2, TR2, JG1
19   same as 18
20   X: JG1; aX: NM1, NM2, TR2
21   X: JG1; bX: NM1, NM2
22   X: NM1, NM2, JG1
23   X: NM1, NM2
24

25
26
27   aX: TR1; bX: SP1, MTh, NM1, NM2, JG1
28   X: SP1, MTh, NM1, NM2, JG1
29   same as 28
30   X: JG1; aX: SP1, MTh, NM1, NM2
31   X: JG1

32   aX: JG1
33

34

35
36

37
38   cX: TR1
39
```

Look to your little mistress, on whose grace **40**   40
You may depend hereafter. Come, my lord.   41

[Exeunt.

SCENE IV. *Ephesus. A room in Cerimon's house.*

Enter CERIMON *and* THAISA.

Cer. Madam, this letter, and some certain
    jewels,   1
Lay with you in your coffer: which are now   2
At your command. Know you the character?   3
  Thai. It is my lord's.   4
That I was shipp'd at sea, I well remember,   5
Even on my eaning time: but whether there   6
Deliver'd, by the holy gods,   7
I cannot rightly say. But since King Pericles,   8
My wedded lord, I ne'er shall see again,   9
A vestal livery will I take me to,   **10**   10
And never more have joy.   11
  Cer. Madam, if this you purpose as ye speak,   12
Diana's temple is not distant far,   13
Where you may abide till your date expire.   14
Moreover, if you please, a niece of mine   15
Shall there attend you.   16
  Thai. My recompense is thanks, that's all: 17
Yet my good will is great, though the gift small.   18

[Exeunt.

ACT IV.

Enter GOWER.

  Gow. Imagine Pericles arrived at Tyre,   1
Welcomed and settled to his own desire.   2
His woeful queen we leave at Ephesus,   3
Unto Diana there a votaress.   4
Now to Marina bend your mind,   5
Whom our fast-growing scene must find   6
At Tarsus, and by Cleon train'd   7
In music, letters; who hath gain'd   8
Of education all the grace,   9
Which makes her both the heart and place **10**   10
Of general wonder. But, alack,   11
That monster envy, oft the wrack   12
Of earned praise, Marina's life   13
Seeks to take off by treason's knife.   14

40 b<u>X</u>: TR1
41 <u>R</u>: TH1; a<u>X</u>: TR1; b<u>X</u>: NM2; <u>ADD</u> 1: MTh; <u>ADD</u> 2: TR2; <u>ADD</u> 4: TR1; <u>ADD</u> 7:
   JG1; <u>ADD</u> 16: SP1

Scene 34

<u>ALL CUT</u>: SP2, TR1
 1 X: TR2; <u>MOVE</u> 1-11 to follow <u>33</u>: 106: TH1; <u>M OVE</u> 1-18 to follow <u>33</u>:
 2 X: TR2
 3 X: TR2
 4 X: TR2
 5 <u>MOVE</u> 5-11 to follow <u>32</u>: 107: TR2
 6
 7
 8
 9
10
11
12 X: TH1, TR2
13 X: TH1, TR2
14 X: TH1, TR2
15 X: TH1, TR2
16 X: TH1, TR2; <u>ADD</u> 1: DS1
17 X: TH1, TR2
18 X: TH1, TR2; <u>Insert</u> <u>44</u>: 1-9a: TR2

4 PROLOG

<u>ALL CUT</u>: SP1, SP2, MTh
 1
 2
 3
 4
 5
 6
 7
 8
 9
10
11
12 b<u>X</u>: TR1
13 a<u>X</u>: TR1
14

And in this kind hath our Cleon   15
One daughter, and a wench full grown,   16
Even ripe for marriage-rite; this maid   17
Hight Philoten: and it is said   18
For certain in our story, she   19
Would ever with Marina be: 20   20
Be't when she weaved the sleided silk   21
With fingers long, small, white as milk: 22
Or when she would with sharp needle wound   23
The cambric, which she made more sound   24
By hurting it; or when to the lute   25
She sung, and made the night-bird mute,   26
That still records with moan; or when   27
She would with rich and constant pen   28
Vail to her mistress Dian; still   29
This Philoten contends in skill   30   30
With absolute Marina: so   31
With the dove of Paphos might the crow   32
Vie feathers white. Marina gets   33
All praises, which are paid as debts,   34
And not as given. This so darks   35
In Philoten all graceful marks,   36
That Cleon's wife, with envy rare,   37
A present murderer does prepare   38
For good Marina, that her daughter   39
Might stand peerless by this slaughter.   40   40
The sooner her vile thoughts to stead,   40
Lychorida, our nurse, is dead: 42
And cursed Dionyza hath   43
The pregnant instrument of wrath   44
Prest for this blow. The unborn event   45
I do commend to your content: 46
Only I carry winged time   47
Post on the lame feet of my rhyme;   48
Which never could I so convey,   49
Unless your thoughts went on my way.   50   50
Dionyza does appear,   51
With Leonine, a murderer.   [*Exit.*   52

SCENE I. *Tarsus. An open place near the
sea-shore.*

Enter DIONYZA *and* LEONINE.

Dion. Thy oath remember; thou hast sworn
    to do't: 1
'Tis but a blow, which never shall be known.   2

```
15
16
17  X: HIM, EdB
18  X: HIM, EdB
19  X: EdB
20  X: EdB
21  X: EdB
22  X: EdB
23  X: TH1, EdB
24  X: TH1, EdB
52  X: EdB; aX: TH1
26  X: EdB
27  X: EdB; bX: TH1
28  X: TH1, EdB
29  X: EdB; aX: TH1
30  X: EdB
31  X: EdB
32  X: EdB
33  X: EdB
34  X: EdB
35  X: EdB
36  X: EdB
37
38
39
40
40  X: TR1
42  X: TR1
43  X: TR1
44  X: TR1
45  X: TR1
46  X: TR1
47  X: TR1, TR2, EdB
48  same as 47
49  same as 47
50  same as 47
51  X: NM1
52  X: NM1; ADD 29: TH1
```

Scene 41

```
1  X: SP1, TH1
2  X: TH1
```

Thou canst not do a thing in the world so soon,   3
To yield thee so much profit. Let not conscience,   4
Which is but cold, inflaming love i' thy bosom,   5
Inflame too nicely; nor let pity, which   6
Even women have cast off, melt thee, but be   7
A soldier to thy purpose.   8
   Leon. I will do't; but yet she is a goodly
      creature.   **9**   9
   Dion. The fitter, then, the gods should have   10
her. †Here she comes weeping for her only mis-   11
tress' death. Thou art resolved?   12
   Leon. I am resolved.   13

   Enter MARINA, *with a basket of flowers.*

   Mar. No, I will rob Tellus of her weed,   14
To strew thy green with flowers: the yellows,
      blues,   15
The purple violets, and marigolds,   16
Shall as a carpet hang upon thy grave,   17
While summer-days do last. Ay me! poor maid,   18
Born in a tempest, when my mother died,   19
This world to me is like a lasting storm,   **20**   20
Whirring me from my friends.   21
   Dion. How now, Marina! why do you ke-
      alone?   22
How chance my daughter is not with you? Do-   23
Consume your blood with sorrowing: you have   24
A nurse of me. Lord, how your favour's chang-   25
With this unprofitable woe!   26
Come, give me your flowers, ere the sea mar it   27
Walk with Leonine; the air is quick there,   28
And it pierces and sharpens the stomach. Com   29
Leonine, take her by the arm, walk with her.   30
   Mar. No, I pray you;   31
I'll not bereave you of your servant.
   Dion.   Come, come   32
I love the king your father, and yourself,   33
With more than foreign heart. We every day   34
Expect him here: when he shall come and fed   35
Our paragon to all reports thus blasted,   36
He will repent the breadth of his great voyage: 37
Blame both my lord and me, that we have tak-   38
No care to your best courses. Go, I pray you,   39
Walk, and be cheerful once again; reserve   40
That excellent complexion, which did steal   41
The eyes of young and old. Care not for me;   42

```
 3    X: TH1
 4    X: TH1; bX: TR1, TR2
 5    X: TR1, T̄H̄1, TR2
 6    X: TH1, TR2; bX: TR1
 7    X: TH1, TR2
 8    X: TH1

 9    X: TH1
10    bX: TR1
11    X̄: TR1
12    X: TH1; ADD 1: TR1
13    X: TH1


14

15
16
17
18
19
20
21


22
23
24
25
26
27    bX: HIM
28    X̄: HIM
29    X: HIM
30    aX: HIM
31

32
33    R: SP2
34
35
36
37
38
39
40
41
42
```

I can go home alone.

Mar.   Well, I will go;   43
But yet I have no desire to it.   44
   Dion. Come, come, I know 'tis good for you   45
Walk half an hour, Leonine, at the least: 46
Remember what I have said.

Leon.   I warrant you, madam   47
   Dion. I'll leave you, my sweet lady, for a
     while: 48
Pray, walk softly, do not heat your blood: 49
What! I must have a care of you.

Mar.   My thanks, sweet madam   50
             [*Exit Dionyza*
Is this wind westerly that blows?

Leon.   South-west.   51
   Mar. When I was born, the wind was north
   Leon.   .   Was't so!   52
   Mar. My father, as nurse said, did never fear   53
But cried 'Good seamen!' to the sailors, galling   54
His kingly hands, haling ropes;   55
And, clasping to the mast, endured a sea   56
That almost burst the deck.   57
   Leon. When was this?   58
   Mar. When I was born: 59
Never was waves nor wind more violent;   &   60
And from the ladder-tackle washes off   61
A canvas-climber. 'Ha!' says one, 'wilt out!'   62
And with a dropping industry they skip   63
From stem to stern: the boatswain whistles, and   64
The master calls, and trebles their confusion.   65
   Leon. Come, say your prayers.   66
   Mar. What mean you?   67
   Leon. If you require a little space for prayer.   68
I grant it: pray; but be not tedious,   69
For the gods are quick of ear, and I am sworn   70
To do my work with haste.

Mar.   Why will you kill me!   71
   Leon. To satisfy my lady.   72
   Mar. Why would she have me kill'd?   73
Now, as I can remember, by my troth,   74
I never did her hurt in all my life: 75
I never spake bad word, nor did ill turn   76
To any living creature: believe me, la,   77
I never kill'd a mouse, nor hurt a fly: 78
I trod upon a worm against my will,   79
But I wept for it. How have I offended,   &   80

43
44
45
46

47

48
49

50

51

52
53
54
55
56
57
58
59
60
61
62
63
64
65
66
67
68
69
70

71
72
73
74
75
76
77   bX: TH1
78   $\overline{\text{X}}$: TH1
79   X: TH1
80   X: TH1

Wherein my death might yield her any profit, 81
Or my life imply her any danger? 82
  Leon. My commission 83
Is not to reason of the deed, but do it. 84
  Mar. You will not do 't for all the world, I 85
  hope.
You are well favour'd, and your looks foreshow 86
You have a gentle heart. I saw you lately, 87
When you caught hurt in parting two that fought: 88
Good sooth, it show'd well in you: do so now: 89
Your lady seeks my life; come you between, 90 90
And save poor me, the weaker.
  Leon.   I am sworn, 91
And will dispatch.   *[He seizes her.* 92

Enter Pirates.

First Pirate. Hold, villain! 93
                [Leonine runs away.
Sec. Pirate. A prize! a prize! 94
Third Pirate. Half-part, mates, half-part. 95
Come, let's have her aboard suddenly. 96
      [Exeunt Pirates with Marina.

Re-enter LEONINE.

  Leon. These roguing thieves serve the great
    pirate Valdes; 97
And they have seized Marina. Let her go: 98
There's no hope she will return. I'll swear she's
  dead, 99
And thrown into the sea. But I'll see further: 100 100
Perhaps they will but please themselves upon her, 101
Not carry her aboard. If she remain, 102
Whom they have ravish'd must by me be slain. 103
            [Exit.

SCENE II. *Mytilene. A room in a brothel.*

Enter PANDAR, Bawd, *and* BOULT.

Pand. Boult! 1
Boult. Sir? 2
Pand. Search the market narrowly: Mytilene 3
is full of gallants. We lost too much money this 4
mart by being too wenchless. 5
  Bawd. We were never so much out of crea- 6
tures. We have but poor three, and they can do no 7

81 X: TH1
82 X: TH1
83
84

85
86
87
88
89
90

91
92

93 X: TH1

94
95 X: TH1
96 X: TH1

97
98 aX: TH1

99
100 bX: HIM, NM2
101 X: SP1, HIM, NM2
102 same as 101
103 same as 101; Insert 43: 1-51, add 1: TR1

Scene 42

ALL CUT: HIM
1 X: SP1, MTh
2 X: SP1, MTh
3 X: SP1, MTh
4 X: SP1, MTh
5 X: SP1, MTh
6 X: SP1, SP2, MTh
7 same as 6, NM1

more than they can do; and they with continual 8
action are even as good as rotten. 9 9

Pand. Therefore let's have fresh ones, what- 10
e'er we pay for them. If there be not a con- 11
science to be used in every trade, we shall never 12
prosper. 13

Bawd. Thou sayest true: 'tis not our bringing 14
up of poor bastards,—as, I think, I have brought 15
up some eleven— 16

Boult. Ay, to eleven; and brought them down 17
again. But shall I search the market? 18

Bawd. What else, man? The stuff we have, 19
a strong wind will blow it to pieces, they are so 20
pitifully sodden. 21 21

Pand. Thou sayest true; they're too unwhole- 22
some, o' conscience. The poor Transylvanian is 23
dead, that lay with the little baggage. 24

Boult. Ay, she quickly pooped him, she made 25
him roast-meat for worms. But I'll go search the 26
market. [*Exit.* 27

Pand. Three or four thousand chequins were 28
as pretty a proportion to live quietly, and so give 29
over. 30

Bawd. Why to give over, I pray you? is it a 31
shame to get when we are old? 32

Pand. O, our credit comes not in like the 33
commodity, nor the commodity wages not with 34
the danger: therefore, if in our youths we could 35
pick up some pretty estate, 'twere not amiss to 36
keep our door hatched. Besides, the sore terms 37
we stand upon with the gods will be strong with 38
us for giving over. 39 39

Bawd. Come, other sorts offend as well as we. 40

Pand. As well as we! ay, and better too: we 41
offend worse. Neither is our profession any trade; 42
it's no calling. But here comes Boult. 43

Re-enter BOULT, *with the* Pirates *and* MARINA.

Boult. [*To Marina*] Come your ways. My 44
masters, you say she's a virgin? 45

First Pirate. O, sir, we doubt it not. 46

Boult. Master, I have gone through for this 47
piece, you see: if you like her, so; if not, I have 48
lost my earnest. 49

Bawd. Boult, has she any qualities? 50 50

```
 8   same as 7; bX: NM2
 9   X: SP1, SP2, MTh, NM1, NM2
10   X: SP1, SP2, MTh
11   same as 10; bX: TR2
12   same as 10, TR2
13   same as 10
14   same as 10; bX: NM1
15   same as 10, NM1
16   same as 15
17   same as 15
18   same as 10
19   same as 10; bX: NM1
20   X: SP1, SP2, NM1; bX: NM2
21   X: SP1, SP2, MTh, NM1
22   same as 21
23   same as 21
24   same as 21
25   same as 21
26   X: SP1, MTh, NM1; aX: SP1
27   same as 26; less aX
28   X: SP1, MTh
29   X: SP1, MTh
30   X: SP1, MTh
31   X: SP1, MTh
32   X: SP1, MTh; ADD 2: JG1
33   X: SP1, MTh, JG1
34   same as 33
35   X: SP1, MTh
36   X: SP1, MTh
37   X: SP1, MTh
38   X: SP1, MTh
39   X: SP1, MTh
40   X: SP1, MTh
41   X: SP1, MTh; bX: NM2; cX: TR1
42   X: SP1, MTh; aX: NM2
43   X: SP1, MTh


44   X: SP1, MTh
45   bX: SP1, MTh
46   X: SP1, MTh
47   X: SP1, MTh
48   X: SP1, MTh
49   X: SP1, MTh
50   aX: SP1, MTh
```

Boult. She has a good face, speaks well, and 51
has excellent good clothes: there's no further 52
necessity of qualities can make her be refused. 53
   Bawd. What's her price, Boult? 54
   Boult. I cannot be bated one doit of a thou- 55
sand pieces. 56
   Pand. Well, follow me, my masters, you shall 57
have your money presently. Wife, take her in: 58
instruct her what she has to do, that she may not 59
be raw in her entertainment.   **6o** 60

          [Exeunt Pandar and Pirates.
   Bawd. Boult, take you the marks of her, the 61
colour of her hair, complexion, height, age, with 62
warrant of her virginity; and cry ' He that will 63
give most shall have her first.' Such a maiden- 64
head were no cheap thing, if men were as they 65
have been. Get this done as I command you. 66
   Boult. Performance shall follow.   *[Exit.* 67
   Mar. Alack that Leonine was so slack, so
     slow! 68
He should have struck, not spoke; or that these
     pirates, 69
Not enough barbarous, had not o'erboard thrown
     me   •   **7o** 70
For to seek my mother! 71
   Bawd. Why lament you, pretty one? 72
   Mar. That I am pretty. 73
   Bawd. Come, the gods have done their part 74
in you. 75
   Mar. I accuse them not. 76
   Bawd. You are light into my hands, where 77
you are like to live. 78
   Mar. The more my fault 79
To scape his hands where I was like to die.   **8o** 80
   Bawd. Ay, and you shall live in pleasure. 81
   Mar. No. 82
   Bawd. Yes, indeed shall you, and taste gen- 83
tlemen of all fashions: you shall fare well: you 84
shall have the difference of all complexions. What! 85
do you stop your ears? 86
   Mar. Are you a woman? 87
   Bawd. What would you have me be, an I be 88
not a woman? 89
   Mar. An honest woman, or not a woman. **9o** 90
   Bawd. Marry, whip thee, gosling: I think I 91
shall have something to do with you. Come, 92

51
52
53
54 <u>b</u>X: SP1
55
56
57 <u>b</u>X: SP1, MTh; <u>ADD</u> 1: MTh
58 X̄: SP1, MTh; b<u>X</u>: SP2
59 X: SP1, SP2, M̄Th
60 same as 59

61 X: SP1, SP2, MTh, NM1
62 same as 61
63 same as 61
64 same as 61; <u>B</u>: NM2
65 same as 61
66 same as 61; <u>b</u>X: JG1; <u>Insert</u> 150-156a: JG1
67 same as 61, J̄G1

68

69

70
71
72
73
74
75 X: TR1
76 X: TR1
77

78
79
80
81
82 X: SP1, MTh, TR1
83 X: SP1, MTh; <u>a</u>X: TR1; <u>b</u>X: SP2, NM1
84 X: SP1; <u>a</u>X: SP̄2, NM1
85 <u>a</u>X: SP1, M̄Th
86
87
88
89
90
91
92

you're a young foolish sapling, and must be 93
bowed as I would have you. 94
   Mar. The gods defend me! 95
   Bawd. If it please the gods to defend you by 96
men, then men must comfort you, men must feed 97
you, men must stir you up. Boult's returned. 98

Re-enter BOULT.

Now, sir, hast thou cried her through the market! 99
   Boult. I have cried her almost to the number 100
of her hairs; I have drawn her picture with my 101
voice. 102
   Bawd. And I prithee tell me, how dost thou 103
find the inclination of the people, especially of 104
the younger sort? 105
   Boult. 'Faith, they listened to me as they 106
would have hearkened to their father's testament. 107
There was a Spaniard's mouth so watered, that 108
he went to bed to her very description. 109 109
   Bawd. We shall have him here to-morrow 110
with his best ruff on. 111
   Boult. To-night, to-night. But, mistress, do 112
you know the French knight that cowers i' the 113
hams? 114
   Bawd. Who, Monsieur Veroles? 115
   Boult. Ay, he: he offered to cut a caper at 116
the proclamation; but he made a groan at it, and 117
swore he would see her to-morrow. 118
   Bawd. Well, well; as for him, he brought his 119
disease hither: here he does but repair it. I know 120
he will come in our shadow, to scatter his crowns 121
in the sun. 122
   Boult. Well, if we had of every nation a tra- 123
veller, we should lodge them with this sign. 124
   Bawd. [*To Mar.*] Pray you, come hither 125
awhile. You have fortunes coming upon you. 126
Mark me: you must seem to do that fearfully 127
which you commit willingly, despise profit where 128
you have most gain. To weep that you live as 129
ye do makes pity in your lovers: seldom but that 130
pity begets you a good opinion, and that opinion 151
a mere profit. 132
   Mar. I understand you not. 133
   Boult. O, take her home, mistress, take her 134
home: these blushes of hers must be quenched 135

```
92
94
95   ADD 13: SP1, MTh
96   X: SP1, SP2, MTh
97   same as 96
98   same as 96; aX: NM2, DS1; bX: NM1, TH1


99   X: SP1, SP2, MTh, NM1
100  same as 99, NM2
101  same as 99; aX: NM2
102  sameas 99
103  same as 99
104  same as 99
105  same as 99
106  same as 99
107  same as 99
108  same as 99
109  same as 99
110  same as 99
111  same as 99
112  same as 99, NM2
113  same as 112
114  same as 112
115  same as 112
116  same as 112
117  same as 112
118  same as 112; ADD 1: TR2
119  same as 112; cX: TR1
120  same as 112; bX: TH1; cX: TR1
121  X: SP1, SP2, MTh, NM1, NM2, TH1
122  same as 121
123  X: SP1, SP2, MTh, NM1
124  sameas 123
125  same as 123; bX: TH1
126  X: SP1, MTh
127  X: SP1, SP2, MTh
128  same as 127
129  same as 127
130  same as 127
131  same as 127
132  same   as 127
133  same as 127
134  same as 127
135  same as 127; bX: NM2
```

with some present practice.   136
   Bawd. Thou sayest true, i' faith, so they   137
must; for your bride goes to that with shame   138
which is her way to go with warrant.   ɪ39   139
   Boult. 'Faith, some do, and some do not. But,   140
mistress, if I have bargained for the joint,—   141
   Bawd. Thou mayst cut a morsel off the spit.   142
   Boult. I may so.   143
   Bawd. Who should deny it? Come, young   144
one, I like the manner of your garments well.   145
   Boult. Ay, by my faith, they shall not be   146
changed yet.   147
   Bawd. Boult, spend thou that in the town: 148
report what a sojourner we have; you'll lose   149
nothing by custom. When nature framed this   150
piece, she meant thee a good turn; therefore say   151
what a paragon she is, and thou hast the harvest   152
out of thine own report.   153
   Boult. I warrant you, mistress, thunder shall   154
not so awake the beds of eels as my giving out   155
her beauty stir up the lewdly-inclined. I'll bring   156
home some to-night.   157
   Bawd. Come your ways; follow me.   158
   Mar. If fires be hot, knives sharp, or waters
     deep,   159
Untied I still my virgin knot will keep.   ℟   160
Diana, aid my purpose!   161
   Bawd. What have we to do with Diana? Pray   162
you, will you go with us?   [*Exeunt*   163

SCENE III *Tarsus. A room in Cleon's house.*

Enter CLEON *and* DIONYZA.

   Dion. Why, are you foolish? Can it be un-
     done?   1
   Cle. O Dionyza, such a piece of slaughter   2
The sun and moon ne'er look'd upon!
   Dion.   I think   3
You'll turn a child again.   4
   Cle. Were I chief lord of all this spacious
     world,   5
I'd give it to undo the deed. O lady,   6
Much less in blood than virtue, yet a princess   7
To equal any single crown o' the earth   8
I' the justice of compare! O villain Leonine!   9
Whom thou hast poison'd too: ɪo   10

```
136   X: SP1, SP2, MTh, NM1, NM2
137   same as 136; bX: TR1
138   same as 136, T̄R̄1
139   same as 138
140   same as 136; aX: TR1
141   same as 136
142   same as 136
143   same as 136
144   X: SP1, MTh, NM1, NM2; aX: SP2; bX: TR1
145   X: SP1, MTh, NM1, NM2, T̄R̄1; ADD 1̄: SP2
146   same as 145, SP2
147   X: SP1, SP2, MTh, NM1, TR1
148   X: SP1, SP2, MTh; bX: TH1
149   same as 148; less bX̄; abX: TH1
150   X: SP1, SP2, MTh, N̄M̄2; aX: TH1; MOVE 150-156a to follow 66a: JG1
151   X: SP1, SP2, MTh; aX: N̄M̄2
152   same as 151; less aX̄
153   same as 152
154   same as 152
155   same as 152
156   same as 152; bX: JG1
157   same as 152, J̄Ḡ1
158   X: SP1, MTh

159   X: SP1, MTh, NM1, NM2
160   same as 159
161   X: SP1, MTh
162   X: SP1, MTh; ADD 20: TH1
163   X: SP1, MTh, T̄H̄1; ADD 1: TR2; Insert 44: 1-14: DS1
```

Scene 43

```
 1   X: TH1; MOVE 1-51 to follow 46: 210: NM2; MOVE 1-51 to follow 41:103:TR1
 2   X: TH1

 3   aX: TH1
 4

 5
 6
 7   aX: TR1
 8
 9   bX: TR1
10   X̄: TR1
```

If thou hadst drunk to him, 't had been a kindness 11
Becoming well thy fact: what canst thou say 12
When noble Pericles shall demand his child? 13
   Dion. That she is dead. Nurses are not the
     fates, 14
To foster it, nor ever to preserve. 15
She died at night: I'll say so. Who can cross it! 16
Unless you play the pious innocent, 17
And for an honest attribute cry out 18
'She died by foul play.'
   Cle. O, go to. Well, well, 19
Of all the faults beneath the heavens, the gods 20 20
Do like this worst.
   Dion. Be one of those that think 21
The petty wrens of Tarsus will fly hence, 22
And open this to Pericles. I do shame 23
To think of what a noble strain you are, 24
And of how coward a spirit.
   Cle. To such proceeding 25
Who ever but his approbation added, 26
Though not his prime consent, he did not flow 27
From honourable sources.
   Dion. Be it so, then: 28
Yet none does know, but you, how she came dead 29
Nor none can know, Leonine being gone. 30
She did distain my child, and stood between 31
Her and her fortunes: none would look on her, 32
But cast their gazes on Marina's face; 33
Whilst ours was blurted at and held a malkin 34
Not worth the time of day. It pierced me
     thorough; 35
And though you call my course unnatural, 36
You not your child well loving, yet I find 37
It greets me as an enterprise of kindness 38
Perform'd to your sole daughter.
   Cle. Heavens forgive it! 39
   Dion. And as for Pericles, 40
What should he say? We wept after her hearse, 41
And yet we mourn: her monument 42
Is almost finish'd, and her epitaphs 43
In glittering golden characters express 44
A general praise to her, and care in us 45
At whose expense 'tis done.
   Cle. Thou art like the harpy, 46
Which, to betray, dost, with thine angel's face, 47
Seize with thine eagle's talons. 48

```
11    X: T.R1, TR2
12    aX: TR1, TR2
13    bX: SP2

14    R: DS1
15
16
17
18

19    R: JG1; bX: TH1
20

21
22
23
24

25    bX: TR2
26    X: TR2
27    X: TR2
      X: TR2
28
29
30    bX: TR1
31
32
33
34

35
36
37
38

39
40
41    bX: TR1; ADD 1: JG1
42    X: TR1
43    R: TR1
44
45

46
47
48
```

Dion. You are like one that superstitiously **49**   49
Doth swear to the gods that winter kills the flies: 50
But yet I know you'll do as I advise.   *[Exeunt.*   51

Scene IV.

Enter Gower, *before the monument of* Marina *at Tarsus.*

Gow. Thus time we waste, and longest
    leagues make short;   1
Sail seas in cockles, have an wish but for't;   2
Making, to take your imagination,   3
From bourn to bourn, region to region.   4
By you being pardon'd, we commit no crime   5
To use one language in each several clime   6
Where our scenes seem to live.   I do beseech
    you   7
To learn of me, who stand i' the gaps to teach
    you,   8
The stages of our story.   Pericles   9
Is now again thwarting the wayward seas,   **10**   10
Attended on by many a lord and knight,   11
To see his daughter, all his life's delight.   12
Old Escanes, whom Helicanus late   13
Advanced in time to great and high estate,   14
Is left to govern.   Bear you it in mind,   15
Old Helicanus goes along behind.   16
Well-sailing ships and bounteous winds have
    brought   17
This king to Tarsus,—think his pilot thought: 18
So with his steerage shall your thoughts grow
    on,—   **19**   19
To fetch his daughter home, who first is gone.   20
Like motes and shadows see them move awhile;   21
Your ears unto your eyes I'll reconcile.   22

Dumb Show.

Enter Pericles, *at one door, with all his train;* Cleon *and* Dionyza, *at the other.* Cleon *shows* Pericles *the tomb; whereat* Pericles *makes lamentation, puts on sackcloth, and in a mighty passion departs. Then exeunt* Cleon *and* Dionyza.

See how belief may suffer by foul show!   23

49
50
51   ADD Song: TR2

Scene 44

ALL CUT: SP1, SP2, MTh
 1   X: TR1; MOVE 1-14 to follow 42: 163: DS1; MOVE 1-9a to follow 34:18:TR2
 2   X: TR1; bX: NM2
 3   X: NM2, TR1
 4   X: NM2, TR1
 5   X: NM2, TR1
 6   X: NM2, TR1

 7   X: TR1; aX: NM2

 8   X: TR1
 9   aX: TR1
10
11   X: NM2
12   X: NM2,
13   X: NM2, TH1; bX: TR2, JG1
14   X: NM2, TR1, TR2, JG1, TH1
15   same as 14, DS1
16   X: NM2, DS1, TR2, JG1, TH1

17   X: NM2, DS1
18

19   X: TR1
20
21
22   X: TR1; Insert 34-43: TR2; ADD 9: TH1

23   X: TR2; MOVE 23-31a to follow 41: TR1

This borrow'd passion stands for true old woe;   24
And Pericles, in sorrow all devour'd,   25
With sighs shot through, and biggest tears o'er-
    shower'd,   26
Leaves Tarsus and again embarks. He swears   27
Never to wash his face, nor cut his hairs: 28
He puts on sackcloth, and to sea.   He bears   29
A tempest, which his mortal vessel tears,   30   30
And yet he rides it out.   Now please you wit   31
The epitaph is for Marina writ   32
By wicked Dionyza.   33

[Reads the inscription on Marina's
monument.

'The fairest, sweet'st, and best lies here,   34
Who wither'd in her spring of year.   35
She was of Tyrus the king's daughter,   36
On whom foul death hath made this slaughter: 37
Marina was she call'd; and at her birth,   38
Thetis, being proud, swallow'd some part o'
    the earth: 39
Therefore the earth, fearing to be o'erflow'd,   40   40
Hath Thetis' birth-child on the heavens be-
    stow'd: 41
Wherefore she does, and swears she'll never
    stint,   42
Make raging battery upon shores of flint.'   43
No visor does become black villany   44
So well as soft and tender flattery.   45
Let Pericles believe his daughter's dead,   46
And bear his courses to be ordered   47
By Lady Fortune; while our scene must play   48
His daughter's woe and heavy well-a-day   49
In her unholy service.   Patience, then,   50   50
And think you now are all in Mytilene. [Exit. 51

Scene V. *Mytilene.   A street before the brothel.*

Enter, from the brothel, two Gentlemen.

First Gent.   Did you ever hear the like?   1
Sec. Gent.   No, nor never shall do in such a   2
place as this, she being once gone.   3
First Gent.   But to have divinity preached   4
there! did you ever dream of such a thing?   5
Sec. Gent.   No, no.   Come, I am for no more   6
bawdy-houses: shall's go hear the vestals sing?   7

```
24  X: TR2
25

26
27  bX: NM2, DS1, TR2
28  X: NM2, DS1, TR2, JG1
29  X: NM2; aX: DS1, JG1
30  X: NM2
31  X: NM2; bX: TR2
32  X: NM2, TR2
33  X: NM2, TR2


34  MOVE 34-43 to follow 22: TR2
35
36  X: JG1
37  X: JG1
38  X: JG1; bX: NM2

39  X: NM2, JG1; bX: TH1
40  X: NM2, JG1, TH1

41  X: NM2, JG1; TH1; Insert 23-31a: TR1

42  X: NM2, TR1, JG1, EdB , TH1
43  same as 42
44  X: NM2, TR2, EdB
45  same as 44
46  X: HIM, TR2
47  X: HIM, TR2
48  X: HIM; aX: TR2
49  X: HIM
50  X: HIM
51  X: HIM; ADD 1: JG1 ; Insert 46, 185-190a: TR2
```

Scene 45

```
ALL CUT: SP1, HIM, MTh, NM1, NM2, EdB
 1
 2
 3
 4
 5
 6
 7
```

First Gent. I'll do any thing now that is vir- 8
tuous; but I am out of the road of rutting for 9
ever. [*Exeunt.* 10 10

SCENE VI. *The same. A room in the brothel.*

Enter Pandar, Bawd, *and* BOULT.

Pand. Well, I had rather than twice the worth 1
of her she had ne'er come here. 2
Bawd. Fie, fie upon her! she's able to freeze 3
the god Priapus, and undo a whole generation. 4
We must either get her ravished, or be rid of her. 5
When she should do for clients her fitment, and 6
do me the kindness of our profession, she has me 7
her quirks, her reasons, her master reasons, her 8
prayers, her knees: that she would make a puri- 9
tan of the devil, if he should cheapen a kiss of her. 10
Boult. 'Faith, I must ravish her, or she'll 11
disfurnish us of all our cavaliers, and make our 12
swearers priests. 13
Pand. Now, the pox upon her green-sickness 14
for me! 15
Bawd. 'Faith, there's no way to be rid on't 16
but by the way to the pox. Here comes the Lord 17
Lysimachus disguised. 18
Boult. We should have both lord and lown, 19
if the peevish baggage would but give way to 20
customers. 21 21

Enter LYSIMACHUS.

Lys. How now! How a dozen of virginities? 22
Bawd. Now, the gods to-bless your honour! 23
Boult. I am glad to see your honour in good 24
health. 25
Lys. You may so; 'tis the better for you that 26
your resorters stand upon sound legs. How now! 27
wholesome iniquity have you that a man may 28
deal withal, and defy the surgeon? 29
Bawd. We have here one, sir, if she would— 30
but there never came her like in Mytilene. 31 31
Lys. If she'ld do the deed of darkness, thou 32
wouldst say. 33
Bawd. Your honour knows what 'tis to say 34
well enough. 35
Lys. Well, call forth, call forth. 36
Boult. For flesh and blood, sir, white and red, 37

8
9
10

Scene 46

ALL CUT : HIM
1   SP1, MTh, NM1, NM2
2   same as 1
3   same as 1
4   same as 1; aX: SP2
5   same as 1; b$\overline{X}$: TR2
6   X: SP1, SP2, MTh, NM1, NM2, TR1, TR2
7   same as 6
8   same as 6
9   X: SP1, MTh, NM1, NM2; aX: SP2, RT2
10 X: SP1, MTh, NM1, NM2
11 same as 10, SP2
12 same as 11
13 same as 11
14 same as 11
15 same as 11
16 X: SP1, SP2, MTh, NM1
17 X: SP1, MTh; aX: SP2, WM1
18 X: SP1, MTh
19 X: SP1, MTh, TR2
20 same as 19
21 X: SP1; bX: MTh; ADD 1: MTh

22 X: SP1
23 X: SP1, SP2
24 X: SP1, SP2
25 X: SP1, SP2; ADD 1: MTh
26 X: SP1, SP2, $\overline{MTh}$; bX: NM1
27 same as 26 NM1; less bX
28 same as 27
29 same as 27; bX: NM2
30 X: SP1
31 X: SP1; ADD 4: MTh
32 X: SP1, $\overline{SP2}$, MTh, NM1
33 same as 32
34 same as 32
35 same as 32
36 X: SP1, MTh, NM1
37 same as 36;

you shall see a rose; and she were a rose indeed,   38
if she had but— 39
   Lys. What, prithee?   40   40
   Boult. O, sir, I can be modest.   41
   Lys. That dignifies the renown of a bawd, no   42
less than it gives a good report to a number to be   43
chaste.   [*Exit Boult.*   44
   Bawd. Here comes that which grows to the   45
stalk; never plucked yet, I can assure you.   46

     Re-enter BOULT *with* MARINA.

Is she not a fair creature?   47
   Lys. 'Faith, she would serve after a long   48
voyage at sea. Well, there's for you: leave us.   49
   Bawd. I beseech your honour, give me leave: 50
a word, and I'll have done presently.   51   51
   Lys. I beseech you, do.   52
   Bawd. [*To Marina*] First, I would have you   53
note, this is an honourable man.   54
   Mar. I desire to find him so, that I may   55
worthily note him.   56
   Bawd. Next, he's the governor of this coun-   57
try, and a man whom I am bound to.   58
   Mar. If he govern the country, you are bound   59
to him indeed; but how honourable he is in that,   60
I know not.   61   61
   Bawd. Pray you, without any more virginal   62
fencing, will you use him kindly? He will line   63
your apron with gold.   64
   Mar. What he will do graciously, I will thank-   65
fully receive.   66
   Lys. Ha' you done?   67
   Bawd. My lord, she's not paced yet: you   68
must take some pains to work her to your manage.   69
Come, we will leave his honour and her together.   70
Go thy ways.   71
     [*Exeunt Bawd, Pandar, and Boult.*
   Lys. Now, pretty one, how long have you   72
been at this trade?   73
   Mar. What trade, sir?   74
   Lys. Why, I cannot name't but I shall offend.   75
   Mar. I cannot be offended with my trade.   76
Please you to name it.   77
   Lys. How long have you been of this profession?   78
   Mar. E'er since I can remember.   79
   Lys. Did you go to't so young? Were you a   80

```
38   same as 36; bX: SP1
 39  X: SP1, SP2, MTh, NM1
 40  same as 39; R: DS1
 41  same  as 39
 42  same as 39; bX: TR1
 43  same as 39; bX: TR1
 44  same as 39; R: TR1
 45  X: SP1, SP2, MTh
 46  same as 45


 47  X: SP1, MTh, TR1
 48  same as 47; bX: SP2
 49  X: SP1, MTh; R: TR2; aX: SP2
 50  X: SP1, MTh
 51  X: SP1, MTh
 52  X: SP1, MTh
 53  X: MTh
 54  X: MTh
 55  X: MTh
 56  X: MTh
 57  X: MTh
 58  X: MTh
 59  X: MTh
 60  X: MTh
 61  X: MTh
 62  X: MTh; bX: SP1; B: SP2
 63  X: MTh; aX: SP1
 64  X: MTh
 65  X: MTh
 66  X: MTh; ADD 2: SP1
 67  X: SP1, MTh
 68  X: SP1, MTh; bX: SP2, NM1; cX: NM2
 69  X: SP1, MTh
 70  X: MTh; aX: SP1; B: JG1
 71  X: MTh


 72  X: MTh
 73  X: MTh; R: SP1
 74  X: 'MTh; R: SP1
 75  X: MTh
 76  X: MTh; cX: SP1
 77  X: MTh; ADD 2: SP1
 78  X: SP1, MTh
 79  X: SP1, MTh
 80  X: SP1, MTh
```

gamester at five or at seven?   81   81
   Mar. Earlier too, sir, if now I be one.   82
   Lys. Why, the house you dwell in proclaims   83
you to be a creature of sale.   84
   Mar. Do you know this house to be a place   85
of such resort, and will come into't? I hear say   86
you are of honourable parts, and are the governor   87
of this place.   88
   Lys. Why, hath your principal made known   89
unto you who I am?   90   90
   Mar. Who is my principal?   91
   Lys. Why, your herb-woman; she that sets   92
seeds and roots of shame and iniquity. O, you   93
have heard something of my power, and so stand   94
aloof for more serious wooing. But I protest to   95
thee, pretty one, my authority shall not see thee,   96
or else look friendly upon thee. Come, bring me   97
to some private place: come, come.   98
   Mar. If you were born to honour, show it now :   99
If put upon you, make the judgement good   100   100
That thought you worthy of it.   101
   Lys. How's this? how's this? Some more;
    be sage.
  Mar.   For me,   102
That am a maid, though most ungentle fortune   103
Have placed me in this sty, where, since I came,   104
Diseases have been sold dearer than physic,   105
O, that the gods   106
Would set me free from this unhallow'd place,   107
Though they did change me to the meanest bird   108
That flies i' the purer air !
   Lys.   I did not think   109
Thou couldst have spoke so well; ne'er dream'd
    thou couldst.   110   100
Had I brought hither a corrupted mind,   111
Thy speech had alter'd it. Hold, here's gold
    for thee: 112
Persever in that clear way thou goest,   113
And the gods strengthen thee !
   Mar.   The good gods preserve you!   114
   Lys. For me, be you thoughten   115
That I came with no ill intent; for to me   116
The very doors and windows savour vilely.   117
Fare thee well. Thou art a piece of virtue, and   118
I doubt not but thy training hath been noble.   119
Hold, here's more gold for thee.   120   120

```
 81   X: SP1, MTh
 82   X: SP1, MTh
 83   X: SP1; bX: MTh
 84   X: SP1, M̄T̄h
 85   bX: SP1
 86   ā X̄: SP1
 87
 88
 89   X: SP1, MTh
 90   X: SP1, MTh
 91   X: SP1, MTh
 92   X: SP1, MTh; bX: TR2
 93   X: SP1; aX: M̄T̄h, TR2
 94   X: SP1
 95   X: SP1
 96   X: SP1
 97   X: SP1; bX: SP2, MTh, NM1, NM2
 98   X: SP1, M̄T̄h, NM1, NM2; aX: SP2
 99
100
101   ADD 25: EdB


102   X: DS1, EdB; bX: SP1, MTh, TR1 ; ADD 58 from George Wilkins: JG1
103   X: SP1, MTh, J̄Ḡ1, EdB
104   same as 103
105   same as 103
106   X: JG1, EdB
107   X: JG1, EdB
108   X: JG1, EdB

109   X: JG1, EdB

110   X: JG1, EdB; ADD 3: DS1
111   X: DS1, TR2, J̄Ḡ1̄, EdB

112   X: JG1, EdB; aX: DS1, TR2
113   X: TR2, JG1, Ēd̄B

114   same as 113
115   same as 113, DS1
116   same as 115
117   same as 115
118   X: TR1, JG1, EdB
119   same as 18
120   X: TR1, JG1
```

A curse upon him, die he like a thief, 121
That robs thee of thy goodness! If thou dost 122
Hear from me, it shall be for thy good. 123

Re-enter BOULT.

Boult. I beseech your honour, one piece for 124
me. 125
Lys. Avaunt, thou damned door-keeper! 126
Your house, but for this virgin that doth prop it, 127
Would sink and overwhelm you. Away! [*Exit.* 128
Boult. How's this? We must take another 129
course with you. If your peevish chastity, 130
which is not worth a breakfast in the cheapest 131
country under the cope, shall undo a whole 132
household, let me be gelded like a spaniel. 133
Come your ways. 134
Mar. Whither would you have me? 135
Boult. I must have your maidenhead taken 136
off, or the common hangman shall execute it. 137
Come your ways. We'll have no more gentle- 138
men driven away. Come your ways, I say. 139

Re-enter Bawd.

Bawd. How now! what's the matter? 140
Boult. Worse and worse, mistress: she has 141
here spoken holy words to the Lord Lysimachus. 142
Bawd. O abominable! 143
Boult. She makes our profession as it were to 144
stink afore the face of the gods. 145
Bawd. Marry, hang her up for ever! 146
Boult. The nobleman would have dealt with 147
her like a nobleman, and she sent him away as 148
cold as a snowball; saying his prayers too. 149
Bawd. Boult, take her away; use her at thy 150
pleasure: crack the glass of her virginity, and 151
make the rest malleable. 152
Boult. An if she were a thornier piece of 153
ground than she is, she shall be ploughed. 154
Mar. Hark, hark, you gods! 155
Bawd. She conjures: away with her! Would 156
she had never come within my doors! Marry, 157
hang you! She's born to undo us. Will you 158
not go the way of women-kind? Marry, come 159
up, my dish of chastity with rosemary and bays! 160
[*Exit.*

```
121    X: DS1, JG1
122    X: JG1; aX: DS1
123    X: JG1



124
125
126
127
128
129
130    bX: SP1, SP2, MTh
131    X: SP1, SP2, MTh ; bX: NM1
132    same as 131; aX: NM1
133    X: SP2; aX: SP1, MTh
134    X: SP1
135    X: SP1, SP2, MTh, JG1
136    same as 135, NM2; bX: NM1
137    X: SP1,  SP2, MTh, JG1; aX: NM1, NM2
138    X: SP1, SP2, MTh, JG1
139    same as 138


140    X: SP1, SP2, MTh
141    same as 140
142    same as 140
143    same as 140; Insert 155: TH1
144    X: SP1, SP2, MTh, TH1
145    same as 144
146    same as 144; bX: NM1
147    same as 144, NM1
148    same as 147
149    same as 147
150    X: SP1, SP2, MTh
151    same as 150, N M2; bX: NM1
152    X: SP1, SP2, MTh, NM1, NM2
153    same as 152
154    same as 152
155    X: SP1, SP2, MTh; MOVE 155 to follow 143: TH1
156    same as 155; less MOVE
157    X: SP1, SP2, MTh, TH1; bX: TR2
158    same as 157; less bX; aX: TR2
159    same as 157; less bX
160    same as 159
```

Boult. Come, mistress ; come your ways with 161
me. 162
Mar. Whither wilt thou have me? 163
Boult. To take from you the jewel you hold 164
so dear. 165
Mar. Prithee, tell me one thing first. 166
Boult. Come now, your one thing. 167
Mar. What canst thou wish thine enemy to be? 168
Boult. Why, I could wish him to be my 169
master, or rather, my mistress. 170 170
Mar. Neither of these are so bad as thou art, 171
Since they do better thee in their command. 172
Thou hold'st a place, for which the pained'st fiend 173
Of hell would not in reputation change : 174
Thou art the damned doorkeeper to every 175
Coistrel that comes inquiring for his Tib ; 176
To the choleric fisting of every rogue 177
Thy ear is liable : thy food is such 178
As hath been belch'd on by infected lungs. 179 179
Boult. What would you have me do? go to 180
the wars, would you? where a man may serve 181
seven years for the loss of a leg, and have not 182
money enough in the end to buy him a wooden 183
one? 184
Mar. Do any thing but this thou doest. Empty 185
Old receptacles, or common shores, of filth : 186
Serve by indenture to the common hangman : 187
Any of these ways are yet better than this : 188
For what thou professest, a baboon, could he
speak, 189
Would own a name too dear. O, that the gods 190
Would safely deliver me from this place ! 191 191
Here, here's gold for thee. 192
If that thy master would gain by me, 193
Proclaim that I can sing, weave, sew, and dance, 194
With other virtues, which I'll keep from boast ; 195
And I will undertake all these to teach. 196
I doubt not but this populous city will- 197
Yield many scholars. 198
Boult. But can you teach all this you speak of? 199
Mar. Prove that I cannot, take me home again, 200
And prostitute me to the basest groom 201 201
That doth frequent your house. 202
Boult. Well, I will see what I can do for thee : 203
if I can place thee, I will. 204
Mar. But amongst honest women. 205

```
161   X SP1, SP2, MTh
162   same as 161
163   sameas 161, NM1
164   same as 163
165   same as 163; ADD 5: JG1
166
167
168
169
170
171
172
173
174
175   X: SP1
176   X: SP1
177   X: SP1
178   X: SP1
179   X: SP1
180
181
182
183
184
185   bX: SP1, MTh
186   X: SP1, MTh; bX: NM1; cX: NM2
187
188

189   X: SP1, MTh
190   aX: SP1, MTh
191   X: JG1
192
193
194
195   X: TR1, TH1; MOVE 185b-191 to open play: TR2
196
197
198
199   X: SP2, NM1
200   X: SP2, NM1; R: SP1
201   X: SP1, SP2, NM1
202   same as 201
203   bX: SP1, MTh
204   X: SP1, MTh
205   X: SP1, MTh
```

Boult. 'Faith, my acquaintance lies little   206
amongst them. But since my master and mis-   207
tress have bought you, there's no going but by   208
their consent: therefore I will make them ac-   209
quainted with your purpose, and I doubt not but   210
I shall find them tractable enough. Come, I'll   211
do for thee what I can; come your ways.   212

[Exeunt.

ACT V.

Enter GOWER.

Gow. Marina thus the brothel 'scapes, and
    chances   1
Into an honest house, our story says.   2
She sings like one immortal, and she dances   3
As goddess-like to her admired lays: 4
Deep clerks she dumbs; and with her neeld com-
    poses   5
Nature's own shape, of bud, bird, branch, or berry,   6
That even her art sisters the natural roses: 7
Her inkle, silk, twin with the rubied cherry: 8
That pupils lacks she none of noble race,   9
Who pour their bounty on her: and her gain   10   10
She gives the cursed bawd.   Here we her place: 11
And to her father turn our thoughts again,   12
Where we left him, on the sea. We there him
    lost;   13
Whence, driven before the winds, he is arrived   14
Here where his daughter dwells: and on this coast   15
Suppose him now at anchor.   The city strived   16
God Neptune's annual feast to keep: from whence   17
Lysimachus our Tyrian ship espies,   18
His banners sable, trimm'd with rich expense;   19
And to him in his barge with fervour hies.   20   20
In your supposing once more put your sight   21
Of heavy Pericles: think this his bark: 22
Where what is done in action, more, if might,   23
Shall be discover'd; please you, sit and hark.   24

[Exit.

SCENE I. *On board Pericles' ship, off Mytilene.*
A close pavilion on deck, with a curtain before
it; Pericles within it, reclined on a couch.
A barge lying beside the Tyrian vessel.

```
206    X: SP1, MTh
207    X: TR1; aX: MTh
208    X: TR1
209    X: TR1
210    X: TR1; ADD 1, insert 43: 1-51: MTh
211    R: MTh; aX: TR1
212    X: MTh
```

5 PROLOG

```
ALL CUT: SP1, SP2, HIM, MTh
  1    B: NM1
  2
  3
  4

  5    X: NM1, NM2, Ed8
  6    same as 5
  7    same as 5
  8    same as 5, TH1
  9
 10
 11
 12


 13
 14
 15
 16    bX: NM1, NM2, TR1, TH1
 17    X: NM1, NM2, TR1, TH1
 18    X: NM1,  NM2, TR1
 19    X: NM1, NM2
 20    X: NM1, NM2, TR1
 21    same as 20
 22    X: TH1; aX: NM1, NM2
 23    X: TH1
 24    X: TH1
```

Scene 51

Enter two Sailors, *one belonging to the Tyrian vessel, the other to the barge; to them* HELICANUS.

Tyr. Sail. [*To the Sailor of Mytilene*]
Where is lord Helicanus? he can resolve you. 1
O, here he is. 2
Sir, there's a barge put off from Mytilene, 3
And in it is Lysimachus the governor, 4
Who craves to come aboard.   What is your will? 5
Hel.   That he have his.   Call up some gentlemen. 6
Tyr. Sail.   Ho, gentlemen! my lord calls. 7

Enter two or three Gentlemen.

First Gent.   Doth your lordship call? 8
Hel.   Gentlemen, there's some of worth would come aboard: 9
I pray ye, greet them fairly.   10   10
[*The Gentlemen and the two Sailors descend.
and go on board the barge.*

Enter, from thence, LYSIMACHUS *and* Lords: *with the* Gentlemen *and the two* Sailors.

Tyr. Sail.   Sir, 11
This is the man that can, in aught you would, 12
Resolve you 13
Lys.   Hail, reverend sir! the gods preserve you! 14
Hel.   And you, sir, to outlive the age I am, 15
And die as I would do.
Lys.   You wish me well. 16
Being on shore, honouring of Neptune's triumphs, 17
Seeing this goodly vessel ride before us, 18
I made to it, to know of whence you are. 19
Hel.   First, what is your place?   20 20
Lys.   I am the governor of this place you lie before. 21
Hel.   Sir, 22
Our vessel is of Tyre, in it the king: 23
A man who for this three months hath not spoken 24
To any one, nor taken sustenance 25
But to prorogue his grief. 26
Lys.   Upon what ground is his distemperature? 27
Hel.   'Twould be too tedious to repeat; 28
But the main grief springs from the loss 29
Of a beloved daughter and a wife.   30 30

```
1    X: DS1, TR1, TH1
2    X: EdB; aX: DS1, TR1, JG1
3    X: EdB; b̄X̄: NM1, NM2
4    X: EdB; āX̄: NM1, NM2
5    X: EdB

6    X: NM1, NM2, EdB; bX: TR1, TH1, JG1
7    X: NM1, NM2, TR1, T̄H̄1, JG1, EdB


8    same as 7

9    X: NM1, NM2, TR1, TH1, EdB
10   X: TR1, TH1, EdB; aX̄: NM2




11   X: NM1, TR1, EdB
12   X: NM1, NM2, TR1, EdB
13   same as 12

14
15

16
17
18
19
20   X: TR1, TR2, JG1

21   same as 20
22
23
24
25
26
27
28   X: TH1; R̲: JG1
29
30   b̲X̲: MTh; A̲D̲D̲ 5: MTh; A̲D̲D̲ 10: SP1
```

Lys. May we not see him? 31

Hel. You may; 32
But bootless is your sight: he will not speak 33
To any. 34

Lys. Yet let me obtain my wish. 35

Hel. Behold him. [*Pericles discovered.*] This
was a goodly person, 36
Till the disaster that, one mortal night, 37
Drove him to this. 38

Lys. Sir king, all hail! the gods preserve you! 39
Hail, royal sir! **40** 40

Hel. It is in vain; he will not speak to you. 41

First Lord. Sir, 42
We have a maid in Mytilene, I durst wager, 43
Would win some words of him.

Lys. 'Tis well bethought. 44
She questionless with her sweet harmony 45
And other chosen attractions, would allure, 46
And make a battery through his deafen'd parts, 47
Which now are midway stopp'd: 48
She is all happy as the fairest of all, 49
And, with her fellow maids, is now upon **50** 50
The leafy shelter that abuts against 51
The island's side. 52

[*Whispers a Lord, who goes off in the
barge of Lysimachus.*

Hel. Sure, all's effectless; yet nothing we'll
omit 53
That bears recovery's name. But, since your
kindness 54
We have stretch'd thus far, let us beseech you 55
That for our gold we may provision have, 56
Wherein we are not destitute for want, 57
But weary for the staleness.

Lys. O, sir, a courtesy 58
Which if we should deny, the most just gods 59
For every graff would send a caterpillar, **60** 60
And so afflict our province. Yet once more 61
Let me entreat to know at large the cause 62
Of your king's sorrow.

Hel. Sit, sir, I will recount it to you: 63
But, see, I am prevented.

Re-enter, from the barge, Lord, *with* MARINA,
and a young Lady.

Lys. O, here is 64

31
32
33
34
35

36
37
38
39
40
41
42
43

44
45
46
47
48   <u>Insert</u> 67-69: DS1
49   <u>X</u>: NM1, NM2
50   X: NM1, NM2
51   X: NM1, NM2
52   X: NM1, NM2

53

54   <u>bX</u>: NM1, N M2, TH1
55   <u>X</u>: NM1, NM2, TH1
56   same as 55
57   same as 55

58   same as 55; <u>bX</u>: TR2
59   same as 55, $\overline{\text{TR2}}$
60   same as 59
61   X: NM1, NM2; <u>aX</u>: TH1; <u>bX</u>: JG1
62   X: NM1, NM2, $\overline{\text{JG1}}$

63   X: NM1, NM2·

64   <u>aX</u>: NM1, NM2, JG1

The lady that I sent for. Welcome, fair one!   65
Is't not a goodly presence?

Hel.   She's a gallant lady.   66

Lys. She's such a one, that, were I well
    assured   67
Came of a gentle kind and noble stock,   68
I'ld wish no better choice, and think me rarely
    wed.   69
Fair one, all goodness that consists in bounty 70   70
Expect even here, where is a kingly patient: 71
If that thy prosperous and artificial feat   72
Can draw him but to answer thee in aught,   73
Thy sacred physic shall receive such pay   74
As thy desires can wish.

Mar.   Sir, I will use   75
My utmost skill in his recovery,   76
Provided   77
That none but I and my companion maid   78
Be suffer'd to come near him.

Lys.   Come, let us leave her;   79
And the gods make her prosperous!   80   80

                    [*Marina sings.*

Lys. Mark'd he your music?
Mar.   No, nor look'd on us   81
Lys. See, she will speak to him.   82
Mar. Hail, sir! my lord, lend ear.   83
Per. Hum, ha!   84
Mar. I am a maid,   85
My lord, that ne'er before invited eyes,   86
But have been gazed on like a comet: she speaks   87
My lord, that, may be, hath endured a grief   88
Might equal yours, if both were justly weigh'd.   89
Though wayward fortune did malign my state, as   90
My derivation was from ancestors   91
Who stood equivalent with mighty kings: 92
But time hath rooted out my parentage,   93
And to the world and awkward casualties   94
Bound me in servitude. [*Aside*] I will desist: 95
But there is something glows upon my cheek.   96
And whispers in mine ear 'Go not till he speak'   97

Per. My fortunes—parentage—good parent-
    age—   98
To equal mine!—was it not thus? what say ye!   99
Mar. I said, my lord, if you did know my
    parentage,   100
You would not do me violence.   101

```
65

66

67    MOVE 67-69 to follow 48: DS1
68

69
70
71
72    X: TH1
73
74

75
76    bX: TR1
77    X: TR1
78    aX: TR1

79
80    ADD 8: TR1, JG1; ADD 9 and song: TR2

81    X: TR1, TH1, JG1, EdB
82    X: TR1, TH1, EdB
83
84    X: EdB
85
86
87
88
89
90
91
92
93
94
95
96
97

98    X: TH1
99    X: TH1

100   X: TH1
101   X: TH1
```

Per. I do think so.   Pray you, turn your eyes
    upon me.   102
You are like something that— What country-
    woman?   103
Here of these shores?
Mar.   No, nor of any shores: 104
Yet I was mortally brought forth, and am   105
No other than I appear.   106
   Per. I am great with woe, and shall deliver
    weeping.   107
My dearest wife was like this maid, and such
    a one   108
My daughter might have been: my queen's
    square brows: 109
Her stature to an inch; as wand-like straight; so 110
As silver-voiced; her eyes as jewel-like   111
And cased as richly; in pace another Juno: 112
Who starves the ears she feeds, and makes them
    hungry,   113
The more she gives them speech.   Where do
    you live?   114
   Mar. Where I am but a stranger: from the
    deck   115
You may discern the place.
   Per.   Where were you bred   116
And how achieved you these endowments, which 117
You make more rich to owe?   118
   Mar. If I should tell my history, it will
    seem   119
Like lies disdain'd in the reporting.
   Per.   Prithee, speak: re 120
Falseness cannot come from thee; for thou
    look'st   121
Modest as Justice, and thou seem'st a palace 122
For the crown'd Truth to dwell in: I will believe
    thee,   123
And make my senses credit thy relation   124
To points that seem impossible; for thou look'st 125
Like one I loved indeed. What were thy friends 126
Didst thou not say, when I did push thee back— 127
Which was when I perceived thee—that thou
    camest   128
From good descending?
   Mar.   So indeed I did.   129
   Per. Report thy parentage. I think thou
    said'st   B   130

102 a̲X: TH1

103 b̲X: TH1

104 X: TH1
105 X: TH1
106 X: TH1

107

108

109
110
111
112 b̲X: TR1

112 X: TR1

114 a̲X: TR1

115

116 b̲X: TH1
117 X̅: TH1
118 X: TH1

119 X: TH1

120 X: TH1

121 X: TH1; b̲X: TR2
122 X: TH1, T̅R̅2

123 X: TH1, TR2
124 X: TH1, TR2
125 X: TH1, TR2
126 X: TH1; a̲X: TR2
127 X: TH1

128 X: TH1

129 X: TR1

130

Thou hadst been toss'd from wrong to injury, 131
And that thou thought'st thy griefs might equal
   mine, 132
If both were open'd.
  Mar.   Some such thing 133
I said, and said no more but what my thoughts 134
Did warrant me was likely.
  Per.   Tell thy story: 135
If thine consider'd prove the thousandth part 136
Of my endurance, thou art a man, and I 137
Have suffer'd like a girl: yet thou dost look 138
Like Patience gazing on kings' graves, and
   smiling 139
Extremity out of act. What were thy friends? 140 140
How lost thou them? Thy name, my most kind
   virgin? 141
Recount, I do beseech thee: come, sit by me. 142
  Mar. My name is Marina.
  Per.   O, I am mock'd, 143
And thou by some incensed god sent hither 144
To make the world to laugh at me.
  Mar.   Patience, good sir, 145
Or here I 'll cease.
  Per.   Nay, I 'll be patient. 146
Thou little know'st how thou dost startle me, 147
To call thyself Marina. 148
  Mar. The name 149
Was given me by one that had some power, 150 150
My father, and a king.
  Per.   How! a king's daughter? 151
And call'd Marina?
  Mar.   You said you would believe me; 152
But, not to be a troubler of your peace, 153
I will end here.
  Per.   But are you flesh and blood? 154
Have you a working pulse? and are no fairy? 155
Motion! Well; speak on. Where were you
   born? 156
And wherefore call'd Marina?
  Mar.   Call'd Marina 157
For I was born at sea.
  Per.   At sea! what mother? 158
  Mar. My mother was the daughter of a king; 159
Who died the minute I was born,   160 160
As my good nurse Lychorida hath oft 161
Deliver'd weeping.

131

132

133
134   b̲X: TH1

135   a̲X: TH1
136
137
138

139
140   b̲X: TH1

141   X: TH1
142   b̲X: JG1; ab̲X: TH1

143
144

145

146   X: TH1
147
148
149
150

151   b̲X: TH1; A̲D̲D̲ 1: TH1

152   X: TH1
153   X: TH1

154   a̲X: TH1
155   b̲X̲: TH1

156   a̲X: TH1

157   X: SP2

158   X: SP2
159   X: SP2
160
161   X: SP2

Per.   O, stop there a little!   162

[*Aside*] This is the rarest dream that e'er dull
   sleep   163
Did mock sad fools withal: this cannot be: 164
My daughter's buried. Well: where were you
   bred?   165
I'll hear you more, to the bottom of your story,   166
And never interrupt you.   167

   Mar. You scorn: believe me, 'twere best I
   did give o'er.   168

   Per. I will believe you by the syllable   169
Of what you shall deliver. Yet, give me leave: 170   170
How came you in these parts? where were you
   bred?   171

   Mar. The king my father did in Tarsus leave
   me: 172
Till cruel Cleon, with his wicked wife,   173
Did seek to murder me: and having woo'd   174
A villain to attempt it, who having drawn to do't,   175
A crew of pirates came and rescued me: 176
Brought me to Mytilene. But, good sir,   177
Whither will you have me? Why do you weep?
   It may be,   178
You think me an impostor: no, good faith;   179
I am the daughter to King Pericles,   180   180
If good King Pericles be.   181

   Per. Ho, Helicanus!   182

   Hel. Calls my lord?   183

   Per. Thou art a grave and noble counsellor,   184
Most wise in general: tell me, if thou canst,   185
What this maid is, or what is like to be,   186
That thus hath made me weep?   187

   Hel.   I know not; but   187
Here is the regent, sir, of Mytilene   188
Speaks nobly of her.   189

   Lys.   She would never tell   189
Her parentage; being demanded that,   190   190
She would sit still and weep.   191

   Per. O Helicanus, strike me, honour'd sir;   192
Give me a gash, put me to present pain: 193
Lest this great sea of joys rushing upon me   194
O'erbear the shores of my mortality,   195
And drown me with their sweetness. O, come
   hither,   196
Thou that beget'st him that did thee beget;   197
Thou that wast born at sea, buried at Tarsus,   198

162

163
164

165   b̲X: TH1
166   c̲X̲: TH1
167

168   a̲X: TH1
169
170   X: TH1

171

172
173
174
175   b̲X: TH1
176   c̲X̲: TH1
177

178   a̲X: TH1
179
180
181
182   X: TH1
183   X: TH1
184
185
186

187
188

189
190
191
192   a̲X: TH1
193
194
195

196
197
198

And found at sea again!   O Helicanus,   199
Down' on thy knees, thank the holy gods as
    loud   **200**   200
As thunder threatens us: this is Marina.   201
What was thy mother's name? tell me but that,   202
For truth can never be confirm'd enough,   203
Though doubts did ever sleep.
   Mar.   **First, sir, I pray,**   204
What is your title?   205
   Per.   I am Pericles of Tyre: but tell me now   206
My drown'd queen's name, as in the rest you
    said   207
Thou hast been godlike perfect,   208
†The heir of kingdoms and another like   209
To Pericles thy father.   **210**   210
   Mar.   Is it no more to be your daughter than   211
To say my mother's name was Thaisa?   212
Thaisa was my mother, who did end   213
The minute I began.   214
   Per.   Now, blessing on thee! rise; thou art
    my child.   215
Give me fresh garments.   Mine own, Helicanus: 216
She is not dead at Tarsus, as she should have
    been,   217
By savage Cleon: she shall tell thee all: 218
When thou shalt kneel, and justify in knowledge   219
She is thy very princess.   Who is this?   **220**   220
   Hel.   Sir, 'tis the governor of Mytilene,   221
Who, hearing of your melancholy state,   222
Did come to see you.
   Per.   I embrace you.   223
Give me my robes.   I am wild in my be-
    holding.   224
O heavens bless my girl! But, hark, what
    music?   225
Tell Helicanus, my Marina, tell him   226
O'er, point by point, for yet he seems to doubt,   227
How sure you are my daughter.   But, what
    music?   228
   Hel.   My lord, I hear none.   229
   Per.   None!   **230**   230
The music of the spheres!   List, my Marina.   231
   Lys.   It is not good to cross him; give him
    way.   232
   Per.   Rarest sounds!   Do ye not hear?
   Lys.   My lord, I hear. [*Music.*   233

199 b̲X: TH1

200
201
202 R̲: TR2
203

204
205
206

207
208
209 a̲X: JG1; A̲D̲D̲ 2: JG1
210
211
212
213 X: SP1
214 X: SP1

215 b̲X: TR1
216 a̲X: TR1, JG1; b̲X: TH1

217
218
219
220 M̲O̲V̲E̲ 220b-223 to follow 256: TR1
221
222 X: TH1

223 a̲X: TH1

224 a̲X: JG1

225
226
227

228
229
230
231

232 X: TH1

233

Per. Most heavenly music! 234
It nips me unto listening, and thick slumber 235
Hangs upon mine eyes: let me rest. [*Sleeps.* 236
Lys. A pillow for his head: 236
So, leave him all. Well, my companion friends, 238
If this but answer to my just belief, 239
I'll well remember you. 240 240
[*Exeunt all but Pericles.*

DIANA *appears to* PERICLES *as in a vision.*

Dia. My temple stands in Ephesus: hie thee
thither, 241
And do upon mine altar sacrifice. 242
There, when my maiden priests are met together, 243
Before the people all, 244
Reveal how thou at sea didst lose thy wife: 245
To mourn thy crosses, with thy daughter's, call 246
And give them repetition to the life. 247
Or perform my bidding, or thou livest in woe; 248
Do it, and happy; by my silver bow! 249
Awake, and tell thy dream. [*Disappears.* 250 250
Per. Celestial Dian, goddess argentine, 251
I will obey thee. Helicanus!

Re-enter HELICANUS, LYSIMACHUS, *and*
MARINA.

Hel. Sir? 252
Per. My purpose was for Tarsus, there to
strike 253
The inhospitable Cleon; but I am 254
For other service first: toward Ephesus 255
Turn our blown sails; eftsoons I'll tell thee why. 256
[*To Lysimachus*] Shall we refresh us, sir, upon
your shore, 257
And give you gold for such provision 258
As our intents will need? 259
Lys. Sir, 260 260
With all my heart: and, when you come ashore, 261
I have another suit. 262
Per. You shall prevail, 262
Were it to woo my daughter; for it seems 263
You have been noble towards her.
Lys. Sir, lend me your arm. 264
Per. Come, my Marina. [*Exeunt.* 265

234
235
236
237 X: NM2, JG1
238 X: NM1, NM2, TH1; bX: TR1, TR2, JG1
239 X: NM1, NM2, TH1, TR2, JG1
240 same as 239

241
242
243 X: TR2
244 X: TR2
245
246 X: TR1
247 X: TR1
248 X: TR1
249 bX: TR1, TH1
250
251

252 bX: TH1

253 X: TR1
254 X: TR1
255 X: TR1
256 Insert 220b-223: TR1

257
258
259
260
261

262
263 bX: TR1

264 X: TR1
265 ADD 1: JG1

SCENE II. *Enter* GOWER, *before the temple of* DIANA *at Ephesus.*

Gow. Now our sands are almost run: 266
More a little, and then dumb. 267
This, my last boon, give me, 268
For such kindness must relieve me, 269
That you aptly will suppose 270   270
What pageantry, what feats, what shows, 271
What minstrelsy, and pretty din, 272
The regent made in Mytilene 273
To greet the king. So he thrived, 274
That he is promised to be wived 275
To fair Marina; but in no wise 276
Till he had done his sacrifice, 277
As Dian bade: whereto being bound, 278
The interim, pray you, all confound. 279
In feather'd briefness sails are fill'd, 280   280
And wishes fall out as they're will'd. 281
At Ephesus, the temple see, 282
Our king and all his company. 283
That he can hither come so soon, 284
Is by your fancy's thankful doom.   [*Exit.* 285

SCENE III. *The temple of Diana at Ephesus.* THAISA *standing near the altar, as high priestess; a number of Virgins on each side* CERIMON *and other Inhabitants of Ephesus attending.*

Enter PERICLES, *with his train;* LYSIMACHUS, HELICANUS, MARINA, *and a* Lady.

Per. Hail, Dian! to perform thy just command, 1
I here confess myself the king of Tyre; 2
Who, frighted from my country, did wed 3
At Pentapolis the fair Thaisa. 4
At sea in childbed died she, but brought forth 5
A maid-child call'd Marina; who, O goddess, 6
Wears yet thy silver livery. She at Tarsus 7
Was nursed with Cleon; who at fourteen years 8
He sought to murder: but her better stars 9
Brought her to Mytilene; 'gainst whose shore 10
Riding, her fortunes brought the maid aboard us 11
Where, by her own most clear remembrance, she 12
Made known herself my daughter.

Scene 52

266
267
268 X: NM1, NM2
269 X: NM1, N M2
270
271
272
273
274
275
276
277
278 X: TR2; b̲X̲: NM1, NM2, EdB
279 X: NM1, N̄M̄2, TR2, EdB
280 X: TR2
281 X: TR2
282
283
284 X: NM1, NM2
285 X: NM1, NM2; A̲D̲D̲ 1: JG1

Scene 53

1
2
3
4
5
6 b̲X̲: TR1, TR2
7 X̄: TR2; a̲X̲: TR1
8 X: TR2; b̄X̄: TH1
9 a̲X̲: TH1, T̄R̄2
10 b̄X̄: TH1
11 X̄: TH1
12

Thai.   Voice and favor!   13
You are, you are—O royal Pericles!   [*Faint*   14
  Per. What means the nun? she dies. help
    gentlemen!   15
  Cer. Noble sir,   16
If you have told Diana's altar true,   17
This is your wife.
  Per.   Reverend appearer, no: 18
I threw her overboard with these very arms.   19
  Cer. Upon this coast, I warrant you.
  Per.   'Tis most certain.   20
  Cer. Look to the lady: O, she's but o'erjoy'd   21
Early in blustering morn this lady was   22
Thrown upon this shore. I oped the coffin,   23
Found there rich jewels; recover'd her, and
    placed her   24
Here in Diana's temple.
  Per.   May we see them?   25
  Cer. Great sir, they shall be brought you to
    my house,   26
Whither I invite you. Look, Thaisa is   27
Recovered.
  Thai. O, let me look!   28
If he be none of mine, my sanctity   29
Will to my sense bend no licentious ear,   30
But curb it, spite of seeing. O, my lord,   31
Are you not Pericles? Like him you spake,   32
Like him you are: did you not name a tempest,   33
A birth, and death?
  Per.   The voice of dead Thaisa!   34
  Thai. That Thaisa am I, supposed dead   35
And drown'd.   36
  Per. Immortal Dian!
  Thai.   Now I know you better.   37
When we with tears parted Pentapolis,   38
The king my father gave you such a ring.   39
    [*Shows a ring.*
  Per. This, this: no more, you gods! your
    present kindness   40
Makes my past miseries sports: you shall do well   41
That on the touching of her lips I may   42
Melt and no more be seen. O, come, be buried   43
A second time within these arms.
  Mar.   My heart   44
Leaps to be gone into my mother's bosom.   45
    [*Kneels to Thaisa*

13 b̲X̲: TR1, TH1
14 a̲X̲: TR1, TH1

15 b̲X̲: JG1
16
17

18 b̲X̲: TR1, TH1; A̲D̲D̲ 1: TH1
19 X̲: TR1, TH1, TR̅2̅

20 X: TR1, TH1; a̲X̲: TR2
21 X: DS1, TR1, T̅H̅1, JG1, EdB
22 X: TH1
23 X: TH1

24 X: TH1

25 X: TR1, TH1; b̲X̲: TR2, JG1; A̲D̲D̲ 1: JG1

26 X: TR1, TH1, TR2, JG1
27 X: TH1, JG1; a̲X̲: TH1, TR2

28 a̲X̲: TH1, JG1
29 X̲: SP1
30 X: SP1
31 a̲X̲: SP1
32
33

34
35
36

37 X: TH1, JG1; b̲X̲: TR1
38 X: TH1, JG1
39 X: TH1, JG1

40 a̲X̲ : TH1; b̲X̲: SP1, MTh
41 X̲: SP1, MT̅h̅
42 X: SP1, MTh
43 a̲X̲: SP1, MTh

44 b̲X̲: DS1
45 X̲: DS1

Per. Look, who kneels here! Flesh of thy
    flesh, Thaisa;   46
Thy burden at the sea, and call'd Marina   47
For she was yielded there.
Thai.   Blest, and mine own!   48
Hel. Hail, madam, and my queen!
Thai.   -   I know you not.   49
Per. You have heard me say, when I did fly
    from Tyre,   50   50
I left behind an ancient substitute: 51
Can you remember what I call'd the man?   52
I have named him oft.
Thai.   'Twas Helicanus then.   53
Per. Still confirmation: 54
Embrace him, dear Thaisa: this is he.   55
Now do I long to hear how you were found;   56
How possibly preserved: and who to thank,   57
Besides the gods, for this great miracle.   58
Thai. Lord Cerimon, my lord; this man,   59
Through whom the gods have shown their power;
    that can   60   60
From first to last resolve you.
Per.   Reverend sir,   61
The gods can have no mortal officer   62
More like a god than you. Will you deliver   63
How this dead queen re-lives?
Cer.   I will, my lord.   64
Beseech you, first go with me to my house,   65
Where shall be shown you all was found with her;   66
How she came placed here in the temple;   67
No needful thing omitted.   68
Per. Pure Dian, bless thee for thy vision! I   69
Will offer night-oblations to thee. Thaisa,   70   70
This prince, the fair-betrothed of your daughter,   71
Shall marry her at Pentapolis. And now,   72
This ornament   73
Makes me look dismal will I clip to form;   74

46
47 b<u>X</u>: MTh

48 X: MTh; <u>a</u>X: SP1; <u>ADD</u> 10: JG1

49 X: SP1, MTh, TH1, TR2, JG1

50 same as 49
51 same as 49
52 same as 49, TR1

53 same as 49; <u>a</u>X: TR1
54 same as 49, $\overline{\text{TR1}}$
55 X: SP1, MTh, DS1, TH1, TR2, JG1; b<u>X</u>: TR1
56
57
58
59

60

61
62 X: SP1, MTh
63 <u>a</u>X: SP1, MTh; b<u>X</u>: JG1

64 X: JG1
65 X: JG1
66 X: SP1, MTh, JG1
67 same as 66
68 same as 66
69 <u>MOVE</u> 69-70a to follow 89: JG1
70
71 X: JG1
72 X: JG1; b<u>X</u>: SP1, MTh, NM1, NM2, TR2
73 X: SP1, $\overline{\text{MTh}}$, NM1, NM2, TR2, JG1
74 same as 73

And what this fourteen years no razor touch'd, 75
To grace thy marriage-day, I'll beautify. 76
  Thai. Lord Cerimon hath letters of good
    credit, sir, 77
My father's dead. 78
  Per. Heavens make a star of him! Yet there,
    my queen, 79
We'll celebrate their nuptials, and ourselves 80 80
Will in that kingdom spend our following days: 81
Our son and daughter shall in Tyrus reign. 82
Lord Cerimon, we do our longing stay 83
To hear the rest untold: sir, lead's the way. 84
                       [Exeunt.

Enter GOWER.

  Gow. In Antiochus and his daughter you
    have heard 85
Of monstrous lust the due and just reward: 86
In Pericles, his queen and daughter, seen, 87
Although assail'd with fortune fierce and keen, 88
Virtue preserved from fell destruction's blast, 89
Led on by heaven, and crown'd with joy at last: 90
In Helicanus may you well descry 91 91
A figure of truth, of faith, of loyalty: 92
In reverend Cerimon there well appears 93
The worth that learned charity aye wears: 94
For wicked Cleon and his wife, when fame 95
Had spread their cursed deed, and honour'd
  name 96
Of Pericles, to rage the city turn, 97
That him and his they in his palace burn; 98
The gods for murder seemed so content 99a $
To punish them; although not done, but meant. 99b $
So, on your patience evermore attending, 100 100
New joy wait on you! Here our play has ending. 101
                       [Exit.

```
75   same as 73
76   same as 73

77   X: NM1, NM2, DS1, TR1, TH1, TR2
78   same as 77, less TR2

79   same as 78
80   X: TH1; bX: TR2
81   X: TR1, TH1
82   X: TR1, TH1; R: JG1
83
84   Insert 69b-70, add 2: JG1




85   X: SP2, HIM, MTh, NM1, NM2, DS1; ADD 1: TR1
86   same as 85; less ADD
87   X: SP2, HIM, MTh
88   same as 87
89   same as 87
90   same as 87
91   X: SP2, HIM, MTh, NM1, NM2, DS1, TR1
92   same as 91
93   same as 91
94
95   same as 91
     same as 91

96   same as 91
97   same as 91
98   same as 91
99a  same as 91
99b  same as 91
100  X: SP2, HIM, MTh
101  same as 100; ADD 12: TR1; ADD 2 and song: TR2
```

APPENDIX A - <u>ADDITIONAL ACKNOWLEDGEMENTS AND CORRECTIONS</u>

1 wish earnestly to thank the people who have supplied additional informations and service since my initial acknowledgements:

Mrs S. Btreknell, House Manager, Maddermarket Theatre, for the chronology 1953-1975

Meredith Dallas, Professor of English, Antioch College, for the chronology of the Antioch Shakespeare Festival

Frank Hilty, doctoral student at Northwestern University, for supplying the collation of Nugent Monck PBs which I had to skip in 1976

Arthur Lithgow, Amherst, Mass., who supplied a number of PBs of the Antioch Shakespeare Festival, and approved their deposit at the Folger Shakespeare Library.

Gail Shoup, Professor Of Theatre, California State University, Long Beach, and former Dean of the Pasadena Playhouse School of the Theatre, for the chronology of the Pasadena Playhouse

Ms Elizabeth A Swain, Special Collections Librarian, Olin Library, Wesleyan University, for the Two LeGallienne PBs

Gerald Kahn(<u>ETJ</u> 30-4, p 567) points out my misspelling of "Furnivall, Bowmer, Vanderhoff, Mander and Mithcinson, Zeffirelli, Philadelphia, poster, likelihood, <u>bestrafte</u>." Others have called my attention to errors in "Maddermarket," "Levi Fox,""Marian Horn"(now Mrs Pringle.) Dr Fox says that the library of the Birthplace Trust continues to be "The Shakespeare Center Library," though it is now housed in the Nuffield Library.

As I have collated I have realized that I have made errors in the collation, such as recording a one-line deviation in an otherwise traditional test, but I have made no attempt to conceal these divergencies, trusting that the reader will excuse an occasional error in the collation of nearly 2,000,000 lines. One source of error is the numbering of yhe Folger editions. While I have tried always to alter these to the Globe numbers, I fear that I have occasionally recorded a Folger line number. Lat in my collation I realized that I have taken "French edition" too literally, and that sometimes a PB is made in a Cumberland reprint. My failure to catch this more quickly is because the initial French editions were very close to Cumberland/

I soon stopped recording movement of a line when it was moved less than three lines.

My sub-title states that this is a collation of 5000 texts. My bibliographies actually record 5995 items(eliminating those that I list as "not seen.") This total does include some duplicates, so the 5000 remains a good approximation.

I next intend to do a "Statistical History of Acting Editions, as a supplement to the present work. I hope for publication about 1982

wph

APPENDIX B: Additional PBs, and Amplification of Collation of Some PBs and Acting Editions Previously Listed

Additions are scripts which reached me after the original collation of a play. Amplifications are scripts which I could not collate origin- ally, but which have been done in 1979

Plays are listed in alphabetical order. They carry the original Jaggard(J), Shattuck(S), or Shakespeare as Spoken(SS) numbers. Additions are given new SS numbers

AS YOU LIKE IT

S AY57   "Fanny Davenport"(Hand)
          Harvard U TC 3059/500
          PB in French(S); CUT: 11: 135b-138a, 140b-142, 148b-153a,
          159b-161, 178b-180, 249-251a; 27: 173-189; 32: 83-87, 134,
          138, 140, 142, 149-152, 160, 194b-196; 34: 59b-61a; 35: 74b-
          76a; 41: 75b-78, 153b-154a, 168-175a, 178-180; 43: 13-14a,
          23-24a, 86b-89a, 139b-142; 55: 114-121, 143-144; RESTORE:
          11: 222-224; 32: 186-188, 209-215; 54: 100-117; MOVE: 33:
          1-99 to follow 32: 92

S AY59   "Augustin Daly"(Gold) "presented by Ada Rehan"(Hand)
          NYPL TC *NCP 1889 (Ac 686456)
          PB in unidentified text(which puts 22 and 25 ahead of 21);
          CUT: 11: 101b-125, 145-153a; 21: 35b-61; 35: 3b-8, 13-16,
          46b, 85-91a, 109-112; 43: 5-75; 51: all; 52: 56b-59a, 77b-
          78a, 95-99; 54: 74-75, 134-136, 3 added, 114-116, 122-123,
          137-146

J AY75   Sydenham: Crystal Palace, 1874
          BPL S313/1874 (Ac 69789)
          Full text(which I had doubted previously)

CORIOLANUS

S CR21   "Charles Dillon," "Mercer Hampton Simpson, Birmingham Theatre
          Royal," "1831"(Hand)
          BPL S649.5
          PB in unidentified acting edition; HAND CUT: 21: 178-186
          (and other lines inserted here); 31: 177b-180a; probably
          cut 51; hand written 52 and 53(which may be restorations.)
          I believe this is a Roman Matron text

HAMLET

SS HA468 "John Barrymore, direction Arthur Hopkins, 1922"(Hand)
          NYPL TC *NCP 76-2597 (1976 acquisition)
          Enough deviations from Lark Taylor to require complete ver-
          balization; CUT 11: mov e 140b-145 and 127b-132 to follow
          49, 60-63, 70-127a, 133-140a, 146, 149b-157, 174b-175;
          12: 17-41, 46-50a, 81, 95-106a, 127; 13: 10b-18, 22-28, 36-
          44, 53-54, 73-74, 94-97, 103-109, 115b-123a,127b-131a; 14:
          21-38a, 58-62, 73, 74b-78a; 15: 27b-28a, 32-34a, 44-45 a,

47-57, 65-73, 77-78, 80N; <u>21</u>: 1-74a, 101, 103-106, 114-117a,
119b-120; <u>22</u>: 5b-7a, 8b-9, 11-14, 16, 21b-37, 40-43a, 51-55,
58-104, 122b, 125-128a, 129b-139, 157-159a, 164b-167a, 263-
276, 301, 333b-385, 388b-393a, 402-404, 428, 434-439, 440b-
441, 461b-467a, 470b-489, 505b-519, 533-535, 549b-551, 567b-
568a, 572-576a, 591-592, 601a; <u>31</u>: 33-37a, 54, 174-177a,
179-183a; <u>32</u>: 9b-16, 32b-50a, 65-76a, 122-128, 141b-158,
167-168, 173-178, 185-186, 192-193, 198-223, 256-265, move
280 to follow 274, 277, 282-296, 302-389, 405-410a, 411b-412,
416-417; <u>33</u>: 1-35, 46b-51a, 57-64a, 83-84a, 91-93, 96; <u>34</u>:
6, 32b-33, 45b-51a, 71b-76a, 78-81a, 85b-88a, 95-96a, 107-
108, 114, 117-124a,126-130, 142b-144a,147-155, 161-165a,
173b-175, 179, 181-199, 204b-205a; <u>41</u>, <u>42</u>, <u>43</u>, <u>44</u>: all; <u>45</u>:
11-13, 17-20, 33-35, 37-39, 41a, 79b-96a, 97, 103-105, 112b-
115a, 133b-135a, 138-139a, 144b-148, 161-163, 174, 190-194,
206-212a, 214-215; <u>46</u>: all; <u>47</u>: 3-24, 27-29a, 30b-35, 37,
40-41a, 51, 59, 63-64a, 67, 69b-130a, 149b-155a, 176b-185,
189b-190a; <u>51</u>: 26-42, 77-78, 83-126a, 150-153a, 176b-185,
224b-235,
238-239, 281b, 283-286a, 287b, 299, 321-322; <u>52</u>: 1-53a, 58b-
63a , 68b-70, 75-80a, 87b-90, 109-110a, 117-130, 154-171,
193-218, 241b-250, 255b-261, 270a, 279-281, 286-288, 298b,
312, 322, 328b-330a, 335b, 337b, 338b-339, 344b-349a, 355-
356, 372, 374, 378b-386, 391b-397a, 400-406a, 412-413; <u>ADD</u>:
2 after <u>32</u>: 404, 1 after <u>51</u>: 25

JULIUS CAESAR

SS JC313   Edinburgh: Oliver and Boyd, n d
Harvard U TC TS2348/389/2 (formerly 13485/47/12a*) in Gilbert
PB; <u>CUT</u>: <u>11</u>: 62-67, 71-76; <u>12</u>: 51, 171-175, 185-188; <u>13</u>:
59b-71, 126b-130, 137-139a, 152, 157-164; <u>21</u>: 147-149, 229-
233a, 243, 250-251, 306-334; <u>22</u>: 17, 19-24, 44b-48a, 128-
129; <u>23</u>: all; <u>24</u>: 33-38; <u>31</u>: 1-26, 84-95a, 105b-116, 120-127,
145b-146a, 207-210, 275-297; <u>32</u>: 1-10, 56b-57a, 262-264,
266b-276; <u>43</u>: 124-142a, 176-178, 231-232a, 239a, 242-255,
290-309; <u>51</u>: 22-26, 68b-93; <u>52</u>: 1N; <u>53</u>: 47-50, 67-71, 74b-
78a, 94, 102b-104, 112-119; <u>54</u>: 1-15, 16R; <u>55</u>: 2-4a, 8-14,
30-32, 33R, 41-57, 50-67; <u>ADD</u>: 4 after <u>43</u>: 289, 4 after<u>53</u>:
111, 4 after <u>55</u>: 40

SS JC415   "Nugent Monck, Maddermarket Th"(Hand. Productions 1926, 1937)
Nugent Monck Coll, Jack Hall
Memorial PB in Methuen, 2nd ed, 1937; <u>CUT</u>: <u>11</u>: 66-74a; <u>12</u>: 1-
11; <u>32</u>: 5-10, 266, 271-276; <u>33</u>: 1-4; <u>42</u>: 31-36; <u>43</u>: 124-
142a, 182-184; <u>51</u>: 68b-93a, 126b; <u>53</u>: 106b-110

KING HENRY 41

SS H41/306 'Augustin Daly.' NY: privately printed, 1896
BM *955/8
I inadvertently collated 42 again; but did collate 41 starting
with Glendower(31.) I believe Acts 1 and 2 were fairly full.

CUT: 31: 32-271; 33, 34: all; 41: 11-52; 42, 43, 44: all; 51:
15-21, 23=24, 27-28, 33-38, 44-46a, 49-55, 59-64, 69, 71,
77-103, 121-198; 52: 1-29, 32-34, 37-39, 46-82, 84-86, 89, 92,
98-101; 53: 7-15, 17-18, 33b-37a, 38b-58, 62; 54: 3-10, 14-24,
27, 30-34, 39b-41, 43, 45-46, 50-58, 69b-74, 83b-85a, 86-87a,
92b-98, 105-108, 115b-121a, 133-137a, 152b-160, 164-169; 55:
2-40; ADD: 1 after 53: 97

SS H41/430 "Arthur Lithgow, Antioch Shakespeare Festival, 1952"(Hand)
Folger acquisition 1978
CUT: 11: 5-33, 86b-91a; 12: 102b-109, 118-120a, 205-213, 228-
238; 13: 17-21, 37-41, 53-66, 102-112, 116-118a, 130b, 160-
186, 211, 272-276, 289-290; 21: all; 22: 37b-39a, 49b-50, 93b-
96a, 105b-108, 111b-114; 23: 4b-7a, 23b-25a, 31-37a, 59-67,
74, 81b-86, 101b-102; 24: 9b-15a, 18b-22a, 29b-30, 84b-85,
106-107, 112-113a, 131b-132a, 150b-153a, 163b-167a, 198b, 201b-
202, 280b-281a, 297b-298a, 367-368a, 390b-392a, 402b-405a,
449b-453a, 470b-473, 516b-520a, 592b-598a; 31: 27-35a, 36b-
43, 60-61, 74-86, 131-135, 158b-164, 169b-176, 180-189; 32:
32-38, 55-59, 97-121, 143-159, 175-179; 33: 42b-51, 187b-189a,
220b-226; 41: 2-6, 9, 31-41, 61-65, 69-72, 104-110, 112b-123,
124b-125; 42: 13b-53, 62b-63; 43: 41b-45a, 62-64, 70-71, 74-
77, 85-88; 44: 5; 51: 11b-14, 34-41a, 115-117; 52: 8-18, 56-
69, 75-79, 82-89, 91-97; 53: 33b-39a, 59b-61a; 54: 31b-35,
40b-43, 53-57, 88-101, 115b-123a, 160-162; 55: 2-10

KING HENRY 42

SS H42/421 "Arthur Lithgow, Antioch Shakespeare Festival, 1952"(Hand)
Folger 1978 acquisition
CUT: 11: 9-11, 70-75, 87b-90, 94-103, 112-149, 161-179, 186,
192-209; 12: 18b-33a, 40b-55a, 87b-90, 100b-101a, 120b-121;
13: 41b-62, 70-75, 87-100a; 21: 26b-34a, 54b-59, 86b-88a,121b-
143, 145-160a, 166-172a, 191; 22: 13b-30, 35, 191-196a, 245b-
261; 24: 13b-15, 278-304, 307-318, 386b-388, 392-394; 31: 86-
91, 102-106a; 32: 1-3a, 42b-43, 51-57, 81b-84a, 93b, 140b-142,
250-257, 276b-289a, 294b-296, 323b-358; 41: 32n-41a, 54-69,
131-139, 150-158, 227-229; 42: 47, 69a, 71b, 104b; 43: 54b-
59a, 81, 137-142; 44: 1-19, 62-67, 73b-78, 88-90, 93b-96. 100-
101, 113b, 121-128; 45: 16b-17, 139-155, 182-186, 189-202; 51:
72-87a, 91b-94a; 52: 22-42, 47-55, 118-140; 55: 1-4, 108,110;
EPILOG: all

S H42/16   "Douglas Seale, 1954-1955"(Hand)   OLD VIC
Old Vic Archives
PB in unidentified full text; CUT: PRO: all; 11: 1-11a, 13b-59,
97-104, 122-131a, 145b-149, 166-179, 192-200, 202; 12: 24b-28a,
32b-55, 70b-74a, 81b-104, 141-150, 157-162, 165, 173-181, 185-
196a, 213b-214a, 231, 253a, 259-260; 13: 4, 25-33, 36-55; 21:
17b-21, 28-35, 83b-90, 103b-104, 107-109, 118-131, 179; 22:
120b-127a, 163-164; 24: 21b, 52-57, 141b-142, 160-163, 167b-
172a, 288-290, 421b; 31: 94; 32: 133-134, 174-179a, 197b-198a,
294, 329b-330a, 337b-341a, 347b-350a, 352b-353; 41: 1-2, 18b-

24, 30b, 35-37, 64, 79-91, 154-158, 170-177, 199-200, 205-206,
225-228; 42: 11-16, 44b-51, 5-58, 122b, 123b; 43: 14b-15a, 20-
22a, 39b-40a, 54b-60; 44: 21-49, 81-82, 88-90, 94-96, 97b,
100-101, 104, 106a, 107b-108, 112, 121-128, 155; 45: 79b-80,
112-116, 128-129, 148-149, 159-165, 181, 191b-202, 207-213a,
217-218; 51: 71b-86a; 52: 1, 16-19, 51-53, 75-80, 83b-90, 104-
106, 135-319; 53: 11-12; 55: 1-4; ADD: 1 after 41: 78

KING HENRY 5

J H5/52b and S H5/40D 'Charles Calv ert'(1872 production.) Manchester;
    Ireland, n d
    Nuffield 50.10/vers 1872 (Ac 2016-2023)
    CUT: PRO: all; 11: all; 12: 18-22, 30-72, 94b-95, 111-114, 130-
    220, 230-233, 242-243, 266b-288, 309-310; 2PRO : 36-42; 21:
    34-38a, 41N, 55-56, 78-93, 122-133; 22: 1B, 23-24, 32-38,
    130b-140a, 158-165, 192-193 23: 1-3, 8b, 37-41; 24: 9-22, 45-
    64, 74-75a, 99-109, 133-143; 3 PRO: 28-32a, 35; 31: 31b-44a;
    32: 19-57, 74B, 92B, 120b-121; 33: 43; 34: 52-66; 35: 5-10,
    16-35, 73b-86a, 178-181; 37: 20-86a, 118-134; 4 PRO: 15-16,
    36-53; 41: 3b-12, 18-22, 105-116a, 141b-147a, 162b-184, 191b-
    196, 198b, 242-246, 291b-295, 298-301, 320-322; 42: 2ab, 3-6,
    8-13, 22-37, 43-44, 53-54; 43: 5a, 6, 11-16a, 23-33a, 49-51a,
    74B, 95-107, 129-131a; 44: 2-11, 53-61; 45: 12-16; 46: 12-
    13, 20-23, 36-38; 47: 7b-10a, 45b-55a, 57, 72, 77-86a, 90B,
    116B, 121B, 178-191; 48: 2B, 96-106, 116b-117a, 118-126;
    5 PRO: 1-6, 29-45; 51: 71-94; 52: 12-21, 25-31, 41-53, 126b-
    134, 140b-141, 150b-152a, 174b-177, 310b-330a, 338b-353a,
    396b-401a, 407b-446, move 487-496 to follow 502; ADD: 39 af-
    ter 5 PRO: 28; MOVE: 23: 4-36 and 31: 27-57 and 2 PRO: 1-35
    to follow 21: 121; 4 PRO 1-35 to follow 35: 177; 34: 1-51
    to follow 5 PRO: 28; 51: 1-70 to follow 52: 407a

J H5/66   "Rev Charles E Moberly.' London: Rivington, 'New Edition,' n d
    (Hand "1880")
    BPL S322/288 (Ac 107216)
    Full text

S H5/40C   "Anonymous"(A)
    Princeton U, Theatre Coll
    I could find no marked book that was not otherwise identified

SS H5/425 "Meredith Dallas, Antioch Shakespeare Festival, 1952"(Hand)
    Folger, 1978 acquisition
    CUT: 11: all; 12: 13-17, 24-32, 106-114, 150-154, 156-165, 169-
    173, 180-213a, 225b-233, 242-243, 264-279, 290-293; 2 PRO :
    9-40; 21: 7b-11, 25b-27a, 28b-29, 58a, 60b-63, 71-72, 78-84;
    22: 52-57a, 73b-76a, 84-85a, 96-142a, 167-173, 179-181a, 184-
    191; 24: 4-14a, 50-64, 120-126, 137b-139; 3 PRO: 3b, 7-27;
    31: 9-14; 32: 30b, 40-55a, 62b-68, 126b-127, 133b-135a, 147;
    33: 10-41, 51b-52, 54-56; 34: 40b-42, 58b-60a; 35: 18b-26,
    38-55a; 36: 33b-40, 48-51, 73-85, 94b-101, 127b-145, 149-171;
    37: 17b-18, 21b-26, 38-41, 55b-57, 60b-61a, 73N, 92-96, 98b-
    99a, 123-124, 153b-155a, 158-163; 4 PRO: 15-28, 35-51; 41:

> 3-12, 66-75, 149b-153, 167b-196, 209-214a, 255-301; 42: 12-13,
> 15, 19-38; 43: 8-10a, 11N, 12b-16a, 24-43, 51b-63, 83b-88a,
> 95-121a, 130-131a; 44: 5b; 45: 5b, 12-16; 46: 1-34; 47: 27b-
> 36a, 77-84a, 177a, 183b-187, 189; 48: 37b-40, 43-44, 86b-111a;
> 5 PRO : all; 51: 74-84a, 89-91; 52: 14-19a, 85, 93-94, 141b-
> 178, 194b-197, 215b-224, 226-235, 237b-253a, 363-372, 373b-
> 375a, 389-394

KING HENRY 6

SS H 61/410 "Arthur Lithgow, Antioch Shakespeare Festival, 1952"(Hand)
>   Folger 1978 acquisition
>   PB in unidentified full text: USES: H61: 24: 1-51, 86, 99, 104-
>   121, 128-134; 25: 1-2, 17-21, 33, 63-98, 101-103, 107-117,
>   122-129; 31: 41b-61, 65-68, 74-101, 141-177, 179-180, 184-188,
>   195-201; 41: 1-8, 78-122a, 123a, 133-134, 152-155; 53: 1-9,
>   13, 18, 20-24a, 30-32, 34-38, 77-145, 187a, 190-195; 54: 1-2,
>   7-10a, 14-21a, 34-41, 54-67, 113-175
>   H62:
>   11: 24-65a, 75-76, 104-106, 165-180, 205-208, 214-216,
>   218-256; 13: 1-7, 40-63, 104-125, 130-147a, 151-157, 165-173,
>   184-197, 200-225; 14: 1-23, 26-40, 42-44, 46-57, 83-84; 22: 1-
>   55, 63-64; 23: 28-29, 32-36, 39-63, 66-74a, 80-94, 100-108;
>   31: 1-17, 42-44, 58-71, 110-127, 133-135, 139-142, 168-172,
>   178-186, 235-236, 238-256, 266-284, 288-299, 302-304, 310-324,
>   327-354, 376, 380, 381R, 382-383; 51: 35-44, 54-61, 83-89,
>   117-123, 141-216; 52: 8-25, 31-33a, 40b-49a, 62-69, 72-90; 53:
>   1, 6-7a;
>   H63: 11: 1-21, 25-58, 89-94, 98-188, 206-218, 226-231a, 257-
>   265, 270-273; 12: 1-11, 48-61, 66-76; 13: 1-10, 12-15, 18-29,
>   34-39, 43-52; 14: 1-4, 15, 17, 22-23, 25-28, 54-55, 61-69, 73-
>   83, 89-90, 93-112, 137-140, 143-148, 156-159, 167-177, 179-180;
>   21: 1-3, 8-10, 25-28, 45-47, 79-84, 89-156, 201-209; 22: 1-6,
>   9-10, 34-39, 43-44, 54-55, 87-123, 126-145, 163-169, 175-177;
>   23: 23-34, 44-48a, 49; 24: 5, 12-13; 26: 34-35, 37-78, 85-86,
>   99-105, 110; 31: 66-71; 32: 1-78, 93-94, 99-101, 106-195; 33:
>   12-18, 21-29, 34-66, 113-122, 129-149, 151-152, 156-185, 221-
>   225, 227-232, 233b-244, 249-251a, 256, 259, 262-265; 41: 1-21,
>   24-46, 48-64, 96-108, 123-129, 134-135a, 143-149; 43: 49-54,
>   60-64; 46: 1-53, 56-76; 48: 1-18, 25-29; 51: 16-44, 47-57, 100-
>   113; 55: 1, 5-7, 9-16, 51-57, 61-76, 81-90; 56: 1-25, 29, 67-
>   93; 57: 1-8, 21-22, 26-41, 45-46

KING HENRY 8

S H8/75G2 "L R Sherwell"(Hand)
>   Princeton U, Th Coll, H8/5
>   Rolebook marked for Queen in French(J 88/35b--Lac); CUT: 11: 1-
>   128a; 14: 1-38a, 90b-108; 21: 56-136. "End of play" at end of
>   32, but Queen markings continue through 42

SS H 8/421 "Meredith Dallas, Antioch Shakespeare Festival, 1952"(Hand)
>   Folger 1978 acquisition

PB in unidentified full text: CUT: PRO: all; 11: 16b-28a, 42b-45a,
53b-57a, 108b-113, 131b-136a, 141b-148a, 172b-190a; 12: 5b-8,
60b-67a, 118b-124a, 126b-128, 177b-178a; 13: 58; 14: 3b-7a, 31b,
51b-52, 62-63; 21: 4b-5a, 24-27a, 66-78. 84-88a, 95-101, 107-
134, 138-139a, 156b-161a, 166b-167a; 22: 49-56a,, 72-73; 23:
18b-22a, 27-33a, 40b-44a, 47b-49a, 95-98a; 24: 80b-84a, 107b-
110, 146b-148a, 217b-219, 226-230a; 31: 1-14, 22-23a, 48b-50a,
52, 85-87a, 89-101a, 105-111, 134-137, 169b-171a, 177-181a; 32:
22b-23, 48b-52a, 55-56a, 97b-101a, 154b-156a, 160b-161a, 194a,
196a, 206b-208a, 259b-264a, 410-410a; 41: 37-117; 42: 3b-4, 39b-
44a, 57b-63, 73-77, 90-93, 97b-98a, 138b-158a, 165b-167a; 51: 1,
33b-37a, 74b-76a, 79-85, 93-96, 171b-176; 52: 1-3, 10b-13a; 53:
24b-31, 42-45a, 61b-69; 54: all; 55: 15b-17, 21b-33a, 37-55a,
56b-73; EPILOG: all

KING JOHN

S KJ65D4   "Jeanne MacPherson"(S)
            Princeton U, Th Coll, KJ8
            Not on shelf 1979

S KJ58   "B Iden Payne, 1940"(Hand)   STRATFORD-UPON-AVON
            Nuffield 71.21/1940/KJ (Ac 5345, f 91)
            CUT: 21: 1N, 73, 101-103, 186b-190a, 195-197, 213-215, 223-225,
            241-246a, 295-314, 374-376, 378, 434-440, 461-465, 575-580;
            31: 56, 121a, 122a, 167, 215-216, 234-235, 243-248, 270-278,
            281-287; 34: 30-31, 61b-68a, 127-130, 158, 166; 42: 20, 23-27,
            71-72a, 99-100; 43: 44b; 51: 71; 52: 29b-31, 43-53, 113-116,
            139-145; 54: 24-25, 28-29, 39; 57: 13b-20a

KING LEAR

S KL22   "J M Maddox, 1830s"(S) "Princess's Th," "1858"(Hand)
            London Museum 40/10/25/Shelf 96
            PB in Cumberland(J KL76--Cum); no cuts

KING RICHARD 2

SS R2/410 "John Barton, 1973-1974," "Original 1973 copy completely altered
            for restaged 1974 Stratford production. Later amended technical-
            ly for Aldwych production"(Hand)   STRATFORD-UPON-AVON
            Nuffield 71.21/1973-74 (Ac S2597)
            Divergence from 1971 production: CUT: 11: 54-55, 70, 91, 124b,
            125c, 129-131, 182-183; 13: 24-25, 76-77, 93, 102-103, 221-222;
            21: 34-37, 114-115, 151-152, 193-194, 197, 275; 22: 92-93, 95,
            23: 50; 32: 11, 40, 100-101, 130; 33: 3b-4a, 113b-114; 34: 66a,
            82-83; 41: 27-29, 139-141, 156b-157a, 158-161; 52: 57, 59, 85,
            93-94, 104a, 107; 53: 31, 44, 50, 57-58, 67, 84-86, 105-106,
            117-118; 55: 95; RESTORE: 11: 117, 119-120, 128R; 12: 51b-52;
            13: 14, 48-49, 146-147, 223-224, 229-230, 241-242, move 271 to
            follow 307; 21: 192, 255, 274; 23: 131-132; 31: 17-18; 32: 69-
            70; 33: 158-159; 34: 59-63a, 78: 41:"42-89a Text for this page
            in Aldwych edition p 127"," 115-120, 126, 130-131, 172-173; 52;
            9, 29; 55: 43, 68-71; DOES NOT ADD: 1 after 41: 156a, 7 after
            56: 4

J R3/66   NY: C M Baldwin, 1821, 'as performed Drury Lane and NY'
Folger PE2821/1821/Sh Col
CUT: 11: 28-162; 12: 1-20, 26-28, 30-32, 43-48, 50-52, 55-74, 78-
84, 87-100, 102-103, 105, 131-132, 138-139, 145b-150, 154-167,
173, 202-206, 239-250; 13, 14, 21, 23, 23, 24: all; 31: 7-16,
18-19, 22-60, 68-94, 99R, 100R, 107-126, 132-135, 149-150, 158-
200; 32, 33, 34, 35, 36: all; 37: 2R, 3R, 6-14, 43-44, 47R, 52-
55, 57R, 76-77, 80-94, 96-110, 118, 120-121, 123-130, 137-140,
144-150, 155-164, 174-202, 211-213, 219-222, 239, 241-242, 246-
247; 41: all; 42: 3-4, 12-16, 24-46, 49-126; 43: 1-23, 29-43,
51-57; 44: 1-8, 19-135, 137-153, 159, 166, 169, 172-176, 179-
195, 199-202, 206-209, 228-229, 285-411, 416-430, 436-437, 440-
463a, 470-540; 45: all; 51: 1-2, 5-29; 52: all; 53: 1-176, 280-
283, 292-320, 308-314, 320-341, 348-351; 54: 9-13; 55: all;
ADD: 245 to open, 25 after 11: 27, then 53 lines from H63:56,
104 more. In scene 12 add: 3 after 42, 6 after 54, 2 after 132,
1 after 153, 2 after 171, 4 after 179, 6 after 185, 9 after
192, 4 after 201, 2 after 238, 146 after 256. In scene 31 add:
3 after 6, 14 after 8, 15 after 106, 3 after 131, 1 after 148,
67 after 156, 61 after 157. In scene 37 add: 1 after 5, 6 after
51, 4 after 218, 2 after 238, 141 after 245; In scene 42 add:
3 after 2, 1 after 11, 20 after 23, 73 after 48. ADD 15 after
43: 28, 6 after 43: 50. In scene 44 add: 1 after 14, 8 after 18,
28 after 178, 2 after 298, 12 after 284, 10 after 415, 7 after
439, 46 after 469; ADD: 303 after 51: 4, 3 after 53: 291, 13
after 53: 347, 37 after 54: 8

J R3/96   'Cibber.' London: Lacy, n d(J "1857," BPL "1860")
BPL S344/31857 (Ac 69794)
see J R3/93

J R3/110b 'Edwin Booth.' NY: Hinton, n d (production 1872)
Folger PR2821/A36/Copy 1/Sh Col
It is a Booth-Hinton. I had thought it might be Booth-Winter

SS R3/439 "Arthur Lithgow, Antioch Shakespeare Festival, 1952"(Hand)
Folger 1978 acquisition
CUT: 11: 60-61, 66-70, 78-83, 139-141; 12: 46-48, 55-61, 75-77,
185-203, 213-219, 222; 13: 30N, 49-50, 56-61, 63-69, 90-102,
107-109, 111-112, 140-142, 170-173, 217-221, 245-246, 257-258,
270-295, 304-350, 311-312, 324-335; 14: 69-72, 78-83, 101-122,
164, 194-197, 221-225; 21: 1-25, 53-72, 91-94, 121-132, 135-
138; 22: 29-30, 34-70, 80-88, 91-95, 128-131; 23: all; 24: 5-
37a, 45N, 48N; 31: 48-54, 132-135, 174-180; 32: 15-18, 25-33,
85-96, 99-113, 118; 33: 16-17; 34: 8, 24-26, 45-47, 82-93; 35:
25-32, 50-51, 80-94; 36: all; 37: 130-140, 151-164, 177-194,
208-213; 41: 1-12; 42: 20, 31, 43-44, 54-57a, 63-66, 86-97;
43: 12-13, 51-55; 44: 3-8a, 59-113, 177-178, 187-193, 224-234,
242-252, 294-336, 369-373, 378-386, 391-396, 428-429,524-529;
45: 6-8, 19-20; 52: all; 53: 2-3, 22-28, 85b-86, 99-101, 104-
106, 139-166, 230-233, 307-311

LOVE'S LABOURS LOST

S LL6   "Augustin Daly PB"(S)
Folger PB LL3
PB in Daly edition 1874; <u>CUT</u>: <u>52</u>: 256-257

SS LL405   "Gerald Freedman, 1965"(Hand)   <u>SHAKESPEARE IN THE PARK</u>
NY Shakespeare Festival Archives
2 copies of PB in Penguin(Harbage), includes sketches and much
tech; also performance tapes; <u>CUT</u>: <u>12</u>: 57; <u>41</u>: 70b-81a, 83-
84a, 90-93, 96-97; <u>42</u>: 155b-156a; <u>43</u>: 34-37, 53b-54a, 67-71,
113-114; <u>51</u>: 75b-76a, 77b-79a; <u>52</u>: 44b-48, 70b-72, 251-255,
277b, 279-281, 327b-329a, 568-569; final song divided; <u>ADD</u>:
1 after <u>11</u>: 32

SS LL303   'Bernard Beckerman and Joseph Papp, editors.' NY: Macmillan,
n d (copyright 1968), 'Festival Shakespeare,' 'NY Shakespear
Festiv al Series'
Folger PR2822/1968/Sh Col
Long essay by Gerald Freedman. 'Complete text, so marked as to
indicate stage text' (by parentheses which were very hard to
locate) I tried to find all, but mistrust result. <u>CUT</u>: <u>31</u>:
20b-21a; <u>41</u>: 70b-80a, 82b-83a, 89-92; <u>42</u>: 143b-144a; <u>43</u>: 62-
66; <u>51</u>: 64b-65a, 66b-68a; <u>52</u>: 44b-46, 278b, 280-282, 328b-
330a, 412b, 782b

MACBETH

J MC2   London: Cademan, 1673
U Mich RBR PR2823/A2/D35/1673a; Cornmarket
I originally listed it as full text, but: <u>CUT</u>: <u>24</u>: 21b; <u>35</u>: 33-
35; <u>ADD</u>: 15 after <u>22</u>: 74, 16 after <u>23</u>: 152, 34 after <u>35</u>:33
(adds are witch scenes)

J MC78   'Oxberry Edition.' London: Proprietors by Simpkin, 1820
BM 11770/f10
<u>CUT</u>: <u>12</u>: 61b-89, 107-108; <u>13</u>: 98a; <u>21</u>: all; <u>22</u>: 47a, 58-60,
108b-112a, 121b-123a, 182; <u>26</u>: 8b-19, 33-34, 60-68; <u>27</u>: all;
<u>28</u>: 18-24, 28-53; <u>29</u>: all; <u>31</u>: 1-3a, 38-44a, 77-79; <u>32</u>: 7-
10a, 14b-21, 26-33a, 47b-73, 81-99, 169b-201a, 209-210, 213-
214, 216b-230a, 242-247, 259b-269a, 287-293; <u>34</u>: 11b-21, 60b-
80; <u>35</u>: 36b-51a, 78b-88a, 91-95; <u>41</u>: 41-52a, 122-126a; <u>51</u>:
1b-14a, 28N, 30b-33, 49-50, 53-88, 92-110a, 123-132a, 243-
247, 279b; <u>ADD</u>: 6 after <u>25</u>: 57, 12 after <u>26</u>: 25, 11 after
<u>31</u>: 142, 4 after <u>32</u>: 47a, 15 after <u>32</u>: 102, 12 after <u>35</u>: 90

S MC78   "John McCullough, Calif Th, San Francisco"(Hand)
Harvard U TC 13486/12/5
PB in Forrest-Torrey; <u>CUT</u>: <u>14</u>: 111b-114; <u>35</u>: all; <u>41</u>: 39-43
and added lines; <u>51</u>: 77-87

S MC91   "Henry Irving," "Ellen Terry"(Hand)
Smallhythe
Notes in Nassau 1888; <u>CUT</u>: <u>15</u>: 23b-26a; <u>34</u>: 35b-37a, 63b-66a

S MC15 OE2 "T H Evans," "Boston Museum"(Hand)
         Princeton U, Theatre Coll, Macbeth 10
         Rolebook in Philadelpia: Palmer, 1822; marked for Macbeth; no
         cuts

MEASURE FOR MEASURE

J MM 12   Manchester, Dean, Dean's Edition of British Th, 1800
          Folger PR2824/Copy 1/Sh Col
          Full text

S MM24   "Roland Giffin directing Frank McMullan's 1946 production,1947"
             (Hand)   STRATFORD-UPON-AVON
          Nuffield O S 71.21/1947/Sha/MEA (Ac 6381, f 87)
          Deviations from McMullan, 1946; RESTORE: 11: 67b; 21: 32b-33a;
             22: 132; 51: 19a; ADD 1 after 12: 21(I missed that in McMullan)

S MM28   "Michael Benthall, Australian Tour, 1955"(Hand)   OLD VIC
          Old Vic Archives
          PB in New Temple(S); CUT: 11: 3-9a, 12-13a, 33-42, 68b-73a; 12:
             1-44, 48-52, 71a, 82, 124-127, 130-132a, 137-140a, 162-169;
             13: 1-6, 20, 35-39a, 42-43a; 14: 45a, 51-55a; 21: 32b-33a,
             39-40, 167b-201, 262a-265a, 282-283, 290; 22: 1-4, 40b, 56,
             132; 23: 30-36a, 42b; 24: 46b-49, 122-123; 31: 46a, 52-53,
             136b, 154-160, 162b-168a, 171-172a, 175-184a, 189a, 195-197a,
             215-216a, 226b-227a, 228, 229b-230a, 236b-239a, 245-248, 270-
             272, 276b-277a; 32: 3b-4, 7b-11, 21-26, 37b-41, 47-55, 60a,
             62-64a, 69-71, 119, 127b-128, 150b-160, 163b-167a, 196-199,
             226b-297; 41: move 51-52 to follow 26, 50b, 59, 76; 42: 33-
             35a, 45-51, 52b-54, 59-62, 72b, 73b, 82b-90, 91b-94, 113-116,
             136-147, 171-179, 186-189a, 203-207a, 211-218a, 222b-224a;
             43: 4b-10a, 60b-61, 68b, 82-95, 106-107a, 117, 129b-131, 133-
             134a, 136b-150, 152a, 153b, move 141a and 142b-144 to follow
             153a, 157a, 158b; 45: 1, 5b-9a, 11b-12; 46: 12b, 15b; 51: 1-
             18, 22-23, 28b, 30b-32a, 48-50a, 51-68a, 72-95, 98b-99, 110b-
             112a, 114, 116b-123, 126a, 131-133, 137-143, 151-158, 162b-
             167a, 176a, 177b-183, 186b-188, 212, 218b-222a, 224b, 227-
             229, 232, 236b-285, 286b, 287b-288, 302a, 303, 313ab, 314-
             315a, 321b-324, 329-355, 365-367, 369b-371a, 379b-411, 421-
             430a, 443, 447, 459b-478, 483-487a, 497-503, 510b-511a, 518b-
             519, 521b-523, 525-527, 529, 538-540a, move 486b-492a to fol-
             low 537; ADD: 2 after 42: 44, 7 after 51: 537; MOVE: 12: 86-
             115, 45-47, 51-70, 71b-81, 86-123, 128-129, 132b-136, 140b-
             161 to follow 13: 59; 32: 1-200 to follow 23: 42a; 43: 1-21
             to follow 41: 75

MERCHANT OF VENICE

S MV132D5 "Anonymous"(S)
          Folger PB MV31
          PB in Booth-Hinton(J MV95--EBH); CUT: 12: 21-22a

S MV91   "Sothern and Marlowe"(S) "Francis T S Powell"(Hand)
            Folger PB MV43
            Duplicate of Sothern and Marlowe(S MV93--SM2)

SS MV445   "Arthur Lithgow, Antioch Shakespeare Festival, 1954"(Hand)
            Folger 1978 acquisition
            CUT: 12: 82-89, 116-118a; 13: 82-84. 98a, 118-120, 171; 25: 22-
              27; 31: 77-79; 32: 44-60, 92-96, 98b-99a, 117b-121a, 123a,
              124b-126a, 176, 317-326; 33: all; 34: 11b-22; 41: 49-52a, 56-
              58, 77, 147b, 454b; 42: 1-4, 5b, 10b-11, 15-19; 51: 26N, 28N,
              51N, 203-206, 278-279a

MERRY WIVES OF WINDSOR

S MW89E5   "Marcus Moriarty, 1874"(S)
            Folger PB MW28
            PB in French: CUT: 55: 238, 241-243

SS MW413   "David Margulis, 1974"(Hand)   SHAKESPEARE IN THE PARK
            NY Shakespeare Festival Archives
            PB in xeroxed unidentified text; CUT: 11: 12b-13, 16b-30a, 121-
              122a, 184b, 293-299; 13: 50b-51a, 59b-61a, 62b; 21: 52-53,
              122b-124, 126b-127a; 33: 69b-70a, 255-260; 42: 109R, 185b-
              186a; 45: 64-94, 103b-104a; 46: 5b; 55: 65-77, 120, 134a,
              146b, 159-167, 169b-175, 246-248; ADD: 4 after 11: 292
                2nd book: ADDITIONAL CUTS: 13: 54-56; 22: 110b-113a; 55:
              145b-152a; RESTORE: 21: 46b-48; 33: 159b-161a, 258-260; 55:
              147-149

MIDSUMMER NIGHT'S DREAM

S MD15aSup "Charles Kean"(Gold) "T W Edwards"(Hand)
            Harvard U TC TS 2429/120
            Memorial PB in Kean(J MD59--CKC); no cuts. Includes colored
              sketches of scenes and panorama

S MD36   "Henry Jewitt, Boston Opera House, 1915"(S)
            Folger PB MD12
            Typed script; CUT: 11: 47-51, 59-61, 83-90, 95-98, 101-105, 120-
              127, 172-175, 188-191, 214-219, 230-233; 21: 64b-68a, 77-80.
              90-117, 119, 124-134, 189-211, 215-226, 236-242, move 249-250
              and 253-254 to follow 268, 251-252, 255-256; 22: 92-99, 117-
              122, 126-130, 137-142; 31: 25-27; 32: 27-30, 50-62, 69-73, 84-
              87, 139b-143a, 147-154, 177-180, 193-194, 198-201a, 227-242,
              300b-303a, 307-314, 333b-335a; 41: move 29-31 to follow 40a,
              move 204-224 to follow 106, 151-154, 160-163, 175b-180, 183-
              188, 191-203; 51: 1-28, 33-38, 60-70, 93-105, 199-202, 360b-
              361, 368b-369, 408-429, 434-445

SS MD406   "Joel Friedman, 1961"(Hand)   SHAKESPEARE IN THE PARK
            NY Shakespeare Festival Archives
            PB and typed director's notes in unidentified full text; CUT:
              11: 48-51, 74-78, 120, 122b-126, 135-141, 173-174, 196-201,

232-233, 236-241; 12: 80, 92b-100, 114b; 21: 34b-39, 47-50, 93-
102, 103R, 107b-11$\overline{1}$a, 232-234; 22: 20-24, $\overline{46}$, 49-50, 58-59, 94-
97, 117-122, 137-142; 31: 24-27, 137-139; 32: 52b-55, 126-127,
129, 131-133, 177-180, $\overline{1}$98-201a, 203b, 205, 207-208a, 211-214,
218-219, 311-313, 317R, 372-373, 382b-385, 392-393, 463a; 41:
14-17a, 21b, 54-59, 124a, 164-167, 175b-178; 51: 1-31, 35, $\overline{38}$-
41, 46b-55, 62-70, 76-81a, 9-105, 108-125, 13$\overline{4}$-155, 200-211,
213-218a, 232-234a, 242-243, 246-250, 312-314, 316, 355-358a,
359, 361-364, 365b, 382-389

SS MD407   "Peter Hall, 1962," "Revival of 1959"(Hand)   STRATFORD-UPON-AVON
Nuffield O S 71.21/1962/Stratford/MID (Ac 10,$\overline{5}$40)
CUT: 11: 34b-38a, 204-207, 236-239; 21: 230-234; 31: 137-139; 32;
  25-$\overline{30}$, 52b-55, 90-93, 141-142, 179-$\overline{1}$80, 234, 24$\overline{8}$-250, 257b; $\overline{41}$:
162-167; 51: 23-27, 232-242a, 246-247, 250, 265-266a, 275,
312-315, $\overline{3}$22-323a, 324-326, 328

MUCH ADO ABOUT NOTHING

J MA12   'Newly adapted with alterations by J Hatton, Comedian.' Edinburgh:
for Williamson, 1774. "Charles Lefrange"(Hand)
Folger PR2828/1774/Sh Col
Many slight revisions, cuts and adds. Only major cut I noted was
  Scene 52: all cut. Not collated

S MA34   "Kate Terry"(Hand)
Smallhythe
Rolebook in Chapman (arranged for Princess's Th, 1858); many
  notes; CUT: 21: 334-338; 23: 103-105; 32: 98-103; 41: 146-147,
195-202

OTHELLO

S OT88   "Ellen Terry, "My part, Desdemona, Ellen Terry, Ilkley and Aug-
ust 2, ?, 1898"(Hand)
Smallhythe
Rolebook in Dent(1897); notes of business; CUT: 21: 113, 130-148,
  181, 183; 22: all; 31: all; 32: all; 33: $\overline{63}$b-6$\overline{7}$a, 88-89; 34: 1-
22, 110b-12$\overline{2}$a, 141-$\overline{1}$42, 143b-$\overline{1}$54, 169-$\overline{2}$14; 42: 65, 71-76a, $\overline{8}$2b,
83-85, 86B, 128a, 141b-164; 43: 48, 51, 55-$\overline{5}$7, 58n-60a, 66-83,
85-104; 52: 45-46a, 68b-70, $\overline{1}$88-19a, 205-209, 250-271, 305-329

SS OT317   "Ellen Terry,"(Hand)
Smallhythe
Rolebook in Dent; CUT: 11: 43-57, 69-73, 86b-92a, 108n-114, 117b-
  118, 121-130, 14$\overline{1}$b, 154-157a; 12: 40-44, 64-76; 13: 1-12,16-32,
44-46, 96b-103a, 107-110a, 140-$\overline{1}$41, 143-145a, 17$\overline{1}$, 191, 195-
220, 223b-226a, 262-275, 292, 323b-340a, 342b-343a, 346a. 352b-
361a, 373b-378; 2$\overline{1}$: 1-42, 56-57a, 69-70, 76-82, 84, 94-95a, 113,
125-127, 130-148, 155-156, 175b-179a, 198-199, 216b-219a, 229b-
238, 242-249, 264-269, 284-288, 291-293; 22: 24; 23: 1-11, 13b-
14a, 16b-17, 19-20, 28-29a, 129-130, 135-13$\overline{6}$a, 163$\overline{b}$-164, 166-
171,, 180-182, 199, 206-207a, 210b-217, 250-252, 255-258, 260,
272-278, 281-292, 292b-294, 301-303a, 320b-323a, 328b-331, 345b-

256a, 377, 382-383, 386-387; 31, 32: all; 33: 16, 24-25, 63-
67a, 88-89, 138b-141, 180b-183a, 232-233, 273b-278a, 345-347a,
397-408, 422-425; 34: 1-22, 37, 104-106a, 110b-122a, 125-129a,
140a, 141-154, 179-214; 41: 276-283a, 290-291a; 42: 28, 65-
69, 71-72a, 73-76, 81B, 82B, 83-88a, 93, 108-109, 137-138,
144a, 161b-164, 165b, 240b-241a, 249b-250; 43: 33b-34a, 51,
58b-60a, 67b-83, 85-184; 51: 1-5, 11-12a, 14b-22a, 28-36, 38-
40, 42-52, 58b-62, 73-87, 91-125; 52: 24, 37b-38a, 41-46a,
69b-71a, 77B, 79B, 93, 103b-105a, 136, 146b-149, 151-153a, 188-
193, 206b-209, 219-224, 229b-231a, 233-234a, 236-239a, 243a,
246b-248, 288a, 305, 307-318, 324-329, 357, 360-371

S OT93   "Oscar Asche-Lily Brayton; Kennington and Tour"(Hand)
         Nuffield 72.925/AS (Ac 5485, f 92)
         PB in unidentified full text; CUT: 11: 21, 24b-26a, 28-31, 35-
         38a, 44b-55a, 69-74, 75b-77, 87-89a, 109b-114, 117b-118, 130-
         134, 137-139a, 170a; 12: 40-45, 48-53, 72-76; 13: 6-7a, 13-46,
         63, 101-103a, 107-109, 142b-145, 199-219, 223b-226a, 262-275,
         292, 323b-344a, 354-355, 356b-359a, 377-378a; 21: 1-65a, 69-
         70, 76-82a, 94-95a, 113, 116, 130-148, 175b-179a, 198-199,
         204b, 215, 216b-219a, 229b-240a, 241b-249a, 250b-252a, 257b-
         270a, 284b-288; 22: all; 23: 1-11, 14c, 16b-27, 28c, 57-61a,
         100, 126-130, 135, 141-142, 163b-164, 166-168, 175b-176a, 250-
         252, 257-258, 273b-276a, 292b-294, 301-303a, 320b-323a, 328b-
         334, 345b-354a, 377-378, 381-384; 31, 32: all; 33: 16, 64-67a,
         78, 138b-141, 180b-183a, 184c, 273b-277a, 327-329a, 346b,
         375-377, 398b-405a, 422b-425; 34: 1-22, 81-82, 103-131, 132b-
         133, 141-142, 145b-154, 165-201; 41: 1-75a, 77-82a, 95-96a,
         97b-98, 114-115a, 127-135, 137b-140, 143-144a, 160c, 187B,
         192b-194a, 195b-198a, 200-201, 211-215 (page missing contain-
         ing lines 250-289) , 291b-292; 42: 73-76, 83-85, 86B, 87-88,
         89B, 144a, 161b-164, 169-170, 245b-246a; 43: 1-10, 16, 34a,
         53a, 55-57, 75b-77a, 80-106; 52: 24, 102b-103a, 104, 141,
         150-152, 171, 186, 188-193, 204-209, 221-224, 229b-231a, 233-
         234a, 236-239a, 241a, 243a, 246b-248, 252-271, 288a, 304,
         308-318, 335b-337a; 357, 360; ADD: 1 after 42: 245a; MOVE:
         51: 1-12a and 22b-129 to follow 42: 245a

SS OT425 Jan Hus Hall (with E arle Hyman), 1953
         NYPL TC *NCP 751044
         CUT: 11: 13-15, 21, 24b-27a, 29b-31, 34-40a, 42-57, 69b-71a,
         74-77, 86b-92a, 98b-101, 102b-103, 109b-114, 120, 121b-138a,
         141b-142, 148b-154a, 167b-177a, 181-184; 12: 40-44a, 48-53,
         64-79; 13: 9-46, 99-103a, 107-109, 140-145a, 155b-158a, 173-
         175a, 195b-198a, 199-219, 223b-226a, 245-248, 262-266, 270-
         271, 292, 307-311, 324b-333, 346, 352b-361, 369-378a; 21: 10-
         42, 69-70, 76-82a, 94-95a, 127-128a, 130-148, 175b-179a, 189-
         192, 229b-253, 270c, 284b-288; 22: all; 23: 42b-44, 48, 53b-
         61a, 63b-64, 85-87, 96-99, 109b-110a, 124-125, 133b-142, 163b-
         164, 257-258, 267b-270a, 273b-276a, 280b-282, 292b-303a, 309b-
         312, 320b-323a, 328b-331, 345b-354a, 361-364, 382-383; 31, 32:
         all; 33: 136b-141, 180-183a, 186, 234-238a, 273b-277, 319a,
         326-329a, 339-344, 361-363a, 371, 388b-390a, 398b-400a, 401a,
         402-405, 422b-426a; 34: 1-22, 31b-34, 104-106a, 110b-122a,

126-129a, 134-137, 145b-147, 150b-154, 174-175, 180a, 189b-
190a, 192, 201; 41: 7-8, 20b-22a, 24-29a, 47-48a, 54-56a, 62-
65, 66b-75a, 76, 80, 83-84, 94-104a, 110, 114-117, 121, 125-
130, 134-152, 164-165, 192b-215, 277b-279a, 280-283a, 285b-289;
42: 36-37, 74-80, 83-85, 95, 110-171, 241a, 246, 249-250; 43:
1-17, 70-83, 88b-94a; 51: 3, 11-22, 28, 29b-44, 46-52, 58b-59,
73, 78-88a, 91-110, 116-125; 52: 21-22, 34b-39, 41-47, 52-66a,
68b-71a, 74-75, 98-101a, 107-111, 126, 147b-152a, 174-175,
186-193, 198b-209, 218-224, 227-231a, 233-234a, 236-240, 246b-
265, 291b-292, 305-317, 324-329, 335b-337a, 357b, 360-371; ADD:
1 after 33: 273a

SS OT424   "Arthur Lithgow, Antioch Shakespeare Festival, 1954"(Hand)
           Folger 1978 acquisition
           CUT: 11: 11, 13-14, 27-36a, 126-130a, 146-157; 12: 40b-44a; 13:
           13-14; 21: 76-77a, 80-81, 93b, 170b-172a, 174b-178, 189-192,
           198-199; 23: 180-184a, 186-187, 211-217a, 221-224a, 232b-236a.
           31: 1-25a, 28b-32; 33: 145-151, 397-400a; 34: 1-22, 115-122a,
           134b-137; 41: 7-8, 20b-22a, 25b-28, 88a, 95-98, 110, 115, 116b-
           117, 121, 125, 130, 135, 141-142, 145-147, 165; 42: 30, 36-37,
           74-80; 51: 28-37, 46, 104a; 52: 98-101a, 104-105a, 148b-149a,
           259b-265, 313b

SS OT431   Unidentified PB; SS conjecture:"Gladys Vaughn, 1964"(but could
           be Stuart Vaughn, 1958(SS OT438)   SHAKESPEARE IN THE PARK
           NY Shakespeare Festival Archives
           PB in unidentified full text: CUT: 11: 75b, 76c, 113b-114, 124,
           125b, 130b-133, 134b, 154b-158a, 165b-166a, 177a; 12: 57b, 72-
           76; 13: 212-215, 232b-234a; 21: 7, 13-15, 37, 39-40a, 41-42,
           50-51a, 63-65a, 69-71a, 79-81, 106-108, 126b-128a, 144b-145a,
           146b-147, 150-151, 154-155, 239b-240a, 242-248a, 286b-288,
           312b-313a; 22: 2b-4a, 7c, 8b-9a, 12b-13; 23: 58-59, 79b-81,
           129-130, 135-136a, 207b-213a, 233b-236a, 237a, 275b-276a,320b-
           322a, 382-383; 34: 31b, 70-72; 41: 26-28a, 64-66a, 67-75a,
           88a, 97-100a, 102-104a, 114b-115, 119b, 123, 127, 132b, 136-
           137, 282-283a, 289b-291a; 51: 35-36, 90b, 108; 52: 103R, 137-
           139a, 306-317, 323-328, 360-361a

ROMEO AND JULIET

J RJ26   'Garrick.' London: Booksellers, n d (J "1758, n p", Folger "Garrick,
           n d) 'with alterations and an additional scene by D Garrick'
           Folger PR2831/A155/Sh Col
           CUT: PROLOG: all; 11: 1-6, 11-37a, 41-43, 83, 87, 122b, 125N, 160-
           166, 168-174, 191-204, 206-209, 214-230, 234-237, 244; 12: 15,
           18, 23b-33, 38-106; 13: 12R (and many subsequent use of numbers),
           49-57, 79-95, 106-107; 14: 50b-52, 59-94, 101-103, 108-114; 15:
           1-15, 20, 27-28, 43R, 46R, 54R, 55, 74-76, 79-87, 88b, 89b, 97-
           98, 100-101, 105-108, 109R, 110-112, 128-129, 142-143; 2 PROL:
           all; 21: 32-38; 22: 7-11, 53b, 57, 75-78, 108, 157-158; 23: 3-4,
           9-14, 41-47, 53-54, 56, 66-84, 87-88; 24: 10-12, 18, 56-107,
           113b-114, 117-124a, 126-128a, 138b-146, 152a, 180b-181, 206-210,
           219b-228; 25: 16-17, 22-24, 27, 29-34, 40b-46a; 26: 14b-15; 31:

13b-15, 27, 61-62, 78b, 124-125, 141b-145, 151; 32: 34b-36a,
39, 48-51, 62, 66-68. 73-79, 83-84a, 87-89, 132-138; 33: 15-
20, 30b-34, 37-39, 41-43, 46-50, 59, 61-62, 85b-92, 94, 98,
117-134, 136-145, 166-168; 34: 6-7. 10-11; 35: 29-34, 41-42,
66, 72-74, 76-105, 117-118, 122b-124, 127-129, 131-137a,148,
150-151, 157-158, 196-197, 207-210, 213-214a,. 220-227; 41:
24-36, 47-49; 42: 1-10; 44: 11-20; 45: 16a, 24, 30-32, 49-
84, 96-148; 51: 23, 63-65; 53: 13-17, 43-44, 49-53, 60b-63,
66-67, 76-81a, 84-91a, 98-101a, 102b-109a, 112b-115, 123-139,
155-156a, 162, 167, 172-187, 198-205, 219-220, 224-227, 229-
269, 271-290, 293-295, 306-310; ADD: 10 after 11: 159, 5 after 11: 214, 24 after 11: 244, 5 after 12: 38, 7 after 14:
107, 1 after 25: 47, 7 after 23: 45, 1 after 34: 18, 1 after
35: 59, 1 after 45: 29, 6 after 45: 48, 5 after 53: 12, 64
after 53: 112a, 15 after 53: 122, 5 after 53: 228, 6 after
53: 305; MOVE: 11: 166-244 to follow 12: 38; 14: 49b-114 to
follow 12: 38

J JR54   'Adapted by David Garrick, revised by J P Kemble.' London:
          Longman, n d ("1800" hand)
          BPL S345/328 (Ac 107933)
          CUT: PRO: all; 11: 3-6, 11-38, 41-42, 80, 82a, 83-84a, 86b-87,
          90-92, 99-102, 109, 119, 122b, 123N, 125N, 155-165, 168, 172-
          174, 182-183, 186-187, 188R, 189R, 191-204, 206-209, 214-230,
          234-236, 242-244; 12: 15, 24-89, 95, 101, 103b-106; 13: 2B,
          4B,, 12R, 13R, 29b-58a, 80-96, 105b-106; 14: 1-49a, 51-52,
          89-95a, 101-103, 109b-114; 15: 1-17, 27-28, 31-42, 43R, 47R,
          49-51, 54-55, 57, 74-76, 79, 81-88, 89b, 90b, 97-98, 100-101,
          106-112, 120, 128-129, 142-143; 2 PRO: all; 21: 13-16, 20,
          23b-27a, 31-38; 22: 7-11, 15-20, 29R, 30, 39-42, 51R, 53b, 56,
          75-78, 108, 132, 156-157, 180; 23: 3-4, 9-14, 41-47, 53-54,
          56, 58R, 60-61a, 65b-84, 87-88, 89R; 24: 10-12, 19, 29B, 32B,
          35b-37, 48R, 49R, 56-107, 113b-114, 117-124a, 126-128a, 131-
          132, 138R, 139-146, 152a. 170B, 180b-181, 205-210, 219b-227;
          25: 16-17, 18B, 19b-20, 22-24, 27, 29-34, 39b-45a, 73, 77-78;
          26:14b-15, 23, 35b; 31: 4, 13b-15, 22b-26a, 37, 61-62, 72, 78b,
          82-83a, 91-92, 97a, move 101b-102a to follow 113, 118, 124-125,
          133, 134R, 141b-145, 152R, 157b, 183-184, 189-191a, 192R; 32:
          8-16, 20, 27b-28a, 34b-36a, 42, 48-51, 53a, 55b-56a, 62, 66-68,
          71B, 73-79, 83-84a, 87-89, 100-101, 114b-122, 124b-126, 132-
          137, 140; 33: 15-20, 30b-34, 38-39, 41-50, 53, 59, 61-62, 72-
          74a, 85b-92, 94, 96b, 98, 104b-105a, 112-113, 118-134, 136-
          145, 157, 166-168, 175; 34: 6-8, 10-11, 15-17, 18n-19a, 20b-22,
          33b-35; 35: 21R, 23, 29-34, 41-42, 66, 72-74, 76-104, 108-112,
          117-118, 122b-124, 127-129, 131b-138a, 148, 150-153a, 157-158,
          165a, 166B, 169B, 173b-174a, 177B, 178R, 179R, 182-183, 189b-
          190, 192b, 196-197, 207-210, 123-214a, 220-227, 235a; 41: 13-
          14, 21b, 24-36, 41B, 42R, 43, 48-49, 54R, 55B, 63b-67, 75-76,
          79R, 80R, 89b-91, 96b-97, 102-103, 118; 42: 1-10, 28, 29b-30,
          31B, 40, 42b-44a; 43: 14B, 22R, 35, 45-48, 56b-57a; 44: 11-20,
          26b-27; 45: 6, 18b, 24, 30R, 31-32, 38R, 39-40, 43, 49, 65-66a,
          68-79a, 81-93, 96-148; 51: 7, 23, 27R, 33b, 51, 54, 63-65; 53:
          13-17, 20b, 22c, 25R, 49-53, 60b-63, 67, 71, 76-81, 84, 85b-91a,
          98-101a, 102b-109a, 112b-115, 119b, move 112b-114 to follow 119a,

123-139, 142-150, 152, 155-156a, 161b-162, 167a, 172b-187, 198-
207, 219-220, 223b-227a, 229-266, 271-310; ADD: 7 after 11: 152,
5 after 11: 213, 8 after 11: 241; 5 after 12: 23, 6 after 12:
103a, 6 after 14: 100, 1 after 15: 53. 1 after 23: 40, 8 after
23:65a, 4 after 23: 86, 1 after 32: 69, 3 after 33: 4θ, 3 after
33: 85a, 1 after 34: 20a, 1 after 35: 36, 3 after 35: 59, 1 af-
ter41: 89a, 3 after 43: 58, 1 after 45: 64, 1 after 45: 80, 21
line di rge after 45: 95, 4 after 53: 12, 61 after 53: 119a, 14
after 53: 141, 2 after 53: 197, 2 after 53: 228, 6 after 53:
270; MOVE 12: 1-23 to follow 11: 152; 14: 1-109a to follow 12:
103a

J RJ55   London: J Barker, Dramatic Repository, n d (J "1803")
Folger Bd in PR1241/n6/Cage/vol 2
Near duplicate of Dodd(J RJ26), but includes: CUT 12: 34b-37; ADD:
3 after 43: 58

SS RJ312   'Altered by Garrick.' London: Lowndes, 1816
Folger Bd in PR1240/vol 29/Cage
Near duplicate of Dodd(J RJ26), but included ADD 3 after 43: 58

S RJ40   "Junius Brutus Booth, Jr, 1870s"(S) "W C Ford--Ford's Th, Washington"(Hand)
Folger PB RJ4
Rolebook in French(J RJ96--USF), marked for Mercutio; CUT: 12: 25
added after 212, 232-233, 238-241 and 3 added, 2 other added;
13: 24b-45, 47b-48, 58; 15: 1 added; 21: all; 22: 187-190; 23:
3 added; 31: 138b-139a, 141a, 146-202; 35: 60-68a, 79-87; 44.
45, dirge: all; 52: all; 53: 112b-120 and Garrick add, 9 other
added, 171--310; RESTORE: 14: 49b-52; 15: 55; 33: 46

S RJ88b   "Ellen Terry"(Hand)
Smallhythe
Hand-written sides for Nurse in very large ink writing; not col-
lated

SS RJ453   "Arthur Lithgow, Antioch Shakespeare Festival, 1954"(Hand)
Folger 1978 acquisition
PB in unidentified full text; CUT: 11: 69b, 177-178, 184-188, 192-
195, 227-228, 235b-237; 12: 26-33; 14: 5-8; 22: 29-32, 88-89,
102-106, 166-167; 31: 23b-33, 165-179; 32: 40-42, 45b-51, 75-82;
33: 33b-35a, 38-42, 72-73, 122-133; 35: 127-138a, 198-199, 208-
212; 41: 55-65; 45: 24, 26-27, 30-32, 37-40, 43-46, 49-61, 65-
78, 86-90, 96-150; 51: 10-11, 39b-54, 63-65; 53: 1b-2, 37-39,
97-101a, 122b-124, 128-135a, 137-139a, 233b-265a, 271-290

TAMING OF THE SHREW

J TS13   Cobler of Preston, 'Mr Christopher Bullock.' London: Palmer, 1716
'a farce as it is acted at the New Th in Lincoln's Inn Fields'
Folger PR3328/B8/C7/1716/Cage
'story as it was wrote by Shakespeare in The Taming of the Shrew.
and part of his language I have made use of with a little alteration! Shakespeare lines are marked by quote marks. I counted
147 so marked(some revised). All from Induction

S TS80E   "PB and 4 rolebooks for performance of <u>Katherine and Petruchio</u>
           at home of C E Flower, March 4 and 5, 1878 (S) Inclosed program
           gives C E Flower as Petruchio)
           Nuffield 50.30/ vers 1865 (Ac 3517, 4706, 3427, all f 101)
           PB in Lacy(J TS64--Cum); <u>CUT</u>: <u>21</u>: 101; <u>32</u>: 120R; <u>41</u>: 8c, 112,
               181; <u>45</u>: 40-41; <u>RESTORE</u>: <u>21</u>: 175-177; <u>43</u>: 4-10. Rolebooks
               for Petruchio, Bion dello, Curtis, Music Master-Tailor. All
               same or fewer cuts

S TS62   "Barry Jackson"(Hand)
           British Th Assn Library(formerly British Drama League)
           PB in unidentified full text; <u>CUT</u>: <u>IND 1</u>: 35, 79a, 83b-87, move
               102-103 to follow 92, 109-111; <u>2 IND</u>: move 4 to follow 8a,
               37b-48, 51b-62, 65, 69, 89, 127-128a; <u>11</u>: 27-28, 69b-71, 73a,
               84b, 85b, 97b-99, 116b-117, 173-175, 224-225, 241; <u>12</u>: 1R,
               13a, 16-17, 23-25, 27-28a, 32b-33, 46-47, 79c, 98, 110b-116a,
               119, 122, 124, 145-163a, 183, 204-205, 258; <u>21</u>: 113b-114,
               222, 262-263, 290-291, 297-298, 380-382, 407; <u>31</u>: 18, 48-50,
               62b-63; <u>32</u>: 46b-49a, 56b-58a, 62-65, 241, 242b-247, 248-254;
               <u>41</u>: 47b-52a, 136-138, 193-196; <u>42</u>: 1-5, 114-120; <u>43</u>: 158,
               160-164, 195b; <u>44</u>: 1-2, 47, 102-105, 106b-109; <u>45</u>: 77-79;
               <u>51</u>: 90a, 94b, 104-105, 136a; <u>52</u>: 4-6, 9-10a, 148-149; <u>ADD</u>
               6 after <u>31</u>: 92, 1 after <u>32</u>: 56a; <u>MOVE</u>: <u>42</u>: 5-113 to follow
               <u>43</u>: 198

SS TS430   "Arthur Lithgow, Antioch Shakespeare Festival, 1954"(Hand)
           Folger, 1978 acquisition
           <u>CUT</u>: <u>32</u>: 30-41; <u>42</u>: 59-66; <u>44</u>: 8b-17; <u>51</u>: 42-61, 113-114; <u>52</u>:
               158-159; <u>ADD</u>: "Sly ending"(presumably from <u>The Taming of a</u>
               <u>Shrew</u>)

TIMON OF ATHENS

J TM27   "Copy of Phelps," "From Library of W Creswick," "Chalmers"
               (Hand)
           Nuffield 50.32/vers 1805 (Ac 1039)
           PB in vol 7 of a <u>Works</u> ; <u>CUT</u>: <u>11</u>: 41, 210-212, 266N, 270N; <u>12</u>:
               44-47, 50b-53, 136, 139-147, 157=159, 162; <u>22</u>: 45b-132, 141-
               142; <u>34</u>: 89, 99; <u>36</u>: 1N, 2N, 15N, 54-67a, 116-132; <u>41</u>: 6b-
               8a, 12b-13a; <u>43</u>: 3b-20a, 31a, 59b, 61B, 83B, 83b-86a, 111-
               122a, 133b-134a, 141a, 143b-148, 151-164a, 168B, 179b-184,
               192-195, 211b-216a, 242b-249, 256b-257a, 272R, 305b-310a, 318-
               356, 374b-375a, 393b-397, 454-463, 509-513a; <u>51</u>: all; <u>52</u>: 148-
               151, 153-161, 199-200a; <u>53</u>: all; <u>54</u>: 20, 24b-29a, 35b-38a,
               42b-44a, 49b-50, 54b, 64a, 65-69, 79b-84; <u>ADD</u>: 12 at some
               place in <u>54</u>

TITUS ANDRONICUS

SS TA401   "William Humphries, 1922 " (Hand)
           NYPL TC Restricted 6865
           Typed script in 5 booklets, so altered that I could not follow
               after use of following: <u>11</u>: 31-32a, 33b-35a, <u>add</u> 1, 46, <u>add</u>
               14, 56-63, <u>add</u> 8, 66, 68-69, 70b, 77-157, <u>add</u> 3, 159-160, 176-
               178, 189 . . .

SS TA402   "Nugent Monck, Maddermarket TH'(Hand. Production 1931)
           Nugent Monck Coll, Jack Hall
           Memorial PB in Methuen, 2nd ed; CUT: 11: 1-17, 18c, 20R, 21R,
           22R, 23R, 33R, 34a, 38-69, 77-78, 80, 85, 127-129, 143b-144,
           146-149, 157-168, 176-178, 206-207, 287-298, 301-308, 312-314,
           338-398, 402b-427, 432-441, 458-461, 484R, 486-487; 21: 1N, 14a,
           16-17, 18N, 86b-94, 97-102, 117-125, 131-135; 23: 20R, 21-27,
           32-37, 43-45, 49-50, 67B, 85-87, 128-135, 142-152, 175-184,
           196-211, 225-245; 24: 11b-12a, 18b-21a, 22N, 52-57; 31: 10-15,
           44-47, 72-80, 91-102, 116-135, 139-147, 163-167, 189-190, 192,
           196b-206, 207R, 210b-214, 217-218, 220N, 231-234, 235N, 251-252,
           254b-259, 280b-283, 290-296, 300-301; 32: 15-33, 46-51, 84-85;
           41: 1-29, 32-33, 41-44, 88-91, 106-119, 121a; 42: 1-31, 42B,
           49-51a, 61-66, 72, 76-84, 93-96, 120-127, 141c, 142-144, 146-
           151, 162-170a, 177-180; 43: all; 44: 39-55; 51: 53a, 76-77, 78b-
           81a, 99-117, 143--150; 52: 64-66, 121-130, 131N, 135-136, 142-
           143, 169-178, 181b-187a, 197b-206; 53: 30-32, 53-54, 58-60, 62R,
           66-95, 99R, 109-110a, 113-124, 130-136, 142-145, 160-169, 172-
           192, 199-204; ADD: 1 after 53: 198

TROILUS AND CRESSIDA

SS TC401 "Peter Hall and John Barton, Edinburgh Festival, Tour, Aldwych.
           Revival of 1960 Stratford. 1961"(Hand) STRATFORD-UPON-AVON
           Nuffield 71.21/1961/TRO (Ac 10,560)
           Deviation from Hall, 1960: CUT: 11: 45b-47; 12: 8-11a, 12-32,
           107-115, 182a, 189, 205-213, 256b-258, 273b-281; 13: 22-30, 49b-
           53a, 105, 151b-178, 217-218, 231-245, 268, 201-203, 305, 316-320,
           327b-329a, 338b-342, 357, 362b-374a; 21: 6b-7, 71-75a; 22: 14b-
           17a, 33-50, 61-72a, 153b-160a, 176b-177, 180-182; 23: 23b-26,
           29b-31a, 72b-74, 113-114, 115b-116a, 165-166, 178-179, 190, 243b-
           245a; 31: 4-5, 13-17a, 20-21, 31a, 56-57, 94b-95a; 32: 1-4, 6,
           89b-90a; 33: 15-16, 25b-27a, 28b-30a, 84-87a, 100-102a, 161-163a,
           196-200, 249; 41: 12-18a, 27b-31, 41, 63-66; 42: 29b-31a, 37-39,
           82-84; 44: 6-8, 50b-51, 62-64, 111-112; 45: 8-9, 85-86, 95, 104,
           109-112, 142-145, 154-157a; 51: 24-35, 44-45, 54b-58, 63b-64,
           87c, 89b, 91b-93; 52: 120-124, 127-128, 130-135, 193b-194a; 53:
           53-55, 66b-70, 85-86; 54: 5b-8a; 55: 1-5, 20-25, 47; RESTORE: 12:
           262-264a; 21: 79-81a, 85, 87-90; 22: 12-13, 80; 23: 5b-7a; 33:
           251-252a, 259b-262a, 265-268a, 269-291, 294-295a; 45: 47, 100

WINTER'S TALE

SS WT413 "Nugent Monck, Maddermarket Th"(Hand. Productions 1923, 1934, 1942)
           Nugent Monck Coll, Jack Hall
           Memorial PB in Methuen, 2nd ed; CUT: 11: 27b-34a; 12: 71b-75a, 84-
           86a, 124-125a, 128b, 129b-135a, 137b, 140b-142a, 183-185a, 186,
           189b-190a, 190b-207a, 222a, 225b-228, 244-245a, 254b-264a, 268-
           269, 275-296a, 304b-306, 313b-316a, 326b-329; 21: 15b-21a, 60-64,
           70b-76a, 82b-96a, 133b-139a, 147-157a, 161b-172a, 176-179a, 181-
           182a; 22: 58b-64; 23: 3b-7a, 20b-22a, 73b-75a, 100b-108a, 132b-
           141a, 160-162a, 193b-199; 32: 37b-43a, 55b-62a, 82-85a, 86a, 89b-
           90a, 102b-105a, 174-175a, 184-200, 205b-208a; 33: 19b-22a, 23a,

62c, 72b-77a; <u>41</u>: 7b-15a, 25b-27a; <u>42</u>: 12-22a; <u>43</u>: 43b-47,
49b; <u>44</u>: 11, 21-24a, 33-35a, 42b-45a, 53-54, 79b-103a, 114b-
116a, 130b-131a, 162-165, 194-204, 210b-212, 245-247, 265-
278, 283b-285a, 331-352, 363b-367a, 373b-390a, 398b-400a,
407b-417a, 439b-440a, 443b-457a, 468-470a, 477-490, 513b-547a,
560b-565a, 569b-571a, 572, 579b-595a, 622-623, 632-635, 639,
move 682-683 to follow 673, 674-675, 681, 743-752, 768-771,
817b-818a, 848-855a, 868b-873a; <u>51</u>: 29b-49a, 57-68, 95b-112a,
124-126a, 129b-130a, 149b-151a, 174b-176a; <u>52</u>: 47b-53a, 58-
59a, 61b-100, 107b-111a; <u>55</u>: 132b-151a

APPENDIX C. CHRONOLOGICAL LISTS OF PRODUCTIONS AT THE SHAKESPEARE THEATRES

    I have listed here the Shakespeare productions of those theatres which
have completed the Canon(Folio plus PE) and those professional theatres
which have the production of Shakespeare as a long-time objective. I have
underlined the plays which contribute to the completion of the Canon, us-
ing the first production of each play.

    In the lists, when a play is repeated within three years under the same
director, it is cited by underlined sigla, on the assumption that it is in
repertory, and is not a new production. "*" indicated that the PB for the
production is collated or verbalized here. "?" indicated that there is here
a PB by the same director at another theatre or at another date.

    References sometimes disagree. I have chosen that which I consider
the most reliable, most often the John Parker lists in the various editions
of Who'sWho in the Theatre, which give the date and director for every
production in London from 1911, plus a list of 'notable productions' from
the earliest time.'

    As I started checking collations against the records of chronology in
order to indicate the productions for which we have PBs, I sometimes found
that the name on the PB did not match the record of director. I assume that
we sometimes have the copy of the PB held by a person other than the director (often the administrative director of the theatre.) I also believe
that it is possible that Parker and other historians might occasionally
credit "producer" rather than "director," since English usage reverses the
meaning of thse two terms. Specifically, I feel sure that the London production of Hamlet in modern dress, produced("directed") by Sir Barry Jackson, waactually directed by H K Aylift, which he did at the Birmingham Repertory Theatre. (I have not tried to solve these contradictions, but surely
they could be solved if it became historically important to do so.)
    In a few cases, we have PBs of productions not listed by Parker. I have
entered them in paraneheses. In some cases the date of a PB differs from
that given by Parker. I assume that he is usually correct, and so accept
his date.

AMERICAN SHAKESPEARE Festival (Strat-
    ford, Connecticut, USA)
1955 CAESAR, Denis Carey
    TEMPEST, Carey
1956 KING JOHN, John Houseman AND
        Norman Lloyd
    MEASURE, Houseman and Lloyd*
    TAMING, Houseman and Lloyd*
1957 OTHELLO, Houseman nd Jack Lan-
        dau*
    MERCHANT, Houseman and Landau*
    MUCH ADO, Houseman and Landau*
1958 HAMLET, Houseman and Landau*
    MIDSUMMER, Houseman and Landau*
    WINTER'S TALE, Houseman and
        Landau*

1959 MD
    ROMEO, Houseman and Landau*
    MERRY WIVES, Houseman and Lan-
        dau*
    ALL'S WELL, Houseman and Landau*
1960 TWELFTH NIGHT, William Ball and
        Landau
    TEMPEST, Ball and Landau
    ANTONYAND CLEO, Ball and Landau
1960 National Tour: MD, WT*
1961 AS YOU, Word Baker and Landau
    MACBETH, Baker and Landau
    TROILUS. Baker and Landau
1962 HENRY 41, Warren Enters, Allen
        Fletcher and Douglas Seale
    RICHARD 2, Fletcher

1963 LEAR, Fletcher*
COMEDY, Seale ?
HENRY 5, Seale ?
1964 HAMLET, Seale *
MUCH ADO, Fletcher
RICHARD 3, Fletcher*
1965 ROMEO, Fletcher
TAMING, Joseph Antony and Don
Dryver*
CORIOLANUS, Fletcher*
KING LEAR, Antony and Fletch-
er
1966 CAESAR, Antony, Fletcher, Frank
Hauser, Houseman*
TWELFTH NIGHT, Hauser
FALSTAFF(H42), Antony
1967 MIDSUMMER, Cyril Richard*
MERCHANT, Michael Kahn*
MACBETH, Houseman*
1968 AS YOU, Stephen Porter*
LOVE'S LABOURS, Kahn
RICHARD 2, Kahn
1969 HENRY 5, Kahn
MUCH ADO, Peter Gill
HAMLET, John Dexter
1970 HA
OTHELLO, Kahn*
ALL'S WELL, Kahn*
1971 TEMPEST, Edward Payton Call*
MERRY WIVES, Kahn*
1972 CAESAR, Kahn*
ANTONY AND CLEO, Kahn*
1973 JC
MACBETH, Kahn, David Giles,
Garland Wright*
MEASURE, Kahn*
1974 TWELFTH NIGHT, Kahn
ROMEO, Kahn

ANTIOCH SHAKESPEARE FESTIVAL of the
ANTIOCH AREA THEATRE, Yellow
Springs, Ohio, USA
1952 KING JOHN, Arthur Lithgow*
RICHARD 2, Meredith Dallas*
HENRY 41, Lithgow*
HENRY 42, Lithgow*
HENRY 5, Dallas*
HENRY 6, Lithgow*
RICHARD 3, Lithgow*
HENRY 8, Dallas*
1953 TROILUS, Lithgow
CORIOLANUS, Dallas
PERICLES, Dallas

TIMON, Mary Morris
TITUS, Lithgow
CAESAR, David Hooks
ANTONY AND CLEO, Lithgow
1954 TAMING, Lithgow*
TWO Gents, Hooks
ROMEO, Lithgow*
MIDSUMMER, Arthur Oshlag
MERCHANT, Lithgow*
OTHELLO, Lithgow*
TEMPEST, Hooks
1955 MERRY WIVES, Hooks
AS YOU, Dallas
TWELFTH NIGHT, Lithgow
MACBETH, Lack Landau
CYMBELINE, Dallas
WINTER'S TALE, Hooks
TWO NOBLE KIN SMEN, Lithgow
1956 ALL'S WELL, Hooks
MUCH ADO, Lithgow
COMEDY, Reuben Silver
LOVE'S LABOURS, Hooks
LEAR; Lithgow
MEASURE, Ellis Rabb
HAMLET, Lithgow (Canon)
1957 CAESAR, Rabb
HENRY 8, Allen Fletcher
TWELFTH NIGHT, Bill Ball
MIDSUMMER, Rabb

BIRMINGHAM REPERTORY THEATR, Birming-
ham, England(Based on J C Trewin,
Birmingham Repertory Theatre, and
Archives. I may credit Jackson
with some done by others.
1907 TWO GENTS, Barry Jackson*
1913 TWELFTH NIGHT, John Drinkwater
KING JOHN, Jackson
MERRY WIVES, Jackson*
MERCHANT Jackson*
HENRY 41, Jackson*
1914 TN
AS YOU, Harcourt Williams
AS YOU, Jackson
1915 MV
TEMPEST, Jackson*
1916 AY, MV, MW, TE, TN
MACBETH, Jackson*
1917 MV, TN
TWO GENTS, Jackson*
1918 MW, TN
MEASURE, Jackson
TAMING, Drinkwater

1919 AY, MV, TN
     MUCH ADO , Donal O'Riordon*
     LOVE'S LABOURS, Jackson
1920 LL, MA
     OTHELLO, A E Filmer
     HENRY 41, Jackson
     MERRY WIVES, Filmer
1921 H41
     HENRY 42, Jackson*
1922 TWELFTH NIGHT, H K Aylift
     ROMEO, Aylift
1923 CYMBELINE (modern dress) Aylift*
1924 TWO GENTS, Aylift*
1925 LOVE'S LABOURS, F Stuart Vinden
     HAMLET(modern dress), Aylift*
1927 ALL'S WELL(modern dress) Aylift*
1928 MACBETH(modern) Aylift*
     TAMING(modern), Aylift*
1929 OTHELLO(modern) Aylift
1935 HAMLET(modern) Herbert Prentice
     MIDSUMMER
1942 HAMLET(full-2 parts) Basil Lang-
     ston
1943 TS
1944 AS YOU, Aylift*
     WINTER'S TALE, Aylift
1945 KING JOHN, Peter Brook
1946 TWELFTH NIGHT, Willard Stoker
1947 TIMON (modern), Stoker
     LEAR, Stoker*
1948 COMEDY, Duglas Seale*
1949 RICHARD 3, Michael Langham*
1952 HENRY 63, Seale *
1953 H63
     HENRY 61, Seale*
     HENRY 62, Seale*
1954 PERICLES, Seale*
1955 RICHARD 2, Seale*
1956 CAESAR, Bernard Hepton, *
     CORIOLANUS, Hepton*
1957 HENRY 5, Seale*
1958 MACBETH, Hepton*
1959 HAMLET, Hepton*
1960 HENRY 41, Hepton*
     HENRY 42, Hepton*
1961 ANTONY AND CLEO, Hepton*
1962 TEMPEST, John Harrington
1963 HENRY 8, Richard Burton*
     TROILUS, Harrison*
     TITUS, Ronald Eyre(Canon)*
1964 MIDSUMMER, Harrison
1966 TWELFTH NIGHT, Harrison*

1967 RICHARD 2, Peter Dews*
     AS YOU, Dews
1968 OTHELLO, Dews*
     ROMEO, Dews*
     MERCHANT, Dews*
1970 MIDSUMMER, Michael Simpson*
1972 MACBETH, Simpson*
1973 TWELFTH NIGHT, Dews
1974 HENRY 5, Simpson*
1975 AS YOU, Dews*

COLORADO SHAKESPEARE FESTIVAL OF
UNIVERSITY OF COLORADO, Boulder,
Colo, USA
1958 HAMLET, J H Crouch
     CAESAR, Hal J Todd
     TAMING, Gerald Kahan
1959 MIDSUMMER, Howard M Banks
     RICHARD 2, Ralph H R L Symonds
     MACBETH, Crouch
1960 HENRY 41, Francis Hodge
     ANTONY AND CLEO, Crouch
     TWELFTH NIGHT, Kahan
1961 HENRY 5, Banks
     LEAR, Crouch
     LOVE'S LABOURS, James Sandoe
1962 ROMEO, Gordon M Wickstrom
     COMEDY, A lbert N Nadeau
     OTHELLO , Sandoe
1963 MEASURE, Crouch
     RICHARD 3, Dandoe
     MUCH ADO , Banks
1964 AS YOU Nadeau
     KING JOHN, Sandoe
     TROILUS Charles H Shattuck
1965 HAMLET, Sandoe
     TEMPEST, Martin Cobin
     HENRY 42, Edgar Reynolds
1966 MERCHANT, Nadeau
     CORIOLANUS, Reynolds
     MERRY WIVES, Sandoe
1967 MIDSUMMER, Nadeau
     HENRY 61, Robert Benedetti
     TITUS, Sandoe
1968 MACBETH, Nadeau
     TWO GENTS, Theodore Herstand
     HENRY 62, Reynolds
1969 ROMEO, Cobin
     TAMING, Benedetti
     HENRY 63, Michael Addison
1970 OTHELLO, Nadeau
     RICHARD 3, Reynolds
     ALL'S WELL, Sandoe

1971 LEAR, Benedetti
HENRY 8, James Edmondson
LOVE'S LABOURS, Reynolds
1972 ANTONY AND CLEO, Alfred Ross
WINTER'S TALE, Crouch
1973 TWELFTH NIGHT, Daniel S P Yang
HAMLET, Wickstrom
PERICLES, Crouch
1974 MACBETH, Cobin
MIDSUMMER, Robert Barush
TIMON, Ricky Weiser
1975 CYMBELINE), Crouch(Canon)
AS YOU, Wickstrom
ROMEO, Yang

NATIONAL THEATRE, London, England,
  performing at the Old Vic
1963 HAMLET, Laurence Olivier
1964 OTHELLO, John Dexter*
1965 MUCH ADO, Zeffirelli*
1967 AS YOU, Clifford Williams*
1968 LOVE'S LABOURS, Olivier
1970 MERCHANT, JonATHAN Miller*
1971 CORIOLANUS, Manfred Wekweth and
       Joachim Tenschert*
1972 RICHARD 2, David Williams
     MACBETH, Michael Blakemore*
1973 TWELFTH NIGHT, Peter James*
1974 MEASURE, Miller
    · TEMPEST, Peter Hall*
     ROMEO, Bill Bryden
1975 HAMLET, Hall

NEW YORK SHAKESPEARE FESTIVAL,known
  as "Shakespeare in the Park," NY,
  NY, USA
1956 CAESAR, Joseph Papp(East River)
     TAMING, Papp*
1957 ROMEO(Mobile and Schools,Papp
     TWO GENTS, Papp*
     MACBETH, Papp*
     RICHARD 2, Stuart Vaughn(Berk-
       shire Th)*
     AS YOU, Vaughn*
1958 TWELFTH NIGHT, Vaughn(Park)
     OTHELLO, Vaughn*
1959 CAESAR, Vaughn
     TWELFTH NIGHT, Gerald Freedman*
1960 MUCH ADO, Papp (Wollman)
     RICHARD 2, Gladys Vaughn
     MIDSUMMER, Joel Freidman*
     ROMEO(Schools) Papp ?

1961 HENRY 5, Papp*
     TAMING, Freedman*
     MEASURE, Alan Schneider
     CAESAR (Schools) Papp   ?
1962 MACBETH(Schools)
     MERCHANT, Papp(Delancourt)*
     TEMPEST, Papp*
     LEAR, Papp*
1963 TWELFTH NIGHT(Schools)
     ANTONY AND CLEO, Papp*
     AS YOU, Papp*
     WINTER'S TALE, G Vaughn*
1964 MIDSUMMER(Schools),
     HAMLET, Papp
     OTHELLO, G Vaughn*
1965 TAMING(Mobile)
     LOVE'S LABOURS, Freedman
     CORIOLANUS, G Vaughn or Papp*
     TROILUS, Papp*
     ROMEO in Spanish(Mobile) Papp
1966 ALL'S WELL, Papp*
     MEASURE, Michael Kahn
     RICHARD 3, Freedman
     MACBETH(Mobile) G Vaughn
1967 MC(Mobile), G Vaughn
     COMEDY, Freedman
     KING JOHN, Papp
     TITUS, Freedman*
1968 HAMLET(Mobile and Schools)
     HENRY 41, Freedman
     FALSTAFF(H42), Freedman
     ROMEO, Papp*
1969 TWELFTH NIGHT, Freedman*
     TROILUS, Papp*
1970 WAR OF THE ROSES(H61, H62)
         Freedman*
     WAR OF THE ROSES(H62, H63)
         Freedman*
     RICHARD 3, S Vaughn and Papp*
1971 TIMON, Freedman*
     TWO GENTS, Mel Shapiro and others*
     CYMBELINE, adapted by Antoon.
       not done?
     TG(Mobile)
1972 HAMLET, Freedman*
     ANTONY AND CLEO, Kornfeld
     MUCH ADO, J Antoon, Papp* or '73
1973 AS YOU, Papp
     LEAR, Edwin Sherwin*
     TROILUS, David Schweizer(Mitzi
       Newhouse Th)*
1974 PERICLES, Edward Berkeley*
     MERRY WIVES, David Margules*

MACBETH, Berkeley(Newhouse)*
TEMPEST, Berkeley(Newhouse)*
TG(Mobi e)
1975 HAMLET
COMEDY OF ERRORS

NORWICH P. AYERS in/MADDERMARKET TH,
Norwich, EnglAND(List from Philip
Hepworth, City Librarian, Norwich.
Memorial PBs prepared by Monck about
1936, in Monck Coll, Jack Hall. It
is believes Coll also has many of the
original PBs. Data for 1953-1975 sup-
plied by Mrs S Brecknell.
1914 TWELFTH NIGHT, Nugent Monck ?
MERCHANT, Monck ?
1919 MUCH ADO, Monck ?
COMEDY, Monck, ?
1920 LOVE'S LABOURS, Monck, ?
ROMEO, Monck ?
1921 MERRY WIVES ?
MOVE INTO MADDERMARKET THEATRE
AS YOU, Monck *
1922 TAMING, Monck*
TWELFTH NIGHT ?
WINTER'S TALE Monck ?
MERCHANT, Monck, ?
HENRY 41, Monck*
1923 OTHELLO , Monck, ?
MIDSUMMER, Monck, ?
TWO GENTS, Monck *
CYMBELINE, Monck, *
HENRY 42 , Monck *
1924 ANTONY AND CLEO, Monck *
HAMLET , Monck, ?
MERRY WIVES, Monck ?
ALL'S WELL, Monck, ?
1925 ROMEO, Monck *
TEMPEST, Monck, ?
M ACBETH, Monck, ?
MEASURE , Monck, *
1926 CAESAR, Monck*
TWELFTH NIGHT, Monck, ?
LEAR, Monck, *
1927 MUCH ADO, Monck*
KING JOHN, Monck*
TAMING, Monck *
1928 CORIOLANUS, Monck*
TROILUS , Monck*
HENRY 5, Monck*
1929 MERCHANT, Monck*
HENRY 8, Monck*
PETICLES, Monck, *

1930 OTHELLO, Monck*
RICHARD 2, Monck*
LOVE'S LABOURS, Monck*
HAMLET, Monck*
1931 MACBETH, Monck*
TIMON, Monck*
AS YOU, Monck*
TITUS, Monck*
1932 RICHARD 3, Monck*
1933 MIDSUMMER, Monck*
HENRY 61, Monck*
HENRY 62, Monck*
HENRY 63, Monck*(Canon)
1934 WINTER'S TALE, Monck
MUCH ADO, Hugh Hunt
MACBETH, Hunt
ANTONY AND CLEO, Monck*
1935 MERRY WIVES, Monck*
COMEDY, Monck*
TWELFTH NIGHT, Monck*
1936 TEMPEST, Monck*
ALL'S WELL, Monck*
MERCHANT, Monck*
1937 LEAR, Monck*
HENRY 5, Monck*
CAESAR, Monck*
1938 MEASURE, Monck?
RICHARD 2, Monck?
HAMLET, Monck*
1939 AS YOU, Monck*
OTHELLO, Monck*
1940 MUCH ADO, Monck*
TWELFTH NIGHT, Monck*
1941 ROMEO, Monck?
MIDSUMMER, Monck?
1942 TEMPEST, Monck*
WINTER'S TALE, Monck?
1943 HAMLET, Monck*
CYMBELINE, Monck*
MERCHANT, Monck*
1944 MERRY WIVES, Monck*
TAMING, Monck?
1945 AS YOU, Monck?
COMEDY, Monck?
1946 KING JOHN, Monck, ?
MIDSUMMER, Monck?
1947 OTHELLO, Monck*
MUCH ADO, Monck?
TWELFTH NIGHT, Monck?
1948 MACBETH, Monck*
TROILUS, Monck*
TWO GENTS, Monck*

1949 RICHARD 2, Monck*
     TEMPEST, Monck*
     ROMEO, Monck*
1950 WINTER'S TALE, Lionel Dunn
     CORIOLANUS, Dunn
     MERCHANT, Monck?
1951 PERICLES, Monck*
     TAMING, Monck?
     LOVE'S LABOURS, Monck*
1952 HENRY 5, Monck*
     AS YOU, Dunn
1953 MEASURE, Dunn
     HAMLET, Dunn
     MIDSUMMER, Monck?
     TWELFTH NIGHT, Dunn
1954 HENRY 41, James Roose Evans
1955 MACBETH, Evans
     MUCH ADO, Evans
     MERRY WIVES, Frank Harwood
1956 RICHARD 2, Harwood
     O THELLO, Harwood
     WINTER'S TALE, Harwood
1957 COMEDY, Harwood
1958 LOVE'S LABOURS, Ian Emmerson
     TWELFTH NIGHT, Harwood
     TEMPEST, Emmerson
1959 KING JOHN, Emmerson
     CAESAR, Emmerson
1960 M IDSUMMER, Emmerson
     MERCHANT, Emmerson
1961 HAMLET, Emmerson
     HENRY 42, Emmerson
1962 ROMEO, Emmerson
1963 MEASURE, Emmerson
     AS YOU, Emmerson
1964 RICHARD 3, Emmerson
1965 HENRY 5 Emmerson
1966 ANTONY AND CLEO, Emmerson
     MERRY WIVES, Emmerson
1967 TIMON, Emmerson
1968 LEAR, Emmerson
     MUCH ADO, Emmerson
1969 MACBETH, Emmerson
1970 CORIOLANUS, Emmerson
1971 AS YOU, Emmerson
1972 PERICLES, Emmerson
     OTHELLO, Emmerson
1973 WINTER'S TALE, Emmerson
     KING JOHN, Emmerson
1974 TWO GENTS, Emmerson
1975 TEMPEST, Emmerson
     HENRY 41, Emmerson

OLD VIC THEATRE, London, England.
(Based on Parker. He does not list
Old Vic in early volumes, but gives
a list of "firsts" in 6th Ed, so
this list does not record continuations in repertory.

1914 TAMING, Matheson Lang and Hun-
     ter Britton
     HAMLET, Lang and Britton
     MERCHANT, LAng and Britton
     TEMPEST, Ben Greet?
     MERRY WIVES, Estelle Stead and
     Andrew Leigh
     COMEDY, Greet ?
     TWELFTH NIGHT, Greet
1915 MIDSUMMER, Greet ?
     MACBETH, Greet
     AS YOU, Stead and Leigh
     WINTER'S TALE, Greet
     OTHELLO, Greet
     CAESAR, Fisher Whit
     ROMEO, Greet
     HENRY 5, Greet
     RICHARD 3, Greet
1916 MUCH ADO, Greet ?
     HENRY 8, Greet
     RICHARD 2, Greet
     TWO GENTS, Greet
     HAMLET, 2nd Quarto, Greet
1917 KING JOHN, Greet
     HENRY 42, Greet
1918 LEAR, Greet
     CYMBELINE, Greet
     MEASURE, George R Foss
     LOVE'S LABOURS, Foss
1919 HENRY 41, Foss
1920 CORIOLANUS, Russell Thorndike
     and Charles Warburton
1921 PERICLES, Robert Atkins
     ALL'S WELL, Atkins
1922 TIMON, Atkins
     ANTONY AND CLEO, Atkins ?
     HENRY 41, Atkins
1923 HENRY 61 and 62, Atkins
     HENRY 62 and 63, Atkins
     TITUS, Atkins
     TROILUS, Atkins (Canon)
     LOVE'S LABOURS, Atkins
     TWO GENTS, Atkins
1924 CORIOLANUS, Atkins
     OTHELLO, Atkins ?
     MIDSUMMER, Atkins ?

1925 MERCHANT, Andrew Leigh
     RICHARD 3, Leigh
     MEASURE, Leigh
     ANTONY AND CLEO, Leigh
     MERCHANT, Leigh
     MIDSUMMER, Leigh
1926 ROMEO, Leigh
     KING JOHN, Leigh
     TEMPEST, Leigh
     MACBETH, Leigh
1927 TWELFTH NIGHT, Leigh ·
     WINTER'S TALE, Leigh
     OTHELLO, Leigh
     COMEDY, Leigh
1928 TN, RJ
     TWO NOBLE KINSMEN, Leigh
     LOVE'S LABOIRS, Leigh
     AS YOU, Leigh
1930 HENRY 41, E Harcourt Williams
     HAMLET(Gielgud), Williams
     ANTONY AND CLEO   ???
1933 TWELFTH NIGHT, Tyrone Guthrie?
     MEASURE, Guthrie
1934 MACBETH, Guthrie ?
     ANTONY AND CLEO, Henry Cass
     MUCH ADO, Cass
1935 OTHELLO, Cass
     HENRY 42, Cass
     HAMLET, Cass
     CAESAR, Cass
     MACBETH, Cass
1936 RICHARD 3, Cass
     LEAR, Cass
     LOVE'S LABOURS, Guthrie
     AS YOU, Esme Church
     WINTER'S TALE, Cass
1937 HAMLET, Gilbert Miller
     TWELFTH NIGHT, Guthrie ?
     HENRY 5, Guthrie
     MEASURE, Guthrie
     RICHARD 3, Guthrie?
     MACBETH, Michel Saint-Denis
     MIDSUMMER, Guthrie ?
1938 OTHELLO, Guthrie
     CORIOLANUS(Olivier),Lewis Casson
     HAMLET, Guthrie, ?
1939 TAMING, Guthrie?
1940 LEAR, Casson and Granville-
     Barker*
     TEMPEST, George Devine and Mar-
     ius Goring

MOVED TO NEW THEATRE TEMPORARILY
1941 KING JOHN, Guthrie and Casson
1944 HAMLET, Guthrie and Michael
     B enthall
     RICHARD 3(Olivier) John Burrell
1945 HENRY 41, Burrell*
     HENRY 42, Burrell
1946 LEAR, Laurence Olivier
1947 RICHARD 2(Guinness) Ralph Rich-
     ardson
     TAMING, Burrell
     TWELFTH NIGHT, Alec Guinness
1949RICHARD 3(Olivier), Burrell
     LOVE'S LABOURS, Hugh Hunt
1950 HAMLET(Redgrave), Hunt
BACK TO THE OLD VIC
     TWELFTH NIGHT, Hunt
1951 HENRY 5, Glen Byam Shaw*
     MERRY WIVES, Hunt
     OTHELLO, Michael Langham*
     MIDSUMMER, Guthrie?
1952 TWO GENTS, Denis CArey
     LEAR, Hunt
     TIMON, Guthrie*
     TWO GENTS(Bristol Old Vic)
     HENRY 63(Birmingham)Douglas
     Sealr*
     ROMEO(Hunt) Langham*
1953 MERCHANT, Hunt
     CAESAR, Hunt*
     HENRY 8, Guthrie*
     HENRY 5, Denis Carey
     HENRY 61(Birmingham) Seale?
     HENRY 62(Birmingham)Seale?
     HENRY 63(Birmingham)Seale?
     HAMLET, Michael Benthall
     ALL'S WELL, Benthall*
     KING JOHN, George Devine
1954 TWELFTH NIGHT, Carey
     CORIOLANUS, Benthall*
     TEMPEST, Robert Helpman*
     MACBETH, Benthall
     LOVE'S LABOURS, First Banbury*
     TAMING, Carey*
1955 RICHARD 2, Benthall
     AS YOU, Helpman*
     HENRY 41, Seale?
     HENRY 42, Seale*
     CAESAR, Benthall*
     MERRY WIVES, Seale
     WINTER'S TALE, Benthall
     HENRY 5(Burton), Benthall*

1955 Australian Tour
    MERCHANT, Benthall*
    MEASURE, Benthall
    TAMING, Benthall
1956 OTHELLO, Benthall
    TROILUS, Guthrie*
    MACBETH, Benthal
    ROMEO, Helpman
    RICHARD 2, Benthall
    TIMON, Benthall*
    CYMBELINE, Benthall*
    MUCH ADO, Carey*
    MERCHANT, Benthall?
1957 TWO GENTS, Langham*
    ANTONY AND CLEO, Helpman*
    TITUS, Walter Hudd*(Double bill:)
    COMEDY, Hudd
    RICHARD 2, Seale*
    HAMLET(Benthall)John Neville*
    HENRY 61 and 62, Seale*
    HENRY 62 and 63, Seale*
    MEASURE, Margaret Webster*
    MIDSUMMER, Benthall
1958 LEAR, Seale*
    TWELFTH NIGHT, Benthall
    HENRY 8, Benthall*
    CAESAR, Seale*
    MACBETH, Seale*
    (HENRY 5, Benthall*)
959 TEMPEST, DAVENANT, Seale
    AS YOU, Wendy Toye*
    RICHARD 2, John Hale
    MERRY WIVES, Hale*
1960 HENRY 5, John Neville*
    ROMEO, Franco Zefferelli
    MIDSUMMER, Langham*
1961 HENRY 41, Dennis Vance
    TWELFTH NIGHT, Colin Graham*
    MERCHANT, Peter Potter
    KING JOHN, Potter
    MACBETH, Oliver Neville*
1962 TWELFTH NIGHT, Graham
    TEMPEST, O Neville
    MERCHANT, Michael Elliott*
1963 OTHELLO, Casper Wrede*
    MEASURE, Elliott
Old Vic taken over by National Theatre
Following listed by Parker, but not
  in National Theatre list of productions
1964 LOVE'S LABOURS, Val May
    HENRY 5, Stuart Burge
    HAMLeto(Italian),Zeffirelli

1965 CORIOLANUS, Manfred Wewerth and
    Joachim Tenscher
1970 KING LEAR, Jonathan Miller

OREGON SHAKESPEARE FESTIVAL, Ashland, Ore, USA
1935 MERCHANT, Angus Bowmer*
    TWELFTH NIGHT, Bowmer
1936 MV, TN
    ROMEO, Bowmer
1937 RJ, TN
    TAMING, Bowmer
1938 MV, TN, TS
    HAMLET, Bowmer
1939 HA, TS
    COMEDY,Bowmer*
    AS YOU, Bowmer*
1940 MERRY WIVES, William Cottrell*
    COMEDY, Cottrell*
    MUCH ADO, Cottrell
    AS YOU, Cottrell
1947 HAMLET, Frank Lambert-Smith*
    LOVE'S LABOURS, Bowmer*
    MACBETH, Bowmer
    MERCHANT, Bowmer
1948 LL, MV
    OTHELLO, Bowmer
    KING JOHN, Allen Fletcher
1949 ROMEO, Richard Graham
    RICHARD 2, James Sandoe
    MIDSUMMER, Sandoe(Bowmer*)
    OTHELLO, Fletcher
    TAMING, Fletcher
1950 HENRY 41, Fletcher
    AS YOU, Bowmer
    ANTONY AND CLEO, Sandoe*
    COMEDY, Graham*
1951 TWELFTH NIGHT, Graham
    MEASURE, Sandoe*
    LEAR, Bowmer*
    HENRY 42, Philip Hanson
1952 TEMPEST, Graham*
    CAESAR, Fletcher
    HENRY 5, Hanson*
    MUCH ADO, Bowmer*
1953 CORIOLANUS, Fletcher*
    MERCHANT, Graham*
    HENRY 61, Dandoe
    TAMING,, Hanson
1954 HAMLET, Bowmer*
    WINTER'S TALE, H Paul Kliss
    MERRY WIVES, Fletcher*
    HENRY 62, Dandoe

1955 TIMON, Robert B Loper*
     MIDSUMMER, Sandoe
     HENRY 63 , Sandoe*
     MACBETH, Kliss
     ALL'S WELL,   Loper
1956 RICHARD 3, Fletcher*
     LOVE'S LABOURS, Fletcher*
     ROMEO, Hal J Todd*
     CYMBELINE, B Iden Payne*
     TITUS, Todd*
1957 AS YOU, Bowmer*
     OTHELLO, Sandoe*
     TWO GENTS, Sandoe*
     HENRY 8, Loper
     PERICLES, Loper
1958 MUCH ADO, Loper*
     LEAR, Loper*
     MERCHANT, Sandoe
     TROILUS,, Sandoe*(Canon)
     MIDSUMMER, Sandoe*
1959 TWELFTH NIGHT, Bowmer*
     KING JOHN, Richard D Risso*
     MEASURE, Sandoe*
     ANTONY AND CLEO, Sandoe
1960 TAMING, Loper*
     CAESAR, Jerry Turner*
     TEMPEST, Sandoe*
     RICHARD 2, Risso
1961 ALL'S WELL, Charles G Taylor*
     MIDSUMMER, Payne*
     HAMLET, Loper*
      HENRY 41, Rosso*
1962 AS YOU, Turner*
     COMEDY, Rod Alexander*
     HENRY 42, Edward S Brubaker*
     CORIOLANUS, J H Crouch*
1963 MERRY WIVES, Brubaker*
     ROMEO, Loper*
     LOVE'S LABOURS, Alexander
     HENRY 5, Turner*
1964 MERCHANT, Alexander*
     LEAR, Bowmer*
     TWELFTH NIGHT, Loper*
     HENRY 61, Turner*
1965 MUCH ADO, James Moll*
     MACBETH, Risso*
     WINTER'S TALE , Hugh C Evans
     HENRY 62, Brubaker*
1966 MIDSUMMER, Evans*
     OTHELLO, Risso*
     TWO GENTS, Nagle Jackson*
     HENRY 63, Turner,*

1967 PERICLES, Jackson*
     ANTONY AND CLEO, Turner*
     TAMING, Risso*
     RICHARD 3, Evans*
1968 CYMBELINE, Sandoe*
     HAMLET, Patrick Hines*
     AS YOU, William Kinsolving*
     HENRY 8, Risso*
1969 TEMPEST, Risso* (ERROR IN COL-
       LATION: Sandoe dated 1969 in-
       stead of 1960)
     ROMEO, Hines*
     TWELFTH NIGHT, Evans*
     KING JOHN, Brub aker*
1970 COMEDY, Jackson*
     CAESAR, Larry Oliver*
     RICHARD 2, Jackson
     MERCHANT, Bowmer*
1971 MIDSUMMER, Raye Birk*
     MUCH ADO, Oliver*
     MACBETH, Philip Davidson*
     HENRY 41, Pat Patton
1972 TAMING, Robert Benedetti*
     LOVE'S LABOURS, Laird Williamson
     HENRY 42, William Roberts
     TROILUS, Turner*
1973 OTHELLO, Turner*
     AS YOU, Patton*
     MERRY WIVES, Thomas B Markus*
     HENRY 5, Williamson*
1974 TWO GENTS, Williamson
     HAMLET, Turner*
     TITUS, Williamson*
     TWELFTH NIGHT, Jim Edmonson*
1975 WINTER'S TALE, Audrey Stanley
     ROMEO, Edmonson*
     ALL'S WELL, Jon Jory
     HENRY 61, Will Huddleston*

PASADENA PLAYHOUSE, Paradena, Calif,
USA
1918 TWELFTH NIGHT,Gilmor Brown
     TAMING, Brown
1919 MUCH ADO, Brown
1920 TEMPEST, Brown
     MERRY WIVES, Brown
1921 COMEDY, Brown
1922 LEAR, Brown
     AS YOU, Brown
1923 LOVE'S LABOURS, Brown
NEW THEATRE ON EL MOLINO
1927 TWO GENTS, Maurice Wells

1929 CAESAR, Brown
1930 OTHELLO, Morris Ankrum
1932 HENRY 8, Ankrum
1933 HAMLET, Lenore Shorwise
1934 MACBETH, Byron Foulger
1935 KING JOHN, Foulger
     RICHARD 2 , Ankrum
     HENRY 41, Brown
     HENRY 42 , Brown
     HENRY 5, Thomas B Henry
     HENRY 61, Henry
     HENRY 62, Foulger and Shorewise
     HENRY 63, Shorewise and Foulger
     RICHARD 3, Ankrum
     HENRY 8, Ankrum
1936 TROILUS, Henry
     TIMON, Shorewise
     PERICLES, Foulger
     CORIOLANUS, Ankrum
     CAESAR, Brown
     ANTONY AND CLEO, Reginald Pole
       and Henry
     CYMBELINE , Ankrun
1937 WINTER'S TALE , Frederick Blan-
      chard
     MEASURE, Hale McKeen
     ALL'S WELL , Maxwell Sholes
     TITUS, Henry
     ROMEO, Shorewise(Canon)
Subsequent productions not checked

OPEN AIR THEATRE IN REGENT'S PARK,
   London, England(Based on Parker)
1933 TWELFTH NIGHT, Robert Atkins?
     AS YOU, Atkins?
     MIDSUMMER, Atkins?
     TEMPEST, Atkins?
1934 AY, MD, TE, TN
     COMEDY, Atkins
     RICHARD 2, Atkins?
     ROMEO, Atkins?
1935 AY, MD, TN
     LOVE'S LABOURS, Atkins
1936 AY, LL, MD, TE, TN
     HENRY 8, Atkins?
1937 CE, MD, TE, TN
     MERRY WIVES, Atkins
     CAESAR, Atkins
     WINTER'S TALE, Atkins
1938 AY, MD, TE, TN
1939 MD, TN
     MUCH ADO, Atkins?
     PERICLES, Atkins

1940 MD
     TAMING, Aktins*
1941 HENRY 5, Atkins?
1942 MD, TN, TS
1943 AY
     TEMPEST, Atkins
     LOVE'S LABOURS, Atkins
1944 WINTER'S TALE, Stephen Thomas
     TWELFTH NIGHT, Thea Holme
1945 AS YOU, Eric Capon
     MERCHANT, Capon
     MIDSUMMER, Capon
1946 AS YOU, Atkins?
     TROILUS, Atkins
     MIDSUMMER, Atkins?
1947 MD
     TWELFTH NIGHT, Atkins?
1948 AY, MD
     KING JOHN, Atkins
1949 MUCH ADO, Atkins ?
     COMEDY, Atkins
     TEMPEST, Atkins
1950 WINTER'S TALE, Atkins
     MERCHANT, Atkins ?
     TAMING, Atkins ?
1951 MIDSUMMER, Atkins?
1952 AS YOU, Atkins ?
     CYMBELINE, Atkins
1953 TWELFTH NIGHT, Atkins ?
     LOVE'S LABOURS, Hugh Goldie
1955 MD
     TEMPEST, David Willis
1956 AY, TN
1958 MUCH ADO, Atkins?
     TAMING, Leslie French
L959 TN
     MIDSUMMER, Atkins?
1960 TEMPEST, Atkins
1962 MIDSUMMER, David Williams
     TWELFTH NIGHT, Denis Carey or
       Colin Graham
     LOVE'S LABOURS, Williams
1963 MD
     MUCH ADO, Williams
1964 HENRY 5, Williams*
     TAMING, Vladek Sheybal
1965 AS YOU, Harold Lang
1966 MIDSUMMER, Michael Meachim
1967 MD
1968 MERRY WIVES, Richard Digby Day*
     TWO GENTS, Day*
1969 TG
     MERCHANT, Day

1970 MIDSUMMER, Day*
    MUCH ADO, David Conville*
1971 MD
    ROMEO, Day*
1972 TEMPEST, Day*
    TWELFTH NIGHT, Conville*
1973 AS YOU, Day*
    TWELFTH NIGHT, Robert Lang
1974 MIDSUMMER, David Conville*
1975 MD
    TAMING, Mervyn Willis

SADLER'S WELLS, London, England,
    under Phelps. (Extracted from Par-
    ker list of "Notable Productions."
    PBs indicate plays kept in reper-
    tory, not noted by Parker
1844 OTHELLO*
    MERCHANT
    MACBETH
    KING JOHN*
1845 WINTER'S TALE*
    HENRY 8*
    KING LEAR?
    RICHARD 3?
1846 ROMEO*
    CAESAR*
    HENRY41*
    MEASURE*
1847 TEMPEST?
    AS YOU*
    CYMBELINE?
1848 TWELFTH NIGHT?
    CORIOLANUS*
    MUCH ADO
    MERRY WIVES
1849 ANTONY AND CLEO*
    RICHARD 3*
1950 MUCH ADO
    MACBETH*
1851 TIMON?
1852 ALL'S WELL*
    HENRY5*
1853 HENRY 42*
    MIDSUMMER*
1854 CYMBELINE?
    PERICLES*
    (HAMLET? Haywell dates a PB 1854.
    Parker records Phelps at Hay-
    market in 1837 but not at
    Sadler's Wells)
1855 COMEDY*
    TEMPEST*

1856 TIMON*
    TAMING*
1857 AS YOU*
    CYMBELINE*
    LEAR*
    LOVE'S LABOURS*
    MERCHANT
    TWO GENTS*
1858 MUCH ADO*
    Winter'S TALE*
1859 KING JOHN?
    ROMEO*
    TWELFTH NIGHT*
1860 AS YOU?
    CORIOLANUS?
    TEMPEST
1861 RICHARD3?

SAN DIEGO NATIONAL SHAKESPEARE FES-
    TIVAL, San Diego, Calif, USA,
    (Theatre built for use of Globe Th
    Co under Thomas Wood Stevens for
    San Diego World's Fair. New Festi-
    val initiated 1949. Burned 1978)
1949 TWELFTH NIGHT, B Iden Payne
1950 TAMING, Payne
    ROMEO, Payne
1951 MUCH ADO, Payne
    MERRY WIVES, Payne
1952 ALL'S WELL, Payne
    AS YOU, Payne*
    ('MERCHANT, Payne PB*but not list-
    ed in official chronology)
1954 OTHELLO, Frank McMullan
    TWELFTH NIGHT, Patrick Wymark
    MERCHANT, Philip Hanson*
1955 MEASURE, Payne
    HAMLET, Allen Fletcher
    TAMING, Craig Noel*
1956 MIDSUMMER, Peter Bucknell
    RICHARD 2, Hanson
1957 TEMPEST, Payne
    LEAR, Fletcher*
1958 MACBETH, Noel
    MUCH ADO, Fletcher
    ANTONY AND CLEO, Charles McGraw
1959 HENRY 41, William Ball
    ROMEO, Fletcher
    LOVE'S LABOURS, Fletcher
1960 CAESAR, Ball*
    AS YOU, Fletcher*
    HAMLET, Fletcher*

1961 TWELFTH NIGHT, Ball
MERCHANT, Fletcher
RICHARD 3, Fletcher*
1962 TAMING, Noel
HENRY 42, Ball*
OTHELLO, Fletcher
1963 MIDSUMMER, Ellis Rabb*
WINTER'S TALE, Duncan Ross
ANTONY AND CLEO, Fletcher*
1964 MUCH ADO, Payne
MACBETH, Ross*
MEASURE, Fletcher*
1965 MERRY WIVES, Mel Shapiro*
HENRY 8, Philip Minor
CORIOLANUS, Milton Katselas
1966 ROMEO, Shapiro*
TEMPEST, Hal George
TWO GENTS, Fletcher*
1967 TWELFTH NIGHT, Edward Payton
Call*
ALL'S WELL, Malcolm Black
OTHELLO, Katselas*
1968 HAMLET, Rabb*
AS YOU, Robert Moss*
1969 CAESAR, Richard Easton*
COMEDY, Jack O'BRIEN
MACBETH, Rabb*
1970 MUCH ADO, Bridie MacDonald*
RICHARD 2, Stephen Porter
CYMBELINE, Louis Criss
1971 MIDSUMMER, Eric Christmas*
TAMING, Nagle Jackson*
ANTONY AND CLEO, Rabb*
1972 MERRY WIVES, O'Brien*
LOVE'S LABOURS, Christmas*
RICHARD 3, Call*
1973 MERCHANT, Christmas*
TWO GENTS, Fletcher*
LEAR, Call*
1974 TWELFTH NIGHT, Chris tmas and
Noel*
ROMEO, Diana Maddox*
HENRY 42, Call*
1975 TEMPEST, Rabb*
MUCH ADO, O'Brien*
MEASURE, Maddox*

SMOCK ALLEY THEATRE, Dublin, Ireland
(S gives "1670s" for all, and that
does not guarantee production)
COMEDY*
CORIOLANUS*

JULIUS CAESAR*
HENRY 41*
HENRY6*
KING JOHN*
LEAR*
RICHARD 2*
MACBETH*
MIDSUMMER*
MERRY WIVES*
OTHELLO*
ROMEO*
TWELFTH NIGHT*
WINTER's TALE*
1750 AS YOU*

STRATFORD SHAKESPEARE FESTIVAL,
Stratford, Ontario, Canada
1953 ALL'S WELL, Tyrone Guthrie*
RICHARD 3, Guthrie*
1954 MEASURE, Cecil Clarke*
TAMING, Guthrie*
1955 MERCHANT, Guthrie*
CAESAR, Michael Langham*
1956 HENRY 5, Langham*
MERRY WIVES, Langham*
1957 HAMLET, Langham*
TWELFTH NIGHT, Guthrie*
1958 HENRY 41, Langham*
WINTER'S TALE, Doulas Campbell*
MUCH ADO, Langham*
(TWO GENTS, Langham* Perhaps
touring only)
1959 AS YOU, Peter Wood*
OTHELLO, Jean Gascon and George
McGovern*
1960 KING JOHN, Douglas Seale*
MIDSUMMER, Campbell*
ROMEO, Langham*
1961 CORIOLANUS, Langham*
HENRY 8, McGowan*
LOVE'S LABOURS, Langham*
1962 MACBETH, Peter Coe*
TAMING, Langham*
TEMPEST, McGowan*
1963 TROILUS, Langham*
COMEDY, Gascon*
TIMON, Langham*
1964 RICHARD 2, Stuart Burge*
LEAR, Langham*
1965 HENRY 41, Burge*
FALSTAFF(H42), Burge*
CAESAR, Campbell*

1966 HENRY 5, Langham*
    HENRY 61-62, John Hirsch*
    TWELFTH NIGHT, David Williams*
1967 ANTONY AND CLEO, Langham*
    RICHARD 3, Hirsch*
    MERRY WIVES, Williams*
1968 ROMEO, Campbell*
    MIDSUMMER, Hirsch*
1969 HAMLET, Hirsch*
    MEASURE, David Giles✗
1970 MERCHANT, Gascon ✗
    CYMBELINE, Gascon ✗
1971 MUCH ADO, William Hutt*
    MACBETH, Giles*
1972 AS YOU, Hutt*
    LEAR, Williams (Gascon on tour)
    TAMING, Gascon*
1973 PERICLES, Gascon✗
    OTHELLO, Williams*
1974 PE✗
    LOVE'S LABOURS, Gascon*
    KING JOHN, Gascon*
1975 COMEDY, Robin Phillips and David
      Toguri*
    TWO GENTS, Phillips*
    MEASURE, Phillips*
    TWELFTH NIGHT, David Jones

STRATFORD-UPON-AVON(INCLUDING MEMOR-
IAL THEATRE AND ROYAL SHAKESPEARE
THEATRE) Assembled from Shakespeare Memorial Theatre, Day, and
same, Trewin; and from PBs at
Shakespe are Centre Library. Checked partially with Parker
1879 AS YOU, Barry Sullivan
    HAMLET, Sullivan
    MUCH ADO, Sullivan ?
1880 AY, HA, MA
    MERCHANT , Sullivan?
    OTHELLO, Sullivan
1881 MUCH ADO, Edward Compton
    TWELFTH NIGHT, Compton
    AS YOU , Compton
1882 AY, TN
    ROMEO, Compton
    COMEDY, Compton
1883 LEAR, Eddicott Galer
    MACBETH, Galer
    HENRY 41, Galer
    MERCHANT, Galer

1884 CYMBELINE, Charles Barnard
    ROMEO, Bernard
    AS YOU, Bernard
    MEASURE, Bernard
1885 AY, CY, MM, RJ
    LOVE'S LABOURS, Bernard
    MERCHANT, Bernard
1886 HAMLET, F R Benson
    OTHELLO, Benson
    RICHARD 3, Benson
1887 R3
    MERRY WIVES, Benson
    MERCHANT, Benson
1888 HA
    ROMEO, Benson
    MIDSUMMER, Benson*
1889 HENRY 61, Osmond Tearle
    CAESAR, Tearle
1890 KING JOHN, Tearle
    TWO GENTS, Tearle
    OTHELLO, Tearle
    LEAR, Tearle
1891 TEMPEST, Benson
    HAMLET, Benson
    MUCH ADO, Benson
1892 TIMON, Benson
    MIDSUMMER, Benson
    CAESAR, Benson?
    TWELFTH NIGHT, Benson
1893 TN
    TAMING, Benson
    ROMEO, Benson
    MERCHANT, Benson
    MERRY WIVES, Benson
    CORIOLANUS, Benson
1894 MUCH ADO, Benson
    HENRY 42, Benson
    AS YOU, Benson
    RICHARD 3, Benson
1895 WINTER'S TALE, Ben Greet
    AS YOU, Greet
    MUCH ADO, Greet
1896 RICHARD 2, Benson
    TWELFTH NIGHT, Benson
    CAESAR, Benson
    MACBETH, Benson
    TAMING, Benson
    HAMLET, Benson
1897 AY, MA, TS
    HENRY 5, Benson
    TEMPEST, Benson
    MERRY WIVES, Benson
    OTHELLO, Benson

ROMEO, Benson ?
M ERCHANT, Benson?
RICHARD 3, Benson
1898 HA, MV, MW, TN, TS, JC
ANTONY AND CLEO , Benson

CORIOLANUS, Benson
HENRY 42, Benson
1899 AY, H5, R3, MV, MW, TN
HENRY 62 , Benson*
HAMLET(Complete), Benson
RICHARD 2, Benson
1900 AY, MC, MV
PERICLES, John Coleman
OTHELLO, Benson*
1901 AY, H62, R2, R3, MV, MW
KING JOHN, Benson
HENRY 41, Benson
MUCH ADO, Benson
HENRY 5, Greet and William Poel
1902 HA, H5, MW, OT
HENRY 8, Benson
TWELFTH NIGHT, Benson
ROMEO, Benson?
LEAR, Benson
TAMING, Benson
1903 HA, MC, MW
WINTER'S TALE, Benson
MIDSUMMER, Benson
1904 HA, H5, KL, R2, MV, MW,TN,TS,WT
CAESAR, Benson?
AS YOU, Benson*
TEMPEST, Benson
1905 AY, HA, H5, R2, MC, MV, MW, RJ,
TN, TS, MA
COMEDY, Benson
HENRY 41, Benson
HENRY 42, Benson
OTHELLO, Benson
1906, AY, JC, H42, H5, R2, MC, MV,TS
MUCH ADO, Benson
HENRY 61, Benson
HENRY 62, Benson?
HENRY 63, Benson
RICHARD 3, Benson
LEAR, Benson
MIDSUMMER, Benson
1907 AY, HA, H5, R2, MA, MW, OT, TS
CORIOLANUS, Benson
LOVE'S LABOURS, Benson
TWELFTH NIGHT, Benson
1908 H A, JC, H5, R2, MA, MC,MD,MW
ROMEO, Benson
TEMPEST, Benson
WINTER'S TALE, Benson

1909 HA, JC, H5, H62, R2, MA, MW,TN,TS
CORIOLANUS, Benson
CYMBELINE, Benson
HENRY 41, Benson
KING JOHN, Benson
RICHARD3, Benson
OTHELLO, Benson
1910Λ AY, CR, HA, JC, H5, R2, R3,MA,
MC, MW, OT, TN, TS, WT
HENRY 42, Benson
TWO GENTS, Benson
1911 AY, HA, JC, H5, R2, R3, MA, MC,
MW. OT, TE
MIDSUMMER, Benson
ROMEO, Benson
TAMING, Benson
1912 AY, CR, HA, JC, H5, R3, MD, MW
RJ, TN, TS
ANTONY AND CLEO, William Poel
1913 AY, HA, H5, R2, R3, MA, MW, RJ,
TN, TS, H42
KING JOHN, Benson
MERCHANT, Benson ?
1914 AY, HA, JC, H42, H5, R2, R3, MA
MD, MV, MW, RJ, TN, TS
COMEDY, Benson
1915 AY, CR, HA, JC, H42, H5, R2, R3·
MV, MW, RJ, TN, TS
1916 CE, HA, H42, H5, KJ, MA, MD,MV,
MW, TE, TN, TS
ALL'S WELL, Benson
HENRY 8, Ben Greet
MAC BETH, Greet
OTHELLO, Greet
TWO GENTS, Greet
WINTER'S TALE, Greet
1917 COMEDY, Greet
1918 MUCH ADO, Greet
TEMPEST, Greet
HAMLET, Greet
1919 TWELFTH NIGHT, J B Fagan
AS YOU, Nigel Playfair
CORIOLANUS, Bensonians
MERRY WIVES, Bensonians
MERRY WIVES, W Bridges-Adams?
WINTER'S TALE, Bridges-Adams
CAESAR, Bridges-Adams?
MIDSUMMER, Bridges-Adams?
TEMPEST, Bridges-Adams?
ROMEO, Bridges-Adams?
1920 CYMBELINE, Bridges-Adams?
MERCHANT, Bridges-Adams?
MUCH ADO, Bridges-Adams?
TAMING, Bridges-Adams?
RICHARD 2, Bridges-Adams?

HAMLET, Bridges-Adams ?
AS YOU, Bridges-Adams ?
TWELFTH NIGHT, Bridges-Adams ?
HENRY 5, Bridges-Adams
MACBETH, Bridges-Adams

1921 AY, MC, MV, WT
ANTONY AND CLEO, Bridges-Adams ?
MERRY WIVES, Bridges-Adams ?
RICHARD 3, Bridges-Adams ?
MIDSUMMER, Bridges-Adams ?
HENRY 41, Bridges-Adams ?

1922 CY, HA, MA, TN, TS
ALL'S WELL, Bridges-Adams*?
OTHELLO, Bridges-AdAMS, ?
CAESAR, Bridges-Adams ?
TAMING (Boys School, Olivier as
   Katherine)

1923 H41, R3, MA, MC, MD, MW, TS
MEASURE, Bridges-Adams?
HENRY 42, Bridges-Adams?

1924 AC, MD. MV, MW, OT, TS
LEAR, Bridges-Adams*
HAMLET, Bridges-AdAms?
RICHARD II, Bridges-Adams?

1925 JC, MA, MC, TN
KING JOHN ?
WINTER' TALE, Bridges-Adams
AS YOU, Bridges-Adams?
TWO GENTS, Bridges-Adams*

Theatre Burned 1926;moved to cinema

1926 R2, MD, MV, MW
CORIOLANUS, Bridges-Adams ?
CAESAR, Bridges-Adams, ?
HENRY 42, Bridges-Adams ?
ROMEO, Bridges-Adams, ?
TEMPEST, Bridges-Adams*

1927 AY, HA, MA, MC, TN, TS
HENRY 5, Bridges-Adams
ANTONY AND CLEO, Bridges-Adams?

1928 HA, JC, MD, MV
TIMON, Bridges-Adams*
HENRY 41, Bridges-Adams?
RICHARD 3, Bridges-Adams*
MERRY WIVES, Bridges-Adams*

1929 HA, R2, MA,*MC, MV, TN, TS
ROMEO, Bridges-Adams ?

1930 AY, HA, JC, MA, MC, MD, MW,RJ,TN
R2
OTHELLO, Bridges-Adams*
TEMPEST, Bridges-Adams*

1931 MC, MD, MW*, TS
WINTER'S TALE, Bridges-Adams
LEAR, Bridges-Adams*

HENRY 41, Bridges-Adams*
MEASURE, Bridges-Adams*
ANTONY AND CLEO, Bridges-Adams*

1932 IN THE NEW THEATRE
AY, JC, H41, KL, MD, TN, WT
HENRY 42, Bridges-Adams*
MERCHANT, Benson
MIDSUMMER, Benson
MERCHANT, Theodore Komisarjevsky*

1933 MA, MD, MV, TS
CORIOLANUS, Bridges-Adams*
MACBETH, Komisarjevsky*
RICHARD 2, Tyrone Guthrie
ROMEO, Bridges-Adams*
HAMLET, Bridges-AdAMS*
AS YOU, Bridges-Adams*

1934 JC, MA, MD, RJ, TN
LOVE'S LABOURS, Bridges-Adams*
TEMPEST, Bridges-Adams*
HENRY 5, Robert Atkins*

1935 ALL'S WELL, B Iden Payne*
ANTONY AND CLEO, Payne*
MERCHANT, Payne?
AS YOU, Payne*
MERRY WIVES, Komisarjevsky*
HENRY 41, Payne*
TEMPEST, Randle Aryton*
TAMING, Payne*

1936 TROILUS, Payne*
LEAR, Komisarjevsky*
ROMEO, Payne?
CAESAR, John Wyse*
MUCH ADO, Payne*
HAMLET, Payne*

1937 AY, HA, KL*
WINTER'S TALE, Payne
MIDSUMMER, E Martin Browne
HENRY 5, Payne*
MERRY WIVES, H K Aylift*
CYMBELINE, Payne*

1938 MD, RJ
HENRY 8, Payne*
MAC BETH, Payne*
COMEDY, Komisarjevsky?
TWELFTH NIGHT, Payne*
TWO GENTS, Payne*
TEMPEST, Payne*

1939 CE* MA
TAMING, Komisarjevsky*
AS YOU, Baliol Holloway*
RICHARD 3, Payne*
OTHELLO, Atkins*
TWELFTH NIGHT, Irene Hentschel*
CORIOLANUS, Payne*

1940 AY*
MEASURE, Payne?
MERRY WIVES, Payne*
MERCHANT, Payne*
HAMLET, Payne?
KING JOHN, Payne*
1941 MA, RJ1, TE*
RICHARD 2, Payne
TWELFTH NIGHT, Payne?
TAMING, Payne*
CAESAR, Andrew Leigh*
1942 AY, HA, MD, MV*, TE*, TS*, MV
WINTER'S TALE, Payne?
MACBETH, Payne*
1943 HENRY5, Milton Rosmer*
LEAR, Peter Creswell*
TWELFTH NIGHT, Rosmer*
OTHELLO(Rosmer) Atkins*
MIDSUMMER, Rosmer
MERRY WIVES, Rosmer
WINTER'S TALE, Dorothy Green
1944 HAMLET, Robert Atkins*
MERCHANT, Atkins*
TAMING, Atkins*
AS YOU, Atkins*
MACBETH, Atkins*
RICHARD 2, Atkins
MIDSUMMER, Atkins*
1945 ANTONY AND CLEO, Atkins
MERRY WIVES, Atkins*
HENRY 8, Atkins*
ROMEO, Atkins*
TWELFTH NIGHT, Atkins*
OTHELLO, Atkins*
MUCH ADO, Atkins*
1946 CYMBELINE, Nugent Monck
HENRY 5, Dorothy Green*
LOVE'S LABOURS, Peter Brook*
MACBETH, Michael MacOwen
MEASURE, Frank McMullan*
TEMPEST, Eric Crozier*
AS YOU, Herbert Prentice*
1947 MM* (Ronald Giffin) , LL
TWELFTH NIGHT, Walter Hudd*
ROMEO, Brooks*
TEMPEST, Norman Wright*
RICHARD 2, Hudd
MERCHANT, Michael Benthall*
PERICLES, Monck*
1948 MV
HAMLET, Benthall*
KING JOHN, Benthall
TAMING, Benthall

WINTER'S TALE, Anthony Quayle
TROILUS, Quayle*
OTHELLO, Godfrey Tearle*
1949 MACBETH, Quayle*
MUCH ADO. Gielgud and Quayle*
MIDSUMMER(Quayle) Benthall*
CYMBELINE(Quayle) Benthall*
OTHELLO(Quayle) Tearle*
HENRY 8(Quayle), Guthrie*
1950 H8*, MA*
MEASURE, Quayle*
CAESAR, Quayle*
LEAR, Gielgud and Quayle*
1951 RICHARD 2, Quayle*
HENRY 41, Quayle*
HENRY 42(Quayle) Redgrave*
HENRY 5, Quayle*
TEMPEST(Quayle) Benthall*
1952 CORIOLANUS, Glen Byam Shaw *
TEMPEST, Benthall*
AS YOU, Shaw*
MACBETH, Gielgud*
1953 MERCHANT, Shaw
RICHARD 3, Shaw*
ANTONY AND CLEO, Shaw*
TAMING, George Devine*
Lear (Shaw) Devine*
1954 OTHELLO, Quayle*
MIDSUMMER, Devine*
ROMEO, Shaw*
TAMING, Devine*
TROILUS, Shaw*
1955 TWELFTH NIGHT, Gielgud*
ALL'S WLLL, Noel Williams*
M ACBETH, Shaw*
MERRY WIVES(Quayle) Shaw*
TITUS , Brook(Canon)
M UCH ADO, Gielgud
LEAR, Devine
1956 HAMLET, Michael Langham*
MERCHANT, Margaret Webster*
OTHELLO, Shaw*
LOVE'S LABOURS, Peter Hall*
MEASURE, Quayle*
1957 AS YOU, Shaw*
KING JOHN, Douglas Seale
CAESAR, Shaw*
CYMBELINE, Hall*
TEMPEST, Brook*
1958 ROMEO, Shaw*
TWELFTH NIGHT, Hall*
HAMLET, Shaw*
PERICLES, Tony Robertson*
MUCH ADO, eale*
LEAR, Trevor Nunn*

1959 OTHELLO, Ri chardson
     ALL'S WELL, T ryone Guthrie*
     MIDSUMMER, Hall*
     CORIOLANUS, Hall*
     LEAR, Shaw*
1960 TWO GENTS, Hall*
     MERCHANT, Langham*
     TWELFTH NIGHT, Hall*
     TAMING, John Barton
     TROILUS, Hall*
     WINTER'S TALE, Peter Wood
1961 TS*
     MUCH ADO, Langham*
     HAMLET, Wood*
     RICHARD 3, William Gaskill*
     AS YOU, Michael Elliott*
     ROMEO, Hall*
     OTELLO, Franco Zeffirelli*
     TAMING, Maurice Daniels
1962 TS
     MEASURE, John Blatchley*
     MIDSUMMER, Hall*
     MACBETH, Donald McWhinney*
     CYMBELINE, William Gaskill
     COMEDY, Clifford Williams*
     LEAR, Brook *
1963 CE, MD
     TEMPEST, Williams*
     CAESAR, Blatchley*
     HENRY 61, Hall
     EDW ARD 4, Hall* (H62-H63)
     RICHARD 3, Hall*
1964 H6, E4, R3
     RICHARD 2, Hall
     HENRY 41, Hall*
     HENRY 42, Hall*
     HENRY 5, Hall*
     MERRY WIVES, Blatchley*
1965 CE
     LOVE'S LABOURS, Barton*
     MERCHANT, Williams*
     TIMON, John Schlesinger*
     HAMLET, Hall*
1966 HA*
     HENRY 41, Barton*
     HENRY 42, Barton*
     HENRY 5, Barton
     TWELFTG NIGHT, Williams*
1967 TAMING, Trevor Nunn*
     CORIOLANUS, Barton*
     ALL'S WELL, Barton*
     AS YOU, David Jones*
     MACBETH, Hall*
     ROMEO, Karolos Koun*

1968 AY, H5
     CAESAR, Barton*
     LEAR, Nunn
     MERRY WIVES, Terry Hands*
     TROILUS, Barton*
     MUCH ADO, Nunn*
1969 MW
     PERICLES, Hands*
     WINTER'S TALE, Nunn
     TWELFTH NIGHT, Barton*
     HENRY 8, Nunn*
     WHEN THOU ART KING, Ba rton*
1970 TN
/   MEASURE, Barton*
     RICHARD 3, Hands*
     HAMLET, Nunn*
     KING JOHN, Buzz Goodbody*
     TWO GENTS, Robin Phillips*
     MIDSUMMER, Brook*
     TEMPEST, Barton*
     WHEN THOU ART KING, Barton ?
1971 TN
     MERCHANT, Hands*
     RICHARD 2, Barton*
     HENRY 5, Ronald Eyre*
     OTHELLO, Barton*
     MUCH ADO, Eyre*
1972 CORIOLANUS, Nunn*
     CAESAR, Nunn*
     ANTONY AND CLEO, Nunn*
     TITUS, Nunn*
1973 CR
     ROMEO, Hands*
     RICHARD 2, Barton*
     AS YOU, Goodbody*
     LOVE'S LABOURS, David Jones*
     TAMING, Williams*
1974 KING JOHN, Barton*
     CYMBELINE Kyle and Barton*
     TWELFTH NIGHT, Peter Gill*
     MEASURE, Keith Hack*
     MACBETH, Nunn*
     LEAR, Goodbody, Other Place*
     TEMPEST, Hooks, Other Place*
1975 HENRY 5, Hands*
     HENRY 41, Hands*
     HENRY 42, Hands*
     MERRY WIVES, Hands*
     HAMLET, Goodbody, Other Place*
     RICHARD 3, Barry Kyle, Other Place*

TYRONE GUTHRIE THEATRE, Minneapolis,
  Minn, USA
1963 HAMLET, Tyrone Guthrie*
1964 HENRY 5, Edward Payton Call*
1965 RICHARD 3, Guthrie*
1966 AS YOU, Call*
1968 TWELFTH NIGHT, Robert LANCASTER
1969 CAESAR, Call*
1970 TEMPEST, Philip Minor
1971 TAMING, Michael Langham*
1973 MIDSUMMER, John Hirsch*
  MERCHANT, Langham*
1974 LOVE'S LABOURS, Langham*
  LEAR, Langham *

UNIVERSITY PLAYERS, UNIVERSITY OR
  MICHIGAN, Ann Arbor, Mich, USA
1917 MERRY WIVES, Richard D T Hollister and Louis Eich
1923 MUCH ADO, Hollister
1930 ROMEO, Valentine B Windt
1932 TAMING, Windt
1933 MIDSUMMER, Windt and William Halstead
  OTHELLO, Windt
  TWELFTH NIGHT, Windt
1937 HENRY 8, Windt
  TWO GENTS, Windt
1940 CAESAR, Windt
1941 MUCH ADO , Halstead and Windt
1944 COMEDY, Windt
1948 AS YOU , Halstead
1950 LEAR, Halstead
  MIDSUMMER, Windt
1951 ROMEO, Halstead
  RICHARD 2, Claribel Baird
1952 TWELFTH NIGHT, R C Hunter
1954 TAMING, Halstead
  HAMLET, B Iden Payne
1957 RICHARD 3, James Brock
1958 LOVE'S LABOURS , Halstead
1960 AS YOU, Halstead
1961 HENRY 41, Baird
1962 HENRY 42, Halstead
1964 HENRY 5, Halstead
1966 HENRY 61, Halstead and Richard
  Burgwin
  HENRY 62, Burgwin and Halstead
  HENRY 63, Halstead and Burnwin
  WINTER'S TALE, Burgwin
  CORIOLANUS, Halstead
1967 MACBETH, Burgwin
  KING JOHN, Burgwin

1968 TROILUS, Burgwin
  TEMPEST, Halstead
1969 MUCH ADO, Coakley
  TITUS, Halstead
1970 MERCHANT, Burgwin
1971 TIMON, Halstead
  TWELFTH NIGHT, Burgwin
  CYMBELINE, Halstead
1974 PERICLES, Halstead (Canon)

APPENDIX D - INDEX TO SIGLA BY PLAYS

NOTE: In spite of effort to prevent it, I have inadvertently occasionally used the same sigla for two editors. Since this never occurs in the
same play, it should not cause confusion. I altered CKRfor Charles Kemble
Shakespeare Readings to KRe after the first volumes to avoid confusion with
Charles Kean items.

AB1 Angus Bowmer: HA, LL

AD1 Augustin Daly: AW, AW, H42, LL,
    MA, MD, MV, MW, RJ, TC, TE, TN,
    TS

AD2 Augustin Daly: TN

AF1 Allen Fletcher: AC, AY, CR, HA1,
    KL, R3, MA, MM, TS

AF2 Allen Fletcher: R3

Age Age of Kings: H41, H42, H5, H61,
    H62, H63, R2, R3

AJA A J Antoon: CY

Ale Rod Alexander: LL

AL1Arthur Lithgow; KJ, but see also
    Appendix

All Belfast: Allen: HA

An1 Anonymous: AW, H42, H5, H8, KJ,
    LL, MW, OT, TE, TN, TS

An2 Anonymous: AW

AN1 Adelaide Neilsen: RJ, TS

AN2 Adelaide Neilsen: RJ1

Ang Margaret Anglin: RJ

Apo Edinburgh: Apollo Press: MM

AQ1 Anthony Quayle: MM, OT, TC, WT

BA1 W Bridges-Adams: AC, AW, AY, CR,
    CY, H4, H41, H42, KJ, KL, R3,
    LL, MA, MM, MW, OT, RJ, TE,TG,
    TM, TS

BAE Banksside Acting Edition: AY, CE,
    CR, HA, JC, H5, KJ, KL, R2,MC,
    MD, MV, TN

Bak Boston: Baker: CE, JC, MV

Bal Richard Baldridge: MV

Bar London: Barker: AY, CY, H8, KL,
    R3, MC, MM, MV, OT, RJ, TE, TN,
    WT

BaS Barry Sullivan: H41, H5, KJ, MC,
    MV, WT

Bat London: Bathurst: CR, CY, JC ,
    H41, H42, H8, KJ, KL, MC, MM,
    OT, TE, TN

Bel London: Bell: AC, AW, AY, CE,CR,
    CY, HA, JC, H41, H42, H5, H8,
    KJ, KL, R2, R3, LL, MA, MC, MV,
    MW, OT, RJ, TA, TE, TG, TM, WT

Ben Walter Benn : HA

BGr Ben Greet Shakespeare : AY, CE,
    JC, H41, MD, MV, TE

BH1 Bernard Hepton: AC, CR, H42

BJ1 Barry Jackson: HA

BK1 Barry Kyle: CY, R3

Bla John Blatchley: MM, MW

B1B Blanche Bates: AY, RJ

Bou Arthur Bouchier: MV

Bri 'Bridgeman.' London: Linsdale

Bro Dublin: Charles Broad: TE

BT1 Herbert Beerbohm-Tree: AC, HA,H41,
    H8, KJ, R2, MA, MC, MM, MV, MW,
    OT, RJ, TE, TN, WT

BT2 Herbert Beerbohm-Tree: MM, TN

BTN 'H Beerbohm Tree.' London: Nassau:
    JC

Bur: Richard Burton: HA

But London: Butters: AY, CR, JC, H41,
    H5, H8, KJ, KL, MA, MC, OT, TE,TG

BVi Benjamin Victor adaptation: TG

BzG Buzz Goodbody: AY, KJ, KL

C21 'Colley Cibber.' London, n p, 1721:
    R3

Cap David Garrick-Edward Capell PB: AC

CBH Charles B Hanford: MA, WT

CBS Columbia Broadcasting Co: AY, HA,
    H41, KL, MA, TS

CC1 Charlotte Cushman: HA

CC2 Charlotte Cushman: HA

ChC Charles Calvert: AC, H42, H5, H8,
    R3, MD, MV, WT

ChF Charles Frohman: MA

ChM Charles Marsh: CY

Cib Colley Cibber: R3

CiM 'Colley Cibber.' London: Mears: R3

CKB 'Charles Kean.' London: Bradley:
    MC, OT

CK1 Charles Kean PB: MW

CK2: "   "   "   " MW

CKC 'Charles Kean.' London: Chapman:
    HA, H5, H8, KJ, KL, R2, MA, MC,
    MD, MV, TE, WT

CKN 'Charles Kean." London: Nassau: MA

CKP Charles Kean PB: CY, R2, MV, TE,
    TG

CKR <u>Charles Kemble Shakespeare Read-
ings</u> : HA, H41, OT (See <u>KRe</u>
for continuation)

CMe Charles Melville: KJ

CN1 Craig Noel, TS (See also <u>Noe</u>)

Col George Colman: KL

Con <u>Contention</u>: H62

CPr <u>Cromwell</u> Price: KJ

CrP Sydenham: Crystal Palace Co: HA,
MA, MC, MV, RJ, TE

CUM London: Cumberland: AC, AW, AY,
CE, CR, CY, HA, JC, H41,H42,
H5, H8, KJ, KL, R2, R3, LL, MA,
MC, MD, MV, MW, OT, RJ, TC, TE,
TN1

Dav London: Davidson: H61, H62, H63,
MC, MW, TE

DBL David Beatt and James Love: H8

DC1 Dennis Carey: MA, TS

DD1 John Dryden and William Daven-
ant: TE

DD2 Dryden and Davenant: TE

DD3 Dryden and Davenant: TE

Deb London: Debrett: H5, TE

Der Dering ms: H41, H42

GD1 Dorothy Green: H5, WT

DiB Dion Boucicault: MA

DJ1 David Jones: LL

DLo Dublin: Austin Long: AY

DM1 Diana Maddox: MM, RJ

Dnt 'Davenant.' London: Clark: MC

DoC Douglas Campbell: WT

DoF Douai Library, France: AY, MC,
RJ, TN

Dol London: Dolby: CY, H41, H5, H8,
R3, MA, MC, MW, OT, RJ, WT

Don Thomas Donovan, <u>English Histor-
ical Plays</u>: H41, H42, H5, H61,
H62, H63, KJ, R2, R3

Dou John Doud: RJ

DS1 Douglas Seale: HA, H5, H61,H62,
H63, KJ, MV, PE, R2

DuG Dublin: Gilbert: AY

DuW Dublin: Wilkinson: CE

DV1 Denis Vance: H41

DvB David Belasco: MV

DW1 David Williams: H5, KL, R2, MW,
OT

EBA Edwin Booth-Hinton, "Altered:"
R3

EBH Edwin Booth-Henry L Hinton: R3,
MC, MV, OT, RJ

EBP Edwin Booth PB: MV, R2, R3, OT

EBW Edwin Booth-William Winter: HA,
JC, H8, KL, R2, MA, MC, MV,OT

EC1 Edward Payton Call: H41, H5, R3
(see EPC)

EC1 Eric Christmas : LL, MD, MV

EdB Edward Berkeley: PE

Edi Edinburgh: Yair: MA

EDR Edinburgh: Reid: RJ

EdT Edward Tearle: AC

Edw Harry Edwards: AW

EF1 Edwin Forrest: KL

EFT 'Edwin Forrest.' NY: Torrey Bros:
R3, MC

EKi <u>Richard, Duke of York</u>. In <u>Henry
Irving Shakespeare</u>: H62, H63

EHW <u>Richard, Duke of York</u>. London:
White: H61, H62, H63

EPC Edward Payton Call, TE

ER1 Ellis Rabb: AC, HA, MC

ET1 Ellen Terry: CR, MA, MV, MW, OT

F1 Folio: HA,

FB1 Firth Banbury: LL

FB1 Frank Benson: AW, AY, HA, JC,H62,
MC, MD, MV, OT, RJ, TM, TS

Fea 'Cibber.' London: Feales: R3

Fec Charles Fechter: OT

Fil A E Filmer: OT

FGr Fred Grove: MA, TN

FHa Frederick Haywell: H61, H62, H63

FL1 May have been used for Fritz
Leiber, but see FrL

FMc Frank McMullan:MM

FnK Fanny Kemble: MD

FrL Fritz Leiber: AY, HA, KL, R3,MA,
MV, RJ, TN, TS

FRo 'Johnston Forbes-Robertson.'Lon-
don: Nassau: MC

FW1 Frank Wolfe: WT

FW1 May have been used for Frederick
Warde, but see FWa

FWa Frederick Warde: KL, RJ, TM, WT

FQ1 <u>Fairy Queen</u>: MD

FQ2 <u>Fairy Queen</u>: MD

G61 David Garrick, 1761

G&C 'David Garrick and George Colman:
MD

GCa 'David Garrick and Edward Capell!
London: Tonson, 1758: AC

GFr David Garrick, <u>The Fairies</u>: MD

GaK David Garrick PB in London:
Knudson: HA

GaP David Garrick PB, 1773: LL, MC
Gar London: Garland: OT
GaT David Garrick PB in Tonson: H42
GaW David Garrick PB in Witford: HA
GaW David Garrick Works: RJ, TS
GB1 George Becks: H8, MC, MM, TE,TS
GeB George Bartlett: MW
DeD George Devine: KJ, KL, TS
GFC George Frederick Cooke: H8, TM
GFT David Garrick, A Fairy Tale: MD
Gie John Gielgud: HA, MA, TN
GM1 Guthrie McClintic: HA
GMG George McGovern: H8
GoT Godfrey Tearle: OT
GS1 Glen Byam Shaw: AC, AY, CE, HA,JC,
    H5, KL, R3, MW, OT, TC
GTh Globe Theatre Versions; AW, AY,CE,
    HA1, JC, KL, MD, RJ, TE, TN,TS
GV1 Gladys Vaughn: WT
Hac James H Hackett: H42, MC, MW
Ha2 James H Backett: MW
Ha3 James H Hackett: MW
Hal 'Halliday.' London: Tinsley: AC
H&K Hare and Kendal: AY
Han Charles B Hanford: CY, TS
Hat J Hatton: MA
HFa Helen Faucit: CY, RJ
Hel Franklin Heller: CR
HIC 'Henry Irving.' London: Chiswick:
    CR, CY, HA, JC, R3, MA, MV, RJ,
    TN
HIM Henry Irving Shakespeare: All but
    MM, TA, TM, TN
Hin 'Love.' London: Hingeston: TM
Hin Peter Hines: HA
HIN 'Henry Irving.' London: Nassau:
    H8, KL, MC
HIP Henry Irving PB: CY, HA, KJ, KL,
    R3, OT
Hir John Hirsch: HA, H61, H62, R3
His London: Hinds Edition: R3, OT
Hit London: Hitch: H41, H8
HIT Henry Irving Tour: MV
HJ1 Henry Jewitt: AY, CR, HA, MA, MC,
    MM, MV, MW, OT, RJ, TE, TN, TS,
    WT
HKA H K Aylift: AW, HA, MW, TS
HM1 Helena Modjeska: AY, HA, KL, MM,
    MV, RJ, TN
HnB Henry Betty: AY, HA, KL, MM, MV,
    RJ, TE, TG
HnC Henrietta Crosman: AY

Hor Miss A E C Horniman: CE, MA, TN
HT1 Hal J Todd: TA
HTP Henry and Thomas Placide: CE
Hud Will Huddleston: H61
Hul Thomas Hull: CE
HWG Harry Wagstall Gribble: TS
H87 London: Herringman, 1687: ? prob-
    ably JC, MA or MM

ICT Ingratitude of a Commonwealth: CR
Inc 'Mrs Inchbald.' London: Longman:
    AC, AY, CE, CR, CY, HA, JC, H41,
    H42, H5, K8, KJ, KL, R3, MA, MC,
    MM, MV, MW, OT, RJ, TE, TN
IP1 Ben Iden Payne: AC, AW, AY, CR,
    CY, HA, H41, H42, H5, H8, R2,
    R3, MA, MC, MM, MV, RJ, TC,TG,
    WT
IP2 Ben Iden Payne: AY,   , CY, H8,R3,
    MM, RC, WT
IP3 Ben Iden Payne: CY
IRC Ian Richardson-Barry Cole: R3
JaA James Anderson: MV
JaS James Stark : KL
JB1 John Barrymore: HA
JB1 John Barton: AW, CR, H41, H42,KJ,
    R2, R3, LL, MM, OT, TC, TE, TS,
    WT
JBB J B Buckstone: AY
JBB Junius Brutus Booth: R3
JBR James B Roberts: HA, H41, H8, KJ,
    MC, MV, OT, RJ
JBW John B Wright: WT
JCo John Coleman: H5
JD1 John Dexter: OT
JFR Johnston Forbes-Robertson: HA,
    OT, RJ(see also FRo)
JG1 Jean Gascon: CY, KJ, LL, OT, PE
JG1 John Golden: WV
JH1 John Houseman: AW, CR, HA, KJ, KL,
    MA, MC, MM, MW, OT, WT
JHa John Hale: MW
JKC 'J P Kemble.' London: Christie: CR
JKD 'J P Kemble.' London: Rodwell: AW,
    R3, MC, OT
JKL 'J P Kemble.' London: Longman: CR,
    H8, KJ, OT, TE, TN
JKM 'J P Kemble.' London: Miller: AW,
    AY, CE, CR, CY, HA, JC, H41,H42,
    H5, H8, KJ, KL, R3, MA, MC, MD,
    MV, OT, RJ, TE, TG, TN, WT
JKP John Philip Kemble PB: AC, JC, TC,
    TN

JKR 'J P Kemble.' London: Ridgeway: H42, MM, MW

JKR 'J P Kemble.' London: Roach: KL

JKT 'J P Kemble.' London: Theatre: AW, AY, CE, CY, JC, H41, KL, R3, MA, MV, RJ, TC, WT

JKW 'J P Kemble.' London: Lowndes: CR, HA, H5, KJ, KL, MM, MV, MW, WT

JL1 J ean Davenport Lander: AC

JM1 Jonathan Miller: MV

JMH John Martin-Harvey: TS

JMo J ohn Moore: HA, KJ, R2, OT, WT

JN1 J ohn Neville: HA

JnC J ane Cowl: RJ, TN

JnL 'John Lee.' Edinburgh: Ceyne: MC

Jor Jon Jory: AW

JP1 Joseph Papp: AC, AW, CR, HA, H5, R3, JC, MA, MV, TC

JP2 Joseph Papp: TC

JRo John Roberts: R2

JS1 James Sandoe: AC

JT1 Jerry Turner: HA, H61, OT, TC

JTe Joachim Tenscher: CR

JuA Julia Arthur: AY, RJ

JM1 Julia Marlowe: AY, KL, MM, TN, TS(see also Sothern and Mar-Lowe)

JuP Julia Powell: MV

JWa James A Wallace: KL

JWB John Wilkes Booth: R3

JWW James William Wallack: RJ

KAQ John Kidd and Antony Quayle H41

Kat Milton Katselas: OT

KH1 Keith Hook; MM, TE

Kin Edward Henry King: H41

KK1 KAROLOS Koun: RJ

KMi 'Charles Kemble.' London: Miller:H42

Kna London: Knapson: HA

KRe Charles Kemble's Shakespeare Readings: AY, CR, CY, JC, H42, H5, H8, KJ, R3, MA, MC, MV

KyB 'Kyrle Bellew.'London: Kopple: AC

L64 London: Lacy; H41(scene 31 only)

L 69 London: Booksellers, 1769: RJ

L&W 'Lopez and Wemyss.' Philadelpia: Poole: MA

Lac London: Lacy: AC, AY, CE, CR, CY, HA, JC, H41, H42, H5, H8, KL,

R2, MA, MD, MV, MW, OT, RJ, TE, TN

LaK Laura Keene: MD

Lam 'Charles Lamb.' London: Chapple: TM

Lan Jack Landau: MV, RJ(see also JH1)

LBa Lawrence Barrett: KL

Lea Dublin: Leathley: H8

LeA Lena Ashwell: HA, H41, MW, WT

LeG Eva LeGallienne: RJ, TN

Let 'Litton.' London: Letts: AY

LiL 'Mrs Langtry.' London: Leadenhall Press: AC

Lis London: Lister: MC

LK1 Larry Kornfeld: AC

LoC 'Louis Calvert.' Manchester: Broad: AC, H41

Lon London: Longman: MC

Low London: Lowndes: CY, R3, MA, TN

LeH Leslie Howard: HA

LT1 Lark Taylor: TN

LW1 Laird Williamson: H5, TA, TG

LWa Louis Waller: CR, OT

MaA Maude Adams: MV, RJ, TN

Man M Manisoff: CR

Mar London: Martin: HA

MB1 Michael Benthall: AW, CR, CY, HA, JC, H5, H8, KJ, R2, MV, TE, TM, WT

MB2 Michael Benthall: CY

MBr E Martin Browne: OT

McC Guthrie McClintic: RJ

McG George McGowan

McV Chicago: McVickers Th: MD

McV 'McVickers.' Chicago: Jefferson Th: TE

MD1 Meredith Dallas: R2 ;see App

Mei Duke of Saxe-Meiningen: JC

Mel Frederick Melville: H8

MEv Maurice Evans: HA

MgM Maggie Morton: RJ

MHS Michael Hampton Simpson: MV(see/7)

MK1 Michael Kahn: H5, R2, LL, MV,MW, OT, TN

ML1 Michael Langham: AC, CR, HA, JC, H41, H5, KL, R3, LL, MV, MW, OT, RJ, TC, TG, TM

ML2 Michael Langham: H5, LL

MMF Minnie Maddern Fiske: MA, MW

MP1 Motion Picture: JC, RJ

MR1 Michael Redgrave: H42

MR1 Milton Rosmer: H5, TN

MS1 Mel Shapiro and John Guare: TG
MS1 Michael Sampson: H59 (see also MHS)
MsB Mrs Bateman: MC
MTh Memorial Theatre Edition: all
Mur James Murdoch: MC
MW1 Margaret Webster: R2, MM, OT, TE
MyA 'Mary Anderson.' London: Nassau: RJ, WT
NBC National Broadcast Co: JC
NBG Norman Bel Geddes: HA
New NY: Dewitt-Charles Newton: H5
NiW Nicol Williamson: HA
NL1 Norman Lloyd: TS
NM1 Nugent Monck: all
NM2 Nugent Monck: AW, CR, CY, HA, JC, H61, H62, H63, R2, R3, LL, MA, MD, MW, RE, RJ, TA, TC, TE
Noe Craig Noel: KJ(see also CN1)
NTa Nahum Tate: KL
Nur 'Nursery PB': CE
NW1 Noel Willman: AW
OA1 Oscar Asche: AC, AY, JC, MM, MV, TS
O&B Edinburgh: Oliver and Boyd: AY, CR, H41, H8, KL, R3, MA, MC, MV, MW, OT, RJ
Oli Laurence Olivier: +A, H5
ON1 Oliver Neville: MC
OP1 Other Place, Stratford-upon-Avon: HA
Opr Opera based on Tempest: TE
OV1 Old Vic: OT
OW1 Orson Welles: JC, MC, MV, TN
OW2 Orson Welles: MC
OwC F Owen Chambers: MD, MW, TE
Oxb Oxberry Edition. London: Simpkin: AY, CR, CY, HA, JC, H41, H5, H8, KJ, KL, R3, MA, MC, MV, MW, OT, RJ, TE, TN, WT
Ox1 London: Oxlade: CY, MV, RJ, TE
P95 London: Proprietors 1795: CY
Pad U of Padua: MM
Pat London: Pattie: MD
PB1 Peter Brook: MM, TA, TE
PCr Peter Creswell: KL
PD1 Peter Dews: AY, R2
PH1 Peter Hall: CR, CY, HA, H41, H42, H5, H61, H62, H63, R2, R3, LL, MC, MD, TE
PHa Philip Hanson: H5
PhM Philip Merivale: MC
Pla The Players: H41, H42, OT, TC

Plu James Plumptree: MV
PW1 Peter Wood: AY, HA, WT

Q1 First Quarto: HA, H5, KL, R3, OT, RJ
Q2 Second Quarto: RJ

RA1 Robert Atkins: AC, AY, HA1, H8, R2, MC, MD, MV, OT, RJ, TS
Ran London: Randall: MC, MV, TN
Rav Howard Ravenscroft: TA
RB1 Richard Burton: H8
RBM Robert M Mantell: RJ
RBr Robert Breen: HA
RCu 'Richard Cumberland.' London: Proprietors: TM
RD1 Richard Digby Day: TE
RE1 Ronald Eyre: TA
REJ Robert Edmond Jones: MA, OT
Rey 'Reynolds.' London: Miller: MD
RH1 Robert Helpman: AC, AY, TE
Ric Peter Richings: MW
Rig 'George Rignold.' London: Williams: CY, H5
Ris Mme Ristori: MC
Riv London: Rivington: AY, MA, TE
RMa Richard Mansfield: H5, R3
RMM London: Rivington, Monthly Magazine: CR
Roa London: Roach: CY, H41, R2, R3, OT
Rob Romney Brent: MW
RoM Rouben Mamoulion: HA
Ros 'Sig Rossi' London: Drury Lane MC
RP1 Robin Phillips: MM
RR1 Richard Risso: H8, TE

Sab London: Sabine: R3
SaC 'Tommaso Salvini.' London: Clayton: MC
SaE 'Tommaso Salvini.' London: Edmonds: KL
Sak 'Edwin Saker.' Liverpool: Newman: CA, MA, MD, WT
Sal Tommaso Salvini: CR
SaL 'Tommaso Salvini.' London: 1876: OT
SB1 Stuart Burge: H41, H42
Sch John Schlesinger: TM
SFr 'George Skillan.' London: French: HA, JC, H41, H42, H8, MA, MW, OT, RJ
Sim London: Butters for Simmons: MC

SmA Dublin: Smock Alley Th: CE, HA, H8, MC, OT
SM1 Sothern and Marlowe: AC, AY, CY, MA, MC, MV, RJ, TN, TS
SM2 Sothern and Marlowe: MW, RJ, TS,
SM3 Sothern and Marlowe; RJ
SMT Sothern and Marlowe, Lark Taylor:
Sot E H Sothern PB; HA, KL
SP1 Samuel Phelps: AC, AY, CE, CR, JC, H41, H42, KJ, KL, R3, LL, MC, MD, MM, PE, RJ, TE, TG, TM
SP2 Samuel Phelps: PE, R3
SP3 Samuel Phelps: TM
SSd Sarah Siddons: OT
Sta Constantin Stanislavsky: OT
SV1 Stuart Vaughn: H61, H62, H63, R3
SW1 David Schweitzer: TC
Swi John Swinburne: CY

T22 London: Tonson for Chetwood; MM
T34 London: Tonson, 1734: CE, RJ
T50 London: Tonson, 1750: RJ
T63 'Garrick.' London: Tonson, 1763: MD
Tab London: Tabby: CR
TaB Tallulah Bankhead: AC
Tay James Taylor: TG
TG1 Tyrone Guthrie: AW, HA, H8, R3, MV, TM
TG2: Tyrone Guthrie: H8, R3
TH1 Terry Hands: H41, H42, H5, MV, MW, PE
ThB Th omas Betterton, "Sequel":H42
ThC Theophilus Cibber: RJ
ThK Theodore Komisarjevsky: CE, KL, MW, TN
Tho London: Thompson: TE
TM1 Thomas MArcus: MW
TN1 Trevor Nunn: AC, CR, HA, H8, KL, MC, TA
TR1 TR1 Tony Robertson: OT, PE
TR2 Tony Robertson: PE
TSh Thomas Shadwell: TM
TTY True Tragedy . . . York, 1596: H61, H62, H63
Tuc London: Tuck: KJ
Ty1 George C Tyler: MC
Ty2 George C Tyler: MC

USF NY : French: AY, CR, HA, JC, H41, H8, KJ, KL, R3, LL, MA, MC, MD, MV, MW, OT, RJ, TN, WT

US: NY; Longworth: H41, H8, MC, MV, MW, R3, RJ
USN Philadelpia: Near: MW
USR Boston: Richardson: OT
USS Boston: Spencer: CE
USS Boston: West: TN
UST NY; Taylor: TE
UST Philadelpia: Turner: R3
USW Boston: Wells: AY, CR, CY, R3, MV, TN

Val 'Valpy.' Reading School: H42, MW
Ves Elizabeth Vestris: LL
Vez Hermann Vezin: KL
ViA Viola Allen: AY, CY, TN, WT
Vin 'Mr Vining,' London: Johnson: CE

WA1 Winthrop Ames: AC, AY, JC, MA, MV, MW , RJ, TN, WT
Wal London: Walker: CR, HA, H41, MM
WB1 Word Baker and Jack Landau: TC
WBa Wilson Barrett: HA
WEB William E Burton: MD
We1 London: Wellington: HA, KL
Wen London: Wenman: AW, CR, CY, JC, H5, H8, MA, MC, MD, MV, MW, OT, RJ, TE, TM, TN, WT
WG1 William Gaskill: R3
WH1 Walter Hampden: HA, H5, R3, MA, MC, MV, OT, RJ, TS
WhK Whitford Kane: HA
Wit London: Witford: HA
WM1 William Charles Macready: AC, AY, CY, HA, JC, H5, H8, KJ, R2, MA, MC, MV, TG
WMT "Macready.' London: Tallis: MC
WmB William Burton: TE
WmC William Creswick: HA, OT
WmD William Daly: HA
WmS William Seymour: CY
Wog: Dublin: E Wogan: R3
WoR War of the Roses, John Barton, Peter Hall: H61, H62, H63
WP1 William Poel: CR, HA, R2, MM, RJ, TC
WPo William Powell; KJ
WR1 William Roberts: H42
Wro 'Richard Wroughton,' London: Miller: R2
WT1 Wendy Toye: AY
WWB William Warren Ed, Boston:Baker:MW
WWo William B Wood: KJ, KL
Zef Zefferelli: OT

APPENDIX E - INDEX BY PLAYS

Baker(Boston): CE, HA, JC, MA, MD, MV MW, TN, TS
Baker, Arthur(London): RJ
Baker(NY): HA
Bald(London), MD, TS
Baldridge, Richard: MV
Baldwin(London): KL
Baldwin(NY): R3, R3App
Ball, Bill: H42, JC
Ballantyne(London): MV
Balne(London)ł OT
Baltimore Museum(Baltimore): JC
Baltimore Theatre : Baltimore Museum
Banbury, Firth: LL
Bankhead, Tallulah: AC
Banks, John: H8
Bankside Acting Edition(London): AY, CE, CR, HA, JC, H5, KJ, KL, R2, MC, MD, MV, TN
Bankside Restoration Shakespeare(London): TE
Barker, Harley, Granville-: see Granville
Barker(London): AC, AY, CY, HA, KL,R3, MC, MD, MM, MV, OT, RJ, RJApp, TN, WT
Barley(London): CE, R3
Barnaby, Charles: AW
Barnes: T H: MC
Barrell, J B: AY
Barrett, Lawrence: HA, JC, KJ, KL, R3, MC, MV, OT
Barrios(London): HA
Barrow, T, Jr(London): OT
Barrow-Diggers, The: MD
Barry and Burton: MD
Barry, Eleanor: AY
Barry, Thomas: AC, CR, JC, H41, H5, H8, KJ, MD, MM, OT, TE, TN, WT
Barrymore, Ethel: HA, MV
Barrymore, John: HA, HAApp
Bartlett, George: MW
Bartley, George: H41
Barton, John: AW, CR, CY, JC, H41, H42, H5, H61, H62, H63, KJ, R2, R2App, R3, LL, MM, OT, TC, TCApp, TE, TN, TS
Bassett, Russell: H8
Bateman, Mrs: MC
Bates, Blanche: AY, RJ
Bates, James W: R3
Batchelder, J D: HA
Bath Theatre : Th Royal(see name)

Bathurst(London): AY, CR, CY, HA, JC, H41, H62, H63, H8, KJ, KL, MC, MM, MV, MW, OT, TE, TM, TN, TS, WT
Batstead(London): RJ
Baumbauer, Charles: MV
Bax, Peter: MD
Beatrice and Benedick: MA
Beatt, David: H8, MC
Beaumont and Fletcher: H41
Beauty the Best Advocate: MM
Beauty the Conquorer: AC
Becker(London): TM
Beckerman, Bernard: LL, LLApp, TC
Becks, George: AC, CW, AY, CE, HA, JC, H8, KJ, KL, R2, R3, MA, MC,MD, MM, MV, OT, RJ, TE, TG, TN, WT
Bedell(London): MW
Bedford(NY): HA, MC
Beerbohm-Tree, Herbert: AC, HA, JC, H41, AY, KJ, R2, MA, MC, MD, MV,MW, OT, RJ, TE, TN, TS, WT
Begnett(Cork): RJ
Belasco, David: KL, MV
Belfast publishers: Allen, Magee, Mance(see names)
Bell, George Joseph: KL, ML
Bell, Gorman T: MC
Bell:Edinburgh): MM
Bell(London): all
Bell, 2nd edition(London): none
Bell, 1777(London): R2
Bell supplement to Bell's British Farces, 1784(London): WT
Bell and Daldy(London): CR, TE
Bell, H B(London): CY
Bell, Jane(London): KL
Bellamy, Daniel: AY
Bellew, Kyrle: AC
Benedetti, Robert: TS
Ben Greet Shakespeare: AC, CE, JC, MD, MV, TN
Benn, Walter: HA
Bennett, Charles: AW, MC
Bennett, C S: JC, KJ
Bennett, James: KJ
Benson: Frank B: AW, AY, HA, JC, H62, MC, MD, MV, OT, RJ, TN, TS
Benthall, Michael: AC, AW, CR, CY, HA, JC, H5, H8, KJ, R2, MD, MM, MMApp, MV, TE, TN, TS, WT
Bentley(London): AC, CY, H41, H62, H63, KL, OT
Berkeley, Edward: MC, PE, TE

Brooklyn Theatre: Academy of Music (See name)
Brough, Brothers: TE
Brown: KL
Brown and Lemon; RJ
Brown, B K: AW
Brown, F: CY
Brown, George: MW
Brown, John Russell: OT
Brown , Sedley: CE, MC
Brown(London): AW, H8, MD, MM, TN
Brown e , E Martin: KL, OT
Brown e , J H, prompter: KL
Browne(London): H8
Brubaker, Edward: H42, H62, KJ, MW
Bryden, Bill: RJ
Buchanan, C W: OT
Buckingham, Duke of: JC
Buckland, Albert: MV
Buckstone, J B: AY, TN
Bullock, Christopher: TSApp
Burbie(London): TS
Burby(London): LL, RJ
Buchall, James: OT
Burge, Stuart: H41, H42, R2
Burger, Alexander: MA, MC, OT
Burnaby, Charles: TN
Burns and Gates(London): R2
Burrell, George B: MA
Burrell, John: H41
Burto n, Richard: HA, H8
Burton, Thomas: MV
Burto n, William: AY, HA1 JC, H8, KL, MD, MW, RJ, TN
Butcher, C: MC
Butler, Edwin: H8
Butters(London): AY, CR, JC, H5, KJ, KL, R2, MA, MC, OT, PE, RJ, TE, TG
Butts, Alfred: MD
Byrne, C A: MV

C--E S, P: H41
C, S : see Short
Cadell(Edinburgh): CE
Cademan(London): MCApp, MV, OT, WT
Caesar in Egypt: AC
Cast ellani, Renati: RJ
Cairn, Mrs: CY, RJ
Caiu s Marius : RJ
Calcu tta publishers: Englishman's Pr ess, Pereira(see name)
Calcutta Theatre: San Souci(see name)
Cald e r(London): MC

Calhern, Louis: KL
California Th(San Francisco); JC, MC, MCApp
Calkins(London): H41
Call, Edward Payton: AY, JC, H42, H5, KL, R3, TE, TN
Calvert, Charles: AC, H42, H5, H5App, H8, R3, MD, MV, TN, WT
Calvert, Louis: AC, HA, H41
Cambridge, W M: MA
Cambridge publishers: Macmillan, U Press
Camden Society(London): KJ
Campbell, Douglas: JC, MD, RJ, WT
Campbell, Mrs Patrick: HA
Campton, EdwardC: CE
Canfield, Curtis: JC
Capell, Edward: AC, JC
Carano, Guilio: MC
Carey, Denis: MA, MV, TN, TS
Carey, Sidney A: JC
Carhart, James L: AY, MV
Carnegie Tec/(B Iden Payne plus E Martin Browne's KL: AW, AY, CY,H41, H8, KJ, KL, R2, R3, LL, MA, MM, MV, TC, TN, TS
Carnovsky, Morris: KL
Carr, G C, prompter: H62, KL, R2
Carrington, James: AY
Cassell(London): AW, H41, MC, MM
Casen, Lewis: H8, KL, MC
Castle Square Th(Boston): JC
Catherin and Petruchio : TS
Cawthrone(London): AW, CR, HA, R2, PE, TC, TS, TS
Chalmers, Alex: PE
Chalmers(London): PE
Chamberlaine(Dublin): KJ
Chambers, F OWen: HA, MD, MW, RJ, TN, TS
Chapman(London): AC, HA, H5, H8, KJ, KL, R2, LL, MA, MC, MD, MV, TE, WT
Chapple(London): TM
Charles(London): HA
Charles Kemble's Shakespeare Readings: AY, CR, CY, HA, JC, H42, H5, H8, KJ, R3, MC, MV, OT, RJ, WT
Charmock, H C: KL, MC
Chatham publishers: Keekan, McKay (see names)
Chatillon: KJ
Chauncey: AY
Chestnut St Th(Philadelpia): JC, MA

Chetwinde(London): AY, H41, MC, MW
Chetwood(London): AY, JC, H42, H5, MM
Cheyne(Edinburgh): MC
Chicago publishers: Dramatic Publishing Co, Rand-McNally(see names)
Chicago Theatre: McVickers(see name)
Chippendale, F: H41, H5, KL, MW
Chiswick(London): CR, CY, HA, R3, MA, MC, MV, OT, RJ, TN
Christie(London): CR
Christmas, Eric: LL, MD, MV, TN
Chronicle History of Henry the Fifth: H5
Cibber, Colley: H8, KJ, R2, R3, R3App
Cibber, Theophilus: AC, H42, H61,H62, H63, KJ
Cincinnati Dramatic Festival: HA, JC, H41, MA, OT, RJ
Cincinnati publisher: Hawley(see name)
Cincinnati theatre: Wood's(see name)
Civic Repertory Th(NY): TN
Clarendon(London): HA
Clarendon Press(Oxford): H41, H5, LL, MA
Clark(London): MC
Clarke, Annie: MC, KJ
Clarke, Cecil: MM
Clarke, Ernest: TN
Clarke, George H: MC, MW, OT, TS
Clarke, H B : JC, KL
Clarke, John Sleeper: CE
Clarke(London): KJ
Clayton, J: MV
Clayton(London): HA, MC, OT
Clayton, E B(NY): JC
Cleopatra in Judaea: AC
Clifford, Henry Marsh: AY
Cob ler of Preston, The TS, TSApp
Coburn Players: MC
Coburn, Charles Donville: MC
Coe, Peter: JC, MC
Coggins, Gordon: MC
Cohen: Alexander: HA
Cole, Barry: R3
Coleman, John: H5
Coleridge, S T: WT1
Collection of the Best English Plays : JC
Collection of the Most Esteemed Farces : WT

Collier, J P: KJ, PE
Collier, R J, prompter: KJ, R3,MC
Collins, V J: C, HA, MV, TN
Collins(Glasgow): MC
Collins New Shakespeare(London): TN
Colman, George: KL, MD, MW
Colman, George, the elder: WT
Colneighi(London): R3
Colum bia Broadcasting Co: AY, H41, KL, MA, TN, TS
Combe(Dublin): R3
Comical Gallant: MW
Comick Masque of Pyramus and Thisbe: MD
Company(London): MC
Composition anterior to Shakespeare's Tragedy: R2
Conklin, Miss C E: HA
Connell, Ted: HA
Conner, Thomas L: CY
Conspiracy Discovered: H5
Conville, David: MD
Conway, F B: TN
Conway, Mrs F B: TN
Conway, William Angus: CR
Cooke, George Frederick: CY, HA, H8, KL, R3, MC, MM, MW, OT, TN
Cooper, J C: CY
Cooper, Thomas Abthorpe: OT
Copleston, Mr: RJ
Corbell(London): RJ
Corbin, John: WT
Cork publisher: Begnett(see name)
Cornell, Katherine: RJ
Costume for Othello and Merchant: MV
Costume for Shakespeare's Historical Tragedy of King John: KJ
Costume of Shakespeare's Tragedy of Othello and Comedy of Merchant of Venice : OT
Costumes: WT
Costumes . . . Henry IV: H41
Costumes as represented at the Princess's Th: MV
Costumes for As You Like It: AY
Costumes in Winter's Tale: WT
Costumes: Twelve Costumes of Richard the Third: R3
Cotes(London): PE
Cottrell, William: CE, MW
Court of Oberon: MD

Court Th(London): MA
Covent Garden Th(London): MA and
   many more
Cowell, Mr: CE
Cowie(London): AC
Cowl, Jane: RJ, TN
Cowley, Abraham: MD
Cooper, J O: R3, MC
Cox: Robert: MD
Craig, Edith: MC, MV
Craig, Edward Gordon: MA
Craig, Elsie: MC
Craig: W J: CY
Craig(London): R3
Crane and Robson: AW
Crane, W H: CE
Creede(London): H5, H61
Creswell: KL
Creswick, William: HA, H42, KJ, KL,
   R3, LL, MA, MC, MM, MV, OT, PE, RJ,
   TE, TMApp, TN
Crisp, Harry: MA
Crosman, Henrietta: AY, R3, TN
Crouch, J H: CR
Crown , John: H61, H62, H63
Crow St Th(Dublin): HA, KJ
Crozier, Eric: TE
Crystal Palace Co(Sydenham): AY,
   AYA pp, HA, MA, MC, MV, RJ, TE
C uko r, George: RJ
Cumberland, Richard: TM
Cumberland(London): all but PE and TA
Cure f or a Scold, A: T'iS
Cushing and Bardua(NY): H5
Cushman, Asa: AY, HA, KL, R3, MA, MC,
   MV, MW, OT, RJ, TG
Cushm an, Charlotte: AY, HA, JC, H8,
   MA, MC, RJ
Cutter, William: OT

Daggett, Windsor: RJ
Daily Press Steam Printing Works
   (Li verpool): MA, WT
Dale, John: KJ
Daley 's Dramatic Company: HA
Dallas, Meredith: H5App, H8App, R2
Dalton(Dublin): JC, RJ
Daly, Augustin: AW, AY, AYApp, CY,
   H41, H41App, H42, LL, LLApp, MA,MD,
   MV, MW, OT, RJ, TE, TG, TN, TS
Daly, Richard: HA
Daly, William: HA
Daly's Th(NY): LL, MA

Dance, James: TM
Dancer, Nathaniel(London): H41, TS
Dandoe, James: R2
Daniel, T A: RJ
Danter, John(London): RJ, TA
Darby(London): OT
Darton, F J H: AW, CE, CR, HA, JC, KJ,
   KL, R2, MC, MD, MV, TN
D'Avenant's Dramatic Works: MM
Davenant, William: JC, MA, MC, MM, TE
Davenport, E L: JC, H8, KJ, KL, MA,MV,
   OT, TE, TS
Davenport, Fanny: AY, AYApp, KJ, MA,MC
Davenport, Harry: JC
Davenport, Jean: AC, H8(see Lander)
Davenport, May: AY
Davenport, Robert: KJ
Davenport-Rankin Coll: R3
David, C N: MC
David(London): H42
Davidson, D: MC
Davidson(London): AC, AW, AY, CE, CR,
   CY, HA, JC, H41, H5, H61, H62, H63,
   H8, KL, R3, LL, MA, MC, MD, MV, MW,
   OT, RJ, TC, TE, TN
Davidson's Penny Shakespeare: JC, KL,
   R3, RJ
Daviot, Gordon: R2
Davis: A B: RJ
Davis: C B: AY
Davis: Fitzroy: RJ
Davis, H C: KL
Day, Richard Digny: AY, RJ, TE, TG
Dean(Manchester): HA, H8, R3, MC, MM,
   MMApp
Death of Falstaff: H42, H5
Debrett(London): AW, H5, MD, TE
Deeve(London): H41
DeGray, Miss: AY
Dell(NY): TN
Dennis, John: CR, MW
Dent, Alan: HA
Dent(London): H42, MM, PE
Dering, Sir Edward: H41, H42
Deuel, James P: HA
Deveridge, William P: MV
Devine, George: KJ, KL, MD, TN
de Walden, Howard: MD
Dews, Peter: AY, H42, H61, H62, H63,
   R2, MV, OT, RJ
DeWitt(NY): H5
Dexter, John: HA, OT
Dicks(London): H61, R3, OT

French(NY): AW , AY, CE, CR, CY, HA,
JC, H41, H8, KJ, KL, R2, R3, LL,
MA, MC, MD, MV, MW, OT, RJ, TE, TG,
TS, WT
Friedman, Joel: MD, MDApp
Frohman, Charles: MA
Furber, George W: OT
Furnivall, Frederick L; H41, H61

G I Hamlet: HA
Gaiety Th(Manchester): MM, TN
Garland(London): OT, RJ
Garrick, David: AC, CY, HA, H42, KJ, ⟨
KL, LL, MC, MD, OT, RJ, RJApp, TE,
TS, WT
Garrick, George: JC
Gascon, Jean: CE, CY, KJ, KL, LL, MV,
OT, PE, TS
Gaskill, William: R3
Gaspar, P A: JC
Gates, G, prompter: KL
Gay, Walter: HA
Geddes, Norman Bel: HA
Genest, John: CR
Gentleman, Thomas: R2, RJ, and most
of Bell
Gentleman's Magazine: RJ
George, Harry: MV
Gielgud, John: HA, JC, KL, MA, MC, TN
Giffin, Donald: MM, MMApp
Gilbert(Dublin): AY
Gilbert   , John G: AC, AY, CE, CR,
JC, H42, H5, H8, KL, R3, LL, MA,
MC, MM, MW, TE, TS, WT
Gilbert and Fenno: CR
Gilder, Rosamund: HA
Gildon, Charles: MM
Giles, David: MC, MM
Gill, Peter: MA, MC, TN
Gill(London): CR
Gillette, William: AY, HA, JC, H8, MC,
MV, MW, OT, RJ, TS
Gilliss(NY): MC
Ginn(London): H41
Gladstone, M C: RJ
Glasgow publishers: Collins, Knox,
n p, n p 1759(see names)
Glees, Choruses, etc: CY
Glenn, S W: H41
Globe(Boston): KL
Globe Theatre Versions: AW, AY,CE,
CR, HA, JC, KL, MC, MD, RJ, TE,TN,
TS

Glyn, Isabelle: AC
Golden, John: MV
Goldsmith, Dr: H41
Gomez, Thomas: HA
Goodbody, Buzz: AC, AY, CR, HA, JC,
KJ, KL, PE, TA
Goodhall, James: R2
Gosson(London): PE
Gower, John: PE
Graham, Colin: TN
Graham, Frank H: TE
Graham, Richard: CE, MV, TE
Grand Rapids Civic Th: MC
Granville Series: R2
Granville, George, MV
Granville-Barker, Harley: MD, TN, WT
Gray(London): PE
Green, Dorothy: H5, WT
Green, Stephen: CY
Greene, Robert: WT
Greene(Dublin): JC
Greet, Ben: AY, CE, JC, MA, MV, TE
Greg, W W: HA
Griegson(Dublin): OT
Gresham(London): AC, AW, AY, CY, JC,
H61, H62, H63, MC, MM, TC, TM, TS
Gribble, Harry Wagstaff: TS
Grice, James: MC
Griggs(London): HA, H41, H42, R3, LL,
MD, MV, MW, TC
Grosset(NY): MD, MV
Grove, Fred: MA, TN
Gruber(Dublin): CY
Guare, John: TG
Guion, C D: AY, H41, MV, MW
Gulliver(London): TS
Gunne(Dublin): R3
Guthrie, Tyrone: AW, HA, JC, H8, R2,
R3, MC, MD, MV, TC, TM, TN, TS
Gwynn, Miss: MW

H, T(for Meignan): MW
Hack, Keith: MM, TE
Hackett, James H: H ᵎ, H41, H42, KL,
MC, MV, MW, OT
Hackett, Mrs James: MC
Hackney School: CY
Hagen, Uta: OT
Hauge, The, Johnson: JC
Hale, John: MW
Half-Pay Officers: H5, TN
Hall, Peter: CR, CY, HA, H41, H5, H61,
H62, H63, R2, R3, LL, MC, MD,MDApp,
RJ, TC, TCApp, TE, TG, TN

Halliday, Andrew: AC
Halliwell, J O: HA, H62, H63, R2,MD, TS
Hamblin, Eliza A: TN
Hamilton, Robert: RJ
Hampden, Walter: HA, H5, R3, MA, MC, MV, OT, RJ, TS
Hands, Terry: H41, H42, H5, MV, MW, PE, RJ
Hanford, Charles B: AC, CY, MA, MV, OT, TS, WT
Hannen, Nicholas: RJ
Hanson, Philip: H5, MV
Heritage Theatre Edition: OT
Harbert(NY): MW
Harcourt Brace Jonanvich(NY): OT
Hartman, Lady: CR
Hardwicke, Countess of: MD
Hare and Mr Kendal, Mr: AY
Harriette, the Countess of Hard-wicke: MD
Harley, John Pritt: HA, TS
Harper(NY): MV, TA
Harrap(London): JC, MC
Harrington, F: AY
Harris, Frank R: MD
Harris, William: MC
Harrison, John: MD, TC, TN
Harrison(London): AC, AW, CE, CR, HA, JC, KL, MC, MM, MW, OT, TM, TN,WT
Harrop(Manchester): R2
Hart, Charles: RJ
Hart(Dublin): OT
Hart, for Charles(Edinburgh): RJ
Hart(NY): HA, KL, R3, MA, MC, MV,OT, TS
Hart-Davis(London): OT
Harvey, James: KL
Haskins, Dan: R3
Hasselman-Journal(Indianapolis): AY, CY, RJ, TN
Hastings, F C: TE
Hastings, George: MC
Hatton, J: MA, MAApp
Hauser, Frank: JC, TN
Hawes(London): HA, OT
Hawkins, William: CY
Hawkins(London): OT
Haw ley, Frederick: H42, H61, H62, H63, RJ, TE (see also Haywell)
Hawley(Cincinnati): HA, H41, JC,MA, RJ, OT
Hayes(London): MV

Haymarket Th(London): MA
Haywell, Frederick: AW, AY, CE, CY, H5, H8, KJ, KL, R3, MA, MC, MV, OT, RJ, TE, TG, TM, TN, WT, see also Hawley
Hedgeon(London): OT
Heinemann(London): CY, MD, TN, WT
Heller, Frederick: CE, CY, H41, H42, H8, RJ, TE
Helme(London): KJ
Helpman, Robert: AC, TE, WT
Henkins: JC
Henry Irving Shakespeare: all
Hentschel, Irene: TN
Hepton, Bernard: AC, CR, H41, H42,JC, MC
Hereford publisher: Perkins(see name)
Her Majesty's Th(Sidney): JC
Herman, John: H61, H62, H63
Herringman(London): HA, JC, H42, H5,

MC, MM, TE, TN
Hester, Hal: TN
Heywood(Manchester): WT
Hicks, Seymour: R3
Hildebrand, William: MA
Hilgrave(London): MC
Hill, Aaron: H5
Hill, Charles: JC
Hill, Roger: MC, MV, TN
Hills(London): TM
Hinchcliffe(London): TS
Hindemarsh(London): TA
Hind's Acting Edition: HA, R3, MC, OT, TN
Hines, Patrick: HA, RJ
Hingston(London): TM
Hinman, Charleton: H41
Hinton, Henry L: HA, R3, MA, MC, MV, MW, OT, RJ, TN
Hinton, Henry L(NY): HA, MC, MV,OT, R3App
Hirman, Kate: MC
Hirsch, John: HA, H61, H62, R3,MD
Historical Tragedy of the civil wars in the reign of King Henry VI:H61, H62, H63
Historie of Troylus and Cresseida, The: TC
History and Fall of Caius Marius: RJ
History of Henry the Fifth: H5
History of King Lear: KL
His True Chronicle History of the Life and Death of King Lear and His

Three Daughters: KL
Hitch(London): HA, H41
Hitch and Hawes(London), AW, HA, H5,
  H8, KL, MA, MW, OT, TN
Hobbs, John: H62, H63
Hoey(Dublin): KL, TN
Holcroft , Thomas: AY, TM
Holland, George: MA
Holland, H; MW
Hollingow, John: MW
Holliston: H5
Holloway, Baliol: AY
Holman, Joseph George: HA
Holmes, Henry: HA, MA, MC, RJ
Holywood Press(Oxford): WT
Hope(London): LL
Hopkins, Arthur: HAApp
Hopkinson, A F: H61, H62, H63
Horn, Mr: MW
Horne, R H: CE
Hornimann, Miss A E C: CE, MA, MM, TN
Houseman, John: AW, CR, HA, JC, KJ,KL,
  MA, MC, MM, MW, OT, WT
Howard Atheneum(Boston): MC
Ho ward, James: RJ
Howard, Leslie: HA
Howe, E: RJ
Hoyt, Edward N: HA, R3
Hubbell, Walter: AY, CR, HA, KJ, MA
  ; (see also Hubble)
Hubble, Walter: HA, H41(see also Hub-
  bell)
Hubert: KJ
Hudd: Walter: R2, TA, TN
Huddleston, Will: H61
Hudson, Henry B: JC, MW
Hughes(Edinburgh): RJ
Hughes(London): R3
Hull, Mr: CE, CR, HA, TN
Hulio, Thomas: WT
Hummel, A S H: KJ
Humourists, The: H42
Humourous Lieutenant: H41
Humours of Sir John Fals taff : H42
Humphrey, Duke of Gloucester : H61
Humphrey, William: TA, TAApp
Hunt, Hugh: JC
Hunter, John: KJ
Hurd(MY): R3, MC, MV, OT, RJ
Hurst(London): AC, CE, CY, HA, JC,
  H42, H8, KJ, KL, R3, MA, MC, MM,
  MV, OT, RJ, TE, TN, WT
Huston, Walter: OT

Hutt, William: AY, MA
Hyman, Earle: OTApp
Hystorie of Hamblet: HA

Ince, Annette: AY
Inchbald, Mrs: AC, AY, CE, CR, CY,
  HA, JC, H41, H42, H5, H8, KJ, KL,
  R3, MA, MC, MM, MV, MW, OT, RJ, TE,
  TN, TS, WT
Ind ianpolis publisher: Hasselman-
  Journal(see name)
Ingar, David: CR
Ingersoll, Harriett: RJ
Ingratitude of a Commonwealth: CR
Injured Princess: CY
Invader of His Country: CR
Ipswich publisher: East Anglia Press
  (see name)
Ireland(Manchester): H5, H5App, R3,
  MD, MV
Irving, H B: HA
Irving, Henry: all, MCApp
Isaacs, J; HA

J, R: TC
Jack, John: H41
Jackson, Barry: HA, H41, H42, MC, MM,
  MV, MW, TE, TG, TS, TSApp
Jackson, Nagle: CE, R2, PE, TG, TS
Jacobi, Derek: MD, PE
Jaggard (London): all but PE
Jarrett, Henry: WT
James, Louis: HA, R3, MV
James, Peter: TN
Jan Hus Hall(NY): OTApp
Januschek: H8
Javier, Isaac(London): H61
Jealous Captain, The : OT
Jealousy Exemplified in the Awful,
  Tragical and Bloody History of the
  Lives and Deaths of Othello and Des-
  demona: OT
Jeans, Isabel: TN
Jefferson, Joseph: KL
Jennings, Charles: OT
Jennings, J W: MD
Jew of Venice: MV
Jewitt, Henry: AY, CR, HA, JC, MA,MC,
  MD, MDApp, MM, MW, OT, RJ, TE, TN,
  TS, WT
Jo, Allen: TE
Johnson: JC, MV, MW, TE, TS
Johnson, Charles: AY

Lang, Albert: MA, RJ, TN
Lang(London): HA
Langham, Michael: AC, CR, HA, JC, H41,
  H5, KL, R2, LL, MA, MM, MV, MW,OT,
  RJ, TC, TG, TM, TS
Langston, Basil C: RJ
Langtry, Lilly: AC, AY, MC
Landsdown(London): H41
Lansdowne, Baron: MV
Laphore, John T: TN
Lark, George E: MA, MW
Larsen, George: KJ
Late, and much admired play, called
  Pericles, Prince of Tyre, The: PE
Law(london): H41, R2, R3
Law Against Lovers: MA, MM
Lawford, Ernest B: TN
Law of Lombardy: MA
Leacock(London): CE
Leacroft(London): MM
Leadenhall Press(London): AC
Leake(London): MV, OT
Leathley(Dublin): H8
Lee, John: MC, RJ
Lee(London): TC
LeGallienne, Eva: RJ, TN
Leiber, Fritz: AY, HA, JC, KL, R3,MA,
  MC, MV, RJ, TN, TS
Leiber, Virginia: KL
Leigh, Andrew: JC, TN
Leigh, Henry: TS
Leigh, J H: TE
Leigh, Vivian: AC
Leipzig publisher: Tauchnitz(see name)
Lelyveld, Toby: MV
Le mon, Walter, M: RJ
Lemoyne(London): H41
Le Moyne, William: HA, H8, R3
Leveridge, Richard: MD
Lewellyn, W L: OT
Lewis, George W, prompter: CR, JC,H8,
  MC, OT
Lewis, James: AY, HA, MA, MC, OT, TS
Life and Death of Falstaff : H42
Life and Death of Henry the Fifth: H5
Life and Death of King Lear : KL
Life and Death of Sir John Falstaff:
  H42
Life and Humours of Falstaff : H41,
  H42, H5
Life of Henry the Fifth: H5
Life of Sir John Oldcastle: H41

Lilli, Mr: PE
Lilly(Boston): CR
Lincoln Center, Repertory Co(NY); MV
Lindon, M P: MC
Lindsley, A B: KJ
Linley: TE
Linsdale(London): R3
Lintott(london)`: R3, MV
Lisle, Sieur de: TM
Lister(London): MC, MV, RJ
Lithgow, Arthur: H41App, H42APP, H6App
  KJ, R3App, MVApp, OTApp, RJApp, TSApp
Little(London): OT
Little(NY): CY
Litton, Marie: AY
Liverpool publishers: Daily Press,
  Newman(see name)
Liverpool Theatre: Alexandra(see name)
Lloyd, Norman: TS
Locke, Matthew: MC
Lodge, Frank: HA, MA, MC
Logan, Celia: LL, MM
London, n p, 1714(Tonson?): KJ
London, n p, 1736: R2
London, n p, 1757: WT
London publishers: Adams, Adlade. Al-
  bert Steam Press, Allot, Allman,
  Ashbee, British Broadcasting Co,
  Badger, Baker, Bald, Baldin, Ballan-
  tyne, Balne, Bankside Acting Edition,
  Barker, Barrois, Bathurst, Bayler,
  Becket, Bedell, Bell, Bell second ed,
  1774, Bell 1777, H B Bell, Bell and
  Daldy, Jane Bell, Bentley, Bettes-
  worth, Black and White, Blackie, Bog-
  ner, Blount, Bobee, Booksellers, Bow-
  yer, Bradbury, Booth, Bosworth,Bragge,
  Broderip, Brown, Burby, Burbie,Butler,
  Cademan, Calkins, Camden Society, Cas-
  sell, Cawthorne, Chalmers, Chapman,
  Chapple, Chetwood, Chetwynd, Chiswick,
  Christie, Clark,Clarke, Clarendon,
  Clayton, Collins, Colneigh, Company,
  Corbett, Cotes, Cowie, Craig, Creede,
  Cumberland, Dancer, David, Davidson
  Davidson's Penny Shakespeare, Debrett,
  Deeve, Dent, Dicks, Dodd, Dodsley,
  Dolby, Dramatic Repository, Duncombe,
  Eyre, Feales, Field, Fenner, Fisher,
  Flecher, Fletcher, Folio Society,
  French, Garland, Gill, Ginn, Gray,Gos-
  con, Gresham, Griggs, Gulliver, Har-
  rap, Hindemarch, Hedgeon, Harris, Hart-

Davis, Hawes, Hawkins, Helme, Her
ringman, Hilgray, Hingston, Hinch-
cliffe, Hitch, Hitch and Hawes,
Hope, Hughes, Hurst, Jaggard, Jav-
ier, Johnson, Joseph, Kearsley, Knap-
son, Knight, Lackington, Lane, Lang,
Lansdown, Law, Leacock, Leadenhall,
Leake, Lee, LeMoyne, Lintott, Lis-
ter, Long, Longman, Lonsdale, Linsdale, Little, Lopez and Wemyss, Low,
Lowndes, Macmillan, Magnus, March,
Mason, Merritt, Meers, Miller, Mil-
ler 1798, Millington, Mills, Mitchell,
Music Publishing Co, Myers, Nassau
Steam Press, National Acting Drama
Office, New Shakespeare Society,
Nicoll, Oxlade, Noble, Norton, Nutt,
Orr, Owens, Paine and Summers, Part-
ridge, Pattie, Pavier, Pemberton,
Pennychicke, Perry, Pollard, Prae-
torius, Proprietors, Randall, Rich-
ards, Richardson, Ridgeway, Riving-
ton, Roach, Roberts, Robinson, Rod-
well, Routledge, Sabine, Sams,
Saunders, Sedgewick, Shakespeare
Associ·ates, Shakespeare Press,
Shakespeare Society, Sheaves, Sher-
wood, Short, Simmes, Simmers, Simp-
kin, Smethwicke, Smith, Society
for Theatre Research, Sonnenscheim,
Stoddard, Strahan, Swall, Symonds,
Tabby, Tallis, Theatre, Thomas,
Thompson, Tinsley Bros, Tonson,
Tothill, Trubner, Truesdale, Truman,
Tuck, Vickers, Vicker's Penny Shakes-
peare, Virtue, Walker, Walsh, Wal-
thoe, Watts, Warrington, Welling-
ton, Wells-Gardner, Whitlock, Whit-
tington, Williams, Woodfall, Wenman,
White, Whittaker, World Film Pub-
lishing Co, Wilkie, Wise, Wright,
Wrighten, Witford, Barlow(see names)
London Theatres: Covent Garden, Court,
Drury Lane, Middle Temple, Haymarket,
National, Sadler's Wells(see names)
Long(London): TS
Long, Augustus(Dublin): AW
Longman(London): AC, AY, CE, CR, CY, HA,
JC, H41, H42, H5, H61, H63, H8, KJ, KL,
R3, MA, MC, MM, MV, MW, OT, RJ, RJApp,
TE, TN, TS, WT
Longworth(NY): HA, H41, H8, KL, R3, MC,
MV, MW, OT, RJ, TS

Lonsdale(London): TE
Loper, Robert: AW, AY, H8, KL, MA, RJ,
TM, TN, TS
Lopez and Wemyss Edition(London): MA
Los Angeles publisher: U of Calif
Press(see name)
Love, James: H8, MC, TM
Love Betrayed or the Agreeable Dis-
appointment: AW, TN
Love in a Forest : AY
Low(London): MW
Lowell, C D, prompter: JC, MC, MV
Lowe's Incorporated: JC
Lowndes(London): CR, CY, HA, H5, KJ,
KL, R3, MA, MC, MM, MV, MW, RJApp,
TE, TN, WT
Ludlow, H M: H41
Ludlow, Noah: CE, CR, H41, KJ, KL,
MC, MW, TS
Lunt, Alfred: MA, TS

"Macbeth in Modern Dress:" MC
McClintic, Guthrie: HA, RJ
McClure(NY): H5, WT
McCoulock, C W: KL
McCullough, John: KL, MC, MCApp, OT
McDonald, Bridie: MA
Macdonald, Laurence: MV
MacDonald, Melbourne: AY
McGarry, M E: HA
McGlashan(Dublin): DM
McGowan, George: H41, H8, OT, TE
Mack, M: AC
McKay(Chatham): R3
Macleish, Archibald: KL
Macklin: AY
Macmillan(Cambridge): H41
Macmillan(London): HA, H41, H42, H61,
H62, H63, KJ, R2, R3
Macmillan(NY): LL, LLApp, TC
McMonigle(NY): HA, MA, MV, OT
McMullan, Frank: MM, MMApp
Macpherson, Jeanne: KJ, KJApp
Macready, William Charles: AC, AY,
CR, CY, HA, JC, H42, H5, H8, KJ, KL,
R2, R3, MA, MC, MV, OT, RJ, TG, WT
Macready, William, the elder: KL
Macready Produces As You Like It:AY
McVickers Th(Chicago): AY, H8, KL,
R3, MA, MD, OT, TE
McWhinney, Donald: MC
Maddermarket Th(Norwich); all, JCApp
KLApp, WTApp

Moll, James: MA
Molloy, C: H5, TN
Mommsen, Thycho: PE
Monck, Nugent: all, JCApp, TSAop, WTApp
Montagna, Barbara: PE
Monthly Magazine: CR
Moore, John: AY, CR, CY, HA, JC, H41, H8, KJ, KL, R3, MA, MC, MD, MV, OT, RJ, TE, TN, TS, WT
Moore, Sir Thomas: R3
Moore(Dublin): H41
Morgan, Gareth: H42
Morgan, Lydia Eliza: AY
Morgan, M: WT
Moriarty, Marcus: CR, JC, H41, H8, KL, R3, MA, MV, MW, MWApp, OT
Morrison, Priestley: AY, RJ
Morton: Maggie: RJ
Moss, Robert: AY
Mossop, Henry: KJ
Most Esteemed Farces, The: CE
Most Excellent Historie of the Merchant of Venice: MV
Most Lamentable Romaine Tragedie of Titus Andronicus: TA
Motion Pictures: JC, H5
Moulton, Harold M: RJ
Mowatt, Anna Cora: MA
Muir, James: MV
Mulford, B: KL
Muller and Everett: HA, MV
Mullin, Michael: MC
Murdoch, James E: HA, JC, H41, H8, KJ, R3, MA, MC, OT, TS
Murray, A S H: AY, CE, CR, JC, MD, MW
Musgrove, John: MW
Music Publishing Co(London): AW, JC, R2, LL, MA, MD, MV, OT, TN, TS, WT
Myers, Joseph(London): H8

Naked Hamlet: HA
Nantz, Edward Coleman: HA
Nassau Steam Press(London): HA, H5, H8, KL, MC, MV, OT, RJ
National Acting Drama Office(London): AY, MV
National Broadcasting Co: JC
National Th(London): CR, MC, MV, R2, TE
Neal(Philadelpia): MV
Neilsen, Adelaide: AY, CY, MA, MV, RJ, TN, TS

Neilsen, James W: HA, MV
Nelson, Elizabeth: TN
Nelson, Ralph: HA
Nera, La: HA
Nesbitt(NY): HA, OT
Neuffer, D: JC
Neville, John(c 1842): KJ
Neville, John: HS, H5
Neville, Oliver: MC
New Hamlet: HA
Newman(Liverpool): CE
New Shakespeare Society(London): PE
New Stratford Shakespeare: JC, MC, MV, TN
New Th(NY): AC
New Th(Philadelpia): CY
New Version,A: HA
New York publishers: Alford, American Academy of Dramatic Art, Art Age Press, Baker, Baldwin, Bedford, Bernard, Clayton, Cushing, Dell, DeWitt, Dodd-Mead, Doubleday, French, Gilliss, Grisset, Harcourt-Brace, Harper, Hart, Hinton, Hurd, Kopple, Longworth, McClure, Macmillan, McMonigle, Metropolitan Printing Co, Nesbitt, Oxford U Press, Pyramid, Scribners, Sears, Stein and Day, Tallis, Taylor, Torrey, Turner, Whale
New York Shakespeare Festival: AC, AW, AY, CR, HA, JC, H41, H42, H5, H61, H62, H63, KJ, KL, LLApp, R3, MA, MC, MD, MDApp, MM, MV, MVApp, OT, OTApp, PE, RJ, TA, TC, TE, TG, TM, TN, TS, WT, CE, CY, MW
New York theatres: Bowery, Civic Repertory, Daly, Fifth Ave, Jan Hus Hall, Little, Lincoln Center, Mercury, Mitzi Newhouse, NY Shakespeare Festival, New, Phoenix (see names)
Nichols, John: CE, MM, TS
Nicol(London): H5, KJ, KL, MD
Nicholai: MW
Noble(London): KL
Noble Peasant: AY, CY, TM
Noel, Craig: RJ, TS
Morris: Mrs E: MC
Northern, Michael: MM
Norton, John W: MA, MW, OT
Norton(London): R2

Norwich theatre: Maddermarket(see
   Monck)
Novak, Helen: OT
Novelli, Ermete: OT
Nunn, Trevor: AC, CR, HA, JC, H41,
   H42, H5, H8, KL, MA, MC, TA, TS,WT
Nursery PB: CE
Nutt(London): H5

O U D S: see Oxford U
Ober, George A: HA
O'Brien, Jack: CE, MA, MW
Occasional Facsimilies: MD
Ogunquit: TN
Oh, It's Impossible: CE
Old Play ina New Garb, An : HA
Old Vic(London): AC, CY, JC, H5,H62,
   KJ, R2, LL, MC, MM, MMApp, TE, TG,
   TM, TS, WT
Oldenberg publisher: Stalling(see
   name)
Oliver and Boyd(Edinburgh): AY, CR,
   HA, JC, JCApp, H41, H42, H8, KL,R2,
   R3, MA, MC, MV, MW, OT, RJ
Oliver, Larry: JC, MA
Olivier, Laurence: AC, HA, H5, MC, TN
Oregon Shakespere Festival: all
O'Riordon: MA
Orr(London): KL
Orrery, Earl of: AY, H5
Othello, the Moor of Venice: OT
Other Place, The(Stratford-upon-Avon):
   KL, TE
Otway, Thomas: RJ
Owen, William F: H41
Owen(London): JC, MC, OT
Oxberry Edition: AY, CR, CY, HA, JC,
   H42, H5, H8, KJ, KL, R2, R3, MA, MC,
   MCApp, MM, MV, MW, OT, RJ, TE, TG,
   TN, WT
Oxberry, Press of(London): TM
Oxford publishers: Clarendon Press,
   Holywood Press, U Press(see name)
Oxford University Drama Society(O U
   D S): WT
Oxford U Press(London): AY, MA
Oxford U Press(NY): HA
Oxlade(London): AY, CY, HA, KL, R3,MA,
   MC, MV, RJ, TE
Oxley: John H: HA

P, William H: HA
P, T(Thomas Pavier)(London): H41,H5
Padua, U of: MC, WT
Paine and Simmons(London): R3
Painfull Adventures of Pericles,
   Prince of Tyre: PE
Palmer, D L: MW
Palmer, John: MC, OT
Palmer(London): TSApp
Palmer(Philadelphia): CR, MC
Pandora, the Triumph of Peace: WT
Papal Tyranny in the Reign of King
   John: KJ
Papp, Joseph: AC, AW, AWApp, AY, CR,
   HA, JC, H5, KJ, KL, R3, LL, LLApp,
   MA, MC, MD, MV, RJ, TE, TG, TN, TS
Parallel Texts of the First and Sec-
   ond Quartos and the First Folio: H5
Paris publishers: Bernois, Vergie(see
   names)
Parker(Dublin): MA
Parsloe, James, prompter: R3, MV
Partride(London): R3
Pattie(London): AY, HA, H5, KL, MD,
   TE
Patton, Pat: AY
Paulding, Frederick: CE, HA, JC, R3,
   MV, MW, OT
Pavier(London): HA, H62, H63, PE
Payne, Ben Iden: AC, AW, AY, CE, CR,
   CY, HA, H41, H42, H5, H8, KJ, KJApp,
   KL, R2, R3, LL, MA, MC, MD, MM, MV,
   MW, RJ, TC, TE, TG, TN, TS, WT
Payne, John Howard: OT
Peacock, J E: TE
Pearson, J K: TE
Peck, Mrs C M E: R3
Pemberton(London): CR
Penn Publishing Co(Philadelphia): HA,
   JC, H8, KL, R2, R3, MC, MV, OT, TS
Pennell, Nicholas: PE
Pennychicke(London): KJ
Percy, Esme: HA
Pereira(Calcutta): AY
Perkins(Hereford): RJ
Perrin(Dublin): TE
Perry, F W: MW
Perry(London): H41
Petter, Helen F: HA
Phelps, Samuel: AC, AW, AT, CE, CR, CY,
   HA, JC, H41, H42, H5, H8, KJ, KL, R3,
   LL, MC, MD, MM, OT, PE, TE, TG, TM,
   TMApp, TN, TS, WT

Richard III: H63
Richard III Costumes: Twelve Costumes
  of Richard the Third: R3
Richards(London): R2, PE
Richardson, Ian: R3
Richardson, William E: HA
Richardson(Boston): OT
Richard Ye Third : R3
Richings, Peter: MW
Riddle, W: AY
Rider, W: CE
Ridgeway, George Spencer: R3
Ridgeway(London): HA, H41, H42, MC,
  MM, MV
Right, John W: MW
Right excellent and famous historie
  of Promos and Cressida, The: MM
Rignold, George: CE, JC, H5
Ring, James Henry: AY, HA, H41, KL,
  R3, MC, MV, OT, TN, WT
Ring's Tremont Th(Boston): MV
Ripman, R J: R3
Risso, Richard: H8, KJ, R2, MC, OT,
  TE, TS
Ristori, Mme Adelaide: MC
Rivers, Earl: R3
Rivington(London): AY, CE, CR, CY,H41,
  H5, H5App, MA, MC, MM, MV, PE, TE,
  TM, TN
Rivington(Rugby): CR
Roach(London): HA, JC, H41, KL, R2,
  R3, MC, OT, RJ, TE, TS, WT
Robbins, John and Constance: RJ
Roberts, James B: AY, HA, JC, H8, KJ,
  KL, R2, R3, MA, MV, OT, RJ, TS
Roberts(London): H61, MD, MV, MW
Robertson, Tony: OT, PE
Robeson, Paul: OT
Robinson(London): AY, CY, RJ
Robson, Stuart: CE
Roche, Frank: R3
Rodwell(London): HA, R3, MC, OT
Rogers, Paul: LL, MC
Roman, Ernest: H5
Roman Matron : CR
Rose, John, prompter: CY
Rosenthal, H S: MW
Roses, The : H62, H63
Rosmer, Milton: H5, TN
Ross, Duncan: MC, WT
Ross, Fred C: MV
Ross, L D: OT

Rossi, Alfred: HA, MC, RJ
Routledge(London): MA, MD
Rowbottom(Pratt): JC
Rowe-Peterson(Evanston): TS
Ruddiman(Edinburgh): MC
Rugby Edition: AY, CR, HA, H5
Rugby publishers: Billington, Riving-
  ton(See name)
Rush, James: HA
Russel, W S: CE
Russell, T; R3
Russell, Mrs: H8

S, C:(see C Short)
S, P C for E: H41
Sabine(London): HA, R3, OT
Sadler's Wells Th(London): AC, AW,
  AY, CE, CR, CY, HA, JC, H42, H5,
  H8, KJ, KL, R3, LL, MC, MD, MM,OT,
  PE, TE, TG, TM, TN, TS, WT
St Ambry, James: H41
St Clair, Thomas M: KL
St John's College, Cambridge U: H41
Saker, Edward: CE, MA, MD, WT
Salmon, Edward: MC
Salmon, Joseph J: JC
Salvini, Tommaso: CR, HA, KL, MC,OT
Sams(London): OT
San Diego National Shakespeare Fes-
  tival: AC, AY, CR, HA, JC, H42, KJ,
  R2, R3, MC, MD, MV, MW, OT, RJ, TE,
  TG, TN, WT
Sandoe, James: AC, CY, H63, MD, MM,
  OT, TE, TG
Sandweth, Thomas: OT
San Francisco theatres: California,
  Maguire's Opera House(see names)
San Souci Th(Calcutta): MC
Sargent, Epes: KJ, TG
Saunders(London): H5
Sauny the Scot, or the Taming of the
  Shrew: TS
Saxe-Meiningen, Duke of: JC
Scenarius: PE
Schenck(Edinburgh): AC
Schlesinger, John: TM
Schramm, P: R2, R3
Schweitzer, David: TC
Scribners(NY and London): TA
Scrivener: H41
Scofield, Paul: PE
Seabert, Charles: MA

Seale, Douglas: CE, HA, JC, H42, H42-App, H5, H61, H62, H63, KJ, KL, R2 R3, MA, MC, MW, TE
Seare, Thomas James: KJ
Sears(NY): HA, MC, OT
Second Folio: R2
Second Folio, fragment: WT
Second Part of the Troublesome Reign . . .: KJ
Sedley, Sir Charles: AC, R3
Sedley-Smith, W H: HA, H41, KL, MW, TN
See If You Like It: CE
Sefton, A D: H41
Sefton, John: AW, AY, HA, H41, R3
Select British Theatre: CE, CY, JC, KJ, MC, MM, WT
Selections from the Plays of Shakespeare: R2
Sequel of Henry IV: H42
Settle, Elkana: MD, TC
Seymour, James: HA, OT
Seymour, John: AY, HA
Seymour, William: AC, AY, CE, CY, HA, KL, R3, MA, MC, MD, MV, MW, OT, TM, TN, TS
Shadwell, Thomas: H42, TE, TM
Shakespeare Assn(London): MV, PE,TN
Shakespeare Drolls: H41, TS
Shakespeare for Schools: AY, JC, H5, KL, MC, MV
Shakespeare in the Park: see NY Shakespeare Festival
Shakespeare League: RJ
Shakespeare Memorial Theatre(Stratfordupon-Avon): all
Shakespeare Plays of Edwin Booth: R2 MA
Shakespeare Press(London): MD
Shakespeare Promptbooks of the Seventeenth Century: CE, MM, WT
Shakespeare Quarto Facsimiles: HA, H41, H42, H5, H61, H62, H63, KJ,KL, R2, R3, LL, MA, MD, MV, MW, OT, PE, RJ, TC, TS
Shakespeare Readngs: see Charles Kemble
Shakespeare Society(London): H41, H62, H63
Shakespeare Society of NY(NY): HA, RJ
Shannon: RJ
Shapiro, Mel: MV, RJ, TG

Shattuck, Charles: AY, KJ
Shaw, Elizabeth Mary Ann: KJ
Shaw, Glen Byam: AC, AY, CR, HA, JC, H5, R3, MC, MW, OT, RJ, TC
Sheaves(London): H41
Sheep-Shearing: WT
Sheffield, John: JC
Sheridan, Richard Brinsley: TE
Sheridan, Thomas: CR, RJ
Sheridan, W E: KL
Sheriff, Jane: TN
Shervell, L R: H8, H8App
Sherwin, Edwin: KL
Sherwood(London): H5
Sheybal, Vladek: TS
Shields, Henry: TN
Shipwreck, The: TE
Shires, W: KL
Shirley, Thomas: MW
Shirley, William: CE
Shislem, F: MD
Short, C: H41, H42, H5
Short, Peter(London): H61, H62, H63
Shorter Shakespeare, A: H41
Shylock on Stage: MV
Shylock, or the Merchant of Venice Preserved: MV
Sicilian Usurper, The: R2
Siddons, Harry: JC
Siddons, Sarah: CY, H8, MC, OT, WT
Sidgewick(London): HA, KL, MV, PE,TC
Sidney publisher: Dunn(see name)
Sidney theatre: Her Majesty's(see name)
Siege of Troy: TC
Sieur de Lisle: TM
Simpkin(London): AC, CR, CY, HA, JC, H41, H5, H8, KJ, KL, R3, MA, MC, MCApp, MM, MV, MW, OT, RJ, TE, TG, TN, TS, WT
Simms(London): JC, H61, H62, H63
Simmons(London): MC
Simpson, Mercer Hampton: CRApp, and many more
Six Old Plays . . .: CE, H61, H62,H63, KJ, MM
Skillan, George: AC, AY, CY, HA, JC, H41, H42, H5, H8, KL, R2, R3, MA, MC, MV, MW, OT, RJ, TE
Skinner, Otis: RJ
Smallhythe: CY and many more
Smart(Reading): H42, H62, H63, KJ, MV

Smethwicke(London): AC, AY, HA, KL,
    LL, RJ, TS
Smith, Mr: TE
Smith, Chris John: RJ
Smith, Euan: AC, JC, TA
Smith, J C: MD
Smith, J H: HA
Smith, Kegan: MM
Smith, Sol: CE, KJ, KL, MC
Smith, T O: RJ
Smith, William Harby: HA, OT
Smith(London): H5
Smith, Brett(Dublin): MC
Smock Alley Th(Dublin): AY, CE, CR,
    JC, H41, H6, KJ, KL, R2, MC, MD,MW,
    OT, RJ, TN, WT
Snowden, M C: OT
Soane: H61, H62, H63
Society for Theatre Research (London):
    HA, R3
Solomon: RJ
Sonnenschein(London): AY
Sothern and Marlowe: AC, AY, CY, HA,
    M A, MC, MM, MV, MVApp, RJ, TN,TS,
    WT
Sothern, E H: AC, AY, CY, HA, KL, MA,
    MC, MM, RJ, TN, WT
Spelman, John: KJ
Spencer(Boston): CE, CR, LL, MW, WT
Spriggs, Elizabeth: AC
Stafford, Simon: PE
"StageVersions of Romeo and Juliet:"RJ
Stalling (Oldenberg): PE
Stanley, Audrey: WT
Stanislavsky, Constantin: OT
Stanislavsky Produces Othello : OT
Stark, J, prompter: CY, HA,H41, KL,
    MV, OT, TS
Steele, John George: MV
Stein and Day(NY): OT
Stephens, William H: JC, KL, MC
Sterne, Richard L: HA
Stevens, George: HA, H41, H42, H5,
    H61, H62, KJ, KL, R2, R3, LL, MA,
    MD, MV,MW, OT, RJ, TA, TC, TS
Stevens, Thomas Wood: AW, HA, JC,KL,
    MC, RJ, TE, TN, TS
Stewart, Douglas: MA
Stewart, Ogden: TN
Stirling, Earl of: JC
Stirling, William: JC
Stocker, Willard: KL
Stoddard(London): R3

Stoker, Bram: R3
Strahan(London): R2
Strange and Worthy accidents in the
    birth and life of Marina: PE
Stratford-upon-Avon: all, KJApp,R2App
    MDApp, MMApp, TAApp
Stratford-upon-Avon publisher: Boy-
    den(see name)
Stratford Shakespeare Festival: all
    except H63 and TA
Strolling Players: MA
Students, The : LL
Sullivan, Barry: H42, H5, KJ, MA, MC,
    MV, RJ, TS, WT
Sullivan, P E: MC
Sutherland: OT
Swall, Abel(London): TC
Swinburne, Algernon Charles: PE
Swinburne, John: CY
Switch, E T: OT
Sydenham publisher: Crystal Palace
    Co(see name)
Symonds, Arthur: AC, TN
Symonds(London): HA

Tabby(London): KL
Taber, Robert S: OT
Talbot, Henry: R3
Talfour, Francis: MV
Tallis(London): MC
Tallis(NY): MC
Talmon, Joseph J: HA
Tate, Nahum: CR, KL, R3, MC
Tauchnitz(Leipzig): R2
Tavener, William: AY, HA, JC, H8,R3,
    OT, RJ, WT
Taylor Charles G: AW
Taylor, E F: R3, MA, MV, OT
Taylor, Henry S: H41
Taylor, James: AC, CY, HA, JC, H8,KL,
    MA, MD, MM, OT, TE, TG
Taylor, Lark: AY, CE, HA, MA, MC, MM,
    MV, RJ, TN, TS, WT
Taylor, Stoddard: MC
Taylor, Tell: R3
Taylor, Tom: HA
Taylor(NY): AY, HA, JC, H41, H8, KJ,
    KL, R3, MA, MC, MV, OT, RJ, TE, TG,
    TN, TS
Teare, Edmund: AC
Tearle, G Osmund: JC, H61
Tearle, Godfrey: OT
Tegg(London): RJ, TM

Tenscher, Joachim: CR
Terry, Ellen: CR, CY, HA, H8, KL, MA,
  MC, MCApp, MM, MV, WM, OT, OTApp,
  RJ, RJApp, WT
Terry, Kate: MA, MAApp
Thalberg: RJ
Thayer(Boston): MC
Theatre(London): AW, AY, CE, CR, CY,
  HA, JC, H41, H42, H5, KL, R3, MA,
  MV, RJ, TG, TN, TS, WT
Theatre-Go-Round: KJ, R2
Theatre Guild: MA, TS, WT
Theatre of Ingenuity: H41, TS
Theatre Royal(Bath): HA, KL
Theatre Royal(Birmingham): CE, CRApp,
  HA, H41, OT, TS
Theatre Royal(Edinburgh): JC
Theatre Royal(Melbourne): AC, KL
Theatrical Magazine: AW, AY, CE, CR,
  HA, H8, MA, MD, MM, MV, MW, OT,TE,
  TN, WT
Thieme, P A(Arnheim): MC
Theobold, Mr: R2
Third Folio: WT
Thomas, Richard(London): MM
Thomas's Burlesque Drama(London): TS
Thompson(London): R3, TE
Thomson, James: CR
Thorndike, Sybil: OT
Thornton, Henry: MD
Tichnor(Boston): HA
Tilden, stage manager: TN
Timon in Love: TM
Timon misanthrope : TM
Tinsley Brothers(London): AC
Todd, Hal J: RJ, TA
Tomkins, C F: R3
Tonson(London): all
Tonson and Draper(London): MD
Toohey, J M M: AY, HA
Torrey(NY): KL, R3, MC, OT
Tothill(London): RJ
Toye, Wendy: AY
Tracey, Thomas F: R3
Tragedies (Dublin): H5
Tragedy of King Richard the Second: R2
Tragedy of Othello: OT
Tragical History of Piramus and This-
  be: MD
Tragical History of Romeus and Juliet:
  RJ
Tragical History of the Life and Reign
  of Richard the Third: R3

Tree: see Beerbohm-Tree
Tremont Th(Boston): CE
Trentsendry(Vienna): WT
Troilus and Cressida, or Truth found
  too late: TC
Troublesome Reigne of John, King of
  England: KJ
Trubner(London): CY, RJ
True Chronicle History of King Lear
  and His Three Daughters, The: KL
True Tragedy of Richard, Duke of York:
  H61, H62, H63
True Tragedy of Richard the Third: R3
Truman(London): WT
Tuck(London): OT
Turner, Jerry: AY, HA, JC, H61, OT,TC
Turner(Philadelphia): HA, R3, OT, RJ
Twelve Costumes of Richard III: R3
Twenty of the Plays . . : H61, H62,R2
Twins, The: CE
Tyler, George C: MC
Tynan, Kenneth: OT
Tyrone Guthrie Th(Minneapolis): AY,
  HA, JC, R3, KL, LL, MD, MV, TE, TN,
  TS
Tyrell, T W: R3
Tyson, Molly: CR

Universal Passion, The: MA
University of California Press(Los
  Angeles): HA
University of Illinois Press(Urbana):
  KJ
University of Virginia Press(Charlottes-
  ville): MD
Urbana publishers: Beta Phi Mu, U of
  Ill Press (see name)
Urhamlet: HA

Valpy, Richard: H42, H62, H63, KJ, R3,
  MV
Vance, C W: R3
Vance, Denis: H41
Vanderhoff, George: HA
Vanderhoff, May: MV
Vardeau School(Brighton): JC
Vaughn, Gladys: MC, OT, OTApp, WT
Vaughn, Stuart: AY, H61, H62, H63, R3,
  OT
Vergie(Paris): R2, RJ
Verner, Elaine: RJ
Vestris, Elizabeth: LL, MW, TN
Vezin, Hermann: AY, HA, JC, KJ, KL,
  R3, MA, MV, OT, TS

Vickers(London): H61, MA, MC, RJ
Vickers' Penny Shakespeare(London):
    CY, MC, RJ
Victor, Benjamin: TG
Vienna publisher: Trentsendry(see
    name)
Vietor, Wilhelm: HA
Viehman, Theodore: MD
Vincent, Felix A: MA, MC
Vincent, Leon James: AY, H41, H5,OT
Vining, Frederick: MA
Vining, George: CE
Virtue(London): HA
Virtue Betray'd or Anne Bullen: H8
Vivian, Percival: MV

Walker(London): all
Walker, Robin: AT
Walkins, Sidney: JC
Wallack, J W: AY, HA, JC, H41, KJ,MA,
    MV, OT
Wallack, James W, Jr: KL
Wallack, Lester: AY, MA
Wallack, Mrs: CR
Waller, David: HA
Waller, Louis: RJ
Waller, M: JC
Walnut St Th(Philadelphia): JC
Walsh(Cork): KL
Walsh(London): MD, TE
Walthoe, J, Jr(London): H61, H62,H63
Walter, J H: AC
Ward, Genevieve: H8
Ward, John: HA
Ward, William: MM, MV, WT
Warde, Frederick: HA, JC, KL, MV, OT,
    RJ, TM, WT
War of the Roses: H61, H62, H63, R3
Warren, Leslie: MA
Warren, William: CR, CY, HA, H61, H62,
    H63, H8, MA, MM, MV, RJ, TM, WT
Warrington(London): AC
Washington theatre : Ford's(see name)
Waterbury, Helen: TN
Watts(Dublin): CR, CY, RJ
Watts(London): AC, KL, MA, TM
Waverly, Charles: MC
Webster, Benjamin: HA, MV, TS
Webster, Margaret: HA, R2, MC, MM, MV,
    OT, TE
Weing(Dublin): CR
Wekworth, Manfred: CR
Welles, Organ: JC, MC, MV, TN

Wellington(London): OT
Wells, Charles B: HA
Wells, Stanley: R2
Wells(Boston): AY, CR, CY, HA, KJ, KL,
    R3, MC, MD, MV, OT, TN
Wells and Lilly(Boston): CR
Wells Gardner(London): AY, CE, CR, HA,
    JC, H5, KJ, KL, R2, MC, MD, MV, TN
Wellwood, S: PE
Wemyss, F C: MA, TS
Wenman(London): AW, AY, CE, CR, CY,
    HA, JC, H8, KL, R3, MA, MC, MD, MM,
    MV, MW, OT, RJ, TE, TM, TN, WT
Wenning: MA
West, Charles, MV
West, W H: MW
West(Boston): HA, MV, OT, TN
Whale(NY): MC
When Thou Art King: H42
Whetstone, George: MM
Which Is Which: CE
White(London): H61, H62, H63, TA
Whitehouse(Dublin): H8
Whitestone(Dublin): MC, RJ
Whitlaw: CR
Whitlock(London): TS
Whittaker(London): MD
Whittington(London) TS
Whitworth(London): MC, MM, RJ
Whytal, Russ: KL, R3, MC, MV
Whole Contention, The: H61, H62, H63
Wigley, Alfred: JC
Wilkie(London): H42
Wilkins, George: PE
Wilkinson, Tate: HA
Wilkinson(Dublin): R3
Wilkinson(Manchester): H42
Williams, prompter: AC
Williams, Clifford: AY, CE, CR, H41,
    H42, R3, MV, TE, TN, TS
Williams, David: H5, KJ, R2, MV, OT,
    TN
Williams, Espy: HA
Williams, Fred: JC
Williams, Harcourt: AY
Williams, Noel: AW
Williams, W C: R3
Williams(London): CY, JC
Williamson, David: LL
Williamson, Laird: H5, TA, TG
Williamson, Nicol: HA
Williamson(Dublin): CR
Williamson(Edinburgh): MA, MAApp

APPENDIX F - INDEX BY PAGE

Barnes, T H: 787w
Barois(London): ¢10n
Barrett, Lawrence: 180o,s,v,331n,
  555u,x, 763n-q, 787u-w, 787u-w,
  810aa-cc, 846ww, 878x
Barrett, Wilson: 710ii
Barrow, T, Jr(London): 878k
Barrow-Diggers, The: 160h
Barry, Eleanor: 204u
Barry, Thomas: lii, 66g, 160j, 204n,
  280g, 303n, 441h,j, 381o, 438f,
  591j, 653i, 763i,k-m, 878g
Barrymore, Ethel: 180cc, 810ss
Barrymore, John: 810rr, 1001
Bartlet, George: 41j
Bartlett, Henrietta C: xxxvii
Bartlett, Mary Jane: xi
Bartley, George: 381i
Barton, John: lx, 66m, 134i, 228x,
  253q, 280u,x, 331k, 355o-p, 381u,
  408-1, 438nn, 468f-g,i, 495b,e,
  525f, 555cc, 621f-g, 653n, 711jj,
  763z,878gg, 943o, 1006, 1017
Bass, Charles: 41i
Bassett, Russell: 591-1
Batchelder, J D: 810aa
Bateman, Mrs: 787u
Bates, Blanche: 204u, 711w
Bates, James W: 555p, 947e
Bath: 355t
Bath publishers: Carrington, Rodd
  (see name)
Bath Theatre: Th Royal(see name)
Bathurst(London): xlvii, 41p, 61ff,
  180d, 204e, 228b, 280c, 303f, 331e,
  381g, 468d, 495b, 525a, 591d, 653e,
  740d, 763f, 787g, 810b, 846w, 878b,
  943e
Batstead(London): 711dd
Baudry Librarie Europeene: x1
Baumbaugh, Charles: 180r
Bax, Peter: 160o
Bayler(London): 555j
Baylor U: 810ww
Beatrice and Benedick : 110bb
Beatt, David: 591d, 787e
Beaumont and Fletcher: 381f
Beauties of the English Stage: 810e
Beauty the Conquerer or the Death
  of Mark Antony: 910b
Beck, Mrs Martha: xi
Beckerman, Bernard: 134i, 621f, 1008
Becket(London): &40d

Becks, George: xviii, liv, lvi, 20g,
  66b, 110i,k,n, 160i-k,m,s, 180p,w,
  204j,r, 253d, 280j, 303k,p, 331f,n,
  235g, 381n,q, 555nn, 591i-j, 711y,
  740f, 763p, 787w-x,z, 810t,y, 846aa-
  bb, gg, jj-kk, 878d, s
Bedell(London): 41b
Bedford(NY): 787o, 810f
Beerbohm-Tree, Herbert: xviii, lv,
  lvii, 41o-p, 110w, 160m-n, 180aa-bb,
  228g, 280-1, 303g, 331p, 355-1,
  381s, 591p, 711bb, 763s-t, 787cc-dd,
  810kk, 878bb-cc, 910h-i
Belasco, David: 180cc, 846pp
Belfast publishers: Allen, Magee,
  Mance(see names)
Bel Geddes: see Geddes
Bell, George Joseph: 787i, 846y
Bell, Gorman T: 787ii
Bell(London): xxxix, xlvi, lxi, 20d
  41d, 66o, 92e, 110d,m, 134d, 160f,
  180d,o,u, 204d,p,s, 228f-g,i, 253b,
  280c, 303e,o, 336n, 355f, 381qq,
  408f, 438o,u, 468c,h, 490b, 525a,
  555f,t, 591d,n, 621d, 653d,j, 687e,
  711r, 740f, 763f,q, 787f-g,t-u,
  810h,bb, 846vv, 878g,u, 910c, 943d,
  j, 976d
Bell(Edinburgh): 66e
Bell and Daldy(London): xl, xli, xliv
Bell, Jane(London): 846t
Bellamy, Daniel: 204c
Bell's British Farces : 303f
Bell's Edition of Shakespeare's Plays:
  xxxix, and most of Bell(London)
Bellew, Kyrle: 910f
Benedetti, Robert: 228y
Ben Greet Shakespeare for Young Peo-
  ple: lvii, 160n, 180bb, 204y, 763u
Benn, Walter: 810x
Barnett, Anne Krooke: ix
Bennett, C M: 787ii
Bennett, Charles: 253e
Bennett, G: 331g
Bennett, James: 331k
Benson, F R: 160h, 180y, 204v, 228r,
  253e, 280-1, 468f, 495d, 711z,
  763v, 787dd, 810gg, 878aa
Benthall, Michael: lix, 66-1, 160p,
  180ff, 228w, 253t, 303t, 331g, 355o,
  438m, 591g, 653m, 740g, 763y, 810vv,
  yy, 910k, 943n, 1009

Boston publishers: Baker, Lilly, Richardson, Spencer, Thayer,Tichner, Wells, West(see names)

Boston Repertory Th: lvii,66-1, 110x, 180u,ii, 303r-s, 763j, 787ee, 810aaa

Boston Theatre(Boston): lii, 41k, 66g, 11-m, 204g, 303w, 331i, 381o, 591j, 763m, 787k, 878q

Boston theatres: Boston Museum, Boston Opera House, Boston Repertory Th, Boston Th, Castle Square, Globe,Hillis St, Howard Atheneum, National, Tremond (see names)

Bosworth, Halliam: xix, 110f, 180bb, 204t,v, 763p,u, 787aa, 810jj,878cc

Bosworth(London): 787t

Boucicault, Dion: 110e

Bouncing Knight, The: 381o

Bourchief, Arthur: 180x

Bowdler, Thomas: xxv

Bowery Th(NY): 180j, 381k, 555r,653h, 763j-k

Bowmer, Angus: 92m, 110aa, 134b, 160p, 180bb, 204z,bb, 280w, 810vv, 846uu-ww

Bowyer(London): 763f

Boyden(Stratford-upon-Avon): xli,lvi, 41c, 66i, 92-1, 110b, 134f, 160-1 180v, 204p,u,x, 228p, 253e, 280i, 303o, 331o, 355k, 381r, 408j,428-1, y, 468e,i, 495d, 525e, 555x, 621e, 653k, 711a, 740g, 763r, 787u, 846pp, 878u, 943j, 976e

Boyle,R W: 787o

Boyle, Fernand: 878o

Boyle, L: 787k

Boyle, Roger: 204d

Br, Ar(London): 711c

Bradbury(London): 110-1, 160k, 331m, 355i, 591-1, 787r, 810x

Bradley, A D: 41-1, 404m

Bradley, Albert: 110k

Bradley(Dublin): 41c, 66d, 204d

Bragge(London): 228e

Br anan, Goerge C: xxxvii

Brayton, Lily: 763u, 910j, 1012

Breckness, Mrs H: 1000

Breen, Robert: 810vv

Breeze, Edmund: 180ii

Brent, Romney: 41y

Bridgeman, T: 555i

Bridges-Adams, W: lvii, lviii, 20h, 41q-s, 66f, 110y, 134g, 160o, 240z, 228u, 253e, 280s-t, 331p, 355n, 381s, 408j, 555z-aa, 653-1, 711cc, 740q, 763w, 810tt, 846ss, 878cc, 910j, 943-1

Brighton: 810-1

Brighton: Varnead School: 763w

Brison(Dublin): 711d

British Broadcasting Co: xl, 355o, 381u, 408k, 438n, 468f-g,j. 495d-e, 525f, 555b,cc, 653j

British Museum Library: xl

Broad(Manchester): 910g

Broadhurst Th(NY): 180cc,ss

Broadway Th(NY): 160i, 180m-n, 591j, 621e, 787o,q-r, 810i,ii, 846ff, 989q,aa

Broderip(London): 787e

Brokaw, Charles: 110x

Broke, Arthur: 711c

Bromley, Edward: 711cc

Brood, Charles: xlix

Brook, Peter: lix, lx, 66k, 134g,1, 160r-s, 331p, 687f, 711ee, 846vv-ww

Brooke, Henry: 943d

Brooklyn: 355p

Brooklyn Th(Brooklyn): 438j, 910e

Brooklyn theatres: Academy of Music, Brooklyn Th, Park (see names)

Brooks, Henry: 910c

Brothers Brough: li

Brown: 846y

Brown, B K: 253d

Brown, F: 943g

Brown, George: 41j, 204m

Brown, John Russell: 878gg

Brown, Maurice: 878dd

Brown, Sedley: 92j, 787v

Brown(London): 66d, 253b, 280b, 591-1

Brown and Lemon(London): 761-1

Brown U: x

Browne, E Martin: 846rr

Browne, J H, prompter: 846jj

Browne(London): 591c

Browning Society(Philadelphia): 110u

Brubaker, Edward: 41u, 331m, 408-1, 468g, 495o

Bryce(Glasgow): xlii

Bryden, Bill: 711kk

Buchanan, C W: 878bb

Korzanjewski, B: 621f
Koun, Karolos: 711ii
Kyle, Barry: 555dd, 943o
Kynge Johan: 331h

L N: see N
l, N(London): 810b
Lackington(London): 846x
Lacy, John: 303d
Lacy, Thomas: xli, 303v
Lacy, Walter: 110-1
Lacy(London): xv, xx, xxi, xli, liv,
  20f, 41i,m, 66h, 92k, 110k,m,o,
  160j, 180h,l,   204m,o, 228e,1-n,
  253d, 280g-i, 3 3n-o, 331m, 355-1
  387g,o, 438g, 555g,t, 591k-1, 653h,
  j,711o,q-r, 763m-n, 787g,s, 810w,
  z,bb, 846bb,gg, 878r,t, 910d,943i,
  1007
Lady's Advice to Froward Women: 228m
Lafayette Th(NY): 787gg
Lahr, Bert: 303t
Lamb, Charles: 740e
Lambe, J F: 160d
.ambert, Charlotte: 228q
Lancaster, Robert: 280y
Lanc ster theatre: Fulton Opera
  House (see name)
Landau, Jack: 41f,u, 66-1, 110aa,
  160p-q, 180gg, 280w, 303f, 331g,
  621f, 711gg, 787ii
Landdown: 381f
Landdown, Baron: 180b
ander, Mrs F W: 591m
Lander, Jean Davenport: 591m,910e-f
Landor, W S: 910f
Lane, John: 787ii
Lane, R J: xl, 180o, 787t, 810bb,
  878a
Lane Allen(London): 810zz
La Nera: 810jj
Lang, Albert: 110x, 280r, 711bb
Langham, Michael: 20i, 110aa-bb,
  134h-i, 160g, 180gg-hh, 228x-y,
  381u, 438m,o, 555bb, 621f, 653m ,
  711ff, 740g, 763x, 810w,y, 846xx,
  878ee, 910-1
Langton, Basil C: 711ee
Langtry, Mrs Lily: 204r, 787y,910g
 Laphore, John T: 280-1
Lark, George E: 41r, 110c
Last words: xxxiv

Late, and much admired Play called
  Pericles, Prince of Tyre, The:
  976c-d
Lathrop, Alan: x
Laura Keene's h(NY): 160j
Law Against Lovers: 66d,h, 110c,h,
  311j, 711g
Law(London): 355d,f, 381e, 355c-d,f,
  y
Lawford, Ernest: 280p
Law of Lombardy: 110d
Leacroft(London): 66e, 92e
Leadenhall Press(London): 910g
Leake(London): 180b, 878d
Leamington Spa: 41s, 228w, 280t,
  810m-n
Lear: see King
Leathley(Dublin): 591c
Lee, John: 787e
Lee(London): 621c
LeGallienne, Eva: 280r, 711cc
Legrange, Charles: 1011
Leiber, Fritz: 110u,x, 180dd, 204y-z,
  228t, 280s, 555aa, 711bb, 763u,
  787ff, 810cc, 846ss
Leiber, Vir.ginia: 846ss
Leigh, Andrew: 763x
Leigh, Henry: 228-1
Leigh, J H: 1v
Leigh, Vivian: 910k
Lelyweld, Toby: 180gg
 emon: Mark: 381g
LeMoyne, William: 555dd, 591v, 810w
Lennep: see Van Lennep
L'Estrange, Robert: see Estrange
Letts(London): 204q
Leveridge, Richard: 160d
Lewis, George, prompter: 591i, 653h,
  711e; 763k; 787n,q, 846ee, 878g
Lewis, James: 110i, 204t, 228-1,787n,
  810s, 878o
Lewelyn, W H: 878s
Library of Congress: x
Life and Death of Falstaff: 408k
Life and Death of Henry the Fifth:
  438d
Life and Death of King Lear: 846u
Life and Death of Sir John Falstaff:
  381j, 408h, 438q
Life of Henry the Fifth: 438d
Life of Sir John Oldcastle: 381e
Lillo: 986d
Lilly(Boston): 653g

Lilly Library: x
Lincoln Center Th(NY): 180bb, 208z
Lincoln's Inn Fields(London): 66d,
  160d, 381t
Lind Theatre: see Jenny
Lindo, M P: 787t
Ling(London): 228d,f, 810b
Linley: xlvi
Linsdale(London): 555i
Lindsley, A B: 331h
Lintott(London): 180b, 555d
Lippencott(Philadelphia): xl
Liquid Paper Corporation: xi
Lisle, Sieur de: 740c
Lister(London): 180d, 711b, 787g
Literary and Philosophical Society:
  x
Lithgow, Arthur: xix, 331g, 1000,
  1003, 1005, 1007, 1010, 1013,
  1015-16
Little(London): 878v
Little(NY): 653k, 878y
Litton, Marie: 204q
Liverpool publishers: Daily Post
  Steam Printing, Newman(see name)
Liverpool theatres: Alexandria, Th
  Royal(see names)
Lloyd, Norman: 228w,x
Locke, Matthew: 787e
Lodge, Frank: 110o, 787w, 810jj
Logan, Celia: 66g, 134d
Long, Augustus(Dublin): 204d
Longman(London): xl, xlviii, xlix,
  41d-e, 66f, 92f, 110e, 180e,n,
  204f, 228i, 280d, 303h, 331f,n,
  381h-i,p, 408g, 438e, 468d,525e,
  555g-h, 591e, 653e-f, 711j-k, 763g,
  787h-i, 810k, 846x, 878i, 910c,
  943f, 1014
Longworth(NY): 41f, 180f, 228i, 381h,
  555g-h, 591f, 711k, 787j, 810k-m,
  846y, 878i,y, 910f
London Museum: x
London, n p: 110p, 160c,h, 180e,g,o,
  204c,f, 228e-f,j, 303d-e, 331n,p,
  355f-g, n, 381f, 468d,i, 495b,525e,
  555d,s, 711e,g,l, 763e, 810n,878d-
  e,i,l, n-o, 943c,e-f
London publishers: Adams, Adlard,
  Allman, Allot, Alson, Aubert's
  Steam Press, BBC, J B, R B, Richard Badger, Arthur Baker, Bald,
  Baldwin, Ballantyne, Balne, Barbie,

Barker, Barley, Barlow, Barois,Bar-
row, Bathurst, Batstead, Bayler,
Becket, Bedell, Bell, Jane Bell,
Bell and Daldy, Bentley, Bettes-
worth, Black and White, Blackie,
Blount, Boboe, Bogus, Bonian and
Watley, Booksellers, Booth, Bos-
worth, Bowyer, Bradbury, Bragge,
Broderip, Brown, Browne, Burbie,
Burby, Burns and Gates, Butters,
P C, T C, Cademan, Cadman, Calder,
Calkins, Camden Society, Cassell,
Cawthorne, Chapman, Chapple, Chet-
win, Chetworth and Watts, Chetwinde,
Chetwynd, Chiswick, Christie, Clar-
endon Press, Clark, Clarke, Clayton,
Collins, Colneighi, Company, Coope,
Corbett, Votes, Cowie, Cr aig,Creed,
Cumberland, Daldy, Nathaniel Dan-
cer, Darby, David, Davidson, David-
son's Penny Shakespeare, Darkes,
Debrett, Deeve, Dent, Dicks, Dodd,
Dodsley, Dolby, Dramatic Repository,
Draper, Dring, Drury Lane Th, Cun-
combe, G Eld, Everyman Th, Eyre and
S, Feales, Fenworth, Field and Tuer,
Fisher, Flesher, Fletcher, Folio
Society, Samuel French, Garland,
Gill, Ginn, Globe, Gosson, Grey,
Griggs, Grewsham, H H,'H H Jr, Har-
per, Harrap, Harrison, Hart-Davis,
Hawes, Hawkins, Hedgeon, Heinemann,
Harrington, Helme, Hayes, Hills,
Hindemarch, Hingston, Hitch, Hitch
and Hawes, Hope, Hughes, Hurst,
Hutcher, Jaggard, Jakes, Johnson,
Johnson 1888, Joseph, Kearsley,Ken-
dal, Knapson, Knight, N L, Lacking-
ton, Lacy, Allen L Lane, Law, Lea-
croft, Leadenhall Press, Leake,Lee,
Lemoyne, Letts, Ling, Linsdale,Lin-
tott, Lister, Little, Longman,Lons-
dale, Lopez and Wemyss, Low, Samp-
son Low, Lowndes, A M, J M, Macmillan, Magnus, Meighan, Marlebourne,
Martin, Mason, Mears, Meers, Merritt, Miles, Miller, Millington,
Mills, Mitchell, Music Publishing
Co, Josephine Myers, I W, L W, Nassau Steam Press, National Acting
Drama Office, Neale, Nelson, New
Shakespeare Society, Nichols,Nicol,
Niles, Noble, Norton, Nutt, N O, Oxberry, Oxlade, Orr, Owen, Oxford

New Hamlet, The: 810mm
New Haven publisher: Yale U Press
  (see name)
Newhouse Theatre: see Mitzi
New Introduction to Bibliography:
  xxxvii
Newlin, Ms Jean T: x
New Look at Shakespeare's Quartos:
  xxxvii
Newman(Liverpool): 92-1
New National Th(Washinton): 943k
New Orleans: 555t, 653i
New San Souci Th(Calculla): 787m
New Shakespeare Company: x, xvii,
  xlii, 1k, 20i, 160s, 204ee, 228x-y,
  280w, 438n, 711i-j
New Shakespeare Society(London):711c,
  r, 943j, 976e
New Stratford Shakespeare: 160s,
  180ii, 280w, 763x, 787ii
New Theatre(Cambridge): 160o
New Theatre(NY): 41p, 280q, 303r,
  910i-j
New Theatre(Philadelphia): 843e
New Variorum: xxii
New Version, A: 810yy
New York publishers: Alford, Amer-
  ican Academy of Dramatic Art, Ap-
  pleton, Art Age Press, Baker, Bald-
  win, Bedford, Bernard, Century
  Edition, Crowell, Cushing and Bar-
  da, Clayton, Dell, DeWitt, Dodd-:
  Mead, Douglas, Doubleday, Dramatic
  Repository, Samuel French, Gilliss,
  Golden Press, Grosset, Herbert, Har-
  court-Brace, Harper, Hart, Hinton,
  Hurd, Little, Longworth, McClure,
  Macmillan, McMonigle, Metropoli-
  tan Job Printing, Modern Language
  Assn, Moore, NBC, Nesbitt, Norton,
  Oxford U Press, Pyramid Books, Ran-
  dom House, Roorbach, Routledge,
  Russell, Sanford, Sc ribners,
  Sears, Shakespeare Society of NY,
  Society Library, Stein and Day,
  Taylor, Torrey Bros, Turner,Whale
  (see names)
New York Shakespeare Festival: x,
  xliii, lx, l i, 20i-j, 41w, 66n,
  110bb,dd, 134-1, 160r, 180gg,204cc
  229y, 253q, 280w-y, 303u, 331r,
  381v, 408-1, 438n, 468g,o, 495e,

525f, 555bb-cc, 610g, 621f-g, 653m,
  687f, 711hh-ii, 740h, 763y, 787hh,
  jj, 810s,aa,xx, 846vv,xx, 878ff,
  910-1, 943o, 976b,g, 1008, 1010,
  1013,1023
New York theatres: Academy of Music,
  Astor Place, Bowery, Broadhurst,
  Broadway, Burton's, Chatham, Civic
  Repertory, Cort, Daly's, Empire,
  Fifth Ave, Fourteenth St, Gander
  Garden, Hudson, Jan Hus Hall, Jol-
  son, Knickerbocher, Lafayette,
  Laura Keene's, Lincoln Center, Ly-
  ceum, Lyric, National, New Bowery,
  New Century, New, NY Shakespeare
  Festival, Niblo's Gardens, Palmer's,
  Park, Phoenix, Republic, St James,
  San Harris, Star, Theatre Guild,
  Wallack's, Winter Garden(see names)
New Zealand: 204bb
Niblo's Gardens(NY): 92j, 555s, 653j,
  878s
Nichols, John: 66e, 93e, 228f
Nichols(London): xxxviii, 311e,h,1,
  438c,e, 846t,w, 878d
Nicholson, Mrs Ruth: x
Nicol(London): 160h
Nicolai: 41k
Niles(London): 1v
"Nineteenth Century Proprietory Act-
  ing Editions of Shakespeare;"
  xxxviii
Noble(London): 846v
Noble Peasant: 204e, 740d, 943e
Noel, Craig: 222w, 331r
Norfolk Public Library: x
Norris, Mrs E: 787n
Northern, Michael: 66k
Norton, John: 41v, 110i, 878o
Norton(London): 355e, 381e-f, 555c
Norton(NY): xxii, xl
Norton Facsimile of the First Folio:
  xl
Novelli, Ermete: 878bb
Norwick theatre: Maddermarket (see
  name)
Nuffield Library: x, xvii, liii,
  1000
Nugent Monck Collection: xlii and
  see Monck
Nunn: Trevor: 110cc, 228x, 303u, 381u,
  408-1, 438n, 591r, 653n, 687f
  763aa, 787jj, 810aaa, 846ww, 910f,1

DATE DUE

HIGHSMITH 45-220